Switching to the Mac _Snow Leopard Edition_

THE MISSING MANUAL

The book that
should have been
in the box®

Switching to the Mac *Snow Leopard Edition*

David Pogue

POGUE PRESS™

O'REILLY®

Beijing • Cambridge • Farnham • Köln • Paris • Sebastopol • Taipei • Tokyo

Switching to the Mac: The Missing Manual, Snow Leopard Edition
by David Pogue

Published by O'Reilly Media, Inc., 1005 Gravenstein Highway North,
Sebastopol, CA 95472.

O'Reilly Media books may be purchased for educational, business, or sales
promotional use. Online editions are also available for most titles: *safari.oreilly.
com*. For more information, contract our corporate/institutional sales department:
800-998-9938 or *corporate@oreilly.com*.

December 2009:   First Edition.

 This book uses RepKover™, a durable and flexible lay-flat binding.

ISBN-13: 978-0-596-80425-1

Table of Contents

Part Three: Making Connections

Part Four: Putting Down Roots

The Missing Credits

About the Author

David Pogue (author) is the weekly tech columnist for *The New York Times*, Emmy-winning correspondent for *CBS News Sunday Morning*, weekly CNBC contributor, and the creator of the Missing Manual series. He's the author or coauthor of 50 books, including 25 in this series, six in the "For Dummies" line (including *Macs, Magic, Opera,* and *Classical Music*), two novels, and *The World According to Twitter*. In his other life, David is a former Broadway show conductor, a piano player, and a magician. He lives in Connecticut with his wife and three awesome children.

Links to his columns and funny weekly videos await at *www.davidpogue.com.* He welcomes feedback about his books by email at *david@pogueman.com.*

About the Creative Team

Julie Van Keuren (copy editor) is a freelance editor, writer, and desktop publisher who runs her "little media empire" from her home in Billings, Montana. In her spare time she enjoys swimming, biking, running, and (hey, why not?) triathlons. She and her husband, M.H., have two sons, Dexter and Michael. Email: *little_media@yahoo.com.*

Phil Simpson (design and layout) works out of his office in Southbury, Connecticut, where he has had his graphic design business since 1982. He is experienced in many facets of graphic design, including corporate identity/branding, publication design, and corporate and medical communications. Email: *pmsimpson@earthlink.net.*

Brian Jepson (technical consultant) is a senior editor for O'Reilly Media. He cowrote *Mac OS X for Unix Geeks* and has written or edited a number of other tech books. He's the cofounder of Providence Geeks and serves as an all-around geek for AS220, a nonprofit, unjuried, and uncensored arts center in Providence, R.I. Email: *bjepson@ oreilly.com.*

Acknowledgments

The Missing Manual series is a joint venture between the dream team introduced on this page and O'Reilly Media. I'm grateful to all of them, and also to a few people who did massive favors for this book. The prose of Joseph Schorr and Adam Goldstein, contributors to earlier editions, lives on in this one. Lesa Snider put in a gruelling week, brilliantly getting this puppy ready for the printer. And Kellee Katagi cheerfully proofed hundreds of pages on a tight deadline. Thanks also to David Rogelberg for believing in the idea, and above all, to Jennifer, Kelly, Tia, and Jeffrey, who make these books—and everything else—possible.

—David Pogue

The Missing Manual Series

Missing Manuals are witty, superbly written guides to computer products that don't come with printed manuals (which is just about all of them). Each book features a handcrafted index; cross-references to specific page numbers (not just "see Chapter 14"); and an ironclad promise never to put an apostrophe in the possessive word *its*.

Here's a partial list of current and upcoming titles.

- *iPhone: The Missing Manual*, 3rd Edition by David Pogue
- *iPod: The Missing Manual*, 8th Edition by J.D. Biersdorfer
- *David Pogue's Digital Photography: The Missing Manual* by David Pogue
- *Photoshop CS4: The Missing Manual* by Lesa Snider King
- *JavaScript: The Missing Manual* by David Sawyer McFarland
- *CSS: The Missing Manual*, 2nd Edition, by David Sawyer McFarland
- *Dreamweaver 8: The Missing Manual* by David Sawyer McFarland
- *Flash CS4: The Missing Manual* by E. A. Vander Veer and Chris Grover
- *Netbooks: The Missing Manual* by J.D. Biersdorfer
- *Home Networking: The Missing Manual* by Scott Lowe
- *Your Brain: The Missing Manual* by Matthew MacDonald
- *Your Body: The Missing Manual* by Matthew MacDonald
- *Facebook: The Missing Manual* by E.A. Vander Veer
- *Photoshop Elements for Mac: The Missing Manual* by Barbara Brundage
- *iMovie '09 & iDVD: The Missing Manual* by David Pogue and Aaron Miller
- *iPhoto '09: The Missing Manual* by David Pogue and J.D. Biersdorfer
- *iWork '09: The Missing Manual* by Josh Clark
- *Office 2008 for Macintosh: The Missing Manual* by Jim Elferdink et al.
- *FileMaker Pro 10: The Missing Manual* by Geoff Coffey and Susan Prosser
- *Windows 7: The Missing Manual* by David Pogue
- *Windows Vista: The Missing Manual* by David Pogue
- *Office 2007: The Missing Manual* by Chris Grover, Matthew MacDonald, and E. A. Vander Veer
- *Photoshop Elements 8: The Missing Manual* by Barbara Brundage
- *Quicken 2009: The Missing Manual* by Bonnie Biafore

Introduction

What's going on with the Mac these days?

Apple was the only computer company whose sales actually increased during the recession. The Mac's market share has tripled since 2005. And Mac how-to book sales are up about 35 percent over two years ago (woo-hoo!).

And then there's the most significant statistic of all: you, sitting there reading this book—because, obviously, you intend to switch to (or add on) a Mac.

What's going on?

Maybe the coolness of all those iPods and iPhones is rubbing off onto the rest of Apple's product line. Maybe people have grown weary of boring beige and black boxes. Maybe it was the "I'm a Mac/ I'm a PC" ads on TV, or the convenience of the Apple Stores. Maybe potential switchers feel more confident to take the plunge now that Macs (because they contain Intel chips) can run Windows programs.

Or maybe people have just spent one Saturday too many dealing with viruses, worms, spyware, crapware, excessive startup processes, questionable firewalls, inefficient permissions, and all the other land mines strewn across the Windows world.

In any case, there's never been a better time to make the switch. Mac OS X version 10.6 (Snow Leopard) is gorgeous, easy to understand, and virus-free. Apple's computers are in top form, too, complete with features like built-in video cameras, built-in Ethernet, DVD burners, illuminated keyboards, and two different kinds of wireless connections. If you're talking laptops, the story is even better: Apple's laptops generally cost less than similarly outfitted Windows laptops, and weigh less, too. Plus, they look a lot cooler.

And then there's that Intel processor that sizzles away inside today's Macs. Yes, it lets you *run Windows*—and Windows programs—at blazing speed, right there on your Macintosh. (Hell really has frozen over.) Chapter 8 has the details.

That's not to say, however, that switching to the Mac is all sunshine and bunnies. The Macintosh is a different machine, running a different operating system, and built by a company with a different philosophy—a fanatical perfectionist/artistic zeal. When it comes to their missions and ideals, Apple and Microsoft have about as much in common as a melon and a shoehorn.

In any case, you have three challenges before you. First, you'll probably want to copy your Windows stuff over to the new Mac. Some of that is easy to transfer (photos, music, Microsoft Office documents), and some is trickier (email messages, address books, buddy lists).

Second, you have to assemble a suite of Macintosh programs that do what you're used to doing in Windows. Most programs from Microsoft, Adobe, and other major players are available in nearly identical Mac and Windows formats. But occasionally, it's more difficult: Many second-tier programs are available only for Windows, and it takes some research (or Chapter 7 of this book) to help you find Macintosh replacements.

Finally, you have to learn Mac OS X itself; after all, it came preinstalled on your new Mac. In some respects, it resembles the latest versions of Windows: There's a taskbar-like thing, a Control Panel–like thing, and, of course, a Trash can. At the same time, hundreds of features you thought you knew have been removed, replaced, or relocated. (If you ever find yourself groping for an old favorite feature, see Appendix B, The "Where'd It Go?" Dictionary.)

Note: In Mac OS X, the X is meant to be a Roman numeral, pronounced "ten." Unfortunately, many people see "Mac OS X" and say "Mac Oh Ess Sex." That's a sure way to get funny looks in public.

All About "Snow Leopard"

What's this business about big cats?

Most software companies develop their wares in secret, using code names for new products to throw outsiders off the scent. Apple's code names for Mac OS X and its descendants have been named after big cats: Mac OS X was Cheetah, 10.1 was Puma, 10.2 was Jaguar, 10.3 was Panther, 10.4 was Tiger, and 10.5 was Leopard. Since 10.6 is considered "only" a refinement of the existing Leopard version, it's called Snow Leopard.

(The real snow leopard is an endangered species, native to Central Asia. It has no larynx and so it can't roar. It can kill animals three times its size. Insert your own operating-system metaphor here.)

Usually, the code name is dropped as soon as the product is complete, whereupon the marketing department gives it a new name. In Mac OS X's case, though, Apple thinks its cat names are cool enough to retain for the finished product.

You do have to wonder what Apple plans to call future versions. Apple increases only the decimal point with each major upgrade, which means it has four big cats to go before it hits Mac OS XI.

Let's see: Bobcat, Cougar, Lion…um…Ocelot?

What Mac OS X Gives You

These days, a key attraction of the Mac—at least as far as switchers are concerned—is security. There isn't yet a single widespread Mac OS X virus. (Even Microsoft Word macro viruses don't run in Mac OS X.) For many people, that's a good enough reason to move to Mac OS X right there.

Along the same lines, there have been no reported sightings of *spyware* (malicious software that tracks your computer use and reports it back to a shady company) for Mac OS X. Mail, Mac OS X's built-in email program, deals surprisingly well with *spam*—the unsolicited junk email that's become the scourge of the Internet.

If you ask average people why the Mac isn't overrun by viruses and spyware, as Windows is, they'll probably tell you, "Because the Mac's market share is too small for the bad guys to write for."

That may be true (although 50 million machines isn't too shabby, as targets go). But there's another reason, too: Mac OS X is a very young operating system. It was created only a few years ago, and with security in mind. (Contrast that with Windows, whose original versions were written before the Internet even existed.) Mac OS X is simply designed better. Its built-in firewall makes it virtually impossible for hackers to break into your Mac, and the system insists on getting your permission before *anything* gets installed on your Mac. Nothing can get installed behind your back, as it can in Windows.

But freedom from gunkware and viruses is only one big-ticket item. Here are a few other joys of becoming a Mac fan:

- **Stability.** Underneath the shimmering, translucent desktop of Mac OS X is Unix, the industrial strength, rock-solid OS that drives many a Web site and university. It's not new by any means; in fact, it's decades old, and has been polished by generations of programmers. That's precisely why Apple CEO Steve Jobs and his team chose it as the basis for the NeXT operating system, which Jobs worked on during his 12 years away from Apple and which Apple bought in 1997 to turn into Mac OS X.

- **No nagging.** Unlike Windows, Mac OS X isn't copy-protected. You can install the same copy on your desktop and laptop Macs, if you have a permissive conscience. When you buy a new Mac, you're never, ever asked to type in a code off a sticker. Nor must you "register," "activate," sign up for ".NET Passport," or endure any other friendly suggestions unrelated to your work. And you won't find any cheesy software demos from other companies clogging up your desktop when you buy a new Mac, either. In short, Mac OS X leaves you alone.

- **Sensational software.** Mac OS X comes with several dozen useful programs, from Mail (for email) to a 3-D, voice-activated Chess program. The most famous programs, though, are the famous Apple "iApps": iTunes for working with audio files, iMovie for editing video, iPhoto for managing your digital photos, GarageBand for creating and editing digital music, and so on. You also get iChat (an AOL-,

Jabber-, and Google Talk-compatible instant messaging program that also offers videoconferencing) and iCal, a calendar program.

- **Simpler everything.** Most applications in Mac OS X show up as a single icon. All the support files are hidden away inside, where you don't have to look at them. There's no Add/Remove Programs program on the Macintosh; in general, you can remove a program from your Mac simply by dragging that one application icon to the Trash, without having to worry that you're leaving scraps behind.

- **Desktop features.** Microsoft is a neat freak. Windows XP, for example, is so opposed to your using the desktop as a parking lot for icons that it actually interrupts you every 60 days to sweep all your infrequently used icons into an "Unused" folder.

  The Mac approach is different. Mac people often leave their desktops absolutely littered with icons. As a result, Mac OS X offers a long list of useful desktop features that will be new to you, the Windows refugee.

  For example, *spring-loaded* folders let you drag an icon into a folder within a folder within a folder with a single drag, without leaving a wake of open windows. An optional second line under an icon's name tells you how many items are in a folder, what the dimensions of a graphic are, and so on. And there's a useful column view, which lets you view the contents of many nested folders at a glance. (You can think of it as a horizontal version of Windows Explorer's folder tree.)

  When your screen gets cluttered with windows, you can temporarily hide all of them with a single keystroke. If you want to see *all* the windows on your screen without any of them overlapping, Mac OS X's Exposé feature is your best friend (page 127).

  A speedy, system-wide Find command called Spotlight is accessible from any program. It searches not only the names of your files and folders, but also the words *inside* your documents, and can even search your email, calendar, address book, Web bookmarks, and about 100 other kinds of data, all at once.

  Finally, Mac OS X offers the Dashboard (which inspired the Sidebar in Windows Vista and Windows 7). It lets you summon dozens of miniprograms—a calculator, weather forecaster, dictionary, and so on—with a single keystroke, and dismiss them just as easily. You can download thousands more of these so-called widgets from the Internet, making it even easier to find TV listings, Google search results, local movie showtimes, and more, no matter what program you're using at the moment.

- **Advanced graphics.** Mac programmers get excited about the set of advanced graphics technologies called *Quartz* (for two-dimensional graphics) and *OpenGL* (for three-dimensional graphics). For the rest of us, these technologies translate into a beautiful, translucent look for the desktop, smooth-looking (*antialiased*) onscreen lettering, and the ability to turn any document on the screen into an Adobe Acrobat (PDF) file. And then there are the slick animations that permeate every aspect of Mac OS X: the rotating-cube effect when you switch from one logged-in person to another, the "genie" effect when you minimize a window to the Dock, and so on.

- **Advanced networking.** When it comes to hooking up your computer to others, including those on the Internet, few operating systems can touch Mac OS X. It offers advanced features like *multihoming,* which lets your laptop switch automatically from its cable modem settings to its wireless or dial-up modem settings when you take it on the road.

  If you're not so much a switcher as an *adder* (you're getting a Mac but keeping the PC around), you'll be happy to hear that Macs and Windows PCs can "see" each other on a network automatically, too. As a result, you can open, copy, and work on files on both types of machines as though the religious war between Macs and PCs had never even existed.

- **Voice control, keyboard control.** You can operate almost every aspect of every program entirely from the keyboard—or even by voice. These are terrific timesavers for efficiency freaks. In fact, the Mac can also read aloud *any text in any program,* including Web pages, email, your novel, you name it.

- **Full buzzword compliance.** You can't read an article about Mac OS X without hearing certain technical buzzwords that were once exclusively the domain of computer engineers: *preemptive multitasking, multithreading, symmetrical multiprocessing, dynamic memory allocation,* and *memory protection,* for example.

  What it all adds up to is that Mac OS X is very stable, that a crashing program can't crash the whole machine, that the Macintosh can exploit multiple processors, and that the Mac can easily do more than one thing at once—downloading files, playing music, and opening a program, for example—all simultaneously.

- **A command-line interface.** In general, Apple has completely hidden from you every trace of the Unix operating system that lurks beneath Mac OS X's beautiful skin. For the benefit of programmers and other technically oriented fans, however, Apple left uncovered a tiny passageway into that far more complex realm: Terminal, a program in your Applications→Utilities folder.

  This isn't a Unix book, so you'll find only the basics of using Terminal here. Still, if the idea of an all-text operating system gets you going, you can capitalize on the *command-line interface* of Mac OS X by typing out commands in the Terminal window, which the Mac executes instantly and efficiently. Think DOS prompt, just faster and more useful.

What Mac OS X Takes Away

Besides quirks like viruses, spyware, and the Start menu, there are some substantial things on a PC that you lose when you switch to the Mac:

- **Programs.** As mentioned above, there are certain programs that are stubbornly Windows-only. You can always search for replacements—using Chapter 7 of this book as a guide, for example—but you may end up having to pay for them. And, of course, there are *certain* programs—like some proprietary accounting and laboratory software, and lots of games—where the Windows versions are simply irreplaceable. For those, you have to keep a PC around or run Windows on your Mac (Chapter 8).

- **Peripherals.** Most add-on devices nowadays work equally well on both Windows PCs and Macs. That includes printers, scanners, digital cameras (still- and video-varieties), and "multifunction" devices that incorporate several of those attributes into one machine.

Unfortunately, not every company is that enlightened. Sometimes the Mac software for a gadget isn't as full-featured as the Windows version. Sometimes some of the features on a multifunction printer/scanner aren't available on the Mac. If you have a device made by an obscure manufacturer—especially if the device is more than a few years old—it may not work with your Mac at all.

Still, all hope is not lost. Chapter 9 can get you out of most hardware ruts you may find yourself in while making the Big Switch.

About This Book

Switching to the Mac: The Missing Manual is divided into five parts, each containing several chapters:

- Part 1, **Welcome to Macintosh,** covers the essentials of the Macintosh. It's a crash course in everything you see onscreen when you turn on the machine: the Dock, Sidebar, icons, windows, menus, scroll bars, Trash, aliases, menu, and so on.

- Part 2, **Moving In,** is dedicated to the actual process of hauling your software, settings, and even peripherals (like printers and monitors) across the chasm from the PC to the Mac. It covers both the easy parts (copying over your documents, pictures, and music files) and the harder ones (transferring your email, address books, buddy lists, and so on). It also covers the steps for running Windows on your Mac, which is an extremely attractive option.

- Part 3, **The Mac Online,** walks you through the process of setting up an Internet connection on your Mac. It also covers Apple's Internet software suite: Mail, Address Book, Safari, and iChat.

- Part 4, **Putting Down Roots**, deals with more advanced topics—and aims to turn you into a Macintosh power user. It teaches you how to set up private accounts for people who share a Mac, create a network for file sharing and screen sharing, navigate the System Preferences program (the Mac equivalent of the Windows Control Panel), and operate the 50 freebie bonus programs that come with Mac OS X.

Note: Some of the material in this book is adapted from the bestselling *Mac OS X Snow Leopard: The Missing Manual*. That book is a much fatter, more in-depth guide to Mac OS X (and a worthy investment if you grow into a true Macoholic).

• Part 5. At the end of the book, you'll find three appendixes. The first covers installation and troubleshooting. The second is the "Where'd It Go?" Dictionary—an essential reference for anyone who occasionally (or frequently) flounders to find some familiar control in the new, alien Macintosh environment. The last is a master keyboard-shortcut list for the entire Mac OS X universe.

About→These→Arrows

Throughout this book—and throughout the Missing Manual series—you'll find sentences like this one: "Open the System→Libraries→Fonts folder." That's shorthand for a much longer instruction that directs you to open three nested folders in sequence, like this: "On your hard drive, you'll find a folder called System. Open that. Inside the System folder window is a folder called Libraries; double-click it to open it. Inside *that* folder is yet another one called Fonts. Double-click to open it, too."

Similarly, this kind of arrow shorthand helps to simplify the business of choosing commands in menus, as shown in Figure I-1.

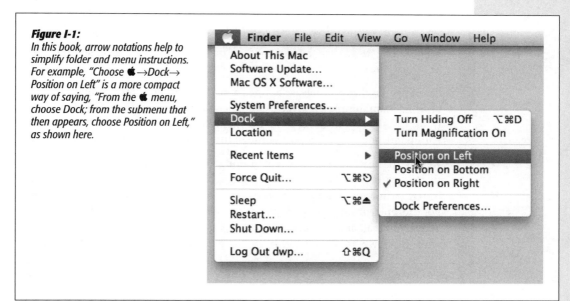

Figure I-1:
In this book, arrow notations help to simplify folder and menu instructions. For example, "Choose →Dock→ Position on Left" is a more compact way of saying, "From the menu, choose Dock; from the submenu that then appears, choose Position on Left," as shown here.

About MissingManuals.com

If you visit *www.missingmanuals.com,* click the "Missing CD-ROM" link, and then click the title of this book, you'll find a neat, organized, chapter-by-chapter list of the shareware and freeware mentioned in this book. (As noted on the inside back cover, having the software online instead of on a CD-ROM saved you $5 on the cost of the book.)

The Web site also offers corrections and updates to the book (to see them, click the book's title, and then click Errata). In fact, you're encouraged to submit such corrections and updates yourself. In an effort to keep the book as up-to-date and accurate as possible, each time we print more copies of this book, we'll make any confirmed corrections you've suggested. We'll also note such changes on the Web site, so that you can mark important corrections into your own copy of the book, if you like.

The Very Basics

To use this book, and indeed to use a Macintosh, you need to know a few basics. This book assumes you're familiar with a few terms and concepts:

- **Clicking.** This book gives you three kinds of instructions that require you to use the Mac's mouse. To *click* means to point the arrow cursor at something on the screen and then—without moving the cursor—press and release the clicker button on the mouse (or your laptop trackpad). To *double-click*, of course, means to click twice in rapid succession, again without moving the cursor at all. And to *drag* means to move the cursor while holding down the button.

  When you're told to ⌘-*click* something, you click while pressing the ⌘ key (which is next to the space bar). *Shift-clicking, Option-clicking,* and *Control-clicking* work the same way—just click while pressing the corresponding key.

- **Menus.** The *menus* are the words at the top of your screen: , File, Edit, and so on. Click one to make a list of commands appear.

  Some people click and release to open a menu and then, after reading the choices, click again on the one they want. Other people like to press the mouse button continuously after the initial click on the menu title, drag down the list to the desired command, and only then release the mouse button. Either method works fine.

- **Keyboard shortcuts.** If you're typing along in a burst of creative energy, it's disruptive to have to grab the mouse to use a menu. That's why many computer fans prefer to trigger menu commands by pressing certain combinations on the keyboard. For example, in word processors, you can press ⌘-B to produce a **boldface** word. When you read an instruction like "press ⌘-B," start by pressing the ⌘ key, then, while it's down, type the letter B, and finally release both keys.

Tip: You know what's really nice? The keystroke to open the Preferences dialog box in every Apple program—Mail, Safari, iMovie, iPhoto, TextEdit, Preview, and on and on—is always the same: ⌘-comma. Better yet, that standard is catching on with other software companies, too; Word, Excel, Entourage, and PowerPoint use the same keystroke, for example.

- **Icons.** The colorful inch-tall pictures that appear in your various desktop folders are the graphic symbols that represent each program, disk, and document on your computer. If you click an icon one time, it darkens, indicating that you've just *highlighted* or *selected* it. Now you're ready to manipulate it by using, for example, a menu command.

SWITCHING TO THE MAC: THE MISSING MANUAL

Part One:
Welcome to Macintosh

1

How the Mac Is Different

W hen you get right down to it, the job description of every operating system is pretty much the same. Whether it's Mac OS X, Windows Vista, or Billy Bob's System-Software Special, any OS must serve as the ambassador between the computer and you, its human operator. It must somehow represent your files and programs on the screen so you can open them; offer some method of organizing your files; present onscreen controls that affect your speaker volume, mouse speed, and so on; and communicate with your external gadgets, like disks, printers, and digital cameras.

In other words, Mac OS X offers roughly the same features as recent versions of Windows. That's the good news.

The bad news is that these features are called different things and parked in different spots. As you could have predicted, this rearrangement of features can mean a good deal of confusion for you, the Macintosh foreigner. For the first few days or weeks, you may instinctively reach for certain familiar features that simply aren't where you expect to find them, the way your tongue keeps sticking itself into the socket of a newly extracted tooth.

To minimize the frustration, therefore, read this chapter first. It makes plain the most important and dramatic differences between the Windows method and the Macintosh way.

Power On, Dude

As a critic might say, Apple is always consistent with its placement of the power button: It's different on every model.

On iMacs and Mac Minis, the power button is on the back panel. On the Mac Pro, it's on the front panel. And on laptop Macs, the button is near the upper-right corner of the keyboard. (Then again, if you have a laptop, you should get into the habit of just closing the lid when you're done working and opening it to resume; the power button rarely plays a role in your life.)

In every case, though, the power button looks the same (Figure 1-1): it bears the ⏻ logo.

Figure 1-1:
Every Mac's power button looks like this, although it might be hard to find. The good news: Once you find it, it'll pretty much stay in the same place.

That One-Button Mouse

You can get terrific mileage out of *shortcut menus* on the Mac, just as in Windows (Figure 1-2).

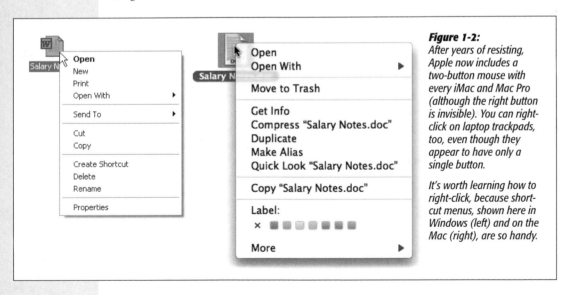

Figure 1-2:
After years of resisting, Apple now includes a two-button mouse with every iMac and Mac Pro (although the right button is invisible). You can right-click on laptop trackpads, too, even though they appear to have only a single button.

It's worth learning how to right-click, because short-cut menus, shown here in Windows (left) and on the Mac (right), are so handy.

Shortcut menus are so important, in fact, that it's worth this ink and this paper to explain the different ways you can trigger a right-click (or a *secondary click,* as Apple calls it, because not all these methods actually involve a second mouse button, and it doesn't *have* to be the right-side one):

- **Control-click.** You can open the shortcut menu of something on the Mac screen by Control-clicking it. That is, while pressing the Control key (bottom row), click the mouse on your target.

- **Right-click.** Windows veterans have always used the one-handed method: right-clicking. That is, clicking something by pressing the *right* mouse button on a two-button mouse.

  "Ah, but that's what's always driven me nuts about Apple," goes the common refrain. "Their refusal to get rid of their stupid one-button mouse!"

  Well, not so fast.

  First of all, you can attach any old $6 USB two-button mouse to the Mac, and it'll work flawlessly. Recycle the one from your old PC, if you like.

  Furthermore, if you've bought a desktop Mac since late 2005, you probably already *have* a two-button mouse—but you might not realize it. Is your mouse a white shiny plastic capsule with tiny gray scrolling track-pea on the far end? That would be what Apple calls the Mighty Mouse. Or is it a sculpted, winglike, wireless mouse with a wide top surface? That would be the newer Magic Mouse.

  Both of them have a secret: an invisible right mouse button. It doesn't work until you ask for it.

  To do that, choose →System Preferences. Click Mouse. There, in all its splendor, is a diagram of the mouse. (There's a picture on page 493.)

  Your job is to choose Secondary Button from the pop-up menu that identifies the right side of the mouse. (The reason it's not called a "right button" is because left-handers might prefer to reverse the right and left functions.)

  From now on, even though there aren't two visible mouse buttons, your mouse does, in fact, register a left-click or a right-click depending on which side of the button you push down. It actually works a lot more easily than it sounds like it would.

- **Use the trackpad (old way).** If you have a Mac laptop, you can "right-click" right there on the trackpad.

  To do that, point to whatever you want to click. Rest two fingers on the trackpad— and then click. (You turn this feature on and off in System Preferences→Trackpad, where you can also see a little video on how to do it.)

- **Use the trackpad (new way).** Two fingers plus thumb? That *is* quite a lot of digits just to get a right-click, and Apple knows it. So on the latest Mac laptops, you can "right-click" by clicking either the lower-right or lower-left corner of the track-pad—one finger only.

(Your laptop is eligible if it has no separate clicker button. Instead, the *whole trackpad surface* is a clicker. You turn on this clicking method in System Preferences→Trackpad, as shown in Figure 1-3.)

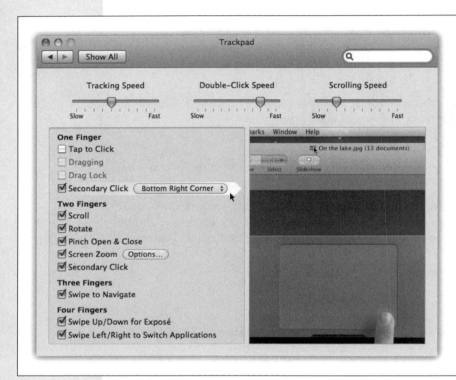

Figure 1-3:
The Trackpad pane of System Preferences looks different depending on your laptop model. But this one shows the two ways to get a "right-click."

On, Off, and Sleep

If you're the only person who uses your Mac, finishing up a work session is simple. You can either turn off the machine or simply let it go to sleep, in any of several ways.

Sleep Mode

It's clear that Apple expects its customers *not* to shut down their machines between sessions, because the company has gone to great lengths to make doing so inconvenient. (For example, you have to save your work in all open programs before you can shut down.)

That's OK. *Sleep mode* (called Standby on the PC) consumes very little power, keeps everything you were doing open and in memory, and wakes the Mac up almost immediately when you press a key or click the mouse. To make your machine sleep, use any of these techniques:

- **Close the lid.** (Hint: This tip works primarily on laptops.)

- **Choose ⌘→Sleep.** Or press Option-⌘-⏏.

- **Press Control-⏏** (or Control-F12, if you don't have a ⏏ key). In the dialog box shown in Figure 1-4, click Sleep (or type *S*).

- **Press the power button (⏻) on your machine.** On desktop models, doing so makes it sleep immediately; on laptops, you get the dialog box shown in Figure 1-4.

Figure 1-4:
Once the Shut Down dialog box appears, you can press the S key to choose Sleep, R for Restart, Esc for Cancel, or Return for Shut Down.

Are you sure you want to shut down your computer now?

Restart | Sleep | Cancel | Shut Down

- **Hold down the Play/Pause button on your remote for 3 seconds.** Many Mac models come, or used to come, with Apple's tiny white remote control.

- **Just walk away,** confident that the Energy Saver setting described on page 488 will send the machine off to dreamland automatically at the specified time.

Restart

You shouldn't have to restart the Mac very often—only in times of severe trouble-shooting mystification, in fact. Here are a few ways to do it:

- **Choose ⌘→Restart.** A confirmation dialog box appears; click Restart (or press Return).

Tip: If you press Option as you release the mouse on the ⌘→Restart command, then you won't be bothered by an "Are you sure?" confirmation box.

- **Press Control-⌘-⏏.** (If you don't have that key, substitute F12.)

- **Press Control-⏏** to summon the dialog box shown in Figure 1-4; click Restart (or type *R*).

Shut Down

To shut down your machine completely (when you don't plan to use it for more than a couple of days, when you plan to transport it, and so on), do one of the following:

- **Choose ⌘→Shut Down.** A simple confirmation dialog box appears; click Shut Down (or press Return).

Tip: Once again, if you press Option as you release the mouse, no confirmation box appears.

- **Press Control-Option-⌘-⏏.** (It's not as complex as it looks—the first three keys are all in a tidy row to the left of the space bar.)
- **Press Control-⏏ (or Control-F12)** to summon the dialog box shown in Figure 1-4. Click Shut Down (or press Return).
- **Wait.** If you've set up the Energy Saver preferences (page 490) to shut down the Mac automatically at a specified time, then you don't have to do anything.

Log Out

If you share your Mac with other people, then you should *log out* when you're done. Doing so ensures that your stuff is safe from the evil and the clueless when you're out of the room. To do it, choose →Log Out (or press Shift-⌘-Q). When the confirmation dialog box appears, click Log Out (or press Return), or just wait for 2 minutes. The Mac hides your world from view and displays the login dialog box, ready for the next victim.

Another option is to use *fast user switching*—a feature that lets you switch from one user to another without actually logging out, just as in Windows XP or Vista. With fast user switching turned on, your Mac can have several people logged in at once, although only one person at a time actually sees his own desktop.

In either case, this whole accounts system is described in much more detail in Chapter 13.

Tip: If you press the Option key as you release the mouse when choosing the Restart, Shut Down, or Log Out commands, you eliminate the "Are you sure?" confirmation dialog box. The mouse clicks you save each time can really add up.

The Menu Bar

It won't take you long to discover that on the Macintosh, there's only one menu bar. It's always at the top of the screen. The names of these menus, and the commands inside them, change to suit the window you're currently using. That's different from Windows, where a separate menu bar appears at the top of *every* window.

Mac and Windows devotees can argue the relative merits of these two approaches until they're blue in the face. All that matters, though, is that you know where to look when you want to reach for a menu command. On the Mac, you always look upward.

Finder = Windows Explorer

In Mac OS X, the "home base" program—the one that appears when you first turn on the machine and shows you the icons of all your folders and files—is called the Finder. This is where you manage your folders and files, throw things away, manipulate disks, and so on. (You may also hear it called the *desktop,* since the items you find there mirror the files and folders you might find on a real-life desktop.)

Getting used to the term "Finder" is worthwhile, though, because it comes up so often. For example, the first icon on your Dock is labeled Finder, and clicking it always takes you back to your desktop.

Dock = Taskbar

At the bottom of almost every Mac OS X screen sits a tiny row of photorealistic icons. This is the Dock, a close parallel to the Windows taskbar. (As in Windows, it may be hidden or placed on the left or right edge of the screen instead—but those are options primarily preferred by power users and eccentrics.)

The Dock displays the icons of all your open windows and programs, which are denoted by small, glowing dots beneath their icons. Clicking these icons opens the corresponding files, folders, disks, documents, and programs. If you click and hold (or right-click) an open program's icon, you'll see a pop-up list of the open windows in that program, along with Quit and a few other commands.

When you close a program, its icon disappears from the Dock (unless you've secured it there for easy access, as described on page 70).

Tip: You can cycle through the various open programs on your Mac by holding down the ⌘ key and pressing Tab repeatedly. (Sound familiar? It's just like Alt-Tabbing in Windows.) And if you just *tap* ⌘-Tab, you bounce back and forth between the two programs you've used most recently.

What you may find confusing at first, though, is that the Dock also performs one function of the Windows Start menu: It provides a "short list" of programs and files that you use often, for easy access. To add a new icon to the Dock, just drag it there (put programs to the left of the divider line; everything else goes on the right). To remove an icon from the Dock, just drag it away. As long as that item isn't actually open at the moment, it disappears from the Dock with a little animated puff of smoke when you release the mouse button.

The bottom line: On the Mac, a single interface element—the Dock—exhibits characteristics of *both* the Start menu (it lists frequently used programs) and the taskbar (it lists currently open programs and files). (The Windows 7 taskbar does the same thing.)

If you're still confused, Chapter 2 should help clear things up.

Menulets = Tray

Most Windows fans refer to the row of tiny status icons at the lower-right corner of the screen as the *tray,* even though Microsoft's official term is the *notification area.* (Why use one syllable when eight will do?)

Macintosh fans wage a similar battle of terminology when it comes to the little menu-bar icons shown in Figure 1-5. Apple calls them Menu Extras, but Mac fans prefer to call them *menulets.*

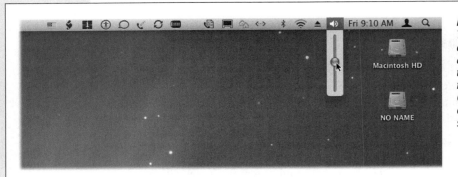

Figure 1-5:
These little guys are the direct descendants of the controls once found on the Mac OS 9 Control Strip or the Windows system tray.

In any case, these menu-bar icons are cousins of the Windows tray—that is, each is both an indicator and a menu that provides direct access to certain settings in System Preferences. One menulet lets you adjust your Mac's speaker volume, another lets you change the screen resolution, another shows you the remaining power in your laptop battery, and so on.

Making a menulet appear usually involves turning on a certain checkbox. These checkboxes lurk on the various panes of *System Preferences* (Chapter 15), which is the Mac equivalent of the Control Panel. (To open System Preferences, choose its name from the menu, or click the gears icon on the Dock.)

Here's a rundown of the most useful Apple menulets, complete with instructions on where to find this magic on/off checkbox for each.

Tip: The following descriptions indicate the official, authorized steps for installing a menulet. There is, however, a folder on your hard drive that contains *25 of them* in a single window, so that you can install any of them with a quick double-click. To find them, open your hard drive→System→Library→CoreServices→Menu Extras folder.

- **AirPort** lets you turn your WiFi (wireless networking) circuitry on or off, join existing wireless networks, and create your own private ones. *To find the "Show" checkbox:* Open System Preferences→Network. Click AirPort.

Tip: Once you've installed this menulet, you can Option-click it to produce a secret menu full of details about the wireless network you're on right now. You see its channel number, password-security method (WEP, WPA, None, whatever), speed, and such geeky details as the MCS Index and RSSI.

- **Battery** shows how much power remains in your laptop's battery, how much time is left to charge it, whether it's plugged in, and more. Using the Show submenu, you can control whether the menulet appears as an hours-and-minutes-remaining display (2:13), a percentage-remaining readout (43%), or a simple battery-icon gauge that hollows out as the charge runs down. *To find the "Show" checkbox:* Open System Preferences→Energy Saver.

- **Bluetooth** connects to Bluetooth devices, "pairs" your Mac with a cellphone, lets you send or receive files wirelessly (without the hassle of setting up a wireless network), and so on. *To find the "Show" checkbox:* Open System Preferences→Bluetooth.

- **Clock** is the menu-bar clock that's been sitting at the upper-right corner of your screen from Day One. Click it to open a menu where you can check today's date, convert the menu-bar display to a tiny analog clock, and so on. *To find the "Show" checkbox:* Open System Preferences→Date & Time. On the Clock tab, turn on "Show the date and time." That's where you can also opt to display the date and the day of the week.

- **Displays** adjusts screen resolution. On Macs with a projector or second monitor attached, it lets you turn *screen mirroring* on or off—a tremendous convenience to anyone who gives PowerPoint-type presentations. *To find the "Show" checkbox:* Open System Preferences→Displays→Display tab.

- **iChat** is a quick way to let the world know, via iChat and the Internet (Chapter 12), that you're away from your keyboard, or available and ready to chat. Via the Buddy List command, it's also a quick way to open iChat itself. *To find the "Show" checkbox:* Open iChat; it's in your Applications folder. Choose iChat→Preferences→ General.

- **Spaces** ties into Snow Leopard's virtual-screens feature (called Spaces and described in Chapter 4). The menulet lets you choose which of your multiple virtual screens you want to see. *To find the "Show" checkbox:* Open System Preferences→Spaces.

- **Sync** is useful only if you have a MobileMe account (Chapter 10)—but in that case, it's *very* handy. It lets you start and stop the synchronization of your Mac's Web bookmarks, Calendar, Address Book, Keychains, and email with your other Macs, Windows PCs, and iPhones across the Internet, and it always lets you know the date of your last sync. *To find the "Show" checkbox:* Open System Preferences→MobileMe, and then click Sync.

Tip: If you Option-click this menulet, you get a breakdown of data types—Calendar, Address Book, bookmarks, and so on—and a listing of when each was last synchronized with MobileMe.

- **TextInput** switches among different *text input modes.* For example, if your language uses a different alphabet, like Russian—or thousands of characters, like Chinese—this menulet summons and dismisses the alternative keyboards and input methods you need. Details are on page 166. *To find the "Show" checkbox:* Open System Preferences→Language & Text→Input Sources.

- **Time Machine** lets you start and stop Time Machine backups (see page 277). *To find the "Show" checkbox:* Open System Preferences→Time Machine.

- **User** identifies the account holder (Chapter 13) who's logged in at the moment. To make this menulet appear (in bold, at the far-right end of the menu bar), turn on *fast user switching,* which is described on page 427.

- **Volume,** of course, adjusts your Mac's speaker or headphone volume. *To find the "Show" checkbox:* Open System Preferences→Sound.

- **VPN** stands for virtual private networking, which allows you to tap into a corporation's network so you can, for example, check your work email from home. You can use the menulet to connect and disconnect, for example. *To find the "Show" checkbox:* Open System Preferences→Network. Click the name of your VPN.

- **WWAN** is useful only if you've equipped your Mac with one of those glorious *cellular modems,* sold by Verizon, Sprint, AT&T, or T-Mobile. These little USB sticks get you onto the Internet wirelessly at near-cable-modem speeds (in big cities, anyway), no WiFi required—for $60 a month. And this menulet lets you start and stop that connection. *To find the "Show" checkbox:* Open System Preferences→Network. Click the name of your cellular modem.

To remove a menulet, ⌘-drag it off your menu bar, or turn off the corresponding checkbox in System Preferences. You can also rearrange menulets by ⌘-dragging them horizontally.

These little guys are useful, good-looking, and respectful of your screen space. The world could use more inventions like menulets.

Keyboard Differences

Mac and PC keyboards are subtly different. Making the switch involves two big adjustments: Figuring out where the special Windows keys went (like Alt and Ctrl)—and figuring out what to do with the special Macintosh keys (like ⌘ and Option).

Where the Windows Keys Went

Here's how to find the Macintosh equivalents of familiar PC keyboard keys:

- **Ctrl key.** The Macintosh offers a key labeled Control (or, on laptops, "ctrl"), but it isn't the equivalent of the PC's Ctrl key. The Mac's Control key is primarily for helping you "right-click" things, as described earlier.

Instead, the Macintosh equivalent of the *Windows* Ctrl key is the ⌘ key. It's right next to the space bar. It's pronounced "command," although novices can often be heard calling it the "pretzel key," "Apple key," or "clover key."

Most Windows Ctrl-key combos correspond perfectly to ⌘ key sequences on the Mac. The Save command is now ⌘-S instead of Ctrl+S, Open is ⌘-O instead of Ctrl+O, and so on.

Note: Mac keyboard shortcuts are listed at the right side of each open menu, just as in Windows. Unfortunately, they're represented in the menu with goofy symbols instead of their true key names. Here's your cheat sheet to the menu keyboard symbols: ⇧ represents the Shift key, ⌥ means the Option key, and ^ refers to the Control key.

- **Alt key.** On North American Mac keyboards, a key on the bottom row of the Macintosh keyboard is labeled both Alt and Option. This is the closest thing the Mac offers to the Windows Alt key.

   In many situations, keyboard shortcuts that involve the Alt key in Windows use the Option key on the Mac. For example, in Microsoft Word, the keyboard shortcut for the Split Document Window command is *Alt*+Ctrl+S in Windows, but *Option*-⌘-T on the Macintosh.

   Still, these two keys aren't exactly the same. Whereas the Alt key's most popular function is to control the menus in Windows programs, the Option key on the Mac is a "miscellaneous" key that triggers secret functions and secret characters.

   For example, when you hold down the Option key as you click the Close or Minimize button on a Macintosh window, you close or minimize *all* open desktop windows. And if you press the Option key while you type *R*, *G*, or *2*, you get the ®, ©, and ™ symbols in your document, respectively. (See page 170 to find out how you can see which letters turn into which symbols when you press Option.)

- ⊞ **key.** As you probably could have guessed, there is no Windows-logo key on the Macintosh. Then again, there's no Start menu to open by pressing it, either.

Tip: Just about any USB keyboard works on the Mac, even if the keyboard was originally designed to work with a PC. Depending on the manufacturer of the keyboard, the Windows-logo key may work just like the Mac's ⌘ key.

- **Backspace and Delete.** On the Mac, the backspace key is labeled Delete, although it's in exactly the same place as the Windows Backspace key.

   The Delete key in Windows (technically, the *forward delete* key, because it deletes the character to the right of the insertion point) is a different story. On a desktop Macintosh, it's labeled with *Del* and the ⌦ symbol.

   On small Mac keyboards (like laptop keyboards), this key is missing. You can still perform a forward delete, however, by pressing the regular Delete key while pressing the Fn key in the corner of the keyboard.

• **Enter.** Most full-size Windows keyboards have *two* Enter keys: one at the right side of the alphabet keyboard, and one in the lower-right corner of the number pad. They're identical in function; pressing either one serves to "click" the OK button in a dialog box, for example.

On the Mac, the big key on the number pad still says Enter, but the key on the alphabet keyboard is labeled Return. Most of the time, their function is identical—once again, either can "click" the OK button of a dialog box. Every now and then, though, you'll run across a Mac program where Return and Enter do different things. In Microsoft Word for Mac OS X, for example, Shift-*Return* inserts a line break, but Shift-*Enter* creates a page break.

'What the Special Mac Keys Do

So much for finding the Windows keys you're used to. There's another category of keys worth discussing: those on the modern Macintosh keyboard you've never seen before.

To make any attempt at an explanation even more complicated, Apple's keyboards keep changing. The one you're using right now, however, is probably one of these models:

• **The current keyboard,** usually aluminum, where the keys are flat little jobbers that poke up through square holes in the keyboard (Figure 1-6). That's what you get on current laptops, wired keyboards, and Bluetooth wireless keyboards.

Figure 1-6:
On the top row of aluminum Mac keyboards, the F-keys have dual functions. Ordinarily, tapping the F1 through F4 keys correspond to Screen Dimmer, Screen Brighter, Exposé, and Dashboard. Pressing the Fn key in the corner changes their personalities.

• **The older, plastic desktop keyboard,** or the white or black plastic laptop one.

Tip: To see closeups of Apple's current wired and wireless keyboards, visit www.apple.com/keyboard.

Here, then, is a guided tour of the non-typewriter keys on the modern Mac keyboard.

- **Fn.** How are you supposed to pronounce Fn? Not "function," certainly; after all, the F-keys on the top row are already known as function keys. And not "fun"; goodness knows, the Fn key isn't particularly hilarious to press.

  What it *does,* though, is quite clear: It changes the purpose of certain keys. That's a big deal on laptops, which don't have nearly as many keys as desktop keyboards. So for some of the less commonly used functions, you're supposed to press Fn and a regular key. (For example, Fn turns the ↑ key into a Page Up key, which scrolls upward by one screenful.)

Note: On most Mac keyboards, the Fn key is in the lower-left corner. The exception is the full-size Apple desktop keyboard (the one with a numeric keypad); there, the Fn key is in the little block of keys between the letter keys and the number pad.

You'll find many more Fn examples in the following paragraphs:

- **Numeric keypad.** The number-pad keys do exactly the same thing as the numbers at the top of the keyboard. But with practice, typing things like phone numbers and prices is much faster with the number pad, since you don't have to look down at what you're doing.

- ☼, ☀ **(F1, F2).** These keys control the brightness of your screen. Usually, you can tone it down a bit when you're in a dark room, or when you want to save laptop battery power; you'll want to crank it up in the sun.

- ▦ **(F3).** This one fires up Exposé, the handy window-management feature described on page 121.

- ☉ **(F4).** Tap this key to open Dashboard, the archipelago of tiny, single-purpose widgets like Weather, Stocks, and Movies. Dashboard is described in detail beginning on page 148.

- ☼, ☼ **(F5, F6).** Most recent Mac laptops have light-up *keys,* which is very handy indeed when you're typing in the dark. The key lights are supposed to come on automatically when it's dark out, but you can also control the illumination yourself by tapping these keys. (On most other Macs, the F5 and F6 keys aren't assigned to anything. They're free for you to use as you see fit.)

- ◄◄, ►ıı, and ►► **(F7, F8, F9).** These keys work in the programs you'd expect: iTunes, QuickTime Player, DVD Player, and other programs where it's handy to have Rewind, Play/Pause, and Fast-forward buttons.

Tip: Tap the ◄◄ or ►► key to skip to the previous or next track or chapter. Hold it down to rewind or fast-forward.

Weirdly, the ►ıı key is hard-wired to open the iTunes program. And no, you can't change that assignment! (Fortunately, when you're already in a playback program like DVD Player or QuickTime Player, the key resumes its duties as the Play/Pause control.)

- ◀, ◀), ◀)) (F10, F11, F12). These three keys control your speaker volume. The ◀ key means Mute; tap it once to cut off the sound completely and again to restore its previous level. Tap the ◀) repeatedly to make the sound level lower, the ◀)) key to make it louder.

  With each tap, you see a big white version of each key's symbol on your screen, and you hear a little audio pop—your Mac's little nod to let you know it understands your efforts. (Press Shift to silence the pop sound.)

- ⏏. This is the Eject key. When there's a CD or DVD in your Mac, tap this key to make the computer spit it out. If your Mac has a DVD *tray* (rather than just a slot), then hold down this button for about a second to make the tray slide open.

- **Home, End.** "Home" and "End" mean "jump to the top or bottom of the window." If you're looking at a list of files, the Home and End keys jump to the top or bottom of the list. In iPhoto, they jump to the first or last photo in your collection. In iMovie, the Home key jumps your movie to the very beginning. In Safari, they take you to the top or bottom of the Web page.

  (In Word, they jump to the beginning or end of the line. But then again, Microsoft has always had its own ways of doing things.)

  On keyboards without a dedicated block of number keys, you get these functions by holding down Fn as you tap the ← and → keys.

- **Pg Up, Pg Down.** These keys scroll up or down by one screenful. The idea is to let you scroll through word processing documents, Web pages, and lists without having to use the mouse.

  On keyboards without a numeric keypad, you get these functions by pressing Fn plus the ↑ and ↓ keys.

- **Clear.** Clear (on the full-size desktop keyboard only) gets rid of whatever you've highlighted, but without putting a copy on the invisible Clipboard, as the Cut command would do.

- **Esc.** Esc stands for Escape, and it means "cancel." It's fantastically useful. It closes dialog boxes, closes menus, and exits special modes like Quick Look, Front Row, slideshows, screen savers, and so on. Get to know it.

- **Delete.** The backspace key.

- ⌦. Many a Mac fan goes for years without discovering the handiness of this delightful little key: the Forward Delete key. Whereas Delete backspaces over whatever letter is just to the *left* of the insertion point, this one (labeled Del on older keyboards) deletes whatever is just to the *right* of the insertion point. It really comes in handy when, for example, you've clicked into some text to make an edit—but wound up planting your cursor in just the wrong place.

  The full-size Apple keyboard has a dedicated key for this. On all other keyboards, you get this function by holding down Fn as you tap the regular Delete key.

- **Return and Enter.** In almost all programs, these keys do the same thing: wrap your typing to the next line. When a dialog box is on the screen, tapping the Return or Enter key is the same as clicking the confirmation button (like OK or Done). Very few programs treat these keys differently, although Microsoft Excel is one of them.

- ⌘. This key triggers keyboard shortcuts for menu items.

- **Control.** The Control key triggers shortcut menus, as described on page 13.

- **Option.** The Option key (labeled Alt in some countries) is sort of a "miscellaneous" key. It's the equivalent of the Alt key in Windows.

  It lets you access secret features—you'll find them described all through this book— and type special symbols. For example, you press Option-4 to get the ¢ symbol and Option-y to get the ¥ (yen) symbol.

- **Help.** In the Finder, Microsoft programs, and a few other places, this key opens up the electronic help screens. But you'd guessed that.

The Complicated Story of the Function Keys

As the previous section makes clear, the F-keys at the top of modern Mac keyboards come with predefined functions. They control screen brightness, keyboard brightness, speaker volume, music playback, and so on.

But they didn't always. Before Apple gave F9, F10, and F11 to the fast-forward and speaker-volume functions, those keys controlled the Exposé window-management function described on page 121.

So the question is: What if you don't *want* to trigger the hardware features of these keys? What if you want pressing F1 to mean "F1" (which opens the Help window in some programs)? What if you want F9, F10, and F11 to control Exposé's three modes, as they once did?

For that purpose, you're supposed to press the Fn key. The Fn key (lower-left on small keyboards, center block of keys on the big ones) switches the function of the function keys. In other words, pressing Fn *and* F10 triggers an Exposé feature, even though the key has a Mute symbol (◄) painted on it.

But here's the thing: What if you decide that you use those F-keys for software features (like Cut, Copy, Paste, and Exposé) *more often* than the hardware features (like brightness and volume)?

In that case, you can reverse the logic, so that pressing the F-keys *alone* triggers software functions, and they govern brightness and audio only when you're pressing Fn. To do that, choose →System Preferences→Keyboard. Turn on the checkbox "Use all F1, F2, etc. keys as standard function keys."

And that's it. From now on, you press the Fn key to get the functions painted on the keys (◄◄, ►ıı, ►►, ◄, ◄ı), ◄ı))↑ ⁙, ⁙, and so on).

Disk Differences

Working with disks is very different on the Mac. Whereas Windows is designed to show the names (letters) and icons for your disk *drives,* the Mac shows you the names and icons of your *disks.* You'll never, ever see an icon for an empty drive, as you do on Windows.

As soon as you insert, say, a CD, you see its name and icon appear on the screen. In fact, *every* disk inside, or attached to, a Macintosh is represented on the desktop by an icon (see Figure 1-7). (Your main hard drive's icon may or may not appear in the upper-right corner, depending on your settings in Finder→Preferences.)

Figure 1-7:
You may see all kinds of disks on the Mac OS X desktop (shown here: hard drive, CD, iPod, iDisk)—or none at all, if you've chosen to hide them using the Finder→Preferences command. But chances are pretty good you won't be seeing many floppy disk icons.

If you do decide to hide your disk icons, you can always get to them as you do in Windows: by opening the Computer window (Go→Computer).

If you prefer the Windows look, in which no disk icons appear on the desktop, it's easy enough to recreate it on the Mac; choose Finder→Preferences and turn off the four checkboxes you see there ("Hard disks," "External disks," "CDs, DVDs, and iPods," and "Connected servers.")

Ejecting a disk from the Mac is a little bit different, too, whether it's a CD, DVD, USB flash drive, shared network disk, iDisk, iPod, or external hard drive. You can go about it in any of these ways:

• Hold down the ⏏ key on your keyboard (CDs and DVDs only).

• Right-click the disk's desktop icon. From the shortcut menu that appears, choose "Eject [whatever the disk's name is]."

• Click the disk's icon and then choose File→"Eject [disk's name]" (or press ⌘-E).

- Drag the icon of the disk onto the Trash icon at the end of the Dock. (You'll see its icon turn into a giant ⏏ symbol, the Mac's little acknowledgment that it knows what you're trying to do.)

For you, the Windows veteran, the main thing to remember here is that you *never eject a Macintosh disk by pushing the Eject button* on the disk drive itself (if there even is one). Doing so usually has no effect, but on the rare occasion that it does, you could end up seriously confusing Mac OS X.

Where Your Stuff Is

If you open the icon for your main hard drive (Macintosh HD), from the Go→ Computer window, for example, all you'll find in the Macintosh HD window is a set of folders called Applications, Library, and Users.

Most of these folders aren't very useful to you, the Mac's human companion. They're there for Mac OS X's own use (which is why Apple no longer puts the Macintosh HD icon on the desktop of a new Mac, as it did for 25 years). Think of your main hard drive window as storage for the operating system itself, which you'll access only for occasional administrative purposes.

In fact, the folders you really do care about boil down to these:

Applications Folder

Applications is Apple's word for *programs*.

When it comes to managing your programs, the Applications folder (which you can open by choosing Go→Applications) is something like the Program Files folder in Windows—but without the worry. You should feel free to open this folder and double-click things. In fact, that's exactly what you're supposed to do. This is your complete list of programs. (What's on your Dock is more like a Greatest Hits subset.)

Better yet, on the Mac, programs bear their real, plain-English names, like *Microsoft Word,* rather than eight-letter abbreviations, like *WINWORD.EXE.* Most are self-contained in a single icon, too (rather than being composed of hundreds of little support files), which makes copying or deleting them extremely easy.

Home Folder

Your documents, files, and preferences, meanwhile, sit in an important folder called your *Home folder.* Inside (Figure 1-8) are folders that closely resemble the My Documents, My Pictures, and My Music folders on the Windows versions of old. (The "My" prefix disappeared in Windows Vista, but you get the point.)

Mac OS X is rife with shortcuts for opening this all-important folder.

- Choose Go→Home.

- Press Shift-⌘-H.

- Click the Home icon in the Sidebar (page 33).

• Click the ⌂ icon on the Dock. (If you don't see it there, choose Finder→Preferences→Sidebar and turn on the ⌂ checkbox in the list of Places.)

Within your Home folder, you'll find another set of standard Mac folders. (You can tell the Mac considers them holy because they have special logos on their folder icons.) Except as noted, you're free to rename or delete them; Mac OS X creates the following folders solely as a convenience:

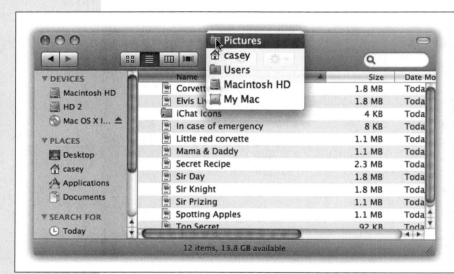

Figure 1-8:
Control-click (or right-click, or ⌘-click) a Finder window's title bar to summon the hidden folder hierarchy menu. This trick also works in most other Mac OS X programs. For example, you can ⌘-click a document window's title to find out where the document is actually saved on your hard drive.

• **Desktop.** When you drag an icon out of a folder or disk window and onto your Mac OS X desktop, it may appear to show up on the desktop. But that's just an optical illusion, a visual convenience. In truth, nothing in Mac OS X is really on the desktop. It's actually in this Desktop folder, and mirrored on the desktop area.

You can entertain yourself for hours by proving this point to yourself. If you drag something out of your Desktop folder, it also disappears from the actual desktop. And vice versa. (You're not allowed to delete or rename this folder.)

• **Documents.** Apple suggests that you keep your actual work files in this folder. Sure enough, whenever you save a new document (when you're working in Keynote or Word, for example), the Save As box proposes storing the new file in this folder, as described in Chapter 4.

Your programs may also create folders of their own here. For example, you may find a Microsoft User Data folder for your Entourage email, a Windows folder for use with Parallels or VMWare Fusion (Chapter 8), and so on.

• **Library.** The main Library folder (the one in your main hard drive window) contains folders for your Mac's system-wide fonts, preferences, help files, and so on.

You have your *own* Library folder, too, right there in your Home folder. It stores the same kinds of things—but they're *your* fonts, your preferences, and so on.

- **Movies, Music, Pictures.** These folders, of course, are designed to store multimedia files. The various Mac OS X programs that deal with movies, music, and pictures will propose these specialized folders as storage locations. For example, when you plug a digital camera into a Mac, the iPhoto program automatically begins to download the photos on it—and stores them in the Pictures folder. Similarly, iMovie is programmed to look for the Movies folder when saving its files, and iTunes stores its MP3 files in the Music folder.

- **Public.** If you're on a network, or if others use the same Mac when you're not around, this folder can be handy: It's the "Any of you guys can look at these files" folder. Other people on your network, as well as other people who sit down at this machine, are allowed to see whatever you've put in here, even if they don't have your password. (If your Mac isn't on an office network and isn't shared, you can throw this folder away.) More details on sharing and networking on the Mac are in Chapter 14.

- **Sites.** Mac OS X has a built-in Web server: software that turns your Mac into a Web site that people on your network—or, via the Internet, all over the world—can connect to. This Mac OS X feature relies on a program called the Apache Web server, which is so highly regarded in the Unix community that programmers lower their voices when they mention it. This is the folder where you will put the actual Web pages you want to make available to the Internet at large.

The rationale for forcing you to keep all of your stuff in a single folder is described in Chapter 13. (Windows 2000, XP, Vista, and 7 work very similarly.) For now, it's enough to note that the approach has some major advantages. Most notably, by keeping such tight control over which files go where, Mac OS X keeps itself pure—and very, very stable.

System Folder

This folder is the same idea as the Windows or WINNT folder on a PC, in that it contains hundreds of files that are critical to the functioning of the operating system. These files are so important that moving or renaming them could render the computer useless, as it would in Windows. And although there are thousands of files within, many are hidden for your protection.

For maximum safety and stability, you should ignore Mac OS X's System folder just as thoroughly as you ignored the old Windows folder.

Window Controls

As in Windows, a window on the Mac is framed by an assortment of doodads and gizmos (Figure 1-9). You'll need these to move a window, close it, resize it, scroll it, and so on. But once you get to know the ones on a Macintosh, you're likely to be pleased by the amount of thought those fussy perfectionists at Apple have put into their design.

Here's an overview of the various Mac OS X window-edge gizmos and what they do.

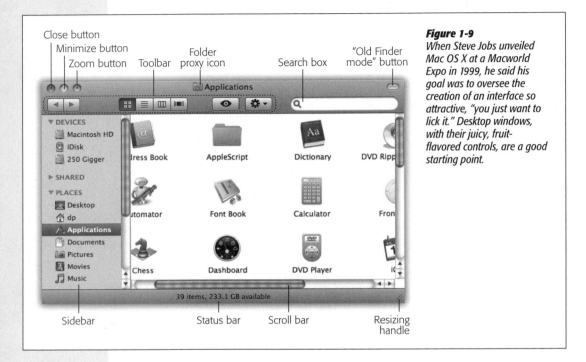

Close button
Minimize button
Zoom button   Toolbar   Folder proxy icon   Search box   "Old Finder mode" button

Figure 1-9
When Steve Jobs unveiled Mac OS X at a Macworld Expo in 1999, he said his goal was to oversee the creation of an interface so attractive, "you just want to lick it." Desktop windows, with their juicy, fruit-flavored controls, are a good starting point.

Sidebar   Status bar   Scroll bar   Resizing handle

Title Bar

When several windows are open, the darkened window name and colorful upper-left controls tell you which window is *active* (in front). Windows in the background have gray, dimmed lettering and gray upper-left control buttons. As in Windows, the title bar also acts as a *handle* that lets you move the entire window around on the screen.

Tip: Here's a nifty keyboard shortcut with no Windows equivalent: You can cycle through the different open windows in one program without using the mouse. Just press ⌘-` (that's the tilde key, to the left of the number 1 key). With each press, you bring a different window forward within the current program. It works both in the Finder and in your programs.

Perhaps more usefully, you can use Control-F4 to cycle through the open windows in *all* programs.

After you've opened one folder inside another, the title bar's secret *folder hierarchy menu* is an efficient way to backtrack—to return to the enclosing window. Figure 1-8 reveals everything about the process after this key move: pressing the ⌘ key as you click the name of the window. (You can release the ⌘ key immediately after clicking.)

Tip: Instead of using this title bar menu, you can also jump to the enclosing window by pressing ⌘-↑. Pressing ⌘-↓ takes you back into the folder you started in. (This makes more sense when you try it than when you read it.)

One more title bar trick: By double-clicking the title bar, you *minimize* the window (see page 32).

Tip: The Option key means "apply this action to all windows." For example, Option-double-clicking any title bar minimizes *all* desktop windows, sending them flying to the Dock. Option-clicking the Close button closes all open desktop windows, and so on. (The Option-key trick doesn't close all windows in every program, however—only those in the current program. Option-closing a Safari window closes *Safari* windows, but your desktop windows remain open. Moreover, Option-closing doesn't work at all in Microsoft Office programs.)

The Folder Proxy Icon

Virtually every Macintosh title bar features a small icon next to the window's name (Figure 1-10), representing the open window's actual folder or disk icon. In the Finder, dragging this tiny icon (technically called the *folder proxy icon*) lets you move or copy the folder to a different folder or disk, to the Trash, or into the Dock, without having to close the window first. (When clicking this proxy icon, hold down the mouse button for half a second, or until the icon darkens. Only then are you allowed to drag it.) It's a handy little function with no Windows equivalent.

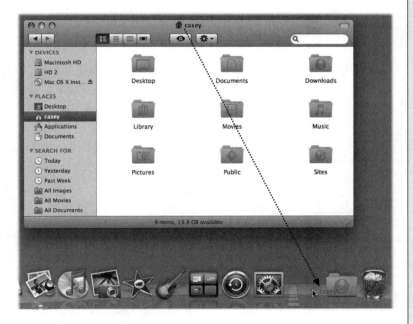

Figure 1-10:
When you find yourself confronting a Finder window that contains useful stuff, consider dragging its proxy icon to the Dock. You wind up installing its folder or disk icon there for future use. That's not the same as minimizing the window, which just puts the window icon into the Dock, and only temporarily at that. (Note: Most Mac OS X document windows also offer a proxy-icon feature, but produce only an alias when you drag the proxy to a different folder or disk.)

Tip: In some programs, including Microsoft Word, dragging this proxy icon lets you move the *actual file* to a different disk or folder—without even leaving the program. It's a great way to make a backup of the document you're working on without interrupting your work.

Close Button

As the tip of your cursor crosses the three buttons at the upper-left corner of a window, tiny symbols appear inside them: **✕**, **–**, and **+**. The most important one is the Close button, the red, droplet-like button in the upper-left corner (see Figure 1-10). It closes the window, exactly like the ✕ button at the upper-*right* corner in Windows. Learning to reach for the upper-left corner instead of the upper-right will probably confound your muscle memory for the first week of using the Macintosh.

If you can't break the old habit, learn the keyboard shortcut: ⌘-W (for *window*)—an easier keystroke to type than the Windows version (Alt+F4), which for most people is a two-handed operation. If you get into the habit of dismissing windows with that deft flex of your left hand, you'll find it far easier to close several windows in a row, because you don't have to aim for successive close buttons.

Tip: If, while working on a document, you see a tiny dot in the center of the Close button, Mac OS X is trying to tell you that you haven't yet saved your work. The dot goes away when you save the document.

Minimize Button

Click this yellow drop of gel to minimize any Mac window, sending it shrinking, with a genie-like animated effect, into the right end of the Dock, where it now appears as

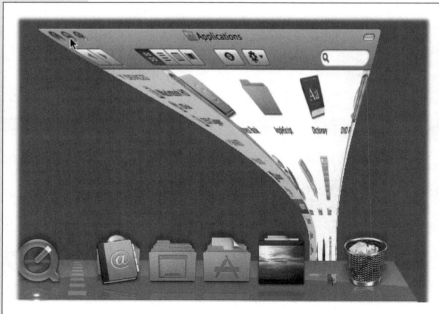

Figure 1-11:
Clicking the Minimize button sends a window scurrying down to the Dock, collapsing in on itself as though being forced through an invisible funnel. A tiny icon appears on the lower-right corner of its minimized image to identify the program it's running in.

an icon. It's exactly like minimizing a window in Windows, except that the window is now represented by a Dock icon rather than a taskbar button (Figure 1-11). To bring the window back to full size, click the newly created Dock icon. See Chapter 2 for more on the Dock.

Tip: You actually have a bigger target than the tiny minimize button. The entire striped title bar is a giant minimize button when you double-click anywhere on it. Or just press ⌘-M for Minimize.

Zoom Button

A click on this green geltab (see Figure 1-10) makes a desktop window just large enough to show you all the icons inside it. If your monitor isn't big enough to show all the icons in a window, then the zoom box resizes the window to show as many as possible. In either case, a second click on the zoom button restores the window to its original size. (The Window→Zoom Window command does the same thing.)

This should sound familiar: It's a lot like the Maximize button at the top right of a Windows window. On the Macintosh, however, the window rarely springs so big that it fills the *entire* screen, leaving a lot of empty space around the window contents; it only grows enough to show you as much of the contents as possible.

The Finder Sidebar

The Sidebar is the pane at the left side of every Finder window (and, by the way, also at the left side of every Open dialog box and full-sized Save dialog box). It's a list (identified in Figure 1-9) with as many as four different sections, each preceded by a collapsible heading:

* **Devices.** This section lists every storage device connected to, or installed inside, your Mac: hard drives, CDs, DVDs, iPods, memory cards, USB flash drives, and so on. The removable ones (CDs, DVDs, iPods, and so on) bear a little gray ⏏ logo, which you can click to eject that disk.

* **Shared.** Here it is: a complete list of the other computers on your network whose owners have turned on File Sharing, ready for access. See Chapter 14 for details.

POWER USERS' CLINIC

Smarter Minimized Document Windows

In the bad old days (up to late 2009), minimizing a bunch of documents could get really messy. Each one flew onto the Dock, creating a new icon there, creating a tighter and tighter squeeze, shrinking the Dock's icons until they were the size of Tic Tacs.

In Snow Leopard, you can have your document windows minimize themselves into their *program's* Dock icon, rather

than creating *new* Dock icons for themselves. That way, your Dock doesn't get any more crowded, and the icons on it don't keep shrinking away to atoms.

To turn on this feature, choose →System Preferences→ Dock. Turn on "Minimize windows into application icon."

So how do you get those windows back *out* of the Dock icon? You use Dock Exposé, which is described on page 125.

- **Places.** This primary section of the sidebar lists *places* (in this case, folders) where you might look for files and folders. Into this list, you can stick the icons of anything at all—files, programs, folders, disks, or whatever—for easy access.

  Each icon is a shortcut. For example, click the Applications icon to view the contents of your Applications folder in the main part of the window. And if you click the icon of a file or program here, it opens.

- **Searches.** The "folders" in this Sidebar section are actually canned searches that execute instantly when you click one. If you click Today, for example, the main window fills with all files and folders on your computer that you've changed today. Yesterday and Past Week work the same way.

  The All Images, All Movies, and All Documents searches round up everything in those file-type categories, no matter what folders they're actually sitting in.

  These insta-searches are very useful all by themselves, but what's even better is how easy it is to make your *own* search folders to put here. Page 114 has the details.

Fine-tuning the Sidebar

The beauty of this parking lot for containers is that it's so easy to set up with *your* favorite places. For example:

- **Remove** an icon by dragging it out of the Sidebar entirely. It vanishes with a puff of smoke (and even a little *whoof* sound effect). You haven't actually removed anything from your *Mac;* you've just unhitched its alias from the Sidebar.

Tip: You can't drag items out of the Shared list. Also, if you drag a Devices item out of the list, you'll have to choose Finder→Preferences→Sidebar (and turn on the appropriate checkbox) to put it back in.

- **Rearrange** the icons by dragging them up or down in the list. (You're not allowed to rearrange the computers listed in the Shared section, though.)

- **Install a new icon** by dragging it off your desktop (or out of a window) into any spot in the Places list of the Sidebar.

Tip: You can also highlight an icon wherever it happens to be and then choose File→Add to Sidebar, or just press ⌘-T.

- **Adjust the width** of the Sidebar by dragging its *right edge*—either the skinny divider line or the extreme right edge of the vertical scroll bar, if there is one. You "feel" a snap at the point when the line covers up about half of each icon's name. Any covered-up names sprout ellipses (…) to let you know (as in "Secret Salaries Spreadsh…").

- **Hide the Sidebar** by pressing ⌘-Option-S, which is the shortcut for the new View→Hide Sidebar command. Bring it back into view by pressing the same key combination (or using the Show Sidebar command).

Window Management

Mac OS X prefers to keep only one Finder window open at a time. That is, if a window called United States is filled with folders for the individual states, double-clicking the New York folder doesn't open a second window. Instead, the New York window replaces the United States window. Modern versions of Windows work exactly the same way (Figure 1-12).

So what if you've now opened inner folder B, and you want to backtrack to outer folder A? In that case, just click the tiny ◀ (Back) button or use one of these alternatives:

• Choose Go→Back.

• Press ⌘-[(left bracket).

• Press ⌘-↑.

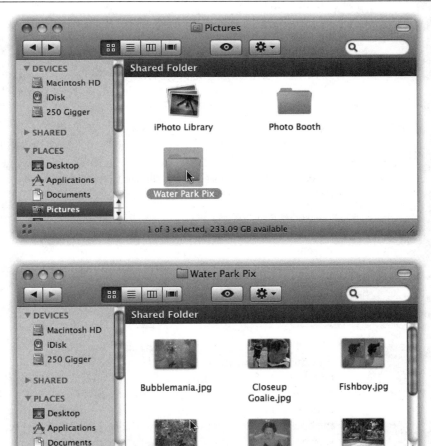

Figure 1-12:
To help you avoid window clutter, Apple has designed Mac OS X windows so that double-clicking a folder in a window (top) doesn't actually open another window (bottom). Every time you double-click a folder in an open window (except in column view), its contents replace whatever was previously in the window. If you double-click three folders in succession, you still wind up with just one open window.

None of that helps you, however, if you want to copy a file from one folder into another, or to compare the contents of two windows. In such cases, you'll probably want to see both windows open at the same time.

You can open a second window using any of these techniques:

• Choose File→New Finder Window (⌘-N).

Tip: The window that appears when you do this is your Home folder by default, but you can change that setting in Finder→Preferences→General.

• ⌘-double-click a disk or folder icon.

• Choose Finder→Preferences, and turn on "Always open folders in a new window." Now when you double-click a folder, it always opens into a new window.

Another alternative is to switch to "Old Finder mode" (not the official Apple terminology). When you click this button (shown in Figure 1-9), you enter a hidden-toolbar, hidden-Sidebar mode. (You can also enter this mode by pressing Option-⌘-T, the equivalent for the View→Hide Toolbar command.)

In this mode, two things happen. First, the Finder window toolbar slides out of sight, along with the Sidebar on the left. Second, double-clicking a folder now opens a new corresponding window.

You can return to regular Mac OS X mode by clicking the toolbar button again, by pressing Option-⌘-T again, or by choosing View→Show Toolbar.

Note: You'll find this little white toolbar-control nubbin in a number of toolbar-endowed programs, including Mail, Preview, and others. Clicking it always makes the toolbar go away.

Scroll Bars

In general, scroll bars work on the Mac just as they do in Windows.

Tip: One key difference: Out of the box, the Mac's scroll-up arrow and scroll-down arrow are nestled together, at the same end of the scroll bar. To "fix" them so that they sit at opposite ends as in Windows, choose ⌘→System Preferences. Click Appearance. Where it says "Place scroll arrows," click "At top and bottom."

Mac OS X, however, offers an option called "Scroll to here." Ordinarily, when you click into the scroll-bar track above or below the gelatinous handle, the window scrolls by one screenful. But your other option is to turn on "Scroll to here" mode in the Appearance panel of your System Preferences (see page 474). Now when you click in the scroll-bar track, the Mac considers the entire scroll bar a proportional map of the document and scrolls directly to the spot you clicked. That is, if you click at the very bottom of the scroll-bar track, you see the very last page.

It's worth noting, however, that the true speed expert eschews scroll bars altogether. The Mac has the usual complement of navigation keys: Page Up, Page Down, Home, and End. And if your mouse has a scroll wheel on the top, you can use it to scroll windows, too, without pressing any keys at all.

Resize Box

The lower-right corner of every standard Mac OS X window is ribbed, a design that's meant to imply that you can grip it by dragging. Doing so lets you resize and reshape the window, just as on the PC. One little bummer: You can't also change the shape of a Macintosh window by dragging its *edges,* as you can in Windows.

Path Bar

This little item appears when you choose View→Show Path Bar. It's a tiny map at the bottom of the window that shows where you are in the folder hierarchy. If it says Casey▸Pictures▸Picnic, well, then, by golly, you're looking at the contents of the Picnic folder, which is inside Pictures, inside your Home folder.

Tip: Each tiny folder icon in this display is fully operational. You can double-click it to open it, right-click it to open a shortcut menu, or even drag things into it.

Status Bar

The information strip at the bottom of a window tells you how many icons are in it ("14 items," for example) and the amount of free space remaining on the disk.

Terminology Differences

There are enough other differences between Mac and Windows to fill 15 pages. Indeed, that's what you'll find the end of this book: an alphabetical listing of every familiar Windows feature and where to find its equivalent on the Mac.

As you read both that section of the book and the chapters that precede it, however, you'll discover that some functions are almost identical in Mac OS X and Windows, but have different names. Here's a quick-reference summary:

Windows term	Macintosh term
Control Panel	System Preferences
Gadget	Widget
Drop-down menu	Pop-up menu
Program	Application
Properties	Get Info
Recycle Bin	Trash
Search command	Spotlight
Shortcuts	Aliases
Sidebar	Dashboard
Taskbar	Dock
Tray (notification area)	Menulets
Windows Explorer	Finder
Windows folder	System folder

With that much under your belt, you're well on your way to learning the ways of Mac OS X.

Folders, Dock, & Windows

Getting into Mac OS X

When you first turn on the Mac, an Apple logo greets you, soon followed by an animated, rotating "Please wait" gear cursor—and then you're in. No progress bar, no red tape.

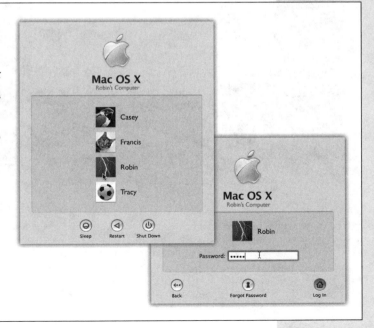

Figure 2-1:
Left: On Macs configured to accommodate different people at different times, this is one of the first things you see upon turning on the computer. Click your name. (If the list is long, you may have to scroll to find your name–or just type the first few letters of it.)

Right: At this point, you're asked to type in your password. Type it, and then click Log In (or press Return or Enter; pressing these keys usually "clicks" any blue, pulsing button in a dialog box). If you've typed the wrong password, the entire dialog box vibrates, in effect shaking its little dialog-box head, suggesting that you guess again. (See Chapter 13.)

CHAPTER 2: FOLDERS, DOCK, & WINDOWS

Logging In

What happens next depends on whether you're the Mac's sole proprietor or have to share it with other people in an office, school, or household.

- **If it's your own Mac,** and you've already been through the Mac OS X setup process described in Appendix A, no big deal. You arrive at the Mac OS X desktop.

- **If it's a shared Mac,** you may encounter the Login dialog box, shown in Figure 2-1. Click your name in the list (or type it, if there's no list).

If the Mac asks for your password, type it and then click Log In (or press Return). You arrive at the desktop. Chapter 13 offers much more on this business of user accounts and logging in.

The Elements of the Mac OS X Desktop

The *desktop* is the shimmering, three-dimensional Mac OS X landscape shown in Figure 2-2. On a new Mac, it's covered by a starry galaxy photo.

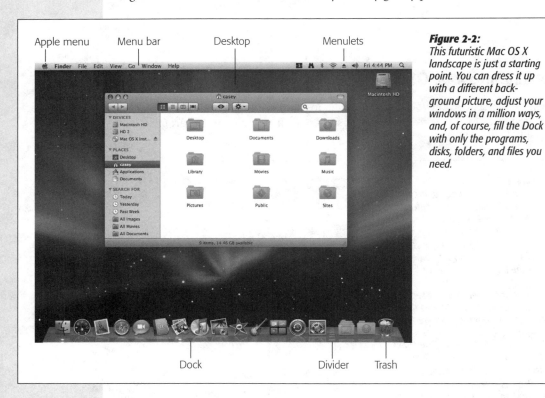

Apple menu   Menu bar   Desktop   Menulets

Dock   Divider   Trash

Figure 2-2:
This futuristic Mac OS X landscape is just a starting point. You can dress it up with a different background picture, adjust your windows in a million ways, and, of course, fill the Dock with only the programs, disks, folders, and files you need.

Most of the objects on your screen are nothing more than Mac versions of familiar elements. Here's a quick tour.

Disk icons

In the Mac world, the icons of your hard drive and any other disks attached to your Mac generally appear on your desktop for quick access.

Note: If you prefer the setup in Windows, where disks remain safely caged in the My Computer window—Snow Leopard can accommodate you. Choose Finder→Preferences, click General, and turn off the checkboxes of the disks whose icons you don't want on the desktop: hard disks, external disks, and so on.

From now on, you'll have to look in the Sidebar (page 33) or the Computer window (Go→Computer) to find those disk icons.

The Dock

This row of translucent, almost photographic icons is a launcher for the programs, files, folders, and disks you use often—and an indicator to let you know which programs are already open. They rest on what appears to be a polished, highly reflective shelf.

Because the Dock is such a critical component of Mac OS X, Apple has decked it out with enough customization controls to keep you busy experimenting for months. You can change its size, move it to the sides of your screen, hide it entirely, and so on. Page 62 begins a complete discussion of using and understanding the Dock.

The menu

The menu at the top left of the screen houses important Mac-wide commands like Sleep, Restart, and Shut Down. In a sense, it's like the Start menu on a diet: It lists recent programs, system-wide functions, and includes a quick way to jump to System Preferences.

The menu bar

The first menu in every program, in boldface, tells you at a glance what program you're in. The commands in this Application menu include About (which tells you what version of the program you're using), Preferences, Quit, and others like Hide Others and Show All (which help you control window clutter, as described on page 170).

The File and Edit menus come next, exactly as in Windows. The last menu is almost always Help. It opens a miniature Web browser that lets you search the online Mac Help files for explanatory text.

The Four Window Views

You can view the files and folders in a desktop window in any of four ways: as icons; as a single, tidy list; in a series of neat columns; or as giant document icons that you flip through like they're CDs in a record-store bin (called Cover Flow view). Some of these are sort of like the corresponding views in Windows; others, not so much. Figure 2-3 shows the four different views.

Every window remembers its view settings independently. You might prefer to look over your Applications folder in list view (because it's crammed with files and folders), but you may prefer to view the Pictures folder in icon or Cover Flow view, where the larger icons serve as previews of the photos.

To switch a window from one view to another, just click one of the four corresponding icons in the window's toolbar, as shown in Figure 2-3.

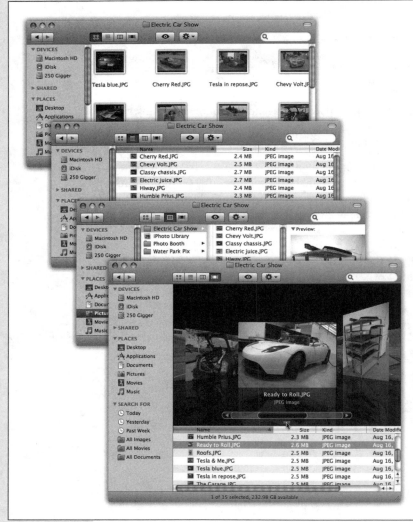

Figure 2-3:
From the top: The same window in icon, list, column, and Cover Flow views. Very full folders are best navigated in list or column views, but you may prefer to view emptier folders in icon or Cover Flow views, because larger icons are easier to preview and click.

Remember that in any view (icon, list, column, or Cover Flow), you can highlight an icon by typing the first few letters of its name. In icon, list, or Cover Flow view, you can also press Tab to highlight the next icon (in alphabetical order), or Shift-Tab to highlight the previous one.

You can also switch views by choosing View→as Icons (or View→as Columns, or View→as List, or View→as Cover Flow), which can be handy if you've hidden the toolbar. Or, for less mousing and more hardbodied efficiency, press ⌘-1, ⌘-2, ⌘-3, or ⌘-4 for icon, list, column, or Cover Flow views, respectively.

The following pages cover each of these views in greater detail.

Note: One common thread in the following discussions is the availability of the View Options palette, which lets you set up the sorting, text size, icon size, and other features of each view, either one window at a time or for *all* windows.

Apple gives you a million different ways to open View Options. You can choose View→Show View Options, or press ⌘-J, or choose Show View Options from the ✿ menu at the top of every window.

Icon View

In icon view, every file, folder, and disk is represented by a small picture—an *icon*. This humble image, a visual representation of electronic bits and bytes, is the cornerstone of the entire Macintosh religion. (Maybe that's why it's called an icon.)

Icon Size

You can scale your icons to almost any size without losing any quality or clarity. Just use the size slider at the bottom of any icon-view window, shown in Figure 2-4. Drag it to the right or left to make that window's icons larger or smaller. (For added fun, make little cartoon sounds with your mouth.)

Tip: Got a laptop? Then you can also make the icons larger or smaller by pinching or spreading two fingers on the trackpad, which may be quicker than fussing with the slider. Details on this feature (and the location of the on/off switch for it) are revealed on page 498.

Figure 2-4:
The Size slider (bottom right) lets you choose an icon size to suit your personality. For picture folders, it can often be very handy to pick a jumbo size, in effect creating a slide-sorter "light table" effect. In Snow Leopard, icons can be an almost ridiculously large 512 pixels square.

Best of the Summer

Aquarium Love.jpg
1,024 × 681

Bee Movie.mov
00:03

Florence & Pisa.jpg
1,024 × 681

Biker Man.jpg
1,024 × 768

True Love.jpg
1,024 × 681

Super Trouper.mp3
04:14

8 items, 11.57 GB available

Icon Previews

Snow Leopard expands the notion of "an icon is a representation of its contents" to an impressive extreme. As you can see in Figure 2-5, each icon actually looks like a miniature of the first page of the *real document.*

THE HALF STEP.pdf

Kelly Balloons.mov

Figure 2-5:
You can actually page through PDF and presentation icons, or play movies and sounds, right on their icons. During movie playback, you even get a circular progress bar around the Play/Pause button to let you know where you are in the movie.

Because you can make icons so enormous, you can actually watch movies, or read PDF and text documents, *right on their icons.*

To check out this feature, make the icons at least about an inch tall (64 pixels square). A Play button (▶) appears on any movie or sound file; as shown in Figure 2-5, ◀ and ▶ page buttons appear on a multipage document (like PDF, Pages, or even presentation documents like PowerPoint and Keynote). You can actually page through one of these documents right there on its icon, without having to open the program!

Tip: If you Option-click the little ◀ and ▶ buttons on a PDF, PowerPoint, or Keynote icon preview, you jump to the first or last page or slide in the document.

Icon View Options

Mac OS X offers a number of useful icon-view options, all of which are worth exploring. Start by opening any icon view window, and then choose View→Show View Options (⌘-J).

Always open in icon view

It's easy to set up your preferred look for *all folder windows* on your entire system. With one click on the "Use as Defaults" button (described below), you can change the window view of 20,000 folders at once—to icon view, list view, or whatever you like.

The "Always open in icon view" option lets you *override* that master setting, just for *this* window.

For example, you might generally prefer a neat list view with large text. But for your Pictures folder, it probably makes more sense to set up icon view, so you can see a thumbnail of each photo without having to open it.

That's the idea here. Open Pictures, change it to icon view, and then turn on "Always open in icon view." Now every folder on your Mac is in list view *except* Pictures.

Note: The wording of this item in the View Options dialog box changes according to the view you're in at the moment. In a list-view window, for example, it says "Always open in list view." In a Cover Flow–view window, it says "Always open in Cover Flow." And so on. But the function is the same: to override the *default* (master) setting.

Icon size

As noted, Snow Leopard makes it super easy to make all your icons bigger or smaller; just drag the "Icon size" slider in the lower-right corner of the window.

But for the benefit of old-timers who expect to find that slider *here,* in the View Options window, well, there's an identical slider here.

Grid spacing

You can control how closely spaced icons are in a window. If you want to see a lot of them without making the window bigger, you can pack 'em in like sardines. Figure 2-6 shows all.

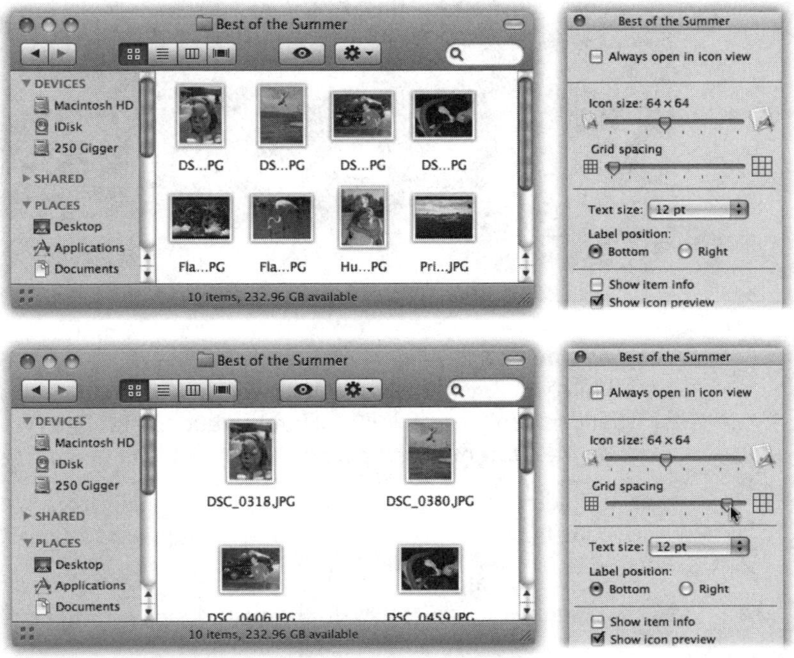

Figure 2-6:
Drag the "Grid spacing" slider to specify how tightly packed you want your icons to be. At the minimum setting (top), they're so crammed that it's almost ridiculous; you can't even see their names. But sometimes, you don't really need to. At more spacious settings (bottom), you get a lot more "white space."

Text size

Using this slider, you can adjust the type *size* for your icons. And for people with especially big or especially small screens—or people with aging retinas—this feature is handy indeed.

Label position

Click either Bottom or Right to indicate where you want an icon's *name* to appear, relative to its *icon*. As shown in Figure 2-7, it lets you create, in effect, a multiple-column list view in a single window.

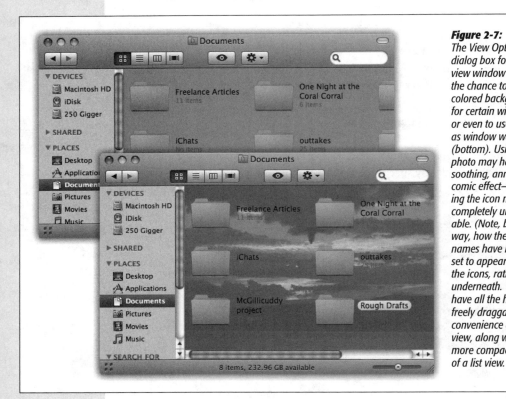

Figure 2-7:
The View Options dialog box for an icon view window offers the chance to create colored backgrounds for certain windows or even to use photos as window wallpaper (bottom). Using a photo may have a soothing, annoying, or comic effect—like making the icon names completely unreadable. (Note, by the way, how the icons' names have been set to appear beside the icons, rather than underneath. You now have all the handy, freely draggable convenience of an icon view, along with the more compact spacing of a list view.

Show item info

While you've got the View Options palette open, try turning on "Show item info." Suddenly you get a new line of information (in tiny blue type) for certain icons, saving you the effort of opening up the folder or file to find out what's in it. For example:

- **Folders.** The info line lets you know how many icons are inside each without having to open it up. Now you can spot empties at a glance.

- **Graphics files.** Certain other kinds of files may show a helpful info line, too. For example, graphics files display their dimensions in pixels.

- **Sounds and QuickTime movies.** The light-blue bonus line tells you how long the sound or movie takes to play. For example, an MP3 file might say "03' 08"," which means 3 minutes, 8 seconds.

- **.zip files.** On compressed archives like .zip files, you get to see the archive's total size on disk (like "48.9 MB").

You can see some of these effects illustrated in Figure 2-7.

Show icon preview

This option is what makes icons display their contents, as shown in Figure 2-5. If you turn it off, then icons no longer look like miniature versions of their contents. Photos no longer look like tiny photos, PDF and Word documents no longer display their contents, and so on. Everything takes on identical, generic icons (one for all text documents, one for all JPEG photos, and so on).

You might prefer this arrangement when, for example, you want to be able to pick out all the PDF files in a window full of mixed document types. Thanks to the matching icons, it's easy now.

Arrange by

For a discussion of this pop-up menu, see page 49.

Background

Here's another Mac OS X luxury that other operating systems can only dream about: You can fill the background of any icon view window on your Mac with a certain color—or even a photo.

Color-coordinating or "wallpapering" certain windows is more than just a gimmick. In fact, it can serve as a timesaving psychological cue. Once you've gotten used to the fact that your main Documents folder has a sky-blue background, you can pick it out like a sharpshooter from a screen filled with open windows. Color-coded Finder windows are also especially easy to distinguish at a glance when you've minimized them to the Dock.

Note: Background colors and pictures disappear in list, column, and Cover Flow views.

Once a window is open, choose View→View Options (⌘-J). The bottom of the resulting dialog box offers three choices, whose results are shown in Figure 2-7.

- **White.** This is the standard option (not shown).

- **Color.** When you click this button, you see a small rectangular button beside the word "Color." Click it to open the Color Picker (page 167), which you can use to choose a new background color for the window. (Unless it's April Fool's Day, pick a light color. If you choose a dark one—like black—you won't be able to make out the lettering of the icons' names.)

• **Picture.** If you choose this option, a Select button appears. Click it to open the Select a Picture dialog box, already open to your Library→Desktop Pictures folder. Now choose a graphics file—one of Apple's in the Desktop Pictures folder, or one of your own. When you click Select, you see that Mac OS X has superimposed the window's icons on the photo. As you can see in Figure 2-7, low-contrast or light-background photos work best for legibility.

Incidentally, the Mac has no idea what sizes and shapes your window may assume in its lifetime. Therefore, Mac OS X makes no attempt to scale down a selected photo to fit neatly into the window. If you have a high-res digital camera, therefore, you see only the upper-left corner of a photo in the window. For better results, use a graphics program to scale the picture down to something smaller than your screen resolution.

Use as Defaults

This harmless-looking button can actually wreak havoc—or restore order to your kingdom—with a single click. It applies the changes you've just made in the View Options dialog box to *all* windows on your Mac (instead of only the *frontmost* window).

If you set up the frontmost window with a colored background, big icons, small text, and a tight grid, and then you click Use as Defaults, you'll see that look in *every* disk or folder window you open.

You've been warned.

Fortunately, there are two auxiliary controls that can give you a break from all the sameness.

First, you can set up individual windows to be weirdo exceptions to the rule; see "Always open in icon view," above.

Second, you can *remove* any departures from the default window view—after a round of disappointing experimentation on a particular window, for example—using a secret button. To do so, choose View→Show View Options to open the View Options dialog box. Now hold down the Option key. The Use as Defaults button magically changes to say "Restore to Defaults," which means "Abandon all the changes I've foolishly made to the look of this window."

Keeping Icons Neat and Sorted

In general, you can drag icons anywhere within a window. For example, some people like to keep current project icons at the top of the window and move older stuff to the bottom.

If you'd like Mac OS X to impose a little discipline on you, however, it's easy enough to request a visit from an electronic housekeeper who tidies up your icons by aligning them neatly to an invisible grid. In Snow Leopard, you can even specify how tight or loose that grid is.

Grid alignment

Mac OS X offers an enormous number of variations on the "snap icons to the under-lying rows-and-columns grid" theme:

- **Aligning individual icons to the grid.** Press the ⌘ key while dragging an icon or several highlighted icons. (Don't press the key until after you begin to drag.) When you release the mouse, the icons you've moved all jump into neatly aligned positions.

- **Aligning all icons to the grid.** Choose View→Clean Up (if nothing is selected) or View→Clean Up Selection (if some icons are highlighted). Now all icons in the window, or those you've selected, jump to the closest positions on the invisible underlying grid.

    These same commands appear in the shortcut menu when you right-click anywhere inside an icon-view window, which is handier if you have a huge monitor.

Tip: If you press Option, you swap the wording of the command. Clean Up changes to read Clean Up Selection, and vice versa.

Note, by the way, that the grid alignment is only temporary. As soon as you drag icons around, or add more icons to the window, the newly moved icons wind up just as sloppily positioned as before you tidied up.

If you want the Mac to lock *all* icons to the closest spot on the grid *whenever* you move them, choose View→Show View Options (⌘-J); from the "Arrange by" pop-up menu, choose Snap to Grid.

Even then, though, you'll soon discover that none of these grid-snapping techniques move icons into the most compact possible arrangement. If one or two icons have wandered off from the herd to a far corner of the window, they're merely nudged to the grid points closest to their current locations. They aren't moved all the way back to the group of icons elsewhere in the window.

To solve that problem, use one of the sorting options described next.

Tip: You can always override the grid setting by pressing the ⌘ key when you drag. In other words, when grid-snapping is turned *off*, ⌘ makes your icons snap into position; when grid-snapping is turned *on*, ⌘ lets you drag an icon freely.

Sorted alignment

If you'd rather have icons sorted and bunched together on the underlying grid—no strays allowed—make a selection from the View menu:

- **Sorting all icons for the moment.** If you choose View→Arrange By→Name, all icons in the window snap to the invisible grid *and* sort themselves alphabetically. Use this method to place the icons as close as possible to one another within the window, rounding up any strays.

The other subcommands in the View→Arrange By menu work similarly (Size, Date Modified, Label, and so on), but sort the icons according to different criteria.

As with the Clean Up command, View→Arrange By serves only to reorganize the icons in the window at this moment. If you move or add icons to the window, they won't be sorted properly. If you'd rather have all icons remain sorted *and* clustered, try this:

- **Sorting all icons permanently.** You can also tell your Mac to maintain the sorting and alignment of all icons in the window, present *and* future. Now if you add more icons to the window, they jump into correct alphabetical position; if you remove icons, the remaining ones slide over to fill in the resulting gap. This setup is perfect for neat freaks.

  To make it happen, open the View menu, hold down the Option key, and choose from the "Keep Arranged By" submenu (choose Name, Date Modified, or whatever sorting criterion you like). Your icons are now locked into sorted position, as compactly as the grid permits.

List View

In windows that contain a lot of icons, the list view is a powerful weapon in the battle against chaos. It shows you a tidy table of your files' names, dates, sizes, and so on. In Snow Leopard, alternating blue and white background stripes help you read across the columns in a list-view window.

You have a great deal of control over your columns, in that you get to decide how wide they should be, which of them should appear, and in what order (except that Name is always the first column). Here's how to master these columns:

Sorting the List

Most of the world's list-view fans like their files listed alphabetically. It's occasionally useful, however, to view the newest files first, largest first, or whatever.

When a desktop window displays its icons in a list view, a convenient new strip of column headings appears (Figure 2-8). These column headings aren't just signposts; they're buttons, too. Click Name for alphabetical order, Date Modified to view newest first, Size to view largest files at the top, and so on.

It's especially important to note the tiny, dark gray triangle that appears in the column you've most recently clicked. It shows you *which way* the list is being sorted.

When the triangle points upward, the oldest files, smallest files, or files beginning with numbers (or the letter A) appear at the top of the list, depending on which sorting criterion you have selected.

Tip: It may help you to remember that when the *smallest* portion of the triangle is at the top (▲), the *smallest* files are listed first when viewed in size order.

To reverse the sorting order, click the column heading a second time. Now the newest files, largest files, or files beginning with the letter Z appear at the top of the list. The tiny triangle turns upside-down.

Figure 2-8:
You control the sorting order of a list view by clicking the column headings (top). Click a second time to reverse the sorting order (bottom).

You'll find the identical ▲ or ▼ triangle—indicating the identical information—in email programs, in iTunes, and anywhere else where reversing the sorting order of the list can be useful.

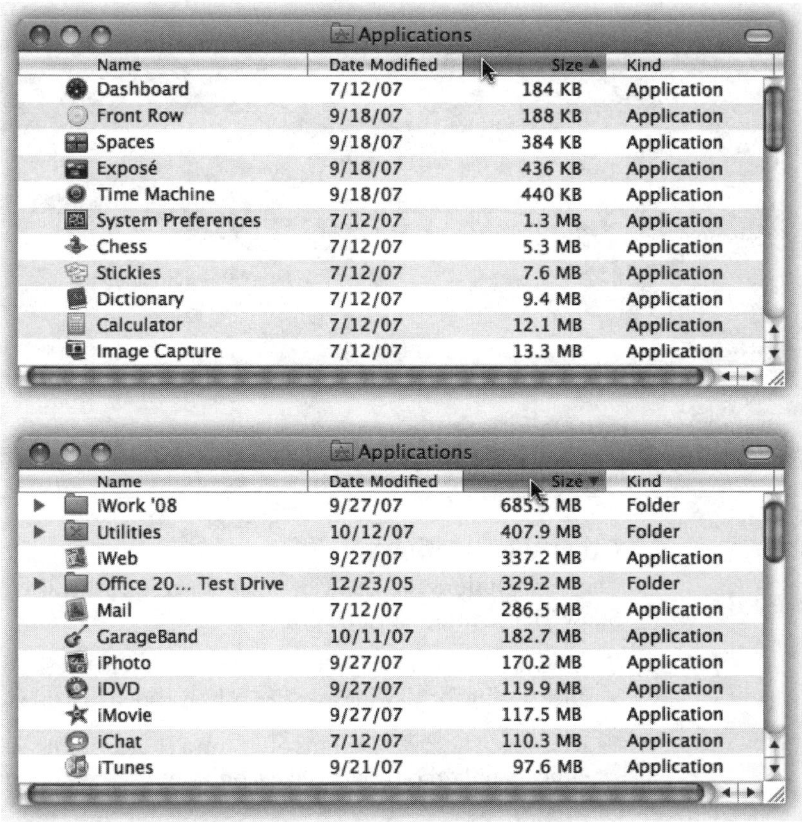

Name	Date Modified	Size ▲	Kind
Dashboard	7/12/07	184 KB	Application
Front Row	9/18/07	188 KB	Application
Spaces	9/18/07	384 KB	Application
Exposé	9/18/07	436 KB	Application
Time Machine	9/18/07	440 KB	Application
System Preferences	7/12/07	1.3 MB	Application
Chess	7/12/07	5.3 MB	Application
Stickies	7/12/07	7.6 MB	Application
Dictionary	7/12/07	9.4 MB	Application
Calculator	7/12/07	12.1 MB	Application
Image Capture	7/12/07	13.3 MB	Application

Name	Date Modified	Size ▼	Kind
▶ iWork '08	9/27/07	685.5 MB	Folder
▶ Utilities	10/12/07	407.9 MB	Folder
iWeb	9/27/07	337.2 MB	Application
▶ Office 20... Test Drive	12/23/05	329.2 MB	Folder
Mail	7/12/07	286.5 MB	Application
GarageBand	10/11/07	182.7 MB	Application
iPhoto	9/27/07	170.2 MB	Application
iDVD	9/27/07	119.9 MB	Application
iMovie	9/27/07	117.5 MB	Application
iChat	7/12/07	110.3 MB	Application
iTunes	9/21/07	97.6 MB	Application

Flippy Triangles

One of the Mac's most attractive features is the tiny triangle that appears to the left of a folder's name in a list view. In its official documents, Apple calls these buttons *disclosure triangles;* internally, the programmers call them *flippy triangles.*

Either way, these triangles are very useful: When you click one, the list view turns into an outline, which displays the contents of the folder in an indented list, as shown in Figure 2-9. Click the triangle again to collapse the folder listing. You're saved the trouble and clutter of opening a new window just to view the folder's contents.

By selectively clicking flippy triangles, you can, in effect, peer inside two or more folders simultaneously, all within a single list view window. You can move files around by dragging them onto the tiny folder icons.

Your Choice of Columns

Choose View→Show View Options. In the dialog box that appears, you're offered on/ off checkboxes for the different columns of information Mac OS X can show you: Date Modified, Size, Kind, Comments, and so on.

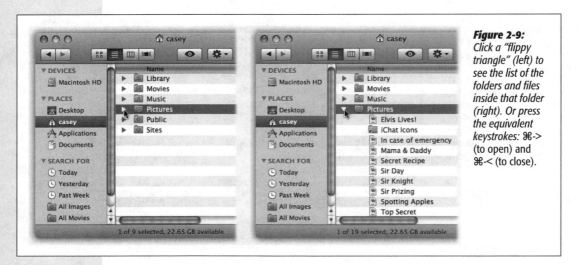

Figure 2-9:
Click a "flippy triangle" (left) to see the list of the folders and files inside that folder (right). Or press the equivalent keystrokes: ⌘-> (to open) and ⌘-< (to close).

Other View Options

The View Options for a list view include several other useful settings; choose View→ Show View Options, or press ⌘-J:

- **Always open in list view.** Turn on this option to override your system-wide preference setting for all windows. See "Always open in icon view" on page 44 for details.

- **Icon size.** These two buttons offer you a choice of icon size for the current window: either standard or tiny. Unlike icon view, list view doesn't give you a size slider.

  Fortunately, even the tiny icons aren't so small that they show up blank. You still get a general idea of what they're supposed to look like.

- **Text size.** You can change the type size for your icon labels, either globally or one window at a time.

- **Show columns.** Turn on the columns you'd like to appear in the current window's list view, as described in the previous section.

- **Use relative dates.** In a list view, the Date Modified and Date Created columns generally display information in a format like this: "Sunday, March 9, 2010." (As noted below, the Mac uses shorter date formats as the column gets narrower.) But when the "Use relative dates" option is turned on, the Mac substitutes the word "Yesterday" or "Today" where appropriate, making recent files easier to spot.

- **Calculate all sizes.** See the box on the facing page.

- **Show icon preview.** Exactly as in icon view, this option turns the icons of graphics files into miniatures of the photos or images within.

- **Use as Defaults.** Click to make your changes in the View Options box apply to *all* windows on your Mac. (Option-click this button to restore a wayward window *back* to your defaults.)

Rearranging Columns

You're stuck with the Name column at the far left of a window. However, you can rearrange the other columns just by dragging their gray column headers horizontally. If the Mac thinks you intend to drop a column to, say, the left of the column it overlaps, you'll actually see an animated movement—indicating a column reshuffling—even before you release the mouse button.

Adjusting Column Widths

If you place your cursor carefully on the dividing line between two column headings, you'll find that you can drag the divider line horizontally. Doing so makes the column to the *left* of your cursor wider or narrower.

FREQUENTLY ASKED QUESTION

Calculate All Sizes

When I sort my list view by size, I see only dashes for folder sizes. What am I doing wrong?

Nothing at all; that's normal. When viewing a Finder window, you see a Size statistic for each file. For folders and disks, however, you're shown only an uninformative dash.

Most Mac fans study this anomaly only momentarily, scratch their chins, and then get back to their work. Former Windows users don't even scratch their chins; Windows PCs *never* show folder-size or disk-size information in list views.

Here's what's going on: It can take a computer a long time to add up the sizes of all files inside a folder. Your System→Library folder alone, for example, contains over 1,500 files. Instead of making you wait while the Mac does all of this addition, Mac OS X simply shows you a dash in the Size column for a folder.

On occasion, however, you really do want to see how big your folders are. In such cases, choose View→Show View Options and turn on "Calculate all sizes." You see the folder sizes slowly begin to pop onto the screen, from the top of the window down, as the Mac crunches the numbers of the files within.

In fact, you can even turn on the "Calculate all sizes" option *globally*—that is, for all windows. In the Mac operating systems of days gone by, this act would have caused a massive slowdown of the entire computer. But remember that Mac OS X is multithreaded—that is, it has the opposite of a one-track mind. It's perfectly capable of devoting all its attention to calculating your folder sizes and all its attention to whatever work you're doing in the foreground.

Now consider this anomaly: Suppose you've opted to sort a particular window by folder size—in other words, you've clicked the word Size at the top of the column. Turning on "Calculate all sizes" bewilders the unprepared, as folders arbitrarily begin leaping out of order, forcing the list to rearrange itself a couple of times per second.

What's happening, of course, is that all folders begin at the bottom of the list, showing only dashes in the Size column. Then, as the Mac computes the size of your folders' contents, they jump into their correct sorted order at what may seem to be random intervals.

What's delightful about this activity is watching Mac OS X scramble to rewrite its information to fit the space you give it. For example, as you make the Date Modified (or Created) column narrower, "Tuesday, March 9, 2010, 2:22 PM" shrinks first to "Tue, Mar 9, 2010, 2:22 PM," then to "3/9/10, 2:22 PM," and finally to a terse "3/9/10."

If you make a column too narrow, Mac OS X shortens the file names, dates, or whatever by removing text from the *middle*. An ellipsis (…) appears to show you where the missing text would have appeared. (Apple reasoned that truncating the *ends* of file names, as in some other operating systems, would hide useful information like the number at the end of "Letter to Marge 1," "Letter to Marge 2," and so on. It would also hide the three-letter *extensions*, such as Thesis.*doc*, that may appear on file names in Mac OS X.)

For example, suppose you've named a Word document "Ben Affleck—A Major Force for Humanization and Cure for Depression, Acne, and Migraine Headache." (Yes, file names can really be that long.) If the Name column is too narrow, you might see only "Ben Affleck—A Major…Migraine Headache."

Tip: You don't have to make the column mega-wide just to read the full text of a file whose name has been shortened. Just point to the icon's name without clicking. After a moment, a yellow, floating balloon appears—something like a tooltip in Windows—to identify the full name.

And if you don't feel like waiting, hold down the Option key. As you whip your mouse over truncated file names, their tooltip balloons appear instantaneously. (Both of these tricks work in list, column, or Cover Flow views—and in Save and Open dialog boxes, for that matter.)

Column View

The goal of column view is simple: to let you burrow down through nested folders without leaving a trail of messy, overlapping windows in your wake.

The solution is shown in Figure 2-10. It's a list view that's divided into several vertical panes. The first pane (not counting the Sidebar) shows whatever disk or folder you first opened.

When you click a disk or folder in this list (once), the second pane shows a list of everything in it. Each time you click a folder in one pane, the pane to its right shows what's inside. The other panes slide to the left, sometimes out of view. (Use the horizontal scroll bar to bring them back.) You can keep clicking until you're actually looking at the file icons inside the most deeply nested folder.

If you discover that your hunt for a particular file has taken you down a blind alley, it's not a big deal to backtrack, since the trail of folders you've followed to get here is still sitting before you on the screen. As soon as you click a different folder in one of the earlier panes, the panes to its right suddenly change, so that you can burrow down a different rabbit hole.

Furthermore, the Sidebar is always at the ready to help you jump to a new track; just click any disk or folder icon there to select a new first-column listing for column view.

The beauty of column view is, first of all, that it keeps your screen tidy. It effectively shows you several simultaneous folder levels, but contains them within a single window. With a quick ⌘-W, you can close the entire window, panes and all. Second, column view provides an excellent sense of where you are. Because your trail is visible at all times, it's much harder to get lost—wondering what folder you're in and how you got there—than in any other window view.

Note: You can change how Column view is sorted; it doesn't have to be alphabetical. Press ⌘-J to open the View Options dialog box, and then choose the sorting criterion you want from the "Arrange by" pop-up menu (like Size, Date Created, or Label).

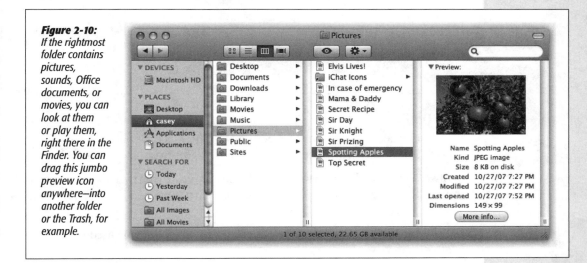

Figure 2-10:
If the rightmost folder contains pictures, sounds, Office documents, or movies, you can look at them or play them, right there in the Finder. You can drag this jumbo preview icon anywhere—into another folder or the Trash, for example.

Manipulating the Columns

The number of columns you can see without scrolling depends on the width of the window. In no other view are the zoom and resize controls as important as they are here.

That's not to say, however, that you're limited to four columns (or whatever fits on your monitor). You can make the columns wider or narrower—either individually or all at once—to suit the situation, according to this scheme:

To make a single column wider or narrower, drag its right-side handle (circled in Figure 2-11).

To make *all* the columns wider or narrower simultaneously, hold down the Option key as you drag that right-side handle.

And here's the tip of the week: *Double-click* one of the right-side handles to make the column *precisely* as wide as necessary to reveal all the names of its contents.

Best of all, you can *Option*-double-click any column's right-side handle to make *all* columns just as wide as necessary.

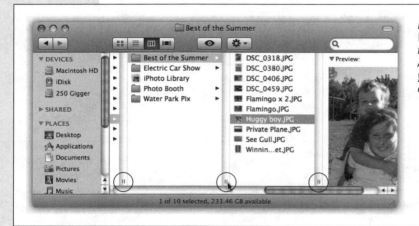

Figure 2-11:
What you want to do most of the time is adjust one column. Adding the Option key as you drag the handle lets you adjust all columns at once.

View Options

Just as in icon and list view, you can choose View→Show View Options to open a dialog box—a Spartan one, in this case—offering additional control over your column views.

• **Always open in column view.** Once again, this option lets you override your system-wide preference setting for all windows. See "Always open in icon view" on page 44 for details.

• **Text size.** Whatever point size you choose here affects the type used for icons in *all* column views.

• **Show icons.** For maximum speed, turn off this option. Now you see only file names—not the tiny icons next to them—in all column views. Weird!

• **Show icon preview.** Turn off this option if you *don't* want the tiny icons in column view to display their actual contents—photos showing their images, Word and PDF documents showing their first pages, and so on. You get generic, identical icons for each file type (text, photo, or whatever).

• **Show preview column.** The far-right Preview column can be handy when you're browsing graphics, sounds, or movie files. Feel free to enlarge this final column when you want a better view of the picture or movie; you can make it *really* big. Almost Quick Look big.

The rest of the time, though, the Preview column can get in the way, slightly slowing down the works and pushing other, more useful columns off to the left side of the window. If you turn off this checkbox, the Preview column doesn't appear.

Tip: No matter what view you're in, remember this if you ever start dragging an icon and then change your mind: Press the Esc key or ⌘-period, even while the mouse button is still down. The icon flies back to its precise starting place. (Too bad real life doesn't have a similar feature.)

Cover Flow View

As you can sort of see from Figure 2-12, Cover Flow is a visual display that Apple stole from its own iTunes software, where Cover Flow simulates the flipping "pages" of a jukebox, or the CDs in a record-store bin. There, you can flip through your music collection, marveling as the CD covers flip over in 3-D space while you browse.

Cover Flow button

Figure 2-12:
The bottom half of a Cover Flow window is identical to list view. The top half, however, is an interactive, scrolling "CD bin" full of your own stuff. It's especially useful for photos, PDF files, Office documents, and text documents. And when a movie comes up in this virtual data jukebox, you can point to the little ▶ button and click it to play the video, right in place.

The idea is the same in Mac OS X, except that now it's not CD covers you're flipping—it's gigantic file and folder icons.

To fire up Cover Flow, open a window. Then click the Cover Flow button identified in Figure 2-12, or choose View→as Cover Flow, or press ⌘-4.

Now the window splits. On the bottom: a traditional list view, complete with sortable columns, exactly as described above.

On the top: the gleaming, reflective, black Cover Flow display. Your primary interest here is the scroll bar. As you drag it left or right, you see your own files and folders float by and flip in 3-D space. Fun for the whole family!

The effect is spectacular, sure. It's probably not something you'd want to set up for every folder, though, because browsing is a pretty inefficient way to find something. But in folders containing photos or movies (that aren't filled with hundreds of files), Cover Flow can be a handy and satisfying way to browse.

And now, notes on Cover Flow:

- **You can adjust the size of Cover Flow display** (relative to the list-view half) by dragging up or down on the grip strip area just beneath the Cover Flow scroll bar.

- **Multipage PDF documents are special.** When you point to one, circled arrow buttons appear on the jumbo icon. You can click them to page through the document—without even opening it for real (Figure 2-13).

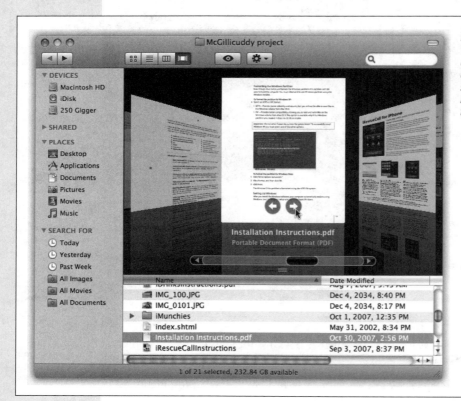

Figure 2-13:
When you point to a PDF file without clicking, you get special arrow buttons that let you turn pages.

- **QuickTime movies are special, too.** When you point to its jumbo display, a ▶ button appears. Click it to play the movie, right there in the Cover Flow window (Figure 2-12).

- **You can navigate with the keyboard, too.** Any icon that's highlighted in the list view (bottom half of the window) is also front and center in the Cover Flow view. Therefore, you can use all the usual list-view shortcuts to navigate both at once. Use the up or down arrow keys, type the first few letters of an icon's name, press Tab or Shift-Tab to highlight the next or previous icon alphabetically, and so on.

- **Cover Flow shows whatever the list view shows.** If you expand a flippy triangle to reveal an indented list of what's in a folder, the contents of that folder now become part of the cover flow.

- **The previews are actual icons.** When you're looking at a Cover Flow minidocument, you can drag it with your mouse—you've got the world's biggest target—anywhere you'd like to drag it: another folder, the Trash, whatever.

Quick Look

As the preceding several thousand pages make clear, there are lots of ways to view and manage the seething mass of files and folders on a typical hard drive. Some of them actually let you see what's in a document without having to open it—the Preview column in column view, the giant icons in Cover Flow, and so on.

Quick Look, a star feature of Mac OS X, takes this idea to another level. It lets you open and browse a document nearly at full size—without switching window views or opening any new programs. You highlight an icon (or several), and then press the space bar (or click the ● button at the top of the window, or choose File→Quick Look).

The Quick Look window now opens, showing a nearly full-size preview of the document (Figure 2-14). Rather nice, eh?

The idea here is that you can check out a document without having to wait for it to open in the traditional way. For example, you can find out what's in a Word, Excel, or PowerPoint document without actually having to *open* Word, Excel, or PowerPoint, which saves you about 45 minutes.

What Quick Look Knows

You might wonder: How, exactly, is Quick Look able to display the contents of a document without opening it? Wouldn't it have to somehow understand the internal file format of that document type?

Exactly. And that's why Quick Look doesn't recognize *all* documents. If you try to preview, for example, a Final Cut Pro video project, a sheet-music file, a .zip archive, or a database file, all you'll see is a 6-inch-tall version of its generic icon. You won't see what's inside.

Over time, people will write plug-ins for those nonrecognized programs. Already, plug-ins that let you see what's inside folders and .zip files await at *www.qlplugins.com*. In the meantime, here's what Quick Look recognizes right out of the box:

- **Graphics files and photos.** This is where Quick Look can really shine, because it's often useful to get a quick look at a photo without having to haul iPhoto or

Photoshop out of bed. Quick Look recognizes all common graphics formats, including TIFF, JPEG, GIF, PNG, Raw, and Photoshop documents (except really huge Photoshop files).

Quick Look

Figure 2-14:
Once the Quick Look window is open, you can play the file (movies and sounds), study it in more detail (most kinds of graphics files), or even read it (PDF, Word, and Excel documents).

You can also click another icon, and another, and an-other, without ever closing the preview; the contents of the window simply change to reflect whatever you've just clicked.

Supertip: Quick Look even works on icons in the Trash, too, so you can figure out what something is before you nuke it forever.

Full Screen   Add to iPhoto

- **PDF and text files.** Using the scroll bar, you can page through multipage documents, right there in the Quick Look window.

- **Audio and movie files.** These begin to play instantly when you open them into the Quick Look window. Most popular formats are recognized (MP3, AIFF, AAC, MPEG-4, H.264, and so on). A scroll bar appears so that you can jump around in the movie or song.

- **Pages, Numbers, Keynote, and TextEdit documents.** Naturally, since these are Apple programs, Quick Look understands the document formats.

- **Saved Web pages from Safari.** That's a new one in Snow Leopard.

- **Microsoft Word, Excel, and PowerPoint documents.** Because these formats are so common, Mac OS X comes with a Quick Look plug-in to recognize them. Move through the pages using the vertical scroll bar; switch to a different Excel spreadsheet page using the Sheet tabs at the bottom.

- **Fonts.** Totally cool. When you open a font file in Quick Look, you get a crystal-clear, huge sampler that shows every letter of the alphabet in that typeface.

- **vCards.** A *vCard* is an address-book entry that people can send each other by email to save time in updating their Rolodexes. When you drag a name out of Apple's or Microsoft's address books and onto the desktop, for example, it turns into a vCard document. In Quick Look, the vCard opens up as a handsomely formatted index card that displays all the person's contact information.

- **HTML (Web pages).** If you've saved some Web pages to your hard drive, here's a great way to inspect them without firing up your Web browser.

To exit the Quick Look display, press the space bar again.

Fun with Quick Look

Here are some stunts that make Quick Look even more interesting.

- **Zoom in or out.** Option-click the preview to magnify it; drag inside the zoomed-in image to scroll; Shift-Option-click to zoom back out. Or press Option as you turn your mouse's scroll wheel. (PDF documents have their own zoom in/zoom out keystrokes: ⌘-plus and ⌘-minus.)

- **Full screen.** When you click the Full Screen arrows (identified in Figure 2-14), your screen goes black, and the Quick Look window expands to fill it. Keep this trick in mind when you're trying to read Word, Excel, or PDF documents, since the text is usually too small to read otherwise. (When you're finished with the closeup, click the Full Screen button again to restore the original Quick Look window, or the ⊗ button to exit Quick Look altogether.)

Tip: How's *this* for an undocumented shortcut?

If you *Option-click* the eyeball icon in any Finder window, you go straight into Full Screen mode without having to open the smaller Quick Look window first. Kewl.

- **Add to iPhoto.** This icon appears in the Quick Look windows of graphics files that you're examining. Click it to add the picture you're studying to your iPhoto photo collection.

- **Keep it going.** Once you've opened Quick Look for *one* icon, you don't have to close it before inspecting *another* icon. Just keep clicking different icons; the Quick Look window changes instantly with each click to reflect the new document.

The Quick Look Slideshow

Highlight a *bunch* of icons, and then open Quick Look. The screen goes black, and the documents begin their slideshow. Each image appears on the screen for about 3 seconds before the next one appears. (Press the Esc key or ⌘-period to end the show.)

Note: If you press the Option key as you start Quick Look—for example, as you hit the space bar, or as you click the Quick Look button—you get a full-screen version of that slideshow.

It's a useful enough feature when you've just downloaded or imported a bunch of photos or Office documents and want a quick look through them. Use the control bar shown in Figure 2-15 to manage the playback.

Note: This same slideshow mechanism is available for graphics in Preview and Mail.

Figure 2-15:
Once the slideshow is under way, you can use this control bar. It lets you pause the slideshow, move forward or backward manually, enlarge the current "slide" to fill the screen, or end the show.

The Index view is especially handy. (You can press ⌘-Return to "click" the Index View button.) It displays an array of labeled miniatures, all at once—a sort of Exposé for Quick Look. Click a thumbnail to jump directly to the Quick Look document you want to inspect.

Previous Pause Next Index View Add to iPhoto Exit Full Screen Exit Quick Look

The Dock

For years, most operating systems maintained two different lists of programs. One listed *unopened* programs until you needed them, like the Start menu in Windows. The other kept track of which programs were *open* at the moment for easy switching, like the Windows taskbar.

In Mac OS X, Apple combined both functions into a single strip of icons called the *Dock*. (And soon thereafter, Microsoft adopted the idea in Windows 7. But that's another book.)

Setting Up the Dock

Apple starts the Dock off with a few icons it thinks you'll enjoy: Dashboard, QuickTime Player, iTunes, iChat, Mail, the Safari Web browser, and so on. But using your Mac without putting your own favorite icons in the Dock is like buying an expensive suit and turning down the free alteration service. At the first opportunity, you should make the Dock your own.

The concept of the Dock is simple: Any icon you drag onto it (Figure 2-16) is installed there as a button.

A single click, not a double-click, opens the corresponding icon. In other words, the Dock is an ideal parking lot for the icons of disks, folders, documents, programs, and Internet bookmarks that you access frequently.

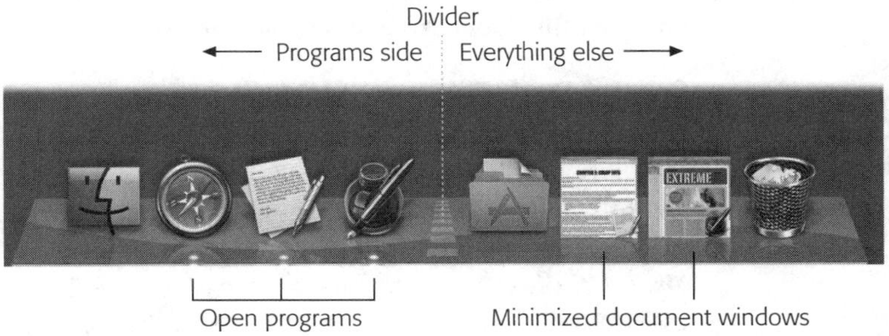

Figure 2-16:
To add an icon to the Dock, simply drag it there. You haven't moved the original file; when you release the mouse, it remains where it was. You've just installed a pointer—like a Macintosh alias or Windows shortcut.

Divider

←—— Programs side ⦙ Everything else ——→

Open programs   Minimized document windows

Here are a few aspects of the Dock that may throw you at first:

- **It has two sides.** See the whitish dotted line running down the Dock? That's the divider (Figure 2-16). Everything on the left side is an application—a program. Everything else goes on the right side: files, documents, folders, disks, and minimized windows.

  It's important to understand this division. If you try to drag an application to the right of the line, for example, Mac OS X teasingly refuses to accept it. (Even aliases observe that distinction. Aliases of applications can go only on the left side, and vice versa.)

- **Its icon names are hidden.** To see the name of a Dock icon, point to it without clicking. You'll see the name appear above the icon.

  When you're trying to find a certain icon in the Dock, run your cursor slowly across the icons without clicking; the icon labels appear as you go. You can often identify a document just by looking at its icon.

- **Folders and disks sprout lists of their contents.** If you click a folder or disk icon in the Dock, a list of its contents sprouts from the icon. It's like X-ray vision without the awkward moral consequences. Turn the page 64 for details.

- **Programs appear there unsolicited.** Nobody but you (and Apple) can put icons on the right side of the Dock. But program icons appear on the left side of the Dock automatically whenever you open a program, even one that's not listed in the Dock. Its icon remains there for as long as it's running.

Organizing and Removing Dock Icons

You can move the tiles of the Dock around by dragging them horizontally. As you drag an icon, the other icons scoot aside to make room. When you're satisfied with its new position, drop the icon you've just dragged.

To remove a Dock icon, just drag it away. (You can't remove the icons of the Finder, the Trash, the Dock icon of an open program, or any minimized document window.) Once your cursor has cleared the Dock, release the mouse button. The icon disappears, and the other Dock icons slide together to close the gap.

Pop-up Dock Folders ("Stacks")

When you click a disk or folder icon on the Dock, you'll witness the effect shown in Figure 2-17. In essence, Mac OS X is fanning out the folder's contents so you can see all of them. If it could talk, it would be saying, "Pick a card, any card."

Tip: You can change how the icons in a particular stack are sorted: alphabetically, chronologically, or whatever. Use the "Sort by" section of the shortcut menu (Figure 2-17, top left).

Pop-up folders are a great idea, because they save you time and clicking. Click a folder to see what's in it; click the icon you want inside; and you're off and running, without having had to open, manage, and close a window.

Fan vs. grid vs. list

When you click a disk or folder icon on the Dock, you see its contents, arrayed in your choice of three displays:

- **Fan.** The fan is a single, gently curved column of icons that pops out of the disk or folder icon. It's ideal for folders that contain very few icons, because there's room for only a handful of items in a fan (the exact number depends on your screen size). After the first few, you see only a "31 more in Finder" button, which you can click to see *everything* in that folder—but now you've *wasted* time, not saved it.

Note: When your Dock is positioned on a side of the screen instead of the bottom, the fan option isn't available.

- **Grid.** If you've set a folder to open as a grid, you get to see the icons in a big rectangular window. File names often get abbreviated because there's not enough horizontal room, but you get to see many more icons this way. Actually, thanks to the scroll bar (or the type-selecting trick described on page 67), you get to see *all* the icons this way.

- **List.** If you don't care about seeing the actual icons, you can also opt for a simple list of the folder's contents, like a pop-up menu. After all, if the folder contains nothing but a bunch of identical-looking audio or database icons, then seeing their icons isn't going to help you much—and a list appears much faster than a fan or a grid does.

There's no scroll bar in a list balloon, but you can scroll the list nonetheless just by pointing to the top or bottom of it with your mouse. And, again, you can type-select as described on page 67.

Figure 2-17:
What happens when you click a folder in the Dock? You see its contents in one of three views.

Top left: Here's how you choose which view you want: fan, grid, list, or automatic. In list view, the folder contents appear as a menu; you can "drill down" into subfolders, and you open something by choosing its name.

Top right: In fan view, click an icon to open it.

Bottom: In grid view, many more icons appear than can fit in Fan view.

List view

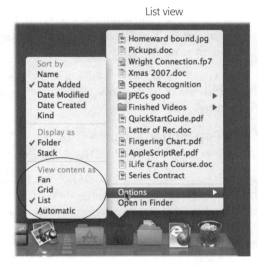

Fan view

Grid view

Tip: The list view also displays a little ▸ to the right of each folder within the Dock folder. That is, it's a hierarchical list, meaning that you can burrow into folders within folders, all from the original Dock icon, all without opening a single new window. You can stick your entire Home folder, or even your whole hard drive icon, onto the Dock; now you have complete menu access to everything inside, right from the Dock.

- **Automatic.** There's a fourth option in the shortcut menu for a Dock folder, too: automatic. If you turn this on, then Mac OS X chooses either fan or grid view, depending on how many icons are in the folder.

So how do you choose which display you want? Right-click the Dock folder's icon, and make a selection from the shortcut menu. Each disk or folder icon remembers its own fan/grid/list setting.

The Finer Points of Pop-up Dock Folders

Those were the basics of pop-up Dock folders. Here's the advanced course:

- **Ever-Changing Folder-Icon Syndrome (ECFIS).** When you add a folder or disk icon to the Dock, you might notice something wildly disorienting: Its icon keeps *changing* to resemble whatever you most recently put into it. For example, your Downloads folder might look like an Excel spreadsheet icon today, a PDF icon tonight, or a photo tomorrow—but never a folder. The annoying part is that you can't get to know a folder by its icon.

  Fortunately, this problem is easy to fix. Right-click the Dock folder. From the shortcut menu, in the "Display as" section, you can choose either Folder (which looks like a folder forever) or Stack (which changes to reflect its contents).

- **Ready-made pop-up folders.** When you first start out with Mac OS X 10.6, you get a couple of starter Dock folders, just to get you psyched. One is Downloads; the other is Documents. (Both of these folders are physically inside your Home folder. But you may well do most of your interacting with them on the Dock.)

  The Downloads folder collects three kinds of Internet arrivals: files you download from the Web using Safari, files you receive in an iChat file-transfer session, and file attachments you get via email using Mail. Unless you intervene, they're sorted by the date you downloaded them.

  It's handy to know where to find your downloads, and nice not to have them all cluttering your desktop.

Tip: Once you've opened a stack's fan or grid, you can drag any of the icons right out of it. Just drag your chosen icon onto the desktop or into any visible disk or folder. In other words, what lands in the Downloads folder doesn't have to stay there. (You can't drag out of a list, however.)

- **Hierarchical folders.** The fans and grids are hierarchical—that is, you can drill down from their folders into *their* folders. Figure 2-18 makes this concept clearer.

Tip: Figure 2-17 shows you how to open a folder in a grid or fan using the mouse—but you can do it all from the keyboard, too. Once a folder is selected, press Return, ⌘-O, or ⌘-↓ to see what's inside it; press ⌘-↑ to backtrack to the original display. When a folder is highlighted, you can press ⌘-Return to open it in a Finder window; add the Option key to open that Finder window without closing the grid or fan.

Figure 2-18:
If you spot a folder inside a fan or grid (left), click it once. You're now looking at a fan or grid of its contents (right). You can also "back out" again by clicking the Back button in the upper-left corner, indicated here by the cursor.

- **Type selecting.** Once a list, fan, or grid is on the screen, you can highlight any icon in it by typing the first few letters of its name. For example, once you've popped open your Applications folder, you can highlight Safari by typing *sa*. (Press Return to open the highlighted icon.)

Tip: Alternatively, you can "walk" through the fan, grid, or list by pressing the arrow keys. A highlighting effect makes it crystal clear which icon you're selecting. Once an icon is selected, press Return to open it.

- **Two ways to bypass the pop-up.** If you just want to see what's in a folder, without all the graphic overkill of the fan or the grid, then right-click the Dock folder's icon and choose "Open 'Applications' " (or whatever the folder's name is) from the shortcut menu. You go straight to the corresponding window.

  Actually, if you *really* value your time, you'll learn the shortcut: Option-⌘-click the Dock folder's icon. That accomplishes the same thing.

  (You jump immediately to the window that *contains* that folder's icon. That's not exactly the same thing as opening the Dock folder, but it's sometimes even more useful.)

Tip: Alternatively, you can ⌘-click a folder on the Dock—or, indeed, any icon on the Dock—to jump to the window that contains that folder's icon. (Bonus: This same ⌘-clicking trick also works in the menu of Spotlight search results.)

Three Ways to Get the Dock Out of Your Hair

The bottom of the screen isn't necessarily the ideal location for the Dock. All Mac screens are wider than they are tall, so the Dock eats into your limited vertical screen space. You have three ways out: Hide the Dock, shrink it, or rotate it 90 degrees.

Auto-hiding the Dock

To turn on the Dock's auto-hiding feature, choose ⌘→Dock→Turn Hiding On (or press Option-⌘-D).

When the Dock is hidden, it doesn't slide into view until you move the cursor to the Dock's edge of the screen. When you move the cursor back to the middle of the screen, the Dock slithers out of view once again. (Individual Dock icons may occasionally shoot upward into Desktop territory when a program needs your attention—cute, very cute—but otherwise, the Dock lies low until you call for it.)

On paper, an auto-hiding Dock is ideal; it's there only when you summon it. In practice, however, you may find that the extra half-second the Dock takes to appear and disappear makes this feature slightly less appealing.

Many Mac fans prefer to hide and show the Dock at will by pressing the hide/show keystroke, Option-⌘-D. This method makes the Dock pop on and off the screen without requiring you to move the cursor.

Shrinking and enlarging the Dock

Depending on your screen's size, you may prefer smaller or larger Dock buttons. The official way to resize them goes like this: Choose ⌘→Dock→Dock Preferences. In the resulting dialog box, drag the Dock Size slider, as shown in Figure 2-19.

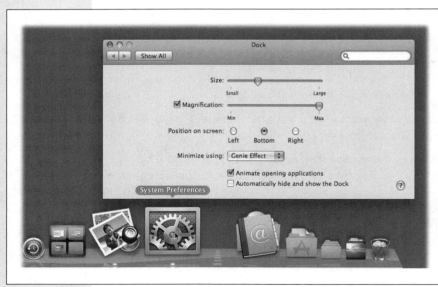

Figure 2-19:
To find a comfortable setting for the Magnification slider, choose ⌘→Dock→Dock Preferences. Leave the Dock Preferences window open on the screen, as shown here. After each adjustment of the Dock Size slider, try out the Dock (which still works when the Dock Preferences window is open) to test your new settings.

There's a much faster way to resize the Dock, however: Just position your cursor carefully in the Dock's divider line, so that it turns into a double-headed arrow. Now drag up or down to shrink or enlarge the Dock.

You may not be able to *enlarge* the Dock, especially if it contains a lot of icons. But you can make it almost infinitely *smaller*. This may make you wonder: How can you distinguish between icons if they're the size of molecules?

The answer lies in the →Dock→Turn Magnification On command. What you've just done is trigger the swelling effect shown in Figure 2-19. Now your Dock icons balloon to a much larger size as your cursor passes over them. It's a weird, magnetic, rippling, animated effect that takes some getting used to. But it's another spectacular demonstration of the graphics technology in Mac OS X, and it can actually come in handy when you find your icons shrinking away to nothing.

Moving the Dock to the sides of the screen

Yet another approach to getting the Dock out of your way is to rotate it, so that it sits vertically against a side of your screen. You can rotate it in either of two ways:

- **The menu way.** From the →Dock submenu, choose "Position on Left," "Position on Right," or "Position on Bottom," as you see fit.

- **The mouse way.** While pressing Shift, drag the Dock's divider line, like a handle, to the side of the screen you want.

You'll probably find that the right side of your screen works better than the left. Most Mac OS X programs put their document windows against the left edge of the screen, where the Dock and its labels might get in the way.

Note: When you position your Dock vertically, the "right" side of the Dock becomes the bottom of the vertical Dock. In other words, the Trash now appears at the bottom of the vertical Dock. So as you read references to the Dock in this book, mentally substitute the phrase "bottom part of the Dock" when you read references to the "right side of the Dock."

Using the Dock

Most of the time, you'll use the Dock as either a launcher (you click an icon once to open it) or as a status indicator (the tiny, shiny reflective spot, identified in Figure 2-16, indicates which programs are running).

But the Dock has more tricks than that up its sleeve. Observe:

Switch applications

The Dock isn't just a launcher; it's also a switcher. For example, it lets you perform the following tricks:

- Jump among your open programs by clicking their icons.

- Drag a document (such as a text file) onto a Dock application (such as the Microsoft Word icon) to open the former with the latter. (If the program balks at opening the document, yet you're sure the program *should* be able to open the document, then add the ⌘ and Option keys as you drag.)

• Hide all windows of the program you're in by Option-clicking another Dock icon.

• Hide all *other* programs' windows by Option-⌘-clicking the Dock icon of the program you *do* want (even if it's already in front).

Secret menus

Each Dock icon has its own very useful shortcut menu (Figure 2-20). If you've clicked a minimized window icon, this shortcut menu says only Close (unless it's a minimized Finder window, in which case it also says Open).

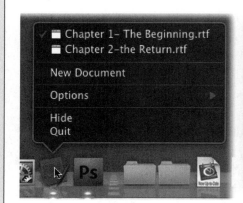

Figure 2-20:
Left: Right-click a Dock icon to open the secret menu.

Right: Right-click the divider bar to open a different hidden menu. This one lists a bunch of useful Dock commands, including the ones listed in the ⌘→Dock submenu.

But if you've clicked any other kind of icon, you get some very useful hidden commands. For example:

• **[Window names.]** The secret Dock menu of a *running program* usually lists at least one tiny, neatly labeled window icon, like those shown in Figure 2-20. This useful feature means you can jump directly not only to a certain program, but also to a certain *open window* in that program.

For example, suppose you've been using Word to edit three different chapters. You can use Word's Dock icon as a Window menu to pull forward one particular chapter, or (if it's been minimized) to pull it up—even from within a different program. (The checkmark indicates the *frontmost* window, even if the entire program is in the background at the moment. A diamond symbol means the window is minimized and therefore not visible on the screen at the moment.)

• **Options.** This submenu contains a bunch of miscellaneous commands. For example:

Options→Keep In Dock. Whenever you open a program, Mac OS X puts its icon in the Dock—marked with a shiny, white reflective spot—even if you don't normally keep its icon there. As soon as you quit the program, its icon disappears again from the Dock.

If you understand that much, then the Keep In Dock command makes a lot of sense. It means, "Hello, I'm this program's icon. I know you don't normally keep me in your Dock, but I *could* stay here even after you quit my program. Just say the word." If you find you've been using, for example, Terminal a lot more often than you thought you would, then this command may be the ticket.

Tip: Actually, there's a faster way to tell a running application to remain in the Dock from now on. Just drag its icon off the Dock and then right back onto it—yes, while the program is running. You have to try it to believe it.

Options→Remove From Dock. On the other hand, what if a program's icon is always in the Dock (even when it's not running) and you *don't* want it there? This command gets the program's icon off the Dock, thereby returning the space it was using to other icons. (You can achieve the same result by dragging the icon away from the Dock.)

Use this command on programs you rarely use. When you *do* want to run those programs, you can always use Spotlight to fire them up.

Note: If the program is already running, using Remove From Dock does not immediately remove its icon from the Dock, which could be confusing. That's because a program always appears in the Dock when it's open. What you're doing here is saying, "Disappear from the Dock when you're not running"—and you'll see the proof as soon as you quit that program.

Options→Open at Login. This command lets you specify that you want this icon to open itself automatically each time you log in to your account. It's a great way to make sure your email Inbox, your calendar, or the Microsoft Word thesis you've been working on is fired up and waiting on the screen when you sit down to work.

To make this item *stop* auto-opening, choose this command again so that the checkmark no longer appears.

Options→Show In Finder. This command highlights the actual icon (in whatever folder window it happens to sit) of the application, alias, folder, or document you've clicked. You might want to do this when, for example, you're using a program that you can't quite figure out, and you want to jump to its desktop folder in hopes of finding a Read Me file there.

Tip: Once again, there's a much faster way to reveal a Dock icon in its enclosing window: ⌘-click its Dock icon.

- **Hide/Show.** Snow Leopard is crawling with ways to hide or reveal a selected batch of windows. Here's a case in point: You can hide all traces of the program you're using by choosing Hide from its Dock icon.

  What's cool here is that (a) you can even hide the Finder and all *its* windows, and (b) if you press Option, the command changes to say Hide Others. This, in its way, is a much more powerful command. It tells all the programs you're *not* using—the ones in the background—to get out of your face. They hide themselves instantly.

Note: Once you've hidden a program's windows, this command changes to say Show, which is how you make them reappear.

- **Quit.** You can quit any program directly from its Dock shortcut menu. (Finder and Dashboard are exceptions.) The beauty of this feature is that you don't have to switch first into a program to get to its Quit command. (Troubleshooting moment: If you get nothing but a beep when you use this Quit command, it's because you've hidden the windows of that program, and one of them has unsaved changes. Click the program's icon, save your document, and then try to quit again.)

Tip: If you hold down the Option key—even after you've opened the pop-up menu—then the Quit command changes to say Force Quit. That's your emergency hatch for jettisoning a locked-up program.

- **Miscellaneous.** You might find other commands in Dock shortcut menus; software companies are free to add specialty options to their own programs.

Tip: If you Control-⌘-click a program's Dock icon, you get only the Options, Hide, and Quit commands in the shortcut menu—not the usual list of windows. If all you want to do is quit a program or something, this abbreviated menu is faster and easier to comprehend.

Drag and Drop

Dock icons are spring-loaded. That is, if you drag any icon onto a Dock icon and pause—or, if you're in a hurry, tap the space bar—the Dock icon *opens* to receive the dragged file.

Note: It opens, that is, *if* the spring-loaded folder feature is turned on in Finder→Preferences.

This technique is most useful in these situations:

- **Drag a document icon onto a Dock folder icon.** The folder's Finder window pops open so you can continue the drag into a subfolder.

- **You drag a document into an application.** The classic example is dragging a photo onto the iPhoto icon. When you tap the space bar, iPhoto opens automatically. Since your mouse button is still down, and you're technically still in mid-drag, you can now drop the photo directly into the appropriate iPhoto album or Event. You can drag an MP3 file into iTunes or an attachment into Mail or Entourage the same way.

Do Your Filing

Once you've tried stashing a few important folders on the right side of your Dock, there's no going back. The folders you care about are always there, ready for opening with a single click.

Better yet, they're easily accessible for *putting away* files; you can drag files directly into the Dock's folder icons as though they were regular folders.

In fact, you can even drag a file into a *subfolder* in a Dock folder. That's because the Dock's folders are spring-loaded. When you drag an icon onto a Dock folder and pause, the folder's window appears around your cursor, so you can continue the drag into an inner folder (and even an *inner* inner folder, and so on). Page 85 has the details on spring-loaded folders.

Tip: When you try to drag something into a Dock folder icon, the Dock icons scoot out of the way; the Dock assumes you're trying to put that something *onto* the Dock. But if you press the ⌘ key as you drag an icon to the Dock, the existing Dock icons freeze in place. Without the ⌘ key, you wind up playing a frustrating game of chase-the-folder.

The Finder Toolbar

At the top of every Finder window is a small set of function icons, all in a gradient-gray row (Figure 2-21). The first time you run Mac OS X, you'll find only these icons on the toolbar:

Figure 2-21:
If you ⌘-click the upper-right toolbar button repeatedly, you cycle through six combinations of large and small icons and text labels. (Three examples are shown here.) Tip: This same ⌘-clicking business cycles through the same toolbar variations in Mail, Preview, and other programs that have toolbars.

- **Back, Forward.** The Finder works something like a Web browser. Only a single window remains open as you navigate the various folders on your hard drive.

The Back button (◀) returns you to whichever folder you were just looking at. (Instead of clicking ◀, you can also press ⌘-[, or choose Go→Back—particularly handy if the toolbar is *hidden*, as described below.)

The Forward button (▶) springs to life only after you've used the Back button. Clicking it (or pressing ⌘-]) returns you to the window you just backed out of.

- **View controls.** The four tiny buttons next to the ▶ button switch the current window into icon, list, column, or Cover Flow view, in that order. And remember, if the toolbar is hidden, you can get by with the equivalent commands in the View menu at the top of the screen—or by pressing ⌘-1, ⌘-2, ⌘-3, or ⌘-4 (for icon, list, column, and Cover Flow view, respectively).

- **Quick Look.** The eyeball icon opens the Quick Look preview for a highlighted icon (or group of them).

- **Action (✿).** This little pop-up menu contains the same commands you'd see if you right-clicked something.

- **Search bar.** This little round-ended text box is yet another entry point for the Spotlight feature described in Chapter 3.

GEM IN THE ROUGH

Menu Help in the Help Menu

Mac OS X contains a weird, wonderful little enhancement to its online help system. It helps you find menu commands you can't find.

You're floundering in some program. You're *sure* there's a Page Numbering command in those menus somewhere. But there are 11 menus hiding 143 submenus, and you haven't got time for the pain.

That's when you should think of using the Help menu. When you type *page number* (or whatever) into its Search box, the results menu lists, at the top, the names of any menu commands in that program that contain the words you typed. Better still, it actually *opens that menu* for you, and displays a big, blue, animated, floating arrow pointing to the command you wanted. You'd have to have your eyes closed to miss it.

Slide your cursor over, click the menu command, and get on with your life.

Supertip: This feature is especially helpful in Web browsers like Safari and Firefox, because it even finds entries in your Bookmarks and History menus!

In Safari, for example, you can pluck a recently visited site out of the hundreds in the daily History submenus, like the

"Wednesday, January 9" submenu. You've just saved yourself a *lot* of poking around menus, trying to find the name of a site you know you've seen recently.)

Ultratip: If you think about it, this feature also means you have complete keyboard power over every menu in every program in the world. Hit ⌘-? to open the Help search box, type a bit of the command's name, and then use the arrow keys to walk down the results. Hit Return to trigger the command you want.

Removing or Shrinking the Toolbar

Between the toolbar, the Dock, the Sidebar, and the large icons of Mac OS X, it almost seems like there's an Apple conspiracy to sell big screens.

Fortunately, the toolbar doesn't have to contribute to that impression. You can hide it by choosing View→Hide Toolbar or pressing Option-⌘-T. (The same keystroke, or choosing View→Show Toolbar, brings it back.)

But you don't have to do without the toolbar altogether. If its consumption of screen space is your main concern, you may prefer to collapse it—to delete the pictures but preserve the text buttons; see Figure 2-21.

Rearranging or Removing Toolbar Icons

You can drag toolbar icons around, rearranging them horizontally, by pressing ⌘ as you drag. Taking an icon off the toolbar is equally easy. While pressing the ⌘ key, just drag the icon clear away from the toolbar. (If the Customize Toolbar sheet is open, you can perform either step *without* the ⌘ key.)

You can also get rid of a toolbar icon by right-clicking it and choosing Remove Item from the shortcut menu.

Getting Help in Mac OS X

It's a good thing you've got a book about Mac OS X in your hands, because the only user manual you get with Mac OS X is the Help menu. You get a Web browser–like program that reads a set of help files that reside in your System→Library folder.

Tip: In fact, you may not even be *that* lucky. In Snow Leopard, the general-information Help page about each topic is on your Mac, but thousands of more nichey or more technical pages actually reside online, and require an Internet connection to read.

You're expected to find the topic you want in one of these three ways:

Figure 2-22:
You don't have to open the Help program to begin a search. No matter what program you're in, typing a search phrase into the box shown here produces an instantaneous list of help topics, ready to read.

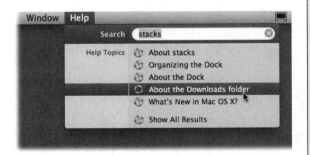

- **Use the new Search box.** When you click the Help menu , a tiny search box appears just beneath your cursor (Figure 2-22). You can type a few words here to specify what you want help on: "setting up printer," "disk space," whatever.

Tip: You can also hit ⌘-Shift-/ (that is, ⌘-?) to open the Help search box.

The menu now becomes a list of Apple help topics pertaining to your search. Click one to open the Help browser described next; you've just saved some time and a couple of steps.

Tip: The results menu does not, however, show *all* of Help's results—only the ones Apple thinks are most relevant. If you choose Show All Results at the bottom of the menu, the Help browser opens (described below). It shows a more complete list of Help-search results.

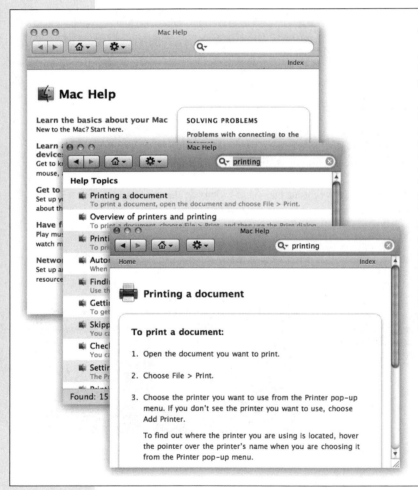

Figure 2-23:
The Mac OS X Help system doesn't bunch together the help pages from every program on your Mac. When you're in the Finder, you get the general Macintosh Help screens. When you're in iPhoto, you get only iPhoto help screens. And so on. But using the Home pop-up menu, you can switch to another program's help system even if that program isn't open.

Double-click a topic's name to open the Help page. If it isn't as helpful as you'd hoped, click the ◄ button at the top to return to the list of relevant topics. Click the little Home button to return to the Help Center's welcome screen.

- **Drill down.** Alternatively, you can begin your quest for assistance the old-fashioned way: by opening the Help browser first. To do that, choose Help→Mac Help. (This works only in the Finder, and only when nothing is typed in the Search box. To empty the Search box, click the ⊗ button at the right end.)

After a moment, you arrive at the Help browser program shown in Figure 2-23. The starting screen offers several "quick click" topics that may interest you. If so, keep clicking text headings until you find a topic that you want to read.

You can backtrack by clicking the ◄ button at the top of the window. And you can always return to the starting screen by clicking the little Home icon at the top.

Tip: Annoyingly, the Snow Leopard Help window insists on floating in front of all other windows; you can't send it to the back like any normal program. Therefore, consider making the window tall and skinny, so you can put it *beside* the program you're working in. Drag the ribbed lower-right corner to change the window's shape.

- **Use the "Ask a Question" blank.** Type the phrase you want, such as *printing* or *switching applications,* into the Search box at the top of the window, and then press Return. The Mac responds by showing you a list of help-screen topics that may pertain to what you need (Figure 2-23).

This Search box usually gives you a more complete list of results than you'd have gotten by using the Search box in the Help *menu,* as described above.

Files, Icons, & Spotlight

E very document, program, folder, and disk on your Mac is represented by an *icon:* a colorful little picture that you can move, copy, or double-click to open. In Mac OS X, icons look more like photos than cartoons, and you can scale them to practically any size.

This chapter is all about manipulating those icons—that is, your files, folders, and disks. It's all about naming them, copying them, deleting them, labeling them—and then, maybe most important of all, finding them, using the Mac's famous Spotlight instant-search feature.

Renaming Icons

A Mac OS X icon's name can have up to 255 letters and spaces. If you're accustomed to the 31-character or even eight-character limits of older computers, that's quite a luxurious ceiling.

As a Windows veteran, furthermore, you may be delighted to discover that in Mac OS X, you can name your files using letters, numbers, punctuation—in fact, any symbol except for the colon (:), which the Mac uses behind the scenes for its own folder-hierarchy designation purposes. And you can't use a period to *begin* a file's name.

To rename a file, click its name or icon (to highlight it) and then press Return. (Or, if you have time to kill, click once on the name, wait a moment, and then click a second time.)

In any case, a rectangle now appears around the name (Figure 3-1). At this point, the existing name is highlighted; just begin typing to replace it. If you type a very long name, the rectangle grows vertically to accommodate new lines of text.

Tip: If you simply want to add letters to the beginning or end of the file's existing name, press the left or right arrow key immediately after pressing Return. The insertion point jumps to the corresponding end of the file name.

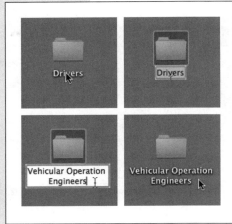

Figure 3-1:
Click an icon's name (top left) to produce the renaming rectangle (top right), in which you can edit the file's name. Snow Leopard is kind enough to highlight only the existing name, and not the suffix (like .jpg or .doc).

Now just begin typing to replace the existing name (bottom left). When you're finished typing, press Return, Enter, or Tab to seal the deal, or just click somewhere else.

When you're finished typing, press Return, Enter, or Tab—or just click somewhere else—to make the renaming rectangle disappear.

As you edit a file's name, remember that you can use the Cut, Copy, and Paste commands in the Edit menu to move selected bits of text around, just as though you're word processing. The Paste command can be useful when, for instance, you're renaming many icons in sequence (*Quarterly Estimate 1, Quarterly Estimate 2,* and so on).

And now, a few tips about renaming icons:

- When the Finder sorts files, a space is considered alphabetically *before* the letter A. To force a particular folder to appear at the top of a list view window, insert a space before its name.

- Older operating systems sort files so that 10 and 100 come before 2, the numbers 30 and 300 come before 4, and so on. You wind up with alphabetically sorted files like this: "1. Big Day," "10. Long Song," "2. Floppy Hat," "20. Dog Bone," "3. Weird Sort," and so on. Generations of computer users have learned to put zeros in front of their single-digit numbers just to make the sorting look right.

  In Mac OS X, though, you get exactly the numerical list you'd hope for: "1. Big Day," "2. Floppy Hat," "3. Weird Sort," "10. Long Song," and "20. Dog Bone." At long last, you can get out of the habit of putting zeros in front of file names to make them sort properly.

Selecting Icons

To highlight a single icon in preparation for printing, opening, duplicating, or deleting, click the icon once. Both the icon and the name darken in a uniquely Snow Leopardish way.

Tip: You can change the color of the oval highlighting that appears around the name of a selected icon. Choose →System Preferences, click Appearance, and use the Highlight Color pop-up menu.

That much may seem obvious. But lots of people have no idea how to manipulate *more* than one icon at a time—an essential survival skill. These techniques are essentially the same as in Windows, except that the keys you hold down are different.

Selecting by Clicking

To highlight multiple files in preparation for moving or copying, use one of these techniques:

- **To highlight all the icons.** To select all the icons in a window, press ⌘-A (the equivalent of the Edit→Select All command).

- **To highlight several icons by dragging.** You can drag diagonally to highlight a group of nearby icons, as shown in Figure 3-2. In a list view, in fact, you don't even have to drag over the icons themselves—your cursor can touch any part of any file's row, like its modification date or file size.

Tip: If you include a particular icon in your diagonally dragged group by mistake, ⌘-click it to remove it from the selected cluster.

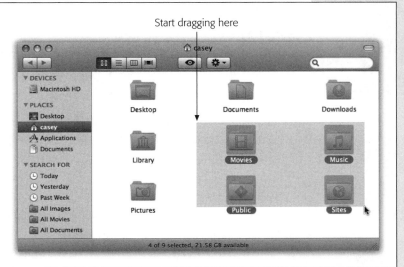

Figure 3-2:
You can highlight several icons simultaneously by dragging a box around them. To do so, drag from outside of the target icons diagonally across them (right), creating a translucent gray rectangle as you go. Any icons or icon names touched by this rectangle are selected when you release the mouse. If you press the Shift or ⌘ key as you do this, any previously highlighted icons remain selected.

Start dragging here

- **To highlight consecutive icons in a list.** If you're looking at the contents of a window in list view or column view, you can drag vertically over the file and folder names to highlight a group of consecutive icons, as described above. (Begin the drag in a blank spot.)

  There's a faster way to do the same thing: Click the first icon you want to highlight, and then Shift-click the last file, just as in Windows. All the files in between are automatically selected, along with the two icons you clicked.

- **To highlight random icons.** If you want to highlight only the first, third, and seventh icons in a window, for example, start by clicking icon No. 1. Then ⌘-click each of the others (or ⌘-drag new rectangles around them). Each icon darkens to show that you've selected it.

  If you're highlighting a long string of icons and click one by mistake, you don't have to start over. Instead, just ⌘-click it again, so that the dark highlighting disappears. (If you do want to start over, you can deselect all selected icons by clicking any empty part of the window—or by pressing the Esc key.)

  The ⌘ key trick is especially handy if you want to select *almost* all the icons in a window. Press ⌘-A to select everything in the folder, then ⌘-click any unwanted icons to deselect them.

Once you've highlighted multiple icons, you can manipulate them all at once. For example, you can drag them en masse to another folder or disk by dragging any *one* of the highlighted icons. All other highlighted icons go along for the ride. This technique is especially useful when you want to back up a bunch of files by dragging them onto a different disk, delete them all by dragging them to the Trash, and so on.

When multiple icons are selected, the commands in the File and Edit menus—such as Duplicate, Open, and Make Alias—apply to all of them simultaneously.

Selecting Icons from the Keyboard

For the speed fanatic, using the mouse to click an icon is a hopeless waste of time. Fortunately, you can also select an icon by typing the first couple letters of its name.

When looking at your Home window, for example, you can type *M* to highlight the Movies folder. And if you actually intended to highlight the Music folder instead, press the Tab key to highlight the next icon in the window alphabetically. Shift-Tab highlights the previous icon alphabetically. Or use the arrow keys to highlight a neighboring icon.

(The Tab-key trick works only in icon, list, and Cover Flow views—not column view, alas. You can always use the ← and → keys to highlight adjacent columns, however.)

After highlighting an icon this way, you can manipulate it using the commands in the File menu or their keyboard equivalents: Open (⌘-O), put it into the Trash (⌘-Delete), Get Info (⌘-I), Duplicate (⌘-D), or make an alias (⌘-L), as described later in this chapter. By turning on the special disability features described on page 504, you can even *move* the highlighted icon using only the keyboard.

Moving and Copying Icons

In Mac OS X, there are two ways to move or copy icons from one place to another: by dragging them, or by using the Copy and Paste commands.

Copying by Dragging

You can drag icons from one folder to another, from one drive to another, from a drive to a folder on another drive, and so on. (When you've selected several icons, drag any *one* of them; the others tag along.) While the Mac is copying, you can tell that the process is still under way even if the progress bar is hidden behind a window, because the icon of the copied material shows up *dimmed* in its new home, darkening only when the copying process is over. You can cancel the process by pressing either ⌘-period or the Esc key.

Tip: If you're copying files into a disk or folder that already contains items with the same names, Mac OS X asks you individually about each one. ("An older item named 'Fiddlesticks' with extension '.doc' already exists in this location.") Note that, thank heaven, Mac OS X tells you whether the version you're replacing is *older* or *newer* than the one you're moving.

Turn on "Apply to all" if all of the incoming icons should (or should not) replace the old ones of the same names. Then click Replace or Don't Replace, as you see fit, or Stop to halt the whole copying business.

Understanding when the Mac *copies* a dragged icon and when it *moves* it bewilders many a beginner. However, the scheme is fairly simple when you consider the following:

• Dragging from one folder to another on the same disk *moves* the icon.

UP TO SPEED

The Wacky Keystrokes of Mac OS X

Mac OS X offers a glorious assortment of predefined keystrokes for jumping to the most important locations on your Mac: your Home folder, the Applications folder, the Utilities folder, the Computer window, your iDisk, the Network window, and so on.

Better yet, the keystrokes are incredibly simple to memorize: Just press Shift-⌘ and the first letter of the location you want. Shift-⌘-H opens your Home folder, Shift-⌘-A opens the Applications folder, and so on. You learn one, you've learned 'em all.

The point here is that Shift-⌘ means *places*.

The other system-wide key combo, Option-⌘, means *functions*. For example, Option-⌘-D hides or shows the Dock, Option-⌘-H is the Hide Others command, Option-⌘-+ magnifies the screen (if you've turned on this feature), Option-⌘-Esc brings up the Force Quit dialog box, and so on. Consistency is always nice.

• Dragging from one disk (or disk partition) to another *copies* the folder or file. (You can drag icons either into an open window or directly onto a disk or folder *icon.*)

• If you press the Option key as you release an icon you've dragged, you *copy* the icon instead of moving it. Doing so within a single folder produces a duplicate of the file called "[Whatever its name was] copy."

• If you press the ⌘ key as you release an icon you've dragged from one disk to another, you *move* the file or folder, in the process deleting it from the original disk.

Tip: This business of pressing Option or ⌘ *after* you begin dragging is a tad awkward, but it has its charms. For example, it means that you can change your mind about the purpose of your drag in mid-movement, without having to drag back and start over.

And if it turns out you just dragged something into the wrong window or folder, a quick ⌘-Z (the shortcut for Edit→Undo) puts it right back where it came from.

Copying by Using Copy and Paste

Dragging icons to copy or move them probably feels good because it's so direct: You actually see your arrow cursor pushing the icons into the new location.

But you pay a price for this satisfying illusion. You may have to spend a moment or two fiddling with your windows to create a clear "line of drag" between the icon to be moved and the destination folder. (A background window will courteously pop to the foreground to accept your drag. But if it wasn't even open to begin with, you're out of luck.)

There's a better way. Use the Copy and Paste commands to move icons from one window into another (just as you can in Windows—except you can only copy, not cut, Mac icons). The routine goes like this:

FREQUENTLY ASKED QUESTION

Printing a Window—or a List of Files

I'd like get a neat list of the files that I can use as a label for a CD I was going to burn, or whatever. How do I print a Finder window in Mac OS X? (The File→Print command prints a selected document, not the list of files in a window.)

It's easy enough to make a list of files for printing. Once the window is open on your screen, choose Edit→Select All. Choose Edit→Copy. Now switch to a word processor and paste. (If you're using TextEdit, use Edit→Paste and Match Style instead.) You get a tidy list of all the files in that window, ready to format and print.

This simple file name list still isn't the same as printing a window, that's true; you don't get the status bar showing how many items are on the disk and how full the disk is. For that purpose, you can always make a screenshot of the window (page 566), and print that. Of course, that technique's no good if the list of files is taller than the window itself.

Really, what you want is Print Window, a handy shareware program dedicated to printing out your Finder windows, without any of these workarounds or limitations. You can download it from the "Missing CD" page at *www.missingmanuals.com.*

---

1. **Highlight the icon or icons you want to move.**

   Use any of the techniques described on page 81.

2. **Choose Edit→Copy.**

   Or press the keyboard shortcut: ⌘-C.

Tip: You can combine steps 1 and 2 by right-clicking an icon and choosing the Copy command from the shortcut menu that appears—or by using the ✿ menu. If you've selected several icons, say five, the command will say "Copy 5 items."

---

3. **Open the window where you want to put the icons. Choose Edit→Paste.**

   Once again, you may prefer to use the keyboard equivalent: ⌘-V. And once again, you can also right-click inside the window and then choose Paste from the shortcut menu that appears, or you can use the ✿ menu.

A progress bar may appear as Mac OS X copies the files or folders; press Esc or ⌘-period to interrupt the process. When the progress bar goes away, it means you've successfully transferred the icons, which now appear in the new window.

Spring-Loaded Folders: Dragging Icons into Closed Folders

Here's a common dilemma: You want to drag an icon not just into a folder, but into a folder nested *inside* that folder. This awkward challenge would ordinarily require you to open the folder, open the inner folder, drag the icon in, and then close both of the windows you opened. As you can imagine, the process is even messier if you want to drag an icon into a sub-subfolder or even a *sub*-sub-subfolder.

Fortunately, there's a better way: Use the *spring-loaded folders* feature (Figure 3-3).

With a single drag, drag the icon onto the first folder—but keep your mouse button pressed. After a second, the window opens automatically, centered on your cursor.

Still keeping the button down, drag onto the inner folder; its window opens, too. Now drag onto the *inner* inner folder—and so on. (If the inner folder you intend to open isn't visible in the window, you can scroll by dragging your cursor close to any edge of the window.)

Tip: You can even drag icons onto disks or folders whose icons appear in the Sidebar (Chapter 1). When you do so, the main part of the window flashes to reveal the contents of the disk or folder you've dragged onto. When you let go of the mouse, the main window changes back to reveal the contents of the disk or folder where you *started* dragging.

In short, Sidebar combined with spring-loaded folders make a terrific drag-and-drop way to file a desktop icon from anywhere to anywhere—without having to open or close any windows at all.

When you finally release the mouse, you're left facing the final window. All the previous windows closed on the way. You've neatly placed the icon into the core of the nested folders.

Making Spring-Loaded Folders Work

That spring-loaded folder technique sounds good in theory, but it can be disconcerting in practice. For most people, the long wait before the first folder opens is almost enough wasted time to negate the value of the feature altogether. Furthermore, when the first window finally does open, you're often caught by surprise. Suddenly your cursor—mouse button still down—is inside a window, sometimes directly on top of another folder you never intended to open. But before you can react, its window, too, has opened, and you find yourself out of control.

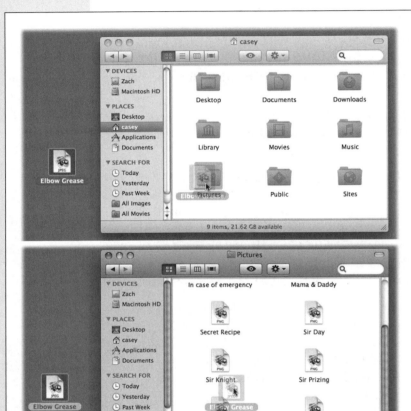

Figure 3-3:
Top: To make spring-loaded folders work, start by dragging an icon onto a folder or disk icon. Don't release the mouse button. Wait for the window to open automatically around your cursor.

Bottom: Now you can either let go of the mouse button to release the file in its new window or drag it onto yet another, inner folder. It, too, will open. As long as you don't release the mouse button, you can continue until you've reached your folder-within-a-folder destination.

Fortunately, you can regain control of spring-loaded folders using these tricks:

- Choose Finder→Preferences. On the General pane, adjust the "Spring-loaded folders and windows" delay slider to a setting that drives you less crazy. For example, if you find yourself waiting too long before the first folder opens, drag the slider toward the Short setting.

- You can turn off this feature entirely by choosing Finder→Preferences and turning off the "Spring-loaded folders and windows" checkbox.

- Tap the space bar to make the folder spring open at your command. That is, even with the Finder→Preferences slider set to the Long delay setting, you can force each folder to spring open when *you* are ready by tapping the space bar as you hold down the mouse button. True, you need two hands to master this one, but the control you regain is immeasurable.

Tip: The space bar trick works even when "Spring-loaded folders and windows" checkbox (in Finder→Preferences) is turned off. That's a handy arrangement, because it means folder windows never pop open accidentally.

- Whenever a folder springs open into a window, twitch your mouse up to the newly opened window's title bar or down to its information strip. Doing so ensures that your cursor won't wind up hovering on, and accidentally opening up, an inner folder. With the cursor parked on the gradient gray, you can take your time to survey the newly opened window's contents, and plunge into an inner folder only after gaining your bearings.

Tip: Email programs like Entourage and Mail have spring-loaded folders, too. You can drag a message out of the list and into one of your filing folders, wait for the folder to spring open and reveal its subfolders, and then drag it directly into one of them.

POWER USERS' CLINIC

Designing Your Own Icons

You don't have to be content with the icons provided by Microsoft, Apple, or whoever wrote your software. You can paste new icons onto your file, disk, and folder icons to help you pick them out at a glance.

The easiest way to replace an icon is to copy it from another icon. To do so, highlight the icon, hold down the Option key and choose File→Show Inspector. In the resulting window, click the existing icon, and then choose Edit→Copy.

Next, click the icon to which you want to transfer the copied picture. Its icon now appears in the Info dialog box that's still open on the screen. Click the icon in the dialog box, and this time choose Edit→Paste.

If you'd rather introduce all-new icons, you're welcome to steal some of the beautifully designed ones waiting at *www. iconfactory.com* and the icon sites linked to it. Once you've

downloaded these special icon files, you can copy their images from the Get Info window as you would any icon.

To design a Mac OS X icon from scratch, use a graphics program like Photoshop or the shareware favorite GraphicConverter.

Once you've saved your icon file, select it, and then copy and paste its icon using the Show Inspector method described above.

Note that you can't change certain folder icons that Mac OS X considers important, such as Applications or System.

You can, however, change the special Mac OS X folder icons in your Home folder—Pictures, Documents, and so on, and your hard drive icon. You're also not allowed to change icons that belong to other people who share your Mac and sign in under a different name (Chapter 13).

Aliases: Icons in Two Places at Once

Highlighting an icon and then choosing File→Make Alias (or pressing ⌘-L), generates an *alias,* a specially branded duplicate of the original icon (Figure 3-4). It's not a duplicate of the *file*—just of the *icon;* therefore it requires negligible storage space. When you double-click the alias, the original file opens. A Macintosh alias, in other words, is essentially the same as a Windows *shortcut.*

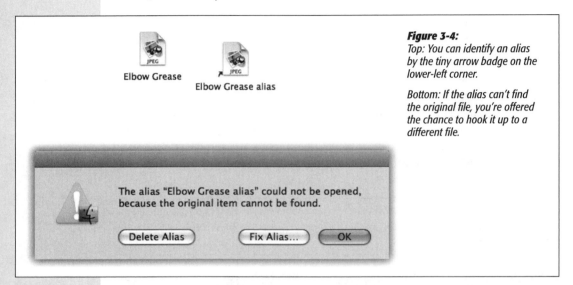

Figure 3-4:
Top: You can identify an alias by the tiny arrow badge on the lower-left corner.

Bottom: If the alias can't find the original file, you're offered the chance to hook it up to a different file.

Elbow Grease

Elbow Grease alias

The alias "Elbow Grease alias" could not be opened, because the original item cannot be found.

Delete Alias   Fix Alias...   OK

Because you can create as many aliases as you want of a single file, aliases let you, in effect, stash that file in many different folder locations simultaneously. Double-click any one of them, and you open the original icon, wherever it may be on your system.

Tip: You can also create an alias of an icon by Option-⌘-dragging it out of its window. (Aliases you create this way lack the word *alias* on the file name—a distinct delight to those who find the suffix redundant and annoying.) You can also create an alias by right-clicking a normal icon and choosing Make Alias from the shortcut menu that appears, or by highlighting an icon and then choosing Make Alias from the ✿ menu.

What's Good about Aliases

An alias takes up almost no disk space, even if the original file is enormous. Aliases are smart, too: Even if you rename the alias, rename the original file, move the alias, and move the original around on the disk, double-clicking the alias still opens the original icon.

Here are a few ways you can put aliases to work:

• You may want to file a document you're working on in several different folders, or place a particular folder in several different locations.

- You can use the alias feature to save you some of the steps required to access another hard drive on the network. (Details on this trick in Chapter 14.)

Tip: Mac OS X makes it easy to find the file to which an alias "points" without actually having to open it. Just highlight the alias and then choose File→Show Original (⌘-R), or choose Show Original from the ✿ menu. Mac OS X immediately displays the actual, original file, sitting patiently in its folder, wherever that may be.

Broken Aliases

An alias doesn't contain any of the information you've typed or composed in the original. Don't email an alias to the Tokyo office and then depart for the airport, hoping to give the presentation upon your arrival in Japan. When you double-click the alias, now separated from its original, you'll be shown the dialog box at bottom in Figure 3-4.

If you're on a plane 3,000 miles away from the hard drive on which the original file resides, click Delete Alias (to delete the orphan alias you just double-clicked) or OK (to do nothing, leaving the orphaned alias where it is).

In certain circumstances, however, the third button—Fix Alias—is the most useful. Click it to summon the Fix Alias dialog box, which you can use to navigate your entire Mac. When you click a new icon and then click Choose, you associate the orphaned alias with a different original icon.

Such techniques become handy when, for example, you click your book manuscript's alias on the desktop, forgetting that you recently saved it under a new name and deleted the older draft. Instead of simply showing you an error message that says " 'Enron Corporate Ethics Handbook' can't be found," the Mac displays the box that contains the Fix Alias button. By clicking it, thus reassociating it with the new document, you can save yourself the trouble of creating a new alias. From now on, double-clicking your manuscript's alias on the desktop opens the new draft.

Tip: You don't have to wait until the original file no longer exists before choosing a new original for an alias. You can perform alias reassignment surgery any time you like. Just highlight the alias icon and then choose File→Get Info. In the Get Info dialog box, click Select New Original. In the resulting window, find and double-click the file you'd now like to open whenever you double-click the alias.

Color Labels

This feature lets you tag selected icons with one of seven different labels, each of which has both a text label and a color associated with it. There's nothing exactly like it in Windows, but it can be very handy.

To do so, highlight the icons. Open the File menu (or the ✿ menu, or the shortcut menu that appears when you right-click the icons). There, under the heading Color Label, you'll see seven colored dots, which represent the seven different labels you can use. Figure 3-5 shows the routine.

What Labels Are Good For

After you've applied labels to icons, you can perform some unique file-management tasks—in some cases, on all of them simultaneously, even if they're scattered across multiple hard drives. For example:

Figure 3-5:
Use the File menu, ✿ menu, or shortcut menu to apply label tags to highlighted icons.

Instantly, the icon's name takes on the selected shade. In a list or column view, the entire row takes on that shade, as shown in Figure 3-6. (If you choose the little ×, you're removing any labels that you may have applied.)

Compressing, Zipping, and Archiving

Mac OS X comes with a built-in command that compresses a file or folder down to a single, smaller icon—an archive—suitable for storing or emailing.

Mac OS X creates .zip files, the same compression format used in Windows. That means you can now send .zip files back and forth to PC owners without worrying that they won't be able to open them. In Snow Leopard, these files open even more reliably in Windows. (Pre-Panther/Tiger/Leopard Mac owners can open .zip files, too. They just use the free StuffIt Expander as usual.)

The software that does the compressing is built right in. Right-click a file or folder, and choose "Compress [the icon's name]" from the shortcut menu. (Of course, you can use the File menu or ✿ menu instead.) Mac OS X thoughtfully creates a .zip archive, but leaves the original behind so you can continue working with it.

Opening a .zip file somebody sends you is equally easy: Just double-click it. Zip!—it opens.

On the other hand, Snow Leopard does not come with StuffIt Expander, the free unstuffing program that recognizes .zip files, .sit files, and just about any other form of compressed files.

If you don't already have a copy of Expander, you can download and install it yourself, which is worth doing. You can get it from, for example, this book's "Missing CD" page at *www.missingmanuals.com*.

- **Round up files with Find.** Using the Find command described in Chapter 3, you can round up all icons with a particular label. Thereafter, moving these icons at once is a piece of cake—choose Edit→Select All, and then drag any one of the highlighted icons out of the results window and into the target folder or disk.

  Using labels in conjunction with Find this way is one of the most useful and inexpensive backup schemes ever devised—whenever you finish working on a document that you'd like to back up, right-click it and apply a label called, for example, Backup. At the end of each day, use the Find command to round up all files with the Backup label—and then drag them as a group onto your backup disk.

- **Sort a list view by label.** No other Mac sorting method lets you create an arbitrary order for the icons in a window. When you sort by label, the Mac creates alphabetical clusters *within* each label grouping, as shown in Figure 3-6.

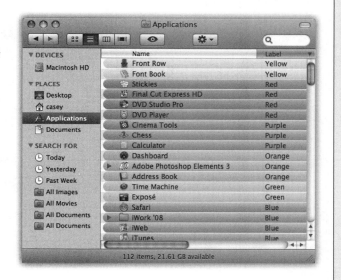

Figure 3-6:
Sorting by label lets you create several different alphabetical groups within a single window. In Snow Leopard, in fact, you can sort by labels in any view (icon, column, whatever), using the View→Show View Options palette.

In a list view, the quickest way to sort by label is to first make the label column visible. Do so by choosing View→Show View Options and turning on the Label checkbox.

This technique might be useful when, for example, your job is to process several different folders of documents; for each folder, you're supposed to convert graphics files, throw out old files, or whatever. As soon as you finish working your way through one folder, flag it with a label called Done. The folder jumps to the top (or bottom) of the window, safely marked for your reference pleasure, leaving the next unprocessed folder at your fingertips, ready to go.

- **Track progress.** Use different color labels to track the status of files in a certain project. The first drafts have no labels at all. Once they've been edited and approved, make them blue. Once they've been sent to the home office, they turn purple. (Heck, you could have all kinds of fun with this: Money-losing projects get red tints; profitable ones get green; things that make you sad are blue. Or maybe not.)

Changing Labels

In Mac OS X's factory settings, the seven labels in the File menu are named for the colors they show: Red, Orange, Yellow, and so on. Clearly, the label feature would be much more useful if you could rewrite these labels, tailoring them to your purposes.

Doing so is easy. Choose Finder→Preferences. Click the Labels button. Now you see the dialog box shown in Figure 3-7, where you can edit the text of each label.

Figure 3-7:
Top left: In the Labels tab of the Preferences dialog box, you can change the predefined label text. Each label can be up to 31 letters and spaces long.

Bottom right: Now your list and column views reveal meaningful text tags instead of color names.

The Trash

No single element of the Macintosh interface is as recognizable or famous as the Trash can, which appears at the end of the Dock. It is, of course, the inspiration for the Windows Recycle Bin.

You can discard almost any icon by dragging it onto the Trash icon (actually a wastebasket, not a trash can, but let's not quibble). When the tip of your arrow cursor touches the Trash icon, the little wastebasket turns black. When you release the mouse, you're well on your way to discarding whatever it was you dragged. As a convenience, Mac OS X even replaces the empty-wastebasket icon with a wastebasket-filled-with-crumpled-up-papers icon, to let you know there's something in there.

Tip: Learn the keyboard alternative to dragging something to the Trash: Highlight the icon, and then press ⌘-Delete. This technique is not only far faster than dragging, but requires far less precision, especially if you have a large screen. Mac OS X does all the Trash-targeting for you.

Rescuing Files and Folders from the Trash

File and folder icons sit in the Trash forever—or until you choose Finder→Empty Trash, whichever comes first.

If you haven't yet emptied the Trash, you can open its window by clicking the wastebasket icon once. Now you can review its contents: icons that you've placed on the waiting list for extinction. If you change your mind, proceed thusly:

- **Use the Put Back command.** This feature flings the trashed item back into whatever folder it came from, even if that was weeks ago—just as it does in Windows.

  You'll find the Put Back command wherever fine shortcut menus are sold. For example, it appears when you right-click the icon or click the icon and then open the ✿ menu.

Tip: The same keystroke you use to hurl something *into* the trash—⌘-Delete—also works to hurl it back out again. That is, you can highlight something in the Trash and press ⌘-Delete to put it back where it once belonged.

- **Hit Undo.** If dragging something to the Trash was the most recent thing you've done, you can press ⌘-Z—the keyboard shortcut for the Edit→Undo command. That keystroke not only removes it from the Trash, but also returns it to the folder from which it came. This trick works even if the Trash window isn't open.

- **Drag it manually.** Of course, you can also drag any icon out of the Trash with the mouse, which gives you the option of putting it somewhere new (as opposed to back in the folder it started from).

Emptying the Trash I: Quick and Easy

If you're confident that the items in the Trash window are worth deleting, use any of these three options:

- Choose Finder→Empty Trash.

GEM IN THE ROUGH

Opening Things in the Trash

Now and then, it's very useful to see what some document in the Trash *is* before committing it to oblivion—and the only way to do that is to open it.

Trouble is, you can't open it by double-clicking; you'll get nothing but an error message.

Or at least that's what Apple *wants* you to think. There is, of course, a workaround or two. First of all, you can use Quick Look (page 59) to inspect something in the Trash.

Or, if Quick Look can't open the file—or if you want to *edit* it instead of just reading it—drag the document onto the icon of a program that can open it.

That is, if a file called Don't Read Me.txt is in the Trash, you can drag it onto, say, the Word or TextEdit icon in your Dock.

The document dutifully pops open on the screen. Inspect, close, and *then* empty the Trash (or rescue the document).

- Press Shift-⌘-Delete. Or, if you'd just as soon not bother with the "Are you sure?" message, throw the Option key in there, too.

- Right-click the wastebasket icon; choose Empty Trash from the shortcut menu.

Tip: This last method has two advantages. First, the Mac doesn't bother asking "Are you sure?" (If you're clicking right on the Trash and choosing Empty Trash from the pop-up menu, it's pretty darned obvious you *are* sure.) Second, this method nukes any locked files without making you unlock them first.

If you use either of the first two methods, the Macintosh asks you to confirm your decision. Click OK. (Figure 3-8 shows both this message and the secret for turning it off forever.)

Either way, Mac OS X now deletes those files from your hard drive.

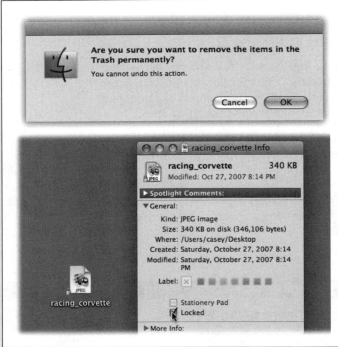

Figure 3-8:
Top: Your last warning. Mac OS X doesn't tell you how many items are in the Trash or how much disk space they take up.

If you'd rather not be interrupted for confirmation every time you empty the Trash, you can suppress this message permanently.

To do that, choose File→Preferences, click Advanced, and turn off "Show warning before emptying the Trash."

Bottom: The Get Info window for a locked file. Locking a file in this way isn't military-level security by any stretch—any passing evildoer can unlock the file in the same way. But it does trigger an "operation cannot be completed" warning when you try to put it into the Trash—or indeed when you try to drag it into any other folder—providing at least one layer of protection against mistakes.

Emptying the Trash II: Secure and Forever

When you empty the Trash as described above, each Trashed icon sure looks like it disappears. The truth is, though, that the data *in* each file is still on the hard drive. Yes, the space occupied by the dearly departed is now marked with an internal "This space available" message, and in time, new files that you save may overwrite that spot. But in the meantime, some future eBay buyer of your Mac—or, more imminently, a savvy family member or office mate—could use a program like Norton Utilities to resurrect those deleted files. (In more dire cases, companies like DriveSavers.com can use sophisticated clean-room techniques to recover crucial information—for several hundred dollars, of course.)

That notion doesn't sit well with certain groups, like government agencies, international spies, and the paranoid. As far as they're concerned, deleting a file should *really, really* delete it, irrevocably, irretrievably, and forever.

Mac OS X has a command, therefore, called *Secure* Empty Trash. When you choose this command from the Finder menu, the Mac doesn't just obliterate the parking spaces around the dead file. It actually records *new* information over the old—random 0's and 1's. Pure static gibberish.

The process takes longer than the normal Empty Trash command, of course. But when it absolutely, positively has to be gone from this earth for good (and you're absolutely, positively sure you'll never need that file again), Secure Empty Trash is secure indeed.

Locked Files: The Next Generation

By highlighting a file or folder, choosing File→Get Info, and turning on the Locked checkbox, you protect that file or folder from accidental deletion (see Figure 3-8 at bottom). A little padlock icon appears on the corner of the full-size icon, also shown in Figure 3-9.

Locked files in Snow Leopard behave like this:

- Dragging the file into another folder makes a copy; the original stays put.

- Putting the icon into the Trash produces a warning message: "Item 'Shopping List' is locked. Do you want to move it to the Trash anyway?" If so, click Continue.

- Once a locked file is in the Trash, you don't get any more warnings. When you empty the Trash, that item gets erased right along with everything else.

You can unlock files easily enough. Press Option as you choose File→Show Inspector. Turn off the Locked checkbox in the resulting Info window. (Yes, you can lock or unlock a mass of files at once.)

Get Info

By clicking an icon and then choosing File→Get Info, you open an important window like the one shown in Figure 3-9. It's a collapsible, multipanel screen that provides a wealth of information about a highlighted icon. In essence, this is the Properties window for the icon. For example:

- For a document icon, you see when it was created and modified, and what programs it "belongs" to.

- For an alias, you learn the location of the actual icon it refers to.

- For a program, you see whether or not it's been updated to run on Intel-based Macs. If so, the Get Info window says *Kind: Universal.* If not, it says *Kind: PowerPC,* and will probably run slower than you'd like because it must be translated by Rosetta (page 150).

• For a disk icon, you get statistics about its capacity and how much of it is full.

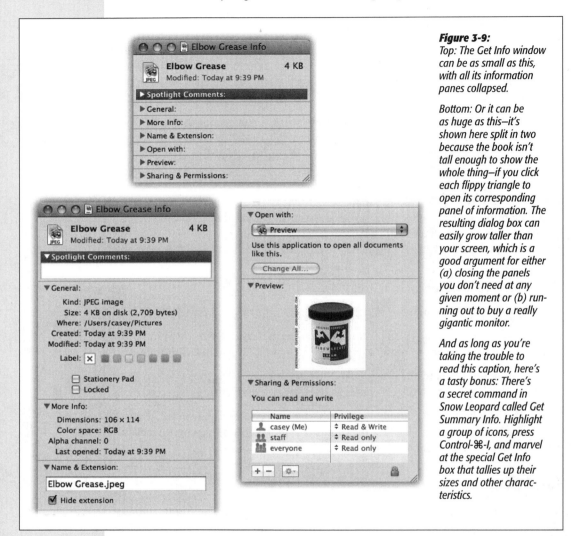

Figure 3-9:
Top: The Get Info window can be as small as this, with all its information panes collapsed.

Bottom: Or it can be as huge as this—it's shown here split in two because the book isn't tall enough to show the whole thing—if you click each flippy triangle to open its corresponding panel of information. The resulting dialog box can easily grow taller than your screen, which is a good argument for either (a) closing the panels you don't need at any given moment or (b) running out to buy a really gigantic monitor.

And as long as you're taking the trouble to read this caption, here's a tasty bonus: There's a secret command in Snow Leopard called Get Summary Info. Highlight a group of icons, press Control-⌘-I, and marvel at the special Get Info box that tallies up their sizes and other characteristics.

• If you open the Get Info window when *nothing* is selected, you get information about the desktop itself (or the open window), including the amount of disk space consumed by everything sitting on or in it.

• If you highlight 11 icons or more simultaneously, the Get Info window shows you how many you highlighted, breaks it down by type ("23 documents, 3 folders," for example), and adds up the total of their file sizes. That's a great opportunity to change certain file characteristics on numerous files simultaneously, such as locking or unlocking them, hiding or showing their filename extensions (page 136), changing their ownership or permissions (page 452), and so on.

If you highlight fewer than 11 icons, Mac OS X opens up individual Get Info windows for each one.

The Get Info Panels

Apple built the Get Info window out of a series of collapsed "flippy triangles," as shown in Figure 3-9. Click a triangle to expand a corresponding information panel.

Depending on whether you clicked a document, program, disk, alias, or whatever, the various panels may include the following:

- **Spotlight Comments.** Here, you can type in random comments for your own reference. Later, you can view these remarks in any list view, if you display the Comments column (see page 52)—and find them when you conduct Spotlight searches.

- **General.** Here's where you can view (and edit) the name of the icon, and also see its size, creation date, most recent change date, locked status, and so on.

  If you click a disk, this info window shows you its capacity and how full it is. If you click the Trash, you see how much stuff is in it. If you click an alias, this panel shows you a Select New Original button and reveals where the original file is. The General panel always opens the first time you summon the Get Info window.

- **More Info.** Just as the name implies, here you'll find more info, most often the dimensions and color format (graphics only) and when the icon was last opened. These morsels are also easily Spotlight-searchable.

- **Name & Extension.** On this panel, you can read and edit the name of the icon in question. The "Hide extension" checkbox refers to the suffix on Mac OS X file names (the last three letters of *Letter to Congress.doc,* for example).

  Many Mac OS X documents, behind the scenes, have filename extensions of this kind—but Mac OS X comes factory-set to hide them. By turning off this checkbox, you can make the suffix reappear for an individual file. (Conversely, if you've elected to have Mac OS X *show* all file name suffixes, this checkbox lets you hide filename extensions on individual icons.)

- **Open with.** This section is available for documents only. Use the controls on this screen to specify which program will open when you double-click this document, or all documents of its type. (Details on page 138.)

- **Preview.** When you're examining pictures, text files, PDF files, Microsoft Office files, sounds, clippings, and movies, you see a magnified thumbnail version of what's actually *in* that document. This Preview is like a tiny version of Quick Look (page 59). A controller lets you play sounds and movies, where appropriate.

- **Languages.** The menus and dialog boxes of well-written Mac OS X programs (iMovie and iPhoto, for example) appear by magic in whatever language you choose. The trouble is, your hard drive carries a lot of baggage as a result; it must store the wording for every menu and dialog box in every language.

If you're pretty sure you do most of your computing in just one language, expand the Languages tab, select all of the languages you *don't* speak, and click Remove. You can reclaim a *lot* of hard-drive space this way.

- **Sharing & Permissions.** This is available for all kinds of icons. If other people have access to your Mac (either from across the network or when logging in, in person), this panel lets you specify who is allowed to open or change this particular icon. See Chapter 14 for a discussion of this hairy topic.

Here and there, you may even see other panels in the Get Info window, especially when you get info on application icons. For example, iPhoto and iDVD each offer a Plugins panel that lets you manage add-on software modules.

Tip: The title-bar hierarchical menu described on page 28 works in the Get Info dialog box, too. That is, ⌘-click the Get Info window's title bar to reveal where this icon is in your folder hierarchy.

The Spotlight Menu

Every computer offers a way to find files. And every system offers several different ways to open them. But Spotlight, a star feature of Mac OS X, combines these two functions in a way that's so fast, so efficient, so spectacular, it reduces much of what you've read in the previous chapters to irrelevance.

That may sound like breathless hype, but wait till you try it. You'll see.

See the little magnifying-glass icon in your menu bar? That's the mouse-driven way to open the Spotlight search box.

The other way is to press ⌘-space bar. If you can memorize only one keystroke on your Mac, that's the one to learn. It works both at the desktop and when you're in other programs. In any case, the Spotlight text box appears just below your menu bar (Figure 3-10).

Begin typing to identify what you want to find and open. For example, if you're trying to find a file called *Pokémon Fantasy League.doc,* typing just *pok* or *leag* would probably suffice. (Spotlight doesn't find text in the *middles* of words, though; it searches from the beginnings of words.)

A menu immediately appears below the search box, listing everything Spotlight can find containing what you've typed so far. (This is a live, interactive search; that is, Spotlight modifies the menu of search results *as you type.*) The menu lists every file, folder, program, email message, address book entry, calendar appointment, picture, movie, PDF document, music file, Web bookmark, Microsoft Office (Word, PowerPoint, Excel, Entourage) document, System Preferences panel, To Do item, chat transcript, Web site in your History list, photo (according to who is in them or where it was taken, using iPhoto's Faces and Places features) iChat buddy name (Chapter 12), and even font—that contains what you typed, regardless of its name or folder location.

If you see the icon you were hoping to dig up, just click it to open it. Or use the arrow keys to "walk down" the menu, and then press Return to open the one you want.

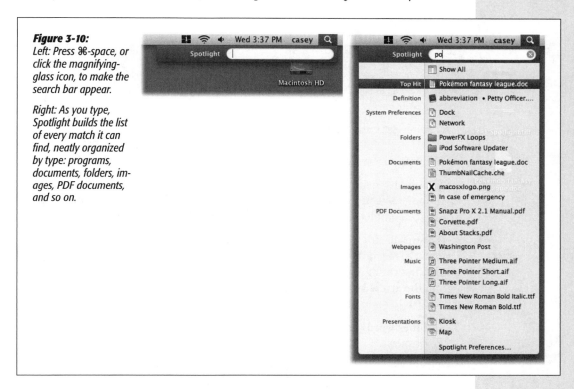

Figure 3-10:
Left: Press ⌘-space, or click the magnifying-glass icon, to make the search bar appear.

Right: As you type, Spotlight builds the list of every match it can find, neatly organized by type: programs, documents, folders, images, PDF documents, and so on.

If you click an application, it pops onto the screen. If you select a System Preferences panel, System Preferences opens and presents that panel. If you choose an appointment, the iCal program opens, already set to the appropriate day and time. Selecting an email message opens that message in Mail or Entourage. And so on.

Spotlight is so fast, it eliminates a lot of the folders-in-folders business that's a side effect of modern computing. Why burrow around in folders when you can open any file or program with a couple of keystrokes?

Spotlight-Menu Tips

It should be no surprise that a feature as important as Spotlight comes loaded with options, tips, and tricks. Here it is—the official, unexpurgated Spotlight Tip-O-Rama:

- If the very first item—labeled Top Hit—is the icon you were looking for, just press Return to open it. This is a huge deal, because it means that in most cases, you can perform the entire operation without ever taking your hands off the keyboard.

To open Safari in a hurry, for example, press ⌘-space bar (to open the Spotlight bar), type *safa,* and hit Return, all in rapid-fire sequence, without even looking. Presto: Safari is before you.

And what, exactly, is the Top Hit? Mac OS X chooses it based on its *relevance* (the importance of your search term inside that item) and timeliness (when you last opened it).

Tip: Spotlight makes a spectacular application launcher. That's because Job One for Spotlight is to display the names of matching *programs* in the results menu. Their names appear in the list nearly instantly–long before Spotlight has built the rest of the menu of search results.

If some program on your hard drive doesn't have a Dock icon, for example–or even if it does–there's no faster way to open it than to use Spotlight.

- To jump to a search result's Finder icon instead of opening it, ⌘-click its name.

- Spotlight's menu shows you only 20 of the most likely suspects, evenly divided among the categories (Documents, Applications, and so on). The downside: To see the complete list, you have to open the Spotlight *window* (page 104).

  The upside: It's fairly easy to open something in this menu from the keyboard. Just press ⌘-↓ (or ⌘-↑) to jump from category to category. Once you've highlighted the first result in a category, you can walk through the remaining four by pressing the arrow key by itself. Then, once you've highlighted what you want, press Return to open it.

  In other words, you can get to anything in the Spotlight menu with only a few keystrokes.

- The Esc key (top-left corner of your keyboard) offers a two-stage "back out of this" method. Tap it once to close the Spotlight menu and erase what you've typed, so that you're all ready to type in something different. Tap Esc a *second* time to close the Spotlight text box entirely, having given up on the whole idea of searching.

  (If you just want to cancel the whole thing in *one* step, press ⌘-space bar again, or ⌘-period, or ⌘-Esc.)

- Think of Spotlight as your little black book. When you need to look up a number in Address Book, don't bother opening Address Book; it's faster to use Spotlight. You can type somebody's name or even part of someone's phone number.

- Spotlight is also a quick way to adjust one of your Mac's preference settings. Instead of opening up the System Preferences program, type the first few letters of, say, *volume* or *network* or *clock* into Spotlight. The Spotlight menu lists the appropriate System Preferences panel, so you can jump directly to it.

- If you point to an item in the Spotlight menu without clicking, a tooltip balloon appears. It tells you the item's actual name—which is useful if Spotlight listed something because of text that appears *inside* the file, not its name—and its folder path (that is, where it is on your hard drive).

- The Spotlight menu lists 20 found items. In the following pages, you'll learn about how to see the rest of the stuff. But for now, note that you can eliminate some of the categories that show up here (like PDF Documents or Bookmarks), and even rearrange them, to permit more of the *other* kinds of things to enjoy those 20 seats of honor.

- Spotlight shows you only the matches from *your account* and the public areas of the Mac (like the System, Application, and Developer folders)—but not what's in anyone else's Home folder. If you were hoping to search your spouse's email for phrases like "meet you at midnight," forget it.

- If Spotlight finds a different version of something on each of two hard drives, it lets you know by displaying a faint gray hard drive name after each such item in the menu.

- Spotlight works by storing an *index,* a private, multimegabyte Dewey Decimal System, on each hard drive, disk partition, or USB flash (memory) drive. If you have some oddball type of disk, like a hard drive that's been formatted for Windows, Spotlight doesn't ordinarily index it—but you can turn on indexing by using the File→Get Info command on that drive's icon.

- If you point to something in the results list without clicking, you can press ⌘-I to open the Get Info window for that item.

Advanced Menu Searches

Most people just type the words they're looking for into the Spotlight box. But if that's all you type, you're missing a lot of the fun.

Use quotes

If you type more than one word, Spotlight works just the way Google does. That is, it finds things that contain both words *somewhere* inside.

But if you're searching for a phrase where the words really belong together, put quotes around them. You'll save yourself from having to wade through hundreds of results where the words appear *separately.*

For example, searching for *military intelligence* rounds up documents that contain those two words, but not necessarily side-by-side. Searching for *"military intelligence"* finds documents that contain that exact phrase. (Insert your own political joke here.)

Limit by kind

You can confine your search to certain categories using a simple code. For example, to find all photos, type *kind:image.* If you're looking for a presentation document, but you're not sure whether you used Keynote, iWork, or PowerPoint to create it, type *kind:presentation* into the box. And so on.

Here's the complete list of kinds. Remember to precede each keyword type with *kind* and a colon.

To find this:	Use one of these keywords:
a program	app, application, applications
someone in your Address Book	contact, contacts
a folder	folder, folders
a message in Mail	email, emails, mail message, mail messages
an iCal appointment	event, events
an iCal task	to do, to dos, todo, todos
a graphic	image, images
a movie	movie, movies
a music file	music
an audio file	audio
a PDF file	pdf, pdfs
a System Preferences control	preferences, system preferences
a Safari bookmark	bookmark, bookmarks
a font	font, fonts
a presentation (PowerPoint, etc.)	presentation, presentations

---

GEM IN THE ROUGH

Sweet Spotlight Serendipity: Equations and Definitions

Spotlight has two secret features that turn it into a different beast altogether.

First, it's a tiny pocket calculator, always at the ready. Click in the Search box (or press ⌘-space bar), type or paste *38*48.2-7+55,* and marvel at the first result in the Spotlight menu: *1879.6.* There's your answer—and you didn't even have to fire up the Calculator.

(For shorter equations—only a few characters long—the first result in the Spotlight menu shows the *entire* equation, like *.15*234=35.1.*)

And it's not just a four-function calculator, either. It works with square roots: Type *sqrt(25),* and you'll get the answer 5. It also works with powers: Type *pow(6,6)*—that is, 6 to

the power of 6—and you'll get 46656. You can even type *pi* to represent, you know, pi.

For a complete list of math functions in Spotlight, open Terminal (page 570), type *man math,* and press Return.

Second, the Spotlight menu is now a full-blown English dictionary. Or, more specifically, it's wired directly into Mac OS X's *own* dictionary, which sits in your Applications folder.

So if you type, for example, *schadenfreude* into the Search box, you'll see, to your amazement, the beginning of the actual definition right there in the menu. Click it to open Dictionary and read the full-blown entry. (In this example, that would be: "noun: pleasure derived by someone from another person's misfortune.")

You can combine these codes with the text you're seeking, too. For example, if you're pretty sure you had a photo called "Naked Mole-Rat," you could cut directly to it by typing *mole kind:images* or *kind:images mole*. (The order doesn't matter.)

Limit by recent date

You can use a similar code to restrict the search by chronology. If you type *date: yesterday*, Spotlight limits its hunt to items you last opened yesterday.

Here's the complete list of date keywords you can use: *this week, this month, this year; today, yesterday, tomorrow; next week, next month, next year.* (The last four items are useful only for finding upcoming iCal appointments. Even Spotlight can't show you files you haven't created yet.)

Limit by metadata

If your brain is already on the verge of exploding, now might be a good time to take a break.

In Snow Leopard, you can limit Spotlight searches by *any* of the 125 different info-morsels that may be stored as part of the files on your Mac: Author, Audio bit rate, City, Composer, Camera model, Pixel width, and so on. Here are a few examples:

- *author:casey*. Finds all documents with "casey" in the Author field. (This presumes that you've actually *entered* the name Casey into the document's Author box. Microsoft Word, for example, has a place to store this information.)

- *width:800*. Finds all graphics that are 800 pixels wide.

- *flash:1*. Finds all photos that were taken with the camera's flash on. (To find photos with the flash *off*, you'd type *flash:0*. A number of the yes/no criteria work this way: Use 1 for yes, 0 for no.)

- *modified:3/7/10-3/10/10*. Finds all documents modified between March 7 and March 10.

  You can also type *created:=6/1/10* to find all the files you created on June 1, 2010. Type *modified:<=3/9/10* to find all documents you edited *on or before* March 9, 2010.

  As you can see, three range-finding symbols are available for your queries: <, >, and -. The < means "before" or "less than," the > means "after" or "greater than," and the hyphen indicates a range (of dates, size, or whatever you're looking for).

Tip: Here again, you can string words together. To find all PDFs you opened today, use *date:today kind:PDF.* And if you're looking for a PDF document that you created on July 4, 2010, containing the word *wombat,* you can type *created:=7/4/10 kind:pdf wombat,* although at this point, you're not saving all that much time.

Now, those examples are just a few representative searches out of the dozens that Mac OS X makes available.

It turns out that the search criteria codes that you can type into the Spotlight box (*author:casey, width:800,* and so on) correspond to the master list that appears when you choose Other in the Spotlight *window,* as described on page 104. In other words, there are *125 different* search criteria.

Boolean searches

Spotlight searches also permit what comp sci professors call *Boolean* searches. These are search terms that round up results containing *either* of two search terms, or *both* search terms, or one term but *not* another.

To go Boolean, you're supposed to incorporate terms like AND, OR, or NOT into your search queries.

For example, you can round up a list of files that match *two* terms by typing, say, *vacation AND kids.* (That's also how you'd find documents coauthored by two specific people—you and a pal, for example. You'd search for *author:Casey AND author:Chris.* Yes, you have to type Boolean terms in all capitals.)

Tip: You can use parentheses instead of AND, if you like. That is, typing *(vacation kids)* finds documents that contain both words, not necessarily together.

If you use OR, you can find icons that match *either* of two search criteria. Typing *kind:jpeg OR kind:pdf* turns up photos and PDF files in a single list.

The minus sign (hyphen) works, too. If you did a search for *dolphins,* hoping to turn up sea-mammal documents, but instead find your results contaminated by football-team listings, by all means repeat the search with *dolphins -miami.* Mac OS X eliminates all documents containing "Miami."

Tip: The word NOT works the same way. You could type *dolphins NOT miami* to achieve the same effect. But the hyphen is faster to type.

The Spotlight Window

As you may have noticed, the Spotlight menu doesn't list *every* match on your hard drive. Unless you own one of those extremely rare 60-inch Apple Skyscraper Displays, there just isn't room.

Instead, Spotlight uses some fancy behind-the-scenes analysis to calculate and display the *20 most likely* matches for what you typed. But at the top of the menu, it usually says something like "Show All," meaning that there are other candidates.

There is, however, a second, more powerful way into the Spotlight labyrinth. And that's the Spotlight *window,* shown in Figure 3-11.

Spotlight Window from Spotlight Menu

If the Spotlight menu—its Most Likely to Succeed list—doesn't include what you're looking for, then click Show All. You've just opened the Spotlight window.

Now you have access to the *complete* list of matches, neatly listed in what appears to be a standard Finder window.

Opening the Spotlight Window Directly

When you're in the Finder, you can also open the Spotlight window *directly*, without using the Spotlight menu as a trigger. Actually, there are three ways to get there (Figure 3-11):

- ⌘-F (for *Find*, get it?). When you choose File→Find (or press ⌘-F), you get an *empty* Spotlight window, ready to fill in for your search.

Tip: When the Find window opens, what folder does it intend to search? That's up to you. Choose Finder→Preferences→Advanced. From the "When performing a search" pop-up menu, you can choose Search This Mac, Search the Current Folder (usually what you want), or Use the Previous Search Scope (that is, *either* "the whole Mac" or "the current folder," whichever you set up last time).

Figure 3-11:
The Spotlight window either lists nothing (top)—or everything on your hard drive (bottom), depending on how you open it. Either way, it's ready to search your entire hard drive (except other people's Home folders). But Spotlight has many tricks up its software sleeve.

- **Option-⌘-space bar.** This keystroke opens the same window. But it always comes set to search everything on your Mac (except other people's Home folders, of course), regardless of the setting you made in Preferences (as described in the previous paragraphs).

• **Open any desktop window, and type something into the Search box at upper right.** Presto—the mild-mannered folder window turns into the Spotlight window, complete with search results.

Tip: You can change the Find keystrokes to just about anything you like. See page 114.

The Basic Search

When the Spotlight window opens, you can start typing whatever you're looking for into the Search box at the upper right.

As you type, the window fills with a list of the files and folders whose names contain what you typed. It's just like the Spotlight menu, but without the 20-item results limit (Figure 3-11).

While the searching is going on, a sprocket icon whirls away in the lower-right corner. To cancel the search and clear the box (so you can try a different search), click the ⊗ button next to the phrase you typed. Or just hit the Esc key.

Power Searches

The real beauty of the Spotlight window, though, is that it can hunt down icons using extremely specific criteria; it's much more powerful (and complex) than the Spotlight menu. If you spent enough time setting up the search, you could use this feature to find a document whose name begins with the letters *Cro,* is over a megabyte in size, was created after 10/1/09 but before the end of the year, was changed within the past week, has the file name suffix *.doc,* and contains the phrase "attitude adjustment." (Of course, if you knew *that* much about a file, you'd probably know where it is without having to use the Searching window. But you get the picture.)

To use the Spotlight window, you need to feed it two pieces of information: *where* you want it to search, and *what* to look for. You can make these criteria as simple or as complex as you like.

Where to Look

The three phrases at the top of the window—This Mac, "Folder Name," and Shared— are buttons. Click one to tell Spotlight where to search:

• **This Mac** means your *entire* computer, including secondary disks attached to it (or installed inside)—minus other people's files, of course.

• **"Letters to Congress"** (or whatever the current window is) limits the search to whatever window was open. So if you want to search your Pictures folder, open it first and *then* hit ⌘-F. You'll see the "Pictures" button at the top of the window, and you can click it to restrict the search to that folder.

Tip: Remember: You can save yourself this click by visiting Finder→Preferences→Advanced and choosing "Search the Current Folder" from the pop-up menu.

- **Shared.** Click this button to expand the search to your *entire network* and all the computers on it. (This assumes, of course, that you've brought their icons to your screen as described in Chapter 14.)

If the other computers are Macs running Leopard or Snow Leopard, Spotlight can search their files just the way it does on your own Mac—finding words inside the files, for example. If they're any other kind of computer, Spotlight can search for files only by name.

Tip: If the object of your quest doesn't show up, you can adjust the scope of the search with one quick click on another button at the top of the window, like This Mac or Shared. Spotlight updates the results list.

Search by Contents/Search by Name

The two other buttons at the top of the Spotlight window are also very powerful:

- **Contents.** This button, the factory setting, searches for the words *inside* your files, along with all the metadata attached to them.

- **File Name.** There's no denying that sometimes you already know a file's *name*—you just don't know where it is. In this case, it's far faster to search by name, just as people did before Spotlight came along. The list of results is far shorter, and you'll spot what you want much faster. That's why this button is so welcome.

Tip: If you press Shift as you open the File menu (or as you press ⌘-F), the Find command changes to Find by Name. It opens the Find window, preset to search for icons by name. What a shortcut!

Complex Searches

If all you want to do is search your entire computer for files containing certain text, you might as well use the Spotlight *menu* described at the beginning of this chapter.

The power of the Spotlight *window,* though, is that it lets you design much more specific searches, using over 125 different search criteria: date modified, file size, the "last opened" date, color label, copyright holder's name, shutter speed (of a digital photo), tempo (of a music file), and so on. Figure 3-12 illustrates how detailed this kind of search can be.

To set up a complex search like this, use the second row of controls at the top of the window.

And third, and fourth, and fifth. Each time you click one of the **+** buttons at the right end of the window, a new criterion row appears; use its pop-up menus to specify *what* date, *what* file size, and so on. Figure 3-12 shows how you might build, for example, a search for all photo files that you've opened within the last week that contain a Photoshop layer named *Freckle Removal.*

To delete a row, click the **−** button at its right end.

Tip: If you press Option, the **+** button changes into a … button. When you click it, you get sub-rows of parameters for a single criterion. And a pop-up menu that says Any, All, or None appears at the top so you can build what are called exclusionary searches.

The idea here is that you can set up a search for documents created between November 1 and 7 or documents created November 10 through 14. Or files named Complaint that are also either Word or InDesign files.

The mind boggles.

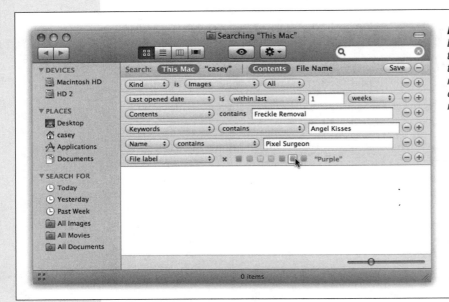

Figure 3-12:
By repeatedly clicking the + button, you can turn on as many criteria as you'd like; each additional row further narrows the search.

Here's a rundown of the ways you can restrict your search, according to the options in the first pop-up menu of a row. Note that after you choose from that first pop-up menu (Last Opened, for example), you're supposed to use the additional pop-up menus to narrow the choice ("within last," "2," and "weeks," for example), as you'll read below.

Kind

When the first pop-up menu says Kind, you can use the second pop-up menu to indicate what kind of file you're looking for: Applications, Documents, Folders, Images, Movies, Music, PDF files, Presentations, Text files, or Other.

And what if the item you're looking for isn't among those nine canned choices? What if it's an alias, or a Photoshop plug-in, or some other type?

That's what the Other option is all about. Here, you can type in almost anything that specifies a kind of file: *Word, Excel, TIFF, JPEG, AAC, final cut, iMovie, alias, zip, html,* or whatever.

Last opened date/Last modified date/Created date

When you choose one of these options from the first pop-up menu, the second pop-up menu lets you isolate files, programs, and folders according to the last time you opened them, the last time you changed them, or when they were created.

- **Today, yesterday, this week, this month, this year.** This second pop-up menu offers quick, canned time-limiting options.

- **Within last, exactly, before, after.** These let you be more precise. If you choose before, after, or exactly, then your criterion row sprouts a month/day/year control that lets you round up items that you last opened or changed before, after, or on a specific day, like 5/27/10. If you choose "within last," then you can limit the search to things you've opened or changed within a specified number of days, weeks, months, or years.

  These are awesomely useful controls, because they let you specify a chronological window for whatever you're looking for.

Tip: You're allowed to add two Date rows—a great trick that lets you round up files that you created or edited between two dates. Set up the first Date row to say "is after," and the second one to say "is before."

In fact, if it doesn't hurt your brain to think about it, how about this? You can even have more than two Date rows. Use one pair to specify a range of dates for the file's creation date and two other rows to limit when it was modified.

Science!

Name

Spotlight likes to find text *anywhere* in your files, no matter what their *names* are. But when you want to search for an icon by the text that's in only its *name*, this is your ticket. (Capitalization doesn't matter.)

Wouldn't it be faster just to click the File Name button at the top of the window? Yes—but using the Spotlight window offers you far more control, thanks to the second pop-up menu that offers you these options:

- **Contains.** The position of the letters you type doesn't matter. If you type *then*, you find files with names like "Then and Now," "Authentic Cajun Recipes," and "Lovable Heathen."

- **Starts with.** The Find program finds only files beginning with the letters you type. If you type *then*, you find "Then and Now," but not "Authentic Cajun Recipes" or "Lovable Heathen."

- **Ends with.** If you type *then*, you find "Lovable Heathen," but not files called "Then and Now" or "Authentic Cajun Recipes."

- **Is.** This option finds only files named *precisely* what you type (except that capitalization still doesn't matter). Typing *then* won't find any of the file names in the previous examples. It would unearth only a file called simply "Then." In fact, a file with a file name suffix, like "Then.doc," doesn't even qualify.

(If this happens to you, though, here's a workaround: From the first pop-up menu, choose Other; in the dialog box, pick Filename. The Filename criterion ignores extensions; it would find "Then.doc" even if you searched for "then.")

Contents

You can think of this option as the opposite of Name. It finds *only* the text that's inside your files, and completely ignores their icon names.

That's a handy function when, for example, a document's name doesn't match its contents. Maybe a marauding toddler pressed the keys while playing Kid Pix, renaming your doctoral thesis "xggrjpO#$5%////." Or maybe you just can't remember what you called something.

Other

If this were a math equation, it might look like this: *options × options = overwhelming.*

Choosing Other from the first pop-up menu opens a special dialog box containing at least 125 *other* criteria. Not just the big kahunas like Name, Size, and Kind, but far more targeted (and obscure) criteria like "Bits per sample" (so you can round up MP3 music files of a certain quality), "Device make" (so you can round up all digital photos taken with, say, a Canon Rebel camera), "Key signature" (so you can find all the GarageBand songs you wrote in the key of F sharp), "Pages" (so you can find all Word documents that are really long), and so on. As you can see in Figure 3-13, each one comes with a short description.

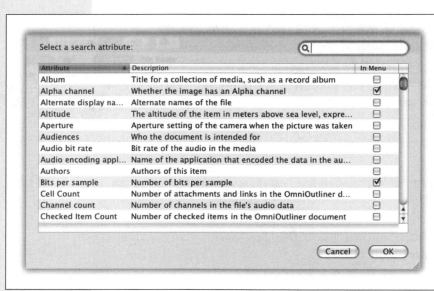

Figure 3-13:
Here's the master list of search criteria. Turn on the "In menu" checkboxes of the ones you'll want to reuse often, as described in the box on the previous page. Once you've added some of these search criteria to the menu, you'll get an appropriate set of "find what?" controls ("Greater than"/"Less than" pop-up menus, for example).

You may think Spotlight is offering you a staggering array of file-type criteria. In fact, though, big bunches of information categories (technically called *metadata*) are all hooks for a relatively small number of document types. For example:

- **Digital photos and other graphics files** account for the metadata types alpha channel, aperture, color space, device make, device model, EXIF version, exposure mode, exposure program, exposure time, flash, FNumber, focal length, ISO speed, max aperture, metering mode, orientation, pixel height, pixel width, redeye, resolution height, resolution width, and white balance.

- **Digital music files** have searchable metadata categories like album, audio bit rate, bits per sample, channel count, composer, duration, General MIDI sequence, key signature, lyricist, musical genre, recording date, sample rate, tempo, time signature, track number, and year recorded. There's even a special set of parameters for GarageBand and Soundtrack documents, including instrument category, instrument name, loop descriptors, loop file type, loop original key, and loop scale type.

- **Microsoft Office documents** can contain info bits like authors, contributors, fonts, languages, pages, publishers, and contact information (name, phone number, and so on).

This massive list also harbors a few criteria you may use more often, like Size, Label, and Visibility (which lets you see all the invisible files on your hard drive). If you turn on their checkboxes, they'll be more easily available for future searches.

Now, you could argue that in the time it takes you to set up a search for such a specific kind of data, you could have just rooted through your files and found what you wanted manually. But hey—you never know. Someday, you may remember *nothing* about a photo you're looking for except that you used the flash and an f-stop of 1.8.

Tip: Don't miss the Search box in this dialog box. It makes it super-easy to pluck one useful criterion needle–Size, say–out of the haystack. Also don't forget about the "In menu" checkbox in the right column. It lets you add one of these criteria to the main pop-up menu, so you don't have to go burrowing into Other again the next time.

What to Do with Search Results

The results window is a regular old Finder window, with all the usual views and controls (Figure 3-14).

You can work with anything in the results window exactly as though it were a regular Finder window: Drag something to the Trash, rename something, drag something to the desktop to move it there, drag something onto a Dock icon to open it with a certain program, Option-⌘-drag it to the desktop to create an alias, and so on.

Or you can proceed in any of these ways:

- **Change the view** by clicking one of the View icons or choosing from the View menu. You can switch between icon, list, or Cover Flow views (see Chapter 2). Actually, Cover Flow is a *great* view for search results; since this list is culled from folders all over the computer, you otherwise have very little sense of context as you examine the file names.

- **Sort the results** by clicking the column headings. It can be especially useful to sort by Kind, so that similar file types are clustered together (Documents, Images, Messages, and so on).

Tip: You can sort the search results even in icon view. True, there are no column headings to click—but you can use the ✿ menu to choose "Keep Arranged by" [whatever criterion you like]. Mac OS X will remember this sort order the next time you do an icon-view search.

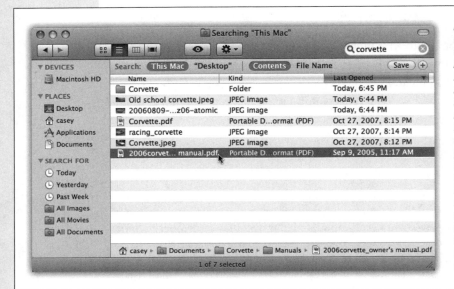

Figure 3-14:
Click a result to see where it sits on your hard drive (bottom). If the window is too narrow to reveal the full folder path, run your cursor over the folder names without clicking. As your mouse moves from one folder to another, Snow Leopard briefly reveals its name, compressing other folders to make room. (Sub-tip: You can drag icons into these folders, too.)

- **Get a Quick Look at one result** by clicking it and then hitting the space bar. If it's a document type that Mac OS X understands, you get the big, bold Quick Look preview window.

- **Find out where it is.** It's nice to see all the search results in one list, but you're not actually seeing them in their native habitats: in the Finder folder windows where they physically reside.

  If you click once on an icon in the results, the bottom edge of the window becomes a folder map that shows you where that item is.

- **Open the file (or open one of the folders it's in).** If one of the found files is the one you were looking for, double-click it to open it (or highlight it and press either ⌘-O or ⌘-↓). In many cases, you'll never even know or care where the file was—you just want to get into it.

- **Move or delete the file.** You can drag an item directly out of the found-files list and into a different folder, window, or disk—or straight to the Dock or the Trash.

- **Give up.** If none of these avenues suits your fancy, you can close the window as you would any other (⌘-W).

Customizing Spotlight

You've just read about how Spotlight works fresh out of the box. But you can tailor its behavior, both for security reasons and to fit it to the kinds of work you do.

Here are three ways to open the Spotlight preferences center:

- **Choose Spotlight Preferences** at the bottom of the Spotlight menu just after you've performed a search.

- **Use Spotlight itself.** Hit ⌘-space bar, type *spotl,* and press Return.

- **Choose **→System Preferences.** Click Spotlight.

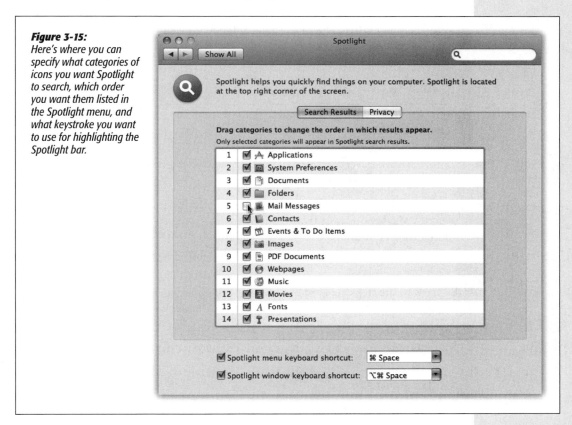

Figure 3-15:
Here's where you can specify what categories of icons you want Spotlight to search, which order you want them listed in the Spotlight menu, and what keystroke you want to use for highlighting the Spotlight bar.

In any case, you wind up face-to-face with the dialog box shown in Figure 3-15. You can tweak Spotlight in three ways here, all very useful:

- **Turn off categories.** The list of checkboxes identifies all the kinds of things Spotlight tracks. If you find that Spotlight uses up valuable menu space listing, say, Web bookmarks or fonts—stuff you don't need to find very often—then turn off their checkboxes. Now the Spotlight menu's precious 20 slots are allotted to icon types you care more about.

- **Prioritize the categories.** This dialog box also lets you change the *order* of the category results; just drag an individual list item up or down to change where it appears in the Spotlight menu.

- **Change the keystroke.** Ordinarily, pressing ⌘-space bar highlights the Spotlight search box in your menu bar, and Option-⌘-space bar opens the Spotlight window described above. If these keystrokes clash with some other key assignment in your software, though, you can reassign them to almost any other keystroke you like.

  Click inside the white box that lists the keystroke and then press *any* key combination—Control-S, for example—to choose something different. Whatever keystroke you choose *must* include at least one of the modifier keys (Option, Control, or ⌘) or one of the F-keys (such as F4).

Note: Apple assumes no responsibility for your choosing a keystroke that messes up some other function on your Mac. ⌘-S, for example, would not be a good choice.

Privacy Settings

Ordinarily, Spotlight doesn't consider any corner of your hard drive off-limits. It looks for matches wherever it can except in other people's Home folders. (That is, you can't search through other people's stuff).

But even within your own Mac world, you can hide certain folders from Spotlight searches. Maybe you have privacy concerns—for example, you don't want your spouse Spotlighting your stuff while you're away from your desk. Maybe you just want to create more focused Spotlight searches, removing a lot of old, extraneous junk from its database.

Either way, the steps are simple. Open the Spotlight panel of System Preferences, as described above. Click the Privacy tab. Figure 3-16 explains the remaining steps.

Once you've built up your list of private disks and folders, close System Preferences. Spotlight now pretends the private items don't even exist.

Smart Folders

You may remember from Chapter 1 (or from staring at your own computer) that the Sidebar at the left side of every Snow Leopard desktop window contains a set of little folders under the Searches heading. Each is actually a *smart folder*—a self-updating folder that, in essence, performs a continual, 24/7 search for the criteria you specify.

(Smart folders are a lot like smart albums in iPhoto and iTunes, smart mailboxes in Mail, and so on.)

Note: In truth, the smart folder performs a search for the specified criteria *at the moment you open it*. But because it's so fast, and because it's always up to date, it feels as though it's been quietly searching all along.

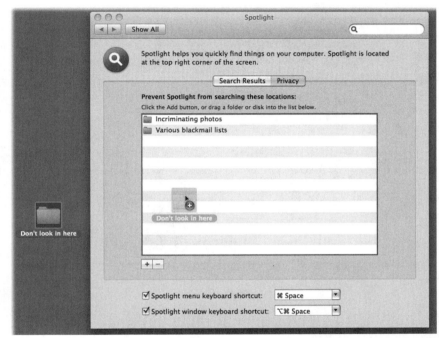

Figure 3-16:
You can add disks, partitions, or folders to the list of non-searchable items just by dragging them from the desktop into this window. Or, if the private items aren't visible at the moment, you can click the + button, navigate your hard drive, select the item, and click Choose. To re-move something from this list, click it and then press the Delete key or click the – button.

As it turns out, the ones installed there by Apple are meant to serve as inspiration for you to create your *own* smart folders. The key, as it turns out, is the little Save button in the upper-right corner of the Spotlight window.

Here's a common example of how you might use it. You choose File→Find. You set up the pop-up menus to say "last opened date" and "this week." You click Save. You name the smart folder something like Current Crises, and you turn on "Add to Sidebar" (Figure 3-17).

From now on, whenever you click that smart folder, it reveals all of the files you've worked on in the past week or so. The great part is that these items' *real* locations may be all over the map, scattered in folders all over your Mac and your network. But through the magic of the smart folder, they appear as though they're all in one neat folder.

Tip: If you decide your original search criteria need a little fine-tuning, click the smart folder. From the ✿ menu, choose Show Search Criteria. You're back on the original setting-up-the-search window. Use the pop-up menus and other controls to tweak your search setup, and then click the Save button once again.

To *delete* a smart folder, just drag its icon out of the Sidebar. (Or if it's anywhere else, like on your desktop, drag it to the Trash like any other folder.)

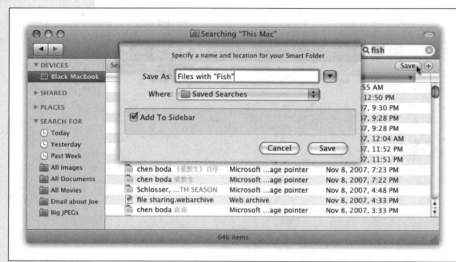

Figure 3-17:
Mac OS X can preserve your search as a smart folder listed in the Sidebar (lower left)—at least, it does as long as "Add To Sidebar" is turned on. You can stash a smart folder in your Dock, too, although it doesn't display a stack of its contents, as normal folders do.

Documents, Programs, & Spaces

The beauty of life in the Era of Switchers is that most of the big-boy programs are available in nearly identical versions for both the Mac and Windows. Word, Excel, and PowerPoint; Photoshop, Illustrator, and InDesign; FileMaker Pro; Dreamweaver; and many other programs are available for both Mac and Windows. Sometimes you have to buy the Mac version separately; sometimes it's on the same CD.

The best part: The documents you create with the Mac versions are generally *identical in format* to the ones created in Windows. A Microsoft Word document, for example, requires no conversion when transferred from a Mac to a PC or vice versa. It is what it is—a .doc or .docx file.

Same thing with Excel spreadsheets (.xls), PowerPoint slideshows (.ppt), Photoshop documents (.psd), and on and on. You may occasionally encounter a tiny formatting difference—a line thickness change, a movie file that requires a plug-in—but most documents open flawlessly when moved between Macs and PCs. (Chapter 7 offers more detail on finding Mac versions of your favorite PC programs.)

But even if switching to the Mac OS X versions of your programs is relatively easy, learning how Mac OS X programs *in general* operate may require some study. As this chapter will make clear, the relationship between programs and their documents differs in several substantial ways from the way things work in Windows.

Opening Mac OS X Programs

Many of the techniques for launching (opening) a program work just as they do in Windows. For example:

- Click a program's icon on the Dock, the Sidebar, or the Finder toolbar.

- Use Spotlight. Hit ⌘-space bar, type the first letters of the program's name, and then press Return.

- Double-click an application's icon in the Finder.

- Highlight an application icon and then press ⌘-O (short for File→Open) or ⌘-↓.

- Use the submenus of the menu's Recent Items→Applications command.

- Open a *document* icon in any of these ways, or drag a document onto the icon of a program that can open it (whether in the Dock, the Finder toolbar, the Sidebar, or in a folder window).

When you launch a program, the Mac reads its computer code, which lies on your hard drive's surface, and feeds it quickly into RAM (memory). During this brief interval, the icon of the opening program jumps up and down eagerly in your Dock.

What happens next depends on the program you're using. Most present you with a new, blank, untitled document. Some, like iDVD, automatically open the last file you worked on. Some, like FileMaker and PowerPoint, ask if you want to open an existing document or create a new one.

And a few oddball programs don't open any window at all when first launched.

The Application Menu

In each case, however, the very first menu after the appears with bold lettering and identifies the program you're using. It might say iTunes, or Microsoft Word, or Stickies.

FREQUENTLY ASKED QUESTION

What's with the Big "Duh"?

So, I've just bought a Mac, I'm all excited, and I double-click an Excel document. And now the Mac asks me: "You are opening Microsoft Excel for the first time. Do you want to continue?" Well, HELLO! I double-clicked the icon, didn't I? Does Apple think I'm some kind of idiot?

It's not you Apple's worried about. It's the silent parade of evil hackers, lurking out there in Internet Land, waiting for the right moment to bring down the Mac.

See, in the Windows world, spyware authors have to be sneaky about how they install their stuff on your PC. You wouldn't be so stupid as to double-click an application called Spyware Installer™, of course. So the spyware tricks you into

running its installer. It commandeers a certain document type (like MP3 or JPEG), reassigning it to its installer. You innocently double-click some document, but an unanticipated program opens—and you've just opened Pandora's box.

In Mac OS X, that can't happen. When double-clicking some document opens a program for the first time, this dialog box appears, just to let you know what's about to happen. If the program that's about to open isn't the one you were expecting, well, you've got a chance to back out of it.

And if it *is* the program you were expecting, click Continue. You won't be asked again about this version of this particular program.

This Application menu (Figure 4-1) offers a number of commands pertaining to the entire program and its windows, including About, Quit, and Hide.

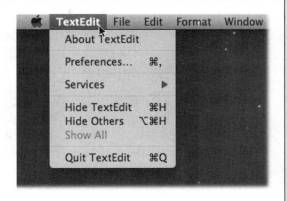

Figure 4-1:
The first menu in every program lets you know, at a glance, which program you're actually in. It also offers overall program commands like Quit and Hide.

Quitting Programs

In Macintosh lingo, you don't "exit" a program when you're finished with it, you "quit" it. And the command to do so isn't in the File menu—it's at the bottom of the Application menu.

But Mac OS X offers two much more fun ways to quit a program:

- Right-click a program's Dock icon and then choose Quit from the pop-up menu.

- When you've pressed ⌘-Tab to summon the "heads-up display" of open programs, type the letter Q without releasing the ⌘ key. The highlighted program quits without further ado.

Force-Quitting Programs

Mac OS X is a rock-solid operating system, but that doesn't mean *programs* never screw up. Individual programs are as likely as ever to freeze—or, rather, to *hang* (to lock up and display the "spinning beach ball of death" cursor). In such cases, you have no choice but to *force-quit* the program—or, in Windows lingo, to terminate it or "end its task."

Doing so doesn't destabilize your Mac; you don't have to restart it. In fact, you can usually reopen the very same program and get on with your life.

You can force-quit a stuck program in any of several ways:

- Click-and-hold on the program's Dock icon. That triggers the Exposé function, of course, but it also offers a Quit button just above your cursor. Press the Option key to make the button say Force Quit (Figure 4-2, left). Click it.

• Control-click (right-click) its Dock icon. Once the shortcut menu appears, press Option so that the Quit command now says Force Quit (Figure 4-2, bottom). Bingo—that program is outta here.

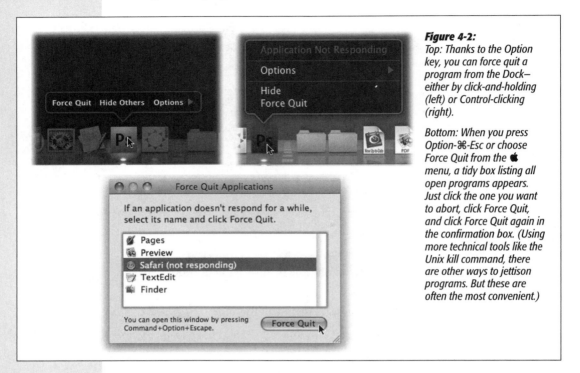

Figure 4-2:
Top: Thanks to the Option key, you can force quit a program from the Dock— either by click-and-holding (left) or Control-clicking (right).

Bottom: When you press Option-⌘-Esc or choose Force Quit from the menu, a tidy box listing all open programs appears. Just click the one you want to abort, click Force Quit, and click Force Quit again in the confirmation box. (Using more technical tools like the Unix kill command, there are other ways to jettison programs. But these are often the most convenient.)

• Press Option-⌘-Esc, the traditional Mac force-quit keystroke, or choose →Force Quit. Either way, proceed as shown in Figure 4-2.

Again, force-quitting is not bad for your Mac. The only downside to force-quitting a program is that you lose any unsaved changes to your open documents, along with any preference settings you may have changed while the program was open.

The New, Improved "Alt-Tab"

Just as in Windows, there's a handy keystroke for switching from one open program to another; it's the ⌘-Tab keystroke (see Figure 4-3).

You can use this feature in three different ways, which are well worth learning:

• If you keep the ⌘ key pressed, each press of the Tab key highlights the Dock icon of another program, in left-to-right Dock order. Release both keys when you reach the one you want. Mac OS X brings the corresponding program to the front. (To move backward through the open programs, press Shift-⌘-Tab.)

- If you leave the ⌘ key pressed, you can choose a program by clicking its icon with your mouse.

- A single press of ⌘-Tab takes you to the program you used most recently, and another, separate ⌘-Tab bounces back to the program you started in.

Figure 4-3:
Apple calls this row of open program icons a "heads-up display," named after the projected data screens on a Navy jet windshield that lets pilots avoid having to look down at their instruments.

Imagine you're doing a lot of switching between two programs—your Web browser and your email program, for example. If you have five other programs open, you don't waste your time ⌘-Tabbing your way through all open programs just to "get back" to your Web browser.

Tip: Here's a related keystroke, equally awesome. If you press ⌘-tilde (the ~ key next to the 1 key), you switch to the next *window* in the *same* program.

Exposé: Death to Window Clutter

Managing all the open windows in all the open programs used to be like herding cats. Off you would go, burrowing through the microscopic pop-up menus of your Dock, trying to find the window you want.

Exposé represents the first fresh look at this problem in decades. The concept is delicious: With the one mouse click or keystroke, Mac OS X shrinks all windows in all programs to a size that fits on the screen (Figure 4-4), like index cards on a bulletin board. You click the one you want, and you're there. It's fast, efficient, animated, and a lot of fun.

Now, this is going to get very mind-blowing very fast, so read slowly and keep your shoulders relaxed.

There are actually three different Exposé modes. One shows you miniatures of *all* windows in *all* programs; one shows you miniatures of all the windows in *just one program;* and one *hides* all windows in all programs so you can see the desktop.

Each of these three modes, moreover, can be triggered using different combinations of the mouse and keyboard. The following pages will cover all of them, but you're not expected to learn all that. Just find the *one* trigger that seems most convenient, and stick with it.

All-Apps Exposé

The first and most famous Exposé method is shown in Figure 4-4. *Every* window in *every* program is arrayed before you, nothing covered up, nothing hidden. It's a great way to get your bearings in a hurry.

Here are the best ways to get this effect:

- **Current keyboards: Press F3 (▣).** On recent Apple laptop and desktop keyboards—aluminum with very flat, thin keys poking up—the F3 key is dedicated

Figure 4-4:
Top: Quick! Where's System Preferences in all this mess?

Bottom: With a tap of the F3 key, you can spot that window, shrunken but not overlapped. Each thumbnail window offers a label to help you identify it. These aren't static snapshots of the windows at the moment you Exposé'd them. They're live, still-updating windows, as you'll discover if one of them contains a playing QuickTime movie or a Web page that's still loading. If you're not pointing to a window, tapping F3 again turns off Exposé without changing anything; if you're pointing to a window, tapping F3 again brings it forward.

to Exposé. It's even painted with a special Exposé logo (⌘). Tap that key to get the all-apps Exposé effect.

Note: There are other key combinations available, too. See the box below for details on the built-in alternative—but you can use the System Preferences→Keyboard→Keyboard Shortcuts panel to make up any keystroke you want.

• **Plastic keyboards: Press F9.** On older keyboards, the white or black plastic ones, press F9 instead.

• **Laptops: Swipe downward with four fingers.** Sounds contrived, it's true. But giving your trackpad a four-finger swipe is a quick and easy way to trigger all-apps Exposé. (Then you can get back to what you were doing by swiping *upward* with four fingers.)

Note: Older Mac laptops don't have multitouch trackpads and therefore don't offer this four-finger option. To find out if yours is eligible—and to make sure the four-finger swiping feature is turned on—open System Preferences→Trackpad. Confirm that there's a list of gestures at the left side of the panel, as shown on page 14.

As you can read later in this section, you can also trigger all-apps Exposé by pressing special buttons on your mouse, or by flinging the cursor into a specified corner of the screen. But start with baby steps.

TROUBLESHOOTING MOMENT

A Tedious Side Note about the Aluminum Apple Keyboards

In previous Mac versions, you could trigger the three Exposé modes described on these pages with three simple keystrokes: F9, F10, and F11.

Then the new-style aluminum keyboards and laptops came along. On these, Apple devoted the F3 key to Exposé functions—and reassigned the F9, F10, and F11 keys to speaker-volume control!

You *can* make them operate Exposé as in the days of yore—by adding the Fn key. That is: Fn-F9 for all-apps Exposé, Fn-F10 for one-app Exposé, and Fn-F11 for desktop Exposé. (Details on the Fn key appear on page 23.)

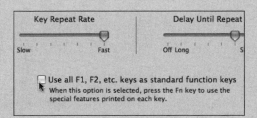

So here's the point: On modern Macs, you have a choice of two Exposé keystroke suites: the F3 key (by itself, with Control, and with ⌘)—or the Fn key plus F9, F10, and F11.

Actually, it's even more complicated than that. If you find yourself using *Exposé* more than you use the volume keys, you can get rid of the requirement to press Fn. Open System Preferences→Keyboard. Here you'll find a checkbox that reverses this logic. It's called "Use all F1, F2, etc. keys as standard function keys."

If that checkbox is *on,* then you can use F9, F10, and F11 to trigger Exposé. Now you need the Fn key only when you want those keys to adjust the *volume.*

To exit Exposé, click one of the miniaturized windows, or repeat any of the Exposé triggers.

Note: If you've *minimized* a program's windows, they now show up in Exposé, too—as miniatures below a fine horizontal line. You can see the effect in Figure 4-4.

One-App Exposé

A second Exposé function is designed to present miniatures of all windows *only in the program you're using*—great when you're Web browsing or word processing. All the program's windows spread out, and shrink if necessary, so you can click the one you want (Figure 4-5, top).

Figure 4-5:
Top: When you trigger one-app Exposé, you get a clear shot at any window in the current program (Safari, in this example). In the meantime, the rest of your screen attractively dims, as though someone has just shined a floodlight onto the windows of the program in question. It's a stunning effect.

Bottom: Trigger desktop Exposé when you need to duck back to the desktop for a quick administrative chore. Here's your chance to find a file, throw something away, eject a disk, or whatever, without having to disturb your application windows.

In either case, tap the same function key again to turn off Exposé. Or click one of the window edges, which you can see peeking out from all four edges of the screen.

Here's how Apple intends most people to trigger this option:

- **Current keyboards: Press Control-F3.** That's the keystroke on current laptops and desktops, the ones with aluminum keyboards.

Tip: As noted in the box on page 123, you can also press Fn-F10, or with some tweaking, F10 alone. Or you can change the keystroke altogether as described on page 143.

- **Plastic keyboards: Press F10.**
- **Use Dock Exposé.** That is, click any program's Dock icon and hold the button down for half a second.

  This feature has one chief advantage over the keystroke method: You can Exposé-ize any program's windows, not just the one you're using at the moment.

Desktop Exposé

The third flavor of Exposé is surprisingly handy. It sends *all* windows in *all* programs cowering to the edges of your screen, revealing the desktop beneath in all its uncluttered splendor (Figure 4-5, bottom).

Here's the keystroke scheme:

- **Current keyboards: Press ⌘-F3.** That's the trigger for aluminum keyboards and laptops.

Note: Once again, you can also press Fn-F11, or (if you set it up) F11 by itself. See the box on page 123.

- **Plastic keyboards: Press F11.**

The windows fly off to the edges of the screen, where they remain—forever, or until you tap the keystroke again, click a visible window edge, double-click an icon, or take some other window-selection step.

This is a spectacular opportunity to save headache and hassle in situations like these:

- You're writing an email message, and you want to attach a file. Tap the desktop Exposé keystroke, root around in the Finder until you locate the file you want. Begin to drag it, and then, without releasing the mouse button, tap the desktop Exposé keystroke again to bring back your email window. (Or drag the attachment directly onto your email program's icon on the Dock and pause until its window thumbnails appear.)

  Move your cursor, with the file in mid-drag, directly over the outgoing message window; release the cursor to create the attachment. You've just added an attachment from the desktop in one smooth motion.

Tip: You can apply the same life-changing shortcut to dragging a graphic into a page-layout program, a folder of photos into iPhoto, a sound or graphic into iMovie, and so on.

• **You want to open a different document.** For many people, having access to the entire Finder beats the pants off having to use the Open dialog box. Double-clicking the icon you want automatically opens it and turns off Exposé.

• **You're on the Web, and you want to see if some file has finished downloading.** Trigger desktop Exposé to survey the situation on your desktop.

If the layer of open programs is the atmosphere, the Finder is the earth below—and the ability to teleport you back and forth is a huge timesaver.

Tip: You can switch among the three Exposé modes (all-apps, one-app, or desktop), even after you've triggered one. For example, if you click-and-hold a Dock icon to shrink only *that* program's windows, you can then press ⌘-F3 to see the desktop, and then press F3 to shrink *all* programs' windows.

Exposé Tip-O-Rama

Just having your world o' windows spread out like index cards is magic enough. But these windows are *live*. You can work with them. Let us count the ways:

• **Tab through Exposé'd apps.** Once you've started one-app Exposé, and a program's windows are arrayed before you, tap the Tab key to switch to the *next* running program. All *its* windows spring to the fore. Tab, Tab, Tab through all your open programs. (Shift-Tab, as usual, cycles through the programs in the opposite direction.)

Tip: You can also switch to another app's micro-windows by clicking its Dock icon.

• **Enter Exposé from the heads-up display.** Page 120 describes the heads-up display—the Mac OS X application switcher, the row of "these are your open programs" icons—which appears when you press ⌘-Tab.

The cool thing is that once you've got that heads-up display open, you can press ↑ or ↓ to enter Exposé for whatever program's icon is highlighted! From there, release the keys and hit Tab to cycle through your open apps.

• **Hold down instead of two presses.** Most of the time, you'll probably use Exposé in two steps. You'll tap the keystroke once to get the windows out of the way, and tap it again to bring them back (if, indeed, you haven't *clicked* a window to bring them back).

In some cases, though, you may find it easier to hold down the relevant key. For example, hold down ⌘-F3 to see if a file is finished copying to the desktop, then release the keys to bring back all of the windows. (Actually, you can let go of the ⌘ key as soon as you've entered Exposé.) For quick window-clearing situations, that method saves you the step of having to press the key a second time to turn off Exposé.

• **Use the spring-loaded Dock.** This trick is great when you want to drop a file from one program into a particular window belonging to another.

The most common example: You want to add an attachment to an outgoing email message. In the Finder, locate the file's icon. Drag it directly onto your email program's Dock icon—and pause with your finger still on the button. After a half second, Exposé happens, showing all your email program's open windows. Now continue your drag onto the miniaturized window of the outgoing message so it's highlighted, tap the space bar to open it, and release. Presto! The file is attached.

This trick also works great when you want to drop a photo into a newsletter, for example, or a text clipping into a word processing document.

- **Sort the windows.** That's right: you can *sort* the windows as they appear on the screen. Press ⌘-1 to sort the window names alphabetically, or ⌘-2 to sort them according to the programs they belong to.

Exposé Meets Quick Look

The trouble with miniaturized windows is that, well, they're miniaturized. The more windows you've Exposé'd, the smaller they are, and the harder it is to see what's in them.

Fortunately, your old friend Quick Look (page 59) is standing by to help.

Once you've got shrunken windows on the screen (using all-apps Exposé or one-app Exposé), tap your arrow keys to highlight a window (or point with your mouse without clicking). You'll see a bright-blue border move from window to window.

At any point, you can press the space bar to make that one window return to life size. You haven't really activated it—you can't edit it—but at least you can see it at full size.

And here's the very cool part. Once you've triggered Quick Look like this, you can press the arrow keys to zap *other* mini windows back to full size, without having to exit Quick Look. Or, again, point to other windows without clicking. Each zooms in to 100 percent size. (All of this is much easier to do than to imagine.)

You can keep examining your windows at full size until you spot the one you're after; now tap Return (or click the mouse in the window) to exit Quick Look *and* Exposé. You've just opened that window, and you're ready to roll.

More Triggers for Exposé

Exposé is wonderful and all, but the standard keys for triggering its three functions may leave something to be desired. For one thing, they might already be "taken" by other functions in your programs (like Microsoft Word) or even by your computer. For another thing, those keys are at the top of the keyboard where your typing fingers aren't used to going, and you may have to hunt to make sure you're pressing the right one.

Fortunately, you can reassign the Exposé functions to a huge range of other keys, with or without modifiers like Shift, Control, and Option. To view your options, choose →System Preferences and then click the Exposé & Spaces icon (Figure 4-6).

Here, you'll discover that you can trigger Exposé's functions in any of three ways:

Screen corners

The four pop-up menus (Figure 4-6) represent the four corners of your screen. Using these menus, you can assign an Exposé trigger to each corner; for example, if you choose Desktop from the first pop-up menu, when your pointer hits the upper-left corner of the screen, you'll hide all windows and expose the desktop. (To make the windows come back, click any visible edge of a window, highlight a window thumbnail and press Return, or twitch the cursor back into the same corner.)

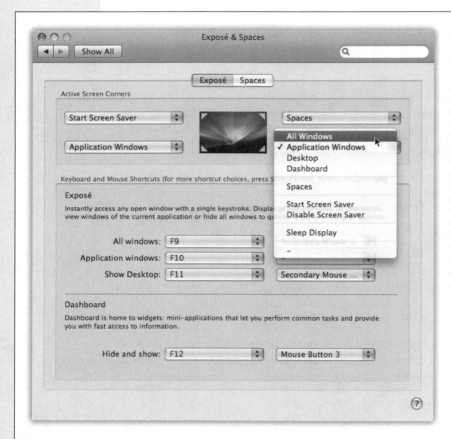

Figure 4-6:
You can trigger Exposé in any of three ways: by twitching your cursor into a certain corner of the screen (top), pressing a key (lower left), or clicking the extra buttons on a multibutton mouse (lower right), including Apple's Mighty Mouse or Magic Mouse. Of course, there's nothing to stop you from setting up all three ways, so you can press in some situations and twitch or click in others.

Depending on the size of your screen, this option can feel awkward at first. But if you've run out of keystrokes that aren't assigned to other functions, be glad that Apple offers you this alternative.

Keystrokes

Also in the Exposé preferences, you'll find three pop-up menus—"All windows," "Application windows," and "Show Desktop"—that correspond to the three functions of Exposé as described above. (The fourth pop-up menu, Dashboard, is described at the end of this chapter.) You can't assign *any* old keystroke to Exposé, but you have far more options than the puny F9, F10, and F11 keys (or the variations on F3).

Within each pop-up menu, for example, you'll discover that all your F-keys—F1, F2, F3, and so on—are available as triggers. If, while the pop-up menu is open, you press one or more of your modifier keys (Shift, Option, Control, or ⌘), all these F-key choices *change* to reflect the key you're pressing; now the pop-up menu says Shift-F1, Shift-F2, Shift-F3, and so on. That's how you can make *Shift*-F1 trigger the hide-all-windows function, for example.

These pop-up menus also contain choices like Left Shift, which refers to the Shift key on the left side of your keyboard. That is, instead of pressing F9 to make all your windows shrink, you could simply tap the Shift key.

Note: This is only an example. Repeat: This is only an example. *Actually* using the Shift key to shrink all your windows is a terrible, terrible idea, as you'll quickly discover the next time you try to type a capital letter. This feature is intended exclusively for hunt-and-peck typists who never use the Shift key on one side.

If you have a laptop, you'll also find out that you can tap the Fn key *alone* for Exposé—and this time, it's a *great* choice, because Fn otherwise has very little direction in life.)

Multiple-button mouse clicks

If your mouse has more than one button, you see a second column of pop-up menus in System Preferences. Each pop-up menu offers choices like Right Mouse Button, Middle Mouse Button, and so on. Use these pop-up menus to assign the three Exposé modes (or Dashboard) to the various clickers on your mouse: right-click to hide *all* windows, left-side click to reveal the desktop, and so on.

Note, by the way, that on a laptop, for example, the wording isn't "right mouse button"—it's "secondary mouse button." Which means "right-click." Which means that on a laptop, you can set it up so that a "right-click" *trackpad gesture* triggers Exposé. See page 12 for all the different ways you can trigger a right-click.

Tip: No matter how you trigger Exposé, try holding down the Shift key as you do it. You'll enjoy watching all your windows shift around with Mac OS X's patented slow-motion animation, which can be quite a sight.

Spaces: Your Free Quad-Display Mac

Exposé is pretty darned cool. But Mac OS X offers another radical step forward in window management that you may even come to prefer. It's called Spaces.

This feature gives you two, four, six, eight, or even 16 *full-size monitors*. Ordinarily, of course, attaching so many screens to a single computer would be a massively expensive proposition, not to mention the number it would do on your living space and personal relationships.

But the bonus monitors that Spaces gives you are *virtual*. They exist only in the Mac's little head. You can look at only one at a time; you switch using a keystroke, a menu, or the mouse. Instead of shuffling through your windows using Exposé, you can now leave them all spread out over a much larger virtual desktop.

Just because the Spaces screens are simulated doesn't mean they're not useful, though. You can dedicate each one to a different program or *kind* of program. Screen 1 might contain your email and chat windows, arranged just the way you like them. Screen 2 can hold Photoshop, with an open document and the palettes carefully arrayed. On Screen 3: your Web browser in full-screen mode.

You can also have the *same* program running on multiple screens—but different documents or projects open on each one.

Now, virtual screens aren't a new idea—this sort of software has been available for the Mac and Windows for years. But it's never before been a standard feature of an operating system.

Turning on Spaces

To "install" your new monitors, start by choosing →System Preferences. Click the Exposé & Spaces icon, then click the Spaces tab. You see something like Figure 4-7.

The setup ritual goes like this:

- **Turn Spaces on.** The "Enable Spaces" checkbox is the master on/off switch.

- **Add the menulet.** Turn on "Show Spaces in menu bar" to make a menu of your virtual screens appear in the menu bar. It not only lets you switch screens, but the numeral on it also reminds you which screen you're *on*.

Tip: Consider turning on this option, if only at first, as a safety net. Otherwise, if you don't remember the keystroke for switching screens, you might lose one of your programs on another screen and not be able to find it!

- **Add rows or columns.** Click the **+** and **−** buttons to add rows or columns of virtual monitors. There's a difference between rows and columns, by the way. Not only will you eventually learn to sense where your various window setups live, but you can also move from one screen to another by bumping the mouse against the corresponding edge of your *current* screen—and you'll need to know which edge.

- **Set up program auto-screen assignments.** Spaces starts to become truly useful only when you make it part of your routine. You'll eventually memorize where everything is: Web stuff, top left. Email, top right. Photoshop, lower left. Finder with Applications folder open, lower right.

For that reason, you can use the controls in the center of the System Preferences pane to specify onto which screen certain programs *automatically* go when they open. Click the **+** button to view your Applications folder. Double-click a program's icon to make it appear in the list. Now use the pop-up menu in the Space column to indicate which space you want this program to live on, as shown in Figure 4-7.

Tip: You can also choose All Spaces, meaning that this program's windows are available on *every* virtual screen. That's handy if it's something you use constantly, like a stock ticker or your phone-book program.

Figure 4-7:
Use the controls at the top to specify how many virtual screens you want— how many rows, how many columns, up to 16 in all. Use the middle section to specify where you want particular programs to appear (that is, on which screen) when they open. Use the bottom controls to set up how you want to move from one screen to another.

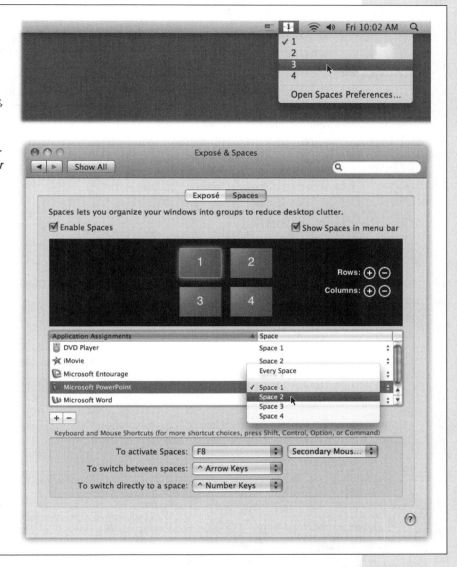

To make a program stop opening into a certain screen, click its name, and then click the **–** button.

- **Set up keyboard or mouse triggers.** Once you've got your majestic array of Cineplex Displays assembled, you need a way to move among them.

Spaces comes set up with the Control key as the "I'm switching screens" key. For example, press Control-↑ to move up one screen, Control-→ to move one screen to the right, and so on. Or, if you have tons of screens, you can jump to one by number (as indicated in the map shown in Figure 4-7): Control-1, Control-4, Control-9, or whatever.

You're welcome to change these keyboard assignments, however, especially if you're already using the Control key for other functions. Use the two bottom pop-up menus.

For example, suppose you want to switch screens by pressing the Option key rather than Control. In that case, you'd open the "To switch between Spaces" pop-up menu, press Option, and choose "⌥ Arrow Keys." (In these pop-up menus, ⌥ means the Option key, ⌘ is the Command key, and ^ means Control.)

Tip: The pop-up menu at the bottom of the window, "To activate Spaces," lets you choose a keystroke that opens up the master map of all your screens. (See Figure 4-9.)

Using Spaces

Once you've got Spaces set up and turned on, the fun begins. Start by moving to the virtual screen you want. Here are some ways to do that:

- Choose a virtual screen's number from the Spaces menulet, shown in Figure 4-7.

- Press Control-arrow key, or whatever keystroke you set up as described above. Or hold down Control and keep tapping the arrow key to scroll through all your screens.

- Press Control-number key to jump to a screen without having to scroll.

- Use the heads-up switcher (page 120), or the Dock, to select a program; Spaces switches to the proper screen automatically.

When you make a switch, you see a flash of animation as one screen flies away and another appears. You also see the display shown in Figure 4-8 to help you orient yourself among your magnificent array of virtual monitors.

Figure 4-8:
This display appears momentarily when you switch screens. The arrow shows you the screens you're moving to and from.

You can even move diagonally. While pressing Control, press two arrow keys on your keyboard at once (like ↓ and →).

Now that you're "on" the screen you want, open programs and arrange windows onto it as usual.

The big picture

The Fn-F8 key opens up a gigantic miniature (if there is such a thing) of your entire Spaces universe (Figure 4-9).

Clicking the Spaces icon in the Dock brings up the same display.

Note: As usual, you may run into trouble with this key if you're using Apple's aluminum, superflat keyboard. See the box on page 123.

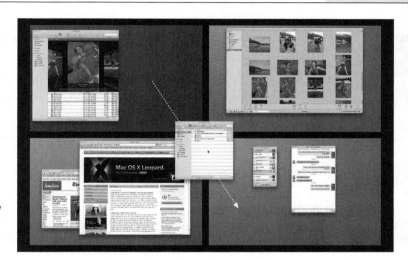

Figure 4-9:
Press F8, or click Spaces in your Dock, to open this live master view of all the windows on all the screens. (The windows update in real time—if you're in a chat or playing a movie, for example.) You can actually drag individual windows from one of these "window panes" (actually virtual screens) to another. In fact, you can even use the Exposé keystrokes to make all the windows on all the screens visible at once, for ease in moving them around the screens.

So what can you do here?

- **Get oriented.** You could have sworn you opened your favorite Web site—where the heck is it? Pressing Fn-F8 gives you an instant readout of where all your windows are sitting at the moment.

- **Switch screens.** Click any "pane" of the big-picture view to jump to the screen.

- **Reorder the screens.** Using any blank background spot as a handle, you can drag the actual panes of the big-picture view around to rearrange them. If you decide that your email screen should really be at top left, drag it there.

- **Move windows around.** Here's the real power of the big-picture view. As shown in Figure 4-9, you can actually drag windows from one screen to another. You can use any part of the window as a handle, not just the title bar.

Tip: If you press Shift as you drag, you move *all* windows that belong to the same program simultaneously.

• **Hit an Exposé keystroke.** You can actually use the F9 and F10 Exposé keystrokes *while* you're in the Fn-F8 big-picture view.

Yes, this gets kind of meta, but it's useful when you're trying to arrange your windows and programs among your screens. Once you're in the big-picture view, for example, you can hit F9 to see *all* windows on *all* screens scurry apart, so that nothing is covered up. Then start dragging windows onto different screens as necessary.

Moving windows among screens

One way to move a particular window to a different screen is to drag it in big-picture view, as shown in Figure 4-9.

But there are two other ways that don't require entering the Fn-F8 big-picture view:

• Drag a window (using its title bar as a handle) all the way to the edge of the screen. Stay there with the mouse button still down. After about a second, you'll see the adjacent screen slide into view; you've just moved the window.

• Click anywhere inside a window, and keep the mouse button down. Now press your screen-switching keystroke (Control-←, for example, or Control-3). You've just moved the window to the designated screen.

To be sure, these are power-user techniques that may not come naturally. But the Fn-F8 big-picture view is always waiting should you become befuddled.

Tip: What if you want to drag something from one screen (like a photo in iPhoto) into a window that's on a different screen (like an outgoing email message)?

Two ways; take your pick. First, you can start dragging whatever it is—and then, in mid-drag, press F8 to open the big-picture view, and complete the drag directly onto the other Space (and even into the relevant window *in* that Space).

Another approach: Start dragging. With the mouse still down, press ⌘-Tab to open the application switcher. Continue the drag onto the *icon* of the receiving program, and still keep the mouse button down. Mac OS X switches to the appropriate virtual screen automatically.

Hiding Programs the Old-Fashioned Way

When it comes to getting windows out of your way, nothing can touch Exposé and Spaces for speed and entertainment value. Once you've mastered those features, the traditional rituals of hiding windows will seem charmingly quaint. "When I was your age," long-time Mac people will tell their grandchildren, "we used to have to *hold down the Option key* to hide windows!"

But you know the drill at software companies: They addeth, but they never taketh away. All the old techniques are still around.

Hiding the Program You're Using

For the purposes of this discussion, when a program is *hidden,* all its windows, tool palettes, and button bars disappear. You can bring them back only by bringing the program to the front again (by clicking its Dock icon again, for example).

If your aim is to hide only the program you're currently using, Mac OS X offers a whole raft of approaches to the same problem. Many of them involve the Option key, as listed here:

- **Option-click any visible portion of the desktop.** The program you were in vanishes, along with all its windows.

- **Option-click any other program's icon on the Dock.** You open that program (or bring all its windows to the front) *and* hide all the windows of the one you were using.

- **Option-click any visible portion of another program's windows.** Once again, you switch programs, hiding the one you were using at the time.

- **From the Application menu, choose Hide iPhoto (or whatever the program is).** The Application menu is the boldfaced menu that bears the program's name.

GEM IN THE ROUGH

Using the Dock or Sidebar for Drag-and-Drop

The Mac is smart about the relationship between documents and applications. If you double-click a TextEdit document icon, for example, TextEdit opens automatically and shows you the document.

But it's occasionally useful to open a document using a program *other* than the one that created it. Perhaps, as is often the case with downloaded Internet graphics, you don't *have* the program that created it, or you don't know which one was used. This technique is also useful when opening a Read Me file into your word processor, such as Word, instead of the usual TextEdit program.

In such cases, the Dock is handy: Just drag the mystery document onto one of the Dock's tiles, as shown here. Doing so forces the program to open

the document—if it can. (Dragging onto a program's icon in the Sidebar or even the Finder toolbar works just as well.)

Incidentally, in general, only the Dock icons of programs that can, in fact, open the file you're dragging onto them become highlighted. The others just shrug indifferently or even scoot aside, thinking maybe you're trying to drag the file *into* the Dock.

Pressing Option-⌘ as you drag forces Dock icons to be more tolerant. Now *all* of them "light up" as your document touches them, indicating that they'll *try* to open your file. Even so, a "could not be opened" error message may result. As they say in Cupertino, sometimes what a can really needs is a can opener.

CHAPTER 4: DOCUMENTS, PROGRAMS, & SPACES

- **When you've highlighted a Dock icon by pressing ⌘-Tab to rotate through the running programs, press the letter H key.** The program hides itself instantly. Leave the ⌘ key down the whole time, and after pressing the H, press Tab again to move on to the next program. If you release the keys while "stopped" on the program instead, you'll bring it forward rather than hiding it.

- **Press ⌘-H.** This may be the easiest and most useful trick of all (although it doesn't work in every program). Doing so hides the program you're in; you then "fall down" into the next running program.

To unhide a program and its windows, click its Dock icon again, choose the Show All command in the Application menu, or press ⌘-Tab to summon the heads-up application display.

Hiding (Minimizing) Individual Windows

In Mac OS X, there's more to managing your window clutter than simply hiding entire programs. You can also hide or show *individual windows* of a single program. In fact, Apple must believe that hiding a window will become one of your favorite activities, because it offers at least four ways to do so:

- Choose Window→Minimize Window, if your program offers such a command, or press ⌘-M.

- Click the Minimize button on the window's title bar, as shown in Figure 4-10.

- Double-click the window's title bar.

In any case, the affected window shrinks down until it becomes a new icon in the right side of the Dock. Click that icon to bring the window back.

How Documents Know Their Parents

Every operating system needs a mechanism to associate documents with the applications that created them. When you double-click a Microsoft Word document icon, for example, it's clear that you want Microsoft Word to launch and open the document.

So how does Mac OS X know how to find a document's mommy?

It actually has two different mechanisms.

- **Filename extensions.** A *filename extension* is a suffix following a period in the file's name, as in *Letter to Mom.doc*. (It's usually three letters long, but doesn't have to be.) These play a role in determining which documents open into which programs.

  That's how Windows identifies its documents, too. If you double-click something called memo.doc, it opens in Microsoft Word. If you double-click memo.wri, it opens in Microsoft Write, and so on.

Note: Mac OS X comes set to hide most filename extensions, on the premise that they make the operating system look more technical and threatening. If you'd like to see them, however, choose Finder→Preferences, click the Advanced button, and then turn on "Show all file extensions." Now examine a few of your documents; you'll see that their names now display the previously hidden suffixes.

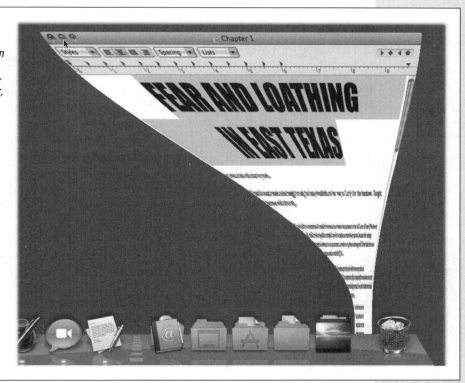

Figure 4-10:
When you click the center button on a window title bar, double-click the title bar, or press ⌘-M, you minimize that window, getting it out of your way and off your screen. Minimizing on the Mac is a lot like minimizing in Windows; the minimized window is now represented by an icon on your Dock, which you can click to reopen the window.

You can hide or show these suffixes on an icon-at-a-time basis, too (or a clump-at-a-time basis). Just highlight the icon or icons you want to affect, and then choose File→Get Info. In the resulting Info window, proceed as shown in Figure 4-11.

- **Your preferences.** If you've used the "Always Open with" command to *specify* which program opens your document (described next), that's the one that opens; this preference *overrides* the filename extension system. Snow Leopard memorizes that new pairing in an internal Unix database. (If you're a Unix geek, you can actually open and inspect that database.)

It's possible to live a long and happy life without knowing anything about these suffixes and relationships. Indeed, the vast majority of Mac fans may never even encounter them. But if you're prepared for a little bit of technical bushwhacking, you may discover that understanding document-program relationships can be useful in troubleshooting, keeping your files private, and appreciating how Mac OS X works.

Reassigning Documents to Programs

Filename extensions don't know which parent program should open a particular document. Suppose you've downloaded a graphic called Sunset.jpg. Well, almost any program these days can open a JPEG graphic—Photoshop, Word, Preview, Safari, and so on. How does Mac OS X know which of these programs to open when you double-click the file?

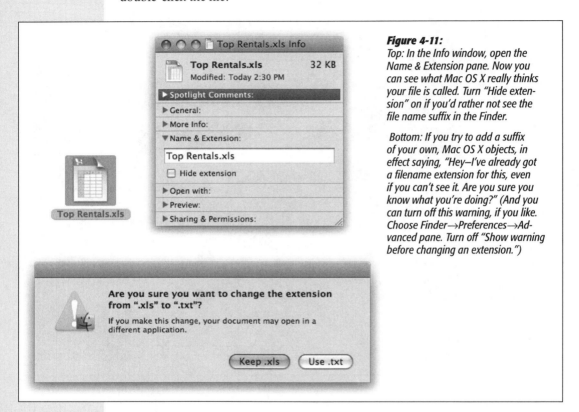

Figure 4-11:
Top: In the Info window, open the Name & Extension pane. Now you can see what Mac OS X really thinks your file is called. Turn "Hide extension" on if you'd rather not see the file name suffix in the Finder.

Bottom: If you try to add a suffix of your own, Mac OS X objects, in effect saying, "Hey—I've already got a filename extension for this, even if you can't see it. Are you sure you know what you're doing?" (And you can turn off this warning, if you like. Choose Finder→Preferences→Advanced pane. Turn off "Show warning before changing an extension.")

Fortunately, *you* can decide. You can *reassign* a document (or all documents of its kind) to a specific program. Here's the rundown.

Reassigning a certain document—just once

Double-clicking a graphics file generally opens it in Preview, the graphics viewer included with Mac OS X. Most of the time, that's a perfectly good arrangement. But Preview has only limited editing powers. What if you decide to edit a graphics file more substantially? You'd want it to open, just this once, into a different program— Photoshop Elements, for example.

To do so, you must access the Open With command. You can find it in two places:

• Highlight the icon, and then choose File→Open With.

- Right-click the file's icon. Or, in a Finder window, highlight the icon and then open the ✿ menu. In the shortcut menu, choose Open With.

Study the submenu for a moment (Figure 4-12, top). The program whose name says "(default)" indicates which program usually opens this kind of document.

Figure 4-12:
Top: The shortcut menu offers a list of programs capable of opening an icon. If you were to press the Option key right now, the words Open With would suddenly change to say Always Open With.

Bottom: If you choose Other, you're prompted to choose a different program. Turn on Always Open With if you'll always want this document to open in the new parent program. Otherwise, this is a one-time reassignment.

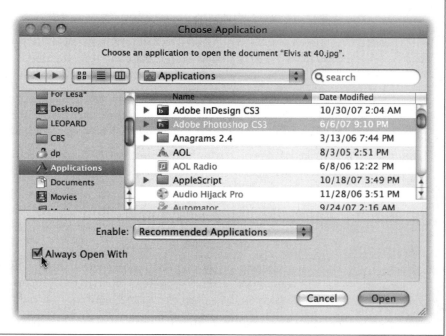

From this pop-up menu, choose the name of the program you'd rather open this particular file, right now, just this once.

Reassigning a certain document—permanently

After opening a TIFF file in, say, Photoshop Elements for editing, you haven't really made any changes in the fabric of your Mac universe. The next time you double-click that file, it opens once again in Preview.

If you wish this particular file would *always* open in Photoshop Elements, the steps are slightly different. In fact, there are three different ways:

- In the Choose an Application dialog box (the one that appears when you double-click a document whose "parent" program isn't clear), turn on "Always Open With" (shown at bottom in Figure 4-12).

- Start out with one of the previously described techniques (File→Open With, or Control-click/right-click the file's icon and choose Open With)—but after you see the menu, press the Option key, too. Before your very eyes, the Open With command changes to say *Always* Open With.

- Highlight the icon, and then choose File→Get Info. Open the "Open with" panel. Choose a new "parent" program's name from the pop-up menu. You'll see that the word "(default)" changes position, now tacking itself onto the name of the program you've chosen.

Reassigning all documents of one type

So much for reassigning one document (or a group of documents) at a time. What if you're writing, say, a book about Mac OS X, and you've been taking a lot of screenshots? Mac OS X saves each captured screen illustration as a graphics file in something called PNG format. That's all fine, except that every time you double-click one of these, it opens into Preview, where you can't paint out unwanted details.

You could reassign all these files, one at a time, to a different program, but your grandchildren would have grandchildren by the time you finish. In this case, you want to tell Mac OS X, "For heaven's sake, make *all* PNG files open in Photoshop from now on!"

To make it happen, start by highlighting *any* PNG file. Choose File→Get Info. (The shortcut menus won't help you in this case.) Open the "Open with" panel.

From its pop-up menu, choose the program you want to open this kind of document from now on. (If the one you prefer isn't listed, use the Other option, which opens the Choose an Application dialog box so you can navigate to the one you want. Find and double-click the program.)

This time, follow up by clicking Change All beneath the pop-up menu. (This button is dimmed until you've actually selected a different program from the pop-up menu.) Mac OS X asks you to confirm by clicking Continue or pressing Return.

From now on, double-clicking any similar kind of document opens it in the newly selected program.

Keyboard Control

In Windows, of course, you can operate every menu in every program from the keyboard—and every control in every dialog box—thanks to the power of the Alt key.

Mac OS X offers full keyboard control, too. You can operate every control in every dialog box from the keyboard, including pop-up menus and checkboxes. And you can even *redefine* many of the keyboard shortcuts in Mac OS X and even your programs. In short, if you were a keyboard power-user in Windows, you'll feel right at home in Mac OS X.

Here are some of the ways you can control your Mac mouselessly. In the following descriptions, you'll encounter the factory settings for the keystrokes that do the magic—but as you'll see in a moment, you can change these key combos to anything you like. (The System Preferences→Keyboard→Keyboard Shortcuts tab contains the on/off switches for these features.)

Note: On modern-day, aluminum keyboards, the keystrokes described below may not work unless you also press the Fn key simultaneously.

If that seems just a *tad* clumsy, you can eliminate the Fn-key requirement either by using the "Use all F1, F2, etc. keys as standard function keys" option described on page 25—or by choosing a different keystroke altogether (page 143).

Control the Menus

When you press Control-F2, the menu is highlighted. At this point, you can "walk" to another menu by pressing the ← or → keys (or Tab and Shift-Tab). When you reach the menu you want, open it by pressing ↓, space, Return, or Enter.

Walk down the commands in the menu by pressing ↑ or ↓, or jump directly to a command in the menu by typing the first couple of letters of its name. Finally, "click" a menu command by pressing Enter, Return, or the space bar.

You can also close the menu without making a selection by pressing Esc or ⌘-period.

Control the Dock

Once you've pressed Control-F3, you can highlight *any* icon on the Dock by pressing the appropriate arrow keys (or, once again, Tab and Shift-Tab).

Then, once you've highlighted a Dock icon, you "click it" by pressing Return or the space bar. Again, if you change your mind, press Esc or ⌘-period.

Tip: Once you've highlighted a disk or folder icon, you can press the ↑ or ↓ keys to make its shortcut menu appear. (If you've positioned the Dock vertically, use ← or → instead!)

Cycle Through Your Windows

Every time you press Control-F4, you bring the next window forward, eventually cycling through *every window in every open program*. Add the Shift key to cycle through them in the opposite order.

You may remember that Mac OS X offers a different keystroke for cycling through the different windows in your *current* program (it's ⌘-~, the tilde symbol at the upper left of your keyboard). Control-F4, on the other hand, tours all windows in *all* programs. Both keystrokes are useful in different situations.

Control the Toolbar

This one is on the unpredictable side, but it more or less works in most programs that display a Mac OS X–style toolbar: the Finder, System Preferences, and so on.

When you press Control-F5, you highlight the first button on that toolbar. Move the "focus" by pressing the arrow keys or Tab and Shift-Tab. Then tap Return or the space bar to "click" the highlighted button.

Control Tool Palettes

In a few programs that feature floating tool palettes, you can highlight the frontmost palette by pressing Control-F6. At this point, use the arrow keys to highlight the various buttons on the palette. You can see the effect when, for example, you're editing text in TextEdit and you've also opened the Font palette. Pressing Control-F6 highlights the Font palette, taking the "focus" off your document.

Control Menulets

You can even operate *menulets*—those menu-bar status indicators for your speaker volume, wireless networks, and so on—from the keyboard.

This time, the trick is to hit Control-F8. That highlights the leftmost Apple menulet. Now you can use your ← and → arrow keys to move around the menu bar; when you've highlighted the one you want, press Return or the space bar to "click" that menu and open it.

Control Dialog Boxes

You can also navigate and manipulate any *dialog box* from the keyboard.

See the dialog box shown in Figure 4-13 If you turn on "All controls" at the bottom, then pressing the Tab key highlights the next control of any type, whatever it may be—radio button, pop-up menu, and so on. Press the space bar to "click" a button or open a pop-up menu. Once a menu is open, use the arrow keys (or type letter keys) to highlight commands on it, and the space bar to "click" your choice.

Tip: Press Control-arrow keys to "click" the different tabs of a dialog box.

Changing a Menu Keyboard Shortcut

Suppose you love iPhoto (and who doesn't?) but one thing drives you crazy: The Revert to Original command, which discards all the changes you've ever made since taking the photo, has no keyboard equivalent. You must trek up to the menu bar every time you need that command.

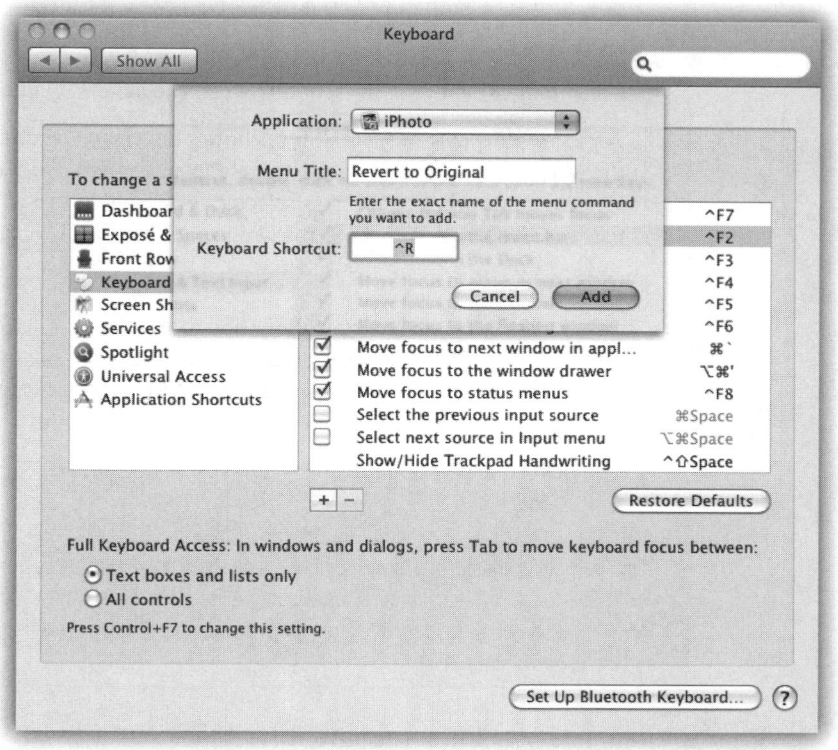

Figure 4-13:
If you choose All Applications from the top pop-up menu, you can change the keyboard combo for a certain command wherever it appears. You could, for example, change the keystroke for Page Setup in every program at once. (Beware the tiny yellow triangles; they let you know if a chosen keystroke conflicts with another Mac OS X keystroke.)

This is why Mac OS X lets you add keyboard shortcuts to menu commands that lack them—or change the command in programs whose key assignments break with tradition. (It works in any program that uses the standard Mac OS X menu software, which rules out Microsoft Word and the other Office programs.) Here's the routine:

1. **Choose →System Preferences→Keyboard. Click the Keyboard Shortcuts tab.**

   You're shown a list of all of Mac OS X's built-in keyboard assignments.

2. **Click the + button just beneath the list.**

   The dialog box shown in Figure 4-13 appears.

3. **Indicate which program needs behavior modification.**

In this example, you'd choose iPhoto from the Application pop-up menu. (If the program's name doesn't appear in the pop-up menu, choose Other; navigate to, and double-click, the program you want.)

4. **Carefully type in the name of the menu command whose keyboard shortcut you want to change or add.**

Type it *exactly* as it appears in the menu, complete with capitalization and the little ellipsis (…) that may follow it. (You make the ellipsis character by pressing Option-semicolon.)

5. **Click in the Keyboard Shortcut box. Press the new or revised key combo you want.**

For example, press Control-R for iPhoto's Revert to Original command. You'll see the Mac's notation of your keystroke appear in the Keyboard Shortcut box—unless, of course, the combo you selected is already in use within that program. In that case, you hear only an error sound that means "Try again."

6. **Click Add.**

The dialog box closes. By scrolling down in your Keyboard Shortcuts list, you'll see that the keystroke you selected has now been written down for posterity under the appropriate program's flippy triangle. (To get rid of it, click its name and then click the − button beneath the list.)

The next time you open the program you edited, you'll see that the new keystroke is in place.

Tip: To delete or change one of your custom menu shortcuts, open System Preferences→Keyboard→Keyboard Shortcuts. Click Application Shortcuts in the list at left. Click the command you'd like to edit. Press Delete to get rid of it; or, to try a different key combo, click where the existing keyboard shortcut appears, and then press a new one.

Redefining a Snow Leopard Keystroke

As you've no doubt become painfully aware, there are *hundreds* of keyboard combinations for the various Mac OS X functions and settings. That's good, because keyboard shortcuts are efficient and quicker than using the mouse. But that's also bad, because there's no *way* you'll be able to remember all of them—and some of most useful shortcuts are ridiculous, multikey affairs that you'll never remember at all.

Snow Leopard comes with a keyboard-shortcut center, shown in Figure 4-14. Here, you can look over all of the common Mac OS X hidden keyboard functions—for Exposé, Spotlight, Spaces, the Dashboard, the Dock, and many others—and *change them*.

Here's how it goes:

1. **Choose →System Preferences. Click Keyboard. Click the Keyboard Shortcuts tab.**

You arrive at the dialog box shown in Figure 4-14.

2. In the left-side list, click the category or function you want.

Your choices include Dashboard & Dock, Exposé & Spaces, Front Row, Keyboard & Text Input, and so on. When you click a category name, you see the available keyboard shortcuts.

Tip: You don't have to be content with *changing* one of these keyboard shortcuts. You can also *turn it off* by clicking the corresponding checkbox. That's great if one of Apple's predefined keystrokes—for a function you don't even use—is interfering with one in a program you like.

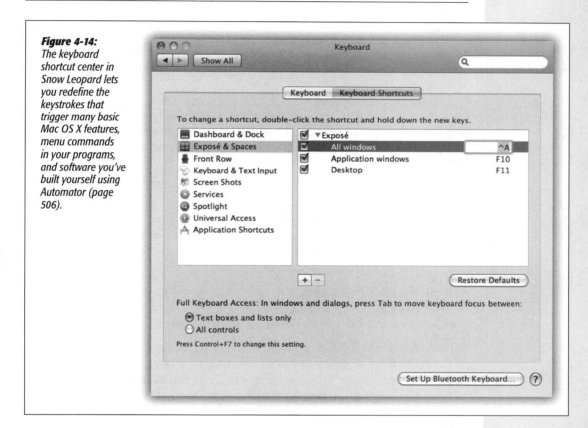

Figure 4-14:
The keyboard shortcut center in Snow Leopard lets you redefine the keystrokes that trigger many basic Mac OS X features, menu commands in your programs, and software you've built yourself using Automator (page 506).

3. Click the command you want to change. Then click the current keyboard combination.

Suppose, for example, that you wished that the All-Apps Exposé keystroke were something easier to remember, like Control-A. So in step 2, you'd click Exposé & Spaces. In this step, you'd click "All windows," as shown in Figure 4-14. Then you'd click where it currently says F9.

4. Press a new key combination.

In this example, you'd press Control-A.

Be careful, though. Mac OS X keystrokes take precedence over *all others*. So if you choose a keystroke like ⌘-P for something, well, by golly, you'll no longer be able to use ⌘-P to print anything in any of your programs. Think before you assign. Run a couple of tests afterward.

The Save and Open Dialog Boxes

When you choose File→Save, you're asked where you want the new document stored on your hard drive. The resulting dialog box is crystal-clear—more than ever, it's a miniature Finder. All the skills you've picked up working at the desktop come into play here.

To give it a try, launch any Mac OS X program that has a Save or Export command—TextEdit, for example. Type a couple of words, and then choose File→Save. The Save sheet appears (Figure 4-15).

Tip: In Mac OS X, a quick glance at the Close button in the upper-left corner of a document window tells you whether it's been saved. When a small dot appears in the red button, it means you've made changes to the document that you haven't saved yet. (Time to press ⌘-S!). The dot disappears as soon as you save your work.

Sheets

In the days of operating systems gone by, the Save dialog box appeared dead center on the screen, where it commandeered your entire operation. Moreover, because it seemed stuck to your *screen* rather than to a particular *document,* you couldn't actually tell which document you were saving—a real problem when you quit out of a program that had three unsaved documents open.

In most Mac OS X programs, there's no mystery regarding which document you're saving, because a little Save dialog box called a *sheet* slides directly out of the document's title bar. Now there's no mistaking which document you're saving.

Better still, this little Save box is a sticky note attached to the document. It stays there, neatly attached and waiting, even if you switch to another program, another document, the desktop, or wherever. When you finally return to the document, the Save sheet is still there, waiting for you to type a file name and save the document.

The Mini Finder

Of course, *you,* O savvy reader, have probably never saved a document into some deeply nested folder by accident, never to see it again. But millions of novices (and even a few experts) have fallen into this trap.

When the Save sheet appears, however, a pop-up menu shows you precisely where Mac OS X proposes putting your newly created document: usually in the Documents folder of your own Home folder. For many people, this is an excellent suggestion. If you keep everything in your Documents folder, it will be extremely easy to find, and you'll be able to back up your work just by dragging that single folder to a backup disk.

As shown at top in Figure 4-15, the Where pop-up menu gives you direct access to some other places you might want to save a newly created file. (The keystrokes for the most important folders work here, too—Shift-⌘-H for your Home folder, for example.)

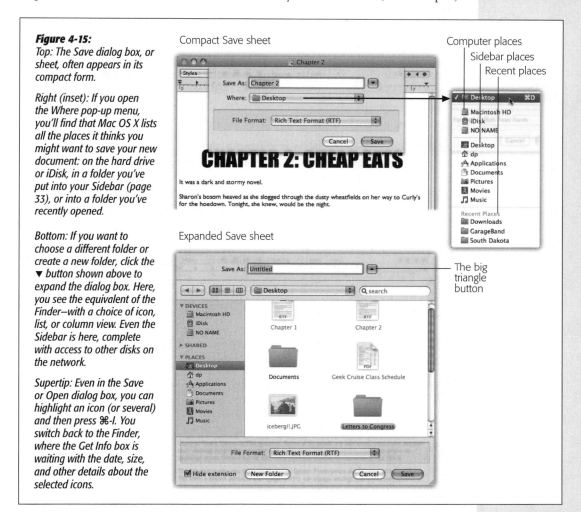

Figure 4-15:
Top: The Save dialog box, or sheet, often appears in its compact form.

Right (inset): If you open the Where pop-up menu, you'll find that Mac OS X lists all the places it thinks you might want to save your new document: on the hard drive or iDisk, in a folder you've put into your Sidebar (page 33), or into a folder you've recently opened.

Bottom: If you want to choose a different folder or create a new folder, click the ▼ button shown above to expand the dialog box. Here, you see the equivalent of the Finder—with a choice of icon, list, or column view. Even the Sidebar is here, complete with access to other disks on the network.

Supertip: Even in the Save or Open dialog box, you can highlight an icon (or several) and then press ⌘-I. You switch back to the Finder, where the Get Info box is waiting with the date, size, and other details about the selected icons.

In any case, when you save a file, the options in the Where pop-up menu have you covered 90 percent of the time. Most people work with a limited set of folders for active documents.

But when you want to save a new document into a new folder, or when you want to navigate to a folder that isn't listed in the Where pop-up menu, all is not lost. Click the ▼ button identified in Figure 4-15. The Save sheet expands miraculously into a very familiar sight: a miniature version of the Finder.

There's your Sidebar, complete with access to the other computers on your network. There's the Back button. There's your toggle switch between views; in Snow Leopard, you can even switch to *icon* view here, in addition to the traditional list and column views.

Tip: In column view, your first instinct should be to widen this window, making more columns available. Do so by carefully dragging the lower-right corner of the dialog box. Mac OS X remembers the size you like for this Save sheet independently in each program.

Most of the familiar Finder-navigation shortcuts work here, too. For example, press the right and left arrow keys to navigate the columns, or the up and down arrow keys to highlight the disk and folder names *within* a column. Once you've highlighted a column, you can also type to select the first letters of disk or folder names.

Highlight the name of the folder in which you want to save your newly created document. Alternatively, you can click the New Folder button to create a new folder *inside* whatever folder is highlighted in the column view. (The usual New Folder keystroke works here, too: Shift-⌘-N.) You'll be asked to type the new name for the folder. After you've done so, click Create (or press Return). The new folder appears in the rightmost pane of the column view. You can now proceed with saving your new document into it, if you like.

The next time you save a new document, the Save sheet reappears in whatever condition you left it. That is, if you used column view the last time, it's still in column view. At any time, you can collapse it into simplified view, shown at top in Figure 4-15, by clicking the ▲ button to the right of the Where pop-up menu.

Tip: The Save box always displays whatever places you've put in your Sidebar. (In compact view, the Where pop-up menu lists them; in expanded view, you see the Sidebar itself.)

The bottom line: If, on some project, you find yourself wanting to save new documents into the same deeply buried folder all the time, press F11 to duck back to the Finder, and add it to your Sidebar. From now on, you'll have quick access to it from the Save dialog box.

Spotlight

The Search bar at the top of the Open and Save dialog box is a clone of the Finder's Search bar (Chapter 3). Press ⌘-F to make your insertion point jump there. Type a few letters of the name of the file or folder you're looking for, and up it pops, regardless of its actual hard-disk location.

Your savings: five minutes of burrowing through folders to find it, and several pages of reading about how to navigate the Save and Open boxes.

The File Format Pop-up Menu

The Save dialog box in many programs offers a pop-up menu of file formats below the Save As box. Use this menu when preparing a document for use by somebody else—somebody whose computer doesn't have the same software. For example, if you've used a graphics program to prepare a photograph for use on the Web, this menu is where you specify JPEG format (the standard Web format for photos).

The Open File Dialog Box

The dialog box that appears when you choose File→Open is almost identical to the expanded Save File sheet. Because you encounter it only when you're opening an existing file, this dialog box lacks the Save button, file name field, and so on.

Note: Furthermore, the Open dialog box shows you only icons for disks, folders, and documents that you can actually open at this moment. For example, when you're using GarageBand, picture files show up dimmed.

But it does have a new Sidebar category called Media, which gives you direct access to all your photos, music, and movies. The premise is that Apple figures you might want to import these items *into* a document you're working on.

Most of the other Save File dialog box controls, however, are equally useful here. That handy Spotlight search bar is still there, only a ⌘-F away. Once again, you can begin your navigation by seeing what's on the desktop (press ⌘-D) or in your Home folder (press Shift-⌘-H). Once again, you can find a folder or disk by beginning your quest with the Sidebar, and then navigate using either list or column view. And once again, you can drag a folder, disk, or file icon off your desktop directly into the dialog box to specify where you want to look. (If you drag a *file* icon, you're shown the folder that contains it.)

When you've finally located the file you want to open, do so by double-clicking it or highlighting it (which you can do from the keyboard), and then pressing Return, Enter, or ⌘-O.

In general, most people don't encounter the Open File dialog box nearly as often as the Save File dialog box. That's because the Mac offers many more convenient ways to *open* a file—double-clicking its icon in the Finder, choosing its name from the →Recent Items command, and so on—but only a single way to *save* a new file.

Universal Apps (Intel Macs)

By the end of 2006, Apple had abandoned the PowerPC processors (made by IBM and Motorola) that had been in Macs since the beginning. It switched its entire Macintosh product line over to Intel's Core Duo processors (the successor to the Pentium).

Yes, *that* Intel. The company that Mac partisans had derided for years as part of the Dark Side. The company that Steve Jobs routinely belittled in his demonstrations of PowerPC chips. The company whose marketing mascot Apple lit on fire in a 1996 attack ad on TV.

Why the change? Apple's computers can only be as fast as the chips inside them, and the chips that IBM had in the works just weren't keeping up with the industry. As one editorial put it, "Apple's doing a U-turn out of a dead-end road."

And sure enough, Intel-based Macs start up and run much faster than the old Macs, thanks to the endless march of speed improvements in the chip-making world. And thanks to that Intel chip, today's Macs can even run Microsoft Windows and all of the thousands of Windows programs. (Chapter 8 has details.)

At the time, though, there was a small glitch: *Existing Mac software didn't run on Intel chips.*

Apple would have to ask the world's software companies to rewrite their programs *yet again*, after already having dragged them through the Mac OS 9-to-Mac OS X transition only a few years earlier.

Fortunately, the transition wasn't as gruesome as you might expect. First, Apple had already secretly recompiled (reworked) Mac OS X itself to run on Intel chips.

Furthermore, Apple wrote an invisible translation program, code-named Rosetta, which permits the existing library of Mac OS X programs—Photoshop, Word, and so on—to run, unmodified, on Intel Macs.

Note: When you install Snow Leopard, as described in Appendix A, you have the option to install Rosetta, so you'll have it just in case you want to run a pre-Intel program. (All software that's still on the market has long since been updated to the so-called Universal versions–that is, Intel-compatible. But plenty of older programs, long since abandoned, or whose software companies have gone under, are still around.)

But if it's too late to install Rosetta along with Snow Leopard, or if you bought a new Mac with Snow Leopard already installed, don't worry. When the day comes that you *try* to run a pre-Intel program, Snow Leopard offers to grab Rosetta for you. It says: "To open BeeKeeper Pro, you need to install Rosetta. Would you like to install it now?" When you click Install, Snow Leopard downloads it for you automatically.

They do not, however, run especially fast on Intel Macs. In fact, many of them run *slower* than they did on pre-Intel Macs.

To make their programs perform at *full speed* on Intel-based Macs, programmers have to update their wares. All the big software companies promised to make their

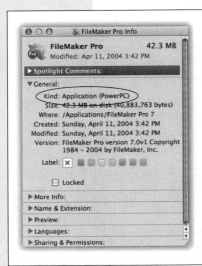
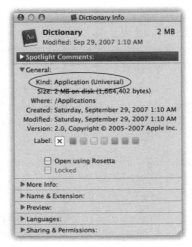

Figure 4-16:
Here's a quick way to tell if a program is an old one that will run slowly on an Intel Mac (instead of a Universal or Intel one that won't require the Rosetta software translation). Highlight its icon and choose File→Get Info. Near the top, you see either "Application: PowerPC" (old and slow), "Application: Intel" (runs only on Intel Macs), or "Application: Universal" (runs fast on both Intel and PowerPC machines).

programs into *universal binaries*—programs that run equally well on PowerPC- *and* Intel-based Macs with a double-click on the very same Finder icon.

It took two years for all the big-name programs to fall in line, but they finally did. Photoshop, Microsoft Office, Final Cut Pro, QuarkXPress, FileMaker, Firefox…one by one, the world's most popular Mac programs were reworked into Universal versions. (There's even a list of them—over 7,000 so far—at *www.apple.com/universal/.*)

You have only two indications that you're using a program originally designed for PowerPC-based Macs: First, you'll see a notation in the program's Get Info window (see Figure 4-16). Second, you'll probably discover that the program isn't as fast as it used to be.

If all this talk about architectures and chips makes your brain hurt, you can at least take comfort in one fact: No matter which kind of Mac you've got Snow Leopard installed on, every feature, tip, and trick you've learned from this book will work exactly the same.

Installing Mac OS X Programs

In general, new programs arrive on your Mac via one of two avenues: on a CD or DVD, or via an Internet download. The CD method is slightly simpler; see "Performing the Installation" later in this section.

For help installing downloaded programs, on the other hand, read on.

.sit, .zip, .tar, .gz, and .dmg

Programs you download from the Internet generally arrive in a specially encoded, compressed form. (And unless you've changed the settings, they arrive in the Downloads folder stack on your Dock.)

The downloaded file's name usually has one of these filename extensions:

- **.sit** indicates a *StuffIt* file, the standard Macintosh file-compression format of years gone by.

- **.zip** is the standard Windows compression file format. And because Snow Leopard has a built-in Compress command right in the File menu (and *doesn't* come with StuffIt Expander), .zip is the *new* standard Macintosh compression format. It certainly makes life easier for people who have to exchange files with the Windows crowd.

- **.tar** is short for *tape archive*, an ancient Unix utility that combines (but doesn't compress) several files into a single icon, for simplicity in sending.

- **.gz** is short for *gzip*, a standard Unix compression format.

- **.tar.gz** or **.tgz** represents one *compressed* archive containing *several* files.

- **.dmg** is a disk image, described below.

Fortunately, if you use Safari (Chapter 12) as your Web browser, you don't have to worry about all this, because it automatically unzips and unstuffs them.

If you use some other browser, *StuffIt Expander* can turn all of them back into usable form when you download a file. (StuffIt Expander doesn't come with Mac OS X, but you can download it for free from, for example, this book's "Missing CD" page at *www.missingmanuals.com.*)

Disk Images (.dmg files)

Once you've unzipped a downloaded program, it often takes the form of a disk image file, whose name ends with the letters *.dmg* (second from top in Figure 4-17). Some files arrive as disk images straight from the Web, too, without having been compressed first.

Disk images are extremely common in Mac OS X. All you have to do is double-click the .dmg icon. After a moment, it magically turns into a disk icon on your desktop, which you can work with just as though it's a real disk (third from top in Figure 4-17). For example:

• Double-click it to open it. The software you downloaded is inside.

• Remove it from your desktop by dragging it to the Trash (whose icon turns into a big silver Eject key as you drag), highlighting it and pressing ⌘-E (the shortcut for File→Eject), clicking its ⏏ button in the Sidebar, or right-clicking it, and then choosing Eject from the shortcut menu. (You've still got the original .dmg file you downloaded, so you're not really saying goodbye to the disk image forever.)

Cleaning Up after Decompression

When you've finished unzipping or unstuffing a downloaded file, you may have several icons on your desktop or in the Downloads folder. Some are useful; some you're free to trash:

• **The original compressed file.** It's safe to throw away the .sit, .tar, .gz, or .tgz file you originally downloaded (after it's decompressed, of course).

• **The .dmg file.** Once you've turned it into an actual disk-drive icon, installed the software from it, and "ejected" the disk-drive icon, you can delete the .dmg file. Keep it only if you think you might need to reinstall the software someday.

Note: If you try to trash the .dmg file *before* removing the disk-drive icon from the screen, you'll get a "file in use" error message when you try to empty the Trash.

• **The disk image itself.** This final icon, the one that contains the actual software or its installer (third from top in Figure 4-17), doesn't exist as a file on your hard drive. It's a phantom drive, held in memory, that will go away by itself when you log out. So after installing its software, feel free to drag it to the Trash (or highlight it and press ⌘-E to "eject" it).

Performing the Installation

Working with .tar, .gz, and .dmg files are all skills unique to downloading Mac OS X programs from the Internet. Installing software from a CD or DVD is much more straightforward.

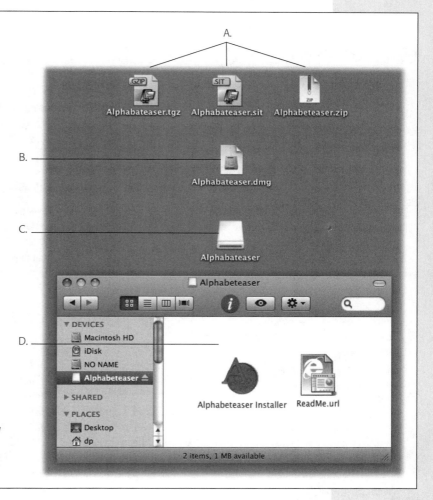

Figure 4-17:
Downloading a program may strew your desktop or Downloads folder with icons.

A: These are the original downloaded files. Delete them after they're decompressed.

B: The compressed file turns into this .dmg file. Double-click it to "mount" the disk image (if it didn't appear automatically).

C: And now, the disk image itself. Double-click it to open the software installer window. "Eject" it after the installation is complete.

D: Here's the actual software installer window. Drag the software's icon to your Applications folder, or double-click the installer, if you see one here. After the installation is complete, you can delete all of this stuff (except maybe the .dmg file, if you think you might want to install the software again later).

In either case, once you've got a disk icon on your desktop (either a pseudo-disk from a disk image or a CD or DVD you've inserted), you're ready to install the software. You can install many Mac OS X programs just by dragging their icons or folders to your hard drive (usually the Applications folder). Others offer a traditional installer program that requires you to double-click, read and accept a license agreement, and so on.

In both cases, *where* you decide to install the new program is suddenly a big issue. You have two alternatives:

• **In the Applications folder.** Most programs, of course, sit in your Applications folder. Most of the time, this is where you'll want to install new programs. Putting them in the Applications folder makes them available to anyone who uses the Mac.

Note: You can't put anything in your Applications folder unless you have an Administrator account, as described on page 407.

A Little Bit About 64 Bits

It's one of the most-advertised features of Snow Leopard: The thing is now almost completely 64-bit.

Right. 64-what?

If you want your eyes to glaze over, you can read the details on 64-bit computing in Wikipedia. But the normal-person's version goes like this:

For decades, the roadways for memory and information passed through Macs or Windows PCs were 32 "lanes" wide—they could manage 32 chunks of data at once. It seemed like plenty at the time. But as programs and even documents grew enormous, and computers came with the capacity to have more and more memory installed, engineers began to dream of 64-lane circuitry.

In the short term, the most visible effect of having a 64-bit computer is that you can install a lot more memory. Today's top-of-the-line Mac Pro, for example, is limited to 32 GB of RAM. That once seemed like a lot, but don't say that to today's video editors, game designers, and number-crunchy engineers.

A 64-bit computer, though, can have just a tad bit more: 16 *million* gigs, to be precise. (That's 16 exabytes, in case you were wondering. And that's a theoretical number; no modern personal computer even has that many RAM slots.)

Eventually, there may be other benefits to a 64-bit Mac. Programs can be rewritten to run faster. Security can be better, too. Unfortunately, getting there requires rewriting huge chunks of the operating system—and all your programs.

Almost all of Snow Leopard is 64-bit software. You may have some older, non-Apple programs that aren't, but fortunately, they still run without a problem. That's because the kernel of Snow Leopard, the underlying heart of it, still runs in 32-bit mode (yes, even on 64-bit processors), to accommodate all those older programs.

Even so, Snow Leopard runs 64-bit programs seamlessly. On certain Macs, you can make Snow Leopard boot into pure 64-bit mode by holding down the 6 and 4 keys as the computer is starting up. It's not a great idea, though, because all your 32-bit applications will crash.

Ordinarily, you never have to worry about any of this stuff. Every kind of program runs in the right mode automatically. Here and there, though, you'll bump your head on this 32-bit/64-bit difference. You'll try to open something—an old PICT graphic you want to see in Preview, for example, or an add-on System Preferences pane from another company—and you'll see a message telling you to deliberately command your modern, 64-bit app (Preview or System Preferences) to run in the older, 32-bit mode.

To do that, highlight the program's icon. Press ⌘-I (Get Info). Turn on "Open in 32-bit mode." Now you'll be able to run that older software.

Over time, these messages will become less frequent, as more of the world's Mac software is released in 64-bit versions. But in the meantime, you'll be ready.

- **In your Home folder.** Suppose you share your Mac with other people, as described in Chapter 13. If that's your situation, you may occasionally want to install a program privately, reserving it for your own use only. In that case, just install or drag it into your Home folder, or a folder inside it. When other people log onto the machine, they won't even know you've installed that new program, since it doesn't show up in the Applications folder.

If you don't have an Administrator account, in fact, this is your only option for installing new programs.

Uninstalling Software

In Mac OS X, there's generally no Uninstall program, and no Add/Remove Programs window. To uninstall a program, you just drag it (or its folder) from the Applications folder (or wherever it is) to the Trash.

Some programs also leave harmless scraps of themselves behind; to check for them, look for preference files or folders bearing the dearly departed program's name in your Library folders (especially in Application Support) and your Home→Library→ Preferences folder.

Dashboard

The essence of using most operating systems is running *programs,* which often produce *documents.*

In Mac OS X, however, there's a third category: a set of weird, hybrid entities that Apple calls *widgets.* They appear, all at once, floating in front of your other windows, when you press the F4 (⊙) key. Welcome to the Dashboard (Figure 4-18).

Note: The keystroke is F4 if you have a current Apple keyboard—the thin aluminum one on a laptop or desktop Mac. In fact, you can see a tiny Dashboard logo ⊙ painted right on the key.

On older, plastic keyboards, the keystroke is usually F12. Or, on laptops where F12 is the ▲ key, you have to hold down the Fn key (lower-left corner).

In either case, you can change the Dashboard keystroke to whatever you like, as described below.

What are these weird, hybrid entities, anyway? They're not really programs. What they most resemble, actually, is little Web pages. They're meant to display information, much of it from the Internet, and they're written using Web programming languages like HTML and JavaScript.

Mastering the basics of Dashboard won't take you long at all:

- **To move a widget,** drag it around the screen. (Click anywhere but on a button, menu, or text box.)

- **To close a widget,** press the Option key as you move the mouse across the widget's face. You'll see the ⊗ button appear at the widget's top-left corner; click it.

Tip: If the Widget bar is open (as described below), every widget displays its ⊗ close button. You don't need the Option key.

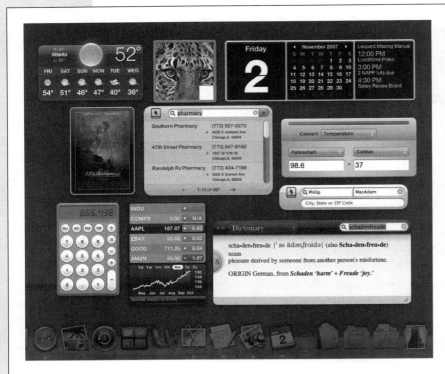

Figure 4-18:
When you summon the Dashboard, you get a fleet of floating miniprograms that convey or convert all kinds of useful information. They appear and disappear all at once, on a tinted translucent sheet that floats in front of all your other windows. You get rid of Dashboard either by pressing the same key again (F12 or whatever) or by clicking anywhere on the screen except on a widget.

- **To open a closed widget,** click the ⊕ button at the bottom of the screen. Now the entire screen image slides upward by about an inch to make room for the Widget bar: a "perforated metal" tray containing the full array of widgets, even the ones that aren't currently on the screen (Figure 4-19). Open one by clicking its icon.

On Macs with newish graphics cards, a new widget appears by splashing down into the center of your screen, sending realistic pond ripples across the liquidy glass of your screen. These widgets really know how to make an appearance, don't they?

- **To hide one of Apple's widgets,** or to delete one you've installed yourself, use the Widget widget described in Figure 4-20.

- **To rearrange your widgets as they appear in the Widget bar,** open your hard drive→Library→Widgets folder. Here you'll find the icons for the standard Apple Dashboard widgets. To rearrange them, you have to rename them; they appear on the Widget bar in alphabetical order. (You can also remove a widget for good by deleting it from this folder, if you must.)

Tip: The Dashboard icon also appears in your Dock, just in case you forget the F4 keystroke. On the other hand, if you prefer the keystroke, you can remove the icon from your Dock to make room for more important stuff. Control-click (or right-click) the icon and, from the shortcut menu, choose Remove from Dock.

Figure 4-19:
You'll probably have to scroll the Widget bar to see all the widgets, by clicking the arrows at either end. When you're finished opening new widgets, close the Widget bar by clicking its ⊗ button at the left side of your screen.

Figure 4-20:
The Widget widget (whose icon appears at lower left in Figure 4-19) opens up this list of widgets. Turn off a checkmark to hide a widget, or click – to completely uninstall any widget you installed yourself. The ones whose boxes aren't checked are the ones that no longer appear on the Widget bar.

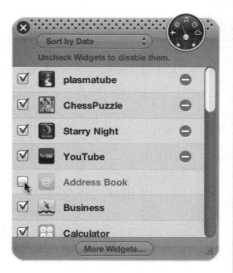

Dashboard Tips

Dashboard is crawling with cool tips and tricks. Here are a few of the biggies:

- If you just *click* an icon on the Widget bar, the widget appears right in the middle of your screen. But if you *drag* the widget's icon off the bar, you can deposit it anywhere you like.

- There's a great keystroke that opens and closes the Widget bar: ⌘-= (equals sign). (This keystroke may be different on non-U.S. keyboard layouts.)

- To refresh a certain widget—for example, to update its information from the Internet—click it and press ⌘-R. The widget instantly *twist-scrambles* itself into a sort of ice-cream swirl (you've got to see it to believe it) and then untwists to reveal the new data.

- You can open more than one copy of the same widget. Just click its icon more than once in the Widget bar. You wind up with multiple copies of it on your screen: three World Clocks, two Stock Trackers, or whatever. That's a useful trick when, for example, you want to track the time or weather in more than one city, or when you maintain two different stock portfolios.

- If you keep the Shift key pressed when you summon Dashboard, the widgets fly onto the screen in gorgeous, translucent, 3-D *slow motion*. Aren't you just glad to be alive?

Dashboard Preferences

To change the Dashboard keystroke to something other than F4 or F12, choose →
System Preferences, and then click Keyboard→Keyboard Shortcuts.

Tip: For faster service, Control-click (right-click) the Dashboard icon on the Dock. Choose Dashboard Preferences from the shortcut menu.

Here, you'll discover that you can choose almost any other keyboard combination to summon and dismiss the Dashboard, or even choose a screen corner that, when your mouse lands there, acts as the Dashboard trigger. This works exactly as described on page 128.

More Widgets

The best part of the Dashboard is that it's expandable. *Thousands* of new widgets, written by other people, are available on the Web: games, chat and email notifiers, gas-price reporters, calculators and translators, news and sports updaters, finance and health trackers, and on and on.

To see Apple's current list of goodies, use one of these tactics:

- **The short way.** Right-click the Dashboard icon in the Dock. From the shortcut menu, choose More Widgets.

- **The long way.** Click the Manage Widgets button that appears whenever the Widget bar is exposed; when the Widgets widget opens, click More Widgets.

Either way, you go to the Apple Dashboard downloads page. (Alternatively, check a Mac-downloads Web site like *www.versiontracker.com* for an even more complete selection.)

Installing a widget

When you download a widget, Mac OS X is smart enough to install it automatically. First, though, it offers you a trial run, as shown in Figure 4-21.

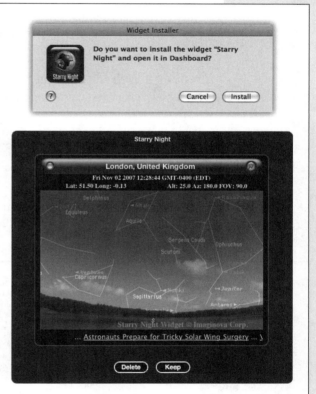

Figure 4-21:
Widgets could, in theory, harbor viruses, so Mac OS X is extremely cautious in downloading them.

Top: When you try to download a widget, the Mac asks if you're sure.

Bottom: After you download a widget and confirm your intention, you meet this test-drive mode for newly downloaded widgets. It's a way to play with new widgets before you actually commit to adding them to your system. Play with the widget, and then click Keep to install it (or Delete, if you think it's evil).

If you click Keep, Mac OS X copies it into your Home→Library→Widgets folder. Only you will see that Dashboard widget, because it's been copied into the Widgets folder of *your account.* Anyone else who has an account on this Mac won't see it.

Unless, of course, you copy or move that widget into the Library→Widgets folder (that is, begin with the Library folder in your main hard drive window). The contents of *that* Widgets folder are available to all account holders.

Web Clips: Make Your Own Widgets

You don't have to be satisfied with Apple's 20 widgets *or* the several thousand that other people have written. You can make a Dashboard widget of your own—in about three clicks.

What if your interest isn't skiing, stocks, or sports? What if it's *The New York Times* front page? Or the bestselling children's books on Amazon? Or the most-viewed video on YouTube? Or some cool Flash game you wish you could summon with the touch of a key?

That's the beauty of Web clips, a joint venture of Dashboard and the Safari Web browser. They let you turn *any section of any Web page* into a Dashboard widget that updates itself every time you open it. It's like having a real-time keyhole peek at all your favorite Web sites at once.

Creating a Web Clip Widget

Here's how you go about creating a do-it-yourself widget:

1. **Open Safari.**

   Safari is the Mac's Web browser. It's in your Applications folder.

2. **Go to the Web page that contains the information you want to snip. Choose File→Open in Dashboard.**

   The screen goes dark, with only a small window of white. As you move your cursor around the page, the small white rectangle conveniently snaps to fit the various rectangular sections of the page.

Clip button   Adjust handles

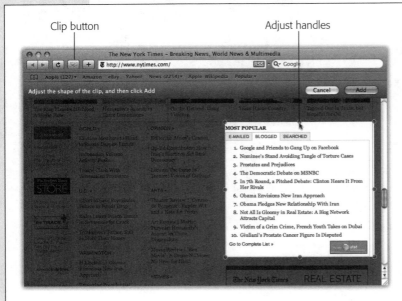

Figure 4-22:
Drag the little round handles to make the white box just big enough to surround the part of the page you want to enshrine. Or drag inside the box to move the whole thing.

As shown in Figure 4-22, your job is to make a frame around the part of the page that usually shows the information you want. If the Web site ever redesigns its pages, it'll wreck your widget—but what the heck. It takes only 5 seconds to make it again.

3. **Adjust the corner or side handles to enclose the piece of page you want. When you're finished, click Add, or press Return.**

Now Dashboard opens automatically. At this point, you can dress up your widget, adding a little polish to this raw clipping you've ripped out of a Web page. Click the ❶ button that appears when you move your mouse to the lower-right corner. The widget flips around to reveal some framing controls; see Figure 4-23.

Figure 4-23:
Top: Here, you can click one of the frame styles to give your widget a better-looking border.

If the widget plays sound, it keeps playing sound when you close the Dashboard unless you turn on "Play audio in Dashboard only."

Click Edit to return to the front of the widget, where you can adjust its position on the underlying Web page.

Bottom: Here's where it gets weird: You can reposition your widget's contents as though they're a window on the Web page that's visible behind it. Drag the widget contents in any direction within the frame, or resize the frame using the lower-right resize handle. Click Done.

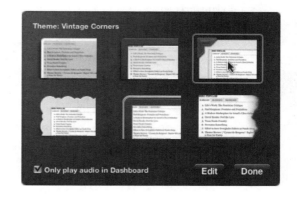

You can make as many Web-clip widgets as you want.

But here's a big screaming caution: If you close one of these homemade widgets, it's gone forever (or at least until you recreate it). They're never represented as icons on the Widget bar, as ordinary widgets are.

Ah, well—easy come, easy go, right?

Power Typing in Snow Leopard

Something strange has been quietly taking place at Apple: *Typing* has been getting a lot of attention.

It starts with Mac OS X's *system-wide* spelling checker. You don't have to maintain a separate spelling checker for each program you use. Now there's just one, and it works in most Apple programs: TextEdit, Stickies, iChat, Mail, iCal, Safari, Pages, iPhoto, iMovie, and so on. Add a word to the dictionary in one program, and it's available to all the others. There's a grammar checker, too.

Snow Leopard also features text substitution, where you type *addr* and the system types out "Irwina P. McGillicuddy, 1293 Eastport Lane, Harborvilletown, MA, 02552." (The same system auto-corrects common typos like *teh* instead of *the.*) There's also a case-flipping feature that can change selected text to ALL CAPS, all lowercase, or First Letter Capped. Both of these new features are available in most Apple programs and in any other programs that tap into Mac OS X's built-in text processing circuitry (although not, alas, Microsoft programs).

The Mac OS X Spelling and Grammar Checker

Mac OS X can give you live, interactive spelling and grammar checking, just as in Microsoft Word and other word processors. That is, misspelled words or badly written sentences or fragments get flagged (with a dashed red underline for spelling problems and a green one for grammar problems) the moment you type them. Here's the crash course:

- **Check the spelling of one word:** Highlight the word. Choose Edit→Spelling and Grammar→Show Spelling and Grammar. The spell-check dialog box opens, with the proposed corrections visible.

- **Check spelling as you type.** Choose Edit→Spelling and Grammar→Check Spelling While Typing. (If Check Grammar With Spelling is turned on in the same submenu, you'll get a grammar check, too.)

  Now, as you type, you'll see those red and green underlines on words the Mac thinks represent spelling or grammar mistakes. To fix one, Control-click (right-click) the underlined word, and proceed as shown in Figure 4-24.

Tip: In TextEdit, you can tell the Mac you always want the error-underlining turned on for all new documents from now on. Choose TextEdit→Preferences, click New Document, and then turn on "Check spelling as you type."

- **Check spelling after the document is finished.** Choose Edit→Spelling and Grammar→Show Spelling and Grammar (or press ⌘-:). The Spelling dialog box appears. The first error it spots appears in the top box, with the proposed corrections in the bottom one.

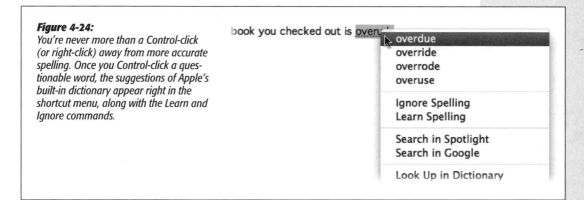

Figure 4-24:
You're never more than a Control-click (or right-click) away from more accurate spelling. Once you Control-click a questionable word, the suggestions of Apple's built-in dictionary appear right in the shortcut menu, along with the Learn and Ignore commands.

If you like one of Apple's proposals, click it and then click Change. If the word was correct already (for example, the guy's last name really is Teh), then click Find Next ("Leave the word as I typed it"), Ignore ("It's OK everywhere in this document"), or Learn ("Never flag this word again").

Handily enough, you can also click Define to look up a highlighted word (one of the spelling suggestions, for example) in the Mac's built-in Dictionary app. Also handily enough, the spelling checker is smart enough to maintain different spelling checkers (dictionaries) for different languages—and to recognize, within a single document, which language you're using!

- **Fix spelling as you type.** Note the difference. *Checking* your spelling just means "finding the misspelled words." *Fixing* means auto-correcting the errors as they occur, as you type. You might not even notice that it's happening!

This most tantalizing option is Edit→Spelling and Grammar→Correct Spelling Automatically. And sure enough, when this option is turned on, common typos like *teh* and *frmo* and *dont* get fixed as you type; you don't have to do anything to make it happen.

It's not perfect. It doesn't correct all errors (or even most of them). It occasionally even corrects a word you didn't mean to have corrected, like turning *brb* (Internet shorthand for "be right back") into *bribe*, or *arent* into *arrant*. (When it makes a mistake, hit ⌘-Z, the Undo command, to restore what you typed.) And sometimes it doesn't make the change until you're halfway through the sentence.

Still, though. Kind of cool.

Text Substitution (Abbreviation Expansion)

This one's kind of cool: a new Snow Leopard feature that auto-replaces *one* thing you type with something else. Why? Because it can do any of these things.

Insert the proper typographical symbols

Snow Leopard can insert attractive "curly quotes" automatically as you type "straight ones," or em dashes—like this—when you type two hyphens (--like that). It can also insert properly typeset fractions (like ½) when you type 1/2.

You can see the list of built-in substitutions—and create your own—in the System Preferences→Language & Text→Text tab, as shown in Figure 4-25.

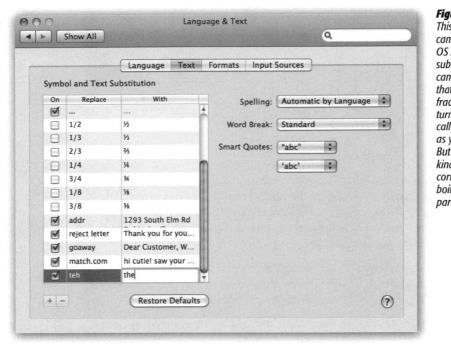

Figure 4-25:
This is where you can manage Mac OS X's typographic substitutions. You can see already that typing common fractions are set to turn into typographically fancy ones as you type them. But you can add all kinds of auto-typo-corrections and even boilerplate text paragraphs.

Apple doesn't want to drive you nuts, though, so it makes sure *you're* sure you really want these swappings to take place. So you have to turn on each of these features manually, in each program. (These commands are available anywhere you do a *lot* of typing, like TextEdit, Mail, and Stickies.)

- **Auto-quotes.** To make the quotes curlify themselves, choose Edit→Substitutions→ Smart Quotes, so that a checkmark appears.

***

Note: In System Preferences→Language & Text→Text tab, you can specify which kind of fancy quotation mark you prefer: «this kind,» „this kind," or whatever. You international thing, you!

- **Auto-dashes.** To turn double hyphens into these (—) long dashes, choose Edit→Substitutions→Smart Dashes, so that a checkmark appears.

- **Smart links.** There's also an option to create Smart Links, where any Web address you type turns into a blue, underlined, *clickable* link to a Web page. Turn on Edit→Substitutions→Smart Links.

Tip: You can also choose Edit→Substitutions→Show Substitutions to make a floating panel appear, complete with on/off checkboxes for all these features.

Replace abbreviations with much longer phrases

You can also program *addr* to type your entire return address. Create two-letter abbreviations for big legal or technical words you have to type a lot. Set up *goaway* to type out a polite rejection letter for use in email. And so on.

This feature has been in Microsoft Office forever (called AutoCorrect), and it's always been available as a shareware add-on (TypeIt4Me and TextExpander, for example). But now it's built right into most Apple programs, plus any others that use Apple's text-input plumbing.

You build your list of abbreviations in the System Preferences→Language & Text→Text tab, shown in Figure 4-25. See the list at left? Click the **+** button to create a new row in the scrolling table of substitutions.

Click in the left column and type the abbreviation you want (for example, *addr*). Click in the right column and type, or paste, the text you want Mac OS X to type instead.

Tip: Don't be shy—you're not limited to short snippets. The replacement text can be pages long, which is handy if you're a lawyer and you build your contracts out of boilerplate chunks of canned text.

You can even create multiple paragraphs—but not by hitting Return when you want a new line; no, hitting Return means, "I'm finished entering this text" and closes up the box. Instead, press Option-Return when you want a paragraph break.

Here again, you have to explicitly *turn on* the text-replacement feature in each program (TextEdit, Mail, Stickies, and so on). To do that, choose Edit→Substitutions→Text Replacement, so that a checkmark appears.

That's it! Now, whenever you type one of the abbreviations you've set up, the Mac instantly replaces it with your substituted text.

Case Swapping

The final new chunk in Snow Leopard's text-massaging tool chest is case swapping—that is, changing text you've already typed (or pasted) from ALL CAPS to lowercase or Just First Letters Capitalized.

This one's simple: Select the text you want to change, and then choose from the Edit→Transformations submenu. Your options are Make Upper Case (all caps), Make Lower Case (no caps), and Capitalize (first letters, like a movie title).

Keep that in mind the next time some raving lunatic SENDS YOU AN EMAIL THAT WAS TYPED ENTIRELY WITH THE CAPS LOCK KEY DOWN.

The Many Languages of Mac OS X Text

In Mac OS X, you can shift from language to language on the fly, as you type, even in midsentence—without reinstalling the operating system or even restarting the computer.

First, tell your Mac which languages you'd like to have available. Open System Preferences→Language & Text. On the Language tab, you see a listing of the different languages the Mac can switch into, in the corresponding languages—Français, Español, and so on. Just drag one of the languages to the top of the list to select it as the target language, as shown in Figure 4-26.

Figure 4-26:
Top: This is the list of the 18 "system localizations" that you get with a standard Mac OS X installation.

Bottom: Here's Safari running in Dutch. Actually understanding Dutch would be useful at a time like this—but even if you don't, it can't help but brighten up your work day to choose commands like Spraak-functie or Knip. (Alas, your success with this trick varies by program.)

Now launch Safari, TextEdit, Mail, or Stickies. Every menu, button, and dialog box is now in the new language you selected! If you log out and back in (or restart) at this point, the entire Finder will be in the new language, too.

Note: Programs differ widely in their "language awareness." If you use a language beyond the 18 in the list, adding it (with the Edit List button) ensures that its relevant features will be available in all programs. (You may still have to add additional language software to make your menus and dialog boxes change.)

Formats Tab

Of course, if you *really* speak French (for example), you'll also want to make these changes:

- On the Formats tab, choose your French-speaking country from the Region pop-up menu, so that time and date formats, number punctuation, and currency symbols also conform to your local customs. (Turn on "Show all regions," if necessary.)

  For example, the decimal and thousands separator characters for displaying large numbers differ from country to country. (The number 25,600.99, for example, would be written as 25 600,99 in France, and as 25.600,99 in Spain.) And what appears to an American to be July 4 (the notation 7/4), to a European indicates April 7.

  If, for some reason, Apple's preprogrammed settings aren't right for your region, you'll see Customize buttons that let you override them.

- Choose the French *keyboard layout* from the Input Menu tab, as explained on the following pages.

GEM IN THE ROUGH

Draw Those Chinese Characters

In Apple's demos, it was one of the coolest features of Snow Leopard: If you want to write in Chinese, you can now *draw* the characters you want, right on your laptop's trackpad. (This trick requires a recent Mac laptop, one of the multitouch models.)

To set this up, turn on Chinese–Simplified, choose the Chinese writing system you prefer, and turn on Trackpad Handwriting, in the System Preferences→Language & Text→Input Sources pane.

Then, when you're actually writing, use the flag (Input) menulet to choose Pinyin–Simplified (or whichever system you like). Now press Shift-Control-space bar to make the writing panel appear, as shown here.

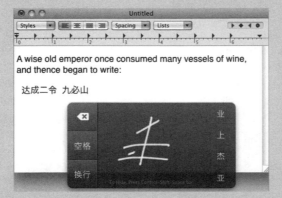

The trick here is to understand that the panel is a *full map* of your trackpad. You can't move the panel. Draw your character by dragging across the trackpad; white lines appear as you go.

On both sides of the on-screen panel, you see the Mac's interpretations of your character; to choose one, tap the corresponding spot on the *outside edges* of your actual trackpad. (Or, to delete your most recent line, tap the upper-left corner of your trackpad.) The Mac drops the character into your document.

Press Shift-Control-space bar again to hide the panel, and shake your head in wonder.

Input Menu Tab

While the Mac can display many different languages, *typing* in those languages is an-other matter. The symbols you use when you're typing in Swedish aren't the same as when you're typing in English. Apple solved this problem by creating different *keyboard layouts*, one for each language. Each rearranges the letters that appear when you press the keys. For example, when you use the Swedish layout and press the semicolon key, you don't get a semicolon (;)—you get an ö.

Use the list in the Input Menu pane to indicate which keyboard layout you want. If you select anything in the list, "Show input menu in menu bar" turns on automatically. A tiny flag icon appears in your menu bar—a keyboard *menulet* that lets you switch from one layout to another just by choosing its name. (To preview a certain keyboard arrangement, launch the Keyboard Viewer program described next.)

GEM IN THE ROUGH

The Character Palette

There you are, two-thirds of the way through your local matchmaker newsletter, when it hits you that you need a heart symbol. Right now.

You know there's one in one of your symbol fonts, but you're not about to type every single key combo until you produce the heart symbol. You can't help wishing there was an easier way to find those special symbols that hide among your fonts—fancy brackets, math symbols, special stars and asterisks, and so on.

The Keyboard Viewer (next page) is one solution. But there's a better one: the Character Palette. To make it appear, choose Edit→Special Characters.

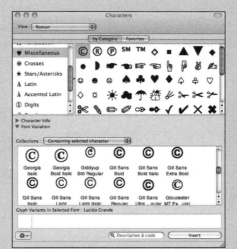

Most modern Mac programs have this command. If yours doesn't, here's the long way: Open System Preferences, click the International icon, click the Input Menu tab, and turn on the Character Palette checkbox.

You've just installed the Keyboard menulet.

Next time you're word processing or doing page layout, choose Show Character Palette from this menu.

The resulting window rounds up all symbols from all your fonts at once. To find a particular symbol, click the "by Category" tab, and then click the various category headings: Arrows, Stars/Asterisks, Math, and so on. Or, for an even more mind-blowing assortment (musical notes, Braille…), choose All Characters from the View pop-up menu.

You can preview variations of the same symbol by opening the Font Variation triangle. You can also use the Search box to find a symbol by name: "heart" or "yen" or "asterisk," for example. When you find the symbol you want, double-click it.

In most Apple programs, the correct symbol pops into your document. (In others, you may get the correct character in the wrong font. In that case, change the font of the inserted character manually. To find out what font it came from, click the Font Variation flippy triangle to see the font name.)

CHAPTER 4: DOCUMENTS, PROGRAMS, & SPACES

Keyboard Viewer: The Return of Key Caps

Keyboard Viewer consists of a single window containing a tiny onscreen keyboard (Figure 4-27). When you hold down any of the modifier keys on your keyboard (like ⌘, Option, Shift, or Control), you can see exactly which keys produce which characters. The point, of course, is to help you learn which keys to press when you need special symbols or non-English characters, such as © or ¢, in each font.

Note: Keyboard Viewer shows only the symbols you can produce by typing keystrokes. A font may contain thousands of other characters that can't actually be typed; the Character Palette (page 169) is the only way to access these other symbols.

It's a great tool—if you can find it.

Here's how. Open System Preferences→Language & Text, click Input Sources, and turn on Keyboard & Character Viewer at the top of the list. The window shown at bottom in Figure 4-27 appears. (Thereafter, you'll be able to choose its name from the Input menulet at the top of the screen, as shown at top in Figure 4-27.)

To see the effect of pressing the modifier keys, either click the onscreen keys or press them on your actual keyboard. The corresponding keys on the onscreen keyboard light up as they're pressed.

Tip: You're not stuck viewing the characters in a 12-point font size—a good thing, because some of them are hard to read when displayed that small. You can make the Keyboard Viewer window as large as you want—fill the screen with it, why don't you?—by clicking its Zoom button or dragging its lower-right corner. That will magnify the Keyboard Viewer window and its font size.

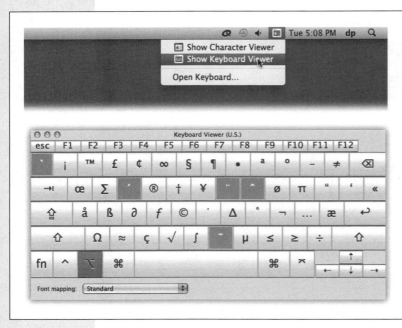

Figure 4-27:
*How do you make a ∏ symbol?
Top: Open Keyboard Viewer by choosing its name from the keyboard (flag) menulet.*

Bottom: Keyboard Viewer reveals the answer. When you press the Option key, the Keyboard Viewer keyboard shows that the pi character (∏) is mapped to the P key. To insert the symbol into an open document, just click it in the Keyboard Viewer window.

Data Detectors

Here's a cool step-saver, something no other operating system offers—a little something Apple likes to call *data detectors*.

In short, Mac OS X recognizes commonly used bits of information that may appear in your text: a physical address, a phone number, a date and time, and so on. With one quick click, you can send that information into the appropriate Mac OS X program, like iCal, Address Book, or your Web browser (for looking up an address on a map).

Here's how it works: When you spot a name, address, date, or time, point to it without clicking. Mail draws a dotted rectangle around it. Control-click inside the rectangle, or right-click, or click the pop-up ▼ at the right side.

As shown in Figure 4-28, a shortcut menu appears. Its contents vary depending on what you're pointing to:

Figure 4-28:
Mail can detect street addresses, phone numbers, dates, and times. When it spots something you may want to add to another program, like Address Book or iCal, it draws a dotted line around the info when you point to it without clicking. Click the little ▼ to get a shortcut menu for further options—like automatically adding the address to your Address Book program or seeing the address pinpointed on a Google map.

- **A mailing address.** You can choose Show Map from the shortcut menu; your Web browser opens automatically and shows you that address on a Google map.

  Alternatively, you can choose Create New Contact (to add an Address Book entry for this address) or Add to Existing Contact (if the *person* is in your Address Book—just not the *address*). Like magic, a little editing box sprouts out of the data-detected rectangle, prefilled with the information from the message, so that you can approve it.

Tip: In Mail, if you highlight some text in the message and then click the pop-up ▼ menu, Mail also fills in the Notes field in this person's Address Book entry with the highlighted text. Wicked cool.

• **A date and time.** The shortcut menu offers two useful commands. Create New iCal Event opens Mac OS X's calendar program and creates a new appointment at the date and time identified in the message. It's up to you to type a name for the date, set an alarm, and do all the other usual appointment-setting things.

Tip: If, while working in iCal, you ever forget where this event came from, double-click it. In the Info balloon, you'll see a link that takes you right back to the original Mail message that started it all.

If you choose Show This Date in iCal, though, you go to iCal, which opens directly to the specified date and/or time. The logic of this feature is overwhelming; after all, when someone emails you to ask if you're free for drinks next Thursday at 10, what's the first thing you usually want to do? Check your calendar, of course.

• **A phone number.** As with mailing addresses, the shortcut menu here offers you things like Create New Contact and Add to Existing Contact. The third one, Large Type, is great when you want to call this person right now—it displays the phone number in *huge* type, filling your screen, so you can see it from across your mansion.

• **A flight number.** There's a new data detector in Mac OS X 10.6: flights. When you highlight flight information in a text document (for example, "AA 152"), the data detector offers a Show Flight Information command. It opens the Flights widget of Dashboard, so you can see the flight's departure time, arrival time, and other details. It works only if the airline is represented as a two-letter code, and as of Mac OS X 10.6.1, only in Mail and iChat.

Part Two:
Making the Move

2

Seven Ways to Transfer Your Files

A huge percentage of "switchers" do not, in fact, *switch*. Often, they just *add*. They may get a Macintosh (and get *into* the Macintosh), but they keep the old Windows PC around, at least for a while. If you're in that category, get psyched. It turns out that communicating with a Windows PC is one of the Mac's most polished talents.

That's especially good news in the early days of your Mac experience. You probably have a good deal of stuff on the Windows machine that you'd like to bring over to the Mac. Somewhere along the line, somebody probably told you how easy this is to do. In fact, the Mac's reputation for simplicity may even have played a part in your decision to switch.

In any case, this chapter describes the process of building a bridge from the PC to the Mac, so that you can bring all your files and settings into their new home. It also tells you where to *put* all of them. (The next chapter is dedicated to the slightly hairier process of getting your email and addresses copied over.)

As it turns out, files can take one of several roads from your old PC to your new Mac. For example, you can transfer them on a disk (such as a CD or iPod), by a network, or as an attachment to an email message.

Tip: The first part of this chapter covers the mechanical aspects of moving files and folders from your Windows PC to the Mac. On page 180, you'll find a more pointed discussion of where to put each kind of data (mail, photos, music, and so on) once it's on the Mac.

Transfers by Apple Genius

By far the easiest way to transfer all the stuff from your PC to your new Mac is to let Apple do it for you. Yes, that's right: Those busy Geniuses who work at the 300 Apple stores around the world are prepared to bring your music, pictures, documents, address book, email, bookmarks, and other stuff to its new home on your Mac.

And believe it or not, you may be able to get this service for free.

It's important to understand, though, that there are two levels of this service:

- **Standard.** This lower-tier service requires some planning. You'll be instructed to put everything that you want rescued into a folder on your Windows desktop called Transfer. Put your Pictures, Music, and Documents folders in there, at the very least.

  If you're smart, you'll also export your address book, email, calendar, and bookmarks from the various Windows programs they're in now, as described in this chapter and the next. Put those exported files into the Transfer folder, too.

  The Apple store will copy that single Transfer folder to the desktop of your new Mac. That's it. They won't put those files in the right places for you (photos into iPhoto, music into iTunes, etc.); that's left for you to do.

  In other words, the Standard service is a great value if you're tech-savvy enough to import and export data into the proper programs. (Although actually, this book describes those steps pretty well.)

  The best part: If you bring in your old PC at the time you buy a new Mac, this service is *free*.

Tip: You don't necessarily have to bring in your PC the day you buy the Mac. If you bring a new Mac to the shop reasonably soon after buying it, even if you bought it online, the Geniuses are generally still willing to do the deed for you.

- **Complete.** Now we're talking. With the Complete service, you just hand over your PC, and the Apple dudes do everything. They take your entire Windows world and transfer everything into the appropriate programs on the Mac.

  For example, all your Windows pictures (even if they're in Picasa or special photo-editing programs from HP or Kodak) get brought over to the Mac and imported into iPhoto. All your music is imported into iTunes on the Mac. Your documents and movies get copied to the Documents and Movies folders on the Mac. Your Web bookmarks from Internet Explorer or Firefox get transferred to Safari on the Mac. Even your email, address book, and calendar get transferred from Outlook or Outlook Express on the PC and brought into Mail and iCal on the Mac.

  When they say complete, they mean complete.

Tip: Behind the scenes, the Apple Geniuses use exactly the same techniques and tools described in this chapter, including the O2M shareware for transferring mail, calendar, and address book out of Outlook.

This service is included with Apple's One to One program, which is itself an amazing deal. One to One gives you weekly private lessons in an Apple store—on any Mac topic—for $100 a year.

The rest of this chapter covers do-it-yourself ways to transfer your stuff. But man, there's nothing like having a professional do it for you.

Transfers by Network

Here's one of the best features of Mac OS X: It can "see" shared disks and folders on Windows PCs that are on the same network (wired or wireless). Seated at the Mac, you can open or copy files from a PC. In fact, you can go in the other direction, too: Your old PC can see shared folders on your Mac.

Chapter 14 offers a crash course in setting up a network. When it's all over, you'll be seated at the Mac, looking at the contents of your Windows PC in a separate window. At that point, you can drag whatever files and folders you want directly to the proper places on the Mac.

Transfers by Disk

Another way to transfer Windows files to the Mac is to put them onto a disk that you then pop into the Mac. (Although Windows can't read all Mac disks without special software, the Mac can read Windows disks.)

This disk can take any of these forms:

- **An external hard drive or iPod.** If you have an external hard drive (USB or IEEE 1394, what Apple calls *FireWire*), you're in great shape. While it's connected to the PC, drag files and folders onto it. Then unhook the drive from the PC, attach it to the Mac, and marvel as its icon pops up on your desktop, its contents ready for dragging to your Mac's built-in hard drive. (Most iPods work great for this process, too; they can operate as external hard drives—even the iPod Nano.)

- **A Time Capsule.** As you can read later in this chapter, an Apple Time Capsule is a sleek white box that contains a huge hard drive+a wireless base station. The idea, of course, is to create a WiFi network for your house or office and include a built-in disk for backing up all of your computers, automatically and wirelessly.

  All of that also means that the Time Capsule makes a great transfer station between a PC and a Mac, since its icon shows up on the desktops of both.

- **A USB flash drive.** These small keychainy sticks are cheap and capacious, and they work beautifully on both Macs and PCs. Like a mini-external hard drive, a flash drive plugs directly into your USB port, at which point it shows up on your desktop just like a normal disk. You copy files to it from your PC, plug it into your

Mac, and copy the files off, just like you would for any other disk. And you're left with a backup copy of the data on the drive itself.

- **A CD or DVD.** If your Windows PC has a CD or DVD burner, here's another convenient method. Burn a disc in Windows, eject it, and then pop it into the Mac (see Figure 5-1). As a bonus, you wind up with a backup of your data on the disc itself.

Note: If you're given a choice of file format when you burn the disc in Windows, choose ISO9660. That's the standard format that the Macintosh can read.

- **Move the hard drive itself.** This is a grisly, technical maneuver best undertaken by serious wireheads—but it can work. You can install your PC's hard drive directly into a Power Mac or Mac Pro, as long as it was prepared using the older FAT or FAT32 formatting scheme. (The Mac can handle FAT hard drives just fine, but chokes with NTFS hard drives.)

When you insert a Windows-formatted disk, whatever the type, its icon appears at the upper-right corner of your desktop, where Mac disks like to hang out. (If it doesn't appear, you or someone you love has probably fiddled with the "Show these items on the Desktop" settings in the Finder→Preferences→General tab.)

Figure 5-1:
Burned CDs generally show up with equal aplomb on both Mac and Windows, regardless of which machine you used to burn it. Here's a CD burned on a Windows XP machine (bottom), and what it looks like on the Mac (top)—same stuff, just a different look and different sorting order. Either way, you can drag files to and from it, rename files, delete files, and so on.

Transfers by File-Sending Web Site

There's a new breed of file-shuttling Web sites prowling the Net—and a new option for transferring large amounts of data between machines.

They're free Web sites, like *yousendit.com* and *sendthisfile.com,* that are specifically designed for sending huge files from one computer to another, without worrying about email file attachments or size limits.

On the Windows PC, zip up your files into a great big .zip file. Upload it to one of these free sites, and provide your Mac's email address.

On the Mac, click the link that arrives by email—and presto, that huge zip file gets downloaded onto your Mac. It's free, there's no file-size limit, and you can download the big file(s) within three days of sending them. The only price you pay is a little bit of waiting while the stuff gets uploaded and then downloaded.

Tip: If you have your own Web site—a *.com* of your own, for example, or a free site through a university—you can also use *that* Web space as a transfer tool. Follow the uploading instructions that you were given when you signed up for the space. (Hint: It usually involves a so-called *FTP* program.) Then, once all your files are on the site, download them onto your Mac.

Transfers by Email

Although sending files as email attachments might seem to be a logical plan, it's very slow. Furthermore, remember that many email providers limit your attachment size to 5 or 10 megabytes. Trying to send more than that at once will clog your system. If you've got a lot of stuff to bring over from your PC, use one of the disk- or network-based transfer systems described earlier in this chapter.

But for smaller transfer jobs or individual files, sending files as plain old email attachments works just fine.

Transfers by iDisk

If your Windows PC isn't in the same building as the Mac, connecting the two using an Ethernet or a wireless network may not be a practical proposition. But even if you can't connect them into *a* network, you can still connect them via *the* network: the Internet.

It turns out that, for $100 per year, Apple will be happy to admit you to a club it calls *MobileMe.* It offers a number of handy Internet features that tie in nicely to Mac OS X, as described on page 306.

For many people, the crown jewel of the MobileMe services is the iDisk, which appears on your desktop as though it's a multigigabyte hard drive. Anything you drag into the folders inside this "drive" gets copied to Apple's secure servers on the Internet. (If that's not enough space for you, Apple will rent you a larger allotment in exchange for more money.)

Because you can use the iDisk as a go-between between Mac and Windows, anywhere in the world, it makes a handy universal transfer disk. Page 310 has details for pulling the iDisk onto the Mac's screen or the PC's screen.

Transfers by Bluetooth

Bluetooth isn't really designed to be a networking technology; it's designed to eliminate cables between various gadgets. But if your Mac and a PC each have Bluetooth adapters, you can share files between them as though there's no language barrier at all. (Bluetooth is built into all Macs, and is available as a USB or internal card for Windows machines.)

Mac OS X comes with a nondenominational file-exchange program called Bluetooth File Exchange (in your Applications→Utilities folder). Not all Windows Bluetooth adapters come with such a program. But if yours does (3Com's adapters do, for example), you should be able to shoot files between the machines with the greatest of ease, if not the greatest of speed.

Where to Put Your Copied Files

Just getting your PC files onto the Mac is only half the battle. Now you have to figure out where they *go* on the Mac.

Tip: For $40, you can buy a program called Move2Mac that takes care of this "where to put it" step for you. You still have to connect the PC to the Mac over a network, or equip yourself with an external USB hard drive. But from there, the software handles putting all of this into the right places on the Mac: files, folders, photos, music, desktop pictures (wallpaper), Internet Explorer bookmarks and home page, and Outlook email, addresses, and calendar appointments.

The short answer is: Everything goes into your Home folder. (Choose Go→Home, or click the ⌂ icon in your Sidebar.)

Some of the more specific "where to put it" answers are pretty obvious:

- **My Documents.** Put the files and folders from the PC's My Documents folder into your Home→Documents folder. Here's where you should keep all your Microsoft Office files, PDF files, and other day-to-day masterpieces, for example.

- **My Music.** Your Windows My Music folder was designed to hold all of your MP3 files, AIFF files, WAV files, and other music. As you could probably guess, you should copy these files into your Mac's Home→Music folder.

  After that, you can import the music directly into iTunes. If you used iTunes on your old PC, for example, just open iTunes on your Mac and choose iTunes→Preferences→Advanced. Then click Change, and navigate to the place where you moved your old iTunes library.

If you used some *other* music program on your PC (like Windows Media Player or MusicMatch), things are a little different. On your Mac, choose iTunes→Import, and navigate to the folder that contains all your music. (In either case, click Choose in the resulting dialog box.)

- **My Pictures.** The latest Windows versions also offer a My Pictures folder, which is where your digital camera photos probably wound up. Mac OS X has a similar folder: the Home→Pictures folder.

  Here again, after copying your photos and other graphics faves over to the Mac, you're only halfway home. If you fire up iPhoto (in your Applications folder), choose File→Import, and choose the Pictures folder, you'll *then* be able to find, organize, and present your photos in spectacular ways.

- **My Videos.** The My Videos folder of Windows XP and later versions contains the video clips you've downloaded from your camcorder (presumably so that you can edit them with, for example, Microsoft's Movie Maker software). Once you've moved them to your Home→Movies folder, though, you're in for a real treat: You can now edit your footage (if it's *digital* footage) with iMovie, which, to put it kindly, runs rings around Movie Maker.

Other elements of your Windows world, though, are trickier to bring over. For example:

Desktop Pictures (Wallpaper)

Especially in recent versions of Windows, the desktop pictures, better known in the Windows world as *wallpaper,* are pretty cool. Fortunately, you're welcome to bring them over to your Mac and use them on your own desktop.

To find the graphics files that make up the wallpaper choices in Windows (version Me or later), proceed like this:

1. **Open My Computer, double-click your hard drive's icon, and open the Windows or WINNT folder.**

   If you see a huge "These files are hidden" message at this point, or if the window appears empty, click "Show the contents of this folder" or "View the entire contents of this folder" at the left side of the window.

2. **In the Windows or WINNT window, open the Web folder.**

   You're looking for a folder inside it called Wallpaper.

3. **Open the Wallpaper folder.**

   It's filled with .bmp or .jpg files ready for you to rescue and use on the Mac. See page 480 for instructions on choosing wallpaper for your Mac.

Note: In Windows 95 or 98, the wallpaper files are in your Program Files→Plus!→Themes folder instead.

Sound Effects

The Mac doesn't let you associate your own sound effects to individual system events, as Windows does (Low Battery Alarm, Maximize, Minimize, and so on). It lets you choose *one* sound effect for all attention-getting purposes (page 496).

Still, there's nothing to stop you from harvesting all of the fun little sounds from your Windows machine for use as the Mac's error beep.

To find them on the PC, repeat step 1 of the preceding instructions. But in the Windows or WINNT folder, open the Media folder to find the WAV files (standard Windows sound files).

Once you've copied them to your Mac, you can double-click one to listen to it. (It opens up in something called QuickTime Player, which is the rough equivalent of Windows Media Player. Press the Space bar to listen to the sound.)

To use these sounds as error beeps, you'll have to convert them from the PC's WAV format into the Mac's preferred AIFF format. You'll find step-by-step instructions in the free downloadable appendix for this chapter, "Converting WAV Sounds to Mac Error Beeps.pdf." You can find it on this book's "Missing CD" page at *www.missing-manuals.com*.

Bookmarks (Favorites)

Moving your Favorites (browser bookmarks) to a Mac is easy. The hardest part is exporting them as a file, and that depends on which browser you've been using on the PC.

- **Internet Explorer.** Fire up Internet Explorer; choose File→Import and Export. (In Internet Explorer 7, click the double-star icon in the upper-left corner of the window. From the pop-up menu, choose Import and Export.)

  When the Import/Export Wizard appears, click Next; on the second screen, click Export Favorites, and then click Next again.

  On the third screen, leave the Favorites folder selected, and click Next. Finally, click Browse to choose a location for saving the exported bookmarks file. For now, save it to your desktop.

  Click Next, Finish, and then OK.

- **Firefox.** In Firefox, choose Bookmarks→Organize Bookmarks. In the Bookmarks Manager window, choose File→Export. Save the Bookmarks file to your desktop.

Now you've got an exported Bookmarks file on your desktop. Transfer it to your Mac using any of the techniques described earlier in this chapter (network, email, whatever).

Now open the Mac's Web browser, Safari (it's in your Applications folder). Choose File→Import Bookmarks. Navigate to, and double-click, the exported Favorites file to pull in the bookmarks.

Tip: Firefox is available for the Mac, too (*www.getfirefox.com*). If your bookmarks are already in Safari, you can import them by choosing File→Import. If not, you can import them from your exported Windows bookmarks file by choosing Bookmarks→Manage Bookmarks; then, in the Bookmarks Manager window, choose File→Import. Find and select the exported bookmarks file.

Everything Else

See Chapter 6 for details on copying your email, Address Book, and Outlook calendar information to the Mac.

Document Conversion Issues

Most big-name programs are sold in both Mac and Windows flavors, and the documents they create are freely interchangeable.

Files in standard exchange formats don't need conversion, either. These formats include JPEG (the photo format used on Web pages), GIF (the cartoon/logo format used on Web pages), PNG (a newer image format used on Web pages), HTML (raw Web-page documents), Rich Text Format (a word-processor exchange format), plain text (no formatting), QIF (Quicken Interchange Format), MIDI files (for music), and so on.

Part of this blessing stems from the fact that both Windows and Mac OS X use file name extensions to identify documents. ("Letter to the Editor.doc", for example, is a Microsoft Word document on *either* operating system.) Common suffixes include:

Kind of document	Suffix	Example
Microsoft Word	.doc, .docx	Letter to Mom.doc
text	.txt	Database Export.txt
Rich Text Format	.rtf	Senior Thesis.rtf
Excel	.xls, .xlsx	Profit Projection.xls
PowerPoint	.ppt, .pptx	Slide Show.ppt
FileMaker Pro	.fp5, fp6, fp7…	Recipe file.fp7
JPEG photo	.jpg, .jpeg	Baby Portrait.jpg
GIF graphic	.gif	Logo.gif
PNG graphic	.png	Dried fish.png
Web page	.htm, .html	Index.htm

Note: Recent versions of Microsoft Office for Mac and Windows offer a more compact file format ending with the letter x. For example, Word files are .docx, Excel files are .xlsx, and so on. The older, more widely compatible format doesn't have the x (.doc, .xls, etc.).

The beauty of Mac OS X is that most Mac programs add these file name suffixes automatically and invisibly—and recognize such suffixes from Windows with equal ease. You and your Windows comrades can freely exchange documents without ever worrying about this former snag in the Macintosh/Windows relationship.

You may, however, encounter snags in the form of documents made by Windows programs that don't exist on the Mac, such as Microsoft Access. Chapter 7 tackles these special cases one by one.

FireWire Disk Mode (Target Disk Mode)

FireWire Disk Mode is by far the fastest method for transferring a lot of data—even faster than copying files over a network—but it works only between two Macs, which is why it occupies this lonely spot at the end of this chapter. FireWire Disk Mode is extremely useful in any of these situations:

- **You're traveling with a laptop.** You want to copy your life onto it from your main Mac, including your entire 2 GB email folder and project files, before taking it on a trip, and then unload it when you return.

Note: The MacBook Air and the less expensive MacBooks don't have FireWire jacks, so they can't do this trick.

- **You have a new Mac.** You want to copy everything off the old one, without having to wait all night.

- **One Mac won't start up.** You want to repair it, using another Mac as a "front end."

In the following steps, suppose your main Mac is an iMac, and you want to use a MacBook Pro laptop as an external hard drive for it.

1. **Using a FireWire cable, connect the FireWire jacks of both computers.**

   For this trick, you need a 6-pin FireWire cable—*not* the one that connects a camcorder to a Mac. The one you need has the same, large connector on both ends.

Note: If both Macs have Apple's new FireWire 800 jacks, use a 9-pin FireWire cable instead for much greater speed. If only one Mac has a FireWire 800 jack, use that computer's traditional FireWire 400 connector instead. Otherwise, you need either a special FireWire 800–to–FireWire 400 cable, or the 400-to-800 adapter that came with your Mac. Yes, it's a confusing hassle, but once you own the cable (or adapter), you're set for life.

2. **On the laptop, choose ⬤→System Preferences. Click Startup Disk. Click Target Disk Mode. In the confirmation box, click Restart.**

   The MacBook Pro turns off, then on again. A giant, yellow, Y-shaped FireWire icon bounces around the laptop screen.

   Now take a look at the iMac's screen: Sure enough, there's the MacBook Pro's hard drive icon on the desktop. You're ready to copy files onto or off of it, at extremely high speeds, and go on with your life.

3. **When you're finished working with the laptop, eject it from the iMac's screen as you would any disk. Then turn off the laptop by pressing the power button.**

   The next time you turn on the MacBook Pro, it will start up from its own copy of Mac OS X, even if the FireWire cable is still attached. (You can disconnect the cable whenever.)

Transferring Email & Contacts

I f you use your PC for email—hey, it could happen—there's good news: Switching to a Mac doesn't mean you have to lose your stash of messages, reconfigure your email accounts from scratch, or manually retype everything in your address book. This chapter covers the secrets of moving your entire email life over to the Mac— messages, addresses, settings, everything—with as little hassle as possible.

As you read this chapter, it's important to keep straight the two leading Windows email programs, which many people don't realize are actually two entirely different beasts:

- **Microsoft Outlook.** This program is part of Microsoft Office for Windows. It's a sprawling, network-based email, contact, and calendar program that's ubiquitous in corporate offices and many schools. You, or somebody who employs you, paid good money for this software.

- **Outlook Express.** This Windows program is a free, scaled-down version of Outlook. It came with Microsoft Windows versions up through Windows Me, and is therefore sitting on practically every PC sold until 2007. It doesn't have a calendar, a To Do list, or other bells and whistles of Outlook—but it's free.

  In Windows Vista, Microsoft renamed this program, calling it Windows Mail. In Windows 7, it's still called Windows Mail, but it doesn't come with Windows; you have to download it from a special Microsoft Web site (don't ask).

  In any case, most people moving to the Mac these days are doing so to *avoid* migrating to Vista or Windows 7, so in this chapter, let's just use the old name: Outlook Express.

Unfortunately, each Windows email program requires a different method of exporting its email and addresses. Each Macintosh email program requires a different piece of go-between Windows software to ease the transition, too.

There are so many permutations of the "to/from" issue, in fact, that you'd practically need a table or two to keep them straight. They might look something like this:

Ways to Move Your Email

	From Outlook	From Outlook Express (Windows Mail)
To Apple Mail	O2M or Thunderbird	Thunderbird
To Entourage (Outlook for Mac)	O2M or Thunderbird	Thunderbird

Tip: If your PC currently connects to your company's Exchange server to get its mail, you don't have to do any transferring at all. Snow Leopard can access exactly the same account, where you'll see exactly the same email folders. See page 200.

Ways to Move Your Address Book

	From Outlook	From Outlook Express (Windows Mail)
To Mac OS X Address Book	O2M or Thunderbird	Thunderbird
To Entourage (Outlook for Mac)	O2M or CSV Method	CSV Method

It's a complex matrix. And it's not helped much by the fact that Microsoft keeps renaming its email programs. (Outlook Express was renamed Windows Mail, and Entourage for the Mac is scheduled to emerge as something called Outlook for Mac at some point in 2010.)

But if you know what program you've been using on the PC, and which one you want to use on the Mac, you'll find the steps you need later in this chapter.

Tip: If you want to transfer your stuff out of *Eudora* for Windows, or into *Eudora* for Mac, you're in the minority—but you're not forgotten. See the free downloadable PDF Appendix, "Moving Email Into or Out of Eudora," on this book's "Missing CD" page at *www.missingmanuals.com* for details.

A Reminder That Could Save You Hours

Remember: For $50, one of the Geniuses at an Apple store will transfer all your mail, settings, and address-book entries from your old PC into Mac OS X Mail for you. Truth is, the Geniuses use exactly the same methods described in this chapter—but the beauty of this concept is that *they* do the work, not you.

Transferring Your Outlook Mail

If Microsoft Outlook has been your Windows address book/email program, you're in luck: You have two options for importing your stuff.

Both of these methods bring over your entire backlog of existing email—the contents of your Inbox, Sent items, archived mail and, perhaps, even deleted items that are still in your email program's Trash.

O2M Method (Quick, Simple, $10)

If you value your time, buy O2M (short for Outlook2Mac)—a $10 utility that stream-lines the process of bringing Outlook data to your Mac. (You can download it right now from *www.littlemachines.com*.)

Tip: This, in fact, is the tool that the Geniuses use at the Apple Store when someone pays them to transfer their stuff from a PC to a new Mac.

With O2M, you're spared the lengthy, sometimes tricky steps required by the free conversion methods described in the following pages. The program takes a wizard-like approach to transferring your Outlook data, gently stepping you through the whole process, as shown in Figure 6-1. It saves all the exported data into one folder (called My_Outlook_Files), making it simple to grab the files you need and move them to your Mac.

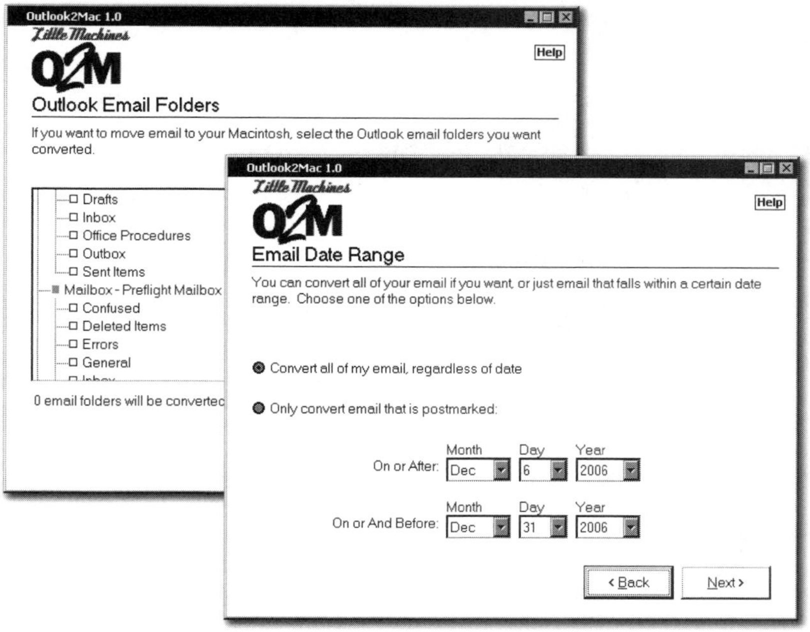

Figure 6-1:
O2M's wizard-like screens take you gently by the hand and walk you step by step through the process of moving mail, contacts, and calendar appointments from Microsoft Outlook to your Mac applications. Options abound. When exporting email, you can select exactly which folder you want included (top) or filter mail based on a specified date range (bottom). O2M even works with iCal, converting Outlook appointments and meetings into entries on an iCal calendar.

O2M also provides far more options than you get using other methods. For example, it lets you choose messages from only a specific date range—the last year's worth of email, for example, but nothing older. It lets you choose whether or not you want to include attachments with the transferred messages. It can even filter out certain attachments based on type.

O2M's other selling point is that it can handle more than just your email messages. It can also convert calendar entries and your address book, which can be imported directly into iCal, Entourage, Outlook for Mac, or the Mac's Address Book.

As a final perk, the program moves email to and from just about any programs: *from* Outlook 97, 98, 2000, 2002, 2003, or 2007 *to* Apple Mail, Entourage, MailSmith, PowerMail, or iCal.

Thunderbird Method (Time-Consuming, Free)

If you're on a *very* tight budget, too tight for a $10 piece of shareware, you can also transfer your email to the Mac for free. The trick is to import it first into—get this— Thunderbird for Windows.

Thunderbird is to email what Firefox is to Web browsers: a free, open-source, high-quality alternative to the Microsoft behemoths. It was put together by Mozilla.org and a team of volunteer programmers all over the world.

Thunderbird effortlessly imports email and address books from Outlook, Outlook Express, or Eudora. It even preserves any hierarchical folders you may have set up to sort and organize your messages. In other words, your email arrives on your Mac just as well organized as it was when it left your Windows machine.

Download your free copy of Thunderbird from *www.getthunderbird.com*. It works with Windows 98 or later. (If your machine has Windows 95, opt for the O2M method described earlier.)

Note: You don't need Thunderbird on the *Mac* for this process. Furthermore, when installing Thunderbird on Windows, you don't have to opt for any of the Custom install options—the default installation will give you everything you need.

When you've got Thunderbird installed on the PC, you're ready to follow the three big steps: First, you import your email into Thunderbird. Next, you copy the Thunderbird email to your Mac. You import the mail into Apple's Mail program—and then, optionally, Microsoft Entourage. Take a deep breath, and read on.

Phase 1: Import to Thunderbird

Your first job is to bring your existing Outlook mail into Thunderbird. (This method also works for transferring Outlook Express or Eudora mail.) Here's how you do it:

1. **Open Thunderbird.**

   Actually, the very first time you open Thunderbird, it offers to do the importing described here. To avoid having to follow two slightly divergent sequences of steps, though, decline that invitation. Go ahead into the program and then proceed as written here.

2. **Choose Tools→Import.**

A dialog box opens, allowing you to select the type of information you want to import.

3. **Choose Mail. Click Next.**

Don't worry about the Address Books or Settings options at this point. You can move those items over separately.

4. **Select the program from which you want to import messages.**

Thunderbird can handle email from Outlook, Outlook Express, Eudora, and easier versions of Netscape Communicator. Pick the appropriate program from among the ones listed.

5. **Click Next to start the import process—and be patient.**

Thunderbird now starts doing its thing, obediently sucking every last email message into its own email folder. If you've got a hefty stash of email—thousands of messages organized in lots of nested folders—this will take a while. It may even look as if Thunderbird has stalled, but it hasn't. Wait patiently as the progress bar creeps forward.

When the process is finally over, Thunderbird displays a dialog box listing all the different mailboxes, folders, and subfolders that it has successfully ingested, as shown in Figure 6-2. Click Finish to wrap things up.

Figure 6-2:
This is Thunderbird's way of telling you that everything went OK when it imported all your mailboxes and messages. Review this list before forging ahead with your Mac migration to make sure Thunderbird grabbed all the mail you want brought over to your Mac.

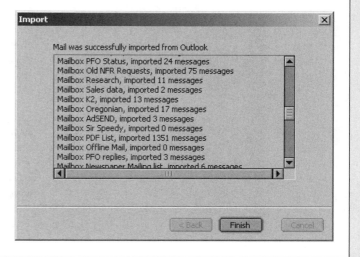

Now you see your imported mailboxes listed in the pane on the left (you might have to expand the Local Folders flippy triangle first). Clicking a mailbox icon displays the corresponding messages in the main window.

Phase 2: Copy to the Mac

Your next task is to transfer Thunderbird's copy of your mail to your Mac.

1. **Open your Application Data folder.**

   The steps depend on your version of Windows. For example:

   Windows 98 or 98SE: Open the My Computer→your hard drive icon→Win98 →Application Data folder.

   Windows Me: Open the My Computer→your hard drive icon→Windows→ Application Data folder.

   Windows 2000: Open the My Computer→your hard drive icon→Documents and Settings→*your name*→Application Data folder, where *your name* is your Windows user account name (the name you use to log into Windows at startup).

   Windows XP and later: Microsoft's assumption is that you, the lowly, technically ignorant PC user, have no business mucking around in the important operating-

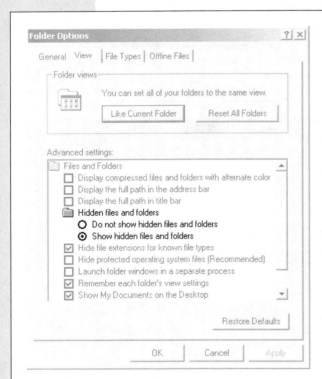

Figure 6-3:
You must uncloak the hidden folders lurking in Windows in order to copy your email files. Here's the trick.

Windows XP: In any open folder window, choose Tools→Folder Options. Switch to the View tab, as shown here.

Windows Vista: Click Start→Control Panel→ Appearance and Personalization→Folder Options.

Windows 7: Click Start→Control Panel→ Appearance and Personalization→Show hidden files and folders.

In each case, you wind up in this dialog box (make sure you're on the View tab. In the Advanced Settings list, turn on "Show hidden files and folders" (or "files, folders, and drives," and then click OK.

Now you can see all the previously hidden folders—including the Thunderbird ones.

system folders—so Windows hides them from you. To expose the hidden files, follow the steps shown in Figure 6-3.

Once that's done, open Computer→your hard drive icon→Documents and Settings→*your name*→Application Data (or AppData), where *your name* is your Windows user account name.

2. **Once you've opened the Application Data folder, open your Thunderbird→Profiles folder.** Finally, open the folder that corresponds with the profile name you chose when you started running Thunderbird. (If you didn't set up a profile, it's just called something like "mx11bvdg. default".)

Inside that folder, you'll find a folder called Mail. That's the one you want.

3. **Copy the Mail folder to your Mac.**

Once again, Chapter 6 describes various ways to go about it.

Once the mail files are on your Mac, you're ready to bring them into the program of your choice. Exactly how you do this depends on the email program you're using; read on.

Phase 3: Import into Mail

Mail, the email program that comes free with Mac OS X, does an elegant job of importing the files generated by Thunderbird. (If you plan to use Microsoft Entourage, you have to start with this step, too; that is, you must first bring the mail into Mail.)

Here are the steps for feeding the mail from your PC to the Mail program. (Note: If Mail won't let you proceed until you've set up a mail account, see page 198.)

1. **Open Mail.**

It's in the Applications folder, and its icon is probably on the Dock.

2. **In Mail, choose File→Import Mailboxes.**

The Import Mailboxes dialog box appears.

3. **Click the Thunderbird/Mozilla radio button.**

You can also import mail from a variety of *Mac* email programs, including Entourage, Outlook Express, and Eudora.

4. **Click the Continue button.**

You're presented with a standard Open dialog box.

5. **Locate and select the Mail folder you brought over from your PC. Click the Choose button.**

Mail displays a list of all the Thunderbird mailboxes it finds, as shown in Figure 6-4.

6. **Turn on the checkboxes of the email folders you want to bring into Mail.**

All the checkboxes start out turned on, meaning that Mail will grab everything you brought over from Thunderbird (including RSS feeds and even what was in the Trash). But if you decide at this point that you don't want to include, say, the messages that were in the Trash folder, you can filter them out by turning off the appropriate checkboxes.

Tip: You can use the up and down arrow keys to navigate through a long list of mailboxes and folders in the Import Mailboxes window.

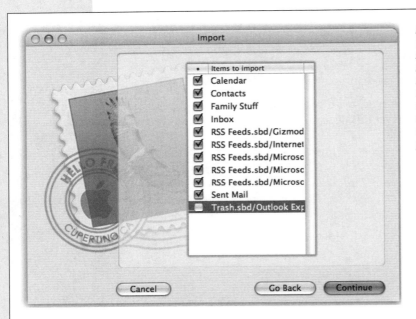

Figure 6-4:
When importing mail messages from Thunderbird, Mail first shows you all the mailboxes it found, ready for import. Turn off the checkboxes next to any folders that you don't want included during the import process.

From the Outlook Archives

I've got about five years' worth of old Outlook email archived on my hard drive. Is there any way to get the contents of these archives into my Mac's email program?

Absolutely.

When you're in Outlook (on your Windows PC), choose File→Open→Personal Folders File to open any of the Outlook-generated archive files that you want to bring over to your Mac. (Outlook archives have *.pst* file name extensions.) Once you open an archive file, a "mailbox" icon called

Archive Folders appears in Outlook's Folder List, allowing you to access any of the individual messages within the archive.

Simply import your Outlook mail into Thunderbird, as explained earlier in this chapter, *after* opening the archive files. Their contents will be included when you bring the mail into Thunderbird and when you later transfer your mail folders to your Mac.

---

7. **Click Continue to start importing.**

The import process now begins. Mail shows you the subject line of each message it brings in.

When the process is complete, your imported mailboxes appear in the Mailboxes column on the left side of the window, in a folder called Import. (See Chapter 11 for more on Mail.) By dragging messages, you can refile them into other mailbox folders, if you like.

Phase 4: Import into Entourage (optional)

If you have Microsoft Office for Macintosh, you may prefer its more powerful Entourage email program. No problem: You can bring the Thunderbird files that you brought over from your PC—and then imported into Mail—into Microsoft Entourage.

1. **In Entourage, choose File→Import.**

The Begin Import dialog box appears.

2. **Click the right arrow. Choose "Import information from a program."**

Since your messages are already stored in Mail—with all the folders and subfolders intact—you can have Entourage go from there.

3. **Click the right arrow. Choose "Apple Mail."**

Make sure Messages and Accounts are turned on. (The other two checkboxes are only useful if you've started customizing Mail as described in Chapter 11.) Click the right arrow again.

4. **Wait until the import is finished, and then click OK.**

If everything went according to plan, your messages now show up in the main pane of Entourage's window.

Outlook and Exchange

If you run Microsoft Outlook on your office PC, you may be able to transfer the contents of your entire mailbox to your Mac *without* going through any of the import-export pyrotechnics described in this chapter.

On most office networks, Outlook accesses mail through a *Microsoft Exchange Server*—a central computer that stores all the email moving through the network. When you use Outlook in conjunction with Exchange, your mail, appointments, and contacts actually reside on the Exchange server itself—not on your PC's hard drive.

The same thing's possible in Entourage and Apple's own Mail program; see page 200.

Transferring Your Outlook Addresses

The contents of your Contacts list may represent years of typing and compiling. The last thing you want to do is leave that valuable info behind or—heaven forbid—manually retype each entry as you set up your Mac email program.

Here are the steps for bringing all those names, phone numbers, email addresses, notes, and other details from Outlook into your favorite Mac contact manager.

O2M Method (Easy, $10)

If you took the wise step of buying the O2M program, you're already done; this ingenious utility brings over both your email *and* your Outlook addresses to your choice of Mac programs.

Thunderbird Method (Time-Consuming, Free)

Once again, Thunderbird for Windows comes to the rescue. Its address book module can extract contact info directly from the most popular PC email programs—not just Outlook, but also Outlook Express and Eudora. Better yet, it converts that data into a format that Apple's Address Book understands perfectly.

Note: These steps guide your little-black-book data into Mac OS X's built-in Address Book program. If your aim is to transfer it into Entourage on the Mac instead, see page 182m.

When you've got Thunderbird installed, you're ready to transfer your contacts, like this:

1. **Import your Outlook contacts into Thunderbird.**

   Follow the "Phase 1" steps described on page 188—but in Step 3, choose Address Books. Along the way, you'll be asked to choose the name of the email program whose addresses you want to snag (Figure 6-5). You can choose Outlook, Outlook Express, Eudora, or Communicator (an earlier version of the Thunderbird software).

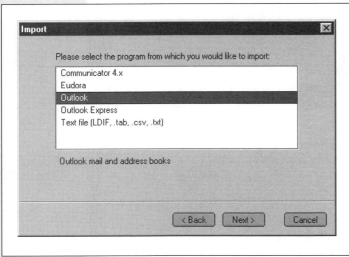

Figure 6-5:
Thunderbird, the Swiss Army software, is happy to open the address book of almost any email program, or even a text file containing addresses (such as tab- or comma-delimited text).

With your contacts safely stored in Thunderbird, you're halfway home. Next, you need to get these contacts out of Thunderbird and onto your Mac. To do this, you must save them into an *LDIF* file. LDIF stands for Lightweight Directory Interchange Format—a text format mostly used by network administrators to synchronize directory information across large networks. It's also a format that Apple's Address Book recognizes.

2. **Click Address Book on the Thunderbird toolbar to view your imported contacts. Choose Tools→Export.**

   The Export dialog box appears.

3. **From the "Save as type" drop-down menu, choose LDIF. Type a name for the file, select a destination, and click Save.**

   Thunderbird writes all your contact data into a single self-contained file with an *.ldif* extension added to the end of its name.

4. **Copy the LDIF file to your Mac.**

   You can use any of the techniques described in Chapter 5.

5. **On the Mac, open Address Book (it's in the Applications folder, and its icon is probably on the Dock). Choose File→Import→LDIF.**

   The Open dialog box appears.

6. **Locate and open the .ldif file you brought over from Windows.**

   Moments later, all the contacts you brought over from your Windows machine are converted into Address Book entries (see Figure 6-6).

Figure 6-6:
Apple's Address Book program can slurp up your Windows contacts in one gulp by importing an LDIF file, which you can easily generate using Thunderbird on Windows.

CSV Method (Free, to Entourage Only)

If your email program of choice on the Mac is Microsoft Entourage (or its successor, Outlook for Mac), and you can't find the $10 you need to buy O2M, the Thunderbird method described above isn't enough. Entourage *can't* import LDIF files.

The best way to transfer contacts into Entourage, then, is to import them in *CSV* format. CSV is short for Comma-Separated Values, and it's a format that many contact programs can import and export these days. (In fact, *Address Book* can attempt to import CSV files, but it's picky to a fault about formatting—which is why the Thunderbird method described above is a lot more reliable if you use Address Book.)

Here's the procedure:

1. **On your PC, export your contacts in CSV format.**

   If you use Outlook Express, for example, choose File→Export Address Book and then select "Text File (Comma Separated Values)." Save the file. (Same goes if you use Outlook.)

   If you use Eudora on Windows, you're in for a bit more fun. Since Eudora can't directly export CSV files, you have to move your contacts into Thunderbird *first*, as described above. When you get to step 3 above, however, choose "Comma Separated" for the type of file you'd like to export, rather than LDIF. You now have a CSV file on your PC with your contacts inside, so read on.

2. **Move the CSV file to your Mac.**

   The file should end in .csv if you did everything right.

3. **Open Entourage and choose File→Import. Click "Import information from a text file."**

   Click the right arrow.

4. **Make sure "Import contacts from a tab- or comma-delimited text file" is selected.**

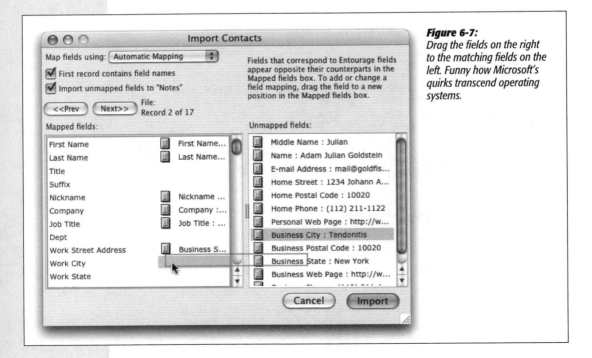

Figure 6-7:
Drag the fields on the right to the matching fields on the left. Funny how Microsoft's quirks transcend operating systems.

Again, click the right arrow.

5. **Select the CSV file you copied to your Mac in step 2.**

   Press Return to dismiss the dialog box.

6. **"Map" any information that's confusing Entourage (Figure 6-7).**

   Even though Entourage and Outlook are both made by Microsoft, there's still room for Entourage to get confused by your contacts—and mapping is how you fix it.

   For instance, if you exported your contacts from Outlook Express, one field on the right might be called "E-mail Address" which confuses Entourage because it's not called "Email Address 1." To eliminate the confusion, drag the gray handle from the E-mail Address line on the right so it's next to the Email Address 1 line on the left. You've just told Entourage, in essence, "'E-mail' and 'Email' are the same thing, so let me get on with my life."

7. **Click Import.**

   Dismiss the dialog box that appears by clicking Don't Save.

8. **Click Finish.**

   Your contacts are now ready and waiting in Entourage.

Transferring from Outlook Express (Windows Mail)

If you've been using Outlook Express (Microsoft's free email program) on the Windows PC, you'll have very little trouble moving into any of the Mac's email programs.

Tip: You can't use that $10 O2M program for this transfer; it works only with Outlook, not Outlook Express. However, Outlook can import mail and addresses from Outlook Express—and O2M can take it from there. So if you have a copy of Outlook somewhere, O2M could still save the day.

Moving Your Address Book

You can use free Windows software as a go-between—but which Mac address book you've adopted will determine which program to use.

- To import your Outlook Express addresses into Apple's *Address Book,* follow the instructions in "Thunderbird Method (Time-Consuming, Free)" on page 194.

- To import them into *Microsoft Entourage* instead, see "CSV Method (Free, to Entourage Only)" on page 195.

Moving Your Mail

Outlook Express is also a pleasant partner when it comes to moving the messages themselves over to the Mac. Here again, you use Thunderbird as a sort of translator. Follow the steps listed under "Thunderbird Method (Time-Consuming, Free)," beginning on page 194.

Email Settings

Chapter 10 guides you through the painless process of plugging your Internet settings—whether by dial-up connection, cable modem, DSL, or network connection—from the PC to your Mac.

But even after you've done that, you can't start sending and receiving email on your Mac until you've transferred some vital email account *settings* from your PC.

Fortunately, there's only a handful of settings you need to grab—and hunting these down and moving them to your Mac is pretty quick work. Here's all the information you need to gather in order to get yourself set up:

- **Account name (or user name).** This is the name you use when you log into your email account, such as *Joe63* or *kjackson*.

- **Password.** This is the password that you have to enter along with your account name to get into your email account. Passwords can't be copied and pasted or directly exported, so you'll need to remember this password and type it in when configuring your Mac email software.

- **Account type.** There are two main kinds of email server protocols—*POP* (which stands for post-office protocol—by far most common) and IMAP (Internet Message Access Protocol). You'll need to know which type you've been using on your PC, so that you can set up accounts on your Mac the same way.

Note: *Exchange* servers are another choice popular in big organizations. If your email is stored on an Exchange server, see page 200.

- **Incoming and outgoing mail servers** are the names of the computers that route email to and from you, such as *mail.earthlink.net* or *mailserve.photorabbit.com*. (The incoming and outgoing servers sometimes have the same address, but they *can* be two different servers with different names.)

Finding the Settings on Windows

Each of the popular Windows email programs stores these nuggets of email account info differently. Here's how to find the items you need:

Outlook

If you're connected to a Microsoft Exchange Server computer—and you probably are if you're running Outlook in a corporate workplace—your user name and password are exactly the same as the ones you use to log into the network when you start up your computer. You'll have to check with your network administrator to get the name of the mail servers being used on the network.

If you're running Outlook in any other situation—at home, for example—choose Tools→E-mail Accounts. Click "View or change existing e-mail accounts," click Next, click your account's name on the E-mail Accounts page, and then click Change. You'll find your name, email address, incoming and outgoing servers, and other key settings staring you in the face. (Click Cancel after you've finished copying it down.)

Outlook Express/Windows Mail

Choose Tools→Accounts→Mail to open the dialog box containing the list of your current email accounts. Select the name of the account you want, then click the Properties button. In the Properties dialog box, click the Servers tab to reveal the Server Information pane, where you'll find all the info you need, as shown in Figure 6-8.

Figure 6-8:
Here's where Outlook Express for Windows keeps all the settings you need to harvest in order to configure your Mac email. Note that you can't copy the contents of the password field—that's prohibited for security reasons. You'll have to type your password in again when moving to your new machine.

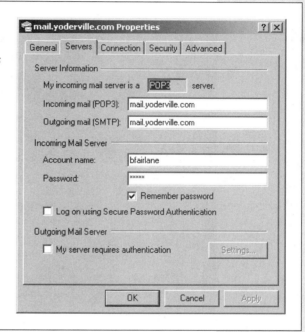

Thunderbird

Choose Tools→Account Settings. Each email account you use is listed in the field on the left side of the window. Click one to display its information on the right.

Configuring the Settings on Your Mac

Once you've found and copied the email settings on your PC, you can plug them into the appropriate places in your Mac email programs:

Apple Mail

Once you've opened Mail (in the Applications folder), choose File→Add Account. Proceed through the various screens, inputting the information from your old PC.

Microsoft Entourage

Choose Tools→Accounts. Click the New button in the Accounts window to start the Account Setup Assistant. Follow the screen-by-screen directions to fill in the user name, password, and server information, as shown in Figure 6-9.

Note: The methods described in this chapter are the least technical ways to get mail, contacts, and settings from the various Windows email apps onto the Mac. But a quick Google search will reveal more technical ones that you may prefer. For example, if you can convert your email account to an IMAP account, no biggie: Your Mac email program reflects your email stash automatically.

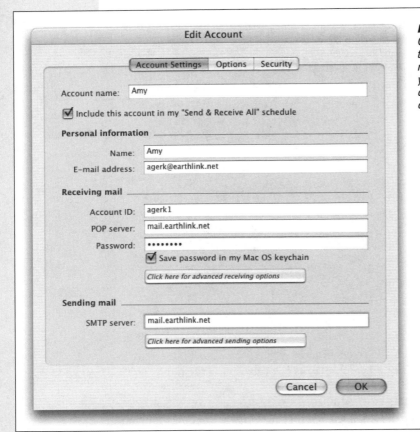

Figure 6-9:
Once you've stepped through the five screens of the Entourage Account Setup Wizard, you end up here, with your account settings all in place and ready to connect up.

Life with Microsoft Exchange

In the corporate world, Microsoft Exchange is the 800-pound gorilla. It's the networking software that runs the email, address book, and calendars for hundreds or thousands of employees. All of this communicates with a central master database whose heart beats away in some closet or back room at your company's headquarters.

For years, Macs have been second-class citizens in Corporate America. As long as they couldn't talk to the Exchange brain, they weren't much use outside of the graphic-design department. (You could buy add-on software or muck about with workarounds, but you always felt like a weirdo.)

In Snow Leopard, for the first time, Exchange compatibility is built in. In iCal, your company's Exchange calendar shows up. In Address Book, your company's names and addresses show up. In Mail, you can get all your corporate email. Best of all, this information shows up side by side with your own personal data, so you can have it all in one place. All the conveniences of Snow Leopard now apply to your corporate email: Spotlight, Quick Look, data detectors, and so on.

The irony is that Mac OS X now comes with built-in Exchange compatibility—and Microsoft Windows *doesn't*. (You have to buy Microsoft Outlook separately.)

If you're lucky—that is, if your company is using Exchange 2007 or later—setting this up could not be easier.

Connecting to Exchange

To connect to your company's Exchange system, open Mail (Chapter 11). Choose Mail→Preferences. Click the **+** below the list of email accounts; proceed as shown in Figure 6-10.

When you click Continue, one of two things happen:

GEM IN THE ROUGH

Delegating Your Calendars

Once you're all Exchanged up, you can even *delegate* your calendar–that is, permit someone else on your corporate network to see (and, if you wish, edit) it from across the network. That's handy when you're a busy executive and you want your personal assistant to help you manage your busy life, or when you're going to be out of town and you've authorized a trusted minion to carry on with your calendar in your absence.

(This is not the same as *publishing* your calendar as de-scribed in Chapter 10. Your Exchange calendar isn't actually going to move. It'll sit right there on the server–you're just giving someone else access to it.)

To set this up, choose iCal→Preferences→Accounts. (If you have more than one account, choose the one you want to share from the Accounts list.)

Click Delegation. Click Edit. On the Manage Account Access screen, click **+**, and then type the name of the person you

want to share your calendar with. You can also specify how much access you want that person to have; "Read Only" means they can just see your life, and "Read & Write" means they can actually edit it. You can grant different levels of access to your calendar and your Tasks list.

Finally, click Done.

Now change hats. Suppose you're the minion–er, trusted assistant.

On your Mac, choose iCal→Preferences→Accounts. Click the account that's been shared with you. Click **+**; type your boss's name.

Finally, turn on the Show checkbox. Close the Preferences dialog box to return to the main iCal display. Here, your boss's calendars (appointment categories) show up in the left-side list; turn on the checkboxes of the ones you want to appear on the calendar grid.

• A message says, "Mail found a server account for the email address you provided. The following account will be set up on your computer." You're all set.

That box offers an "Also set up" item featuring two delicious checkboxes: "Address Book contacts" and "iCal calendars." Hard to think why you'd want to turn these off; they'll do all the work for you.

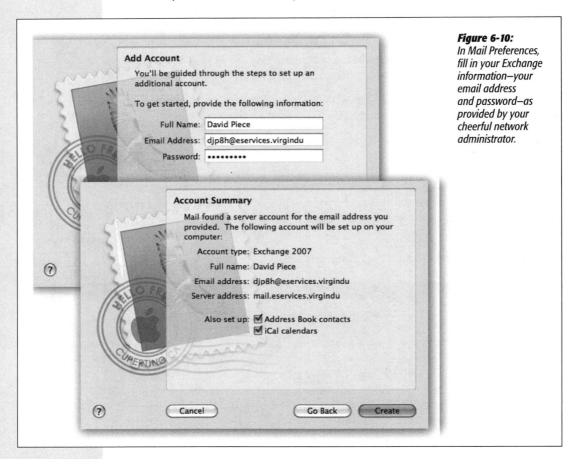

Figure 6-10:
In Mail Preferences, fill in your Exchange information—your email address and password—as provided by your cheerful network administrator.

• Your Mac doesn't find the server. In that case, either (a) your company doesn't use Exchange 2007 or later or (b) your network geek hasn't turned on Exchange *Autodiscovery.* In that case, you have no choice but to call that person over to your desk and either (a) harangue him for not turning on Autodiscovery or (b) have him fill in the server address and other boxes by hand.

Note: Here's a tip for the network administrator who gets to fill in this information, courtesy of Apple: "Enter the fully qualified domain name for the organization's Exchange Client Access Server (CAS). (For example, exchange01.example.com, not exchange01.) Note that the CAS doesn't necessarily share the same address as the Outlook Web Access (OWA) Server—although they often do. Http prefixes are not required." Hope you know what that means.

Exchange in Mail

Once everything's set up, open Mail. If you have a lot of mail, it may take a moment (or several) for Mail to synchronize with the Exchange server and display your messages. But it gets there eventually.

Your Exchange account appears with its own heading, beneath your personal accounts (Figure 6-11).

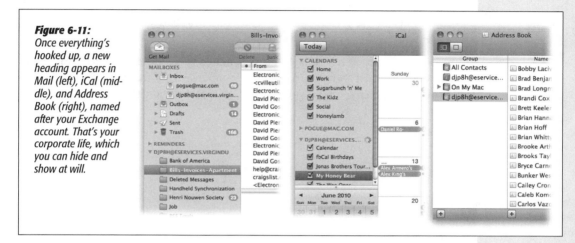

Figure 6-11:
Once everything's hooked up, a new heading appears in Mail (left), iCal (middle), and Address Book (right), named after your Exchange account. That's your corporate life, which you can hide and show at will.

Now you can send and receive email, create notes and to-do items, respond to emailed invitations, and so on. All the Mail features described in Chapter 11 are ready to go: Spotlight can search all your accounts simultaneously, Smart Folders can round up messages from one account or all of them, Quick Look can show you attachments without your having to open them in a separate program, and so on.

Exchange in Address Book

Your company's Global Address Lists show up in Address Book (Chapter 11) in a "folder" on the left side called Exchange, as shown in Figure 6-11. You can work with

---

GEM IN THE ROUGH

Connecting to Exchange from Entourage

To set up your Mac's copy of Microsoft Entourage so that it checks your Exchange email, proceed like this:

1. Open Entourage and choose Tools→Accounts. This is the setup window for all your email accounts.

2. Click the arrow next to New and choose Mail from the pop-up menu. That's how you tell Entourage, "I want to input the settings for an email account."

3. Turn on the "My account is on an Exchange server" checkbox.

4. Call your network administrator over and ask how to fill in all the required fields.

When you're done inputting everything and Entourage is satisfied, you should see a list of all your network-based email—the same messages you saw in Outlook.

---

them just as you would your own addresses: Put them in groups, click an address to see where it is in Google Maps, and so on. When you're addressing an email message or a calendar invitation, the autocomplete feature now proposes names from both your personal and corporate address books.

Exchange in iCal

Your corporate appointments now show up in the Mac's calendar program (Chapter 10), neatly filed under their own heading. Each appointment category shows up with its own checkbox, as usual, so you can hide and show them as you see fit—even when they're mixed right in with your personal agenda.

The big payoff here is scheduling meetings. When you click "add invitees" for an appointment, iCal can show you a graph of your coworkers' free time, and open slots for your conference room, so you can find a time when they're free.

Special Software, Special Problems

Be glad you waited so long to get a Mac. By now, all the big-name programs look and work almost exactly the same on the Mac as they do on the PC. Once you've mastered the basic differences between the Mac and Windows (keyboard shortcuts, the menu bar, and so on), you'll find that programs from Microsoft, Adobe, and other major software companies feel distinctly familiar in their Mac incarnations. In fact, the documents that they create are in the same format and generally need no conversion.

But one fact is unassailable: There are more software programs available for Windows than for the Mac. Sooner or later, you'll probably run into a familiar Windows program for which there's no equivalent on the Mac.

One solution is simply to run those Windows programs *on* the Mac, as described in Chapter 8. For thousands of people, that's the screamingly obvious, and extremely convenient, approach. Each time you read, "There's no Mac equivalent of this program" in this chapter, add, in your head, "but you can always run the Windows version."

Still, in other cases, you may not want to fool around with Windows anymore. You may prefer to identify Mac replacements for your favorite Windows programs. That's the purpose of this chapter: to guide you in finding Mac equivalents for the most popular Windows programs (listed here alphabetically), and to guide you in bringing over your data and settings from Windows to the Mac whenever possible.

ACDSee

As digital photography becomes more popular, so do programs like ACDSee, a popular Windows program that serves as a digital shoebox and basic retouching program for

---

digital photos. Your Mac, of course, stands ready to run a far more elegant equivalent: iPhoto. It's one of the world's most pleasant photo-organizing programs—and it's free.

In its most recent incarnation, iPhoto has a pretty complete set of image-retouching features. Still, if you need more editing power, consider Photoshop Elements, a program that's available for both Mac and Windows and has won rave reviews on both platforms.

In any case, ACDSee doesn't have any documents of its own—it does all its work on your existing digital photos, wherever you keep them on your hard drive. All you have to do, then, is move the photos themselves to the Mac, using any of the techniques described in Chapter 5. From there, drag them into the iPhoto window to import them.

Acrobat Reader

Acrobat Reader, which lets you read Acrobat (PDF) files, works precisely the same on the Mac as it does in Windows. If you like, you can download Acrobat Reader from *www.adobe.com*.

There are fewer and fewer reasons to use Acrobat Reader, though; you have a much nicer PDF-reading program right there in your Applications folder, called Preview.

Preview can read PDFs like the best of them—but it's also got Acrobat Reader covered on several other counts. Preview can annotate PDFs with virtual yellow sticky-notes— a great tool for marking up book layouts before they go to press, for example. Also, Preview's search feature is so fast and convenient, it blows Acrobat Reader out of the water. And finally, Preview opens in a matter of seconds, while Acrobat Reader can take a minute or so to launch. (For more on Preview, see page 534.)

ACT

No Mac version of this address book/calendar program is available, but don't let that stop you. Export and Import commands are the bread and butter of address and calendar programs. Your ACT life can find a happy home in any of several Mac address books:

- Mac OS X's free, built-in Address Book.

Tip: Address Book syncs with Google Calendar on the Web, which opens up a fascinating possibility: All of your computers (Macs, Windows, iPhone) can maintain synchronized calendars, with Google Calendar serving as the mother ship.

- Microsoft Entourage or Outlook for Mac (part of Microsoft Office for Mac).

- BusyCal *(www.busycal.com)*, which is networkable. That is, if you have more than one computer in the house, you can check your Rolodex from any machine on the network.

In any case, here are the instructions for transferring your addresses from ACT (version 5 or later) to the Mac:

1. **In ACT for Windows, start by choosing File→Data Exchange→Export.**

   The Export Wizard dialog box appears.

2. **From the "File type" drop-down list, choose Text-Delimited. Specify a folder location and name for your exported file (call it Exported Contacts, for example). Click Next, and click Next on the next screen, too.**

   Now you're asked "Which contact or group records do you want to export?"

3. **Click "All records," and then click Next.**

   Now you see a list of the *fields* (information tidbits like City, State, and Zip) that ACT is prepared to export. You can save yourself time later if you take a moment now to remove the ones you don't need (click its name and then click Remove Field).

4. **Click Finish.**

   If you plan to import your addresses into a commercial program like BusyCal, transfer the Exported Contacts file to the Mac (see Chapter 5), and then import them into BusyCal.

   If your aim is to import the addresses into Microsoft Entourage on the Mac, or Mac OS X's own Address Book program, though, read on.

5. **Open Outlook Express.**

   Yes, Outlook Express for Windows, the free program that comes on every PC. (The Windows Vista/Windows 7 version is called Windows Mail.) You'll use it as a glorified converter program.

6. **Follow the instructions on page 194 for exporting the contacts into a format suitable for your Mac.**

   That page outlines two ways (one free, one fast) to get your contacts from Outlook Express into Mac OS X's Address Book—your ACT info's final resting place.

Ad Subtract (Pop-up Stopper)

Nothing quite spoils the fun of the Web like pop-ups—those annoying miniature advertising windows that sprout in front of the Web page you're trying to read.

Safari, Mac OS X's Web browser, has a simple menu command for blocking pop-ups: Safari→Block Pop-Up Windows. Nowadays, so does just about every other Web browser made for the Mac—Firefox, Netscape, Camino, and so on. In other words, you don't even *need* Ad Subtract.

If you're interested in some of Ad Subtract's other features, like blocking animated ads or zapping all ads on Web pages, consider SafariBlock (for Safari) or Adblock (for Firefox). Or, for Safari, the awesome Click2Flash, which simply neutralizes all of those annoying *blinking* ads. All three are free and available for download from this book's "Missing CD" at *www.missingmanuals.com.*

Adobe [your favorite program here]

Most of Adobe's bestsellers are available in Mac OS X versions, including Photoshop, Photoshop Elements, After Effects, Illustrator, InDesign, GoLive, Acrobat, Acrobat Reader, Premiere, and so on.

You almost never have to do any document conversion. A Windows Photoshop document is exactly the same thing as a Macintosh Photoshop document, for example.

America Online

Truth is, you don't actually need an AOL *program* on your Mac. You can access all of your AOL mail, as well as all of AOL's features, on the Web at *www.aol.com.*

Still, there is a double-clickable Mac program called AOL Desktop. You can download it from *http://downloads.channel.aol.com/macproducts.*

If you do decide to use it, you'll discover a great feature: AOL stores your mail, address book, buddy list, and favorites *online.* You can check your email one day at the office on a PC and the following night at home on the Mac, and you'll always see the same messages there. It makes no difference if you connect to the service using a Windows PC, a Macintosh, or a kerosene-powered abacus.

Tip: Your Favorites (bookmarks) are stored online only if you use AOL for Windows version 8 and later. If you've been using an earlier version on your PC, your Favorites won't be waiting for you when you switch to the Mac.

If your PC meets the system requirements, you'd be wise to upgrade its copy of America Online to version 8 or later before switching to the Macintosh. (This is a free upgrade; you can download the software at *www. aol.com/downloads*.) If you do so, you'll find the Favorites waiting for you in AOL for Mac OS X.

This is all really good news, of course, but you may have one headache in performing the switch: your Personal Filing Cabinet. If you've been saving email messages into this virtual filing drawer, the news isn't quite as good: These messages are saved on the PC, not online. So when you switch to the Macintosh, your Personal Filing Cabinet will be empty.

Here are your options at this point:

- Be content with only the last 30 days' worth of old mail, and the last week's worth of new mail. This is what lives on the America Online computers, no matter what computer you use to access it. When you move to the Mac, that much email will immediately appear the first time you use AOL.

- Fire up your old PC and open each message in your Personal Filing Cabinet. Click the Forward button, and type in your own AOL address. You're basically emailing each message to yourself.

  Once the messages have arrived on the Mac, you can save them into *its* Personal Filing Cabinet. Of course, you were the sender, so you can no longer click Reply to send a response to whoever originally wrote you. (If that's ever necessary, you can always copy and paste the sender's address into your reply.)

Once all your information is in AOL for Mac OS X, you can, if you want, move the information into Apple's *own* Internet programs: iChat, Address Book, Mail, and Safari. Just download AOL Service Assistant from *http://downloads.channel.aol.com/macproducts,* and click through the various steps.

By the final screen, all your bookmarks, contacts, screen names, and email settings will be waiting for you in Apple's programs, which are a lot more powerful (not to mention attractive) than the AOL software itself.

AIM (AOL Instant Messenger)

If you're an online chat junkie, switching to the Mac involves very little disruption to your routine. AIM is available for the Mac, too, and it awaits your download at *www.aim.com.* Better yet, the minute you fire it up, you'll discover that your entire Windows-version buddy list is intact and ready to use. (That's because it actually lives on the America Online network, not on your Windows PC.)

Tip: Actually, you might have a lot more fun—and save a lot of effort—by just using iChat. It's a free Mac OS X chat program that's compatible with the whole AIM network, as described on page 381.

Children's Software

Thanks to the vast number of Macs in schools, a huge percentage of educational software programs are available in both Mac and Windows versions—often on the same CD. That includes most programs from The Learning Company (including the Arthur, Carmen Sandiego, Little Bear, and Reader Rabbit series), Broderbund (Kid Pix, Mavis Beacon, Print Shop, and so on), Humongous Entertainment (series like Blue's Clues, Dora the Explorer, Putt-Putt, Backyard Sports), and other major educational publishers.

Easy CD Creator

You don't need any add-on software at all to burn CDs in Mac OS X. You can just drag files and folders onto the icon of a blank CD, as described on page 259.

If you want fancier features—recording less common disc formats, for example—what you need is Toast for the Macintosh. It comes from the same company that makes Easy CD Creator.

Its main rival is DiScribe *(www.charismac.com)*. Both programs can create audio CDs, video CDs, data DVDs, and so on. Both come with a program that helps you turn old vinyl records and tapes into digital CDs, too.

The only disappointment: Neither program can treat a CD as a glorified floppy disk, as Easy CD Creator for Windows can, so that you can add and delete files freely (rather than burning the CD all at once).

There's a workaround, though: Copy the contents of a rewriteable CD (a CD-RW disc) to a folder on your desktop; make whatever changes you like to the contents of this folder; and then burn the CD-RW again. (Use the Disk Utility program in your Applications→Utilities folder to erase the disc first.)

Tip: Ordinarily, the CD-burning feature of Mac OS X burns the entire CD each time, even if you've only filled a small portion of it. But if you download the handy $17 shareware program called CD Session Burner, you can perform additional "mini-burns" of new data to the CD until all the space is used up. Each such *session* shows up on your desktop with its own icon, as though it's a separate disc. You can download this program from *http://www.sentman.com/CD_Session_Burner.html.*

Encarta

Microsoft's best-selling encyclopedia program isn't available for the Macintosh. The World Book Encyclopedia is, however. (Details at *www.worldbook.com.*)

Of course, you can also use the Web-based versions of either encyclopedia (or Wikipedia, of course).

Eudora

You want Eudora? You got Eudora! It's available on the Mac, as it is in Windows. Download it from *www.eudora.com.*

Excel

See "Microsoft Office" in this chapter.

Firefox

On Windows, Firefox is a faster, more secure, better-featured Web-browsing alternative to Internet Explorer. If you'd like, you can download the identical Mac version from *www.getfirefox.com,* and then follow the instructions on page 182 for transferring your bookmarks.

Alternatively, you can switch to Mac OS X's built-in, super-fast Safari browser. Chapter 12 houses the coverage of the Safari adventure.

Games

Nobody switches to the Mac to play games; of the top 250 computer games for Windows, only about 150 are available for the Macintosh.

Still, that number includes the majority of the big-name titles and series, including *Guitar Hero, Spore, Civilization, Madden NFL, Tiger Woods PGA*, the various Sims games, *Civilization, Quake, Harry Potter, Spider-Man, Tomb Raider, Warcraft, Jedi Knight, Soldier of Fortune, Max Payne, Links Championship Edition, Age of Empires, Medal of Honor, Return to Castle Wolfenstein*, and hordes of others.

And once you do get these programs going on the Mac, you're likely to be impressed. Recent Macs generally come equipped with pleasantly high-horsepower graphics cards—the kind that serious computer games crave.

If you're a game nut, you can stay in touch with what's new and upcoming by reading the articles (and watching the game "trailers") at *www.apple.com/games*, not to mention *www.insidemacgames.com, macgamer.com*, and *macgamefiles.com*.

Google Desktop Search

Mac OS X's Spotlight feature does everything that Google Desktop does—searching inside files, finding favorite Web sites, and so on. Spotlight just does it better.

ICQ

If you're a fan of this Internet-wide chat program, look no further than ICQ for Mac or one of its many shareware rivals. To grab them, visit *www.versiontracker.com* and perform a search, on the Mac OS X tab, for *ICQ*.

Internet Explorer

Microsoft once wrote an Internet Explorer version for the Mac, but abandoned it years ago. Safari (Apple's built-in Web browser) blocks pop-up windows, loads pages more quickly, and doubles as an RSS reader for news sites. Coverage starts on page 359.

If some Web site (like a banking site) refuses to work with Safari, download Firefox for the Mac instead (*www.getfirefox.com*); it works with almost everything.

iTunes

If you grew used to iTunes on Windows, you'll be glad to know that the Mac version is already sitting in your Applications folder. It works identically to the PC version.

Just move your iTunes Library folder from the Music folder of your old PC into the Music folder on your Mac. That's all there is to it!

Limewire

Limewire, of course, is the "new Napster." People use it to swap music and video files online, hard drive to hard drive—illegally, in many cases. You know who you are.

It runs on something called the Gnutella network—and there's a nice Mac version of the downloading program. You can get it at *www.limewire.com*.

McAfee VirusScan

There's a Mac version of VirusScan, all right—but don't buy it. You don't even need a virus program for Mac OS X. (If you run Windows on your Mac, as described in the next chapter, then install your copy of VirusScan onto that side of the computer, by all means.)

Microsoft Access

Microsoft has never been much interested in creating a Macintosh equivalent of its flagship database program (which comes with the higher-priced versions of Microsoft Office for Windows). FileMaker, a much easier-to-use database program, towers over the Macintosh database market like the Jolly Green Giant (and has a decent following on the Windows side, too). Resistance, Microsoft apparently assumes, is futile.

Tip: FileMaker's little brother, Bento (for the Mac), is even easier to use still.

It's easy enough to get your data out of Microsoft Access; just choose File→Export. In the resulting dialog box, you can choose from a number of common export formats that can serve as intermediaries between the Windows and Mac worlds (see Figure 7-1).

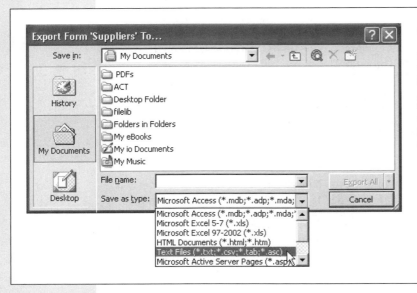

Figure 7-1:
When you export your data from Access, you can choose from any of several formats. The idea is that you'll transfer the resulting exported file onto your Mac, and then import it into a proper database program there.

Among them is Microsoft Excel—that is, you can turn your database into a spreadsheet. The beauty here is that FileMaker on the Macintosh can turn Excel documents into FileMaker databases without even batting an eye. You just drag the exported Excel document onto the FileMaker icon, and FileMaker does the rest.

Unfortunately, there's more to an Access database than just its data. Your database may well have fancy forms (layouts), complete with letterhead and other graphic elements, not to mention relational links between database files. In these situations, the situation isn't quite so hopeful—there's no way to export layouts and relational links to the Macintosh.

In this situation, your best bet might be to run Microsoft Access itself on the Macintosh, as described in Chapter 8.

Microsoft Money

Microsoft has abandoned its Money personal-finance program, so you would have had to export your Money data to Quicken whether you switched to the Mac or not.

It's easy enough to export your Money data into Quicken for the Mac, although not every scrap of information comes through alive. You'll lose your Money abbreviations, comments, and Lifetime Planner information. Fortunately, the important stuff—your accounts and the transactions in them, including categories, classes, and stocks that you've set up—come through in one piece.

Unfortunately, you have to export one account at a time. Furthermore, you'll be creating something called a QIF (Quicken Interchange Format) file as an intermediary between Windows and the Mac—and this file format can't handle category names longer than 15 characters. Before you begin, then, you might want to take a moment either to shorten them or to make a note of which ones might get truncated in the transfer.

Ready? Fire up Money on your Windows PC and then proceed like this:

1. **Choose File→Export.**

   The Export dialog box appears. It wants to know if you are exporting your information to another version of Money ("Loose QIF") or to some other, rival financial program that shall, as far as Microsoft is concerned, remain nameless.

2. **In the resulting dialog box (Figure 7-2), choose Strict QIF, and then click OK.**

   Now you're supposed to name and save the exported file. Make sure you give each account a descriptive name (like Citibank Savings).

3. **Specify a name and folder on your PC for the exported file, and then click OK.**

   Repeat these three steps for each of your Money accounts.

4. **Specify the kind of account (usually you'll want Regular, not Investment), and which one of your accounts to export.**

Click OK when the exporting is done.

5. **Transfer the exported files to the Mac.**

You can do it via network, email, or any of the other techniques described in Chapter 5. Then move to the Macintosh, open Quicken, and create a new file (see the Quicken instructions). Then, once you've got an empty "check register" before you, continue like this:

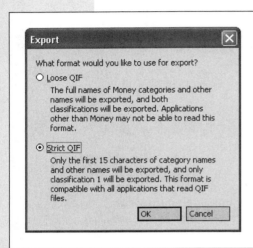

Figure 7-2:
Use the Strict QIF option. It lops off category names longer than 15 characters.

6. Choose File→Import QIF. In the "Select a QIF file" dialog box, navigate to, and open, the first exported account file.

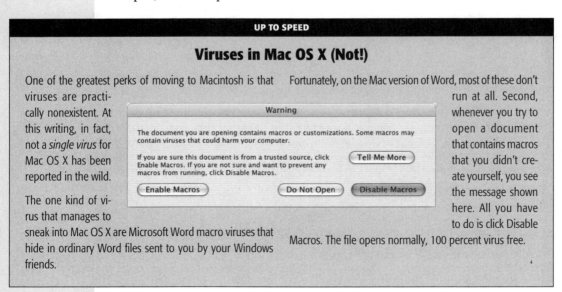

Viruses in Mac OS X (Not!)

One of the greatest perks of moving to Macintosh is that viruses are practically nonexistent. At this writing, in fact, not a *single virus* for Mac OS X has been reported in the wild.

The one kind of virus that manages to sneak into Mac OS X are Microsoft Word macro viruses that hide in ordinary Word files sent to you by your Windows friends.

Fortunately, on the Mac version of Word, most of these don't run at all. Second, whenever you try to open a document that contains macros that you didn't create yourself, you see the message shown here. All you have to do is click Disable Macros. The file opens normally, 100 percent virus free.

If all goes well, you should see a progress bar appear and then disappear. When the dust settles, you'll see your Money transactions safely ensconced in Quicken. (If you see a message that some transactions couldn't be completed, don't worry; it's usually just telling you that some of your category names were longer than 15 characters and have been marked with asterisks to make them easier for you to find and correct.)

If you have more than one account, choose File→New Account to set it up, and then repeat from step 4 to bring in your other Money accounts.

Microsoft Office

Microsoft Office is available for the Mac in what some critics have declared to be a more attractive, less frustrating version than the Windows incarnation. At this writing, the current version is called Office 2008 for Macintosh.

As noted elsewhere in this book, the beauty of Microsoft Word, Excel, and PowerPoint documents is that their format is the same on Mac and Windows. You can freely exchange files without having to go through any kind of conversion. (The big exception, as noted earlier, is Access; Microsoft doesn't make a database program for the Mac.)

In heavily formatted documents, you may occasionally see some strange differences: Windows documents containing many numbered paragraphs sometimes become confused on the Mac, for example. And if the Mac and the originating PC don't have the same fonts installed, you'll see different fonts, too. Otherwise, documents look identical despite having been shuttled to a different kind of computer.

Tip: With Office 2007 for Windows, Microsoft introduced a set of new file formats (.docx for Word, .pptx for PowerPoint, and so on) that's more compact than the previous set (.doc, .ppt, and so on). When you save a document, you can choose which format you want to use: the old one, which 400 million other people can open on their Macs and PCs, or the new one, which nobody but recent upgraders can open.

Exactly the same conundrum presents itself on the Mac. Office 2008 can open and create those same new-fangled files, but the previous versions (like Office 2004 for the Mac) can open only the older formats.

Microsoft Publisher

Microsoft Publisher is a comprehensive page-layout program, complete with canned designs, clip art, and so on.

There's no Mac version of it, but you can perform most of the same tasks using Pages. (Pages is part of Apple's $80 iWork software suite; you can download a 30-day trial from *www.apple.com/iwork*.) Like Publisher, Pages offers dozens of attractive, ready-to-use page-design templates that you can adapt as you see fit.

There are also plenty of standalone page-design programs—this is the Mac, after all—including professional powerhouses like Adobe InDesign and QuarkXPress.

Microsoft Visio

If flowcharts, org charts, network diagrams, family trees, project processes, office layouts and similar diagrams are part of your own personal workflow, you're in luck—at least some luck. Microsoft Visio isn't available in a Macintosh version, but you'll probably find that OmniGraffle for Mac OS X is a satisfactory, even delightful, replacement (see Figure 7-3). The Pro version even lets you import and export Visio documents.

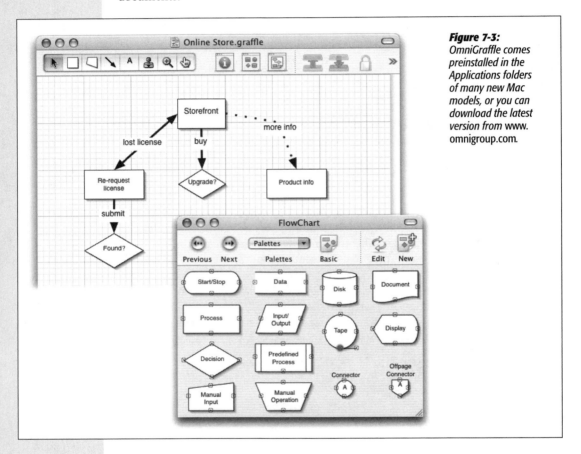

Figure 7-3:
OmniGraffle comes preinstalled in the Applications folders of many new Mac models, or you can download the latest version from www. omnigroup.com.

Minesweeper

Time wasters, rejoice! There are a number of free Minesweeper programs for Mac OS X, including CocoaMines and Aqua Mines. You can download them from a site like *www.versiontracker.com* (search for *minesweeper*).

MSN Messenger

Online chat-aholics have nothing to worry about on the Mac. MSN Messenger, the instant-messaging program, is alive and well in a Mac OS X version that you can download from *www.microsoft.com/mac.* Like AOL Instant Messenger described earlier in this chapter, you don't even have to worry about your carefully assembled buddy list. From the instant you start up MSN Messenger for Mac OS X, you'll see your Buddy list in place (because the list is actually stored on the Internet, not on your computer).

NaturallySpeaking

Speech-recognition programs have traditionally been far more advanced on Windows than on the Macintosh. Windows programs like Dragon NaturallySpeaking transcribe your dictated text with almost Star Trek–like accuracy, and even let you make corrections and manipulate the computer itself using all voice commands.

Fortunately, the Mac program called MacSpeech Dictate uses precisely the same "recognition engine" as NaturallySpeaking (*www.macspeech.com*). If you just can't use the keyboard, or don't want to, you'll be amazed at its speed and accuracy, although it's much younger (and therefore less fully featured) than Naturally Speaking.

Netscape

Netscape, on both Mac and Windows, has grown up into the beloved Web browser called Firefox. It comes in a Mac OS X version—free, of course—from *http://getfirefox. com.*

Newsgroup Readers

If you're a fan of the online bulletin boards known as *newsgroups,* you've come to the right place. The Mac is crawling with newsgroup-reading programs. Microsoft Entourage, for instance, has one built in. In the shareware world (try searching *www. versiontracker.com),* you can take your pick of MT-NewsWatcher X, NewsHunter, and Halime, to name a few.

Norton AntiVirus

You can buy Norton Antivirus for the Macintosh, no problem (*www.symantec.com*). The question is, why? See the box on page 214.

Norton Utilities

On Windows, this program defragments your hard drive, helps recover files in case of disaster, and repairs disk problems. There's no Mac version, but very similar Mac programs are available; for example, Mac veterans swear by DiskWarrior (*www.alsoft.com*).

Notepad

If you're an aficionado of this beloved note-taking tool in the standard Windows Start menu, you're in luck. Mac OS X's Stickies program is even more powerful, because it offers formatting and even graphics. Or, for more of a word-processor effect, check out TextEdit.

Outlook/Outlook Express/Windows Mail

Mac OS X's built-in Mail program is similar to Outlook Express for Windows (or Windows Mail in Vista), just more powerful and a lot better-looking. Chapter 6 describes the process of switching, and Chapter 11 covers the rest of the Mail experience.

If you want all the features from *Outlook,* though, you'd probably be better off using Microsoft Entourage, which is available as part of Microsoft Office for Mac. (In 2010, in fact, Entourage will be upgraded and renamed Outlook for the Mac.)

Paint Shop Pro

If your goal is to retouch and edit digital photos, the closest you can come to Paint Shop on the Mac is probably Photoshop Elements, a terrific Mac OS X program (about $100) that belongs on the hard drive of any serious digital camera owner. (Any digital camera owner who doesn't also own the full-blown Photoshop program, that is.)

If your goal is to organize and *use* your photos, rather than paint on them, remember that iPhoto is already on your hard drive.

Finally, if opening and converting graphics to other formats is your main concern, try Preview (page 534), whose exporting feature is surprisingly powerful. You may also want to investigate the beloved shareware program GraphicConverter (find and download it at *www.versiontracker.com*), which may be the last graphics editing/converting program you'll ever need.

Palm Desktop

If you're still tracking your calendar and address book on an ancient PalmPilot—which you store lovingly next to your gramophone and kerosene lamp—you should have no problem. You can sync your palmtop with the Mac version of Palm Desktop that still lurks at *www.palm.com*. (Getting your data from there to something more modern is another challenge, but not insurmountable. Google can help you.)

If your concern is syncing a smartphone with your Mac (Treo, BlackBerry, whatever), you can buy a utility program called The Missing Sync at *www.markspace.com* that does precisely that.

Picasa

Picasa, one of several Windows photo-organizers, is also available for the Mac. Now, therefore, you have a choice; you can edit, organize, and order prints of your images with either Picasa or iPhoto.

PowerPoint

PowerPoint is available on the Mac; see "Microsoft Office" in this chapter. Remember, too, that Apple's own Keynote presentation program (available as part of iWork for $80) is the same idea as PowerPoint, but with more spectacular graphic effects.

QuickBooks

If you've been happily using QuickBooks for Windows to manage your small business—to prepare estimates and invoices, track bills, maintain lists of inventory and customers, and so on—there's good news and bad news. The good news is that QuickBooks is available on the Mac, and the steps for transferring your company files aren't difficult.

The bad news is that the transfer isn't perfect. Along the way, you might lose your memorized transactions, custom report designs, and reconciliations. Note, too, that you may not be able to send an older Windows file (like QuickBooks 2007) to an older version on the Mac (like QuickBooks 2006).

It's not especially hard; heck, there's a File→Utilities→Copy Company File for Quick-Books Mac command right in QuickBooks for Windows. You can find the rest of the step-by-step instructions in two places:

- Open the electronic Help for QuickBooks for Mac, and search for this topic: "Converting a QuickBooks file from Windows to Mac."

- Follow the do-it-yourself procedure described on Intuit's Support Web page (here's a short link to it: *http://bit.ly/36UiTZ*).

Quicken

If you've been keeping track of your personal finances in Quicken on your PC, you'll feel right at home when you move to the Mac. Quicken 2003 and later versions are available for Mac OS X.

In general, switching over is quick and painless. You can import into the Mac version of Quicken all of the actual transaction information, including accounts, the categories and classes you've used to group them, and stock holdings. Certain kinds of Windows Quicken information—like schedule transactions, QuickFill transactions, online account information, stock histories, and loan information—don't make it, however.

For the official manual on transferring your Quicken data from Windows to the Mac, download this chapter's free PDF Appendix from this book's "Missing CD" at *www.missingmanuals.com*.

If the technology gods are smiling, the Mac version of Quicken should take only a moment to import all of your Windows data, which now appears neatly in your Register windows, ready to use. Make sure the final balances match the final balances in Quicken for Windows. (If they don't, scan your Mac registers for duplicate or missing transactions.)

RealPlayer

Want to listen to Internet music and watch Internet video in Real format, just as you did on your PC? No sweat. Visit *www.real.com* and download RealPlayer for Mac OS X, either in the free basic edition or the fancy paid version.

If you just want to listen to music on your *hard drive*, though, you'd be better off using iTunes (page 263).

RssReader

RSS is a technology for reading quick Web site summaries, and it's taking the Net by storm. RSS returns the Internet to real utility, free from pop-up ads and the other annoyances of Web life.

To take advantage of RSS, however, you need a program to *subscribe* to Web sites that support RSS—and then to display the resulting summaries. On Windows, you might use a program like RssReader, or a Web site like *www.pluck.com*.

On Mac OS X, however, Apple's way ahead of you. Both Safari (Chapter 12), and Mail (Chapter 11) provide fantastic built-in RSS readers; both can subscribe to RSS sites with ease.

Skype

For making Internet-based phone calls, it's hard to beat Skype. If you call from one computer to another, you pay absolutely nothing—no matter how far away your recipient is.

Luckily, you can download a Mac version from *www.skype.com*. From there, you can audio-chat with all your Mac- and PC-using Skype buddies until you lose your voice.

Tip: iChat, Apple's own instant-messaging program, also offers free audio chats. If you and your buddy both have Web cams or video cameras, in fact, you can make free, Internet *video* calls. See Chapter 12 for the details.

SnagIt

If you prepare instructions for using any kind of computer or software—computer books, magazine articles, or how-to materials of any kind—you may already be familiar with this amazing screen-capture program. It captures any window, menu, or area of the Windows screen and saves it as a graphics file that you can print or pop into a layout program.

In Mac OS X, this feature is built right in. Here's how to capture:

- **The whole screen.** Press Shift-⌘-3 to create a picture file on your desktop, in PNG format, that depicts the entire screen image. A satisfying camera-shutter sound tells you that you were successful.

  The file is called *Picture 1*. Each time you press Shift-⌘-3, you get another file, called Picture 2, Picture 3, and so on. You can open these files in Preview, Photoshop, or another graphics program, in readiness for editing or printing.

- **One section of the screen.** You can capture only a rectangular *region* of the screen by pressing Shift-⌘-4. When you drag and release the mouse, you hear the camera-click sound, and the Picture file appears on your desktop as usual.

- **One menu, window, icon (with its name), or dialog box.** Once you've got your menu or window open onscreen, or the icon visible (even if it's on the Dock), press Shift-⌘-4. But instead of dragging diagonally, press the space bar.

  Now your cursor turns into a tiny camera. Move it so that the misty highlighting fills the window or menu you want to capture—and then click. The resulting Picture file snips the window or menu neatly from its background. (Press the space bar a second time to exit "snip one screen element" mode and return to "drag across an area" mode.)

Tip: If you hold down the Control key as you click or drag (using any of the techniques described above), you copy the screenshot to your *Clipboard,* ready for pasting, rather than saving it as a new graphics file on your desktop.

Mac OS X also offers another way to create screenshots: a program called Grab, which offers a timer option that lets you set up the screen before it takes the shot. It's in your Applications→Utilities folder.

But if you're really serious about capturing screenshots, you should opt instead for Snapz Pro X (*www.ambrosiasw.com*), which can capture virtually anything on the screen—even movies of onscreen procedures, along with your narration—and save it in your choice of format.

Solitaire

Ah yes, Solitaire: possibly the most overused Windows software in the world.

The Mac doesn't come with a preinstalled copy of Solitaire, but the Web is crawling with free and shareware solitaire games for the Mac. Luckily, there's a quick way to unearth the most popular 20 or so. On the Web, visit *www.versiontracker.com* (one of the most popular sources for freeware and shareware programs). Click the Mac OS X tab if it's not already selected, and then, in the Search box, type *solitaire.*

When you click Go or press Enter, you'll see a substantial list of solitaire games, ready to download: FreeCell, MacSolitaire, Klondike, and so on.

Street Atlas USA

Mapping software is, alas, a weak spot in the Mac software catalog. Street Atlas USA and Route 66, for example, are no longer available for the Mac.

Until these programs re-emerge in a Mac edition, your best bet is to run the Windows versions in Windows mode on your Mac, as described in Chapter 8.

Tip: If you're looking for driving directions and maps, don't forget about Google Maps (*http://maps.google.com*). It's fast, it's convenient, it works the same on both Mac and Windows, and it's free.

Also, don't forget about the Yellow Pages feature of the Dashboard (page 155). It's ready to print directions and draw maps.

TaxCut, TurboTax

Both TaxCut and TurboTax are available for the Mac. You can even buy state versions of TurboTax for the states that require income tax returns. You can buy them wherever fine Mac programs are sold: *www.macmall.com, www.macwarehouse.com, www.macconnection.com,* and so on.

WinAmp, MusicMatch

When it comes to playing MP3 files, creating MP3 files, burning music CDs, and otherwise organizing your music library, you'd be hard-pressed to beat iTunes, the free Mac OS X program that's already on your Mac (and a free download from *www.apple.com/itunes*).

Windows Media Player

The Macintosh equivalent for Windows Media Player is, of course, QuickTime Player. It handily plays and shows almost any kind of movie, picture, or sound (although you'll want to use iTunes for most music playback).

There are a few entertainment sources that come in the Windows Media format, however, notably Windows Media Video (.wmv) movies that play on Web sites. By itself, QuickTime Player can't play them.

Microsoft actually went to the trouble of creating a Macintosh version of Windows Media Player (never mind the irony of its name). You can download it from *www.microsoft.com/mac,* but it's officially been abandoned.

The more modern, equally free solution is to download and install Flip4Mac. It's technically a plug-in for QuickTime Player, but you don't need to know that. All you need to know is that once you've installed it, you can suddenly play all those Web videos that you couldn't play before. You can download it from this book's "Missing CD" at *www.missingmanuals.com.*

WinZip

In Mac OS X, you create a .zip file by right-clicking any Finder icon and choosing "Compress [the icon's name]" from the shortcut menu. You decompress a .zip file by simply double-clicking its icon in the Finder.

Sometimes, however, you'll encounter compressed files on the Mac that end in *.sit.* You decompress such files with StuffIt Expander, a free download from *www.stuffit.com.*

Word

See "Microsoft Office" in this chapter.

WordPerfect

Unfortunately, WordPerfect lost the battle with Microsoft Word on the Mac side pretty much the same way it did on the Windows side. If you're a die-hard WordPerfect fan, your best bet might be to invest in Microsoft Word and capitalize on its keystroke-customizing features to turn it into a living simulation of WordPerfect.

Or, if you'd rather not spend a significant portion of your life's savings on a word processor, use the free Word-importing and -exporting features of TextEdit (page 550).

Yahoo Messenger

The equivalent chat program on the Mac is, of course, Yahoo Messenger for Mac OS X. It's a free download from *http://messenger.yahoo.com.*

Windows on Macintosh

The very moment Apple announced in 2006 that all new Mac models would come with Intel chips inside, the geeks and the bloggers started going nuts. "Let's see," they thought. "Macs and PCs now use exactly the same memory, hard drives, monitors, mice, keyboards, networking protocols, *and processors.* By our calculations, the Mac should be able to run Windows!"

Now, some in the Cult of Macintosh were revolted by the very idea. Who on earth, they asked, wants to pollute the magnificence of the Mac with a headache like Windows?

Lots of people, as it turns out. Millions of switchers have been tempted by the Mac's sleek looks, yet worried about leaving Windows behind entirely. Then there are the people who love Apple's iLife programs, but have jobs that rely on Microsoft Access, Outlook, or some other piece of Windows corporateware. Even true-blue Mac fans occasionally look longingly at some of the Windows-only games, Web sites, palmtop sync software, or movie download services they thought they'd never be able to use.

Today, there are two ways to run Windows on a Mac with an Intel chip:

• **Restart it in Boot Camp.** Boot Camp lets you *restart* your Mac into Windows. At that point, it's a full-blown Windows PC, with no trace of the Mac on the screen. It runs at 100 percent of the speed of a real PC, because it *is* one. Compatibility with Windows software is excellent. The only drag is that you have to restart the Mac *again* to return to the familiar world of Mac OS X and all your Mac programs and files.

Tip: What's cool, though, is that even when you're running Windows, you can still access your Mac files and folders, as described below.

- **Run Windows in a window.** For $80, you can buy a program like Parallels or VM-Ware Fusion, which lets you run Windows *in a window.*

  You're still running Mac OS X, and all your Mac files and programs are still available. But you've got a parallel universe—Microsoft Windows—running in a window simultaneously.

  Compared with Boot Camp, this *virtualization software* offers only 90 percent of the speed and 90 percent of the software compatibility. But for thousands of people, the convenience of eliminating all those restarts—and gaining the freedom to copy and paste documents between Mac OS X and Windows programs—makes the Windows-in-a-window solution nearly irresistible.

Tip: There's nothing wrong with using *both* on the same Mac, by the way. In fact, the Parallels/VMWare-type programs can use the *same copy of Windows* as Boot Camp, so you save disk space and don't have to manage two different Windows worlds.

Both techniques require you to provide your own copy of Windows. And both are described on the following pages.

Boot Camp

To set up Boot Camp, you need the proper ingredients:

- **An Intel-based Mac.** All Mac models introduced in 2006 and later have Intel chips inside. If you're not sure, choose →About This Mac; if the Processor line says something about Intel, you're good to go.

- **A copy of Windows XP, Windows Vista, or Windows 7.** Windows XP needs Service Pack 2. If you have an earlier copy, you're not *totally* out of luck, but you'll need a hacky approach that you can find online. Let Google be your friend.

  For Windows Vista or Windows 7, you need the Home Basic, Home Premium, Business, or Ultimate Edition. In both cases, an upgrade disc won't work; you need a full-installation copy. Also, Boot Camp requires the normal 32-bit editions of Windows.

Note: The fancy 64-bit versions of Vista and Windows 7 work only on recent Mac models. To find out if yours is eligible, see *http://support.apple.com/kb/HT1846.*

- **At least 10 gigs of free hard drive space** on your built-in hard drive, or a second internal drive. (You can't install Windows on an external drive using Boot Camp.)

- **A wired keyboard and mouse,** at least for the installation process. You can use a Bluetooth keyboard and mouse once the installation is complete.

Then you're ready to proceed.

Installing Boot Camp

Open your Applications→Utilities folder. Inside, open the program called Boot Camp Assistant.

Phase 1: Partition your drive

On the Introduction screen, you can print the instruction booklet, if you like (although the following pages contain the essential info). There's a lot of good, conservative legalese in that booklet: the importance of backing up your whole Mac before you begin, for example.

When you click Continue, you get the dialog box shown in Figure 8-1—the most interesting part of the whole process.

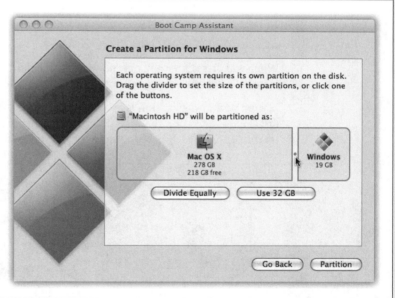

Figure 8-1:
How much hard drive space do you want to dedicate to your "PC"? It's not an idle question; whatever you give Windows is no longer available for your Mac. Drag the vertical handle between the Mac and Windows sides of this diagram.

You're being asked to *partition*—subdivide—your hard drive (which can't already be partitioned), setting aside a certain amount of space that will hold your copy of Windows and all the PC software you decide to install. This partitioning process doesn't involve erasing your whole hard drive; all your stuff is perfectly safe.

The dialog box offers handy buttons like Divide Equally and Use 32 GB, but it also lets you drag a space-divider handle, as shown in Figure 8-1, to divide up your drive space between the Mac and Windows sides. Use your experience using Windows on a real PC, if you have one, to decide how big your Windows "hard drive" should be.

Most people choose to dedicate a swath of the main internal hard drive to the Windows partition. But if you have a second internal hard drive, you can also choose one of these options:

- **Create a Second Partition.** The Boot Camp Assistant carves out a Windows partition from *that* drive.

- **Erase Disk and Create a Single Partition for Windows.** Just what it says.

Phase 2: Install Windows

On the Start Windows Installation screen, you're supposed to—hey!—start the Windows installation. Grab your Windows CD or DVD and slip it into the Mac. Its installer goes to work immediately.

Following the "I agree to whatever Microsoft's lawyers say" screen, Microsoft's installer asks which partition you want to put Windows on. It's *really* important to pick the right one. Play your cards wrong, and you could erase your whole *Mac* partition. So:

- **Windows XP.** Choose the partition (by pressing the up or down arrow keys) that's usually called "C: Partition3 <BOOTCAMP>."

When you press Enter, you may now encounter another frightening-looking screen. Here, Windows invites you to format the new partition.

If your Windows partition is less than 32 gigs, you get to choose between FAT32 or NTFS —a decision that, presumably, you've already made, having read the box on the facing page. Proceed as shown in Figure 8-2.

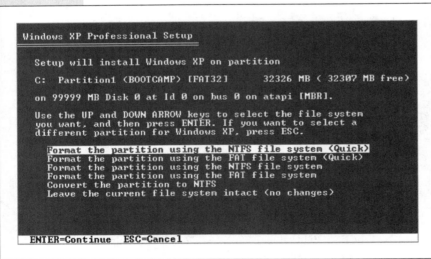

Figure 8-2:
Use the arrow keys to highlight either "Format the partition using the NTFS file system (Quick)" or "Format the partition using the FAT file system (Quick)." Then press Enter. On the following screen, type F to confirm the formatting, then Enter to confirm the whole thing.

- **Windows Vista, Windows 7.** Choose the one called "Disk 0 Partition 3 BOOT-CAMP."

Then click "Drive options (advanced)," click Format, click OK, and finally click Next. Your Windows partition is now formatted for NTFS, like it or not.

Now your Mac looks just like a PC that's having Windows installed. Be patient; sit around for half an hour as the Windows installer flits about, restarts, does what it has to do.

Phase 3: Install the drivers

When it's all over, a crazy, disorienting sight presents itself: your Mac, running Windows. There's no trace of the familiar desktop, Dock, or menu; it's Windows now, baby.

Walk through the Windows setup screens, creating an account, setting the time, and so on.

At this point, your Mac is actually a true Windows PC. You can install and run Windows programs, utilities, and even games; you'll discover that they run *really* fast and well.

But as Windows veterans know, every hardware feature of Windows requires a *driver*—a piece of software that tells the machine how to communicate with its own monitor, networking card, speakers, and so on. And it probably goes without saying that Windows doesn't include any drivers for *Apple's* hardware components.

That's why, at this point, you're supposed to insert your Mac OS X installation DVD; it contains all the drivers for the Mac's graphics card, Ethernet and AirPort networking, audio input and output, AirPort wireless antenna, iSight camera, brightness and volume keys, eject key, multitouch trackpad gestures, and Bluetooth transmitter. When this is all over, your white Apple remote control will even work to operate iTunes for Windows.

POWER USERS' CLINIC

The Skinny on FAT32

If you're installing Windows XP and you choose an amount less than 32 gigabytes, you have a choice of two formatting schemes for your Windows "hard drive."

FAT32 may sound unappetizing, but it will give you one very cool feature that the other available format (NT File System) doesn't: the ability to drag files back and forth from the Windows side to the Mac side. (This works only when you've started up the computer in Mac OS X. When you're in Windows, you'll be able to see and open files on the Mac side of the hard drive, although you won't be able to edit them where they are. At least not without a commercial program like MacDrive [*www.macdrive.com*].)

If you choose a partition size *greater* than 32 GB, or if you're installing Windows Vista or Windows 7, then you *must* use NTFS. It's a more modern, flexible formatting scheme—it offers goodies like file-by-file access permissions, built-in file compression and encryption, journaling (a data-protection feature), and so on.

But on a Boot Camp Mac, NTFS has a drawback. When you're running from the Mac side, you'll be able to see what's on the Windows partition, but you won't be able to add, remove, or change any files.

(It also installs a new Control Panel icon and system-tray pop-up menu, as described later in this chapter.)

Note: Unbeknownst to you, the Snow Leopard DVD is actually a dual-mode disc. When you insert it into a Mac running Mac OS X, it appears as the Snow Leopard installer you know and love. But when you slip it into a PC, its secret Windows partition appears—and automatically opens the Mac driver installer!

When you insert the Mac OS X disc, the driver installer opens and begins work automatically. Click past the Welcome and License Agreement screens, and then click Install. You'll see a lot of dialog boxes come and go; just leave it alone (and don't click Cancel).

A few words of advice:

- If the installation seems to stall, Windows may be waiting for you to click OK or Next in a window that's hidden behind other windows. Inspect the taskbar and look behind open windows.

- Windows XP concludes by presenting the Found New Hardware Wizard. Go ahead and agree to update your drivers.

When it's all over, a dialog box asks you to restart the computer; click Restart. When the machine comes to, it's a much more functional Windows Mac. (And it has an online Boot Camp Help window waiting for you on the screen.)

Forth and Back, Windows/Mac

From now on, your main interaction with Boot Camp will be telling it what kind of computer you want your Mac to be today: a Windows machine or a Mac.

Presumably, though, you'll prefer one operating system *most* of the time. Figure 8-3 (top and middle) shows how you specify your favorite.

Tip: If you're running Windows and you just want to get back to Mac OS X right now, you don't have to bother with all the steps shown in Figure 8-3. Instead, click the Boot Camp system-tray icon and, from the shortcut menu, choose Restart in Mac OS X.

WORKAROUND WORKSHOP

How to Right-Click in Boot Camp

Page 12 offers the full details on right-clicking when your Mac is being a Mac. But how are you supposed to right-click when your Mac is running Windows?

You can use any USB two-button mouse, including the Apple Mighty Mouse or Magic Mouse (page 13) that comes with every desktop Mac.

If you're stuck with a one-button mouse or trackpad, you can highlight whatever you want to right-click and then press Shift-F10.

Or use the Apple Mouse Utility program for Windows. (You can download it from this book's "Missing CD" page at *www. missingmanuals.com.*) It lets you Control-click to simulate a right-click while you're running Windows.

From now on, each time you turn on the Mac, it starts up in the operating system you've selected.

If you ever need to switch—when you need Windows just for one quick job, for example—press the Option key as the Mac is starting up. You'll see something like the icons shown in Figure 8-3 (bottom).

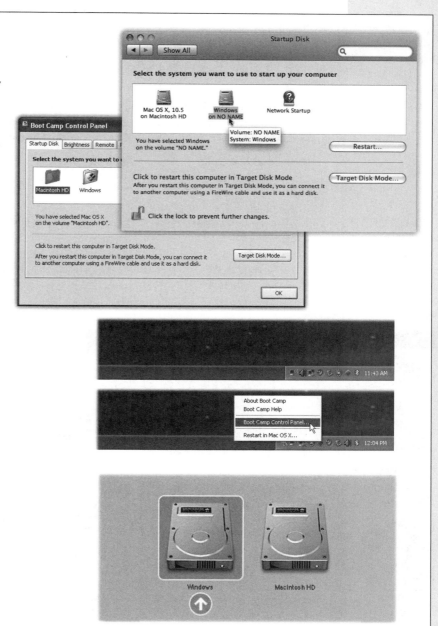

Figure 8-3:
Top: To choose your preferred operating system—the one that starts up automatically unless you intervene—choose ⌘→*System Preferences. Click Startup Disk, and then click the icon for either Mac OS X or Windows. Next, either click Restart (if you want to switch right now) or close the panel.*

The identical controls are available when you're running Windows, thanks to the new Boot Camp Control Panel.

Middle: To open the Boot Camp control panel, choose its name from its new icon in the Windows system tray.

Bottom: This display, known as the Startup Manager, appears when you press Option during startup. It displays all the disk icons, or disk partitions, that contain bootable operating systems. Just click the name of the partition you want, and then click the Continue arrow.

Tip: For nerds only: When you're running Windows, you can now reboot in Mac OS X just by typing a command at the Windows command line (Start→All Programs→Accessories→Command Prompt). Type this, exactly as shown, and then tap Enter. *c:\progra~1\Bootca~1\bootcamp.exe -StartupDisk "Mac OS" Shutdown /r /t 0*

Keyboard Translation Guide

Now, if you really want to learn about Windows, you need *Windows XP: The Missing Manual* (available in Home and Pro editions), *Windows Vista: The Missing Manual,* or *Windows 7: The Missing Manual.*

But suggesting that you go buy *another* book would be tacky. So here's just enough to get by.

First of all, a Mac keyboard and a Windows keyboard aren't the same. Each has keys that would strike the other as extremely goofy. Still, you can trigger almost any keystroke Windows is expecting by substituting special Apple-keystrokes, like this:

Windows keystroke	**Apple keystroke**
Control-Alt-Delete	Control-Option-Delete
Alt	Option
Backspace	Delete
Delete (forward delete)	⌦ (on laptops, Fn-Delete)
Enter	Return or Enter
Num lock	Clear (laptops: Fn-F6)
Print Screen	F14 (laptops: Fn-F11)
Print active window	Option-F14 (laptops: Option-Fn-F11)
⊞ key	⌘

FREQUENTLY ASKED QUESTION

The Virus Question

Doesn't running Windows on my Mac mean I'll be exposed to the nightmare of viruses and spyware, just like the rest of the Windows world?

As a matter of fact, yes.

If you install Windows on your Mac, you should also install Windows antivirus and antispyware software to protect that half of the computer. The world is crawling with commercial programs that do the job. There are also lots of free programs, like Microsoft Defender for spyware, and either AVG Antivirus (*www.free.grisoft.com*) or Avast Antivirus (*www.avast.com*) for viruses.

The good news is that even if your Windows installation gets infected, the Mac side of your computer is unaffected. Just as Mac OS X can't run Windows-only software like, say, Dragon NaturallySpeaking, it also can't run Windows virus software.

Some people, therefore, run Windows naked—*without* virus protection (especially when using Windows-in-a-window programs like Parallels and VMWare Fusion). If a virus does strike, no big deal; they just drag the infected copy of Windows to the Trash and install a fresh one!

The keyboard shortcuts in your programs are *mostly* the same as on the Mac, but you have to substitute the Ctrl key for the ⌘ key. So in Windows programs, Copy, Save, and Print are Ctrl-C, Ctrl-S, and Ctrl-P.

Similarly, the Alt key is the Windows equivalent of the Option key.

Tip: You know that awesome two-finger scrolling trick on Mac laptops (page 499)? Guess what? It works when you're running Windows, too.

Accessing Mac Files from the Dark Side—and Vice Versa

One nice feature in Snow Leopard: When you've started up in one operating system, it's much easier to access documents that "belong" to the other one. For example:

- When you're running Mac OS X, you can get to the documents you created while you were running Windows, which is a huge convenience. Just double-click the Windows disk icon (called NO NAME or Untitled), and then navigate to the Documents and Settings→[your account name]→My Documents (or Desktop).

  If you formatted your Windows XP partition using the FAT format as described earlier, you can copy files to *or* from this partition, and even open them up for editing on the Mac side. If you used NTFS, though, you can only copy them *to* the Mac side, or open them without the ability to edit them.

UP TO SPEED

Removing Windows

Maybe you're a switcher who held onto Windows because you were worried that you'd need it. Maybe you're finished with the project, the job, or the phase of life that required you to use Windows on your Mac. But one way or another, there may come a time when you want to get rid of your Windows installation and reclaim all the hard drive space it was using.

Not only can you do that, but the process won't touch anything that's already on the Mac side. You don't have to erase your entire hard drive or anything—Snow Leopard simply erases what's on the Windows partition of your hard drive, and then adds that disk space back to your main, *Mac* partition.

To do this, start by making sure you've rescued anything worth saving from the Windows side of your computer—it's about to be erased.

Start up in Mac OS X, quit all open programs, and make sure nobody's logged in but you. Now open up the Boot Camp

Assistant program in your Applications→Utilities folder.

On the welcome screen, click "Restore the startup disk to a single volume," and then click Continue. That's all there is to it.

Special notes for special setups: If you installed Windows on a separate hard drive, rather than a partition of your *main* hard drive, don't bother with all this. Just erase the Windows hard drive using Disk Utility, as described in Chapter 10, and format it as a Mac drive.

On the other hand, if your Mac has more than one internal hard drive and you created a Windows partition on one of them (rather than taking it over completely), then open Boot Camp Assistant as described above. This time, though, click "Create or remove a Windows partition," click Continue, click the Windows disk, and then click "Restore to a single Mac OS partition."

Tip: Actually, there's no reason your Windows "drive" has to be called NO NAME or Untitled. You can rename it as you would any other icon, either in Windows or in Mac OS X. (That's if you used the FAT format. If you used NTFS, you can't change the name in Mac OS X.)

- When you're running Windows, you can get to your Mac documents, too (this is the part that's new in Snow Leopard). Click Start→Computer. In the resulting window, you'll see an icon representing your Mac's hard-drive partition. Open it up.

  You can see and open these files. But if you want to edit them, you have to copy them to your Windows world first—onto the desktop, for example, or into a folder. (The Mac partition is "read-only" in this way, Apple says, to avoid the possibility that your Mac stuff could get contaminated by Windows viruses.)

Tip: If you did want to edit Mac files from within Windows, one solution is to buy a $50 program called MacDrive (*www.mediafour.com*). Another solution: Use a disk that both Mac OS X and Windows "see," and keep your shared files on that. A flash drive works beautifully for this. So does your iDisk (page 309) or a shared drive on the network.

Windows in a Window

The problem with Boot Camp is that every time you switch to or from Windows, you have to close down everything you were working on and restart the computer—and reverse the process when you're done. You lose two or three minutes each way. And you can't copy and paste between Mac and Windows programs.

There is another way: an $80 utility called Parallels Desktop for Mac OS X (*www.parallels.com*) and its rival, VMWare Fusion (*www.vmware.com*). These programs let you run Windows and Mac OS X *simultaneously;* Windows hangs out in a window of its own, while the Mac is running Mac OS X (Figure 8-4). You're getting about 90 percent of Boot Camp's Windows speed—not fast enough for 3-D games, but plenty fast for just about everything else.

Once again, you have to supply your own copy of Windows for the installation process. This time, though, it can be any version of Windows, all the way back to Windows 3.1—or even Linux, FreeBSD, Solaris, OS/2, or MS-DOS.

Having virtualization software on your Mac is a beautiful thing. You can be working on a design in iWork, duck into a Microsoft Access database (Windows only), look up an address, copy it, and paste it back into the Mac program.

And what if you can't decide whether to use Boot Camp (fast and feature-complete, but requires restarting) or Parallels/Fusion (fast and no restarting, but no 3-D games)? No problem—install both. They coexist beautifully on a single Mac and can even use the same copy of Windows.

Together, they turn the Macintosh into the Uni-Computer: the single machine that can run nearly 100 percent of the world's software catalog.

Virtualization Tip-O-Rama

Mastering Parallels or Fusion means mastering Windows, of course, but it also means mastering these tips:

- You don't *have* to run Windows in a window. With one keystroke, you can make your Windows simulator cover the entire screen. You're still actually running two operating systems at once, but the whole Mac world is hidden for the moment so you can exploit your full screen. Just choose View→Full Screen.

Tip: Or use the keystroke Alt-Enter (Parallels) or Ctrl-⌘-Return (Fusion) to enter and exit Full Screen mode.

Figure 8-4:
The strangest sight you ever did see: Mac OS X and Windows XP. On the same screen. At the same time. Courtesy of VMWare Fusion. Parallels is very similar.

- Conversely, both Parallels and Fusion offer something called *Coherence* or *Unity* mode, in which there's no trace of the Windows desktop. Instead, each Windows program floats in its own disembodied window, just like a Mac program; the Mac OS X desktop lies reassuringly in the background.

Tip: In Fusion's Unity mode, you can access your Computer, Documents, Network, Control Panel, Search, and Run commands right from Fusion's Dock icon or launch palette, so you won't even care that there's no Start menu.

In Parallels, press Alt+Ctrl+Shift to enter or exit Coherence mode. In Fusion, hit Ctrl-⌘-U for Unity mode.

Tip: In Fusion, in Unity view, you can use the usual Mac keystrokes for Cut, Copy, and Paste within Windows applications (⌘-X, ⌘-C, and ⌘-V). In Parallels, on the other hand, you can remap all Windows Control-key shortcuts to the ⌘ key in Preferences.

- To send the "three-fingered salute" when things have locked up in Windows (usually Ctrl+Alt+Delete), press Control-Option-D (Fusion) or Ctrl+Fn+Alt+Delete (Parallels). Or use the Send Ctrl-Alt-Delete command in the menus.

- You can drag files back and forth between the Mac and Windows universes. Just drag icons into, or out of, the Windows window.

- If you have a one-button mouse, you can "right-click" in Parallels by Control-Shift-clicking. In Fusion, Control-click instead. On Mac laptops, you can right-click by putting two fingers on the trackpad as you click.

- When you quit the virtualization program, you're not really "shutting down" the PC; you're just *suspending* it, or putting it to sleep. When you double-click the Parallels/VMWare icon again, everything in your Windows world is exactly as you left it.

- Your entire Windows universe of files, folders, and programs is represented by a single file on your hard drive. In Parallels, it's in your Home→Library→Parallels folder. In Fusion, it's in your Home→Documents→Virtual Machines folder.

That's super convenient, because it means you can back up your entire Windows "computer" by dragging a single icon to another drive. And if your Windows world ever gets a virus or spyware infestation, you can drag the entire thing to the Trash—and restore Windows from that clean backup.

POWER USERS' CLINIC

Beyond the Big Names

Parallels and VMWare Fusion are bloodthirsty rivals. New versions tumble out with alarming frequency, each designed to one-up its rival.

Still, these products aren't the only options. A program called VirtualBox (*www.virtualbox.org*) is not as polished or full-featured as its big-name rivals, but it's free. That's because it's open-source software, meaning that programmers around the world volunteer to collaborate on it.

Finally, several efforts are afoot to create software that lets you run Windows software *without Windows*. The most

promising one is a $60 program called CrossOver (*www.codeweavers.com*).

Sure enough, CrossOver-compatible Windows programs open up and run in Mac OS X just as though they're real Mac programs—without your having to own, install, or fire up a copy of Windows itself.

Unfortunately, the list of compatible programs is tiny; fewer than 50 Windows programs work flawlessly in CrossOver. The list of programs that *mostly* work is longer, though, so check the list on CrossOver's Web site to see if what you need is CrossOver-friendly.

Hardware on the Mac

M ost of the discussion in this book so far has covered *software*—not only the Mac OS X operating system that may be new to you, but also the programs and documents you'll be using on it. But there's more to life with a computer than software. This chapter covers the finer points of using Macintosh-compatible printers, cameras, disks, monitors, and keyboards—plus a guide to Time Machine, the Mac's automatic backup feature.

Printers and Printing

Printing has always been one of the Mac's strong suits—and you're about to find out why.

Setting Up a Printer

Setting up a printer for the first time is incredibly easy. The first time you want to print something, follow this guide:

1. **Connect the printer to the Mac, and then turn the printer on.**

   Inkjet printers connect to your USB jack. Laser printers hook up either to your USB jack or to your network (Ethernet or wireless).

2. **Open the document you want to print. Choose File→Print. In the Print dialog box, choose your printer's name from the Printer pop-up menu (or one of its submenus, if any, like Nearby Printers).**

   Cool! Wasn't that easy? Very nice how the Mac autodiscovers, autoconfigures, and autolists almost any USB, FireWire, Bluetooth, or Bonjour (Rendezvous) printer.

Have a nice afternoon. The End.

Oh—unless your printer *isn't* listed in the Printer pop-up menu. In that case, read on.

> **Note:** "Nearby Printers" refers to printers that aren't connected directly to your Mac but are accessible anyway: a printer connected to an Apple Time Capsule or AirPort base station, certain network printers that speak Bonjour (a feature that lets networked gadgets introduce each other automatically), or printers connected to other Macs that you've shared, as described later in this chapter.

3. **From the Printer pop-up menu, choose Add Printer (Figure 9-1, top).**

   A special setup window opens (Figure 9-1, bottom), which is even better at auto-detecting printers available to your Mac. If you see the printer's name here, click it, and then click Add (Figure 9-1, bottom).

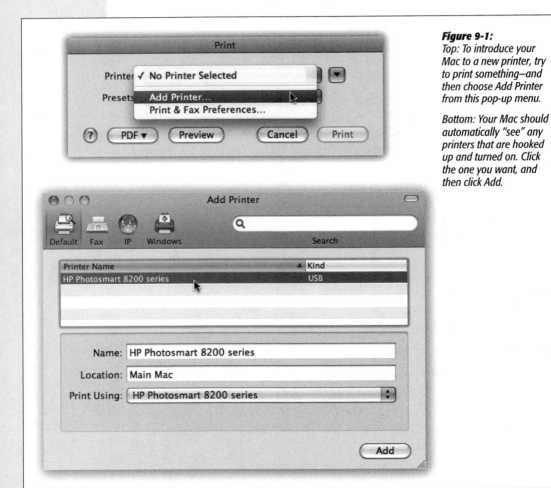

Figure 9-1:
Top: To introduce your Mac to a new printer, try to print something—and then choose Add Printer from this pop-up menu.

Bottom: Your Mac should automatically "see" any printers that are hooked up and turned on. Click the one you want, and then click Add.

You're all set. Have a good time.

Unless, of course, your printer *still* isn't showing up. Proceed to step 4.

4. **Click the icon for the kind of printer you have: Default, IP, or Windows.**

   Default usually does the trick, especially if you have an inkjet printer. Choose **IP** if you have a network printer that's not showing up in Default—especially if you have an old AppleTalk printer (see the box below). And choose **Windows** if there's a Windows-only printer out there on your office network.

   After a moment, the names of any printers that are turned on and connected appear in the printer list. For most people, that means only one printer—but one's enough.

TROUBLESHOOTING MOMENT

The Death of AppleTalk

Like most 800-pound-gorilla computer companies, Apple can be a frustrating partner. It throws its hairy weight behind some technology, gets all the other companies to adopt it—and then moves on to something else.

That's why AppleTalk is no longer with us, much to the dismay of thousands of Mac fans who own Apple-Talk printers.

AppleTalk was a networking system that was part of the Mac since 1984. Hundreds of networkable printer models, especially laser printers, used this scheme to talk to Macs.

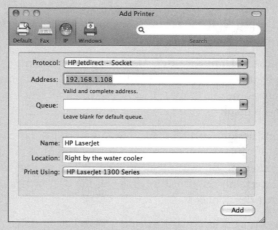

If yours is among them, you can still make your printer work. Follow steps 1 through 4 of "Setting Up a Printer" on these pages; in step 4, choose IP.

From the Protocol pop-up menu, choose HP Jetdirect–Socket (if you have an HP laser printer), or Internet Printing Protocol (IPP) (for most other laser printers). If you and your company's network expert determine that the printer you want

to use is, in fact, an LPR printer, then choose Line Printer Daemon instead.

In any of these cases, you now have to fill in the *IP address* (network address) of the printer. On some printers, you can call up this information on the screen. On others, you have to print out that printer's configuration or test page. (On many HP laser printers, you do that by holding down a button while the printer turns on.) There's no solution to this except to cuddle up with the manual—or, faster yet, Google it ("HP LaserJet 1300 configuration page").

Once you've filled in the IP address, you can make up a name for this printer ("HP Hulk") and a location ("Next to the water cooler"), if you like. The "Print using:" pop-up menu is supposed to fill itself in with the correct printer-driver information; if it doesn't, you can choose the printer model (or, in a pinch, a very similar one) manually.

Click Add. You're off and printing!

---

5. **Click the name of the printer you want to use.**

As an optional step, you can open the Print Using pop-up menu at the bottom of the dialog box. Choose "Select a driver to use," and then, in the list that appears, choose your particular printer's model name, if you can find it. That's how your Mac knows what printing features to offer you when the time comes: double-sided, legal size, second paper tray, and so on.

6. **Click Add.**

After a moment, you return to the main Printer Browser window (Figure 9-1), where your printer now appears. You're ready to print.

Note: If you still don't see your printer's name show up, ask yourself: Is my Mac on a corporate network? Does the network have an LPR (Line Printer Remote) printer? If you and your company's network nerd determine that the printer you want to use is, in fact, an LPR printer, click IP Printing at the top of the Printer Browser dialog box. Fill in the appropriate IP address and other settings, as directed by your cheerful network administrator.

The Printer List

If you're lucky enough to own several printers, repeat the steps above for each one. Eventually, you'll have introduced the Mac to all the printers available to it, so all their names show up in the printer list.

To see the printer list so far, open System Preferences→Print & Fax. You can have all kinds of fun here:

- **Choose a default printer.** Most people don't switch printers much. Still, you can choose one particular printer from this pop-up menu to set it as the *default* printer—the one the Mac uses unless you intervene by choosing from the Printer pop-up menu in the Print dialog box (Figure 9-1).

- **Create desktop printer icons.** From the Print & Fax pane of System Preferences, drag a printer's icon out of the window and onto the desktop (or wherever you like). Repeat for your other printers. From now on, you can print a document on a certain printer just by dragging the document's icon onto the appropriate printer desktop icon.

- **Check the ink level.** Click a printer, then click Options & Supplies, to see how your inkjet ink or laser-printer toner level is. That way, you won't be caught short when you're on a deadline and your printer is out of ink.

Making the Printout

The experience of printing depends on the printer you're using—laser printer, inkjet, or whatever. In every case, however, all the printing options hide behind two commands: File→Page Setup, which you need to adjust only occasionally, and File→Print, which you generally use every time you print. You'll find these two commands in almost every Macintosh program.

Page Setup

The Page Setup box lets you specify some key characteristics about the document you're going to print: orientation, paper dimensions, and so on; see Figure 9-2.

The options here vary by program and printer. The Page Setup options for an Epson inkjet, for example, differ dramatically from those for a laser printer. Only your printer's user manual can tell you exactly what these choices do.

Tip: You configure the Page Setup settings independently in each program you use. And by the way, to change the default paper size for all new documents, choose Save As Default from the Settings pop-up menu. (Mac fans in the UK: You're welcome.)

Figure 9-2:
Here in Page Setup are the controls you need to print a document rotated sideways on the page, so it prints "the long way." The Scale control, which lets you reduce or enlarge your document, can be handy if the program you're using doesn't offer such a control. And the Paper Size pop-up menu, of course, specifies the size of the paper you're printing on—US Letter, US Legal, envelopes, or one of the standard European or Japanese paper sizes (A4 and B5).

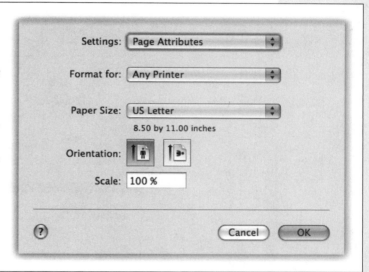

The Print Command

Although you can grow to a ripe old age without ever seeing the Page Setup dialog box, you can't miss the Print dialog box. It appears, like it or not, whenever you choose File→Print in one of your programs.

Once again, the options you encounter depend on the printer you're using. They also depend on whether or not you *expand* the dialog box by clicking the ▼ button; doing so reveals a *lot* of useful options, including a handy preview; see Figure 9-3.

Note: The exact layout of this expanded Print dialog box differs by program, but most modern ones resemble Figure 9-3.

If you expand the box, here's what you may find:

- **Printer.** If you have more than one printer connected to your Mac, you can indicate which you want to use for a particular printout by choosing its name from this pop-up menu.

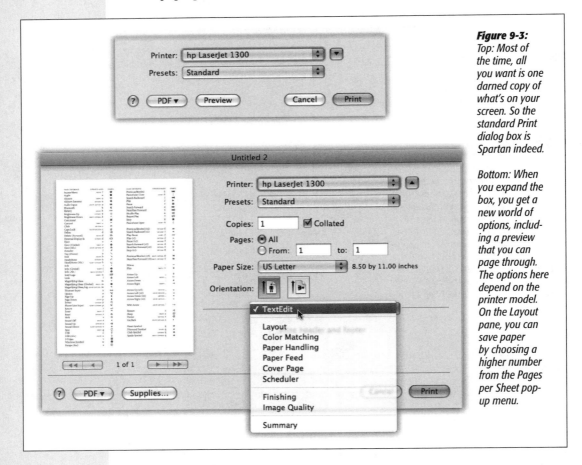

Figure 9-3:
Top: Most of the time, all you want is one darned copy of what's on your screen. So the standard Print dialog box is Spartan indeed.

Bottom: When you expand the box, you get a new world of options, including a preview that you can page through. The options here depend on the printer model. On the Layout pane, you can save paper by choosing a higher number from the Pages per Sheet pop-up menu.

- **Presets.** Here's a way to preserve your favorite print settings: Once you've proceeded through this dialog box, specifying the number of copies, which printer trays you want the paper taken from, and so on, you can choose Save As from the pop-up menu, and then assign your settings set a name (like "Borderless, 2 copies"). Thereafter, you'll be able to recreate that elaborate suite of settings simply by choosing its name from this pop-up menu.

- **Copies.** Type the number of copies you want printed. The Collated checkbox controls the printing order for the various pages. For example, if you print two copies of a three-page document, the Mac generally prints the pages in this order: 1, 2, 3, 1, 2, 3. If you turn off Collated, on the other hand, it prints in this order: 1, 1, 2, 2, 3, 3.

- **Pages.** You don't have to print an entire document—you can print, say, only pages 2 through 15.

- **Paper Size, Orientation.** Somebody at Apple finally realized how frustrating it was to have to open the Page Setup dialog box to change the paper-size and orientation settings, and then open the Print dialog box for other settings. Now, in most programs, these controls are duplicated right in the Print dialog box for your convenience.

- **PDF.** A *PDF* file, of course, is an Adobe Acrobat document—a file that any Mac, Windows, Linux, or Unix user can view, read, and print using either Preview or the free Acrobat Reader (available for Mac or Windows).

  You can easily save any document as a PDF file instead of printing it—a truly beautiful feature that saves paper, ink, and time. The document remains on your hard drive, and the text inside is even searchable using Spotlight.

  But that's just the beginning. Apple has added a long list of additional PDF options (like password-protected PDFs, emailed ones, and so on) in the pop-up *button* shown in Figure 9-3, top. For details on the PDF-related options here, see page 251.

- **Preview.** This button provides a print-preview function to almost every Mac OS X program on earth, which, in the course of your life, could save huge swaths of the Brazilian rain forest and a swimming pool's worth of ink in wasted printouts.

  Technically, the Preview button sends your printout to Preview, the program. Preview lets you zoom in or zoom out, rotate, or otherwise process your preview. When you're satisfied with how it looks, you can print it (File→Print), cancel it (File→Close), or turn it into a PDF file (File→Save as PDF).

- **Supplies.** This feature will strike you either as blissfully convenient or disgustingly mercenary: a button that takes you directly to a Web page where you can buy new cartridges for your specific printer model. It turns yellow and sprouts a "Low Ink" exclamation point when your cartridges are running low.

If you examine the unnamed pop-up menu just below the Presets pop-up menu, you find dozens of additional options. They depend on your printer model and the program you're using at the moment, but here are some typical choices:

- **Layout.** As described in Figure 9-3, you can save paper and ink or toner cartridges by printing several miniature "pages" on a single sheet of paper.

- **Paper Handling.** You can opt to print out your pages in reverse order so they stack correctly, or you can print just odd or even pages so you can run them through again for double-sided printing.

- **Paper Feed.** If you chose the correct printer model when setting up your printer, then this screen "knows about" your printer's various paper trays. Here's where you specify which pages you want to come from which paper tray. (By far the most popular use for this feature is printing the first page of a letter on company letterhead and the following pages on blank paper from a second tray.)

- **Cover Page.** Yes, that throwaway info page has made its way from the fax world into the hard-copy world.

- **Scheduler.** This option lets you specify *when* you want your document to print. Try printing a 400-page catalog in a big office where other people on the network might conceivably resent you for tying up the laser printer all afternoon, and you'll get the idea.

Then, below the light gray line in this pop-up menu, you'll find a few options that are unique to the chosen printer or program. Some HP printers, for example, offer Cover Page, Finishing, and other choices. Other likely guest commands:

- **Quality & Media** (inkjet printers only). Here's where you specify the print quality you want, the kind of paper you're printing on, and so on. (The name of this panel varies by manufacturer.)

- **[Program Name].** Whichever program you're using—Mail, Word, or anything else—may offer its own special printing options on this screen.

- **Summary.** This command summons a text summary of all your settings so far.

Tip: Here's one for the technically inclined. Open your Web browser and enter this address: *http://127.0.0.1:631.* You find yourself at a secret "front end" for CUPS (Common Unix Printing System), the underlying printing technology for Mac OS X. This trick lets your Mac communicate with a huge array of older printers that don't yet have Mac OS X drivers. Using this administration screen, you can print a test page, stop your printer in its tracks, manage your networked printers and print jobs, and more—a very slick trick.

Printing

When all your settings look good, click Print (or press Return) to send your print-out to the printer.

Managing Printouts

After you've used the Print command, you can either sit there until the paper emerges from the printer, or you can *manage* the printouts-in-waiting. That option is attractive primarily to people who do a lot of printing on multiple printers.

Start by opening the printer's window. If you're already in the process of printing, just click the printer's Dock icon. If not, open →System Preferences→Print & Fax, click the printer's name, and then click Open Print Queue.

At this point, you see something like Figure 9-4: The printouts that will soon be sliding out of your printer appear in a tidy list.

Here are some of the ways in which you can control these waiting printouts, which Apple collectively calls the *print queue:*

- **Delete them.** By clicking an icon, or ⌘-clicking several, and then clicking the Delete toolbar button, you remove items from the list of waiting printouts. Now they won't print.

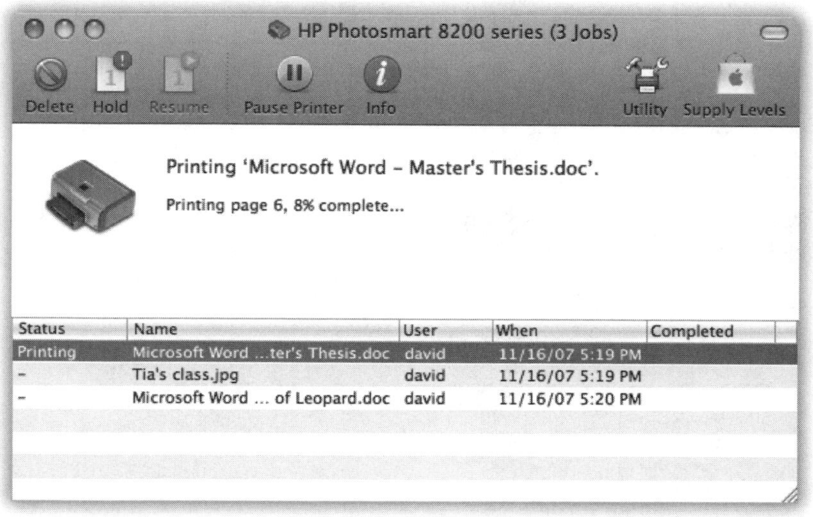

Figure 9-4:
Waiting printouts appear in this window. You can sort the list by clicking the column headings (Name or Status), make the columns wider or narrower by dragging the column-heading dividers horizontally, or reverse the sorting order by clicking the column name a second time. The Supply Level button opens a graph that shows how much ink each cartridge has remaining (certain printer models only).

- **Pause them.** By highlighting a printout and then clicking the Hold button, you pause that printout. It doesn't print out until you highlight it again and then click the Resume button. (Other documents continue to print.) This pausing business could be useful when, for example, you need time to check or refill the printer, or when you're just about to print your letter of resignation as your boss drops by. (Maybe to offer you a promotion.)

- **Halt them all.** You can stop all printouts from a printer by clicking Pause Printer. (They resume when you click the button again, which now says Resume Printer.)

You can't rearrange printouts by dragging them in the queue list. But remember that you can resequence the printing order by choosing the Scheduler option; you can also drag waiting printouts *between* these lists, shifting them from one printer to another.

Tip: As you now know, the icon for a printer's queue window appears automatically in the Dock when you print. But it also stays in the Dock for the rest of the day; it doesn't disappear when the printing is complete.

If you wish it would, Control-click (or right-click) the printer's Dock icon; from the shortcut menu, choose Auto Quit.

Printer Sharing

Printer sharing is for people (or offices) with more than one Mac, connected to a network, who'd rather not buy a separate printer for each machine. Instead, you connect the printer to one Mac, flip a couple of software switches, and then boom: The other Macs on the network can send their printouts to the printer without actually being attached to it—even wirelessly attached, if they're on an AirPort network.

Note: Of course, this feature is most useful when you're sharing printers that can hook up to only one Mac at a time, like USB inkjet photo printers. Office laser printers are often designed to be networked from Day One.

Setting up printer sharing is easy; see Figure 9-5, top. Then, to make a printout from across the network, see the instructions in Figure 9-5, bottom.

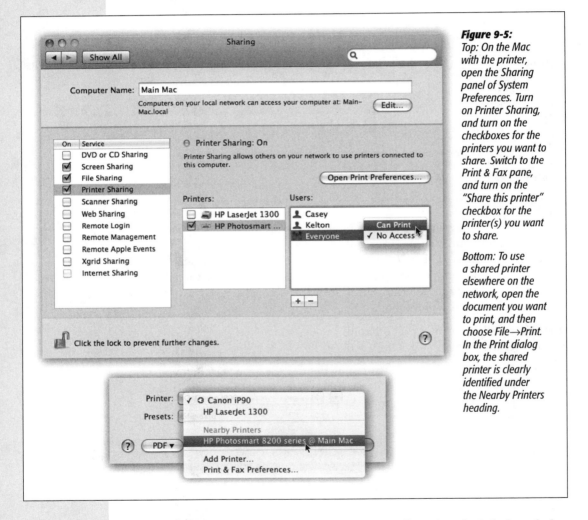

Figure 9-5:
Top: On the Mac with the printer, open the Sharing panel of System Preferences. Turn on Printer Sharing, and turn on the checkboxes for the printers you want to share. Switch to the Print & Fax pane, and turn on the "Share this printer" checkbox for the printer(s) you want to share.

Bottom: To use a shared printer elsewhere on the network, open the document you want to print, and then choose File→Print. In the Print dialog box, the shared printer is clearly identified under the Nearby Printers heading.

If you're still using your Windows PC, you can install Bonjour for Windows (a free download from this book's "Missing CD" page at *www.missingmanuals.com*); then that machine can print to your Mac's shared printer, too.

Tip: Of course, your Mac (the one attached to the printer) must be turned on in order for the other computers to print. In part, that's because the documents-in-waiting from other people pile up on *your* hard drive.

Faxing

Using the Mac as a fax machine saves money on paper and fax cartridges, and spares you the expense of buying a physical fax machine. It also eliminates the silly and wasteful ritual of printing something out just so you can feed it into a fax machine. And because your fax originates directly from the heart of Mac OS X instead of being scanned by a crummy 200-dpi fax-machine scanner, it blesses your recipient with a great-looking document.

Here's the basic idea: When faxes come in, you can read them on the screen, opt to have them printed automatically, or even have them emailed to you so that you can get them wherever you are in the world. (Try *that* with a regular fax machine.)

Setting Up Faxing

Open System Preferences. Click Print & Fax. Click the **+** button, and proceed as shown in Figure 9-6.

Note: Unfortunately, Apple no longer builds fax modems into new Macs—not even laptops. You can buy an external dangly Apple USB Fax/Modem for $50, however. As soon as it's plugged into a USB port, its name appears in the Printers list.

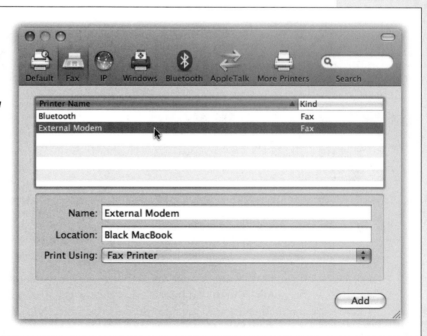

Figure 9-6:
When you click the +
button, this handy list of
fax modems pops up.
Chances are, you have
only one—and it's either
an old Apple Internal or a
USB External model that
you bought from Apple.
Click its name, and then
click Add.

If you intend to *send* faxes from the Mac, type in your return fax number in the Fax Number box. Also turn on "Show fax status in menu bar." It installs a fax menulet that lets you monitor and control your fax sending and receiving.

If you intend to *receive* faxes, click Receive Options, and turn on "Receive faxes on this computer." Then specify how soon the fax machine should pick up the call (after how many rings—you don't want it answering calls before *you* have a chance).

Finally, you can say how you want to handle incoming faxes, as described in Figure 9-7.

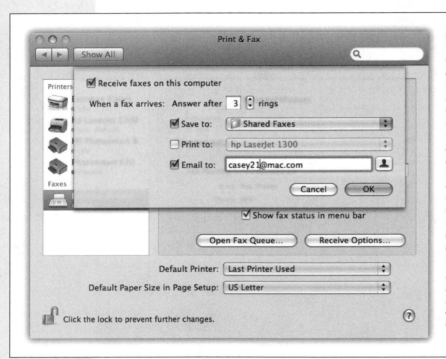

Figure 9-7:
When your Mac answers the fax line, it can do three things with the incoming fax. Option 1: Save it as a PDF file that you open with Preview. (The Mac proposes saving these files into the Users→ Shared→Shared Faxes folder, but you can set up a more convenient folder.) Option 2: Print it out automatically, just like a real fax machine. Option 3: Email it to you, so you can get your faxes even when you're not home (and so you can forward the fax easily).

Sending a Fax

When you're ready to send a fax, type up the document you want to send. Choose File→Print. In the Print dialog box (Figure 9-3), open the PDF pop-up button and choose Fax PDF.

The dialog box shown in Figure 9-8 appears. Here are the boxes you can fill in:

- **To.** If you like, you can simply type the fax number into the To box, exactly the way it should be dialed: *1-212-553-2999,* for example. You can send a single fax to more than one number by separating each with a comma and a space.

  If you fax the same people often, though, you're better off adding their names and fax numbers to the Address Book (Chapter 11). That way, you can click the little silhouette button to the right of the To box and choose the recipient.

- **Settings.** Most of the time, fiddling with the printing pop-up menu isn't relevant to sending a fax. But the standard printing controls are here for your convenience. You can use the Scheduler pane to specify a time for your outgoing fax, the Layout pane to print more than one "page" per sheet, and so on.

- **Use Cover Page, Subject, Message.** If you turn on this checkbox, you're allowed to type a little message into the Subject and Message boxes.

  Beware! Don't press the Return key to add a blank line to your message. Mac OS X thinks you intend to "click" the Fax button—and off it goes!

Tip: Choosing Save as PDF from the little PDF pop-up button, at this moment, is your only chance to keep a copy of the fax you're sending.

Figure 9-8:
When you send a fax, you get a modified Print dialog box. Here is where you specify a cover page (and what you want on it).

You can type a fax number into the To box, or you can click the silhouette head button to open a miniature version of Address Book. It lets you choose someone's name by double-clicking. All phone numbers appear here, so look for those identified as fax numbers. (Chances are that these listings don't include the 1- long-distance prefix, which is why Apple gave you a separate Dialing Prefix box.) If you've built groups in your address book, you can send to everyone in a group at once.

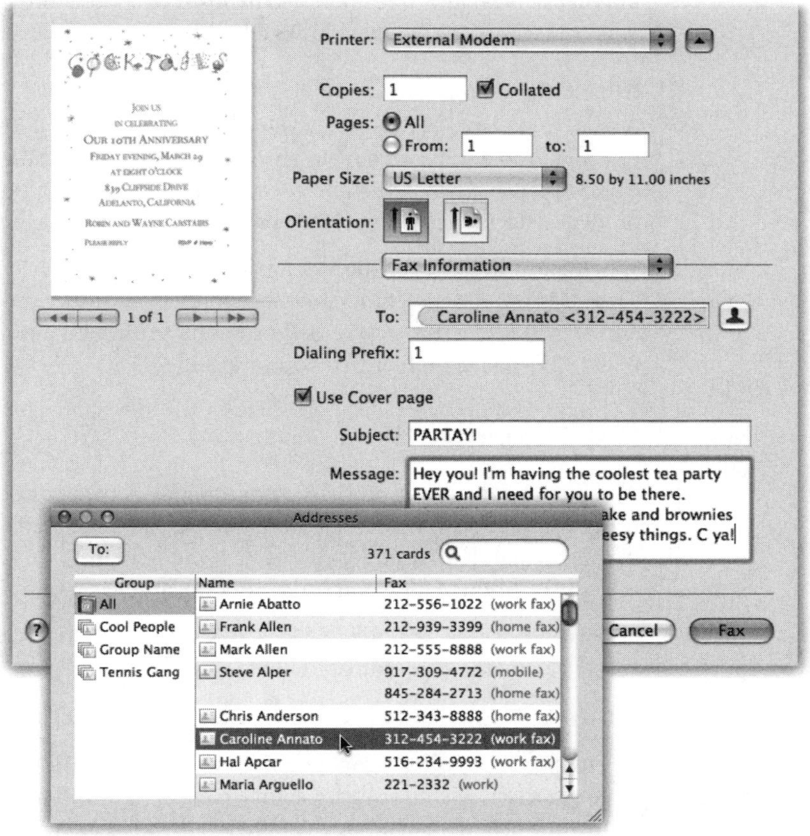

Sending

When everything looks good, hit the Fax button. Although it may look like nothing is happening, check your Dock, where the icon for your fax/modem has appeared. If you click it, you'll see a clone of the dialog box shown in Figure 9-4, indicating the progress of your fax. Here you can pause the faxing, delete it, or hold it, exactly as you would a printout. (Your Fax menulet, if you've installed it, also keeps you apprised of the fax's progress.)

Otherwise, you don't get much feedback on the faxing process. Once the connection sounds are complete, you don't hear anything, see anything, or receive any notice that the fax was successful.

(If your fax was *not* successfully sent for some reason, the modem's window automatically reschedules the fax to go out in five minutes.)

Checking the log, checking the queue

To see the log of all sent and received faxes, choose →System Preferences→Print & Fax. Double-click your fax/modem's name; its fax-management window appears, but that's not what you're interested in. Instead, choose Jobs→Show Completed Jobs. You get a status window that looks a lot like the one for a printer.

Receiving a Fax

A Mac that's been set up to answer calls does a very good impersonation of a fax machine. You don't even have to be logged in to get faxes, although the Mac does have to be turned on. In System Preferences→Energy Saver→Options, turn on "Wake when modem detects a ring" to prevent your Mac from being asleep at the big moment.

When a fax call comes in, the Mac answers it after the number of rings you've specified. Then it treats the incoming fax image in the way you've specified in System Preferences: by sending it to your email program, printing it automatically, or just saving it as a PDF file in a folder that you've specified.

PDF Files

As a PC veteran, you've probably run into PDF (portable document format) files already. Many a software manual, Read Me file, and downloadable "white paper" comes in this format. In Windows, you needed the free program called Acrobat Reader to open or print these files, and some not-free-at-all software program to *create* them.

PDF files, however, are one of Mac OS X's common forms of currency. In fact, you can turn *any document* into a PDF file.

What's the big deal about PDF in Mac OS X? Consider these advantages:

- **Other people see your layout.** When you distribute PDF files to other people, they see precisely the same fonts, colors, page design, and other elements that you put in your original document. And here's the kicker: They get to see all of this even if they don't *have* the fonts or the software you used to create the document.

- **It's universal.** PDF files are very common in the Macintosh, Windows, Unix/Linux, and even smartphone (BlackBerry, iPhone) worlds. When you create a PDF file, you can distribute it (by email, for example) without worrying about what kinds of computers your correspondents are using.

- **It has very high resolution.** PDF files print at the maximum quality of any printer. (Right now you're looking at a PDF file that was printed at a publishing plant.)

- **You can search it.** Behind the scenes, a PDF's text is still text; Spotlight can find a PDF in a haystack in a matter of seconds. That's an especially handy feature when you work with electronic software manuals in PDF format.

Opening PDF Files

There's nothing to opening up a PDF file: Just double-click it. Preview takes over from there, and opens the PDF file on your screen. (See page 537 for details on using Preview to read PDF documents.)

Creating PDF Files

Opening, schmopening—what's really exciting in Mac OS X is the ability to create your *own* PDF files. The easiest way is to click the PDF pop-up button in the standard Print dialog box (visible in Figure 9-3). When you click it, you're offered a world of interesting PDF-creation possibilities, the most useful of which are these:

- **Save as PDF.** Mac OS X saves your printout-to-be to the disk as a PDF document instead of printing it.

- **Fax PDF** *faxes* a document instead of printing it, as described on the preceding pages.

- **Mail PDF** generates a PDF, and then attaches it to an outgoing message in Mail. Great for exchanging layout-intensive documents with collaborators who don't have the same fonts, layout software, or taste as you.

- **Save PDF to iPhoto** creates a PDF version of the document and then exports it to iPhoto. That's not such a bad idea; iPhoto is great at managing and finding any kind of graphics documents, including PDFs.

- **Save PDF to Web Receipts Folder** is one of the simplest and sweetest features in all of Mac OS X.

  You use it when you've just ordered something on a Web site, and the "Print This Receipt" screen is staring you in the face. Don't waste paper and ink (and, later, time trying to find it!). Instead, use this command. You get a perfectly usable PDF version, stored in your Home→Documents→Web Receipts folder, where you can use Spotlight to find it later, when you need to consult or print it because your gray-market goods never arrived.

- **Edit Menu** lets you prune this very list to remove the options you never use.

Fonts—and Font Book

Mac OS X delivers type that is *all smooth, all the time*. Fonts in Mac OS X's formats—called TrueType, PostScript Type 1, and OpenType—always look smooth onscreen and in printouts, no matter what the point size.

Mac OS X also comes with a program that's *just* for installing, removing, inspecting, and organizing fonts. It's called Font Book (Figure 9-9), and it's in your Applications folder.

Figure 9-9:
Each account holder can have a separate set of fonts; your set is represented by the User icon. You can drag fonts and font families between the various Fonts folders represented here—from your User account folder to the Computer icon, for example, making it available to all account holders.

Where Fonts Live

Brace yourself. In Mac OS X, there are *three* Fonts folders. The fonts you actually see listed in the Fonts menus and Font panels of your programs are combinations of these Fonts folders' contents.

They include:

- **Your private fonts (your Home folder→Library→Fonts).** This Fonts folder sits right inside your own Home folder. You're free to add your own custom fonts to this folder. Go wild—it's your font collection and yours alone. Nobody else who uses the Mac can use these fonts; they'll never even know that you have them.

- **Main font collection (Library→Fonts).** Any fonts in this folder are available to everyone to use in every program. (As with most features that affect everybody who shares your Macintosh, however, only people with Administrator accounts can change the contents of this folder.)

- **Essential system fonts (System→Library→Fonts).** This folder contains the 35 fonts that the Mac itself needs: the typefaces you see in your menus, dialog boxes, icons, and so on. You can open this folder to *see* these font suitcases, but you can't do anything with them, such as opening, moving, or adding to them. Remember that, for stability reasons, the System folder is sealed under glass forever.

With the exception of the essential system fonts, you'll find an icon representing each of these locations in your Font Book program, described next.

Note: And just to make life even more exciting, Adobe's and Microsoft's software installers may donate even *more* fonts to your cause, in yet *another* folder: your Home→Application Support folder.

Font Book: Installing and Managing Fonts

One of the biggest perks of Mac OS X is its preinstalled collection of over 50 great-looking fonts—"over $1,000 worth," according to Apple, which licensed many of them from type companies. In short, fewer Mac users than ever will wind up buying and installing new fonts.

But when you do buy or download new fonts, you're in luck. There's no limit to the number of fonts you can install.

Looking over your fonts

Right off the bat, Font Book is great for one enjoyable pursuit: looking at samples of each typeface. Click Computer, for example, click the first font name, and then press the down arrow key. As you walk down the list, the rightmost panel shows you a sample of each font (Figure 9-9).

You can also click any font family's flippy triangle (or highlight its name and then press the right arrow) to see the font *variations* it includes: Italic, Bold, and so on.

Tip: When you first open Font Book, the actual text of the typeface preview (in the right panel) is pretty generic. Don't miss the Preview menu, though. It lets you substitute a full display of every character (choose Repertoire)—or, if you choose Custom, it lets you type your *own* text.

Printing a reference sheet

You can print a handy, whole-font sampler of any font. Click its name and then choose File→Print. In the Print dialog box, click the ▼ button to expand the dialog box, if necessary.

You can use the Report Type pop-up menu to choose from three reference-sheet styles: Catalog, Repertoire, or Waterfall. Choose each to view a preview of the report. When everything looks good, click Print.

Eliminating duplicates

Since your Mac accesses up to three folders containing fonts, you might wonder what happens in the case of *conflicts*. For example, suppose you have two slightly different fonts, both called Optima, which came from different type companies, and are housed in different Fonts folders on your system. Which font do you actually get when you use it in your documents?

The scheme is actually fairly simple: Mac OS X proceeds down the list of Fonts folders in the order shown on pages 252-253, beginning with your own home Fonts folder. It only acknowledges the existence of the *first* duplicated font it finds.

If you'd rather have more control, open Font Book. A bullet (•) next to a font's name is Font Book's charming way of trying to tell you that you've got copies of the same font in more than one of your Fonts folders. You might have one version of Comic Sans in your own Home→Library→Fonts folder, for example, and another in your Mac's main Fonts folder.

Click the one that you want to keep, and then choose Edit→Resolve Duplicates. Font Book turns off all *other* copies, and the bullet disappears.

Adding, removing, and hiding fonts

Here's what you can do with Font Book:

- **Install a font.** When you double-click a font file's icon in the Finder, Font Book opens and presents the typeface for your inspection pleasure. If you like it, click Install Font. You've just installed it into *your account's* Fonts folder, so that it appears in the Font menus of all your programs. (If you'd rather install it so that it appears in *all* account holders' Fonts menus, see Figure 9-9.)

- **Remove a font.** Removing a font from your machine is easy: Highlight it in the Font Book list, and then press the Delete key. (You're asked to confirm the decision.) Before taking such a drastic and permanent step, however, keep in mind that you can simply *disable* (hide) the font instead. Read on.

- **Disable a font.** When you disable a font, you're simply hiding it from your programs. You might want to turn off a font so that you can use a different version of it (bearing the same name but from a different type company, for example), or to make your Font menus shorter, or to make programs like Microsoft Word start up faster. You can always turn a disabled font back on if you ever need it again.

Tip: How's this for a sweet feature? Mac OS X can activate fonts *automatically* as you need them. When you open a document that relies on a font it doesn't have, Leopard activates that font and keeps it available until that particular program quits.

Actually, it does better than that. If it doesn't see that font installed, it actually *searches your hard drive* on a quest to find the font—and then it asks you if you want it installed, so the document will look right.

To disable a font, just click it (or its family name; see Figure 9-9) and then click the checkbox button beneath the list (or press Shift-⌘-D). Confirm your decision by clicking Disable in the confirmation box. (Turn on "Do not ask me again," if you're the confident sort.)

The font's name now appears gray, and the word Off appears next to it, making it absolutely clear what you've just done. (To turn the font on again, highlight its name, and then click the now-empty checkbox button, or press Shift-⌘-D again.)

Note: When you install, remove, disable, or enable a font using Font Book, you see the changes in the Font menus and panels of your modern *Cocoa* programs immediately. You won't see the changes in older Carbon programs, however, until you quit and reopen them.

Font libraries

A font library is a set of fonts *outside* Font Book that you can install or uninstall on the fly. They don't have to be in any of your Fonts folders; Font Book can install them from wherever they happen to be sitting on your hard drive (or even on the network). Font Book never copies or moves these font files as you install or remove them from libraries; it simply adds them to your Font menus by referencing them right where they sit.

Tip: That can be a handy arrangement if you periodically work on different projects for different clients. Why burden your day-to-day Font menu with the 37 fonts used by *Beekeeper Quarterly* magazine, when you need to work with those fonts only four times a year?

Once you've added some fonts to a library, you can even set up collections *within* that library.

To create a library, choose File→New Library; the library appears in the Collection list at the left side of Font Book. Now you can drag fonts into it right from the Finder, or set up collections inside it by highlighting the library's icon and choosing File→New Collection.

The Fonts Panel

In many standard programs—like TextEdit, iMovie, Pages, Keynote, Numbers, iPhoto, and Mail—you get a standard Mac OS X feature called the Fonts panel. If you're seated in front of your Mac OS X machine now, fire up TextEdit or Pages and follow along.

Choosing fonts from the Fonts panel

Suppose you've just highlighted a headline in TextEdit, and now you want to choose an appropriate typeface for it.

In TextEdit, you open the Fonts panel (Figure 9-10) by choosing Format→Font→Show Fonts (⌘-T). If you've ever used Font Book, this display should look familiar. The first column lists your Collections, as described above. The second column, Family, shows the names of the actual fonts in your system. The third, Typeface, shows the various style variations—Bold, Italic, Condensed, and so on—available in that type family. (Oblique and Italic are roughly the same thing; Bold, Black, and Ultra are varying degrees of boldface.)

The last column lists a sampling of point sizes. You can use the size slider, choose from the point-size pop-up menu, or type any number into the box at the top of the Size list.

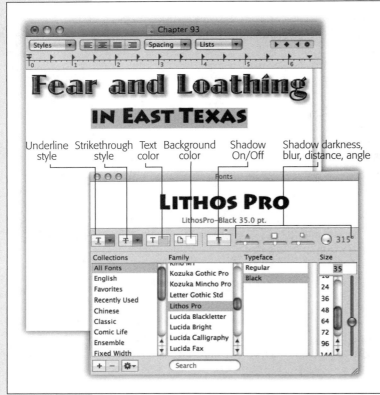

Figure 9-10:
The Fonts panel, generally available only in newer Cocoa programs, offers elaborate controls over text color, shadow, and underline styles. It also contains some of the genetic material of old-style programs like Suitcase and Font Juggler.

See the handy font sample shown here above the font lists? To get it, choose Show Preview from the ✿ pop-up menu. Or use the mousy way: Place your cursor just below the title bar (where it says Fonts) and drag downward.

Digital Cameras

Just like Windows XP and later versions, Mac OS X is extremely camera-friendly. The simple act of connecting a digital camera to its USB cable stirs Mac OS X into action—namely, it opens iPhoto, Apple's digital-photo shoebox program.

If it's a digital *video* camera you plugged in, Mac OS X opens iMovie instead. (Both of these programs are described in this book's free 85-page iLife Appendix, which you can download from this book's "Missing CD" at *www.missingmanuals.com.*)

Disks

Floppy drives disappeared from Macs beginning in 1997—and these days, they're absent from most Windows PCs, too.

In the meantime, there are all kinds of other disks you can connect to a Mac these days: CDs and DVDs, hard drives, iPods, USB flash drives, and so on.

When you insert a disk, its icon shows up in three places (unless you've changed your Finder preferences): on the right side of the screen, in the Computer window, and in the Sidebar (page 33). To see what's on a disk you've inserted, double-click its icon.

Note: You can make the Mac work like Windows, if you choose. For example, to open a single window containing icons of all currently inserted disks, choose Go→Computer (which produces the rough equivalent of the My Computer window).

To complete the illusion that you're running Windows, you can even tell Mac OS X not to put disk icons on the desktop at all. Just choose Finder→Preferences, click General, and turn off the four top checkboxes—"Hard disks," "External disks," "CDs, DVDs, and iPods," and "Connected servers." They'll no longer appear on the desktop—only in your Computer window. (You can stop them from appearing in the Sidebar, too, by clicking the Sidebar button in the Finder preferences and turning off the same checkboxes.)

To remove a disk from your Mac, use one of these methods:

- **Hold down the Eject key on your keyboard.** Mac keyboards, both on laptops and desktops, have a special Eject key (⏏), usually in the upper-right corner. Hold it down for a moment to make a CD or DVD pop out.

- **Drag its icon onto the Trash icon.** For years, this technique has confused and frightened first-time Mac users. Their typical reaction: Doesn't the Trash mean "delete"? Yes, but only when you drag *file or folder* icons there—not *disk* icons.

The Eject Button That Doesn't

When I push the ⏏ key on my keyboard (or the Eject button on my CD-ROM drawer), how come the CD doesn't come out?

There might be three things going on. First of all, some file on the disc might be open—that is, in use by one of your programs. You're not allowed to eject the disc until that file is closed.

Second, to prevent accidental pushings, the Eject key on the modern Mac keyboard is designed to work only when you hold it down steadily for a second or two. Just tapping it doesn't work.

Third, remember that once you've inserted a disk, the Mac won't let go unless you eject it in one of the official ways.

On Mac models with a CD tray (drawer), pushing the button on the CD-ROM door opens the drawer only when it's empty. If there's a disc in it, you can push that button till doomsday, but the Mac will simply ignore you.

That behavior especially confuses people who are used to working with Windows. (On a Windows PC, pushing the CD button does indeed eject the disc.) But on the Mac, pushing the CD-door button ejects an inserted disc only when the disc wasn't seated properly, or the Mac couldn't read the disc for some other reason, and the disc's icon never appeared onscreen.

The Eject key on the modern Mac keyboard, however, isn't so fussy. It pops out whatever CD or DVD is in the drive.

Oh—and if a CD or DVD won't come out at all (and its icon doesn't show up on the desktop), restart the Mac. Keep the mouse button pressed as the Mac restarts to make the disc pop out.

And if even that technique doesn't work, look for a tiny pinhole in or around the slot. Inserting a straightened paper clip, slowly and firmly, will also make the disc pop out.

Dragging a disk icon into the Trash (at the end of the Dock) makes the Mac spit the disk out. (If you've dragged a *disk image* icon or the icon of a networked disk, this maneuver *unmounts* them—that is, gets them off your screen.)

The instant you begin dragging a disk icon, the Trash icon on the Dock changes form, as though to reassure the novice that dragging a disk icon there will only eject the disk. As you drag, the wastebasket icon morphs into a giant-sized ⏏ logo.

- **Highlight the disk icon, and then choose File→Eject (or press ⌘-E).** The disk pops out.

- **Right-click the disk icon.** Choose Eject from the shortcut menu.

- **Use the Sidebar.** Click the ⏏ button next to a disk's name in the Sidebar.

Tip: Any of these techniques also work to get network disks and disk images off your screen.

Startup Disks

When you turn the Mac on, it hunts for a *startup disk*—that is, a disk containing a System folder. If you've ever seen the dispiriting blinking folder icon on a Mac's screen, you know what happens when the Mac *can't* find a startup disk. It blinks like that forever, or until you find and insert a disk with a viable System folder on it.

Creating a startup disk

By installing Mac OS X onto a disk—be it a hard drive or a DVD—you create a startup disk.

Note: Not all external USB disks are capable of starting up the Mac, but any internal hard drive can, and any external FireWire hard drive can.

Selecting a startup disk

It's perfectly possible to have more than one startup disk simultaneously attached to your Mac. If you've set up a Boot Camp partition (Chapter 8), for example, you essentially have a Mac startup disk and a Windows startup disk.

Only one System folder can be operational at a time. So how does the Mac know which to use as its startup disk? You make your selection in the Startup Disk pane of System Preferences (Figure 9-11).

Tip: If you're in a hurry to start the machine up from a different disk, just click the disk icon and then click Restart in the System Preferences window. You don't have to close the System Preferences window first.

Erasing a Disk

When you want to erase a disk (such as a DVD-RW disc), the only tool Apple gives you is Disk Utility, which sits in your Applications→Utilities folder.

Once you've opened Disk Utility, click the name of the disk (in the left-side list), click the Erase tab, and then click the Erase button.

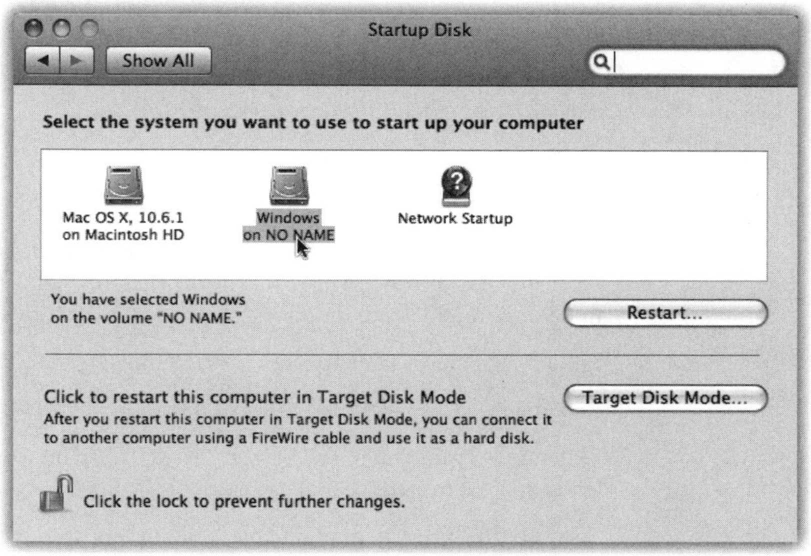

Figure 9-11:
In the Startup Disk pane of System Preferences, the currently selected disk—the one that will be "in force" the next time the machine starts up—is always highlighted. You also see the System folder's version, the name of the drive it's on, and its actual name.

Startup Disk

Show All

Select the system you want to use to start up your computer

Mac OS X, 10.6.1 on Macintosh HD   Windows on NO NAME   Network Startup

You have selected Windows on the volume "NO NAME."

Restart...

Click to restart this computer in Target Disk Mode
After you restart this computer in Target Disk Mode, you can connect it to another computer using a FireWire cable and use it as a hard disk.

Target Disk Mode...

Click the lock to prevent further changes.

Burning CDs and DVDs

Who misses the floppy drive anymore? A blank DVD holds about 3,250 times as many files!

You can buy blank CDs incredibly cheaply in bulk—$20 for 100 discs, for example—via the Web. Blank DVDs are only slightly more expensive—about $30 for 100.

Burning a CD or DVD is great for backing stuff up, transferring stuff to another computer (like a Windows PC), mailing to somebody, or offloading (archiving) older files to free up hard drive space.

You can burn a disc in either of two ways: with the blank disc inserted or without.

Burn Folders: Without the Disc

The *burn folder* is a special folder that you fill up by dragging file and folder icons to it. Then, when you're ready to burn, you just insert the blank disc and go.

The burn-folder concept has a lot going for it:

- **No wasted hard drive space.** When you use a burn folder, you're not using up any additional disk space as you load up a disc with files and folders. Instead, the Mac just sets aside aliases of the files and folders you want to burn. Aliases take up negligible hard drive space. When you finally burn the disc, the designated material is copied directly onto the CD or DVD.

- **Easy reuse.** You can keep a burn folder on your desktop, prestocked with the folders you like to back up. Each time you burn a disc, you get the latest version of those folders' contents, and you're saved the effort of having to gather them each time.

- **Prepare ahead of time.** You can get a CD or DVD ready to burn without having a blank disc on hand.

Here's how you use burn folders:

1. **Create a burn folder.**

   To make a burn folder appear on your desktop, choose File→New Burn Folder. To create one in any other window, Control-click (or right-click) a blank spot inside that window and, from the shortcut menu, choose New Burn Folder.

   Either way, a new folder appears, bearing the universal Mac "burn" symbol (☢).

2. **Rename it.**

   Its name is highlighted, so you can just start typing to rename it. Press Return when you're finished.

3. **Load up the folder by dragging files and folders onto it.**

   If you double-click the burn folder to open its window (Figure 9-12), you'll notice that you're not actually copying huge files. You're simply making a list of aliases.

Tip: At the bottom of the burn folder's window, the "minimum disc size" display keeps track of how much stuff you've loaded up so far, so you can gauge if it will fit on one disc.

---

4. **Decorate the window, if you like.**

   You can choose list view or icon view; you can drag the icons into an arrangement you like; you can change the background color of the window; and so on. One nice feature of the Mac (which is not available on The Other OS) is that the look of a window is preserved when you burn it to CD.

5. **Click the Burn button in the upper-right corner of the window, or choose File→ Burn Disc.**

   The message shown at bottom in Figure 9-12 appears.

6. **Insert a blank disc.**

   If you have a slot-loading Mac, slip the disc into the slot. If your Mac has a sliding CD/DVD tray instead, open it first by pressing the button on the tray, or pressing your ⏏ key for about a second.

Tip: Once you've inserted a CD or DVD into your tray, you can close it either by pushing gently on the tray or by pressing the ⏏ key again.

One last confirmation box appears, where you can name the disc and choose a burning speed for it.

7. **Click Burn (or press Return).**

The Mac's laser proceeds to record the CD or DVD, which can take some time. Feel free to switch into another program and continue using your Mac. When it's all over, you have a freshly minted CD or DVD, whose files and folders you can open on any Mac or Windows PC.

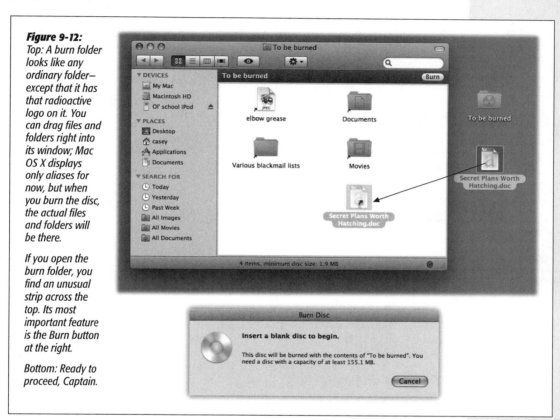

Figure 9-12:
Top: A burn folder looks like any ordinary folder— except that it has that radioactive logo on it. You can drag files and folders right into its window; Mac OS X displays only aliases for now, but when you burn the disc, the actual files and folders will be there.

If you open the burn folder, you find an unusual strip across the top. Its most important feature is the Burn button at the right.

Bottom: Ready to proceed, Captain.

When You Have a Blank Disc on Hand

If you have a blank disc ready to go, burning is even simpler.

Start by inserting the disc. After a moment, the Mac displays a dialog box asking, in effect, what you want to do with this blank disc (unless you've fiddled with your preference settings). See Figure 9-13 for instructions.

If you choose Open Finder, the disc's icon appears on the desktop after a moment; its icon also appears in the Sidebar, complete with the Burn symbol (✪).

At this point, you can begin dragging files and folders onto the disc's icon, or (if you double-click the icon) into its window. You can add, remove, reorganize, and rename the files on it just as you would in any standard Finder window. All you're really doing is dragging aliases (file shortcuts) around; the real files are left untouched on your hard drive. You can also rename the CD or DVD itself just as you would a file or folder.

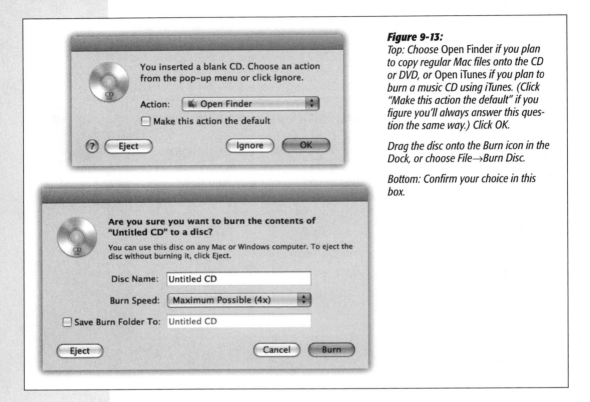

Figure 9-13:
Top: Choose Open Finder *if you plan to copy regular Mac files onto the CD or DVD, or* Open iTunes *if you plan to burn a music CD using iTunes. (Click "Make this action the default" if you figure you'll always answer this question the same way.) Click OK.*

Drag the disc onto the Burn icon in the Dock, or choose File→Burn Disc.

Bottom: Confirm your choice in this box.

When the disc's icon contains the files and folders you want to immortalize, do one of these things:

- Choose File→Burn [the disc's name].

- Click the ☢ button next to the disc's name in the Sidebar.

- Click the Burn button in the upper-right corner of the disc's window.

- Drag the disc's icon toward the Trash icon in the Dock. As soon as you begin to drag, the Trash icon turns into the yellow ☢ logo. Drop the disc's icon onto it.

- Control-click (or right-click) the disc's icon; from the shortcut menu, choose Burn [the disc's name].

In any case, the dialog box shown at bottom in Figure 9-13 now appears. Click Burn. When the recording process is over, you'll have yourself a DVD or CD that works in any other Mac or PC.

The discs that your Mac burns work equally well on Macs and Windows (or Linux) PCs. If you plan to insert a CD or DVD into a PC, however, remember that Windows doesn't permit certain symbols in a Windows filename (\ / : * ? " < > |). You'll run into trouble if any of your file names contain these symbols. In fact, you won't be able to open any folders on your disc that contain illegally named files.

iTunes: The Digital Jukebox

As a Windows veteran, you may already be familiar with iTunes.

This program, which sits in your Applications folder, is the ultimate software jukebox (Figure 9-14). It can play music CDs, tune in to Internet radio stations, load up your iPod music player or iPhone, and play back digital sound files (including the Internet's favorite format, MP3 files) and other popular audio formats. It can also turn selected tracks from your music CDs *into* MP3 files, so that you can store favorite songs on your hard drive to play back anytime—without having to dig up the original.

Figure 9-14:
iTunes has become one of the most popular software programs in the world, because it's useful, it's cross-platform, and, of course, it's free.

It's basically a database that lists all of your music, video, and other playables, but it's full of ways to slice, dice, and export that entertainment to other devices.

iTunes also lets you record your own custom audio CDs that contain only the good songs. Finally, of course, iTunes is the shop window for the online iTunes Store, which sells music, TV shows, and movies.

iTunes can also burn *MP3 CDs:* music CDs that fit much more than the usual 74 or 80 minutes of music onto a disc (because they store songs in MP3 format instead of AIFF). Not all CD players can play MP3 discs, however, and the sound quality is slightly lower than standard CDs.

The first time you run iTunes, you're asked (a) whether you want iTunes to be the program your Mac uses for playing music files from the Internet, (b) whether you want it to ask your permission every time it connects to the Internet, and (c) whether you want the program to scan your Home folder for all music files already on it. (You can decline to have your hard drive scanned at this time. Later, you can always drag it, or any other folder, directly into the iTunes window for automatic scanning.)

Tip: The following pages present a mini-manual on iTunes. For the full scoop, plus coverage of the iPod and the iTunes Store, consult *iPod: The Missing Manual.*

By now, the layout of iTunes should look familiar: a Source list at the left side, acting as a table of contents for the larger window to the right. It's the same layout used in Finder windows (the Sidebar), iPhoto, Image Capture, and other Apple programs.

The major headings in iTunes's list are Library, Store, Devices, Shared, Genius, and Playlists. Here's what they do:

Library

The items in this list represent all your music and videos: Music, Movies, TV Shows, Podcasts, and so on. They include both your own stuff—songs you copied off of music CDs, for example—and material you bought from the iTunes Store online.

Note: When you first open iTunes, it offers to search your hard drive for the kinds of files it can play—every song in formats like MP3, AIFF, WAV, AAC, and Apple Lossless, for example. It then copies all such files into your Home folder→Music→iTunes→iTunes Music folder. But you don't ever need to muck around in there; use iTunes to manage your collection instead.

FREQUENTLY ASKED QUESTION

Auto-Playing Music CDs

How do I make my Mac play music CDs automatically when they're inserted?

First, make sure iTunes is slated to open automatically when you insert a music CD. You do that on the CDs & DVDs panel of System Preferences (use the "When you insert a music CD" pop-up menu).

Then all you have to do is make sure iTunes knows to begin playing automatically once it launches. Choose iTunes→Preferences, click the General icon, and from the On CD Insert pop-up menu, choose Begin Playing. Click OK.

From now on, whenever you insert a music CD, iTunes will launch automatically and begin playing.

When you click Music, the main iTunes window is organized much like a Finder window, with columns indicating the song length, artist, album, and so on. As always, you can rearrange these columns by dragging their headings, sort your list by one of these criteria by clicking its heading, reverse the sorting order by clicking the heading a second time, and so on.

Or click one of the three View buttons next to the Search box to display your music as either a grid of thumbnail album covers—or as Cover Flow, which lets you flip through album covers as though they're sitting in a record-store bin.

To find a particular song or video, just type a few letters into the Spotlight-ish Search box above the list. iTunes hides all but the ones that match.

Store

The iTunes Store is easy to figure out. By clicking the tabs across the top of the window, you can search or browse for music (over 11 million songs, classical pieces, and comedy routines); movies (8,000 and counting); TV shows ($2 an episode, with no ads, from over 500 series); iPhone apps (85,000); free podcasts (75,000); audiobooks (30,000); and more. Sure, you may go broke, but at least you'll be entertained.

Besides, there are no monthly fees, and your downloads don't go *poof!* into the ether if you decide to cancel your subscription, as they do with some rival services.

Use the Search Music Store box (top-right corner) to find the songs or performers you're interested in. Double-click a song or video to hear or view a 30-second excerpt. (For audiobooks, you get a 90-second excerpt.)

If you decide to buy a song, you need an Apple account. Click the Sign In button (upper right) and then Create New Account to get started. (If you've ever bought or registered an Apple product on the company's Web site, signed up for AppleCare, ordered an iPhoto book, or have a MobileMe membership, you have an Apple Account already. All you have to do is remember your name—usually your email address—and password.)

When you click the Buy button next to a song's name, iTunes downloads it to your Mac. Behind the scenes, it goes into your Home→Music→iTunes Music folder. But for your purposes, it shows up in the Store→Purchased category in the Source list for convenient access.

Devices

These icons represent other gadgets that iTunes can talk to. If you insert a CD, it shows up here. If you attach an iPod or iPhone, its icon appears here, too. An Apple TV, if you have one, also appears here. Click any one of these icons to see what's on it.

And if you don't have *any* of these things attached, the Devices category doesn't appear at all.

Shared

If you've taken the trouble to set up a home network, you can share songs and playlists with up to five networked computers. You could, for example, tap into your roommates' jazz collection without getting up from your desk, and they can sample the zydeco and tejano tunes from your World Beat playlist. The music you decide to share is streamed over the network to the other computer. In fact, you can even *copy* songs and videos from one machine to the other, so you can enjoy them even when the original computer is turned off.

Note: This Home Share feature even works between Macs and PCs.

To get started, sit at Computer A. Click Home Sharing in the Source list. You're asked for your Apple account information. Click Create Home Share and then Done.

Now, if you open iTunes on Computer B, you'll see Computer A listed in the Shared category at left. Click it to see what's in its copy of iTunes. You can play that stuff—even sitting at Computer B—and even copy it to Computer A. (Just drag the songs or videos you want into the appropriate category—Music, Movies, TV Shows, and so on—at the top of your Source list.)

Note: There's some fine print. Up to five computers can do this Home Share business. They all have to sign in with the same Apple account, and they all have to be on the same network (meaning inside the same building).

Genius

Genius, according to Apple, assembles lists of "songs that sound great together," whatever that means. (It seems to mean "songs that have the same degree of rockiness").

To get started, choose Store→Turn On Genius (unless it's already on). Click a song in your library that you want to serve as the anchor—the "seed" song—that you want to match. Then proceed in one of these three ways:

- **Create a Genius playlist.** Click the ✳ button at lower right. Presto: a new playlist, filed in your Source list under Genius. (Its name is Genius. Pure genius!) Play it to see how iTunes did at matching your original song's feel.

  At the top of the window, you can use the Limit To pop-up menu to specify how many songs are in this playlist; the Refresh button to try again matching your "seed" song; or the Save Playlist button to turn this iTunes guess into a proper playlist.

- **Create a Genius Mix.** There's also such a thing as a Genius *Mix,* which, unlike a playlist, never ends. It's more like a radio station, eternally plucking songs from your collection that all match each other (or, as Apple would say, "sound great together"). Just click Genius Mixes in the Source list; you'll see a couple of starter mixes to get you going. Click one to hear it.

- **Shop for Genius suggestions.** If you click a song name, and then click the tiny, boxed ▶ button to the *right* of the ✳ button, you get a new Genius panel hugging the right side of the iTunes window. It shows other songs and albums from the iTunes store that Apple thinks you'd like, based on whatever song you clicked.

Playlists

Apple recognizes that you may not want to listen to *all* your songs every time you need some tunes. That's why iTunes lets you create *playlists*—folders in the Source list that contain, and play back, only certain songs (or videos). In effect, you can devise your own albums, like one called Party Tunes, another called Blind Date Music, and so on.

Creating playlists

To create a new playlist, click the **+** button in the lower-left corner of the window, or choose File→New Playlist (⌘-N). Alternatively, if you've already highlighted certain songs—by ⌘-clicking them or Shift-clicking them—you can choose File→New Playlist From Selection.

A new playlist appears as an icon in the Source list. You can rename this playlist by double-clicking it, and add songs to it by dragging them out of the main list into the icon.

Tip: Deleting a song from a playlist doesn't delete it from the Library (or your hard drive). Similarly, it's fine to add the same song to as many different playlists as you like, since you're not actually increasing the size of your Library. (You might be starting to pick up a running theme in Apple's software. Playlists work just like albums in iPhoto, or the Sidebar in the Finder.)

Smart playlists

Smart playlists constantly rebuild themselves according to criteria you specify. You might tell one smart playlist to assemble 45 minutes' worth of songs you've rated higher than four stars but rarely listen to, and another to list your most-often-played songs from the '80s.

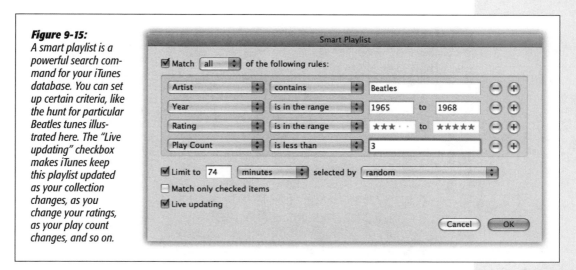

Figure 9-15:
A smart playlist is a powerful search command for your iTunes database. You can set up certain criteria, like the hunt for particular Beatles tunes illustrated here. The "Live updating" checkbox makes iTunes keep this playlist updated as your collection changes, as you change your ratings, as your play count changes, and so on.

Tip: To rate a song, make the window wide enough that you can see the Rating column. (If you don't see this column, Control-click any column heading and choose Rating from the list of options.) Then just click the Rating column for a selected song. The appropriate number of stars appears—one, two, three, four, or five—depending on the position of your click. You can change a song's rating as many times as you like—a good thing, considering the short shelf life of a pop hit these days.

To make a smart playlist, choose File→New Smart Playlist (Option-⌘-N)—or just Option-click the **+** button beneath the Source list. The dialog box shown in Figure 9-16 appears. The controls here are designed to set up a search of your music database. Figure 9-15, for example, illustrates how you'd find up to 74 Beatles tunes released between 1965 and 1968—that you've rated three stars or higher and that you've listened to fewer than three times.

When you click OK, your smart playlist is ready to show off. When you click its name in the Source list, the main song list updates itself according to your criteria and any changes in your music collection. (Smart playlists get transferred to your iPod or iPhone but don't continue to update themselves there.)

Audio CDs

If you insert a music CD while iTunes is open, the songs on it immediately show up in the list.

At first, they may appear with the exciting names "Track 01," "Track 02," and so on. But after a moment, iTunes connects to the Internet and compares your CD with the listings at *www.gracenote.com*, a global database of music CDs and their contents. If it finds a match among the thousands of CDs there, it copies the album and song names into iTunes, where they reappear every time you use this particular CD.

Done

Stop ripping

In progress

Figure 9-16:
Watch the display at the top of the window to see how long the conversion is going to take, and which song iTunes is working on. As iTunes finishes processing each song, you see a small, circled checkmark next to its name in the main list to remind you that you've got it on board and no longer need the CD in your machine.

You can play the CD just as you would anything else in iTunes: by tapping the space bar, for example.

Tip: If you connect an iTunes-compatible portable MP3 player to your Mac (the iPod isn't the only one), its name, too, shows up in the left-side Source list. You can add songs to your player (by dragging them onto its icon), rename or reorder them, and so on.

Copying (ripping) CD songs to your hard drive

Once you copy your favorite audio CDs onto your hard drive, you can play them whenever you like, without the original CD.

To *rip* a CD (as aficionados would say) like this, make sure that only the songs you want to capture have checkmarks in the main list. Choose a format for the files you're about to create, if you like—MP3, for example, or AAC (better quality/size tradeoff, but less compatible with other gadgets)—by clicking the Import Settings button (Figure 9-16). Finally, click the Import CD button at the lower-right corner of the window.

When it's all over, you'll find the imported songs listed in your Library. (Click Music in the left-side Source list.) From there, you can drag them into any other "folder" (playlist), as described above.

The iPod and iPhone

Unless you're just off the shuttle from Alpha Centauri, you probably already know that the iPod is Apple's tiny, elegant music player. It, and its cellular pal the iPhone, are designed to integrate seamlessly with iTunes.

All you have to do is connect the iPod or iPhone to the Mac via its white USB cable. The gadget's icon shows up in the iTunes Source list. Click its icon to view its contents—and click the tabs (Music, TV Shows, Podcasts, and so on) to specify what Mac material you'd like copied over to it.

Playing with Playback

To play a song or video, double-click it. Or click iTunes's Play button (▶) or press the space bar. The Mac immediately begins to play the songs whose names have checkmarks in the main list (Figure 9-16), or the CD that's currently in your Mac.

Tip: The central display at the top of the window shows not only the name of the song and album, but also where you are in the song, as represented by the diamond in the horizontal strip. Drag this diamond, or click elsewhere in the strip, to jump around in the song.

To view the current music's sound levels, click the tiny triangle at the left side of this display to see a pulsing VU meter, indicating the various frequencies.

As music plays, you can control and manipulate the music and the visuals of your Mac in all kinds of interesting ways. Some people don't move from their Macs for months at a time.

Turning on visuals

Visuals are onscreen light shows that pulse, beat, and dance in sync to the music. The effect is hypnotic and wild. (For real party fun, invite some people who grew up in the '60s to your house to watch.)

To summon this psychedelic display, choose View→Turn On Visuals, or just press ⌘-T. The show begins immediately—although it's much more fun if you choose View→Full Screen (⌘-F) so the show takes over your whole monitor. True, you won't get a lot of work done, but when it comes to stress relief, visuals are a lot cheaper than a hot tub.

GEM IN THE ROUGH

Internet Radio and Podcasts

Audio CDs and MP3 files aren't the only sources of musical and spoken sound you can listen to as you work. iTunes also lets you tune in to hundreds of Internet-based radio stations, which may turn out to be the most convenient music source of all. They're free, they play 24 hours a day, and their music collections make yours look like a drop in the bucket. You can also download and listen to podcasts, which are like home-made (sometimes *very* homemade), Web-distributed personal radio shows.

For radio, click Radio in the left-side Source list. (If you don't see Radio there, choose iTunes→Preferences→ General, and turn on Radio.)

In the main list, if you're connected to the Internet, you'll see categories like Blues, Classic Rock, Classical, and so on. Click the flippy triangle to see a list of Internet radio stations in that category.

When you see one that looks interesting, double-click it. (The higher the number in the Bit Rate column, the better the sound quality.) Wait a moment for your Mac to connect to

the appropriate Internet site, and then let the music begin!

Without add-on shareware, there's no easy way to capture Internet broadcasts or save them onto your hard drive. You can, however, drag a radio station's name into the Music list (in the Source list), or even a playlist, to make it easier to access later on.

If you discover other Internet radio stations that sound interesting, choose Advanced→Open Stream, type in the station's Web address (URL), and press Return.

To grab a podcast, click iTunes Store in the Source list. At the top of the screen, click Podcasts. Now iTunes lets you browse a vast list of available podcasts. When you click one that looks promising, you'll see that you can either listen to it on the spot, or—and here's the real fun—click Subscribe.

Once you do that, a new icon called Podcasts appears in your Source list; click it to find the latest episodes of the podcasts you've subscribed to. Sync those babies to your iPod or iPhone, and you've got interesting material—or, at least fresh material—to listen to every day of the week.

If you investigate the View→Visualizer submenu, you'll see that iTunes comes with six different screeensavery modules. Each one has secret keystrokes that trigger secret functions. Press the ? key to see a tiny cheat sheet of the available keyboard commands.

Keyboard control

You can control iTunes' music playback using its menus, of course, but the keyboard can be far more efficient. Here are a few of the control keystrokes worth noting:

Function	Keystroke
Play, Pause	space bar or ▶❚❚ key
Next song/previous song	↑, ↓ or ←, →
Louder, quieter	⌘-↑, ⌘-↓
Rewind, fast-forward	◀◀, ▶▶ keys (or Option-⌘-←, Option-⌘-→)
Eject the CD	⌘-E
Turn Visuals on	⌘-T
Turn Visuals off	⌘-T or mouse click
Full-screen visuals	⌘-F
Exit full-screen visuals	⌘-T, ⌘-F, Esc, or mouse click

Tip: You can also control CD playback from the Dock. Control-click (or right-click) the iTunes icon to produce a pop-up menu offering playback commands like Pause, Next Song, and Previous Song, along with a display that identifies the song currently being played.

Preventing ear-blast syndrome

Here's a clever touch: In iTunes→Preferences→Playback, you see a checkbox called Sound Check. Its function is to keep the playback volume of all songs within the same

---

WORKAROUND WORKSHOP

iPod Independence

Out of the box, the iPod and iTunes come set for automatic synchronization. That is, as soon as you hook them together, iTunes sends your complete music library (the contents of your Library "folder" in iTunes) to the iPod. The iPod's songs and playlists always match the Mac's.

Apple's idea here was to ensure that you don't use the iPod as a convenient piracy machine. Your iPod gets its music from your Mac, it but can't put its songs *onto* a Mac.

At least that's the theory. But what if your hard drive self-destructs, vaporizing the 945 MP3 files that you've made from your paid-for CD collection? You legally own those

copies. Shouldn't you have the right to retrieve them from your own iPod?

If you believe the answer is yes, a quick search at *www. versiontracker.com* for the word "iPod" will bring up a list of programs like Senuti (iTunes spelled backward, get it?), which let you copy music from the iPod to the Mac.

These programs know that the name of the super-secret music folder on the iPod, called iPod_Control, is invisible, which is why you can't see it on your desktop without the help of these utilities.

---

basic level so you don't have to adjust the volume to compensate for different recorded levels. (This setting, too, gets transferred to your iPod or iPhone.)

Come to think of it, you could while away quite a few happy afternoons just poking through the Preferences dialog box. It grows richer with every successive version of iTunes.

Playing with the graphic equalizer

If you choose Window→Equalizer, you get a handsome control console that lets you adjust the strength of each musical frequency independently (Figure 9-17).

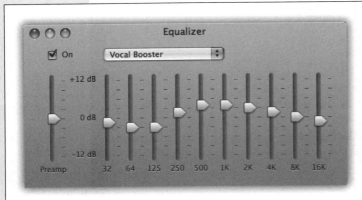

Figure 9-17:
Drag the sliders (bass on the left, treble on the right) to accommodate the strengths and weaknesses of your speakers or headphones (and listening tastes). Or save yourself the trouble— use the pop-up menu above the sliders to choose a canned set of slider positions for Classical, Dance, Jazz, Latin, and so on. These settings even transfer to the iPod.

Burning Music CDs

iTunes can record selected sets of songs, no matter what the original sources, onto a blank CD. When it's all over, you can play the burned CD on a standard CD player, just as you would a CD from the record store—but this time, you hear only the songs you like, in the order you like, with all the annoying ones eliminated.

Start by creating a playlist for the CD you're about to make. Click its icon in the left-side Source list to see the list you've built. Drag songs up or down in the list to change their playback order. Keep these points in mind:

- The readout at the bottom of the list shows how much time the songs will take.

- About 74 or 80 minutes of regular audio files fit on one CD. But if you make an *MP3 CD*, you can fit at least 10 times as much—12 hours of music on a single disc!

  The fine print: Not all CD players can play MP3 CDs (check the manual or the side of the CD player's box). Also note that your MP3 CD can't include songs you've bought on Apple's iTunes music store; iTunes won't convert them into the MP3 format.

  To burn an MP3 CD, see Figure 9-18.

- You can control how many seconds of silence iTunes leaves between tracks on your custom CD, too. Use the Gap Between Songs pop-up menu shown in Figure 9-18.

When everything is set up, click the Burn Disc button in the playlist window. Specify your CD options (Figure 9-18), insert a blank CD into the Mac, and go read a book; the burning process takes some time. Feel free to work in other programs while iTunes chugs away.

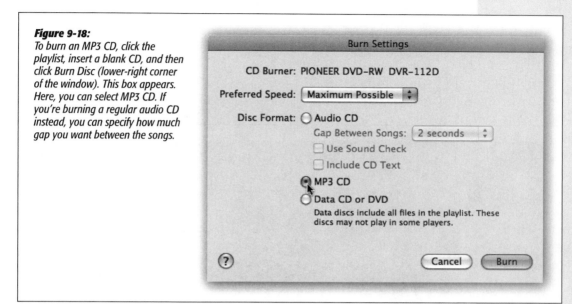

Figure 9-18:
To burn an MP3 CD, click the playlist, insert a blank CD, and then click Burn Disc (lower-right corner of the window). This box appears. Here, you can select MP3 CD. If you're burning a regular audio CD instead, you can specify how much gap you want between the songs.

DVD Movies

Watching movies on your Mac screen couldn't be simpler: Just insert a movie DVD. The Mac detects that it's a video DVD (as opposed to, say, one that's just filled with files). Then, unless you've fiddled with your preference settings, the DVD Player program opens and begins playing the movie in full-screen mode. (Even the menu bar disappears. To make it reappear, move your cursor to near the top of the screen.)

Note: If DVD Player doesn't open automatically when you insert a DVD movie, you can open it yourself. It's sitting there in your Applications folder. (Then fix the problem, using the CDs & DVDs panel of System Preferences.)

Playing a Movie

Once DVD Player starts playing your movie, you can move your mouse to the bottom of the screen, at any time, to bring up the control bar, which is deconstructed in Figure 9-19.

Or just use the keyboard controls, which appear here in this clip 'n' save cheat sheet:

Function	Keystroke
Play, Pause	space bar or ▶॥ key
Fast-forward, rewind	◀◀, ▶▶ (or Shift ⌘-→, Shift-⌘-←); press repeatedly to multiply the speed of scanning
Skip forward/back 5 seconds	Option-⌘-→, Option-⌘-←
Louder, quieter	⌘-↑, ⌘-↓
Mute/Unmute	Option-⌘-↓
Next/previous "chapter"	→, ←
Full-screen mode on/off	⌘-F
Half, normal, maximum size	⌘-1, -2, -3
Eject	⌘-E
Add a bookmark	⌘-= (equal sign)

Figure 9-19:
Top: Even in full-screen mode, you can control the playback and navigate the disc using the translucent pop-up control bar.

Don't miss the scrubber bar at the very bottom. It lets you scroll directly to any spot in the DVD.

Bottom: When you're not in full-screen mode, you get a separate, floating "remote control." It has most of the same controls, but they're arranged with a more 1999 sort of design aesthetic.

Scrubber bar

Languages, Subtitles

Eject DVD

Click to see elasped time/ time remaining

Picture controls

Exit full screen

Slo Mo
Frame Advance
Return to Movie

Subtitles
Language
Angle

Previous chapter/Next chapter
(Hold to scan backward/forward)

Language Fun

Most Hollywood DVDs have been programmed with onscreen subtitles to help those with hearing impairments and people sitting in noisy bars. The Subtitle button offers a pop-up menu of alternative languages and subtitle options.

Tip: For real fun, turn on English subtitles but switch the soundtrack to a foreign language. No matter how trashy the movie you're watching, you'll gain much more respect from your friends and family when you tell them you're watching a foreign film.

Chapter Thumbnails

A standard Hollywood DVD comes programmed with chapters—invisible markers that let you jump from one important scene beginning to the next. To see them in DVD Player, just move your mouse to the top of the screen. A row of chapter thumbnail images appears, which you can click to jump around in.

Parental Controls

The parental controls in DVD Player aren't much. You can't say, for example, "Don't play anything rated PG-13 or above"; you have to rate each DVD yourself, one at a time. But they're better than nothing.

Insert the DVD you're worried about. Choose File→Get Disk Info. Click the Parental Controls tab.

Click the 🔒 button and enter your administrator's password. (Unless, of course, your 8-year-old is the administrator of this Mac instead of you, in which case this DVD is the least of your problems.)

Now you can select either "Always ask for authorization" or "Always allow to be played," depending on your feelings about the movie. Click OK.

All you've done so far, however, is to specify what happens when you turn on parental controls—and you haven't done that yet. Choosing Features→Enable Parental Control does the trick.

When parental control is turned on, nobody's allowed to watch the "Always ask for authorization" DVDs *unless* they correctly input your administrator's password.

Which nobody knows except you. (Right?)

The Big Picture

Now, watching a movie while sitting in front of your Mac is not exactly the great American movie-watching dream. Fortunately, every recent Mac model has a video-output jack; with the proper cables, you can connect the Mac to your TV for a much more comfortable movie-watching experience.

Just be sure to connect the cable *directly* to the TV. If you connect it to your VCR instead, you'll probably get a horrible, murky, color-shifting picture—the result of the built-in copy-protection circuitry of every VCR.

Or what the heck—just ask for an Apple TV for your birthday.

Keyboard

As you know by now, switching to the Mac entails switching your brain, especially when it comes to the old keyboard shortcuts. All of those Ctrl-key sequences become, on the Mac, ⌘-key sequences. (Check your Macintosh keyboard: The ⌘ key is right next to the space bar, usually on both sides.)

But plenty of other Mac keys may seem unfamiliar. For your reassurance pleasure, page 22 offers a rundown of what they do.

Text-Navigation Keystrokes

In Windows, you may have grown accustomed to certain common keystrokes for navigating text—key combinations that make the insertion point jump to the beginning or end of a word, line, or document, for example.

Mac OS X programs offer similar navigation keystrokes, as you can see here:

Function	Windows keys	Mac keys
Move to previous/next word	Ctrl+arrow keys	Option-arrow keys
Move to beginning/end of line	Home/End	Home/End*
Move to previous/next paragraph	Ctrl+up/down arrows*	Option-up/down arrows*
Move to top/bottom of window	Home/End	Home/End (but see below)
Select all text	Ctrl+A	⌘-A
Select text, one letter at a time	Shift+arrow keys	Shift-arrow keys
Select text, one word at a time	Ctrl+Shift+arrow keys	Option-Shift-arrow keys
Undo	Ctrl+Z	⌘-Z
Cut, Copy, Paste	Ctrl+X, C, V	⌘-X, C, V
Close window	Alt+F4	⌘-W
Switch open programs	Alt+Tab	⌘-Tab
Hide all windows	⊞+D	F11

* in some programs

Incidentally, the keystroke for jumping to the *top or bottom* of a window varies, depending on the program. You need ⌘-Home/End in Microsoft Word, ⌘-up/down arrow in TextEdit and Stickies, and Home/End in iPhoto and Finder list windows.

Mouse

Most USB mice work as soon as you plug them into your Mac—even two-button, scroll-wheel mice. Using System Preferences, you can even program your spare mouse buttons to invoke cool features like Exposé and the Dashboard.

That's not to say, however, that you shouldn't install your mouse's driver software. If your mouse *came* with such software (or if you find it on the manufacturer's Web site), you may well find that your mouse learns a few new tricks—making its "back" and "forward" buttons work properly in Safari, for example. Otherwise, a shareware program like USB Overdrive ($20, from *www.usboverdrive.com*) can unlock those features.

(For more on Mac mice, see page 13.)

Monitors

Your Mac can use standard monitors of the type found in the Windows world. Every Macintosh can drive *multiple* screens at the same time, too, meaning that you can generally use your old PC screen either as your Mac's main monitor or as a second, external screen.

If one of those arrangements appeals to you, the only complication might be the connector. Most PC screens, of course, have a standard VGA connector (or a more modern DVI connector) at the tip of their tails. Over the years, however, Apple has "standardized" on enough different screen-plug types to fill a catalog. There's been DVI, Mini-DVI, Micro-DVI, Mini DisplayPort—you get the idea.

For the proper fee, Apple will be happy to sell you whatever adapter cable you need to accommodate the monitor you've got.

Tip: It's even possible to connect *both* your Mac and your PC to the *same* monitor, and switch from one to the other at will. If this arrangement appeals to you, you'll need a so-called KVM switch (which also lets you switch your keyboard and mouse between your two computers). You can find KVM switches for sale at electronics stores, and online from manufacturers like Belkin (*www.belkin.com*).

In any case, once you've hooked up a second monitor or a projector, you can turn Mirroring on or off. Mirroring is when both screens show the same thing—a handy setup in classroom situations; turning it off lets one screen act as additional real estate, an annex to the first. (If you're giving a PowerPoint or Keynote slideshow , you might also want to turn off Mirroring so that your laptop's screen shows your private speaker notes, while the audience's screen shows only your luscious bullet points.)

You specify which mode you want using the Displays pane of System Preferences, or using the Displays menu-bar icon.

Time Machine Backups

As the old saying goes, there are two kinds of people: those who have a regular backup system—and those who *will*.

You'll get that grisly joke immediately if you've ever known the pain that comes with deleting the wrong folder by accident, or making changes that you regret, or worst of all, having your hard drive die. All those photos, all that music you've bought online, all your email—gone.

Yet the odds are overwhelming that, at this moment, you do not have a complete, current, automated backup of your Mac. Despite about a thousand warnings, articles, and cautionary tales a year, guess how many do? About *4 percent.* Everybody else is flying without a net.

If you don't have much to back up—you don't have much in the way of photos, music, or movies—you can get by with burning copies of stuff onto blank CDs or DVDs (Chapter 5) or using the MobileMe Backup program described in Chapter 10. But those methods leave most of your Mac unprotected: all your programs and settings, not to mention Mac OS X itself.

What you really want, of course, is a backup that's rock-solid, complete, and *automatic.* You don't want to have to remember to do a backup, to insert a tape, to find a cartridge. You just want to know that you're safe.

That's the idea behind Time Machine, a marquee feature of Mac OS X. It's a silent, set-it-and-forget-it piece of peace of mind. You sleep easy, knowing there's a safety copy of your *entire* system: your system files, programs, settings, music, pictures, videos, document files—*everything.* If your luck runs out, you'll be *so* happy you set Time Machine up.

Setting up Time Machine

Here's the bad news: Time Machine requires a second hard drive. That's the only way to create a completely safe, automatic backup of your *entire* main hard drive.

That second hard drive can take any of these forms:

- An external USB or FireWire hard drive.

- An Apple Time Capsule. That's an AirPort wireless base station/network backup hard drive in one; it's available in gigantic capacities.

Tip: The Time Capsule also shows up as a hard drive on the screen of your Windows machines, which means that it's another handy way to copy files back and forth between the PC and the Mac. Just use the Time Capsule as a temporary parking place for them on their way between computers. (The Time Capsule comes with a setup CD just for Windows.)

- Another internal hard drive.

- A partition of any one of those drives.

- The hard drive of another Leopard or Snow Leopard Mac on the network. You must first mount its drive on your screen (Chapter 14).

Tip: It's perfectly OK to back up several computers onto the same external hard drive, as long as it's got enough room. You can also back up onto a hard drive that has other stuff on it, although of course that means you'll have less room for Time Machine backups.

In all cases, the backup disk must be bigger than the drive you're backing up (preferably *much* bigger).

Here's what you *can't* use as the backup disk: an iPod, an iDisk, a removable disk (like a CD or flash drive), or your startup drive.

Note: The backup drive must be a standard Mac-formatted hard drive. That's a gotcha that befalls many a Mac fan who buys a new hard drive for backup purposes; many new drives come in Windows format, which Time Machine doesn't recognize.

To make a new, empty drive like this ready for Time Machine, open Disk Utility (page 560). Click the drive's name, click the Erase tab, choose Mac OS Extended (Journaled) from the Volume Format pop-up menu, and then click Erase.

Sure, it sounds like an Apple plot to sell more hard drives. But you'd be surprised at how cheap hard drives are. At this writing, you can buy a 1-*terabyte* hard drive (1,000 gigabytes) for $75, for goodness' sake—and hard drive prices-per-gigabyte go only down.

The first time the Mac sees your second hard drive, it invites you to use it as Time Machine's backup drive (Figure 9-20, top). That could be the moment you connect an external drive, or the first time you turn on the Mac after installing an internal drive.

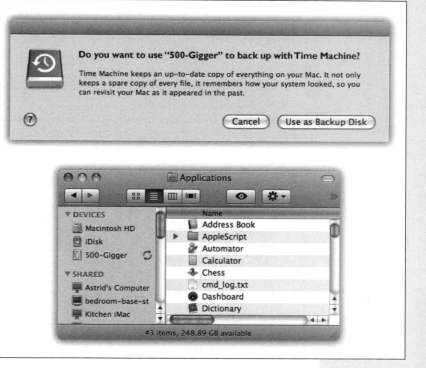

Figure 9-20:
Top: The Mac has just encountered a second hard drive. Time Machine still works if there's other stuff on the drive, but life is simpler if you don't use that drive for anything but Time Machine. The more space Time Machine has to work with, the further back in time you'll be able to go to recover deleted or mangled files.

Bottom: The backup has begun. You know that because you see both a progress message and the ↻ symbol that appears next to the backup drive's name in your Sidebar.

If you click Use as Backup Disk, you're taken immediately to the Time Machine pane of System Preferences (Figure 9-21). It shows that Time Machine is now on, your backup disk has been selected, and the copying process has begun. The Mac copies *everything* on your hard drive, including Mac OS X itself, all your programs, and everyone's Home folders.

Figure 9-21:
Use the big On/Off switch to shut off all Time Machine activity, although it would be hard to imagine why you'd want to risk it. You can click Change Disk to choose a different hard drive to represent the mirror of your main drive (after the first one is full, for example).

Your total involvement has been *one click*. And that, ladies and gentlemen, is the easiest setup for a backup program in history.

Note: Time Machine doesn't use any compression or encoding; it's copying your files exactly as they sit on your hard drive, for maximum safety and recoverability. On the other hand, it does save some space on the backup drive, because it doesn't bother copying cache files, temporary files, and other files you'll never need to restore.

Now go away and let the Mac do its thing. The first backup can take hours as the Mac duplicates your entire internal hard drive onto the second drive (Figure 9-20, bottom). The Mac may feel drugged during this time.

How the Backups Work

From now on, Time Machine quietly and automatically checks your Mac once per hour. If any file, folder, or setting has changed, it gets backed up at the end of the hour. These follow-up backups, of course, take very little time, since Time Machine backs up only what's changed.

So, should disaster strike, the only files you can lose are those you've changed within the past 59 minutes.

Tip: And even then, you can force more frequent backups if you want to. Just choose Back Up Now from the Time Machine menulet. Or choose Back Up Now from the shortcut menu of the Dock's Time Machine icon.

You can pause the backup the same way—if you need to use the backup drive for another quick task, for example. Open System Preferences→Time Machine and turn the big switch Off. Don't forget to turn the backing-up on again when you're finished.

Declaring Stuff Off-Limits to Time Machine

The whole point of Time Machine, of course, is to have a backup of your *entire* hard drive. That's how most people use it.

It's conceivable, though, that you might want to exclude some files or folders from the Time Machine treatment. There are two reasons.

First, you might not want certain, ahem, *private* materials to be part of your incriminating data trail.

Second, you might want to save space on the backup drive, either because it's not as big as your main drive or because you'd rather dedicate its space to *more* backups of the *essential* stuff. For example, you might decide not to back up your collection of downloaded TV shows, since video files are enormous. Or maybe you use an online photo-sharing Web site as a backup for all your photos, so you don't think it's necessary to include those in the Time Machine backup.

To eliminate certain icons from the backup, open the Time Machine panel of System Preferences. Click Options.

In the resulting list, click the + button; navigate your hard drive, and then select the files or folders you don't want backed up. Or just find their actual icons in the Finder and *drag* them into the list here. (Use the — button to *remove* items from the list, thereby excluding them from the excluded list.)

If you're strapped for disk space, one logical candidate to exclude is the System folder on your main hard drive—that is, Mac OS X itself. After all, if you lose your hard drive, you already *have* a copy of Mac OS X: the original installation DVD. (Of course, it doesn't have all the Apple updates that may have come out since the original version.)

When you add the System folder to the exclusion list, Time Machine makes another space-saving offer: "Would you like to also exclude other files installed with Mac OS X, such as system applications and UNIX tools?"

Agreeing (by clicking Exclude All System Files) saves you another several gigabytes of backup space.

By the end of the day, you'll have 24 hourly backups on that second disk, all taking up space. So at day's end, Time Machine replaces that huge stash with a single *daily* backup. You can no longer rewind your system to 3:00 p.m. last Monday, but you can rewind to the way it was at the *end* of that day.

Similarly, after a month, Time Machine replaces all those 30 dailies (for example) with four weekly backups. Now you may not be able to rewind to October 24, but you can rewind to November 1. (Apple assumes it won't take you a whole week to notice that your hard drive has crashed.)

Tip: You can see these backups, if you want. Open your backup drive, open the Backups.backupdb folder, and open the folder named for your computer. Inside, you'll find a huge list of backup folders, bearing names like 2010-03-22-155831. That's the backup from March 22, 2010 at 15:58 (that is, 3:58 p.m.) and 31 seconds.

The point is that Time Machine doesn't just keep *one* copy of your stuff. It keeps *multiple* backups. It remembers how things were in every folder—not just yesterday, but last week, last month, and so on. It keeps on making new snapshots of your hard drive until the backup drive is full.

At that point, the oldest ones get deleted to make room for new ones.

By the way, if a backup is interrupted—if you shut down the Mac, put it to sleep, or take your laptop on the road—no big deal. Time Machine resumes automatically the next time you're home and connected.

FREQUENTLY ASKED QUESTION

The End of Time

What happens when my backup drive gets full?

Good question.

The whole idea of Time Machine is that it preserves multiple backups, so that you can rewind a window or a drive not just to *a* backup, but to *any* date in the past. The bigger the hard drive, the farther back those monthly backups are preserved.

Eventually, of course, your backup drive runs out of space. At that point, Time Machine notifies you and offers you a choice.

You can keep using that drive; Time Machine will begin

deleting the oldest backups to make room for newer ones.

Or you can install a new Time Machine backup drive. New backups will go on that one; your older backups will still be available on the original drive.

If you ever need to retrieve files or folders from the older disk, right-click the Time Machine icon in the Dock; from the shortcut menu, choose Browse Other Time Machine Disks. In the list of disks, choose the older one. Then click the Time Machine icon on the Dock to enter the Restore mode.

Changing Time Machine Settings

Time Machine has four faces. There's the application itself, which sits in your Applications folder; open it only when you want to enter Restore mode. There's its Dock icon, which also enters Restore mode, but which has a shortcut menu containing useful commands like Back Up Now (and Stop Backing Up).

There's the Time Machine menulet, which may be the handiest of all. It identifies the time and date of the most recent backup; offers Back Up Now/Stop Backing Up commands; and has direct access to Time Machine's restore mode and preferences pane.

Finally, there's its System Preferences pane, where you adjust its settings (Figure 9-22). To see it, choose →System Preferences→Time Machine. Or choose Time Machine Preferences from Time Machine's Dock icon or menulet.

Recovering Lost or Changed Files

All right, you've got Time Machine on the job. You sleep easy at night, confident that your life's in order—and your stuff's backed up.

Then, one day, it happens: Your hard drive crashes. Or you can't find a file or folder you know you had. Or you save a document and then wish you could go back to an earlier draft. Some kind of disaster—sunspots, clueless spouse, overtired self—has befallen your files. This is Time Machine's big moment.

Start by pinpointing what you're looking for, in one of these two ways:

- Open the disk or folder window where the missing or changed item was.

- Type what you're looking for into the Search box at the top of any Finder window. Click the location button that makes the most sense: "This Mac" or the name of the window you're in.

 In the case of deleted files or folders, the search will probably come up empty; that's totally OK.

Now click the Time Machine icon on the Dock, or choose Enter Time Machine from the menulet (Figure 9-22, top). Don't look away; you'll miss the show.

Your desktop *slides down the screen* like a curtain that's been dropped from above. And it reveals…outer space. This is it, the ultimate Apple eye candy: an animated starry universe, with bits of stardust and meteors occasionally flying outward from the massive nebula at the center.

Front and center is your Finder window—or, rather, dozens of them, stretching back in time (Figure 9-22, bottom). Each is a snapshot of that window at the time of a Time Machine backup.

You have four ways to peruse your backup universe:

- Click individual windows to see what's in them.

- Drag your cursor through the timeline at the right side. It's like a master dial that flies through the windows into the past.

• Click one of the two big, flat perspective arrows. The one pointing into the past means "Jump directly to the most recent window version that's *different* from the way it is right now."

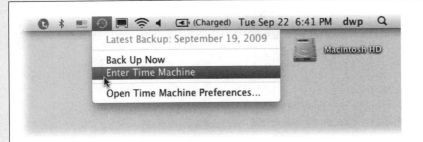

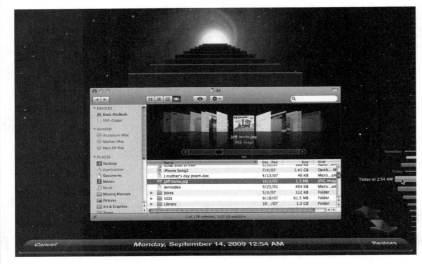

Figure 9-22:
Top: Choose Enter Time Machine from the menulet. (If you don't see this menulet, turn on "Show Time Machine status in the menu bar," shown in Figure 9-21.)

Bottom: This is the big payoff for all your efforts. The familiar desktop slides down, dropping away like a curtain. For the first time, you get to see what's been behind the desktop all this time. Turns out it's outer space. Time Machine shows you dozens of copies of the Finder window, representing its condition at each backup, stretching back to the past.

In other words, it's often a waste of time to go flipping through the windows one at a time, because your missing or changed file might have been missing or changed for the past 25 backups (or whatever). What you want to know is the last time the contents of this window *changed*. And that's what the big flat arrows do. They jump from one *changed* version of this window to another. (Or, if you began with a search, the arrow takes you to the most recent version backup with a matching result.)

• Use the Search box in the corner of the window. You can search for whatever you're missing in the current backup.

As you go, the very bottom of the screen identifies where you are in time—that is, which backup you're examining.

Tip: OK, it's all very dazzling and all. But if you're technically inclined, you don't have to sit still for the big show. Just open the backup disk itself, whose icon appears on your desktop. Inside, you'll find nested folders, neatly representing every computer, every backup, every day and every hour—which you can rummage through by hand.

In many ways, the recovery mode is just like the Finder. You can't actually open, edit, rename, or reorganize anything here. But you can use Quick Look (page 59) to inspect the documents, to make sure you've got the right version. And you can use icon, list, column, or Cover Flow view to sort through the files you're seeing.

If you're trying to recover an older *version* of a file or folder, highlight it and then click the flat arrow button that's pointing away from you; Time Machine skips back to the most recent version that's *different* from the current one.

If you're trying to restore a deleted file or folder that you've now located, highlight it and then click Restore (lower-right). The Mac OS X desktop rises again from the bottom of the screen, there's a moment of copying, and then presto: The lost file or folder is back in the window where it belonged.

Recovering from iPhoto, Address Book, and Mail

The Finder isn't the only program that's hooked into Time Machine's magic. iPhoto, Address Book, and Mail work with Time Machine, too. Other software companies can also revise their own applications to work with it.

In other words, if you want to recover certain photos, addresses, or email messages that have been deleted, you don't start in the Finder; you start in iPhoto, Address Book, or Mail.

Then click the Time Machine icon on the Dock. Once again, you enter the starry recovery mode—but this time, you're facing a strange, disembodied, stripped-down copy of iPhoto, Address Book, or Mail (Figure 9-23).

Tip: Alternatively, in iPhoto, you can also choose File→Browse Backups to enter recovery mode.

You're ready to find your missing data. Click the Jump Back arrow to open the most recent version of your photo library, Address Book file, or email stash that's different from what you've got now. (You can also use the timeline on the right if you remember the date when things went wrong.)

Tip: If you're looking for something particular, specify that before you start clicking. For example, select the iPhoto Event or album first, or type a name into the Address Book search box.

At this point, you can select individual photos (or albums, or events), Address Book entries, or email messages to restore; just click the Restore button.

Often, though, you'd rather reinstate the *entire* iPhoto library, Address Book file, or email collection from the backup. That's what the Restore All button is for.

If you click it, the experience is slightly different. iPhoto asks if you're sure you want to replace your iPhoto library. Address Book may discover a lot of duplicate name-and-address entries and invite you to step through them, deciding which ones "win" (the old or the new).

Note: When you finish restoring in Mail, you'll find the restored messages in the On My Mac→Time Machine→Recovered folder at the left side of the window.

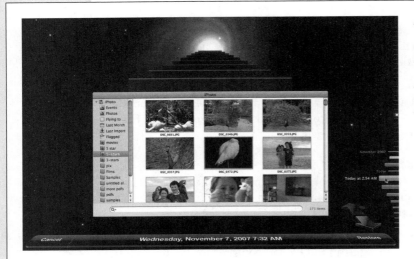

Figure 9-23:
The Time Machine version of iPhoto is a weird, simplified, viewing-only version. You can't do much here besides browse your backups—but when you're in dire straits, that's enough.

Recovering the entire hard drive

Every hard drive will die at some point. You just hope it won't happen while *you* own the computer.

But the great gods of technology have a mean-spirited sense of humor, and hard drives do die. But you, as a Time Machine aficionado, won't care. You'll just repair or replace the hard drive, and then proceed as follows:

1. **Connect the Time Machine backup disk to the Mac. Insert the Snow Leopard installation DVD. Double-click the Install Mac OS X icon.**

   The Mac OS X installer opens up as though it's going to lead you through the process of putting Snow Leopard on the new, empty hard drive. But don't fall for it.

2. **At the Welcome screen, choose Utilities→Restore System from Backup.**

   The Restore Your System dialog box appears.

3. **Click Continue.**

   Now you're shown a list of Time Machine backup disks. You probably have only one.

4. **Click your Time Machine backup disk. In the list of backups, click the most recent one.**

The installer goes about copying *everything* from the backup disk onto your new, empty hard drive. When it's all over, you'll have a perfect working system, just the way it was before your series of unfortunate events.

Tip: You can use these steps to rewind to a previous version of Mac OS X 10.6, too—for example, after you install an Apple software update (10.6.2, say) and discover that it "breaks" a favorite program.

Beware, however: Restoring your earlier version also *erases any files* you've created or changed since you installed the update. Back them up manually before you proceed!

Then follow the steps above; when you're asked to choose a backup to restore, choose the most recent one. When it's all over, copy the latest files (the ones that you manually backed up) back onto the hard drive.

Recovering to another Mac

Weirdly enough, you can also use Time Machine as a glorified data bucket that carries your world from one computer to another. You can bring over some or part of any Time Machine backup to a totally different Mac.

On the new machine, connect your backup disk. In the Applications→Utilities folder, open the program called Migration Assistant. On the first screen, click "From a Time Machine backup." The subsequent screens invite you to choose which backup, which Home folder, and which elements (applications, settings, files) you want to bring over. (You can use the Snow Leopard installation DVD for this purpose, too, as described above.)

Frequently Asked Questions

Time Machine is a very different kind of backup program, and a real departure for longtime PC addicts. A few questions, therefore, are bound to come up—like these:

- **Can I back up more than one Mac onto the same disk?** Yes. Each Mac's backup is stored in a separate folder on that disk.

- **Can I use Time Machine with a Windows PC?** No. However, you can use a Time *Capsule* wireless hard drive to back up your PC, even if it's also being used to back up your Mac.

- **Does the backup disk have to be dedicated to Time Machine?** No. It can have other files and folders on it. Keep in mind, though, that the more space that's available, the further back your backup trail can go.

- **Can I use more than one backup disk—like one at the office and one at home?** Yes. Just use the Time Machine panel of System Preferences (or the Time Machine Dock icon's shortcut menu) to select the new backup drive each time you switch.

- **Can I delete something for good, from all the backups at once?** Yes. Click the Time Machine icon on the Dock to enter the Restore (outer-space) mode. Find and select the file or folder you want to obliterate. From the ✿ menu, choose Delete From All Backups. (Sneaky, huh? That command is never in the ✿ menu *except* when you're in Time Machine restoring mode.)

- **Can Time Machine back up other hard drives besides the main internal one?** Yes. Open System Preferences→Time Machine. Click Options. Your secondary drives are listed here on the excluded-items list. If you want them backed up, too, then *remove* them from the list (click the drive name and then click the — button.)

- **Anything else you want to get off your chest?** Yes. Remember that Time Machine backs up *entire* files at a time—not pieces of files. If you edit huge, multigigabyte files like video files, therefore, keep in mind that each giant file gets recopied to the backup drive every time you change it. That is, one 2-gig video file that you work on all day could wind up occupying 48 gigabytes on the backup drive by the end of the day. Consider adding these files to the exclusion list, as described above.

Part Three:
Making Connections

3

Internet Setup & MobileMe

As Apple's programmers slogged away for months on the massive Mac OS X project, there were areas where they must have felt like they were happily gliding on ice: networking and the Internet. For the most part, the Internet already runs on Unix, and hundreds of extremely polished tools and software chunks were already available.

There are all kinds of ways to get your Mac onto the Internet these days:

- **WiFi.** Wireless hot spots, known as WiFi (or, as Apple calls it, AirPort), are glorious conveniences, especially if you have a laptop. Without stirring from your hotel bed, you're online at high speed. Sometimes for free.

- **Cable modems, DSL.** Over half of the U.S. Internet population connects over higher-speed wires, using *broadband* connections that are always on: cable modems, DSL, or corporate networks. (These, of course, are often what's at the other end of an Internet hot spot.)

- **Cellular modems.** A few well-heeled individuals enjoy the go-anywhere bliss of *USB cellular modems*, which get them online just about anywhere they can make a phone call. These modems are offered by Verizon, Sprint, AT&T, and so on, and usually cost $60 a month.

- **Tethering.** *Tethering* is letting your cellphone act as a glorified Internet antenna for your Mac, whether connected by a cable or a Bluetooth wireless link. In general, the phone company charges you a hefty fee for this convenience.

- **Dial-up modems.** It's true: Plenty of people still connect to the Internet using a modem that dials out over ordinary phone lines. The service is cheap, but the connection is slow, and their numbers are shrinking.

This chapter explains how to set up each one of these. It also describes some of Mac OS X's offbeat Internet featurettes. It tackles MobileMe, Apple's $100-a-year suite of essential and nonessential Internet features; Internet Connection Sharing, which lets several computers in the same household share a single broadband connection; and the system-wide Internet bookmarks known as *Internet location files*.

Network Central—and Multihoming

In this chapter, you'll be spending a lot of time in the Network pane of System Preferences (Figure 10-1). (Choose →System Preferences; click Network.) This list summarizes the ways your Mac can connect to the Internet or an office network—Ethernet, AirPort wireless, Bluetooth, FireWire, cellular modem card, VPN (virtual private networking—a corporate thing), and so on.

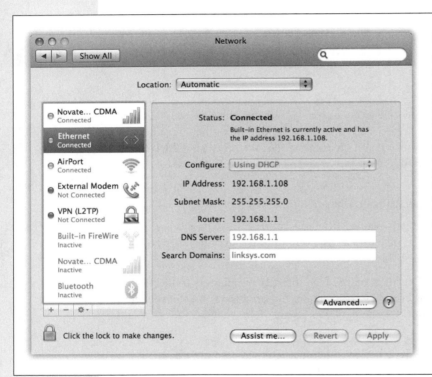

Figure 10-1:
You set up all your network connections here, and you can connect and disconnect to all your networks here. The listed network connections are tagged with color-coded dots. A green dot means turned on and connected to a network; yellow means working, but not connected at the moment; red means you haven't yet set up a connection method.

Multihoming

The *order* of the network connections listed in the Network pane is important. That's the sequence the Mac uses as it tries to get online. If one of your programs needs Internet access and the first method isn't hooked up, then the Mac switches to the next available connection automatically.

In fact, Mac OS X can maintain multiple simultaneous network connections—Ethernet, AirPort, dial-up, even FireWire—a feature known as *multihoming*.

This feature is especially relevant for laptops. When you open your Web browser, your laptop might first check to see if it's at the office, plugged into an Ethernet cable, which is the fastest, most secure type of connection. If there's no Ethernet, it looks for an AirPort network. Finally, if it draws a blank there, the laptop reluctantly dials the modem. It may not be the fastest Internet connection, but it's all you've got at the moment.

Here's how to go about setting up the connection attempt sequence you want:

1. **Open System Preferences. Click the Network icon.**

   The Network Status screen (Figure 10-1) brings home the point of multihoming: You can have more than one network connection operating at once.

2. **From the ✿ pop-up menu, choose Set Service Order.**

   Now you see the display shown in Figure 10-2. It lists all the ways your Mac knows how to get online, or onto an office network.

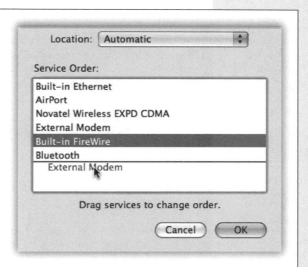

Figure 10-2:
The key to multihoming is sliding the network connection methods' names up or down. Note that you can choose a different connection sequence for each location. (Locations are described later in this chapter.)

3. **Drag the items up and down the list into priority order.**

   If you have a wired broadband connection, for example, you might want to drag Built-in Ethernet to the top of the list, since that's almost always the fastest way to get online.

4. **Click OK.**

   You return to the Network pane of System Preferences, where the master list of connections magically re-sorts itself to match your efforts.

Your Mac will now be able to switch connections even in real time, during a single Internet session. If lightning takes out your Ethernet hub in the middle of your Web surfing, your Mac will seamlessly switch to your AirPort network, for example, to keep your session alive.

All right then: Your paperwork is complete. The following pages guide you through the process of setting up these various connections.

Broadband Connections

If your Mac is connected wirelessly or, um, *wirefully* to a cable modem, DSL, or office network, you're one of the lucky ones. You have a high-speed broadband connection to the Internet that's always available, always on. You never have to wait to dial.

Automatic Configuration

Most broadband connections require *no setup whatsoever*. Take a new Mac out of the box, plug in the Ethernet cable to your cable modem—or choose a wireless network from the ⇧ menulet—and you can begin surfing the Web instantly.

That's because most cable modems, DSL boxes, and wireless base stations use *DHCP.* It stands for *dynamic host configuration protocol,* but what it means is: "We'll fill in your Network pane of System Preferences automatically." (Including techie specs like IP address and DNS Server addresses.)

Manual Configuration

If, for some reason, you're not able to surf the Web or check email the first time you try, it's remotely possible that your broadband modem or your office network *doesn't* offer DHCP. In that case, you may have to fiddle with the Network pane of System Preferences.

On the Network pane, click your Internet connection (AirPort, Built-in Ethernet, cellular modem, whatever). Click Advanced; click TCP/IP. Now you see something like Figure 10-3.

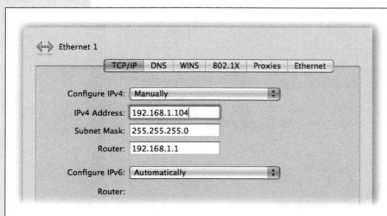

Figure 10-3:
Don't be alarmed by the morass of numbers and periods—it's all in good fun. (If you find TCP/IP fun, that is.)

In this illustration, you see the setup for a cable-modem account with a static IP address, which means you have to type in all these numbers yourself.

To get this information, you can call your Internet provider (cable or TV company) for help—or you can copy your Windows configuration onto the Mac, like this:

Settings from Windows 2000, XP, Vista, or Windows 7

Your first task is to get to the Properties dialog box for your connection. So go like this:

- **Windows 2000.** Choose Start→Settings→Network and Dial-up Connections.

- **Windows XP.** Choose Start→Control Panel. Open Network Connections.

- **Windows Vista.** Choose Start→Control Panel. Open "Network and Sharing Center." Click "Manage network connections."

- **Windows 7.** Choose Start→Control Panel. Open "Network and Sharing Center." Click "Change adapter settings."

Either way, you wind up with a window full of icons that represent the various ways you can connect (3G Connection, Wireless Network Connection, Local Area Connection—that is, Ethernet cable—and so on).

Continue by right-clicking the icon for your broadband connection; from the shortcut menu, choose Properties. (In Windows Vista, you get an "Are you sure?" box at this point; click Continue.)

In the resulting dialog box, click the row that says "Internet Protocol (TCP/IP)."

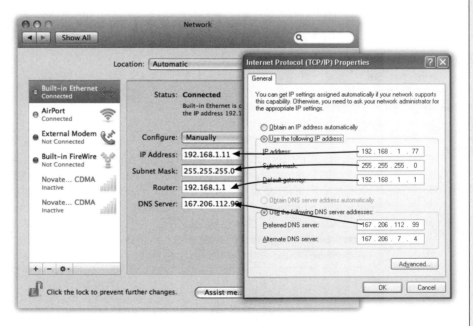

Figure 10-4:
Here you see the setup for a cable-modem account with a static IP address, which means you have to type in these numbers yourself, as guided by the cable company.

If the resulting screen says "Obtain an IP address automatically" (see Figure 10-4), then leave "Using DHCP" selected in the Mac's Configure pop-up menu; your Mac should teach itself the correct settings automatically.

If the Windows screen says, "Use the following IP address" instead, then select Manually from the Mac's Configure pop-up menu, and copy the relevant numbers into the Mac's Network panel like this (see Figure 10-5).

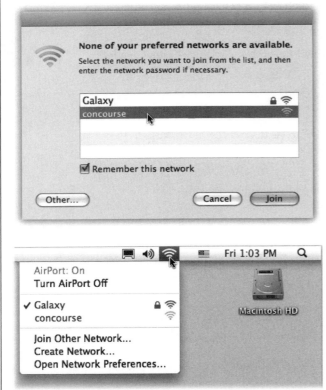

Figure 10-5:
Top: Congratulations—your Mac has discovered new WiFi hot spots all around you! In Snow Leopard, you even get to see the signal strength right in the menu. Double-click one to join it. But if you see a 🔒 icon next to the hot spot's name, beware: It's been protected by a password. If you don't know it, you won't be able to connect.

Bottom: Later, you can always switch networks using the AirPort menulet.

Similarly, if the Internet Protocol (TCP/IP Properties) dialog box says, "Use the following DNS server addresses," then type the numbers from the "Preferred DNS server" and "Alternate DNS server" boxes into the Mac's DNS Servers text box. (Press Return to make a new line for the second number.)

Note: If your Mac plugs directly into the cable modem (that is, you don't use a router), then you'll have to turn the cable modem or DSL box off and then on again when you've switched from the PC to the Mac.

Settings from Windows 98, Windows Me

Choose Start→Settings→Control Panel. In the Control Panel window, double-click Network. Double-click the TCP/IP row that identifies how your PC is connected to the broadband modem. (It may say "TCP/IP→3Com Ethernet Adapter," for example.)

Click the IP Address tab. If it says "Specify an IP address," then copy the IP Address and Subnet Mask numbers into the same ones on the Mac's Network panel. Then click the Gateway tab, and copy the "Installed gateway" number into the Mac's Router box.

Finally, click the DNS Configuration tab. Copy the strings of numbers you see here into the Mac's DNS Servers text box. (Press Return to make a new line for the second number, if necessary.)

Applying the Settings

That's all the setup; on the Mac, in the Network pane of System Preferences, click Apply. If your settings are correct, you're online, now and forever. You never have to worry about connecting or disconnecting.

Ethernet Connections

The beauty of Ethernet connections is that they're super-fast and super-secure. No bad guys sitting across the coffee shop, armed with shareware "sniffing" software, can intercept your email and chat messages, as they theoretically can when you're on wireless.

And 99 percent of the time, connecting to an Ethernet network is as simple as connecting the cable to the Mac. That's it. You're online, fast and securely, and you never have to worry about connecting or disconnecting.

AirPort (WiFi) Connections

AirPort is Apple's term for the 802.11 (WiFi) wireless networking technology. If you have it, your Mac can communicate with a wireless base station up to 300 feet away, much like a cordless phone. Doing so lets you surf the Web from your laptop in a hotel room, for example, or share files with someone across the building from you.

Chapter 14 has much more information about *setting up* an AirPort network. The real fun begins, however, when it comes time to *join* one.

Sometimes you just want to join a friend's WiFi network. Sometimes you've got time to kill in an airport, and it's worth a $7 splurge for half an hour. And sometimes, at some street corners in big cities, WiFi signals bleeding out of apartment buildings might give you a choice of several free hot spots to join.

Your Mac joins WiFi hot spots like this:

- First, it sniffs around for a WiFi network you've used before. If it finds one, it connects quietly and automatically. You're not asked for permission, a password, or anything else; you're just online. (It's that way, for example, when you come home with your laptop every day.) For details on this memorization feature, see the box on the next page.

• If the Mac can't find a known hot spot, but it detects a new hot spot or two, a message appears on the screen (Figure 10-5), displaying their names. Double-click one to connect.

Tip: If you don't want your Mac to keep interrupting you with its discoveries of new hot spots—it can get pretty annoying when you're in a taxi driving through a city—you can shut them off. In System Preferences, click Network, click AirPort, and then turn off "Ask to join new networks."

• If you missed the opportunity to join a hot spot when the message appeared, or if you joined the wrong one or a non-working one, then you have another chance. You can always choose a hot spot's name from the 🛜 menulet, as shown in Figure 10-5 at bottom. A 🔒 icon indicates a hot spot that requires a password, so don't waste your time trying to join those (unless, of course, you *have* the password).

Note: It always takes a computer a few seconds to connect to the Internet over WiFi. In Snow Leopard, the 🛜 menulet itself pulses, or rather ripples, with a black-and-gray animation to let you know you're still in the connection process. It's an anti-frustration aid. (Each hot spot's signal strength appears right in the menulet.)

Before you get too excited, though, some lowering of expectations is in order. There are a bunch of reasons why your 🛜 menulet might indicate that you're in a hot spot, but you can't actually get online:

• **It's locked.** If there's a 🔒 next to the hot spot's name in your 🛜 menulet, then the hot spot has been password protected. That's partly to prevent hackers from "sniffing" the transmissions and intercepting messages, and partly to keep random passersby like you off the network.

POWER USERS' CLINIC

The Super-Secret Hot-Spot Management Box

If you open System Preferences→Network, click AirPort in the left-side list, and then click Advanced, you see the dialog box shown here. It lets you manage the list of WiFi hot spots that Mac OS X has memorized on your travels.

For example, you can delete the old ones. You can also double-click a WiFi net's name to type in and store its password. Finally, you can drag the hot spots' names up and down the list to establish a priority for making connec-

tions when more than one is available.

Ordinarily, Mac OS X memorizes the names of the various hot spots you join on your travels. It's kind of nice, actually, because it means you're interrupted less often by the "Do you want to join?" box.

But if you're alarmed at the massive list of hot spots Mac OS X has memorized—for privacy reasons, say—here's where you turn off "Remember any network this computer has joined."

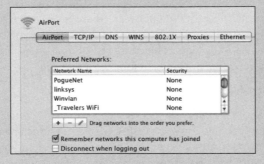

- **The signal's not strong enough.** Sometimes the WiFi signal is strong enough to make the hot spot's name show up in your 🛜 menu, but not strong enough for an actual connection.

- **You're not on the list.** Sometimes, for security, hot spots are rigged to permit only *specific* computers to join, and yours isn't one of them.

- **You haven't logged in yet.** Commercial hot spots (the ones you have to pay for) don't connect you to the Internet until you've supplied your payment details on a special Web page that appears automatically when you open your browser, as described below.

- **The router's on, but the Internet's not connected.** Sometimes wireless routers are broadcasting, but their Internet connection is down. It'd be like a cordless phone that has a good connection back to the base station in the kitchen—but the phone cord isn't plugged into the base station.

Commercial Hot Spots

Choosing the name of the hot spot you want to join is generally all you have to do—if it's a *home* WiFi network.

Unfortunately, joining a *commercial* WiFi hot spot—one that requires a credit card number (in a hotel room or airport, for example)—requires more than just connecting to it. You also have to *sign into* it before you can send so much as a single email message.

To do that, open your Web browser. You'll see the "Enter your payment information" screen either immediately or as soon as you try to open a Web page of your choice. (Even at free hot spots, you might have to click OK on a welcome page to initiate the connection.)

Supply your credit card information or (if you have a membership to this WiFi chain, like Boingo or T-Mobile) your name and password. Click Submit or Proceed, try *not* to contemplate how this $8 per hour is pure profit for somebody, and enjoy your surfing.

Cellular Modems

WiFi hot spots are fast and usually cheap—but they're hot *spots*. Beyond 150 feet away, you're offline.

No wonder laptop luggers across America are getting into *cellular* Internet services. All the big cellphone companies offer ExpressCards or USB sticks that let your laptop get online at high speed *anywhere* in major cities.

No hunting for a coffee shop; with a cellular Internet service, you can check your email while zooming down the road in a taxi. (Outside the metropolitan areas, you can still get online wirelessly, though much more slowly.)

Verizon, Sprint, and AT&T all offer cellular Internet networks with speeds approaching a cable modem. So why isn't the world beating a path to this delicious technology's door? Because it's expensive—at this writing, $60 a month on top of your phone bill.

To get online, insert the card or USB stick; it may take about 15 seconds for the thing to latch on to the cellular signal.

Now you're supposed to make the Internet connection using the special "dialing" software provided by the cellphone company. Technically, though, you may not need it; Snow Leopard comes set to autorecognize most cellular modems. You can start and stop the Internet connection using the menulet—no phone-company software required (see Figure 10-6).

Figure 10-6:
In System Preferences→ Network, click your cellular modem's icon. Click Connect to get online–or, better yet, turn on "Show WWAN status in menu bar." (It stands for Wireless Wide-Area Network, if that helps.) Next time, you'll be able to connect by choosing Connect from this menulet instead of lumbering off to System Preferences.

Dial-up Modem Connections

If you ask Apple, dial-up modems are dead. Macs don't even come with built-in modems anymore. You can get an external USB modem for $50, but clearly, Apple is trying to shove the trusty dial-up technology into the recycling bin.

Still, millions of people never got the memo. If you're among them, you need to sign up for Internet service. Hundreds of companies, large and small, would love to become your *Internet service provider* (ISP), generally charging $20 or so per month for the privilege of connecting you to the Internet.

Once you've selected a service provider, you plug its settings into the Network pane of System Preferences. You get the necessary information directly from your ISP by consulting either its Web page, the instruction sheets that came with your account, or a help-desk agent on the phone.

Note: *The following instructions don't pertain to America Online. It comes with its own setup program and doesn't involve any settings in System Preferences.*

Setting Up the Modem

Open System Preferences and click Network. If your modem isn't already listed, click the **+** button at lower left; from the Interface pop-up menu that appears, choose External Modem, and then click Create.

Your modem connection now appears in the list at the left side of the pane. Click it. Now fill in the blanks like this:

- **Configuration.** It's called Default at first, which is fine. If you like, you can choose Add Configuration from this pop-up menu and then name it after your ISP (*EarthLink,* for example).

- **Telephone Number.** This is the local access number your modem is supposed to dial to connect to your ISP.

Tip: *If you need your Mac to dial a 9 or an 8 for an outside line (as you would from within a hotel), or *70 to turn off Call Waiting, add it to the beginning of the phone number followed by a comma. The comma means "Pause for 2 seconds." You can also put the comma to good use when typing in the dialing sequence for a calling-card number.*

- **Account Name.** This is your account name with your ISP. If you're BillG@earthlink.net, for example, type *BillG* here.

- **Password.** Specify your ISP account password here. Turn on "Save password" if you'd rather not retype it every time you connect.

POWER USERS' CLINIC

PPPoE and DSL

If you have DSL service, you may be directed to create a *PPPoE service.* (You do that on the Network pane of System Preferences; click your Ethernet connection, and then choose Configuration→Create PPPoE Service.)

It stands for PPP over Ethernet, meaning that although your DSL "modem" is connected to your Ethernet port, you still have to make and break your Internet connections manually, as though you had a dial-up modem.

Fill in the PPPoE dialog box as directed by your ISP (usually just your account name and password). From here on in, you start and end your Internet connections exactly as though you had a dial-up modem.

The Advanced Button

Click the Advanced button to bring up a special dialog box filled with tweaky, soon-to-be-obsolete modem settings. Most of the action is on two tabs: Modem (where you can specify Tone or Pulse dialing) and PPP (where you can, and should, turn on "Connect automatically when needed," so you don't have to connect manually each time you want to use email or the Web).

Disconnecting

The Mac automatically drops the phone line 15 minutes after your last activity online. In fact, if other people have accounts on your Mac (Chapter 13), the Mac doesn't even hang up when you log out. It maintains the connection so the next person can surf the Net without redialing.

Of course, if other people in your household are screaming for you to get off the line so they can make a call, you can also disconnect manually. Choose Disconnect from the ☎ menulet.

Tip: If you have more than one ISP, or if you travel between locations with your laptop, don't miss the Location feature. It lets you switch sets of dial-up modem settings—including the local phone number—with a simple menu selection. It's described next.

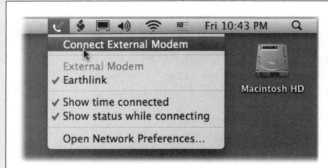

Figure 10-7:
Life is simplest when you've told your Mac to dial automatically when it needs to get online. But you can also go online on command, using this menulet.

Switching Locations

Maybe you visit the branch office from time to time, and you're getting tired of having to change the local access number for your ISP each time you leave home (and return home again). Or maybe you want to use only WiFi when you're home, and a wired connection at work.

The simple solution is the ☐→Location submenu, which appears once you've set up more than one Location. As Figure 10-8 illustrates, all you have to do is tell it where you are. Mac OS X handles the details of switching Internet connections.

Creating a New Location

To create a *Location,* which is nothing more than a set of memorized settings, open System Preferences, click Network, and then choose Edit Locations from the Location pop-up menu. Continue as shown in Figure 10-9.

Tip: You can use the commands in the ✿ menu to rename or duplicate a Location.

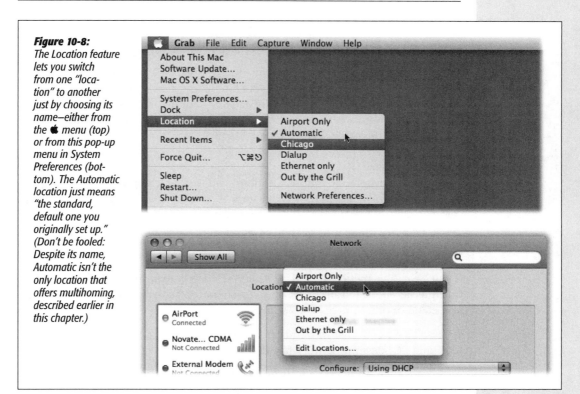

Figure 10-8:
The Location feature lets you switch from one "location" to another just by choosing its name—either from the ❖ menu (top) or from this pop-up menu in System Preferences (bottom). The Automatic location just means "the standard, default one you originally set up." (Don't be fooled: Despite its name, Automatic isn't the only location that offers multihoming, described earlier in this chapter.)

Figure 10-9:
When you choose Edit Locations, this list of existing Locations appears; click the + button. A new entry appears at the bottom of the list. Type a name for your new location, such as Chicago Office or Dining Room Floor.

When you click Done, you return to the Network panel. Take this opportunity to set up the kind of Internet connection you use at the corresponding location, just as described on the first pages of this chapter.

If you travel regularly, you can build a *list* of Locations, each of which "knows" the way you like to get online in each city you visit.

A key part of making a new Location is putting the various Internet connection types (Ethernet, AirPort, Modem, Bluetooth) into the correct order. Your connections will be slightly quicker if you give the modem priority in your Hotel setup, the AirPort connection priority in your Starbucks setup, and so on.

You can even turn off some connections entirely. Use the Make Service Inactive command in the ✿ menu. For example, if your laptop uses nothing but WiFi when you're on the road, your Location could include *nothing* but the AirPort connection. You'll save a few seconds each time you try to go online, because your Mac won't bother hunting for an Internet connection that doesn't exist.

Making the Switch

Once you've set up your various locations, you can switch among them using the ⌘→Location submenu, as shown in Figure 10-8. As soon as you do so, your Mac is automatically set to get online the way you like.

Internet Sharing

If you have cable modem or DSL service, you're a very lucky individual. You get terrific Internet speed and an always-on connection. Too bad only one computer in your household or office can enjoy these luxuries.

It doesn't have to be that way. You can spread the joy of high-speed Internet to every Mac (and PC) on your network in either of two ways:

- **Buy a router.** A *router* is a little box, costing about $50, that connects directly to the cable modem or DSL box. In most cases, it has multiple Internet jacks so you can plug in several Macs, PCs, and/or wireless base stations. As a bonus, a router provides excellent security, serving as a firewall to keep out unsolicited visits from hackers on the Internet.

- **Use Internet Sharing.** Mac OS X's Internet Sharing feature is the software version of a router: It distributes a single Internet signal to every computer on the network. But unlike a router, it's free. You just fire it up on the one Mac that's connected directly to the Internet—the *gateway* computer. (Windows Me and later versions offer a similar feature.)

    But there's a downside: If the gateway Mac is turned off or asleep, the other machines can't get online.

Most people use Internet Sharing to share a broadband connection like a cable modem or DSL. But there are other times when it comes in handy. If you have a cellular modem, for example, you might want to share its signal via WiFi so the kids in the back seat can get online with their iPod Touches. You could even share a tethered Bluetooth cellphone's Internet connection with a traveling companion who needs a quick email check.

The only requirement: The Internet-connected Mac must have some *other* kind of connection (Ethernet, AirPort, Bluetooth, FireWire) to the Macs that will share the connection.

Turning On Internet Sharing

To turn on Internet Sharing on the gateway Mac, open the Sharing panel of System Preferences. Click Internet Sharing, as shown in Figure 10-10, but don't turn on the checkbox yet.

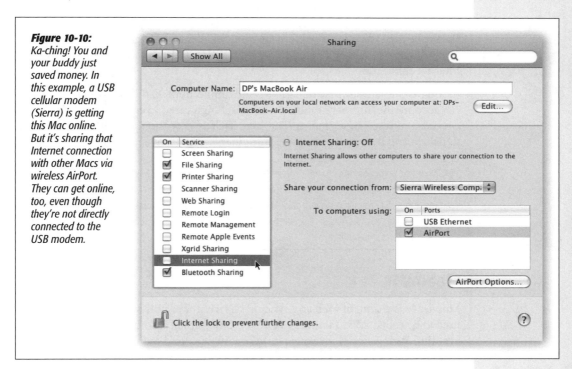

Figure 10-10:
Ka-ching! You and your buddy just saved money. In this example, a USB cellular modem (Sierra) is getting this Mac online. But it's sharing that Internet connection with other Macs via wireless AirPort. They can get online, too, even though they're not directly connected to the USB modem.

Before you do that, you have to specify (a) how the gateway Mac is connected to the Internet, and (b) how it's connected to the other Macs on your office network:

- **Share your connection from.** Using this pop-up menu, identify how *this Mac* (the gateway machine) connects to the Internet—via Built-in Ethernet, AirPort, cellular modem, or Bluetooth DUN (dial-up networking—that is, tethering to your cellphone).

- **To computers using.** Using these checkboxes, specify how you want your Mac to rebroadcast the Internet signal to the others. (It has to be a *different* network channel. You can't get your signal via AirPort and then pass it on via AirPort.)

Note: Which checkboxes appear here depends on which kinds of Internet connections are turned on in the Network pane of System Preferences. If the gateway Mac doesn't have AirPort circuitry, for example, or if AirPort is turned off in the current configuration, then the AirPort option doesn't appear.

Now visit each of the other Macs on the same network. Open the Network pane of System Preferences. Select the network method you chose in the second step above: AirPort, Built-in Ethernet, or FireWire. Click Apply.

If the gateway Mac is rebroadcasting using AirPort—by far the most common use of this feature—you have one more step. In your 🛜 menulet, you'll see a strange new "hot spot" that wasn't there before, bearing the name of the gateway Mac. (It might say, for example, "Casey's MacBook Air.") Choose its name to begin your borrowed Internet connection.

As long as the gateway Mac remains on and online, both it and your other computers can get onto the Internet simultaneously, all at high speed, even Windows PCs. You've created a *software* base station. The Mac itself is now the transmitter for Internet signals to and from any other WiFi computers within range.

Tip: Now that you know how to let a wireless Mac piggyback on a wired Mac's connection, you can let a wired Mac share a wireless connection, too. Suppose, for example, that you and a buddy both have laptops in a hotel lobby. You're online, having paid $13 to use the hotel's WiFi network. If you set up Internet Sharing appropriately, your buddy can connect to yours via an Ethernet cable or even a FireWire cable and surf along with you—no extra charge.

MobileMe

MobileMe is a suite of Web and syncing services that Apple sells for $100 a year. (It used to be called .Mac.) It gives you a Web-based email account, Web-based storage, beautiful Web galleries for your photos and videos, and a universal syncing feature that keeps your Macs, PCs, and iPhones synchronized, so that your Address Book, calendar, and other data are wirelessly updated in every direction.

Much of it is based on the central Web site *www.me.com* (Figure 10-11).

Signing Up for MobileMe

Open System Preferences and click the MobileMe icon. Click Learn More. You now go online, where your Web browser has opened up to the MobileMe sign-up screen. Fill in your name and address, make up an account name and password, turn off the checkbox that invites you to get junk mail, and so on.

Finally, back at System Preferences→MobileMe, fill in the account name and password you just composed, if necessary. Now the preference pane has magically sprouted four tabs, which you'll meet in the following pages.

Let your grand tour of MobileMe's motley features begin.

Figure 10-11:
The MobileMe features appear as buttons on the me.com Web site. Here's all your email, your Address Book, and your calendar, which get auto-synchronized among your Macs, PCs, and iPhones. Here, too, are any photos or videos you've published from Snow Leopard, and any files you've stashed on your iDisk.

MobileMe Sync

For many people, this may be the killer app for MobileMe right here: The me.com Web site, acting as the master control center, can keep multiple Macs, Windows PCs, and iPhones/iPod Touches synchronized.

It works by storing the master copies of your stuff—email, calendars, address books, Web bookmarks, Dock items, passwords, notes, email account details, and Dashboard widgets—on the Web. (Or "in the cloud," as the product managers would say.)

Whenever your Macs, PCs, or iPhones/Touches are online, they connect to the mother ship and update themselves. Edit an address on your iPhone and shortly thereafter, you'll find the same change in Address Book (on your Mac) and Outlook (on your PC). Send an email reply from your PC at the office and you'll find it in your Sent Mail folder on the Mac at home. Add a Web bookmark anywhere and find it everywhere else.

Actually, there's a fourth place where you can work with your data: on the Web. At *www.me.com,* you can log in to find Web-based clones of iCal, Address Book, and Mail; there's even a mini-iPhoto.

To set up syncing, open System Preferences→MobileMe→Sync. Turn on the checkboxes of the stuff you want to be synchronized all the way around:

- **Bookmarks.** If a Web site is important enough to merit bookmarking while you're using your laptop, why shouldn't it also show up in the Bookmarks menu on your desktop Mac at home, your iPhone, or your PC at work?

- **Calendars, Contacts.** This is a big one. There's nothing as exasperating as realizing that the Address Book you're consulting on your home Mac is missing somebody you're *sure* you entered—on your computer at work. This option keeps all your Macs' Address Books and iCal calendars synchronized. Delete a phone number at work, and you'll find it deleted on your Mac at home, too.

- **Dashboard Widgets.** Now the configuration and setup of your widgets on Mac A are synced to Macs B, C, and D, so they all match.

- **Dock Items.** Not the biggest deal in the world, but if you've put some time into setting up your Dock on one Mac, it's nice to find it set up identically on your other Macs.

- **Keychains.** All your Macs can have the same passwords memorized. Worth its weight in gold.

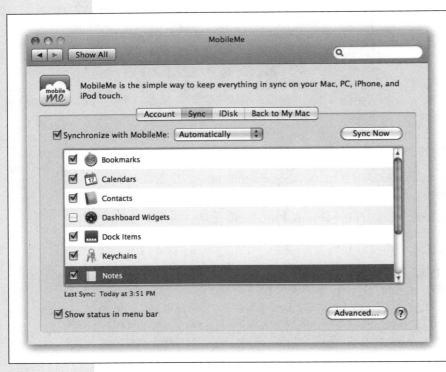

Figure 10-12:
To set up MobileMe sync, open System Preferences. Click MobileMe, and then click the Sync tab. Turn on the checkboxes for the information you want synchronized. Use the pop-up menu at the top to set up an automatic sync schedule. While you're at it, turn on "Show status in menu bar" so you'll be able to start or stop the syncing manually, too.

- **Mail Accounts, Rules, Signatures, and Smart Mailboxes.** These refer to your account settings and preferences from Mac OS X's Mail program, not the email messages themselves.

- **Notes.** This option refers to the notes you enter in Mail's Notes feature (Chapter 11). How great to make a reminder for yourself on one Mac and have it reminding you later on another one. (If you have Microsoft Office, you'll see an Entourage Notes option here, too.)

- **Preferences.** All your System Preferences settings.

- **Other apps.** Non-Apple programs can install their own Sync options at the bottom of this list. Microsoft Entourage offers to sync your notes, for example, and TextExpander (typing-substitution shareware) keeps your list of typing abbreviations in sync among Macs.

To set up MobileMe syncing, turn on the checkboxes for the items you want synced, as shown in Figure 10-12.

After the first sync, you can turn on the checkboxes on the other Macs, too, in effect telling them to participate in the great data-sharing experiment.

The first time they try, they may get confused. "Hold on. *My* address book is empty, but the one I'm downloading from the Internet (from the other Mac) is loaded. Who wins?" You get the dialog box shown in Figure 10-13, which lets you decide how to proceed.

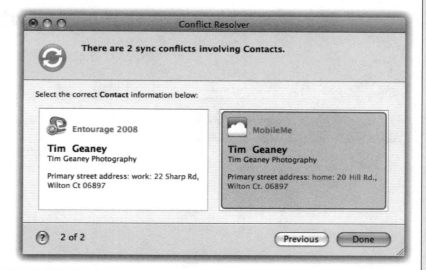

Figure 10-13:
This message lets you decide how to proceed when data on one of the synced Macs is wildly different from what's been "published" by another Mac. You can merge the information from the two (a great way to combine address books or calendars), make this Mac's data wipe out the other's ("Replace data on MobileMe"), or make the Internet-based data replace this computer's ("Replace data on computer").

The iDisk

The iDisk is an Internet-based hard-drive icon on your desktop that makes a perfect intermediate parking place for files you want to shuttle from one computer to another—your old Windows PC and your new Mac, for example. Or you can just use it for offsite backup of your most important files. (Your MobileMe account comes with 20 gigabytes of storage. In your account settings at *www.me.com*, you can decide how to divide up that storage between your iDisk and the other MobileMe stuff, like Mail and your Web sites. And, of course, you can pay more money for more storage.)

Furthermore, you can pull the iDisk onto *any* computer's screen—Mac or Windows—at your office, at your home, at your friend's house, so you don't need to carry around a physical disk to transport important files.

Pulling it onto your screen

Apple must really love the iDisk concept, because it has devised about 300 different ways to pull the iDisk icon onto your screen (Figure 10-14). The simplest is to choose Go→iDisk→My iDisk (or press Shift-⌘-I), or click the iDisk icon in the Sidebar (of a Finder window or a Save or Open dialog box).

At this point, the iDisk behaves like an external hard drive. You can drag files or folders from your hard drive into one of the folders on the iDisk.

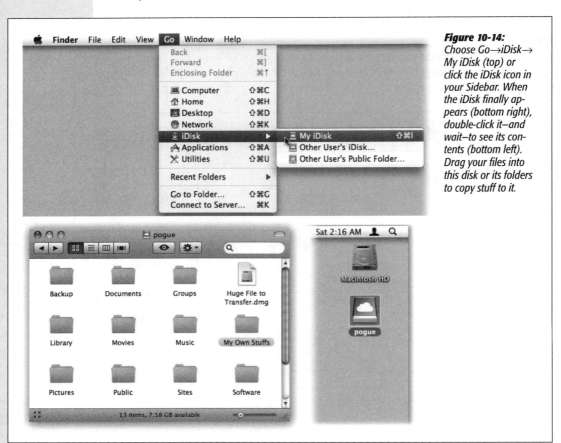

Figure 10-14:
Choose Go→iDisk→ My iDisk (top) or click the iDisk icon in your Sidebar. When the iDisk finally appears (bottom right), double-click it—and wait—to see its contents (bottom left). Drag your files into this disk or its folders to copy stuff to it.

Thereafter, you can retrieve or open whatever you copied to the iDisk. Open one of the folders on it; you can now open, rename, trash, or copy (to your hard drive) whatever you find inside.

Making the iDisk fast and synchronized

Copying files to and from a disk on the Internet is slower than copying them between hard drives on the same Mac. The iDisk has a reputation, therefore, of being sluggish.

But behind the scenes, Mac OS X can keep a full, invisible *copy* of the iDisk's contents on your hard drive. When you add something to the iDisk, therefore, it *seems* to appear there instantly—even when you're not online—because all you've done is copy something onto a secret stash of your own drive. The Mac will begin the process of transmitting the copy to the *online* iDisk at the next opportunity. In short, you can leave the iDisk's icon onscreen for as long as you like, even when you're offline.

To turn on this feature, see Figure 10-15.

Tip: If you have Macs in different locations (home and office, for example), you can keep your key files synchronized among all of them by turning on this automatic iDisk syncing on all the machines. (The option "Always keep the most recent version of a file" makes this arrangement especially worry-free because you no longer have to worry about version conflicts.) You've burned your last "Take Home" CD!

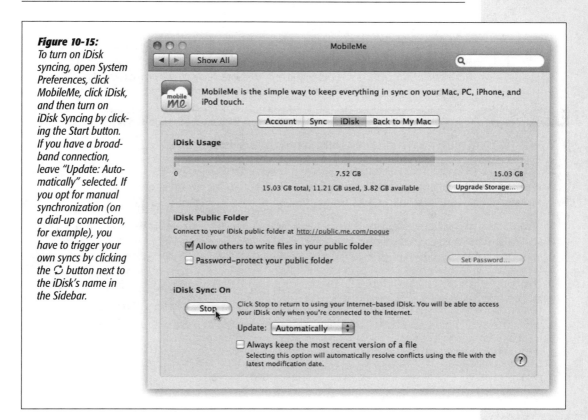

Figure 10-15:
To turn on iDisk syncing, open System Preferences, click MobileMe, click iDisk, and then turn on iDisk Syncing by clicking the Start button. If you have a broadband connection, leave "Update: Automatically" selected. If you opt for manual synchronization (on a dial-up connection, for example), you have to trigger your own syncs by clicking the ↻ button next to the iDisk's name in the Sidebar.

The Public folder

In general, whatever you put onto your iDisk is private and password-protected. There's one exception, however: Whatever you put into the *Public* folder on any iDisk can be seen, opened, and copied by other MobileMe members. All they need is your member name—not your password (although you *can* password-protect it, if you like). Think of the iDisk Public folder as the long-lost twin of the Public folder in your own Home folder.

The Public folder is terrific for storing family photos where anyone who's interested can look at them. It's also handy when you're collaborating; just post the latest drafts of your work in the Public folder for your coworkers to review.

To view someone *else's* Public folder (suppose the person's MobileMe name is Ski-Bunny23), use one of these techniques:

- **From your Mac.** Choose Go→iDisk→Other User's Public Folder. Type *SkiBunny23*, and hit Return.

- **From Windows.** See the box below.

After a minute or so, a new iDisk icon appears on your desktop bearing that member's name. Double-click it to view its contents. You can copy these files to your hard drive or double-click them to open them directly.

Tip: If you have an iPhone or iPod Touch, don't miss the free iDisk App (which you can download from the App Store). It lets you view, open, and forward anything on your iDisk—right from your phone or iPod. (You can't put anything new onto the iDisk this way, but still—in a pinch, how great it would be to pass on the McGillicuddy proposal to a client when you're on a beach somewhere, far from a computer!)

The iDisk from Windows

Once, you could get to your iDisk only from a Macintosh. These days, you can bring your iDisk onto the screen of any computer, even one running Windows or Linux.

Now you can *access* your iDisk files from any computer on earth—just go to *www.me.com* and log in. Doesn't matter if you're on Mac, Windows, or Joe-Bob's Discount OS.

But if you want that iDisk icon *on your desktop* so you can easily drag and drop files, then the procedure is slightly more complex. You're going to create a new "hard drive" in your PC's Computer window, whose icon represents the iDisk.

Choose Start→Computer. In the Computer window, click "Map network drive" in the toolbar. When you're asked for the disk's address, type *http://idisk.me.com/casey* (or whatever your MobileMe name is). Click "Connect using a different user name." Enter your MobileMe member name and password, and then click OK. Your iDisk appears on the desktop; you can work with it as you would any other hard disk.

iDisk options

In System Preferences→MobileMe→iDisk, you're offered these Public-folder options:

- **Allow others to write files in your public folder.** Ordinarily, other people can deposit stuff into your Public folder as well as copy things out. If you'd rather set it up so that only *you* can drop things in there, then turn off this checkbox.

- **Password-protect your Public folder.** Probably a good idea if you decide to make your Public folder available for deposits.

Email

Apple offers an email address to each MobileMe member.

Probably anyone who can *get* to the Apple Web site already *has* an email account. So why bother? The first advantage is the simple address: *YourName@me.com*. (You can also use *YourName@mac.com* interchangeably.)

Second, MobileMe addresses are integrated into Mac OS X's Mail program, as you'll see in the next chapter. And finally, you can read your MobileMe email from any computer anywhere in the world, via the me.com Web site, or on your iPhone/iPod Touch.

Galleries

Within iPhoto, iMovie, Final Cut, and even QuickTime Player, you'll find handy, one-click MobileMe Gallery buttons. They let you post the selected photos or movies on your private corner of the me.com Web site. (You're always shown the Web address of the resulting gallery, so you can tell your friends how to find it.)

GEM IN THE ROUGH

The 20-Gigabyte Email Attachment

People use the iDisk for all kinds of things: as backup, as a bucket to carry files between computers, and so on. But here's one of the coolest features of all: You can *email* anything on your iDisk to anyone.

Ordinarily, you can't attach anything bigger than 5 or 10 megabytes to an email message. But iDisk email "attachments" can be enormous—many gigabytes. That's because they're not really attached to the email at all; you're simply sending your colleague a *link* to download something from your iDisk.

To use this feature, go to *www.me.com.* Log in. Click the iDisk button on the toolbar. In the list of your iDisk contents, click the file you want to send, and then click Share File. Fill in the email address of the recipient; a short message; and, if you like, a password to protect the download.

Once your colleagues receive your email from the me.com Web site, they have but to click the link in the message to download your huge file immediately.

This is not the same as posting to, say, Flickr or YouTube, where a cacophony of ads and blinking and ugly text distracts from the presentation. MobileMe galleries are handsome and classy, with black backgrounds and subtle animations. You get all kinds of interesting options, too—for example, you can offer your fans the chance to download full-quality versions of your photos and movies (so family members can print their own copies, for example). And you can permit other people to post their own photos on your galleries, for a better one-stop nostalgia shopping experience about that wedding or reunion.

Web Sites

If you use Apple's iWeb program to design your own Web sites, then MobileMe provides another one-click publishing opportunity. Your Web pages have a happy, hassle-free home on the Web, without your having to know HTML or work an FTP program to post them online.

Once you've posted Web pages, you'll find the source files at *www.me.com* by clicking the iDisk icon on the toolbar. The Sites heading at left contains the iWeb folder that houses your actual Web-site files.

Internet Location Files

An Internet location file (Figure 10-16) is like a system-wide bookmark: When you double-click one, your Web browser opens to that page, or your email program generates an outgoing message to a predetermined addressee. You could put a folder full of location files for favorite Web sites into the Dock. Do the same with addresses to which you frequently send email. Thereafter, you save a step every time you want to jump to a particular Web page or send email to a particular person—just choose the appropriate name from the Dock folder's Stack. (It's fine to rename them, by the way.)

Figure 10-16:
To create an Internet location file, drag a highlighted address from a program like TextEdit to your desktop. Although Web and email addresses are the most popular types, you can also create location files for the addresses of newsgroups (news://news.apple.com), FTP sites (ftp://ftp.apple.com), AppleShare servers (afp://at/Engineering:IL5 3rd Floor), AppleTalk zones (at://IL5 2nd Floor), and even Web pages stored on your Mac (file://Macintosh HD/Website Stuff/home.html).

Mail & Address Book

Y̶ou know how every copy of Windows comes with a free, basic email program like Outlook Express or Windows Mail? Well, every copy of Mac OS X comes with Mail, a slightly fancier email program that's also free. Mail is a surprisingly complete, refreshingly attractive program, filled with shortcuts and surprises. Together with the high-octane Address Book program included with Mac OS X, you may never pine for your Windows setup again.

Note: This chapter assumes that you've already transferred your email, addresses, and email account settings to Mail and the Address Book, as described in Chapter 6.

Checking Your Mail

You get new mail and send mail you've already written using the Get Mail command. You can trigger it in any of several ways:

• Click Get Mail on the toolbar.

• Choose Mailbox→Get All New Mail (or press Shift-⌘-N).

Note: If you have multiple email accounts, you can also use the Mailbox→Get New Mail submenu to pick just *one* account to check for new mail.

• Right-click Mail's Dock icon, and choose Get New Mail from the shortcut menu. (You can use this method from within any program, as long as Mail is already open.)

- Wait. Mail comes set to check your email automatically every few minutes. To adjust its timing or to turn this feature off, choose Mail→Preferences, click General, and then choose a time interval from the "Check for new messages" pop-up menu.

Now Mail contacts the mail servers listed in the Accounts pane of Mail's preferences, retrieving new messages and downloading any files attached to those messages. It also *sends* any outgoing messages that couldn't be sent when you wrote them.

Tip: The far-left column of the Mail window has a tiny Mail Activity monitor tucked away; click the second tiny button at the lower-left corner of the Mail window to reveal Mail Activity. If you don't want to give up Mailboxes-list real estate, or if you prefer to monitor your mail in a separate window, you can do that, too. The Activity Viewer window gives you a Stop button, progress bars, and other useful information. Summon it by choosing Window→Activity, or by pressing ⌘-0.

Also, if you're having trouble connecting to some (or all) of your email accounts, choose Window→Connection Doctor. There, you can see detailed information about which of your accounts aren't responding. If your computer's Internet connection is at fault, you can click Network Diagnostics to try to get back online.

The Mailboxes List

If you used early versions of Mail, the first thing you may notice is that the Mailbox panel isn't just for mailboxes anymore. Categories like Reminders and RSS Feeds can appear there, too, as shown in Figure 11-1. But the top half of this gray-blue column on the left side lists all your email accounts' folders (and subfolders, and sub-subfolders)

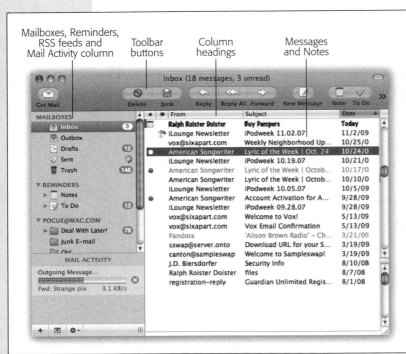

Figure 11-1:
If you've ever used iTunes, you'll notice a lot of similarities with the Mail window. All your information sources— mailboxes, notes, To Do items, and RSS Feeds—are grouped tidily in the far-left column, where you can always see them. Buttons along the top of the Mail window let you create new messages, notes, and tasks with a click. To see what's in one of these folders, click it once. The list of its messages appears in the top half of the right side of the window (the Messages list).

for easy access. Mail looks quite a bit like iTunes (and iPhoto, and the Finder)—except here you have mailboxes where your iTunes Library and connected iPods would be.

In the Mailboxes panel, sometimes hidden by flippy triangles, you may find these folders:

- **Inbox** holds mail you've received. If you have more than one email account, you can expand the triangles to see separate folders for your individual accounts. You'll see this pattern repeated with the Sent, Junk, and other mailboxes, too—separate accounts have separate subheadings.

Tip: If Mail has something to tell you about your Inbox (like, for instance, that Mail can't connect to it), a tiny warning triangle appears on the right side of the Mailboxes column. Click it to see what Mail is griping about.

If you see a lightning-bolt icon, that's Mail's way of announcing that you're offline. Click the icon to try to connect to the Internet.

- **Outbox** holds mail you've written but haven't yet sent (because you were on an airplane when you wrote it, for example). If you have no mail waiting to be sent, the Outbox itself disappears.

GEM IN THE ROUGH

The Mighty Morphing Interface

You don't have to be content with the factory-installed design of the Mail screen. You can control almost every aspect of its look and layout.

For example, you can control the main window's information columns exactly as you would in a Finder list view window—make a column narrower or wider by dragging the right edge of its column heading, rearrange the columns by dragging their titles, and so on.

You can also control *which* columns appear using the commands in the View→Columns menu. Similarly, you can *sort* your email by clicking these column headings, exactly as in the Finder. Click a second time to reverse the sorting order.

The various panes of the main window are also under your control. For example, you can drag the divider bar between the Messages list and the Preview pane up or down to adjust the relative proportions, as shown here. In fact, you can get rid of the Preview pane altogether by double-clicking the divider line, double-clicking just above the vertical scroll

bar, or dragging the divider line's handle all the way to the bottom of the screen. Bring it back by dragging the divider line up from the bottom.

You can also control the Mailboxes pane. Drag the thin vertical line that separates this tinted column from the white messages area to make the column wider or narrower. You can even drag it so tightly that you see only the mailboxes' icons. You can make the column disappear or reappear by choosing View→Hide Mailboxes (or View→Show Mailboxes), or by pressing Shift-⌘-M.

Finally, you have full control over the toolbar, which works much like the Finder toolbar. You can rearrange or remove icon buttons (by ⌘-dragging them); add interesting new buttons to the toolbar (by choosing View→Customize Toolbar); change its display to show *just* text labels or *just* icons—either large or small (by repeatedly ⌘-clicking the white, oval, upper-right toolbar button); or hide the toolbar entirely (by clicking that white button or using the View→Hide Toolbar command).

- **Drafts** holds messages you've started but haven't yet finished and don't want to send just yet.

- **Sent,** unsurprisingly, holds copies of messages you've sent.

- **Trash** works a lot like the Trash on your desktop, in that messages you put there don't actually disappear. They remain in the Trash folder until you permanently delete them or move them somewhere else—or until Mail's automatic trash-cleaning service deletes them for you.

- **Junk** appears automatically when you use Mail's spam filter, as described later in this chapter.

- **Reminders.** Any Notes you've jotted down while working in Mail are here. To Do items hang out here as well. (Both are described later in this chapter.)

- **RSS Feeds.** Who needs to bop into a Web browser to keep up with the news? Mail brings it right to you while you're corresponding, as described in a moment.

- **Mail Activity.** You don't need to summon a separate window to see how much more of that message with the giant attachment the program still has to send. To reveal the Mail activity panel, shown in Figure 11-1, click the second tiny icon in the bottom-left side of the Mail window.

- **Preview pane.** The difference between Figure 11-1 and Figure 11-2 is the Preview pane—the bottom half of the main window, which shows the contents of whatever message you've selected in the list. If you're not already seeing this pane, drag the bottom edge of the window, marked with a dot, upward (as shown in the box on the previous page); that's the movable border between window halves.

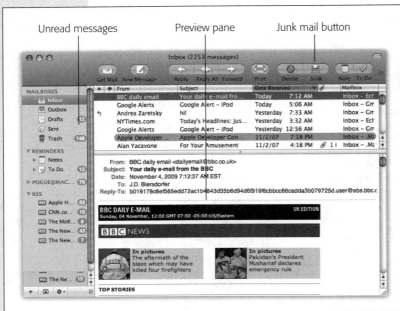

Figure 11-2:
The many panes of Mail. Click an icon in the Mailboxes column to see its contents in the Messages list. When you click the name of a message in the Messages list (or press the ↑ and ↓ keys to highlight successive messages in that list), you see the message itself, along with any attachments, in the Preview pane.

Click one of the column headings (From, Subject, and so on) to sort your mail collection by that criterion.

Tip: You can even drag the mailboxes up and down in the list. Sweet.

Checking Your Mail

Writing Messages

To send an email, click New Message in the toolbar or press ⌘-N. The New Message form, shown in Figure 11-3, opens. Here's how you go about writing a message:

1. **In the "To:" field, type the recipient's email address.**

   If somebody is in your Address Book, type the first couple of letters of the name or email address; Mail automatically completes the address. (If the first guess is wrong, type another letter or two until Mail revises its guess.)

Tip: If you find that Mail constantly tries to autofill in the address of someone you don't really communicate with, you can zap that address from its memory by choosing Window→Previous Recipients. Click the undesired address, and then click Remove From List.

As in most dialog boxes, you can jump from blank to blank (from "To:" to "Cc:," for example) by pressing Tab. To send this message to more than one person, separate the addresses with commas: *bob@earthlink.net, billg@microsoft.com,* and so on.

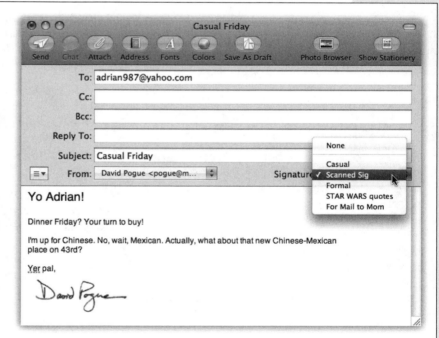

Figure 11-3:
A message has two sections: the header, *which holds information about the message; and the* body, *the big empty area that contains the message itself. In addition, the Mail window has a toolbar, which offers features for composing and sending messages. The Signature pop-up menu doesn't exist until you create a signature; the Account pop-up menu lets you pick which email address you'd like to send the message from (if you have more than one email address).*

Tip: If you send most of your email to addresses within the same organization (like *reddelicious@apple.com,* *grannysmith@apple.com,* and *winesap@apple.com*), Mail can automatically turn all *other* email addresses red. It's a feature designed to avoid sending confidential messages to outside addresses.

To turn this feature on, choose Mail→Preferences, click Composing, turn on "Mark addresses not ending with," and then type the "safe" domain (like *apple.com*) into the blank.

2. **To send a copy to other recipients, enter their addresses in the "Cc:" field.**

Cc stands for *carbon copy.* Getting an email message where your name is in the "Cc:" line implies: "I sent you a copy because I thought you'd want to know about this correspondence, but I'm not expecting you to reply."

UP TO SPEED

Bcc:, Reply-To, and Priority

A *blind carbon copy* is a secret copy. This feature lets you send a copy of a message to somebody secretly, without any of the other recipients knowing that you did so. To view this field when composing a message, choose View→Bcc Address Field.

You can use the "Bcc:" field to quietly signal a third party that a message has been sent. For example, if you send your co-worker a message that says, "Chris, it bothers me that you've been cheating the customers," you could Bcc your supervisor to clue her in without getting into trouble with Chris.

The "Bcc:" box is useful in other ways, too. Many people send email messages (corny jokes, for example) to a long list of recipients. You, the recipient, have to scroll through the long list of names the sender placed in the "To:" or "Cc:" field.

But if the sender used the "Bcc:" field to hold all the recipients' email addresses, you, the recipient, won't see anybody else's names at the top of the email. In the "To:" box, you might see the sender's name, or "undisclosed recipients," or nothing at all. (Spammers have also learned this trick, which is why it usually looks like you're the only recipient of a junk message when there are actually millions of other people who received the same message.)

Another hidden field you can add to your messages is *Reply-To.* (Choose View→Reply-To Address Field.) That field has one simple purpose: to make the recipient's email program reply to a different email address than the one you sent the message from. For example, if your business email address isn't working but you absolutely *have* to send a field report to your boss, you can send the message from your personal email account but put your business address in the Reply-To field. That way, when your boss emails you back to congratulate you, the email goes to your business account.

Finally, if you click the three-line pop-up button on the left side of an email message and choose Customize, you can enable one more hidden header option: *Priority.* (It's the pop-up menu with an exclamation mark in it.) If you turn on the checkbox next to that pop-up menu and click OK, all your email messages let you set how important they are on a three-tiered scale.

The good part about this system is that it lets your recipient see that an email you've sent is, for example, urgent. The bad part is that not every email program displays the priority of email—and even if your recipient's email program *does* display your message's priority, there's no guarantee that it'll make him respond any faster.

Tip: If Mail recognizes the address you type into the "To:" or "Cc:" box (because it's someone in your Address Book, for instance), the name turns into a shaded, round-ended box button. Besides looking cool, these buttons have a small triangle on their right; when you click one, you get a list of useful commands (including Open in Address Book).

These buttons are also drag-and-droppable. For example, you can drag one from the "To:" box to the "Cc:" field, or from Address Book to Mail.

3. Type the topic of the message in the Subject field.

It's courteous to put some thought into the Subject line. (Use "Change in plans for next week," for instance, instead of "Yo.") And leaving it blank only annoys your recipient. On the other hand, don't put the *entire* message into the Subject line, either.

4. Specify an email format.

There are two kinds of email: *plain text* and *formatted* (which Apple calls Rich Text). Plain text messages are faster to send and open, are universally compatible with the world's email programs, and are greatly preferred by many veteran computer fans. And even though the message itself is plain, you can still attach pictures and other files. (If you want to get really graphic with your mail, you can also use the *Stationery* option, which gives you preformatted message templates to drop in pictures, graphics, and text. Flip to page 325 for more on using stationery.)

Resourceful geeks have even learned how to fake some formatting in plain messages: They use capitals or asterisks instead of bold formatting (**man* is he a GEEK!*), "smileys" like this— :-) —instead of pictures, and pseudo-underlines for emphasis (*I _love_ Swiss cheese!*).

By contrast, formatted messages sometimes open slowly, and in some email programs the formatting doesn't come through at all.

To control which kind of mail you send on a message-by-message basis, choose from the Format menu either Make Plain Text or Make Rich Text. To change the factory setting for new outgoing messages, choose Mail→Preferences; click the Composing icon; and choose from the Message Format pop-up menu.

Tip: If you plan to send formatted mail, remember that your recipients won't see the fonts you use unless their machines have the same ones installed. Bottom line: For email to Mac and Windows owners alike, stick to universal choices like Arial, Times, and Courier.

5. Type your message in the message box.

You can use all standard editing techniques, including copy and paste, drag and drop, and so on. If you selected the Rich Text style of email, you can use word processor–like formatting (Figure 11-4).

As you type, Mail checks your spelling, using a dotted underline to mark questionable words (also shown in Figure 11-4). To check for alternative spellings for a suspect word, Control-click it. From the list of suggestions in the shortcut menu, click the word you really intended, or choose Learn Spelling to add the word to the Mac OS X dictionary. You can read much more about Mac OS X's built-in spelling/grammar checker (and typing expander) starting on page 162.

If you're composing a long email message, or if it's one you don't want to send until later, click the Save as Draft button, press ⌘-S, or choose File→Save As Draft. You've just saved the message in your Drafts folder. It'll still be there the next time you open Mail. To reopen a saved draft later, click the Drafts icon in the Mailboxes column and then double-click the message you want to work on.

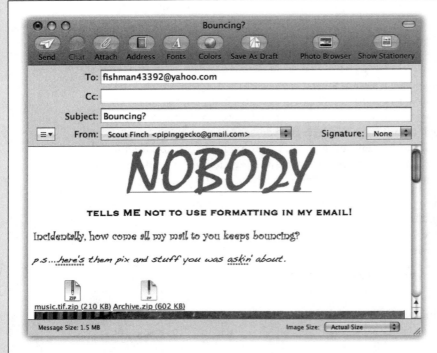

Figure 11-4:
If you really want to use formatting, click the Fonts icon on the toolbar to open the Font panel, or the Colors icon to open the Color Picker dialog box. The Format menu (in the menu bar) contains even more controls: paragraph alignment (left, right, center, or justify), and even Copy and Paste Style commands that let you transfer formatting from one block of text to another.

6. **Click Send (or press Shift-⌘-D).**

   Mail sends the message.

Tip: To resend a message you've already sent, Option-double-click the message in your Sent mailbox. Mail dutifully opens up a brand-new duplicate, ready for you to edit, readdress if you like, and then send again.

(The prescribed Apple route is to highlight the message and then choose Message→Send Again, but that's not nearly as much fun.)

If you'd rather have Mail place each message you write in the Outbox folder instead of connecting to the Net when you click Send, choose Mailbox→Take All Accounts

Offline. While you're offline, Mail refrains from trying to connect, which is a great feature when you're working on a laptop at 39,000 feet. (Choose Mailbox→Take All Accounts Online to reverse the procedure.)

Attaching Files to Messages

Sending little text messages is fine, but it's not much help when you want to send somebody a photograph, a sound, or a Word document. To attach a file to a message you've written, use one of these methods:

• Drag the icons you want to attach directly off the desktop (or out of a folder) into the New Message window. There your attachments appear with their own hyper-linked icons (shown in Figure 11-4), meaning that your recipient can simply click to open them.

Tip: Exposé was *born* for this moment. Hit ⌘-F3 to make all open windows flee to the edges of the screen, revealing the desktop. Root around until you find the file you want to send. Begin dragging it; without releasing the mouse, press ⌘-F3 again to bring your message window back into view. Complete your drag into the message window. (On old plastic keyboards, press F11 instead.)

Attachment Tricks

Nowadays, what's *attached* to an email message is often more important than the message itself. You might send a PowerPoint file to a coworker or send your aunt a picture of your new dog, for example, without bothering to write anything more than "See attached" in the body of the message.

That's why it's such a pain when email attachments don't go through properly—or when they're too big to send at all. Luckily, Mac OS X now provides three tools for making attachments smaller and more compatible with Windows, so you'll never get another angry "I *can't* see attached!" reply again.

If you're sending images along with your message, you can shrink them down right in Mail. Use the Image Size pop-up menu in the lower-right corner of the window to pick a smaller size for the images (like Medium or Small).

You can keep tabs on the total size of your attachments in the lower-left corner of the window, too. Ideally, you should keep the total under 2 MB, so dial-up sufferers don't get annoyed—and so your message doesn't get rejected by your recipient's ISP for being too big.

Use the Finder to compress big files before you send

them. As described on page 90, the Finder creates zip-compressed files, which generally take up much less space than the originals.

You can pick from two different formats for your attachments: normal or Windows-friendly. Normal attachments open correctly on both Macs and PCs. Trouble is, a normal attachment may show up on a PC accompanied by a useless second attachment whose name starts with "._" (which your recipients should just ignore).

Windows-friendly attachments, on the other hand, always work correctly on PCs—but may not open at all on Macs. Unless you work in an all-Windows company, then, stick with the normal setting.

To use the Windows-friendly setting for an open message, choose Edit→Attachments→Send Windows Friendly Attachments. (If no message is open, the command says "*Always Send Windows Friendly Attachments*" instead). You can also adjust the setting on a per-email basis using the Send Windows Friendly Attachments checkbox at the bottom of the attachment dialog box.

Mail makes it look as though you can park the attached file's icon (or the full image of a graphics file) *inside* the text of the message, mingled with your typing. Don't be fooled, however; on the receiving end, all the attachments will be clumped together at the end of the message (unless your recipient also uses Mail or you've sent pictures with Stationery).

- Drag the icons you want to attach from the desktop onto Mail's Dock icon. Mail dutifully creates a new, outgoing message, with the files already attached.

- Click the Attach icon on the New Message toolbar, choose File→Attach File, or press Shift-⌘-A. The standard Open File sheet now appears so you can navigate to and select the files you want to include. (You can choose multiple files simultaneously in this dialog box. Just ⌘-click or Shift-click the individual files you want as though you were selecting them in a Finder window.)

  Once you've selected them, click Choose File (or press Return). You return to the New Message window, where the attachments' icons appear, ready to ride along when you send the message.

To remove an attachment, drag across its icon to highlight it, and then press the Delete key. (You can also drag an attachment icon clear out of the window into your Dock's Trash, or choose Message→Remove Attachments.)

Signatures

Signatures are bits of text that get stamped at the bottom of your outgoing email messages. A signature might contain a name, a postal address, a pithy quote, or even a scan of your *real* signature, as shown in Figure 11-3.

You can customize your signatures by choosing Mail→Preferences and then clicking the Signatures icon. Here's what you should know:

- **To build up a library of signatures that you can use in any of your accounts:** Select All Signatures in the leftmost pane, and then click the **+** button to add each new signature (Figure 11-5). Give each new signature a name in the middle pane, and then customize the signatures' text in the rightmost pane.

Tip: If you ever get tired of a signature, you can delete it forever by selecting All Signatures→[your signature's name], clicking the **−** button, and then clicking OK.

- **To make a signature available in one of your email accounts:** Drag the signature's name from the middle pane onto the name of the account in the leftmost pane. In other words, you can make certain signatures available to only your work (or personal) account, so you never accidentally end up appending your secret FBI contact signature to the bottom of a birthday invitation you're sending out.

- **To assign a particular signature to one account:** In the left pane, click an account; choose from the Choose Signature pop-up menu. Each time you compose a message from that account, Mail inserts the signature you selected.

Tip: To make things more interesting for your recipients, pick At Random; Mail selects a different signature each time you send a message. Or, if you're not that much of a risk-taker, choose In Sequential Order; Mail picks the next signature in order for each new message you write.

Remember that you can always change your signature on a message-by-message basis, using the Signature pop-up menu in any new email message.

- **To use the signature feature as a prefix in replies:** Turn on "Place signature above quoted text." If you turn on this setting, your signature gets inserted *above* any text that you're replying to, rather than below. You'd use this setting if your "signature" said something like, "Hi there! You wrote this to me!"

Tip: If you're into consistent typographical styling, also turn on "Always match my default font." That setting makes sure any messages you send contain the signature in the same font as the rest of the message, lending it an air of professionalism.

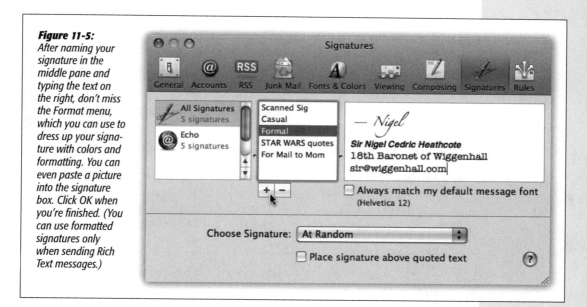

Figure 11-5:
After naming your signature in the middle pane and typing the text on the right, don't miss the Format menu, which you can use to dress up your signature with colors and formatting. You can even paste a picture into the signature box. Click OK when you're finished. (You can use formatted signatures only when sending Rich Text messages.)

Stationery

Rich text—and even plain text—messages are fine for your everyday personal and business correspondence. After all, you really won't help messages like, "Let's have a meeting on those third-quarter earnings results" much by adding visual bells and whistles.

But suppose you have an occasion where you *want* to jazz up your mail, like an electronic invitation to a bridal shower or a mass mail update as you get your kicks down Route 66.

These messages just cry out for Mail's *Stationery* feature. Stationery means colorful, predesigned mail templates that you make your own by dragging in photos from your own collection. Those fancy fonts and graphics will certainly get people's attention when they open the message.

Note: They will, that is, if their email programs understand HTML formatting. That's the formatting Mail uses for its stationery. (If *HTML* rings a bell, it's because this HyperText Markup Language is the same used to make Web pages so lively and colorful.)

It might be a good idea to make sure everyone on your recipient list has a mail program that can handle HTML; otherwise, your message may look like a jumble of code and letters in the middle of the screen.

To make a stylized message with Mail Stationery:

1. **Create a new message.**

   Click File→New Message, press ⌘-N, or click the New Message button on the Mail window toolbar. The choice is up to you.

2. **On the right side of the toolbar on the New Message window, click Show Stationery.**

   A panel opens up, showing you all the available templates, in categories like "Birthday" and "Announcements."

3. **Click a category, and then click a stationery thumbnail image to apply it to your message.**

   The body of your message changes to take on the look of the template.

4. **If you like what you see, click the Hide Stationery button on the toolbar to fold up the stationery-picker panel.**

Tip: If you don't like the background color, try clicking the thumbnail; some templates offer a few different color choices.

Now, without question, Apple's canned stationery looks fantastic. The only problem is, the photos that adorn most of the templates are pictures of *somebody else's* family and friends. Unless you work for Apple's modeling agency, you probably have no clue who they are.

Fortunately, it's easy enough to replace those placeholder photos with your *own* snaps.

5. **Add and adjust pictures.**

Click the Photo Browser icon on the message toolbar to open up a palette that lists all the photos you've stored in iPhoto, Aperture, and Photo Booth (Figure 11-6).

Tip: If you don't keep your pictures in any of those programs, you can drag any folder of pictures onto the Photo Browser window to add them.

Figure 11-6:
To use Stationery, start by clicking a template, then add your own text in place of the generic copy that comes with the template.

Click the Photo Browser button at the top of the message window to open your Mac's photo collections (shown at right), and then drag the images you want into the picture boxes on the stationery template. You don't have to know a lick of HTML to use the templates—it's all drag, drop, and type, baby.

Now you can drag your own pictures directly *onto* Apple's dummy photos on the stationery template. They replace the sunny models.

To resize a photo in the template, double-click it. A slider appears that lets you adjust the photo's size within the message. Drag the mouse around the photo window to reposition the picture relative to its frame.

6. **Select the fake text and type in what you really want to say.**

    Unless you're writing to your Latin students, of course, in which case "Duis nonsequ ismodol oreetuer iril dolore facidunt" might be perfectly appropriate.

    In any case, as you type over the dummy text, your words are autoformatted to match the template design.

Once you've got that message looking the way you want it, address it just as you would any other piece of mail, and then click the Send button to get it on its way.

> **Tip:** You're not stuck with Apple's designs for your Stationery templates; you can make your own. Just make a new message, style the fonts and photos the way you want them, and then choose File→Save as Stationery. You can now select your masterwork in the Custom category, which appears down at the end of the list in the stationery-picker panel.

If you decide the message would be better off as plain old text, click Show Stationery on the message window. In the list of template categories, click Stationery and then Original to strip the color and formats out of the message.

> **Tip:** If you find you're using one or two templates a lot (if, for example, all your friends are having babies these days), then drag your frequently used templates into the Favorites category so you don't have to go wading around for them.
>
> To remove one from Favorites, click it, and then click the ⊗ in the top-left corner of the thumbnail.

Reading Email

Mail puts all incoming email into your Inbox; the statistic after the word *Inbox* lets you know how many messages you haven't yet read. New messages are also marked with light-blue dots in the main list.

UP TO SPEED

All the Little Symbols

The first column of the main email list shows little symbols that let you know at a glance how you've processed certain messages. The most common one is, of course, the light-blue dot (●), which means "new message." (After reading a message, you can mark it once again as an *unread* message by choosing Message→Mark→As Unread [Shift-⌘-U]—or by Control-clicking the message's name and then choosing Mark→As Unread from the shortcut menu.)

You might also see these symbols, which represent messages you've replied to (↩), forwarded (→), redirected (↯), or flagged ⚑.

A well-guarded secret, however, is that the "replied to" and "forwarded" symbols aren't just indicators—they're also *buttons*.

When you see one of these symbols next to your original message, click it to jump straight to your reply (or forwarded message). You're spared the trouble of having to search through all your mailboxes.

Incidentally, you may have noticed that Mail marks a message as having been read the moment you click it. You can change it back to unread by using its shortcut menu—but there's also a more permanent workaround.

If you hide the Preview pane by double-clicking the divider bar just above it, Mail no longer marks messages "read" just because you clicked them in the list. (You can bring back the Preview pane by double-clicking just above the vertical scroll bar, or by dragging the divider bar back up from the bottom.)

Tip: The Mail icon in the Dock also shows you how many new messages you have waiting; it's the number in the red circle.

Click the Inbox folder to see a list of received messages. If it's a long list, press Control-Page Up and Control-Page Down to scroll. (Page Up and Page Down without the Control key scrolls the Preview pane instead.)

Click the name of a message once to read it in the Preview pane, or double-click a message to open it into a separate window. (If a message is already selected, pressing Return also opens its separate window.)

Tip: Instead of reading your mail, you might prefer to have Mac OS X read it *to* you, as you sit back in your chair and sip a strawberry daiquiri. Highlight the text you want to hear (or choose Edit→Select All), and then choose Edit→Speech→Start Speaking. You'll hear the message read aloud, in the voice you've selected on the Speech pane of System Preferences (Chapter 15).

To stop the insanity, choose Edit→Speech→Stop Speaking.

Once you've viewed a message, you can respond to it, delete it, print it, file it, and so on. The following pages should get you started.

Threading

Threading is one of the most useful mail-sorting methods to come along in a long time. When threading is turned on, Mail groups emails with the same subject (like "Raccoons" and "Re: Raccoons") *as a single item* in the main mail list.

To turn on threading, choose View→Organize by Thread. If several messages have the same subject, they all turn light blue to indicate their membership in a thread (Figure 11-7).

Here are some powerful ways to use threading:

- **View a list of all the messages in a thread** by clicking its heading. In the Preview pane, you see a comprehensive inventory of the thread (Figure 11-7). You can click a message's name in this list to jump right to it.

- **Move all the members of a thread to a new mailbox** simply by moving its heading. You might find this useful, for example, when you've just finished a project and want to file away all the email related to it quickly. (As a bonus, a circled number tells you how many messages you're moving as you drag the heading.) You can even delete all the messages in a thread at once by deleting its heading.

- **Examine thread members from multiple mailboxes.** Normally, threads display only messages held in the *same* mailbox, but that's not especially convenient when you want to see both messages (from your Inbox) and your replies (in your Sent box). To work around that problem, click Inbox, and then ⌘-click the Sent mailbox (or any other mailboxes you want to include). Your threads seamlessly combine related messages from all the selected mailboxes.

- **Quickly collapse all threads** by choosing View→Collapse All Threads. If your main list gets cluttered with too many expanded threads, this is a quick way to force it into order. (If, on the other hand, your main list isn't cluttered *enough*, choose View→Expand All Threads.)

- **Send someone all the messages in a thread** by selecting the thread's heading and clicking Forward. Mail automatically copies all the messages of the thread into a new message, putting the oldest at the top. You might find this useful, for instance, when you want to send your boss all the correspondence you've had with someone about a certain project.

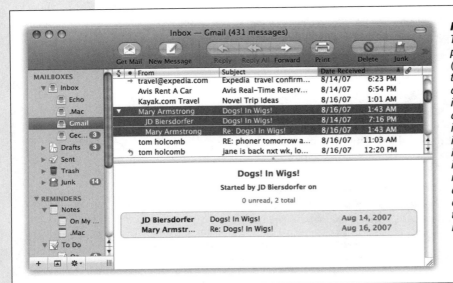

Figure 11-7:
Threads have two parts: a heading (the subject of the thread, listed in dark blue when it's not selected) and members (the individual messages in the thread, listed in light blue and indented). Often, the main list shows only a thread's heading; click the flippy triangle to reveal its members.

Adding the Sender to Your Address Book

When you choose the Message→Add Sender to Address Book command, Mail memorizes the email address of the person whose message is on the screen. In fact, you can highlight a huge number of messages and add *all* the senders simultaneously using this technique.

Thereafter, you'll be able to write new messages to somebody just by typing the first few letters of her name or email address.

Data Detectors

Data detectors are described on page 171. They're what you see when Mac OS X recognizes commonly used bits of written information: a physical address, a phone number, a date and time, a flight number, and so on. With one quick click, you can send that information into the appropriate Mac OS X program, like iCal, Address Book, the Flights widget in Dashboard, or your Web browser (for looking an address up on a map).

This is just a public-service reminder that data detectors are especially useful—*primarily* useful, in fact—in Mail. Watch for the dotted rectangle that appears when you point to a name, address, date, time, or flight number.

Note: When someone sends you what looks like a date and time –"Hey, we're getting together for a luau at my apartment on 6/12/2010 at 8:30 pm! Hope you can come!"– the data detector goes one better. Now the pop-up menu that opens when you click the ▼ button actually proposes, "Create New iCal Event." (It even works for less specific wording, like, "Can you come over Thursday afternoon at 3:30?")

You look over the proposed appointment (you'll probably want to edit the title), and that's it–Mail actually creates an appointment on your iCal automatically!

Opening Attachments

Just as you can attach files to a message, so people often send files to you. Sometimes they don't even bother to type a message; you wind up receiving an empty email message with a file or two attached. Only the presence of the file's icon in the message body tells you there's something attached.

Tip: Mail doesn't ordinarily indicate the presence of attachments in the Messages list. It can do so, however. Just choose View→Columns→Attachments. A new column appears in the email list–at the far right–where you see a paper-clip icon and the number of file attachments listed for each message.

Mail doesn't store downloaded files as normal file icons on your hard drive. They're actually encoded right into the *.mbox* mailbox databases that, behind the scenes, maintain your mail stash. To extract an attached file from this mass of software, you must proceed in one of these ways:

- Click the Quick Look button in the message header. Instantly, you're treated to a nearly full-size preview of the file's contents. Yes, Quick Look has come to email. Its strengths and weaknesses here are exactly as described in Chapter 1.

Tip: If the attachments are pictures, clicking Quick Look gives you a full-screen slideshow of every attached image.

If you jiggle the mouse a little during the slideshow, you get a useful row of slideshow-control buttons along the bottom of the screen, too.

- Click the Save button in the message header to save it to the Mac's Downloads folder, nestled within easy reach in the Dock.

Tip: If you don't want to use the Downloads folder, you can choose a new autosave location for attachments by choosing Mail→Preferences→General→Downloads Folder.

- Control-click (or right-click) the attachment's icon, and choose Save Attachment from the shortcut menu. You'll be asked to specify where you want to put it. Or save time by choosing Save to Downloads Folder, meaning the Downloads folder in the Dock.

- Drag the attachment icon out of the message window and onto any visible portion of your desktop (or any visible folder).

- Click the Save button at the top of the email, or choose File→Save Attachments. (If the message has more than one attachment, this maneuver saves all of them.)

Tip: The Save button at the top of the Preview pane doubles as a pop-up menu; if you click it and keep the mouse button pressed, you can select from several other options for saving the attachments—like importing them into iPhoto or downloading only one of them.

- Double-click the attachment's icon, or single-click the blue link underneath the icon. If you were sent a document (a photo, Word file, or Excel file, for example), it now opens in the corresponding program.

Note: After the attachment is open, use the File→Save As command to save the file into a folder of your choice. Otherwise, any changes you make to the document won't be visible except when you open it from within Mail.

- Control-click the attachment's icon. From the shortcut menu, you can specify which program you want to use for opening it, using the Open With submenu.

Replying to a Message

To answer a message, click the Reply button on the message toolbar (or choose Message→Reply, or press ⌘-R). If the message was originally addressed to multiple recipients, you can send your reply to everyone simultaneously by clicking Reply All instead.

A new message window opens, already addressed. As a courtesy to your correspondent, Mail places the original message at the bottom of the window, set off by a vertical bar, as shown in Figure 11-8.

Tip: If you highlight some text before clicking Reply, Mail pastes *only that portion* of the original message into your reply. That's a great convenience to your correspondent, who now knows exactly which part of the message you're responding to.

At this point, you can add or delete recipients, edit the Subject line or the original message, attach a file, and so on.

Tip: Use the Return key to create blank lines in the original message. Using this method, you can splice your own comments into the paragraphs of the original message, replying point by point. The brackets preceding each line of the original message help your correspondent keep straight what's yours and what's hers.

When you're finished, click Send. (If you click Reply All in the message window now, your message goes to everyone who received the original note, *even* if you began the reply process by clicking Reply. Mac OS X, in other words, gives you a second chance to address your reply to everyone.)

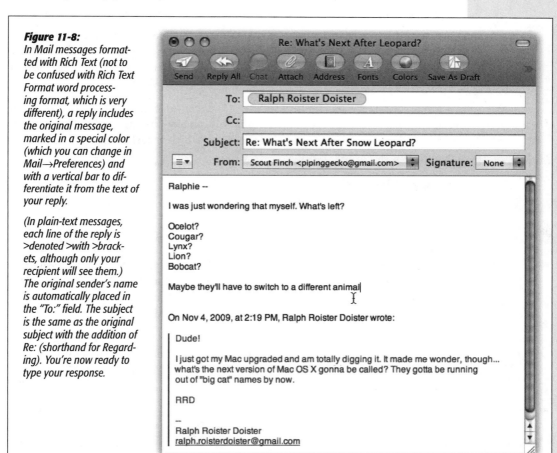

Figure 11-8:
In Mail messages format-ted with Rich Text (not to be confused with Rich Text Format word process-ing format, which is very different), a reply includes the original message, marked in a special color (which you can change in Mail→Preferences) and with a vertical bar to dif-ferentiate it from the text of your reply.

(In plain-text messages, each line of the reply is >denoted >with >brack-ets, although only your recipient will see them.) The original sender's name is automatically placed in the "To:" field. The subject is the same as the original subject with the addition of Re: (shorthand for Regard-ing). You're now ready to type your response.

Forwarding Messages

Instead of replying to the person who sent you a message, you may sometimes want to pass the note on to a third person.

To do so, click the Forward toolbar button (or choose Message→Forward, or press Shift-⌘-F). A new message opens, looking a lot like the one that appears when you reply. You may wish to precede the original message with a comment of your own, along the lines of: "Frank: I thought you'd be interested in this joke about your mom."

Finally, address it as you would any outgoing piece of mail.

Redirecting Messages

A redirected message is similar to a forwarded message, with one useful difference: When you forward a message, your recipient sees that it came from you. When you redirect it, your recipient sees the *original* writer's name as the sender. In other words, a redirected message uses you as a low-profile relay station between two other people.

Treasure this feature. Plenty of email programs, including Outlook and Outlook Express for Windows, don't offer a Redirect command at all. You can use it to transfer messages from one of your own accounts to another, or to pass along a message that came to you by mistake.

To redirect a message, choose Message→Redirect, or press Shift-⌘-E. You get an outgoing copy of the message—this time without any quoting marks. (You can edit redirected messages before you send them, too, which is perfect for April Fools' Day pranks.)

Printing Messages

Sometimes there's no substitute for a printout. Choose File→Print, or press ⌘-P to summon the Print dialog box.

Filing Messages

Mail lets you create new mailboxes in the Mailboxes pane. You might create one for important messages, another for order confirmations from Web shopping, still another for friends and family, and so on. You can even create mailboxes *inside* these mailboxes, a feature beloved by the hopelessly organized.

Mail even offers *smart mailboxes*—self-updating folders that show you all your mail from your boss, for example, or every message with "mortgage" in its subject. It's the same idea as smart folders in the Finder or smart playlists in iTunes: folders whose contents are based around criteria you specify (Figure 11-9).

Figure 11-9:
Mail lets you create self-populating folders. In this example, the "New Mail from Mom" smart mailbox will automatically display all messages from her that you've received in the past week.

The commands you need are all in the Mailbox menu. For example, to create a new mailbox folder, choose Mailbox→New Mailbox, or click the **+** button at the bottom of the Mailboxes column. To create a smart mailbox, choose Mailbox→New Smart Mailbox.

Mail asks you to name the new mailbox. If you have more than one email account, you can specify which one will contain the new folder. (Smart mailboxes, however, always sit outside your other mailboxes.)

Tip: If you want to create a folder-inside-a-folder, use slashes in the name of your new mailbox. (If you use the name *Cephalopods/Squid*, for example, then Mail creates a folder called Cephalopods, with a subfolder called Squid.) You can also drag the mailbox icons up and down in the drawer to place one inside another.

None of those tricks work for smart mailboxes, however. The only way to organize smart mailboxes is to put them inside a smart mailbox *folder*, which you create using Mailbox→New Smart Mailbox. You might do that if you have several smart mailboxes for mail from your coworkers ("From Jim," "From Anne," and so on) and want to put them together in one collapsible group to save screen space.

When you click OK, a new icon appears in the mailbox column, ready for use.

You can move a message (or group of messages) into a mailbox folder in any of three ways:

- Drag it out of the main list onto a mailbox icon.

- In the list pane, highlight one or more messages, and then choose from the Message→Move To submenu, which lists all your mailboxes.

- Control-click (or right-click) a message, or one of several that you've highlighted. From the resulting shortcut menu, choose Move To, and then, from the submenu, choose the mailbox you want.

Of course, the only way to change the contents of a *smart* mailbox is to change the criteria it uses to populate itself. To do so, double-click the smart mailbox icon and use the dialog box that appears.

Flagging Messages

Sometimes you'll receive email that prompts you to some sort of action, but you may not have the time (or the fortitude) to face the task at the moment. ("Hi there… it's me, your accountant. Would you mind rounding up your expenses for 1999 through 2009 and sending me a list by email?")

That's why Mail lets you *flag* a message, summoning a little flag icon in a new column next to a message's name. These indicators can mean anything you like—they simply call attention to certain messages. You can sort your mail list so that all your flagged messages are listed first; click the flag at the top of the column heading.

To flag a message in this way, select the message (or several messages) and then choose Message→Mark→As Flagged, or press Option-⌘-L, or Control-click (right-click) the message's name in the list and, from the shortcut menu, choose Mark→As Flagged. (To clear the flags, repeat the procedure, but use the Mark→As Unflagged command instead.)

Tip: This whole flagging business has another useful side effect. When Mail finds messages it thinks are spam, it marks them with little trash-bag icons in the flag column. If you sort your mail by flag, then all your spam gets grouped together—which is great if you want to do one big spam-cleaning by dragging it all to the Trash.

Finding Messages

When you deal with masses of email, you may come to rely on Mail's *dedicated* searching tools. They're fast and convenient, and when you're done with them, you can go right back to browsing your Message list as it was.

Finding messages within a mailbox

The box in the upper-right corner of the main mail window is Mail's own private Spotlight. You can use it to hide all but certain messages, as shown in Figure 11-10.

Tip: You can also set up Mail to show you only certain messages that you've *manually* selected, hiding all others in the list. To do so, highlight the messages you want, using the usual selection techniques (page 81). Then choose View→Display Selected Messages Only. (To see all of them again, choose View→Display All Messages.)

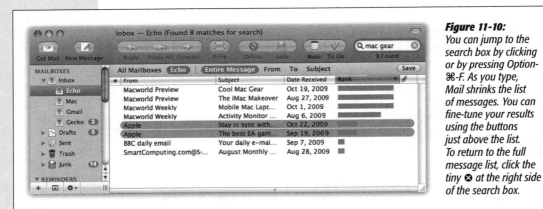

Figure 11-10:
You can jump to the search box by clicking or by pressing Option-⌘-F. As you type, Mail shrinks the list of messages. You can fine-tune your results using the buttons just above the list. To return to the full message list, click the tiny ⊗ at the right side of the search box.

In Snow Leopard, this search box is powerful indeed. For example:

- You have the power of Spotlight charging up your search rankings; the most relevant messages for your search appear high on the list. And Notes and To Do items show up in the search results now, too.

- When you're searching, a thin row of buttons appears underneath the toolbar. You can use these buttons to narrow your results to only messages with your search term in their *subject*, for example, or to only those messages in the currently selected mailbox.

- When you select a message in the search view, the Preview pane pops up from the bottom of the window. If you click Show in Mailbox, on the other hand, you exit the search view and jump straight to the message in whatever mailbox it came from.

That's perfect if the message is part of a thread, since jumping to the message also displays all the other messages from its thread.

- If you think you'll want to perform the current search again sometime, click Save in the upper-right corner of the window. Mail displays a dialog box with your search term and criteria filled in; all you have to do is give it a name and click OK to transform your search into a smart mailbox that you can open anytime.

Finding text within an open message

You can also search for certain text *within* an open message. Choose Edit→Find→Find (or press ⌘-F) to bring up the Find dialog box (Figure 11-11).

Figure 11-11:
The Find box works just as it does in a word processor, except that the Replace function works only on messages you've written yourself—Mail doesn't let you change the words of mail you've received. (Lawyers would have a field day with that one.)

Deleting Messages

Sometimes it's junk mail. Sometimes you're just done with it. Either way, it's a snap to delete a selected message, several selected messages, or a message that's currently before you on the screen. You can press the Delete key, click the Delete button on the toolbar, choose Edit→Delete, or drag messages out of the list window and into your Trash mailbox—or even onto the Dock's Trash icon.

Tip: If you delete a message by accident, the Undo command (Edit→Undo or ⌘-Z) restores it.

All these commands move the messages to the Trash folder. If you like, you can then click its icon to view a list of the messages you've deleted. You can even rescue messages by dragging them back into another mailbox (back to the Inbox, for example).

Method 1: Emptying the Trash folder

Mail doesn't vaporize messages in the Trash folder until you "empty the trash," just like in the Finder. You can empty the Trash folder in any of several ways:

- Click a message (or several) within the Trash folder list, and then click the Delete icon on the toolbar (or press the Delete key). Now those messages are *really* gone.

- Choose Mailbox→Erase Deleted Messages (⌘-K). (If you have multiple accounts, choose Erase Deleted Messages→In All Accounts.)

- Control-click (or right-click) the Trash mailbox icon, and then choose Erase Deleted Messages from the shortcut menu. Or choose the same command from the ✿ pop-up menu at the bottom of the window.

- Wait. Mail will permanently delete these messages automatically after a week.

  If a week is too long (or not long enough), you can change this interval. Choose Mail→Preferences, click Accounts, and select the account name from the list at left. Then click Mailbox Behaviors, and change the "Erase deleted messages when" pop-up menu. If you choose Quitting Mail from the pop-up menu, Mail will take out the trash every time you quit the program.

Method 2: Deleted mail turns invisible

Mail offers a second—and very unusual—method of deleting messages that doesn't involve the Trash folder at all. Using this method, pressing the Delete key (or clicking the Delete toolbar button) simply hides the selected message in the list. Hidden messages remain hidden, but don't go away for good until you use the Rebuild Mailbox command described in the box on page 341.

If this arrangement sounds useful, choose Mail→Preferences; click Accounts and select the account from the list on the left; click Mailbox Behaviors; and then turn off the checkbox called "Move deleted messages to a separate folder" or "Move deleted messages to the Trash mailbox." (The checkbox's wording depends on what kind of account you have.) From now on, messages you delete vanish from the list.

They're not really gone, however. You can bring them back, at least in ghostly form, by choosing View→Show Deleted Messages (or pressing ⌘-L). Figure 11-12 shows the idea.

Figure 11-12:
To resurrect a deleted message (indicated in light gray type), Control-click it and choose Undelete from the shortcut menu.

Using this system, in other words, you never truly delete messages; you just hide them.

At first, you might be concerned about the disk space and database size involved in keeping your old messages around forever like this. Truth is that Mac OS X is perfectly capable of maintaining many thousands of messages in its mailbox databases—and with the sizes of hard drives nowadays, a few thousand messages aren't likely to make much of a dent.

Meanwhile, there's a huge benefit to this arrangement. At some point, almost everyone wishes they could resurrect a deleted message—maybe months later, maybe years later. Using the hidden-deleted-message system, your old messages are always around for reference. (The downside to this system, of course, is that SEC investigators can use it to find incriminating mail that you thought you'd deleted.)

When you do want to purge these messages for good, you can always return to the Special Mailboxes dialog box and turn the "Move deleted mail to a separate folder" checkbox back on.

Archiving Mailboxes

Time Machine (page 277) keeps a watchful eye on your Mac and backs up its data regularly—including your email. If you ever delete a message by accident or otherwise make a mess of your email stash, you can duck into Time Machine right from within Mail.

But not everybody wants to use Time Machine, for personal reasons—lack of a second hard drive, aversion to software named after H. G. Wells novels, whatever.

Yet having a backup of your email is critically important. Think of all the precious mail you'd hate to lose: business correspondence, electronic receipts, baby's first message. Fortunately, there's a second good way to back up your email—*archive it,* like this:

1. **In the Mailboxes column, choose which mailbox or mailboxes you want to archive.**

   If you have multiple mailboxes in mind, Control-click (or right-click) each one until you've selected all the ones you want.

2. **At the bottom of the Mail window, open the ✿ pop-up menu and choose Archive Mailbox(es).**

   You can also get to this command by choosing Mailbox→Archive.

3. **In the box that appears, navigate to the place you want to stash this archive of valuable mail, like a server, flash drive, or folder. Click Choose.**

   Your archived mailboxes are saved to the location you've chosen. You can now go back to work writing new messages.

   Later, if you need to pull one of those archives back into duty, choose File→Import Mailboxes. Choose the "Mail for Mac OS X" option and navigate back to the place you stored your archived mailboxes.

Note: If you archive mailboxes on a regular basis, don't worry about changing the name of the .mbox file to prevent it from overwriting a previous archive. Mail is smart enough to stick a number at the end of the new file name for you.

Message Rules

Once you know how to create folders, the next step in managing your email is to set up a series of *message rules* (filters) that file, answer, or delete incoming messages automatically based on their contents (such as their subject, address, and/or size). Message rules require you to think like the distant relative of a programmer, but the mental effort can reward you many times over. Message rules turn Mail into a surprisingly smart and efficient secretary.

Setting up message rules

Here's how to set up a message rule:

1. **Choose Mail→Preferences. Click the Rules icon.**

The Rules pane appears, as shown at top in Figure 11-13.

2. **Click Add Rule.**

Now the dialog box shown at bottom in Figure 11-13 appears.

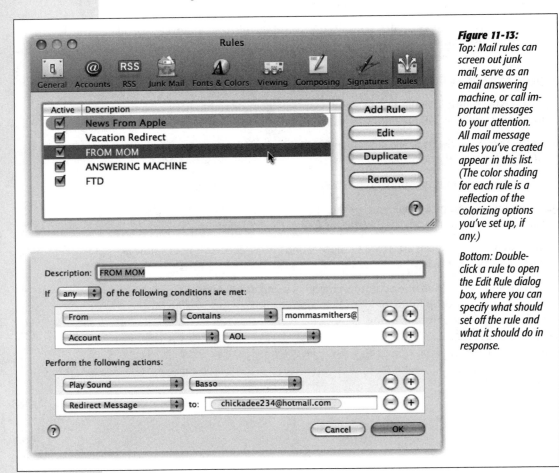

Figure 11-13:
Top: Mail rules can screen out junk mail, serve as an email answering machine, or call important messages to your attention. All mail message rules you've created appear in this list. (The color shading for each rule is a reflection of the colorizing options you've set up, if any.)

Bottom: Double-click a rule to open the Edit Rule dialog box, where you can specify what should set off the rule and what it should do in response.

3. **Use the criteria options (at the top) to specify how Mail should select messages to process.**

   For example, if you'd like the program to watch out for messages from a particular person, you would set up the first two pop-up menus to say "From" and "Contains," respectively.

   To flag messages containing *loan, $$$$, XXXX, !!!!,* and so on, set the pop-up menus to say "Subject" and "Contains."

   You can set up *multiple* criteria here to flag messages whose subjects contain any one of those common spam triggers. (If you change the "any" pop-up menu to say "all," then *all* the criteria must be true for the rule to kick in.)

4. **Specify which words or people you want the message rule to watch for.**

   In the text box to the right of the two pop-up menus, type the word, address, name, or phrase you want Mail to watch for—a person's name, or *$$$$,* in the previous examples.

5. **In the lower half of the box, specify what you want to happen to messages that match the criteria.**

   If, in steps 1 and 2, you've told your rule to watch for junk mail containing *$$$$* in the Subject line, here's where you can tell Mail to delete it or move it into, say, a Junk folder.

   With a little imagination, you'll see how the options in this pop-up menu can do absolutely amazing things with your incoming email. Mail can colorize, delete, move, redirect, or forward messages—or even play a sound when you get a certain message.

   By setting up the controls as shown in Figure 11-13, for example, you'll have specified that whenever your mother *(mom@mcmail.com)* sends something to

---

TROUBLESHOOTING MOMENT

Rebuilding Your Mail Databases

Mail keeps your messages in a series of mailbox database files in your Home→Library→Mail folder.

Over time, as you add and delete hundreds of messages from these database files, some digital sawdust gets left behind, resulting in peculiarities when addressing messages or general Mail sluggishness. You also wind up with *massive* message files hidden on your hard drive, which can consume hundreds of megabytes of disk space. That's a particular bummer if you like to copy your message databases to your laptop when you go on a trip.

Fortunately, it's easy enough to *rebuild the message databases*. Doing so cleanses, repairs, and purges your message files. As a result, you wind up with a much more compact and healthy database.

To rebuild a mailbox, highlight it in the Mailboxes column in Mail. (Highlight several by ⌘-clicking, if you like.) Then choose Mailbox→Rebuild. Mac OS X takes several minutes (or hours, depending on the size of your mailboxes) to repair and compact your database—but if you're experiencing Mail weirdness or slowness, it's well worth the sacrifice.

---

your Gmail account, you'll hear a specific alert noise as the email is redirected to a different email account, *chickadee745@hotmail.com.*

6. In the very top box, name your mail rule. Click OK.

Now you're back to the Rules pane (Figure 11-13, top). Here you can choose a sequence for the rules you've created by dragging them up and down. Here, too, you can turn off the ones you won't be needing at the moment, but may use again one day.

Tip: Mail applies rules as they appear, from top to bottom, in the list. If a rule doesn't seem to be working properly, it may be that an earlier rule is intercepting and processing some messages before the "broken" rule even sees them. To fix this, try dragging the rule (or the interfering rule) up or down in the list.

The Anti-Spam Toolkit

Spam, the junk that now makes up more than 80 percent of email, is a problem that's only getting worse. Luckily, you, along with Mail's advanced spam filters, can make it better—at least for *your* email accounts.

Using the Junk Mail Filter

You'll see the effects of Mail's spam filter the first time you check your mail: A certain swath of message titles appears in color. These are the messages that Mail considers junk.

Note: Out of the box, Mail doesn't apply its spam-targeting features to people whose addresses are in your Address Book, to people you've emailed recently, or to messages sent to you *by name* rather than just by email address. You can adjust these settings in Mail→Preferences→Junk Mail tab.

During your first couple of weeks with Mail, your job is to supervise Mail's work. That is, if you get spam that Mail misses, click the message, and then click the Junk button at the top of its window, or the Junk icon on the toolbar. On the other hand, if Mail flags legitimate mail as spam, slap it gently on the wrist by clicking the Not Junk button. Over time, Mail gets better and better at filtering your mail; it even does surprisingly well against the new breed of image-only spam.

The trouble with this so-called Training mode is that you're still left with the task of trashing the spam yourself, saving you no time whatsoever.

Once Mail has perfected its filtering skills to your satisfaction, though, open Mail's preferences, click Junk Mail, and click "Move it to the Junk mailbox." From now on, Mail automatically files what it deems junk into a Junk mailbox, where it's much easier to scan and delete the messages en masse.

Tip: Don't miss the "Trust Junk Mail headers set by your Internet Service Provider" option in the Junk Mail pane of the preference window. If you turn on that checkbox, Mail takes your ISP's word that certain messages are spam, giving you a *double* layer of spam protection.

More Anti-Spam Tips

The Junk filter goes a long way toward cleaning out the spam from your mail collection—but it doesn't catch everything. If you're overrun by spam, here are some other steps you can take:

- **Don't let the spammers know you're there.** Choose Mail→Preferences, click Viewing, and turn off "Display remote images in HTML messages." This option thwarts a common spammer tactic by blocking graphics that appear to be embedded into a message but are actually retrieved from a Web site somewhere. Spammers use that embedded-graphics trick to know that their message has fallen on fertile ground—a live sucker who actually looks at these messages—but with that single preference switch, you can fake them out.

- **Rules.** Set up some message rules, as described on the preceding pages, that autoflag messages as spam that have subject lines containing trigger words like "Viagra," "Herbal," "Mortgage," "Refinance," "Enlarge," "Your"—you get the idea.

- **Create a private account.** Above all, if you're overrun by spam, consider sacrificing your address to the public areas of the Internet, like chat rooms, online shopping, Web site and software registration, and newsgroup posting. Spammers use automated software robots that scour every public Internet message and Web page, recording email addresses they find. (In fact, that's probably how they got your address in the first place.)

Using this technique, at least you're now restricting the junk mail to a secondary mail account. Reserve a separate email account for person-to-person email.

Here are some suggestions for avoiding spammers' lists in the first place:

- **Don't ask for it.** When filling out forms online, turn off the checkboxes that say, "Yes, send me exciting offers and news from our partners."

- **Fake out the robots.** When posting messages in a newsgroup or message board, insert the letters NOSPAM somewhere into your email address. Anyone replying to you via email must delete the NOSPAM from your email address, which is a slight hassle. Meanwhile, though, the spammers' software robots will lift a bogus email address from your online postings.

- **Never reply to spam.** Doing so identifies your email address as an active one and can lead to even more unwanted mail. Along the same lines, never click the "Please remove me from your list" link at the bottom of an email unless you know who sent the message.

And for goodness' sake, don't *order* anything sold by the spammers. If only one person in 500,000 does so, the spammer makes money.

RSS Feeds

Mail gets more than *mail*. It also helps you keep yourself up to date with the world outside—and within your own little corner of it.

For example, the ability to subscribe to those constantly updating news summaries known as *RSS feeds* has saved a lot of people a lot of time over the years. After all, why waste precious minutes looking for the news when you can make the news find you?

With Mail, you don't even have to waste the seconds switching from your Inbox to your browser or dedicated RSS program to get a fresh dose of headlines. They can appear right in the main Mail window. You don't even have to switch programs to find out which political candidate shot his foot off while it was still in his mouth.

In fact, if you find it too exhausting to click the RSS icon in the Mailboxes list, you can choose instead to have all your RSS updates land right in your Inbox along with all your other messages.

Adding RSS Feeds

With just a few clicks, you can bring the news of the world right in with the rest of your mail. Choose File→Add RSS Feeds, and then proceed as shown in Figure 11-14.

Tip: As you turn on the feeds you want to see in Mail, ⌘-click to select a bunch of feeds at once.

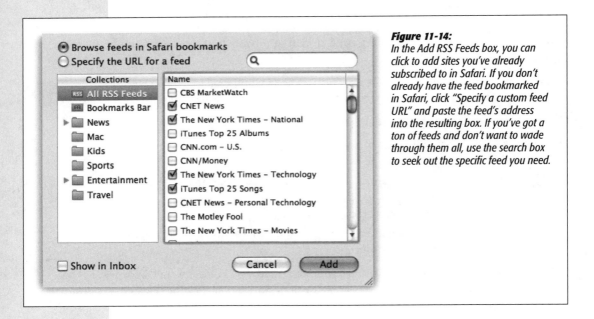

Figure 11-14:
In the Add RSS Feeds box, you can click to add sites you've already subscribed to in Safari. If you don't already have the feed bookmarked in Safari, click "Specify a custom feed URL" and paste the feed's address into the resulting box. If you've got a ton of feeds and don't want to wade through them all, use the search box to seek out the specific feed you need.

If you want the RSS headlines to appear in your Inbox like regular email messages, turn on "Show in Inbox." Finally, once you've chosen the feeds you want to see, click Add. Your feeds now appear wherever you told them to go: either the Inbox or the Mailboxes column.

Now, in the RSS category of your Mailboxes list, the names of your RSS feeds show up; the number in the small gray circle tells you how many unread headlines are in the list. If a feed headline intrigues you enough to want more information, click "Read More…" to do just that. Safari pops up and whisks you away to the Web site that sent out the feed in the first place.

Tip: Click the up arrow button next to a feed's name to move all its updates into your Inbox; there, they appear with the same blue RSS label, but they behave as though they're an Inbox category. This spares you having to flip back and forth between two distant areas of the Mailboxes list.

If you *accidentally* click that arrow, and you don't really want 57 headlines from RollingStone.com peppering your daily dose of mail, click the feed's name and then click the down-pointing arrow next to it; it returns to the RSS section of the list. Alternatively, you can Control-click (or right-click) the feed name under Mailboxes and turn off "Show in Inbox" from the shortcut menu.

Managing Feeds

Now that you've got your feeds in Mail, you may want to fiddle around with them.

- **Updating.** You can change the frequency of your news updates by choosing Mail→Preferences→RSS→Check for Updates. You can automatically update them every half hour, every hour, or every day. You can also command Mail to update a certain feed *right now;* Control-click the feed's name in the Mailboxes list and, from the shortcut menu, choose "Update BBC News" (or whatever its name is).

- **Archiving.** You can save and store a whole batch of feeds in an archive file, just as you can do with regular mailboxes; choose Mailbox→Archive Feed. A dialog box walks you through saving a copy of all the messages to a backup drive or other location for safekeeping.

- **Sharing.** If you want to share the news with a friend, Control-click a headline; from the shortcut menu, choose Forward (or Forward as Attachment) to pop the info into a new Mail message that you can send off to your pal.

- **Renaming.** You don't have to use the site's full name in your Mail window—after all, "WaPo" fits much better in the Mailboxes column than "Washington Post." To rename a feed, select it and then choose Mailbox→Rename Feed. Type in the new name and press Return. (You can also Control-click or right-click the name to bring up the Rename Feed option.)

- **Deleting.** After you've read a news item and are done with it, click the Delete button at the top of the window. You can tell Mail to dump all the old articles after a certain amount of time (a day, a week, a month) in Mail→Preferences→RSS→Remove Articles.

  Or, to get rid of an RSS feed altogether, select it and then choose Maibox→Delete Feed. (Control- or right-clicking the name gives you the same option.)

Notes

Let's face it: No operating system is complete without Notes. You *have* to have a place for little reminders, phone numbers, phone messages, Web addresses, brainstorms,

---

shopping-list hints—anything that's worth writing down, but too tiny to justify heaving a whole word processor onto its feet.

The silly thing is how many people create reminders for themselves by *sending themselves an email message.*

That system works, but it's a bit inelegant. Fortunately, Mac OS X has a dedicated Notes feature. As a bonus, it syncs automatically to the Notes folder of your iPhone's mail program, or to other computers, as long as you have a so-called IMAP email account (like Gmail, for example).

Notes look like actual yellow notepaper with ruled lines, but you can style 'em, save 'em, and even send 'em to your friends. You can type into them, paste into them, and attach pictures to them. And unlike loose scraps of paper or email messages to yourself that may get lost in your mailbox, Notes stay obediently tucked in the Reminders section of the Mailboxes list so you can always find them when you need them.

Tip: Ordinarily, Notes also appear in your Inbox, at the top. If you prefer to keep your Inbox strictly for messages, though, you can remove the Notes. Choose Mail→Preferences→Accounts→Mailbox Behaviors, and then turn off "Store notes in Inbox." The Notes will still be waiting for you in the side column, down in the Reminders area.

To create a Note, click the Note button on the Mail toolbar. You can also choose File→New Note or press Control-⌘-N to pop up a fresh piece of onscreen paper.

Figure 11-15:
They may look like little pads of scratch paper, but Mail Notes let you paste in Web addresses and photos alongside your typed and formatted text. If you want to share, click the Send button to have the entire Note plop into a new Mail message, ready to be addressed.

Once you have your Note, type your text and click the Fonts and Colors buttons at the top of the window to style it. To insert a picture, click the Attach button, and then find the photo or graphic on your Mac you want to use. Figure 11-15 shows an example.

Note: You can also attach other kinds of files to a Note—ordinary documents, for example. But you can't send such Notes to other people—only Notes with pictures.

When you're finished with your Note, click Done to save it. When you look for it in the Reminders category of the Mailboxes list, you'll see that Mail used the first line of the Note as its subject.

To delete a Note for good, select it and press the Delete key.

If you've worked hard on this little Note and want to share it, double-click it to open the Note into a new window. Click the Send button on its toolbar. Mail puts the whole thing into a new Mail message—complete with yellow-paper background—so your pal can see how seriously (and stylishly) you take the whole concept of "Note to self."

To Dos

You've got all this mail piling up with all sorts of things to remember: dinner dates, meeting times, project deadlines, car-service appointments. Wouldn't it be great if you didn't have to remember to look through your mailbox to find out what you're supposed to be doing that day?

It would, and it is, thanks to Mail's To Do feature. And the best part is that Mail accesses the *same* To Do list as iCal. The same task list shows up in both programs.

Creating To Dos

You can use To Dos in several different ways. For example, when you get an email message that requires further action ("I need the photos for the condo association newsletter by Friday"), highlight the important part of the text. Then do any of these things:

• Click To Do in the message window's toolbar.

• Choose File→New To Do.

• Press Option-⌘-Y.

• Control-click (or right-click) the highlighted text, and then choose New To Do from the shortcut menu.

In each case, Mail pops a copy of the selected text into a yellow strip of note-style paper at the top of the message, as shown in Figure 11-16.

That task is also listed in the Reminders area of the Mailboxes list. If you need to see *all* the tasks that await you from all your mail accounts, click the flippy triangle to have it spin open and reveal your chores. The number in the gray circle indicates how many To Do items you still need to do.

Tip: Control-click (or right-click) any item in this To Do list to open a shortcut menu that offers useful controls for setting its due date, priority, and *calendar* (that is, iCal category).

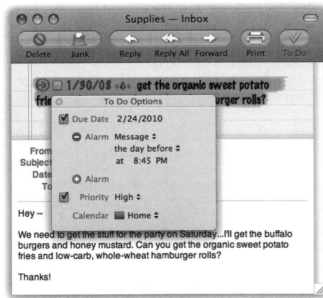

Figure 11-16:
Top: If a message brings a task that you need to complete, you can give yourself an extra little reminder, right in Mail. Highlight the pertinent text and click the To Do button to add a large, colorful reminder to the top of the message.

Bottom: Click the arrow next to the first line of the To Do for a quick and easy way to set a due date/time and alarm, and also to choose which calendar you want to use for this particular chore.

When you click the To Do area of the Mailboxes list, all your tasks are listed in the center of the Mail window. Click the gray arrow after each To Do subject line to jump back to the original message it came from.

Tip: Not all of your life's urgent tasks spring from email messages. Fortunately, you can create standalone To Dos, too. Just click the To Do button at the top of the Mail window when no message is selected. A blank item appears in your To Do list with the generic name "New To Do." Select the name to overwrite it with what this reminder is really about: *"Buy kitty litter TODAY"* (or whatever).

Completing and Deleting To Dos

When you complete a task, click the small checkbox in front of the To Do subject line—either in the message itself or in the Reminders list. Once you've marked a task as Done this way, the number of total tasks in the Reminders list goes down by one, and that's one less thing you have to deal with.

To delete a big yellow To Do banner from a message, point to the left side of the banner until a red handwritten-looking X appears. Click the X to zap the To Do banner from the message.

You can delete a To Do item from the Reminders list by selecting it and then pressing Delete, among other methods.

To Do List: Mail/iCal Joint Custody

Seeing your To Do items in Mail is great—when you're working in Mail. Getting them into iCal is even better, though, because you can see the big picture of an entire day, week, or month. Mail and iCal share the exact same To Do list. Create a To Do in one program, and it shows up *instantly* in the other one.

Tip: You can even set the due date and priority of a task from within Mail. Those controls are in the To Do Options balloon (Figure 11-16, bottom). Open this balloon by Control-clicking the task and choosing Edit To Do, or just click the large arrow button that appears to the left of a To Do banner in an email message window. Later, in iCal, if you double-click a To Do item and then click "Show in Mail," you get whisked back to the original message, sitting right there in Mail.

Address Book

Address Book is Mac OS X's little-black-book program—an electronic Rolodex where you can stash the names, job titles, addresses, phone numbers, email addresses, and Internet chat screen names of all the people in your life (Figure 11-17). Address Book can also hold related information, like birthdays, anniversaries, and any other tidbits of personal data you'd like to keep at your fingertips.

Once you make Address Book the central repository of all your personal contact information, you can call up this information in a number of convenient ways:

- You can launch Address Book and search for a contact by typing just a few letters in the Search box.

- Regardless of what program you're in, you can use a single keystroke (F12 is the factory setting, or the ☉ key on aluminum keyboards) to summon the Address Book Dashboard widget. There, you can search for any contact you want. When you're done, hide the widget with the same quick keystroke.

- When you're composing messages in Mail, Address Book automatically fills in email addresses for you when you type the first few letters.

Tip: If you choose Window→Address Panel (Option-⌘-A) from within Mail, you can browse all your addresses without even launching the Address Book program. Once you've selected the people you want to contact, just click the "To:" button to address an email to them—or, if you already have a new email message open, to add them to the recipients.

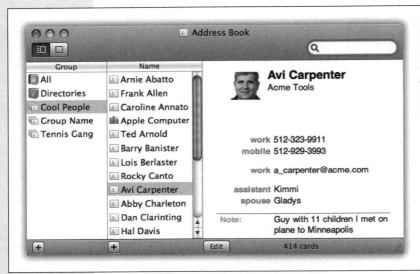

Figure 11-17:
The big question: Why isn't this program named iContact? With its three-paned view, soft rounded corners, and gradient-gray background, it looks like a close cousin of iPhoto, iCal, and iTunes.

- When you use iChat to exchange instant messages with people in your Address Book, the pictures you've stored of them automatically appear in chat windows.

- If you've bought a subscription to the MobileMe service (Chapter 10), you can synchronize your contacts to the Web so you can see them while you're away from your Mac. You can also share Address Books with fellow MobileMe members: Choose Address Book→Preferences→Sharing, click the box for "Share your address book," and then click the **+** button to add the MobileMe pals you want to share with. You can even send them an invitation to come share your contact list. If you get an invitation yourself, open your own Address Book program and choose Edit→Subscribe to Address Book.

- Address Book can send its information to an iPod or an iPhone, giving you a "little black book" that fits in your shirt pocket, can be operated one-handed, and comes with built-in musical accompaniment. (To set this up, open iTunes while your iPod or iPhone is connected. Click the iPod/iPhone's icon; on the Contacts or Info tab, turn on "Synchronize Address Book Contacts.")

You can find Address Book in your Applications folder or in the Dock.

Creating Address Cards

Each entry in Address Book is called a *card*—like a paper Rolodex card, with predefined spaces to hold all the standard contact information.

To add a new person, choose File→New Card, press ⌘-N, or click the **+** button beneath the Name column. Then type in the contact information, pressing the Tab key to move from field to field, as shown in Figure 11-18.

Tip: If you find yourself constantly adding the same fields to new cards, check out the Template pane of Address Book's Preferences (Address Book→Preferences). There, you can customize exactly which fields appear for new cards.

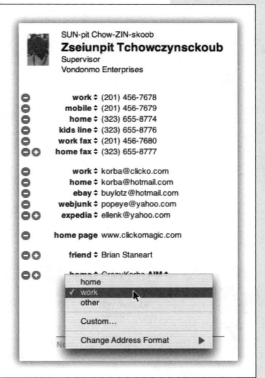

Figure 11-18:
If one of your contacts happens to have three office phone extensions, a pager number, two home phone lines, a cellphone, and a couple of fax machines, no problem—you can add as many fields as you need. Click the little green + buttons when editing a card to add more phone, email, chat name, and address fields. (The buttons appear only when the existing fields are filled.) Click a field's name to change its label; you can select one of the standard labels from the pop-up menu (Home, Work, and so on) or make up your own labels by choosing Custom, as seen in the lower portion of this figure.

This example shows some unusual fields that you can plug into your address cards. The phonetic first/last name fields (shown at top) let you store phonetic spellings of hard-to-pronounce names. The other fields store screen names for instant messaging networks like Jabber and Yahoo. To add fields like these, choose from the Card→Add Field menu.

Each card also contains a free-form Notes field at the bottom, where you can type any other random crumbs of information you'd like to store about the person (pet's name, embarrassing nicknames, favorite Chinese restaurant, and so on).

Editing an address

When you create a new address card, you're automatically in Edit mode, which means you can add and remove fields and change the information on the card. To switch into Browse Mode (where you can view and copy contact information but not change it), click the Edit button or choose Edit→Edit Card (⌘-L). You can also switch *out* of Browse Mode in the same ways.

Tip: Regardless of which mode you're in—Edit or Browse—you can *always* type, drag, or paste text into the Notes field of an address card.

Adding addresses from Mail

You can also make new contacts in the Address Book right in Mail, saving you the trouble of having to type names and email addresses manually. Select a message in Mail, then choose Message→Add Sender to Address Book (Shift-⌘-Y). Presto: Mac OS X adds a new card to the Address Book, with the name and email address fields already filled in. Later, you can edit the card in Address Book to add phone numbers, street addresses, and so on.

Importing Addresses

The easiest way to add people to Address Book is to import them from another program, like Entourage, Outlook Express, or Palm Desktop.

Address Book isn't smart enough to read an Entourage or Outlook Express database—it can only import files in vCard format, the less common LDIF format, or tab-separated or comma-separated database files (described next).

It's a fine art, this importing business; all kinds of things can go wrong. The fields (like Name, Street, Phone) may not be in the right order. Tab-separated export files may not have the right number of empty fields. And so on.

For best results, choose Address Book→Help, and search for "Importing contacts from other applications." The resulting page gives special tips for each kind of export/import file format.

POWER USERS' CLINIC

The Windows-to-Address-Book Journey

Getting names and addresses out of one Mac program and into another is one thing. But what if your contacts are stored on a Windows PC running Microsoft Outlook, the most-used contact manager in the world?

Easy: Use Outlook's Export command to create a tab-delimited text file containing all your contacts. Then copy the text file to your Mac.

In Address Book, choose File→Import→Text File, locate the file you exported from Outlook, and click Open. After a short delay, your new contacts appear, ready to go in Address Book.

About vCards

Address Book exchanges contact information with other programs primarily through *vCards*. vCard is short for *virtual business card*. More and more email programs send and receive these electronic business cards, which you can identify by their .vcf file name extensions (if, that is, you've set your Mac to display these extensions, as described on page 97).

If you ever receive an email with a vCard file attached, drag the .vcf file into your Address Book window to create an instant entry with a complete set of information. You can create vCards of your own, too. Just drag a name out of your Address Book and onto the desktop (or into a piece of outgoing mail).

Tip: In addition to letting you create vCards of individual entries, Address Book makes it easy to create vCards that contain several entries. To do so, ⌘-click the entries in the Name column that you want included, and drag them to the desktop. There, they'll appear all together as a single vCard. You can even drag an item from the Group column to the desktop to make a vCard that contains all the group's entries.

Keep this trick in mind if you ever want to copy all your contacts from an old PC to a new Mac. By creating a single vCard containing all your contacts, you've made it trivial to import them into the copy of Address Book running on your new Mac.

Syncing with Google, Yahoo, MobileMe, or Exchange

Yeah, it's a big deal, baby: Address Book can synchronize its contacts with any of four external Rolodexes that may be very important to you: your Gmail (Google) contacts, Yahoo contacts, MobileMe address book, or your company's Microsoft Exchange master address book.

For details on Exchange, see the end of Chapter 8; for MobileMe, see Chapter 10.

Figure 11-19:
When you turn on one of these checkboxes, you first get a legal disclaimer; ignore it and click Agree.

Now you're asked to enter your Yahoo or Gmail name and password. Once that's done, presto!— your Mac's Address Book and online contacts are kept in sync. Even their photos, if your online address book has them, show up in Address Book!

If you keep an address book in Yahoo or Gmail, choose Address Book→Preferences→Accounts. Click "On My Mac." Turn on the checkbox you want, and proceed as shown in Figure 11-19.

Tip: Once you've set up this online syncing, the two-way updating takes place hourly. If you can't wait that long, here's how to force a sync on command: Open the iSync program in your Applications folder, choose iSync→Preferences, and then select "Show status in menu bar." From now on, you can choose Sync Now from that menulet whenever you want Address Book to check in with its online twin.

Groups

A *group* is a collection of related address cards, saved under a single descriptive name (visible in Figure 11-20).

Organizing your contacts into groups can make them much easier to find and use—especially when your database of addresses climbs into the hundreds. For example, if you regularly send out a family newsletter to 35 relatives, you might gather the address cards of all your assorted siblings, cousins, nieces, nephews, uncles, and aunts into a single group called Family. When addressing an outgoing message using Mail, you can type this group name to reach all your kin at once. A person can be a member of as many different groups as you want.

Tip: When you send an email message to a group en masse, how does Mail know which email address to use for each person?

Because you've *told* it. Choose Edit→Edit Distribution List. A special dialog box appears, listing everyone in each group, along with each person's complete list of email addresses. (Use the tiny pop-up menu above the list to choose Phone or Address; that way, you can also indicate the preferred phone number and mailing address.)

To create a group, click the **+** button at the bottom of the Group column in the Address Book window, or choose File→New Group (Shift-⌘-N.) Type a name for the newly spawned group icon in the Group column, and then populate it with address cards by dragging entries from the Name list into the group. Clicking a group name automatically locates and displays (in the Names column) all the names that are part of that group—and hides any that aren't.

Tip: To turn a set of address cards into a group very quickly, select multiple entries from the Names column—by either Shift-clicking the names (to make contiguous selections) or by ⌘-clicking (for non-contiguous selections)—and then choose File→New Group From Selection. You end up with a new group containing all the selected names.

Removing someone from a group

To take someone out of a group, first click the group name, and then click the person's name in the Name column and press the Delete key. If you want to remove the person from Address Book *itself*, click Delete in the resulting dialog box. Otherwise, just click

"Remove from Group" or press Return. Address Book keeps the card but removes it from the currently selected group.

Note: If you selected All in the Group column, rather than a specific group, you don't get a "Remove from Group" option. Instead, the Mac just asks you to confirm that you do, in fact, want to permanently remove the card.

Adding Pictures

You can dress up each Address Book entry with a photo. Whenever you're editing somebody's address book card, drag a digital photo—preferably 64 pixels square, or a multiple of it—onto the empty headshot square; the image shows up. Or double-click the picture well; now you can either browse to a picture on your hard drive by clicking Choose, or, if this person is *with* you, take a new photo by clicking the camera icon. (Don't miss the swirly button next to it, which lets you apply nutty effects.) At that point, you can enlarge, reposition, and crop the new photo.)

You don't necessarily have to use a photo, of course. You could add any graphic that you want to represent someone, even if it's a Bart Simpson face or a skull and cross-bones. You can use any standard image file in an address card—a JPEG, GIF, PNG, TIFF, or even a PDF.

From now on, if you receive an email from that person, the photo shows up right in the email message.

Tip: If you've got snapshots in iPhoto, it's particularly easy to add a picture to any address card. Just drag a picture directly from the main iPhoto window to the picture frame on the address card to insert it.

Replacing and removing a picture

To replace a photo on an address card, just drag a new image on top of the old one. If you want to get rid of an existing picture without replacing it, select the card, and then choose Card→Clear Custom Image (or, in Edit mode, press Delete).

Finding an Address

You can search for an Address Book entry inside the currently selected group by typing a few letters of a name (or address, or any other snippet of contact information) in the Search box (Figure 11-20). To search *all* your contacts instead of just the current group, click All in the Group list.

Tip: You can press ⌘-F to jump directly to the search field and start typing. Your savings: one mouse click.

If Address Book finds more than one matching card, use the ↓ and ↑ keys, or Return and Shift-Return, to navigate through them.

Once you've found the card you're looking for, you can perform some interesting stunts. If you click the label of a phone number ("home" or "office," for example), you see the Large Type option: Address Book displays the number in an absurdly gigantic font that fills the entire width of your screen, making it possible to read the number as you dial from across the room. You can also click the label of an email address to create a preaddressed email message, or click a home page to launch your Web browser and go to somebody's site.

You can also copy and paste (or drag) address card info into another program or convert it into a Sticky Note.

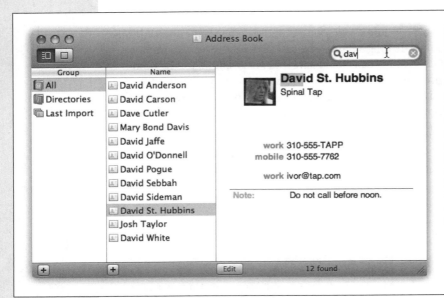

Figure 11-20:
With each letter you type, Address Book filters your social circle and displays the number of matches at the bottom. The matching records themselves appear in the Name column, the first of the matching card entries appears in the far-right pane, and the matching text itself appears highlighted in the matching card.

Figure 11-21:
The options that become available when you click the field labels on an address card vary according to field type. Pop-up menus let you send email, open a Web page, or view a map, depending on the type of field you've clicked.

Tip: Once you find a street address in your Address Book, you can find those coordinates on a map by Control-clicking (or right-clicking) the address part of the card and choosing "Map Of" from the shortcut menu, as shown in Figure 11-21. Your Web browser obediently leaps up to display the address on a Google map.

Changing the Address Book Display

You can't do much to customize Address Book's appearance, but the Preferences pane (Address Book→Preferences) gives you at least a couple of options in the General pane that are worth checking out:

- **Display Order.** Choose to have names displayed with the first name followed by the last name, or vice versa.

- **Sort By.** Sort the entries in Address Book by either first or last name.

- **Font Size.** Choose from Regular, Large, or Extra Large. Unfortunately, you can't change anything else about the font used in the Address Book; the color, face, and style are all locked down.

Printing Options

When you choose File→Print and click the ▼ to expand the Print box, the Style pop-up menu offers four ways to print whatever addresses are selected at the moment:

- **Mailing Labels.** This option prints addresses on standard sheets of sticky mailing labels—Avery, for example—that you buy at office-supply stores.

Tip: As you manipulate settings, you can see your changes in the preview pane on the left. If the preview is too small for you to see, use the Zoom slider. (It doesn't affect your printout.)

- **Envelopes.** This feature is great if you have bad handwriting; rather than hand-addressing your envelopes, you can have Address Book print them out for you. Use the Layout pop-up menu to pick the size of your envelopes—it's usually listed on the outside of the envelope box.

POWER USERS' CLINIC

Automatic Notifications

In Address Book, notifying friends and family that your email address has changed is a piece of cake.

Choose Address Book→Preferences→General and turn on "Notify people when my card changes." From now on, whenever you change the information in your own address card (like home address, email address, or phone number), Address Book asks whether you want to send a notification email–a virtual change-of-address card. If you do, click Notify.

In the resulting dialog box, choose which groups of people you want to notify, and then personalize the outgoing message. When you click Send, Address Book delivers an email to all the people in the groups you chose, attaching your new vCard (page 353). When your recipients get the email, they can simply drag the vCard into their own Address Books to update their information about you.

(If you ever want to send updates to your contacts *manually*, just choose File→Send Updates.)

Note: Both the Mailing Labels and Envelopes options print only the contacts for which you have, in fact, entered physical mailing addresses.

- **Lists.** If all you want is a paper backup of your Address Book entries, use this setting. In the Attributes list, turn on the checkboxes of the fields you want printed—just name and phone number, for example.

- **Pocket Address Book.** This feature prints out a convenient *paper* address book from your virtual one. If you pick Indexed from the Flip Style pop-up menu, each page's edge will even list the first letters of the last names listed on the page, making it a cinch to find the page with the address you want. (Here again, you can pick which fields you'd like to include—phone numbers, addresses, and so on.)

As you fiddle with the options presented here, you get to see a miniature preview, right in the dialog box, that shows what you're going to get.

No matter which mode you choose, the only cards that print are the ones that were selected when you chose File→Print. If you want to print *all* your cards, therefore, click All in the Group column before you print.

Tip: You can combine the smart-groups feature with the printing features in one clever way: to print yourself a portable phone book when you're heading off for a visit to a different city. That is, set up a smart group that rounds up everyone you know who lives in Chicago, and then print that as a pocket address book.

Address-Book Backups

Your Address Book may represent *years* of typing and compiling effort. Losing all that information to a corrupted database or a hard drive crash could be devastating. Here are three ways to protect your Address Book data:

- **Turn on MobileMe syncing.** A MobileMe account has its privileges—and one of them is automatic synchronizing with the MobileMe mothership online.

- **Back up your entire Address Book database.** Open your Home→Library→Application Support folder. Copy the entire Address Book folder to another disk—burn it to a CD, download it to your iPod, or upload it to a file server, for example.

- **Back up your whole Mac with Time Machine.** Chapter 6 tells you how.

Safari & iChat

A pple is obviously intrigued by the possibilities of the Internet. With each new release of Mac OS X, more clever tendrils reach out from the Mac to the world's biggest network.

But Apple's most obvious Internet-friendly creation is Safari, a smartly designed window to the Web (available for both Mac OS X and, believe it or not, Windows). This chapter is all about Safari—the compass icon in the Dock points the way to your Internet adventure—and iChat, the unsung superstar of the chat-and-conferencing universe.

Safari

If you want something done right, you have to do it yourself.

That must be what Apple was thinking when it wrote its own Web browser a few years ago, which so annoyed Microsoft that it promptly ceased all further work on the Mac version of its own Internet Explorer.

Safari is beautiful, fast, and filled with delicious features (Figure 12-1). Safari is not, however, Internet Explorer, and so some Web sites—a few banking sites, for example—refuse to acknowledge its existence. For these situations, you might try the Mac version of Firefox, a free browser available at *www.getfirefox.com*.

To move your Web bookmarks over from Windows to the Mac, see page 182. Then, when you're ready to get going, read on.

Browsing Basics and Toolbars

You probably know the drill when it comes to Web browsers. When you click an underlined *link (hyperlink)* or a picture button, you're transported from one Web page to another. One page might be the home page of General Motors; another might contain critical information about a bill in Congress; another might have baby pictures posted by a parent in Omaha.

Tip: Text links aren't always blue and underlined. In fact, trendy Web designers sometimes make it very difficult to tell which text is clickable and which is just text. When in doubt, move your cursor over some text; if the arrow changes to a pointing-finger cursor, you've found yourself a link.

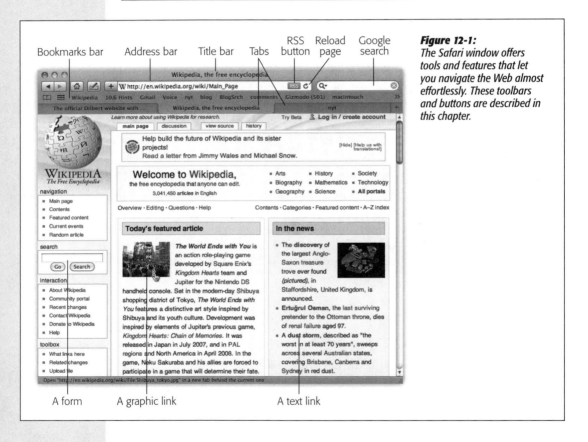

Figure 12-1:
The Safari window offers tools and features that let you navigate the Web almost effortlessly. These toolbars and buttons are described in this chapter.

Some of the other Safari tips may not be obvious:

- **Graphics worth saving.** When you see a picture you'd like to keep, right-click it and choose Save Image to Desktop (or Save Image to iPhoto, or just Save Image) from the shortcut menu. Safari stores it as a new graphics file, freed from its birthplace on the Web. (You can specify where Safari saves downloaded pictures on the Safari→Preferences→General tab. In that case, the shortcut menu's wording changes to say, for example, "Save Image to 'Pictures.' ")

Tip: You can also save a graphic to the desktop just by dragging it there, right out of the Safari window.

- **Scroll bars.** Instead of using the scroll bar to move up and down the page, it's often easier to press the space bar each time you want to see more. Press Shift-space to scroll *up*. (The space bar serves its traditional, space-making function only when the insertion point is blinking in a text box or the address bar.)

  You can also press your ↑ and ↓ keys to scroll one line at a time. Page Up and Page Down scroll in full-screen increments, while Home and End whisk you to the top or bottom of the current Web page. And if your mouse has a scroll wheel, trackball, or multitouch surface (that is, the Magic Mouse), it works, too.

  On a laptop, drag with two fingers to scroll, as usual.

Safari Toolbars

Many of Safari's most useful controls come parked on toolbars and buttons that you can summon or hide by choosing their names from the View menu. Here's what they do:

Address bar

When you type a new Web page address (URL) into this strip and press Return, the corresponding Web site appears.

Because typing out Internet addresses is so central to the Internet experience and such a typo-prone hassle, the address bar is rich with features that minimize keystrokes. For example:

- You don't have to click the address bar before typing; just press ⌘-L.

- You can highlight the entire address (so it's ready to be typed over with a new one) by clicking the small icon just to the left of the current address. Or triple-click the address bar. Or press ⌘-L.

FREQUENTLY ASKED QUESTION

Where to Specify Your Preferred Mail and Browser Programs

Hey! Where the heck do I specify what browser I want to open when, say, I click a link in an email message?

This is going to sound a little odd. But to indicate that you want some other browser to be your favorite, you start by opening Safari. Choose Safari→Preferences, click the

General tab, and choose from the Default Web Browser pop-up menu.

You change email programs using the same twisted logic: You open Mail and then open its Preferences.

- You don't have to type out the whole Internet address. You can omit the *http://*, *www*, and *.com* portions; Safari fills in those standard address bits for you. To visit NYTimes.com, for example, a speed freak might press ⌘-L to highlight the address bar, type *nytimes,* and then press Return.

- When you begin to type into the address bar, the AutoComplete feature compares what you're typing against a list of Web sites that you've recently visited or that you've saved as bookmarks. Safari displays a drop-down list of Web addresses that seem to match what you're typing. To spare yourself the tedium of typing out the whole thing, click the correct complete address with your mouse, or use the ↓ key to reach the desired listing and then press Return. The complete address you select pops into the address bar.

Tip: You might wonder why the View menu even offers you the chance to hide the address bar. If it were hidden, how could you use the Web?

Simple: Even with this bar hidden, you can briefly summon it by pressing ⌘-L. Type the address you want and then press Return to make the bar disappear again. That's good news for people with small screens—and for Mac trivia collectors.

Address-bar buttons

You can summon or dismiss a number of individual buttons on the address bar, in effect customizing it (Figure 12-2). It's worth putting some thought into this tailoring, because some of these buttons' functions are really handy. So here's a catalog of your options:

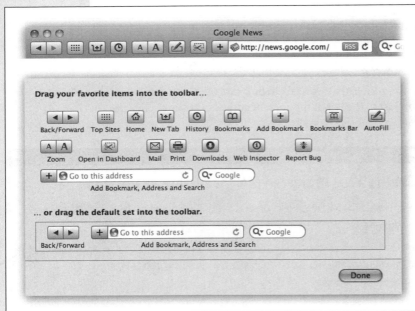

Figure 12-2:
To summon this toolbar-tailoring screen, choose View→Customize Toolbar. Then drag the buttons you want directly onto the address bar. Some of them lack text labels once installed, but all offer tooltip labels you can read by pointing to the button without clicking.

- **Back/Forward.** Click the Back button (◄) to revisit the page you were just on. *Keyboard shortcut:* Delete, or ⌘-←.

  Once you've clicked ◄, you can then click the ► button (or press ⌘-→ to return to the page you were on before you clicked the Back button. Click and hold the ◄ button for a drop-down list of *all* the Web pages you've visited during this online session.

  That pop-up menu lists the sites by name, as in "The New York Times—Breaking News, World News & Multimedia." To view the actual *addresses* instead, Option-click (and hold the mouse down on) the Back or Forward button.

Tip: Instead of clicking and holding the ◄ or ► button for these tricks, you can save half a second of waiting by just Control-clicking.

- **Top Sites.** This feature opens up the highly visual dashboard shown in Figure 12-3. These thumbnails represent what Safari has determined are your favorite Web sites, as calculated by how often and how recently you've visited them.

Figure 12-3:
You can open the Top Sites display either by clicking the Top Sites button on the toolbar or by choosing History→ Top Sites. Click a page to revisit it; a star in the corner means "This page has changed since your last visit."

• **Home.** Click to bring up the Web page you've designated as your home page (in Safari→Preferences→General tab).

• **New Tab.** Creates a new tab (embedded window), described later in this chapter.

• **History.** Click to open the list of Web sites you've visited recently in a window—a much easier-to-navigate display than the History *menu*.

• **Bookmarks, Add Bookmark.** When you find a Web page you might like to visit again, click Add Bookmark. You can also press ⌘-D, choose Bookmarks→Add Bookmark, or drag the tiny icon from the address bar directly onto your Bookmarks bar.

As shown in Figure 12-4, Safari offers to add this Web page's name (or a shorter name that you specify for it) either to the Bookmarks menu or to the Bookmarks bar (described below). The next time you want to visit that page, just select its name in whichever location you chose.

Tip: Press Shift-⌘-D to add the bookmark to the menu instantly—no questions asked, no dialog box presented.

The ⚏ (Bookmarks) button opens the Bookmarks editing window (Figure 12-4). Here you can rearrange the names in your Bookmarks menu easily, or peruse them by scrolling through their giant Cover Flow thumbnails—a great feature in a Web browser, because a visual representation of a page is a lot more helpful than some Web address.

(Even without the ⚏ button, you can get there by choosing Bookmarks→Show All Bookmarks or by pressing Option-⌘-B.)

POWER USERS' CLINIC

Customizing Top Sites

Ordinarily, the Top Sites display changes over time, as your tastes and your activity change. But you can override Safari's attempt to curate this page in various ways. For example, you can pin a certain site so that it never leaves the Top Sites screen, or you can manually add a page.

It all happens when you click the Edit button in the lower left. Each thumbnail sprouts two buttons in the corner: the × button (this page will never again appear on Top Sites) and the thumbtack button (this page will always appear in Top Sites, even if you don't visit it much).

To add a new page to the Top Sites display, first open that page in another Safari window. Then highlight its address in the address bar and drag it right onto the Top Sites page. You can also drag a Web link from an email message, text document, Web page, or any other source to the Top Sites page.

You can reorder the thumbnails, too, just by dragging them around on this screen.

Finally, you can change the thumbnail size on this Edit screen, too. Use the Small/Medium/Large control in the lower right; smaller thumbnails means more of them fit (24, 12, or six, respectively).

In the resulting organization window, drag the bookmarks up and down. Figure 12-4 also shows you how to perform more dramatic management tasks, like editing, renaming, or deleting bookmarks.

Figure 12-4:
Top: Once you've got a juicy Web page on the screen, you can drag its tiny page-logo icon (circled) from the address bar directly onto the Bookmarks bar or menu.

Second from top: Safari realizes that you may prefer a shorter name to appear on the space-limited bar, so it offers you the chance to type in a label you prefer.

Third from top: When you click OK, the new button appears on the bar, as shown here. (You can also drag any link to the bar, such as a blue underlined phrase from a Web page, or even an icon from your desktop!) To remove a button, drag it off the bar; to rearrange the icons, just drag them.

Bottom: Click the ⊞ icon (circled) to open the Organize Bookmarks window. Here, you can drag names up or down to rearrange the list, or drag them into a "folder" that becomes a submenu in the Bookmarks menu. (Create a submenu by clicking the + button below the list.) You can edit a bookmark by clicking once on its name or URL, or delete one by pressing Delete.

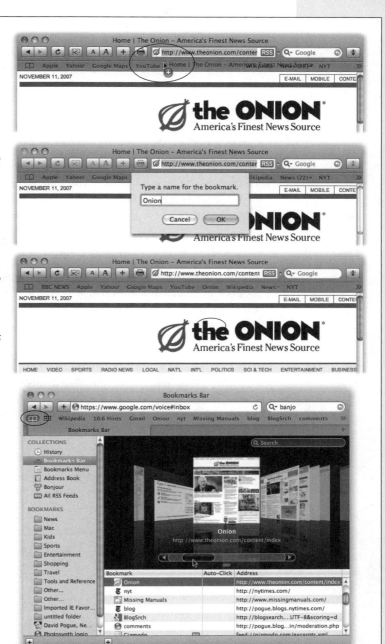

- **Bookmarks Bar.** Hides or shows the horizontal toolbar that lists your favorite bookmarks. (The equivalent of choosing View→Bookmarks Bar).

- **AutoFill.** Click this button to make Safari fill in Web order forms with your name, address, and other information. See the box on the facing page.

- **Text Size.** You can adjust the point size of a Web page's text using these buttons. When you visit a Web site designed for Windows computers—whose text often looks too small on Mac screens—you can use these buttons to bump up the size. The keyboard shortcuts are ⌘-plus or ⌘-minus.

- **Open in Dashboard.** This icon is the key to creating Dashboard *Web clips,* as described on page 160. Click this button, and then select the part of the page you want to widgetize. It's the equivalent of the File→Open in Dashboard command.

- **Mail.** Opens a new, outgoing email message in your email program. The Subject line contains the *name* of the site you were visiting; the body contains a link to it. You can address the message, add a comment ("Re: your comment that 'no expert' recommends trampolines for children"), and send it.

- **Stop/Reload.** Click the Stop button (or Esc, or ⌘-period) to interrupt the downloading of a Web page you've just requested (if you've made a mistake, for instance).

  Once a page has finished loading, the Stop button turns into a Refresh button. Click this circular arrow (or press ⌘-R) if a page doesn't look or work quite right, or if you want to see the updated version of a Web page (such as a breaking-news site) that changes constantly. Safari redownloads the Web page and reinterprets its text and graphics.

- **Google Search.** Here's one of Safari's most profoundly useful features—a Search box that automatically sends your search request to Google.com, the world's most popular Web search page. Press Option-⌘-F to deposit your insertion point inside this rounded text box, type something you're looking for—*phony baloney,* say—and then press Return. Safari takes you directly to the Google results page.

Tip: The tiny ▾ at the left end of the Google bar is a pop-up menu. It offers two categories of listings, in hopes of saving you time and typing. First, there are Suggested Searches (you may notice that these pop up automatically as you type into the Search box, too). These suggestions come from Google's own Suggest feature. The second category: your most recent searches.

Bonus Tip: If you Control-click (or right-click) a highlighted word or phrase on a Web page, you can choose Google Search from the shortcut menu to search for that text. And, even cooler, this trick works in all Cocoa programs—not just Safari.

- **Print.** You can add a printer icon to Safari for point-and-click paper action if you don't want to bother with ⌘-P.

Tip: Safari automatically shrinks your printouts, if necessary, by up to 10 percent, if doing so will avoid printing a second page with just one or two lines of text on it. Nice.

- **Downloads.** This button opens your Downloads window, which shows the progress of whatever file you're downloading, shows your history of recent downloads, and contains double-clickable icons of the downloads that let you jump right to them on the hard drive.

Tip: In Safari→Preferences→General, you can opt to have your download listings removed from the Downloads window as soon as they've been successfully downloaded. You might want to do that for privacy reasons, or just because there's no reason to keep looking at them in the list once they're done.

- **Report Bug.** Ladies and gentlemen, this is Apple at its most humble. This insect-shaped button opens a tiny "Dear Apple" box, where you can tell Apple about a Safari feature or Web page that doesn't work. If you click Options, you can even send Apple a screen illustration of, for example, a screwy Web-page layout that Safari delivered.

Bookmarks bar

The Bookmarks menu is one way to maintain a list of Web sites you visit frequently. But opening a Web page from that menu requires *two mouse clicks*—an exorbitant expenditure of energy. The Bookmarks bar (View→Bookmarks Bar), on the other hand, lets you summon a few *very* favorite Web pages with only one click.

Tip: If you have a bunch of bookmarks stored in another Web browser, use that browser's export feature to save them to a file, and then use Safari's File→Import Bookmarks command to save you the time of re-entering the bookmarks by hand.

GEM IN THE ROUGH

Let AutoFill Do the Typing

Safari can also remember user names, passwords, and other information you type into the text boxes you encounter in your Web travels.

To turn on this great feature, visit the Safari→Preferences→AutoFill tab. If you turn on "Using info from my Address Book card," then whenever you're supposed to fill in your shipping address on a Web form, you can click the AutoFill button in the address bar to have Safari fill in the blanks for you automatically. (If you don't see the AutoFill button—see Figure 12-2—choose its name from the View menu, or use Edit→AutoFill Form to do the deed instead.)

Alternatively, just click a text box—Name, for example—and start typing. As soon as Safari recognizes a familiar scrap of your contact information, it fills out the rest of the word automatically. (If it guessed wrong, just keep typing.)

If, in Preferences, you turn on "User names and passwords," then each time you type a password into a Web page, Safari offers to memorize it for you. It's a great time- and brain-saver, even though it doesn't work on all Web sites. (Of course, use it with caution if you share an account on your Mac with other people.)

When you want Safari to "forget" your passwords—for security reasons, for example—revisit that Safari→Preferences→AutoFill tab. Click one of the Edit buttons, and then delete the Web site names for which your information has been stored.

Turn on Other Forms if you'd like Safari to remember the terms you've typed into search engines, shopping sites, online gaming sites, and so on.

Figure 12-4 illustrates how to add buttons to, and remove them from, this toolbar.

Tip: As shown in Figure 12-4, you can drag a link from a Web page onto your Bookmarks bar. But you can also drag a link directly to the desktop, where it turns into an Internet location file. Thereafter, to launch your browser and visit the associated Web page whenever you like, just double-click this icon.

Better yet, stash a few of these icons in your Dock or Sidebar for even easier access.

Status Bar

The Status bar at the bottom of the window tells you what Safari is doing (such as "Opening page…" or "Done"). When you point to a link without clicking, the Status bar also tells you which URL will open if you click it. For those two reasons, it's a very useful strip, but it doesn't appear when you first run Safari. You have to summon it by choosing View→Show Status Bar.

Tips for Better Surfing

Safari is filled with shortcuts and tricks for better speed and more pleasant surfing. For example:

SnapBack

The little orange SnapBack button (◀), which sometimes appears at the right end of the address bar or Google search bar, takes you instantly back to the Web page whose address you last typed (or whose bookmark you last clicked), or to your first Google results page.

The point here is that, after burrowing from one link to another in pursuit of some Google result or Amazon listing, you can return to your starting point without having to mash the Back button over and over again. (The SnapBack button doesn't appear until you've actually clicked away from the first page you visited.)

Tip: You can hit the Delete key (or ⌘-←) to go back a page, or Shift-Delete (⌘-→) to go forward.

Stifle Pop-Ups and Pop-Unders

The world's smarmiest advertisers inundate us with *pop-up* and *pop-under* ads—nasty little windows that appear in front of the browser window or, worse, behind it, waiting to jump out the moment you close your current window. They're often deceptive, masquerading as error messages or dialog boxes, and they'll do absolutely anything to get you to click inside them.

If this kind of thing is driving you crazy, choose Safari→Block Pop-Up Windows, so that a checkmark appears next to the command. It's a war out there—but at least you now have some ammunition.

Note: This feature doesn't squelch small windows that pop up when you click a link—only windows that appear unbidden.

Even unbidden windows, however, are sometimes legitimate (and not ads)—notices of new banking features, warnings that the instructions to use a site have changed, and so on. Safari can't tell these from ads and stifles them, too. So if a site you trust says, "Please turn off pop-up blockers and reload this page," then you know you're probably missing out on a useful pop-up message.

And one more thing: These days, the evildoers of the Internet have begun to create pop-up windows using nonstandard programming code that Safari and other browsers can't do anything about. Fortunately, they're still fairly rare.

Three Ways to Magnify Web Text

If it seems as though a lot of Web sites are designed with type that's too small to read; it's not just you and your aging eyes. Macs and Windows come with different screen resolutions, so a site designed for one kind of computer may look too small on another.

Fortunately, Safari is extremely well equipped to help you with this problem. In fact, it offers three different solutions:

- **Enlarge the screen.** Press ⌘-plus or ⌘-minus to enlarge or reduce the entire Web page. Or use the two-finger "spread" gesture on your laptop trackpad. Or use the Zoom button, if you've added it to your toolbar. The advantage of this method is that the whole Web page's layout remains proportional.

- **Blow up just the text.** If you turn on View→Zoom Text Only, then all those shortcuts serve to magnify or shrink *only the text* on your page. Graphics remain at their original size. You're now distorting the original layout, but you're maximizing the amount of reading you can do before you have to scroll.

- **Specify a minimum type size.** This may be the best option of all, because it saves you all that zooming. Open Safari→Preferences→Advanced, and set the "Never use font sizes smaller than" option to, for example, 14 points. Now *every* Web page shows up with legible text. (Except a few oddballs that use weird coding to prevent text-size changing.)

Keyboard Control

Efficiency freaks generally prefer keyboard shortcuts to using the mouse, so Safari is filled with them.

Press Tab to jump from one text box or pop-up menu to the next on your Web page. Add the Option key to jump from one *link* to another (and when you highlight a link, press Return to "click" it).

Tip: For a shockingly complete list of Safari's keyboard shortcuts, open the Help menu. In the search box at the top of the menu, type *Safari shortcuts*. Wait a moment. Click "Safari shortcuts" in the list of Help topics.

Impersonating Internet Explorer

Sooner or later, you'll run into a Web site that doesn't work in Safari. Why? When you arrive at a Web site, your browser identifies itself. That's because many commercial Web sites display a different version of the page depending on the browser you're using, thanks to differences in the way various browsers interpret Web layouts.

But because you're one of the minority oddballs using Safari, your otherwise beloved Web site tells you: "Sorry, browser not supported." (Will this problem change now that Apple has released a Windows version of Safari? We can only hope.)

In such times of trouble, you can make Safari *impersonate* any other browser, which is often good enough to fool the picky Web site into letting you in.

The key to this trick is Safari's Develop menu, which is generally hidden. You can make it appear by choosing Safari→Preferences→Advanced tab. Turn on "Show Develop menu in menu bar."

The new Develop menu appears right next to Bookmarks. Most of its commands are designed to appeal to programmers, but the submenu you want—User Agent—is useful to everyone. It lets Safari masquerade as a different browser. Choose User Agent→Internet Explorer 7.0, for example, to assume the identity of a popular Windows browser.

Where am I?

As you dig your way down into a Web site, you may wish you had left a trail of bread crumbs to mark your path. Ah, but Safari has already thought of that. See Figure 12-5.

Figure 12-5:
If you ⌘-click the title bar (centered just above the address bar), Safari displays the "ladder" of pages you descended to arrive at the current one.

Faster Browsing Without Graphics

To turn off graphics, choose Safari→Preferences→Appearance tab. Turn off "Display images when the page opens," and close the Preferences window. Now try visiting a few Web pages and enjoy the substantial speed boost. (If you wind up on a Web page that's nothing without its pictures, then return to Safari→Preferences, turn the same checkbox on, and then reload the page.)

Tip: Can't stand having your Web page blinking like Times Square when you're trying to read? Then download Click2Flash, which omits all animations and blinking from a page unless you click because you want to see them. Or the amazing Readability, which hides *all* clutter–ads, banners, blinking, navigation bars–and presents the article you're reading in a large, clear font on a white background. Both are free and available from this book's "Missing CD" page at *www.missingmanuals.com.*

Expanding Web Forms

If the customer-service comment form on that corporate Web site doesn't give you enough room to rant properly, you can resize the text box right on the page—a *very* welcome feature in Snow Leopard. Figure 12-6 tells all.

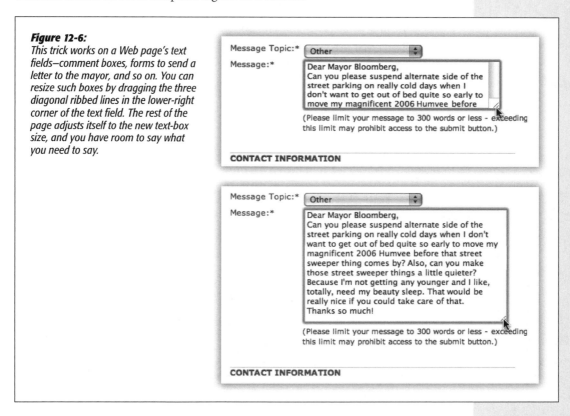

Figure 12-6:
This trick works on a Web page's text fields–comment boxes, forms to send a letter to the mayor, and so on. You can resize such boxes by dragging the three diagonal ribbed lines in the lower-right corner of the text field. The rest of the page adjusts itself to the new text-box size, and you have room to say what you need to say.

Viewing Web Pages Offline

You don't have to be connected to the Net to read a favorite Web page. You can save it on your hard drive so you can peruse it later—on your laptop during your commute, for example—just by choosing File→Save As.

To save the *entire* page, along with all its images, movies, and so on, choose Web Archive from the Format pop-up menu. (Choose Page Source only if you intend to *edit* the raw HTML Web documents and then repost them, or if you just want to study the underlying code.)

As a handy bonus, in Snow Leopard, Quick Look recognizes Safari sites you save in this way.

Tip: When you buy something online, don't waste paper by printing out the final "This is your receipt" page. Instead, choose File→Print and, from the PDF pop-up button, choose Save PDF to Web Receipts folder. Safari saves it as a PDF file into a tidy folder (in your Home→Documents folder) called Web Receipts. Nice touch!

Sending a Page to a Friend

Safari provides two ways of telling a friend about the page you're looking at. You might find that useful when you come across a particularly interesting news story, op-ed piece, or burrito recipe.

- **The send-the-whole-page method.** While looking at a page, choose File→Mail Contents of This Page (⌘-I) to open a new Mail message with a copy of the *actual* Web page in the body. Address the message and click Send.

- **The send-a-link method.** To send just a *link* to the page you're looking at, choose File→Mail Link to This Page (Shift-⌘-I). Then proceed as usual, addressing the message and clicking Send.

  Links take only a split second for your recipient to download, and they're guaranteed to display properly in all email programs. All your recipients have to do is click the link to open it in their Web browsers.

Designate Your Start Page

What's the first thing you see when you open Safari? Is it the Apple news Web site? Is it the Top Sites display (Figure 12-3)?

Actually, that's up to you.

Choose Safari→Preferences→General tab. Here, the "New windows open with" pop-up menu offers choices like these:

- **Top Sites.** The thumbnail view of your favorites sites makes a great starting point.

- **Home Page.** If you choose this option, then Safari will open up with whatever page you've specified in the "Home page" box. Google—or its news page, *http://news.google.com*—is a good starting place. So is your favorite newspaper home page, or *www.macsurfer.com*, a summary of the day's Mac news coverage around the world, or maybe *www.dilbert.com* for today's Dilbert cartoon.

  If you're already *on* the page you like, just click Set to Current Page.

- **Empty Page.** Some people prefer this setup, which makes Safari load very quickly when you first open it. Once this empty window opens, *then* you can tell the browser where you want to go today.

- **Bookmarks.** Whenever you open a new window or launch Safari, you see your full list of bookmarks. You can then choose exactly which page you want to open.

- **Tabs for Bookmarks Bar.** This intriguing new option creates a row of tabs in a single window—one for *every* icon on your Bookmarks bar. The idea, of course, is to have not just one favorite Web page waiting for you in the morning, but *all* the ones you visit frequently, pre-loaded and ready to go.

- **Choose Bookmarks folder.** This option is similar to "Tabs for Bookmarks Bar," except that it starts you off with tabs for *any* random bunch of Web sites—not just the ones on your Bookmarks bar. The trick is to build a *folder* full of bookmarks (Figure 12-4), and choose *that* as the basis for your auto-opening tabs.

Note: An identical pop-up menu is available for "New tabs open window." That is, you can specify one starter-page preference for new tabs and another for new windows.

Finding Text on Web Pages

The Google search bar can help you find Web sites that match your keywords. But some pages are so long, dense, or poorly designed that finding the words *on* the page needs a whole 'nother search engine. Fortunately, Safari's search-within-the-page function shines a light on the words or phrase you're seeking.

To use it, press ⌘-F and then type your search word into the Find box (Figure 12-7). As Safari locates the word or words, it displays them within a bright yellow box and dims the background of the rest of the page. The Find bar also tells you how many times the word or phrase occurs on the page; you can jump to each instance. Click the ⊗ to start over with new search terms, or click Done to close the Find bar and return to your normal browsing activity.

Figure 12-7:
Once you enter your keywords (Eagles, in this case), the browser dims the page and highlights every instance of that word— making it much easier to find what you're looking for across a crowded Web page.

Zoom in on PDF Pages

PDF files are all over the Web as, among other things, forms to download, online brochures, and scanned book pages. But they aren't always especially readable in a browser window.

Unless, that is, you're using Safari. The next time you're squinting at a PDF in the window, point to the bottom edge of the document; you'll see a toolbar appear like the one in Figure 12-8. With these four icons, you can zoom out, zoom in, open the file in Preview, or save the PDF file itself to your Downloads folder.

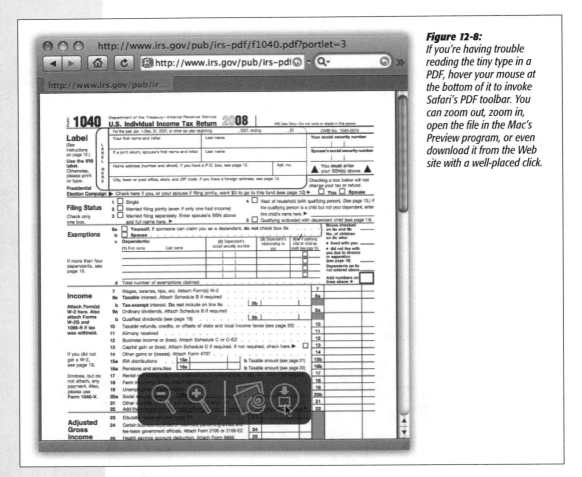

Figure 12-8:
If you're having trouble reading the tiny type in a PDF, hover your mouse at the bottom of it to invoke Safari's PDF toolbar. You can zoom out, zoom in, open the file in the Mac's Preview program, or even download it from the Web site with a well-placed click.

The History Menu

The History menu lists the Web sites you've visited in the past week or so, neatly organized into subfolders like "Earlier Today" and "Yesterday." (A similar menu appears when you click *and hold* on the Back or Forward button.) These are great features if you can't recall the URL for a Web site you remember having visited recently.

Tip: See Safari's Help menu? It features a Search box that lets you search all the menu commands in Safari—including Safari's History menu. That's just a crazy powerful feature. It means you can re-find a site without having to hunt through all the History submenus manually; just search for a word you remember in the title.

You can also view your History in a more expansive view—in Cover Flow view, in fact—by clicking the ⊞ at the left end of your toolbar. You enter the Bookmarks-management view, described in Figure 12-4.

Tabbed Browsing

Beloved by hardcore surfers the world over, *tabbed browsing* is a way to keep a bunch of Web pages open simultaneously—in a single, neat window. Figure 12-9 illustrates.

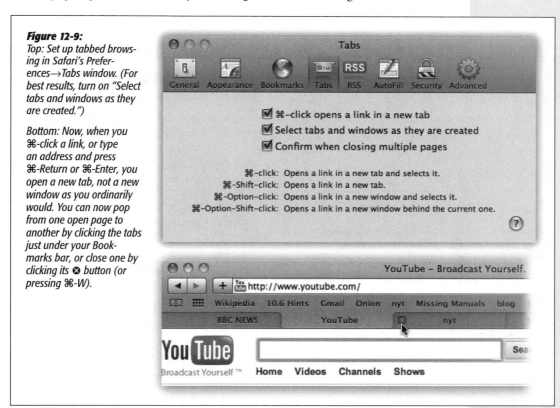

Figure 12-9:
Top: Set up tabbed browsing in Safari's Preferences→Tabs window. (For best results, turn on "Select tabs and windows as they are created.")

Bottom: Now, when you ⌘-click a link, or type an address and press ⌘-Return or ⌘-Enter, you open a new tab, not a new window as you ordinarily would. You can now pop from one open page to another by clicking the tabs just under your Bookmarks bar, or close one by clicking its ⊗ button (or pressing ⌘-W).

Turning on tabbed browsing unlocks a whole raft of Safari shortcuts and tricks, which are just the sort of thing power surfers gulp down like Gatorade:

- If there's a certain set of Web sites you like to visit daily, put the bookmarks into one folder, using Bookmarks→Add Bookmark Folder and the Bookmarks organizer window (Figure 12-4). You can then load all of them into a single tabbed window, simply by selecting the resulting "folder" in the Bookmarks menu—or the Bookmarks bar—and choosing Open in Tabs from the submenu.

The beauty of this arrangement is that you can start reading the first Web page while all the others load into their own tabs in the background.

Tip: Click the 🕮 icon at the left end of the Bookmarks bar. In the Bookmarks organizer, click the Bookmarks Bar item in the left-side list. Now you can see an Auto-Click checkbox for each listed folder.

If you turn on this checkbox, then you'll be able to open all the bookmarks in that folder into tabs, all at once, merely by clicking the folder's name in the Bookmarks bar. (If you want to summon the normal menu from the folder, just hold the mouse button down.)

- A variation on a theme: When you have a bunch of pages open in tabs, you can drag the tabs across the window to rearrange the order. When you have them the

---

FREQUENTLY ASKED QUESTION

Erasing Your Tracks—and Private Browsing

So, about this History menu: I'd just as soon my wife/husband/boss/parent/kid not know what Web sites I've been visiting. Must that History menu display my movements quite so proudly?

Some people find it creepy that Safari maintains a complete list of every Web site they've seen recently, right there in plain view of any family member or coworker who wanders by.

To delete just one particularly incriminating History listing, click the 🕮 icon at the left end of the Bookmarks bar; in the resulting Bookmarks organizer window, click History. Expand the relevant date triangle, highlight the offending address, and then press your Delete key. Click 🕮 again to return to normal browsing. You've just rewritten History!

Or, to erase the entire History menu, choose History→Clear History.

Of course, the History menu isn't the only place where you've left footprints. If you choose Safari→Reset Safari instead, you also erase all other shreds of your activities: any cookies (Web-page preference files) you've accumulated, your list of past downloads, the cache files (tiny Web graphics on your hard drive that a browser stores to save time when you return to the page they came from), and so on. This is good information to know; after all, you might be nominated to the Supreme Court someday.

That's a lot of work just to cover my tracks; it also erases a lot of valuable cookies, passwords, and History entries I'd like to keep. Is all that really necessary just so I can duck in for an occasional look at the Hot Bods of the Midwestern Tax Preparers' Association Web site?

No, it's not. A feature called private browsing lets you surf without adding any pages to your History list, searches to your Google search box, passwords to Safari's saved password list, or autofill entries to Safari's memory. (Apple says this feature is intended for use at public Macs, where you don't want to reveal anything personal to subsequent visitors. Ha!)

The trick is to choose Safari→Private Browsing before you start browsing. Once you OK the explanation box, Safari records nothing while you surf. (Nothing, that is, except cookies. Your tracks, in other words, are not completely hidden. You can erase cookies, if need be, in Safari→Preferences→Security.)

When you're ready to browse "publicly" again, choose Safari→Private Browsing once more so the checkmark goes away. Safari again begins taking note of the pages you visit—but it never remembers the earlier ones.

In other words, what happens in Private Browsing stays in Private Browsing.

---

way you want them, Control-click (or right-click) a tab, and then choose Add Bookmark for These [*Number*] Tabs from the shortcut menu. You can save your saved tabs to the Bookmarks bar and load all those pages with one click.

- If you Option-click a tab's ✖ button, you close all the tabs *except* the one you clicked. The same thing happens if you hold down Option and choose File→Close Other Tabs, or if you press Option-⌘-W.

- If you Option-⌘-click a link, it opens in a separate window, rather than a new tab. (When tabbed browsing is turned *off,* you just ⌘-click a link to open a new window.)

- If you find yourself with a bunch of separate browser windows all over your screen, you can neatly consolidate them all into one nicely tabbed Safari window by choosing Window→Merge All Windows.

- If you Shift-⌘-click a link, Safari opens that page in a tab *behind* the one you're reading. That's a fantastic trick when you're reading a Web page and see a reference

---

FREQUENTLY ASKED QUESTION

Cookie Control

Help! I'm afraid of cookies! The cookies are trying to watch me!

Cookies are something like Web page preference files. Certain Web sites—particularly commercial ones like Amazon.com—deposit them on your hard drive like little bookmarks so that they'll remember you the next time you visit. Most cookies are perfectly innocuous— and, in fact, are extremely helpful, because they help Web sites remember your tastes. Cookies also spare you the effort of having to type in your name, address, credit card number, and so on, every time you visit these Web sites.

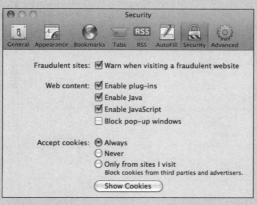

But fear is widespread, and the media fans the flames with tales of sinister cookies that track your movements on the Web. If you're worried about invasions of privacy, Safari is ready to protect you.

Once the browser is open, choose Safari→Preferences→ Security tab. The buttons in this dialog box are like a paranoia gauge. If you click Never, you create an acrylic shield around your Mac. No cookies can come in, and no cookie information can go out. You'll probably find the Web a very inconvenient place; you'll have to re-enter your information upon every visit, and some Web sites may not work properly at all.

A less-drastic choice is "Only from sites I visit," which accepts cookies from sites you want to visit but blocks cookies deposited on your hard drive by sites you're not actually visiting—cookies an especially evil banner ad gives you, for example.

Note, too, the Show Cookies button, which reveals the shockingly complete list of every cookie you've accumulated so far—and offers you the chance to delete the ones that don't look so savory.

---

you want to set aside for reading next, but you don't want to interrupt whatever you're reading now.

RSS: The Missing Manual

In the beginning, the Internet was an informational Garden of Eden. There were no banner ads, pop-ups, flashy animations, or spam messages. Back then, people thought the Internet was the greatest idea ever.

Those days, unfortunately, are long gone. Web browsing now entails a constant battle against intrusive advertising and annoying animations. And with the proliferation of Web sites of every kind—from news sites to personal Web logs (*blogs*)—just reading your favorite sites can become a full-time job.

Enter RSS, a technology that lets you subscribe to *feeds*—summary blurbs provided by thousands of sources around the world, from Reuters to Apple to your nerdy next-door neighbor. You can use a program like Safari to "subscribe" to updates from such feeds and then read any new articles or postings at your leisure (Figure 12-10).

News source   Headline   Date/time posted   RSS button   Article count

Figure 12-10:
The Length slider controls how much text appears for each RSS blurb; if you drag it all the way to the left, you're left with nothing but headlines. To change the number and order of the articles being displayed, use the sort options on the right. And if you feel a sudden desire to tell your friends about an amazing RSS feed you've just discovered, use the "Mail Link to This Page" link in the lower-right section of the window.

The result: You spare yourself the tedium of checking for updates manually, plus you get to read short summaries of new articles without ads and blinking animations. And if you want to read a full article, you can click its link in the RSS feed to jump straight to the main Web site.

Note: RSS stands for either Rich Site Summary or Really Simple Syndication. Each abbreviation explains one aspect of RSS—either its summarizing talent or its simplicity.

Viewing an RSS Feed

So how do you sign up for these free, automatic RSS "broadcasts"? Watch your address bar as you're surfing the Web. When you see a blue RSS button appear (identified back in Figure 12-1), Safari is telling you, "This site has an RSS feed available."

To see what the fuss is all about, click that button. Safari switches into RSS-viewing mode. At this point, you have two choices:

- **Add the RSS feed as a bookmark.** Use the Bookmarks→Add Bookmark command, and add the feed to your Bookmarks menu, Bookmarks bar, or Mail as you would any Web page. From now on, you'll be able to see whether the RSS feed has had any new articles posted—without actually having to visit the site. Figure 12-11 (top) has the details.

- **Close the RSS feed altogether.** To do so, just click the RSS button again. You're left back where you started, at whatever Web page you were visiting.

RSS Tricks

RSS is a tremendously flexible and powerful technology, especially in Safari. The fun never ends, as these tricks illustrate.

Creating RSS summaries

If you create a new bookmark folder and fill it with RSS feeds, you can see the *total* number of new articles right next to the folder's name (Figure 12-11, bottom). You might create a folder of Mac news feeds, for instance, so you know whenever there's a important event in the Mac world.

From then on, by clicking the folder's name (and opening its pop-up menu), you can see which feeds have new articles; they're the ones with numbers next to their names. If you ⌘-click a bookmark folder's name—in either the Bookmarks bar or the Bookmarks menu—Safari shows you *all* the feeds, neatly collated into one big, easily digestible list for your perusing pleasure. (If you're billing by the hour, you can also choose View All RSS Articles from the folder's pop-up menu to achieve the same effect.)

Tip: To make the merged list more useful, click New under the Sort By heading. Now Safari displays any new articles at the top of the list, regardless of what site they came from, so you don't have to hunt through the list for new articles yourself.

The personal clipping service

The search box at the right of any RSS-viewing window works pretty much as you'd expect: It narrows down the list of articles to only those that contain your search terms.

Figure 12-11:
Top: Want to specify when Safari should check for updates to your RSS bookmarks? In Safari→Preferences, click RSS. Turn on Bookmarks Bar and Bookmarks Menu. (If you're an especially impatient person, select "Every 30 minutes" from the "Check for updates" pop-up menu.)

Bottom: Next to your RSS feeds' names (in this screenshot, VersionTracker and Wired), a number tells you how many new articles are waiting for you. If you have a bookmark folder containing several RSS feeds in it (here, Potato News), the number reflects the total number of new articles in that folder's feeds. Never again will you have to check a Web site for updates the old-fashioned way.

But that's barely scratching the surface of the search field's power. If you've adopted the feed-merging trick described above, the Search box can search *several* feeds at once—perfect, for example, if you want to see all the news from Mac sites that has to do with iTunes.

Now how much would you pay? But get this—you can then save the search itself as a bookmark. Use the Bookmark This Search link at the lower-right corner of the window. Give the bookmark a name, choose where it should appear in Safari, and then click Add.

You've just turned Safari into a high-tech personal clipping service. With one click on your new bookmark, you can search all your news sources simultaneously—the feeds you've selected—for the terms you want. You've just saved yourself *hours* of daily searching—not to mention the expense of a real clipping service.

Tip: Mail can display your RSS feeds, too. Flip back to page 343 if you skipped that chapter.

The RSS screen saver

In System Preferences→Desktop & Screen Saver→Screen Saver tab, you'll find the RSS Visualizer screen saver, an impressive display indeed. When you click Options and select an RSS feed, you set up Mac OS X to get news from that feed whenever you're away from your Mac. When the screen saver comes on, you're treated to a 3-D animation of the news from that site—and astonished gazes from coworkers.

If a news story grabs your interest, press the number key mentioned at the bottom of the screen. The screen saver fades out, and Safari displays the associated article.

Tip: But what if the feed you want isn't part of Safari's repertoire? No problem. Add the feed to your Safari bookmarks and relaunch System Preferences.

Make feeds open automatically

It's easy enough to set up any favorite Web site as your start page. But you can also make an RSS feed—or a list of feeds—your home page. Open the feeds you want, choose Safari→Preferences→General tab, click Set to Current Page, and choose "Home Page" from the "New windows open with" pop-up menu.

In other words, suppose you start by opening a list of local, national, international, business, and sports news feeds. In that case, you've just made yourself a fantastic imitation of newspaper headlines, but tailored to *your* interests with spectacular precision: The Francis J. McQuaid (or whatever your name is) Times.

Tip: If you've turned on tabbed browsing, you can Shift-⌘-click headlines. That makes the full articles open in background tabs while you continue to read the headlines.

Articles in this arrangement are timelier than anything you could read in print—and they're free. If you miss a day of reading the headlines, no problem; they stick around for days and disappear only once you've read them. Finally, when you're done reading, you don't have to worry about recycling your "newspaper." No trees were harmed in the making of this publication. Welcome to the future of news: customized, free, up-to-date, and paperless.

Tip: To find more RSS feeds, visit a site like *www.syndic8.com*, or just watch for the appearance of the blue RSS button in the address bar. And if you want more power in an RSS reader, try out a program like NetNewsWire (*http://ranchero.com/netnewswire/*), which offers many more power-user features.

iChat

Somewhere between email and the telephone lies a unique communication tool called *instant messaging*. Plenty of instant messenger programs run on the Mac, but guess what? You don't really need any of them. Mac OS X comes with its very own instant messenger program called iChat, built right into the system and ready to connect to your friends on the AIM, Jabber, or GoogleTalk networks.

To start up iChat, go to Applications→iChat, or just click iChat's Dock icon. This section covers how to use iChat to communicate by video, audio, and text with your online pals.

Three Chat Networks

iChat lets you reach out to chat partners on three networks:

- **The AIM/MobileMe network.** If you've signed up for a MobileMe address (the paid kind or the free kind described below) or a free AOL Instant Messenger (AIM) account, you can chat with anyone in the 150 million-member AOL Instant Messenger network.

Note: If you're on AOL's AIM service, why would you want to use iChat instead? Easy: Because iChat is a nice, cleanly designed program that's free of advertisements, chatbots, and clunky interface elements.

- **The Jabber network.** Jabber is a chat network whose key virtue is its *open-source* origins. In other words, it wasn't masterminded by some corporate media behemoth; it's an all-volunteer effort, joined by thousands of programmers all over the world. There's no one Jabber chat program (like AOL Instant Messenger). There are dozens, available for Mac OS X, Windows, Linux, Unix, iPhone, Palm organizers, and so on. They can all chat with one another across the Internet in one glorious frenzy of typing.

  And now there's one more program that can join the party: iChat.

- **Google Talk.** Behind the scenes, it uses the Jabber network, so Google Talk doesn't really count as a different *network*. But it does mean you can use iChat to converse with all those Google Talkers, too.

- **Your own local network.** Thanks to the Bonjour network-recognition technology, you can communicate with other Macs on your own office network without signing up for anything at all—and without being online. This is a terrific feature when you're sitting around a conference table, idly chatting with colleagues using your wireless laptop (and the boss thinks you're taking notes). It's also handy when you want to type little messages throughout the day to a family member downstairs, or a roommate 15 feet away.

Each network generally has its own separate Buddy List window and its own chat window, but you *can* consolidate all your chats into a single window (iChat→Preferences→Messages→"Collect chats in a single window").

You log into each network separately using the iChat→Accounts submenu, but you can be logged into all of them at once. This is a great option if your friends are spread out among different chat networks.

Otherwise, however, chatting and videoconferencing works identically on all three networks. Keep that in mind as you read the following pages.

Signing Up

When you open iChat for the first time, you see the "Welcome To iChat" window (Figure 12-12). This is the first of several screens in the iChat setup sequence, during which you're supposed to tell it which kinds of chat accounts you have and set up your camera, if any.

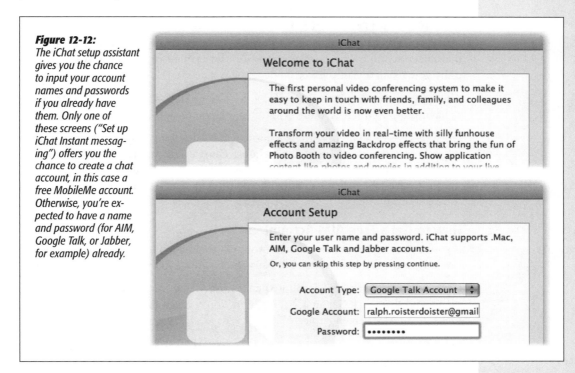

Figure 12-12:
The iChat setup assistant gives you the chance to input your account names and passwords if you already have them. Only one of these screens ("Set up iChat Instant messaging") offers you the chance to create a chat account, in this case a free MobileMe account. Otherwise, you're expected to have a name and password (for AIM, Google Talk, or Jabber, for example) already.

An *account* is a name and password. Fortunately, these accounts are free, and there are several ways to acquire one.

How to Get a Free MobileMe Account

If you're already a member of Apple's MobileMe service (Chapter 10), iChat fills in your member name and password automatically. If not, you can get an iChat-only MobileMe account for free. To get started, do one of these two things:

• Click the "Get an iChat Account" button that appears on the second Setup Assistant screen.

• Choose iChat→Preferences→Accounts, click the **+** button, and click Create New MobileMe Account.

Either way, you go to an Apple Web page, where you can sign up for a free iChat account name. You also get 60 days of the more complete MobileMe treatment (usually

$100 a year) described in Chapter 10. When your trial period ends, you lose all the other stuff MobileMe provides, but you do get to keep your iChat name.

Note: If your MobileMe name is missingmanualguy, you'll appear to everyone else as missingmanualguy@ mac.com. The software tacks on the "@me.com" suffix automatically.

How to Get a Free Jabber (or Gmail) Account

Apple expects that, if you're that interested in Jabber, you already have an account that's been set up by the company you work for (Jabber is popular in corporations) or by you, using one of the free Jabber programs.

Alternatively, you can just sign up for a free Google Talk account, which is the same as having a free Gmail account. (Go to Gmail.com to sign up for one.)

Once you've got a Gmail address, choose iChat→Preferences→Accounts, and click the **+** button. Under Account Type, choose Google Talk and type in your complete Gmail address (like *gwashington@gmail.com)* and password. Your Gmail name pops up on iChat's Jabber list—along with any of your Gmail contacts who are already online and yapping.

How to Get a Free AIM Account

If you're an America Online member, your existing screen name and password work; if you've used AIM before, you can use your existing name and password.

If you've never had an AIM account, then choose AIM from the Account Type pop-up menu, and then click Get an iChat Account. You're taken to the Web, where you can make up an AIM screen name.

The Buddy Lists

Once you've entered your account information, you're technically ready to start chatting. All you need now is a chatting companion. iChat comes complete with a Buddy List window where you can house the chat "addresses" for all your friends, relatives, and colleagues out there on the Internet.

Actually, to be precise, iChat comes with *three* Buddy Lists (Figure 12-13):

- **AIM Buddy List.** This window lists all your chat pals who have *either* MobileMe or AIM accounts; they all share the same Buddy List. You see the same list whether you log into MobileMe or your AIM account.

Tip: You can conduct text, audio, and video chats with other AIM members, Mac or PC. They just need the latest version of the AIM program—and, of course, a Webcam.

- **Jabber List.** Same idea, except that all your contacts in this window must have Jabber or Google Talk accounts.

- **Bonjour.** This list is limited to your local network buddies—the ones in the same building, most likely, and on the same network. You can't add names to your Bonjour list; anyone who's on the network and running iChat appears automatically in the Bonjour list.

Making a List

When you start iChat, your Buddy Lists automatically appear (Figure 12-13). If you don't see them, choose the list you want from the Window menu: [Your MobileMe/AIM account], Bonjour List, or Jabber List. (Or press their keyboard shortcuts: ⌘-1, ⌘-2, or ⌘-3.)

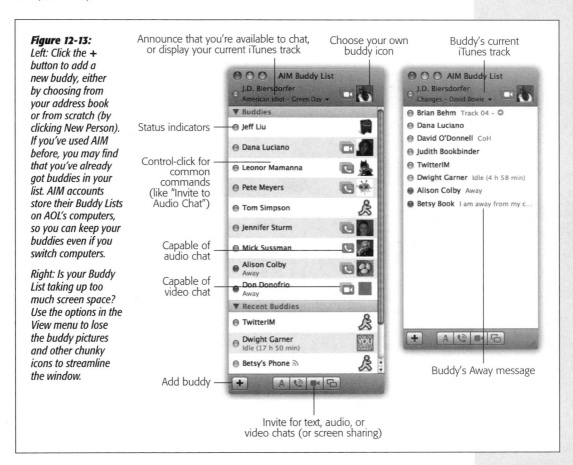

Figure 12-13:
Left: Click the + button to add a new buddy, either by choosing from your address book or from scratch (by clicking New Person). If you've used AIM before, you may find that you've already got buddies in your list. AIM accounts store their Buddy Lists on AOL's computers, so you can keep your buddies even if you switch computers.

Right: Is your Buddy List taking up too much screen space? Use the options in the View menu to lose the buddy pictures and other chunky icons to streamline the window.

Announce that you're available to chat, or display your current iTunes track

Choose your own buddy icon

Buddy's current iTunes track

Status indicators

Control-click for common commands (like "Invite to Audio Chat")

Capable of audio chat

Capable of video chat

Add buddy

Invite for text, audio, or video chats (or screen sharing)

Buddy's Away message

Adding a buddy to this list entails knowing that person's account name, whether it's on AIM, MobileMe, or Jabber. Once you have it, you can either choose Buddies→Add Buddy (Shift-⌘-A) or click the **+** button at the bottom-left corner of the window.

Down slides a sheet attached to the Buddy List window, offering a window into the Address Book program (Chapter 11).

Tip: As you accumulate buddies, your Buddy List may become crowded. If you choose View→Show Offline Buddies and uncheck the box, then only your currently online buddies show up in the Buddy List—a much more meaningful list for the temporarily lonely.

If your chat companion is already in Address Book, scroll through the list until you find the name you want (or enter the first few letters into the Search box), click the name, and then click Select Buddy.

If not, click New Person and enter the buddy's AIM address, MobileMe address, or (if you're in the Jabber list) Jabber address. You're adding this person to both your Buddy List and to your Address Book.

Broadcasting Your Status

Using the pop-up menu just below your name (Figure 12-14, right), you can display your current mental status to *other* people's Buddy Lists. You can announce that you're Available, Away, or Drunk. (You have to choose Edit Status Menu for that last one; see Figure 12-14, left.)

Figure 12-14:

Left: Choose Edit Status Menu from the pop-up menu at the top of the iChat Buddy List to set up more creative alternatives to "Available" and "Away."

Right: Your edited list of status messages is now available. The most interesting one is Invisible. It lets you see your friends online, but they can't see you—great when you're too busy to chat with annoying barely-acquaintances but want to keep an eye out for a particular pal. You can still send and receive messages to chat with anyone on your Buddy List.

Better yet, if you have music playing in iTunes, you can tell the world what you're listening to at the moment by choosing Current iTunes Song. (Your buddy can even click that song's name to open its screen on the iTunes Store, all for Instant Purchase Gratification.)

For some people, by far the juiciest status option is Invisible (available for MobileMe and AIM accounts only). It's like a *Star Trek* cloaking device for your onscreen presence (Figure 12-14). Great for stalkers!

Once you get a lot of people piled on your list, all with their buddy pictures and audio/ video chat icons, you may feel like iChat is taking up way too much screen real estate. If you want a more space-efficient view of your Buddy List (like the one shown on the right in Figure 12-13), go to the View menu and turn off Show Buddy Pictures, Show Audio Status, or Show Video Status. You can turn off Buddy Groups here as well, if you'd prefer to see your buddies in one undivided list.

Let the Chat Begin

As with any conversation, somebody has to talk first. In chat circles, that's called *inviting* someone to a chat.

They Invite You

To "turn on your pager" so you'll be notified when someone wants to chat with you, run iChat. Hide its windows, if you like, by pressing ⌘-H.

When someone tries to "page" you for a chat, iChat comes forward automatically and shows you an invitation message like the one in Figure 12-15. If the person initiating a chat isn't already in your Buddy List, you'll simply see a note that says "Message from *[name of the person]*."

Tip: If you're getting hassled by someone on your AIM/MobileMe Buddy List, click his screen name and choose Buddies→Block Person. If the person isn't online at the time, go to iChat→Preferences→Accounts→Security and click the button for "Block specific people." Click the Edit List button, and then type in the screen name of the person you want out of your IM life.

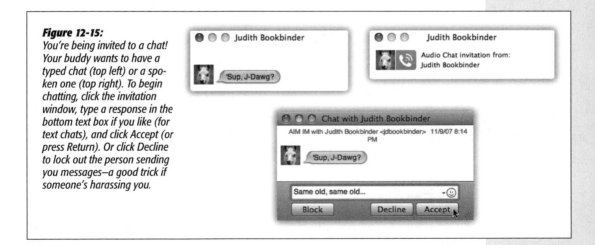

Figure 12-15:
You're being invited to a chat! Your buddy wants to have a typed chat (top left) or a spoken one (top right). To begin chatting, click the invitation window, type a response in the bottom text box if you like (for text chats), and click Accept (or press Return). Or click Decline to lock out the person sending you messages—a good trick if someone's harassing you.

You Invite Them

To invite somebody in your Buddy List to a chat:

- For a text chat, double-click the person's *name,* type a quick invite ("You there?"), and press Return.

You can invite more than one person to the chat. Each time you click the **+** button at the bottom of the Participants list, you choose another person to invite. (Or ⌘-click each name in the Buddy List to select several people at once and then click the A button at the bottom of the list to start the text chat.) Everyone sees all the messages anyone sends.

- To start an audio or video chat, click the microphone or movie-camera icon in your Buddy List (shown in Figure 12-13).

To initiate a chat with someone who *isn't* in the Buddy List, choose File→New Chat With Person. Type the account name, and then click OK to send the invitation.

Either way, you can have more than one chat going at once. Real iChat nerds often wind up with screens overflowing with individual chat windows.

But in modern times, you can now contain all your conversations in a single window. If you like the idea of a consolidated chatspace, choose iChat→Preferences→Messages and slap a checkmark in the "Collect chats in a single window" box. Figure 12-16 shows the result.

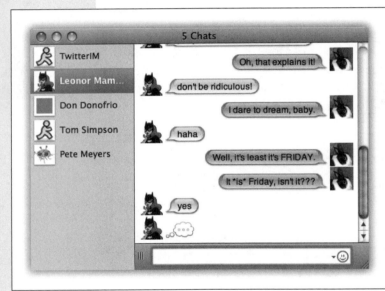

Figure 12-16:
Now, when you're conversing with several buddies, you can bounce between conversations by clicking the buddy names on the side of the window. It's not as adventurous as keeping all your chats going in separate windows, but it's a lot easier to hide when the boss comes your way.

Text Chatting

A typed chat works like this: Each time you or your chat partner types something and then presses Return, the text appears on both of your screens (Figure 12-17). iChat displays each typed comment next to an icon, which can be any of these three things:

- **A picture they added.** If the buddy added her *own* picture to her chat program, it will be transmitted to you, appearing automatically in the chat window. Cool!

- **A picture you added.** If you've added a picture of that person to the Buddy List or Address Book, you see it here instead. (After all, your vision of what somebody looks like may not match his own self-image.)

- **Generic.** If nobody's done icon-dragging of any sort, you get a generic icon.

Figure 12-17:
As you chat, your comments always appear on the right. If you haven't yet created a custom icon, you'll look like a blue globe or an AOL running man. You can choose a picture for yourself either in your own Address Book card or right in iChat. And Web links your pals paste into messages are perfectly clickable—your Web browser leaps right up to take you to the site your friend has shared.

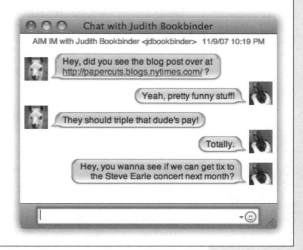

GEM IN THE ROUGH

Making iChat Auto-Answer

When you invite another Mac to a video chat, someone has to be sitting in front of it to accept your invitation. That's an important privacy feature, of course, because it prevents total strangers from peeking in on you when you're walking around in your underwear.

But having to have a live human at the other end is kind of a bummer if you just want to peek in on your house, your kids, or your spouse while you're away, using your iSight camera or camcorder as a sort of security cam or nannycam. In the pre-Leopard days, you

could set up iChat to auto-answer your video-chat invitations only by using add-on software or geekster Terminal commands.

Since Leopard, though, that option has been available right out of the box.

Choose iChat→Preferences→Alerts and then turn on Run AppleScript script. From the adjoining pop-up menu, choose Auto Accept.

From now on, iChat will love all your buddies and accept their invites immediately.

To choose a graphic to use as your own icon, click the square picture to the right of your own name at the top of the Buddy, Jabber, or Bonjour list. From the pop-up palette of recently selected pictures, choose Edit Picture to open a pop-up image-selection palette, where you can take a snapshot with your Mac's camera or choose a photo file from your hard drive. Feel free to build an array of graphics to represent yourself—and to change them in midchat, using this pop-up palette, to the delight or confusion of your conversation partner.

In-chat Fun

Typing isn't the only thing you can do during a chat. You can also perform any of these stunts:

- **Open the drawer.** Choose View→Show Chat Participants to hide or show the "drawer" that lists every person in your current group chat. To invite somebody new to the chat, click the **+** button at the bottom of the drawer, or drag the person's icon out of the Buddy List window and into this drawer.

- **Format your text.** You can press ⌘-B or ⌘-I to make your next typed utterance bold or italic. Or change your color or font by choosing Format→Show Colors or Format→Show Fonts, which summons the standard Mac OS X color or font palettes. (If you use some weird font that your chat partners don't have installed, they won't see the same typeface.)

- **Insert a smiley.** When you choose a face (like Undecided, Angry, or Frown) from this quick-access menu of smiley options (at the right end of the text-reply box), iChat inserts it as a graphic into your response.

  On the other hand, if you know the correct symbols to produce smileys—that :) means a smiling face, for example—you can save time by typing them instead of using the pop-up menu. iChat converts them into smiley icons on the fly, as soon as you send your reply.

GEM IN THE ROUGH

The Chat Transcript

Every now and then, you wish you could preserve a chat for all time–for example, a particularly meaningful conversation with a friend, lover, or customer-service agent.

On the iChat→Preferences→Messages panel, you can turn on "Save chat transcripts to" (and choose a folder on your hard drive). From now on, the text of your conversations is automatically saved in that folder. To view a chat later, double-click its icon. It opens within iChat, compete with all its colors and formatting.

While you're at it, you might also want to turn on a new Snow Leopard feature: "In new chapter window, show." What that means is, the next time you chat with someone, your last chat message with that buddy (or your last five, 25, 100, or 250) pop up automatically in a new window, for your reference. (Bonus tip: Edit→Mark Transcripts stamps the current date and time on each transcript.)

Even if you don't turn on this checkbox, you can save individual chats in progress by choosing File→Save a Copy As.

- **Send a file.** Choosing Buddies→Send File lets you send a file to *all* the participants in your chat.

  Better yet, just drag the file's icon from the Finder into the box where you normally type. (This trick works well with pictures, because your conversation partner sees the graphic right in his iChat window.)

  This is a fantastic way to transfer a file that would be too big to send by email. A chat window never gets "full," and no attachment is too large to send.

  This method halves the time of transfer, too, since your recipients get the file *as* you upload it. They don't have to wait 20 minutes for you to send the file, and then another 20 minutes to download it, as they would with email or FTP.

  Note, though, that this option isn't available in old versions of the AOL Instant Messenger program—only new versions and iChat.

Tip: If you've opened the Participants drawer (View→Show Chat Participants), you can drag files from the Finder onto individual participants' names in this drawer to send files directly to them.

- **Get Info on someone.** If you click a name in your Buddy List, and then choose Buddies→Show Info (or right-click someone's name and choose Show Info from the shortcut menu), you get a little Info window about your buddy where you can edit her name, email address, and picture. (If you change the picture here, you'll see it instead of the graphic your buddy chose for herself.)

  If you click the Alerts tab at this point, you can make iChat react when this particular buddy logs in, logs out, or changes status—for example, by playing a sound or saying, "She's here! She's here!"

- **Send an Instant Message.** Not everything in a chat session has to be "heard" by all participants. If you choose Buddies→Send Instant Message, you get a *private* chat window, where you can "whisper" something directly to a special someone behind the other chatters' backs.

- **Send a Secure Message.** Fellow MobileMe members can engage in encrypted chats that keep the conversation strictly between participants. If you didn't turn on encrypted chats when you set up your MobileMe account in iChat, choose iChat→Preferences→Accounts→Security, and then click Enable.

- **Send Email.** If someone messages you, "Hey, will you email me directions?" you can do so on the spot by choosing Buddies→Send Email. Your email program opens up automatically so you can send the note along; if your buddy's email address is part of his Address Book info, the message is even preaddressed.

- **Send an SMS message to a cellphone.** If you're using an AIM screen name or MobileMe account, you can send text messages directly to your friends' cellphones (in the United States, anyway). Choose File→Send SMS. In the box that pops up, type the full cellphone number, without punctuation, like this: *2125551212.*

Press Return to return to the chat window. Type a very short message (a couple of sentences, tops), and then press Return.

Tip: If iChat rudely informs you that your own privacy settings prevent you from contacting "this person," choose iChat→Preferences, click Accounts, click your chat account, and turn on "Allow anyone."

Obviously, you can't carry on much of an interactive conversation this way. The only response you get is from AOL's computers, letting you know that your message has been sent. But what a great way to shoot a "Call me!" or "Running late—see you tonight!" or "Turn on Channel 4 right now!!!" message to someone's phone.

On the other hand, if you're going to be away from your Mac for a few hours, you can have iChat forward incoming chat messages to *your* cellphone. Choose iChat→Preferences→Accounts and click Configure AIM Mobile Forwarding. In the resulting window, fill in your own cellphone number, so the incoming messages know where to go.

Audio Chats

iChat becomes much more exciting when you exploit its AV Club capabilities. If you have a broadband connection, up to 10 of you can join in one massive, free conference call from across the Internet.

A telephone icon next to a name in your Buddy List tells you that the buddy has a microphone. If you see what appear to be stacked phone icons, then your pal's Mac has enough horsepower to handle a *multiple-person* conference call. (You can see these icons back in Figure 12-13.)

To begin an audio chat, you have three choices:

- Click the telephone icon next to the buddy's name.
- Highlight someone in the Buddy List, and then click the telephone icon at the bottom of the list.
- If you're already in a text chat, choose Buddies→Invite to Audio Chat.

Once your invitation is accepted, you can begin speaking. The bars of the sound-level meter let you know that the microphone—which you've specified in the iChat→Preferences→Audio/Video tab—is working.

Tip: Although the audio is full-duplex (you can hear and speak simultaneously, like a phone but unlike a walkie-talkie), there may be a delay, like you're calling overseas on a bad connection. If you can't hear anything at all, check out iChat's Help system, which contains a long list of suggestions.

Video Chats

If you and your partner both have broadband Internet connections, even more impressive feats await. You can conduct a free video chat with up to four people, who show up on three vertical panels, gorgeously reflected on a shiny black table surface. This isn't the jerky, out-of-audio-sync, Triscuit-sized video of days gone by. If you've got the Mac muscle and bandwidth, your partners are as crisp, clear, bright, and smooth as television—and as big as your screen, if you like.

Apple offers this luxurious experience, however, only if you have luxurious gear:

- **A video camera.** It can be the tiny iSight camera embedded above the screens of iMacs and laptops; an external FireWire iSight camera; an ordinary digital camcorder; or a golf-ball Webcam that connects via FireWire instead of USB.

Tip: You and your buddy don't both need the gear. If only you have a camera, for example, you can choose Buddies→Invite to One-Way Video Chat (or Audio Chat). Your less-equipped buddy can see you, but has to speak (audio only) or type in response.

- **Bandwidth.** You need Internet upload/download speeds of at least 100 kilobits per second for basic, tiny video chats with one other person, and a minimum of 384 Kbps for four-way video chats. And those are for the *smallest* video windows. Starting a video chat at the highest video quality requires 300 Kbps uploading bandwidth. That requirement may be too rich for residential DSL packages.

Tip: As you're beginning to appreciate, iChat's system requirements are all over the map. Some features require very little horsepower; others require tons.

To find out exactly which features your Mac can handle, choose Video→Connection Doctor; from the Show pop-up menu, choose Capabilities. There's a little chart of all iChat features, showing checkmarks for the ones your Mac can manage.

If you see a camcorder icon next to a buddy's name, you can have a full-screen, high-quality video chat with that person, because they, like you, have a suitable camera and a high-speed Internet connection. If you see a *stacked* camcorder icon, then that person has a Mac that's capable of joining a four-way video chat.

To begin a video chat, click the camera icon next to a buddy's name, or highlight someone in the Buddy List and then click the camcorder icon at the bottom of the list. Or, if you're already in a text chat, choose Buddies→Invite to Video Chat.

A window opens, showing *you*. This Preview mode is intended to show what your buddy will see. (You'll probably discover that you need some kind of light in front of you to avoid being too shadowy.) As your buddies join you, they appear in their own windows (Figure 12-18).

And now, some video-chat notes:

- If your conversation partners seem unwilling to make eye contact, it's not because they're shifty. They're just looking at *you*, on the screen, rather than at the camera—and chances are you aren't looking into your camera, either.

- Don't miss the Video→Full Screen command! Wild.

• You can have video chats with Windows computers, too, as long as they're using a recent version of AOL Instant Messenger. Be prepared for disappointment, though; the video is generally jerky, small, and slightly out of sync. That's partly due to the cheap USB Webcams most PCs have, and partly due to the poor video *codec* (compression scheme) built into AIM.

Figure 12-18:
That's you in the smaller window. To move your own mini-window, click a different corner, or drag yourself to a different corner. If you need to blow your nose or do something else unseemly, Option-click the microphone button to freeze the video and mute the audio. Click again to resume.

• If you use iChat with a camcorder, then you can set the camera to VTR (playback) mode and play a tape right over the Internet to a buddy on the other end! (The video appears flipped horizontally on your screen but looks right to the other person.)

• You can capture a still "photo" of a video chat by ⌘-dragging the image to your desktop, or by choosing Video→Take Snapshot (Option-⌘-S).

• Don't want to see yourself in the picture-in-picture window during your video chat? Choose Video→Hide Local Video.

• This cutting-edge technology can occasionally present cutting-edge glitches. The video quality deteriorates, the transmission aborts suddenly, the audio has an annoying echo, and so on. When problems strike, iChat Help offers a number of tips; the Video→Connection Doctor can identify your network speed. (iChat video likes *lots* of network speed.)

• Just as you can save your typed transcripts of instant message conversations, you can record your audio and video chats. Once you start a chat, choose Video→Record Chat. Your buddy is asked if it's OK for you to proceed with the recording (to ward off any question of those pesky wiretapping laws); if permission is granted, then iChat begins recording the call.

When you've got what you want, click Stop. Your recordings are automatically saved into Home→Documents→iChats (AAC files for audio conversations, MPEG-4 files for video chats). From there, you can drag them into iTunes to play or sync them up with an iPod or iPhone. Yes, you can now relive those glorious iChat moments when you're standing in line at the grocery store.

Bluescreen Backdrops and Video FX

If your video chats look like a bunch of cubicle-dwellers sitting around chatting at their desks, you can liven things up with one of iChat's most glamorous and jaw-dropping features: photo or video *backgrounds* for your talking head. Yes, now you can make your video chat partners think you're in Paris, on the moon, or even impersonating a four-panel Andy Warhol silkscreen.

Here's how to prepare your backdrop for a video chat:

1. **Go to iChat→Preferences→Audio/Video.**

   A video window opens so you can see yourself.

2. **Press Shift-⌘-E (or go to Video→Show Video Effects).**

   The Effects box appears. Click the various squares of the tic-tac-toe grid to see how each effect will transform you in real time: making your face bulbous, for example, or rendering you in delicate colored pencil shadings.

   The first two pages of effects all do video magic on *you* and everything else in the picture. If you want one of those, click it; you're done. There's no step 3. Your video-chat buddies now see you in your distorted or artistic new getup.

   The second two pages of effects, however, don't do anything to your image. Instead, they replace the *background*.

   In TV and movies, replacing the background is a common special effect. All you have to do is set up a perfectly smooth, evenly lit, shadowless blue or bright green backdrop behind the subject. Later, the computer replaces that solid color with a new picture or video of the director's choice.

   iChat, however, creates exactly the same special effect (Figure 12-19) without requiring the bluescreen or the greenscreen. Read on.

3. **Click the background effect you want.**

   Suppose, for example, that you've clicked the video loop showing the Eiffel Tower with people walking around. At this point, a message appears on the screen that says, "Please step out of the frame."

4. **Duck out of camera range (or move off to one side).**

See, iChat intends to memorize a picture of the *real* background—without you in it. When you return to the scene, your Mac then compares each pixel of its memorized image with what it's seeing now. Any differences, it concludes, must be *you*.

Note: To make this work, both the camera and the background must be perfectly still. If the lighting or the visuals shift or change in any way, you may get some weird, glitchy effects where your real background bleeds through.

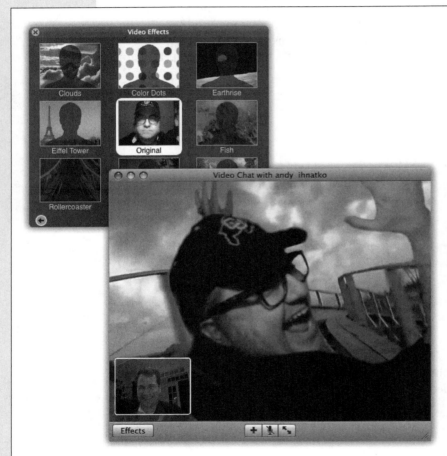

Figure 12-19:
Top left: You have plenty of backgrounds to choose from for your next video chat. Click an effect to add it to your chat window. Click the small arrows at the bottom of the window to advance or retreat through the various effects styles. Click the Original square in the middle of the window to erase the effect and start again from scratch.

Lower right: Let the live bluescreen action begin!

5. **When the screen says, "Background detected," step back into the frame.**

Zut alors! You are now in virtual Paris. Go ahead and start the video chat with your friends, and don't forget your beret.

If you want to clear out the background or change it, click the Original square in the middle of the Effects palette and then choose a different backdrop. (You can also change backdrops in midchat by choosing Video→Show Video Effects to open the Effects palette.)

If things get too weird and choppy onscreen, you can restore the normal background by choosing Video→Reset Background.

Tip: You can use one of your own photos or video clips as iChat backdrops, too. In the Video Effects box, click the arrows on the bottom until you get to the screen with several blank User Backdrop screens. Next, drag a photo or video from the desktop directly onto one of the blank screens. Click it just like you would any of Apple's stock shots.

Sharing Your Screen

iChat's screen sharing feature is a close relative of the *network* screen-sharing feature described in Chapter 14. It lets you see not only what's on a faraway buddy's screen, but *control* it, taking command of the distant mouse and keyboard. (Screen sharing can work the other way, too.)

And if you're the family tech-support specialist—but the family lives all over the country—screen sharing makes troubleshooting a heckuva lot easier. You can now jump on your mom's shared Mac and figure out why the formatting went wacky in her Word document, without her having to attempt to *explain* it to you over the phone. ("And then the little thingie disappeared and the doohickey got scrambled…")

To make iChat screen sharing work, you and your buddy must both be running Macs with Leopard or Snow Leopard. To begin, click the sharee's name in your Buddy List.

- If you want to share *your* screen with this person, choose Buddies→Share My Screen.

- If you want to see *her* screen (because she has all the working files on her Mac), choose Buddies→Ask to Share.

Note: Similar commands are available in the Screen Sharing pop-up button—the one that looks like two overlapping squares at the bottom of the Buddy List window. The commands say "Share My Screen with casey234" and "Ask to Share casey234's screen."

Once the invitation is accepted, the sharing begins, as shown in Figure 12-20. To help you communicate further, iChat politely opens up an audio chat.

If you're seeing someone else's screen, you see his Mac desktop in full-screen view, right on your own machine. You also see a small window showing your own Mac; click it to switch back to your own desktop.

Tip: To copy files from Mac to Mac, drag them between the two windows. Files dragged to your Mac wind up in your Downloads folder.

If something's not right, or you need to bail out of a shared connection immediately, press Control-Escape on the Mac's keyboard.

iChat Theater

iChat Theater turns the chat window into a presentation screen for displaying and narrating your own iPhoto or Keynote slideshows, QuickTime movie files, and even text documents. Your buddy, on the other end of the iChat line, sees these documents at nearly full size—with you in a little picture-in-picture screen in the corner.

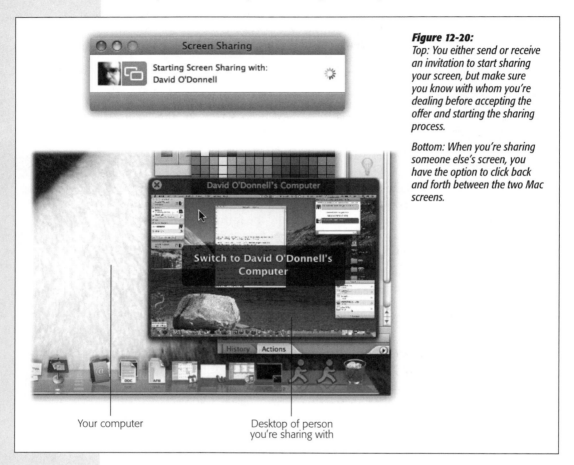

Figure 12-20:
Top: You either send or receive an invitation to start sharing your screen, but make sure you know with whom you're dealing before accepting the offer and starting the sharing process.

Bottom: When you're sharing someone else's screen, you have the option to click back and forth between the two Mac screens.

Your computer

Desktop of person you're sharing with

All you need is:

- **Some stuff to show off.** iChat Theater can display exactly the same kinds of files that Quick Look (Chapter 2) can display: Word, Excel, and PowerPoint documents; photos, text and HTML files; PDF files; audio and movie files; fonts; vCards; Pages, Numbers, Keynote, and TextEdit documents; and so on.

- **A zippy broadband Internet connection.** iChat Theater likes 384 kilobits per second or faster; check with your Internet provider if you aren't sure of your connection speed.

To get the show running, you can take one of two approaches:

- **If a video chat is under way,** you can just drag the file(s) you want to share into the video window. iChat asks if you want to *send* the file to the person or *share* it with iChat Theater (Figure 12-21, top). Click iChat Theater, of course.

- **If no video chat is in progress,** choose File→Share a File in iChat Theater. Locate the file you want to present on your hard drive. When iChat asks you to start a video chat with the buddy who's going to be your audience, click the video-camera icon next to that person's name (or choose Video→Invite to Video Chat).

When your friend accepts, the curtain goes up, as shown the bottom of Figure 12-21. The file you're sharing takes center stage (er, window) and your buddy appears in a little video window off to the side. Click the ■ button to expand the view to full screen.

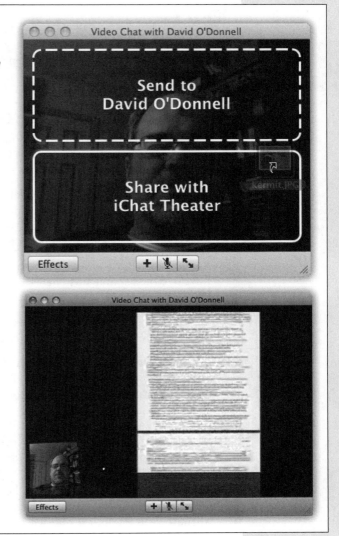

Figure 12-21:
Top: You can start an iChat Theater session by choosing File→Share a File with iChat Theater, or as shown here, by simply dropping the file on an open video chat window and going for the iChat Theater option.

Bottom: Once you've started a Theater show in Chat, the shared file takes center stage so you both can look at it and discuss amongst yourselves.

If you have iPhoto '08 or later, sharing picture albums is one menu command away: Choose File→Share iPhoto with iChat Theater. When the Media Browser pops up, pick the album you want to present. The first picture in the selected album appears in the iChat window before iPhoto itself opens, so you can use iPhoto's nice controls for cruising forward (or backward) through your album.

The same thing happens if you're running a Keynote presentation in iChat Theater: The first slide shows up in the chat window while the Keynote program launches to provide you with the proper controls to click through the rest of the slides in the presentation.

When the show is over, close the window to end the iChat Theater session.

iChat Tweaks

If you've done nothing but chat in iChat, you haven't even scratched the surface. The iChat→Preferences dialog box gives you plenty of additional control. A few examples:

- **General pane.** If you turn on "Show status in menu bar," you bring the iChat *menulet* to your menu bar. It lets you change your iChat status (Available, Away, and so on), whether you're in iChat or not.

  And if you turn off "When I quit iChat, set my status to Offline," then quitting iChat doesn't actually log you out. When someone wants a chat with you, iChat opens automatically.

  The General pane is also where you tell iChat what to do when you're temporarily away from the Mac. You can have it automatically reply to chat invitations with your personalized "I'm not here" message. When you come back to the Mac or wake it up from sleep, you can have iChat flip your status from Away to Available all by itself.

- **Accounts pane.** If you have more than one AIM, Jabber, or MobileMe account, you can switch among them here. Your passwords are conveniently saved in your Mac OS X Keychain.

- **Messages pane.** The Messages preference panel lets you design your chat windows—the background color, word balloon color, and typeface and size of text you type.

  If you want to set a special background image for your chats, you can do that as well—just drag a graphics file into the chat preview box on this pane. You can revert to a white background by choosing View→Clear Background.

Tip: Here's a little tweak, right on the Messages pane, that nobody ever mentions: the preference setting called "Watch for my name in incoming messages." It alerts you anytime anyone, in any of the open chats, types your name, even if you're doing something else on the Mac. (As in, "Casey, are you there? Casey!? CASEY!!")

- **Alerts pane.** Here, you can choose how iChat responds to various events. For example, it can play a sound, bounce its Dock icon, or say something out loud whenever you log in, log out, receive new messages, or run an AppleScript, as described earlier in this chapter.

- **Audio/Video pane.** This is where you get a preview of your own camera's output, limit the amount of *bandwidth* (signal-hogging data) the camera uses (a trouble-shooting step), and specify that you want iChat to fire up automatically whenever you switch on the camera.

Part Four:
Putting Down Roots

4

Accounts, Parental Controls, & Security

I n an era when *security* is the hottest high-tech buzzword, Apple was smart to make
it a focal point for Mac OS X. It was already virus-free and better protected from
Internet attacks than Windows. But Mac OS X 10.6 is the most impenetrable
Mac system yet, filled with new defenses against the dark arts. This chapter covers
the whole range of them.

On the premise that the biggest security threat of all comes from other people in
your home or office, though, the most important security feature in Mac OS X is the
accounts system.

Introducing Accounts

Like the Unix under its skin (and also like Windows), Mac OS X was designed from
the ground up to be a *multiple-user* operating system. That is, you can set up your
Mac OS X so that everyone must log in—click your name, type your password—when
the computer turns on (Figure 13-1).

Upon doing so, you discover the Macintosh universe just as you left it, including
your documents, files, and folders; your preference settings in every program you
use; your Web browser bookmarks and preferred home page; icons on the desktop
and in the Dock; email account(s), including personal information and mailboxes;
your personally installed programs and fonts; your choice of programs that launch
automatically at startup; and so on.

This system lets different people use it throughout the day without disrupting one
another's files and settings. It also protects the Mac from getting fouled up by mischievous (or bumbling) students, employees, and hackers.

If you're the only person who uses your Mac, you can safely skip most of this chapter. The Mac never pauses at startup time to demand the name and password you made up when you installed Mac OS X, because the Mac logs you in automatically. You *will* be using one of these accounts, though, whether you realize it or not.

Tip: Even if you don't share your Mac with anyone and don't create any other accounts, you might still be tempted to learn about the accounts feature because of its ability to password-protect the entire computer. All you have to do is to turn off the automatic login feature described on page 423. Thereafter, your Mac is protected from unauthorized fiddling when you're away from your desk or if your laptop is stolen.

Figure 13-1:
When you set up several accounts, you don't turn on the Mac so much as sign into it. A command in the ⌘ menu called Log Out summons this sign-in screen, as does the Accounts menu described later in this chapter. Click your own name, and type your password (if any), to get past this box and into your own stuff.

The First Account

When you first installed Mac OS X, you were asked for a name and password. You were creating the first *user account* on your Macintosh. Since that fateful day, you may have made a number of changes to your desktop—adjusted the Dock settings, set up your folders and desktop the way you like them, added some bookmarks to your Web browser, and so on—without realizing that you were actually making these changes to only *your account.*

You've probably been saving your documents into your own Home folder, which is the cornerstone of your account. This folder, generally named after you and stashed in the Users folder on your hard drive, stores not only your own work, but also your preference settings for all the programs you use, special fonts you've installed, your own email collection, and so on.

Now then: Suppose you create an account for a second person. When she turns on the computer and signs in, she finds the desktop exactly the way it was factory-installed by Apple—outer-space desktop picture, Dock along the bottom, and so on. No changes *she* makes will affect *your* environment the next time you log in.

In other words, the multiple-accounts feature has two components: first, a convenience element that hides everyone else's junk; and second, a security element that protects both the Mac's system software and everybody's work.

Creating an Account

Suppose somebody new joins your little Mac family—a new worker, student, or love interest, for example. And you want to make that person feel at home on your Mac.

Begin by opening System Preferences (Chapter 15). In the System Preferences window, click Accounts. You have just arrived at the master control center for account creation and management (Figure 13-2).

To create a new account, start by unlocking the Accounts panel. That is, click the 🔒 at lower left, and fill in your own account name and password.

Now you can click the **+** button beneath the list of accounts. The little panel shown at bottom in Figure 13-2 appears.

Phase 1: Choose an Account Type

As though this business of accounts and passwords weren't complicated enough already, Mac OS X offers more *types* of accounts than ever. And you're expected to specify *which* type each person gets at the moment you create an account.

To do that, open the New Account pop-up menu (Figure 13-2, bottom). Its five account types are described on the following pages.

Administrator accounts

If this is your own personal Mac, then just beneath your name on the Accounts pane of System Preferences, it probably says *Admin*. This, as you could probably guess, stands for Administrator.

Because you're the person who originally installed Mac OS X, the Mac assumes you are its *administrator*—the technical wizard in charge of it. You're the teacher, the parent, the resident guru. You're the one who will maintain this Mac. Only an administrator is allowed to:

• Install new programs into the Applications folder.

• Add fonts that everybody can use.

• Make changes to certain System Preferences panes (including Network, Date & Time, Energy Saver, and Startup Disk).

- Use some features of the Disk Utility program.

- Create, move, or delete folders outside of your Home or Shared folder.

- Decide who gets to have accounts on the Mac.

- Open, change, or delete anyone else's files.

- Bypass FileVault using a master password (page 435).

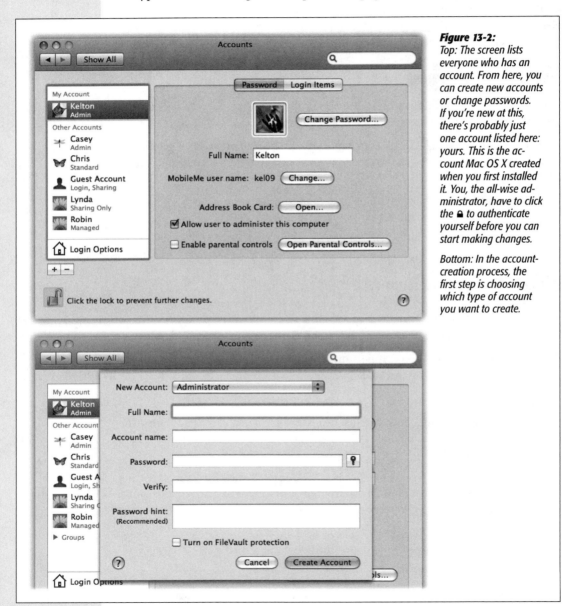

Figure 13-2:
Top: The screen lists everyone who has an account. From here, you can create new accounts or change passwords. If you're new at this, there's probably just one account listed here: yours. This is the account Mac OS X created when you first installed it. You, the all-wise administrator, have to click the 🔒 to authenticate yourself before you can start making changes.

Bottom: In the account-creation process, the first step is choosing which type of account you want to create.

The administrator concept may be new to you, but it's an important pill to swallow. For one thing, you'll find certain settings all over Mac OS X that you can change *only* if you're an administrator—including many in the Accounts pane itself. For another thing, administrator status plays an enormous role when you want to network your Mac to other kinds of computers, as described in the next chapter. And finally, in the bigger picture, the fact that the Mac has an industrial-strength accounts system, just like traditional Unix and recent Windows operating systems, gives it a fighting chance in the corporations of America.

As you create accounts for other people who'll use this Mac, you're offered the opportunity to make each one an administrator just like you. Needless to say, use discretion. Bestow these powers only upon people as responsible and technically masterful as yourself.

Standard accounts

Most people, on most Macs, are ordinary *Standard* account holders (Figure 13-2). These people have everyday access to their own Home folders and to the harmless panes of System Preferences, but most other areas of the Mac are off limits. Mac OS X won't even let them create new folders on the main hard drive, except inside their own Home folders (or in the Shared folder described starting on page 425).

A few of the System Preferences panels display a padlock icon (🔒). If you're a Standard account holder, you can't make changes to these settings without the assistance of an administrator. Fortunately, you aren't required to log out so an administrator can log in and make changes. You can just call the administrator over, click the padlock icon, and let him type in his name and password (if, indeed, he feels comfortable with you making the changes you're about to make).

Managed accounts with Parental Controls

A Managed account is the same thing as a Standard account—except that you've turned on Parental Controls. (These controls are described later in this chapter.) You can turn a Managed account *into* a Standard account just by turning off Parental Controls, and vice versa.

That is, this account usually has even fewer freedoms—because you've limited the programs this person is allowed to use, for example. Use a Managed account for children or anyone else who needs a Mac with rubber walls.

Sharing Only

This kind of account is extremely useful—*if* your Mac is on a network (Chapter 14). See, ordinarily, you can log in and access the files on your Mac in either of two ways:

• In person, seated in front of it.

• From across the network.

This arrangement was designed with families and schools in mind: lots of people sharing a *single* Mac.

The setup gets a little silly, though, when the people on a home or office network each have their *own* computers. If you wanted your spouse or your sales director to be able to grab some files off of your Mac, you'd have to create full-blown accounts for them on *your* Mac, complete with utterly unnecessary Home folders they'd never use.

That's why the *Sharing Only* account is such a great idea. It's available *only* from across the network. You can't get into it by sitting down at the Mac itself—it has no Home folder!

Finally, of course, Sharing Only account holders can't make any changes to the Mac's settings or programs.

In other words, a Sharing Only account exists *solely* for the purpose of file sharing on the network, and people can enter their names and passwords *only* from other Macs.

Once you've set up this kind of account, all the file-sharing and screen-sharing goodies described in Chapter 14 become available.

Group

A *group* is just a virtual container that holds the names of other account holders. You might create one for your most trusted colleagues, another for those rambunctious kids, and so on—all in the name of streamlining the *file-sharing privileges* feature described on page 452. To create a group, click the **+** button as though you're about to create a new account. But from the New Account pop-up menu (shown at bottom in Figure 13-2), choose Group. Type a name for the new group (Accounting, Kids, or whatever), and then click Create Group. Then turn on the checkboxes for the people you consider worthy of being part of this group.

The Guest account

The Guest account is great for accommodating visitors, buddies, or anyone else who was just passing through and wanted to use your Mac for a while. If you let such people use the Guest account, your own account remains private and un-messed-with.

Any changes your guest makes while using your Mac are automatically erased when he logs out. Files are deleted, email is nuked, setting changes are forgotten.

The Guest account is permanently listed in the Accounts panel of System Preferences. Ordinarily, though, you don't see it in the Login screen list; if you're ordinarily the only person who uses this Mac, you don't need to have it staring you in the face every day.

So to use the Guest account, bring it to life by turning on "Allow guests to log into this computer." You can even turn on the parental controls described earlier in this chapter by clicking Open Parental Controls, or permit the guest to exchange files with your Mac from across the network (Chapter 14) by turning on "Allow guests to connect to shared folders."

Just remember to warn your vagabond friend that once he logs out, all traces of his visit are wiped out forever. (At least from your *Mac*.)

Phase 2: Name, Password, and Status

All right. So you clicked the **+** button. And from the New Account pop-up menu, you chose the type of account you wanted to create.

Now, on the same starter sheet, it's time to fill in the most critical information about the new account holder:

- **Name.** If it's just the family, this could be "Chris" or "Robin." If it's a corporation or school, you probably want to use both first and last names.

- **Short Name.** You'll quickly discover the value of having a short name—an abbreviation of your actual name—particularly if your name is, say, Alexandra Stephanopoulos.

  When you sign into your Mac in person, you can use either your long or short name. But when you access this Mac by dialing into it or connecting from across the network (as described in the next chapter), use the short version.

  As soon as you tab into this field, the Mac proposes a short name for you. You can replace the suggestion with whatever you like. Technically, it doesn't even have to be shorter than the "long" name, but spaces and most punctuation marks are forbidden.

- **Password, Verify.** Here's where you type this new account holder's password (Figure 13-2). In fact, you're supposed to type it twice, to make sure you didn't introduce a typo the first time. (The Mac displays only dots as you type, to guard against the possibility that somebody is watching over your shoulder.)

  If you're the only one who uses your Mac, you may want to consider setting up *no* password—leaving both password blanks empty. Later, whenever you're asked for your password, just leave the Password box blank. You'll be able to log in that much faster each day.

- **Password Hint.** If you gave yourself a password, you can leave yourself a hint in this box. If your password is the middle name of the first person who ever kissed you, for example, your hint might be "middle name of the first person who ever kissed me."

  Later, if you forget your password, the Mac will show you this cue to jog your memory.

- **Turn on FileVault protection.** Page 434 has more on this advanced corporate-security feature. (This option isn't available for Sharing Only accounts.)

When you finish setting up these essential items, click Create Account. If you left the password boxes empty, the Mac asks for reassurance that you know what you're doing; click OK.

You then return to the Accounts pane, where you see the new account name in the list at the left side.

Here, three final decisions await your wisdom:

- **MobileMe User Name.** Each account holder might well have his own MobileMe account (especially because Apple offers a family-pack deal on these accounts). Since the MobileMe service is growing in importance and features—email address, Web site, iDisk, syncing, Back to My Mac, and so on—it's convenient to associate each account with its own MobileMe name. (See Chapter 10 for details on MobileMe.)

- **Enable Parental Controls.** "Parental Controls" refers to the Mac OS X feature that limits what your offspring are allowed to do on this computer—and how much time a day they're allowed to spend glued to the mouse. Details are on page 414.

- **Allow user to administer this computer.** This checkbox lets you turn ordinary, unsuspecting Standard or Managed accounts into Administrator accounts, as described above. You know—when your kid turns 18.

Phase 3: Choose a Picture

The usual Mac OS X sign-in screen (Figure 13-1) displays each account holder's name, accompanied by a little picture.

When you click the sample photo, you get a pop-up menu of Apple-supplied graphics; you can choose one to represent you. It becomes not only your icon on the sign-in screen but also your "card" photo in Mac OS X's Address Book program and your icon in iChat.

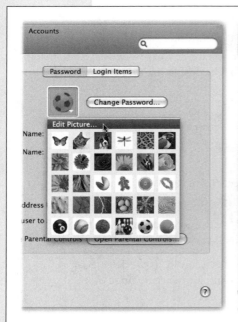

Figure 13-3:
Once you've selected a photo to represent yourself (left), you can adjust its position relative to the square "frame" (right), or adjust its size by dragging the slider. Finally, when the picture looks correctly framed, click Set. (The next time you return to the Images dialog box, you can recall the new image using the Recent Pictures pop-up menu.)

If you'd rather supply your *own* graphics file—a digital photo of your own head, for example—then choose Edit Picture from the pop-up menu. As shown in Figure 13-3, you have several options:

- Drag a graphics file directly into the "picture well" (Figure 13-3). Use the cropping slider below the picture to frame it properly.

- Click Choose. You're shown a list of what's on your hard drive. Find and double-click the image you want.

- Take a new picture. If your Mac has a built-in camera above the screen, or if you have an external Webcam or a camcorder hooked up, click the little camera button. The Mac counts down from three with loud beeps to help you get ready and then takes the picture.

In each case, click Set to enshrine your icon forever (or until you feel like picking a different one).

Phase 4: Startup Items

There's one additional setting that your account holders can set up for themselves: which programs or documents open automatically upon login. (This is one decision an administrator *can't* make for other people. It's available only to whomever is logged in at the moment.)

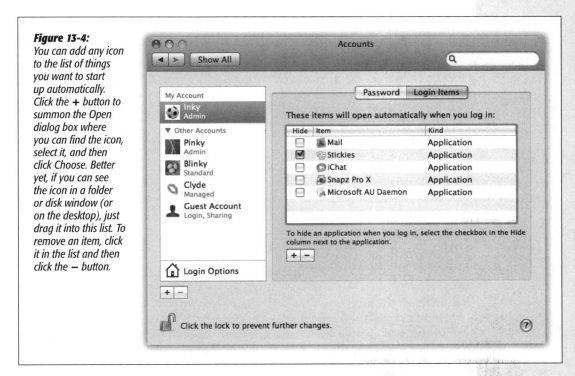

Figure 13-4:
You can add any icon to the list of things you want to start up automatically. Click the + button to summon the Open dialog box where you can find the icon, select it, and then click Choose. Better yet, if you can see the icon in a folder or disk window (or on the desktop), just drag it into this list. To remove an item, click it in the list and then click the – button.

To choose your own crew of self-starters, open System Preferences and click Accounts. Click the Login Items tab. As shown in Figure 13-4, you can now build a list of programs, documents, disks, and other goodies that automatically launch each time you log in. You can even turn on the Hide checkbox for each one so that the program is running in the background at login time, waiting to be called into service with a quick click.

Don't feel obligated to limit this list to programs and documents, by the way. Disks, folders, servers on the network, and other fun icons can also be startup items, so that their windows are open and waiting when you arrive at the Mac each morning.

Tip: Here's a much quicker way to add something to the Login Items list: Control-click (or right-click) its Dock icon and choose "Open at Login" from the shortcut menu.

Parental Controls

If you're setting up a Standard/Managed account, the Parental Controls checkbox affords you the opportunity to shield your Mac—or its very young, very fearful, or very mischievous operator—from confusion and harm. This is a helpful feature to remember when you're setting up accounts for students, young children, or easily intimidated adults. (This checkbox is available for Admin accounts, too, but trying to turn it on produces only a "Silly rabbit—this is for kids!" sort of message.)

You can specify how many hours a day each person is allowed to use the Mac, and declare certain hours (like sleeping hours) off-limits. You can specify exactly who your kids are allowed to communicate with via email (if they use Mail) and instant messaging (if they use iChat), what Web sites they can visit (if they use Safari), what programs they're allowed to use, and even what words they can look up in the Mac OS X Dictionary.

Here are all the ways you can keep your little Managed account holders shielded from the Internet—and themselves. For sanity's sake, the following discussion refers to the Managed account holder as "your child." But some of these controls—notably those in the System category—are equally useful for people of *any* age who feel overwhelmed by the Mac, are inclined to mess it up by not knowing what they're doing, or are tempted to mess it up deliberately.

Note: If you apply any of these options to a Standard account, the account type listed on the Accounts panel changes from "Standard" to "Managed."

System

On this tab, you see the options shown in Figure 13-5. Use these options to limit what your Managed-account flock is allowed to do. You can limit them to using certain programs, for example, or prevent them from burning DVDs, changing settings, or fiddling with your printer setups.

(Limiting what people can do to your Mac when you're not looking is a handy feature under any shared-computer circumstance. But if there's one word tattooed on its forehead, it would be "Classrooms!")

On the panel that pops up when you click Configure, you have two options: "Use Simple Finder" and "Only allow selected applications."

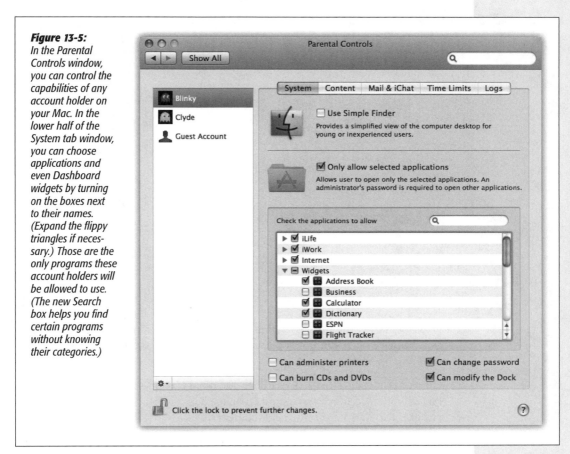

Figure 13-5:
In the Parental Controls window, you can control the capabilities of any account holder on your Mac. In the lower half of the System tab window, you can choose applications and even Dashboard widgets by turning on the boxes next to their names. (Expand the flippy triangles if necessary.) Those are the only programs these account holders will be allowed to use. (The new Search box helps you find certain programs without knowing their categories.)

Use Simple Finder

If you're *really* concerned about somebody's ability to survive the Mac—or the Mac's ability to survive them—turn on Use Simple Finder. Then turn on the checkboxes of the programs that person is allowed to use.

Suppose you've been given a Simple Finder account. When you log in, you discover the barren world shown in Figure 13-6. There are only three menus (, Finder, and File), a single onscreen window, no hard drive icon, and a bare-bones Dock. The only folders you can see are in the Dock. They include:

• **My Applications.** These are aliases of the applications that the administrator approved. They appear on a strange, fixed, icon view, called "pages." List and column views don't exist. As a Simple person, you can't move, rename, delete, sort, or change the display of these icons—you can merely click them. If you have too many to fit on one screen, you get numbered page buttons beneath them, which you can click to move from one set to another.

Figure 13-6:
The Simple Finder doesn't feel like home– unless you've got one of those Spartan, space-age, Dr. Evil– style pads. But it can be just the ticket for less-skilled Mac users, with few options and a basic one-click interface. Every program in the My Applications folder is actually an alias to the real program, which is safely ensconced in the off-limits Applications folder.

- **Documents.** Behind the scenes, this is your Home→Documents folder. Of course, as a Simple Finder kind of soul, you don't *have* a visible Home folder. All your stuff goes in here.

- **Shared.** This is the same Shared folder described on page 425. It's provided so that you and other account holders can exchange documents. However, you can't open any of the folders here, only the documents.

- **Trash.** The Trash is here, but you won't use it much. Selecting or dragging any icon is against the rules, so you're left with no obvious means of putting anything into your Trash.

The only programs with their own icons in the Dock are Finder and Dashboard.

Otherwise, you can essentially forget everything else you've read in this book. You can't create folders, move icons, or do much of anything beyond clicking the icons that your benevolent administrator has provided. It's as though Mac OS X moved away and left you the empty house.

Simple Finder is great for streamlining the Finder, but novices won't get far combating their techno-fear until the world presents us with Simple iMovie, Simple Mail, and Simple Microsoft Word. Still, it's better than nothing.

When Simple people try to save documents, they'll find that although the Save box lists the usual locations (Desktop, Applications, and so on), they can in fact save files only into their own Home folders or subfolders inside them.

Only allow selected applications

By tinkering with the checkboxes here, you can declare certain programs off-limits to this account holder, or turn off his ability to remove Dock icons, burn CDs, and so on.

You can restrict this person's access to the Mac in several different ways:

- **Limit the programs.** At the bottom of the dialog box shown in Figure 13-5, you see a list of all the programs in your Applications folder (an interesting read in its own right). Only checked items show up in the account holder's Applications folder.

Tip: If you don't see a program listed, use the Search box, or drag its icon from the Finder into the window.

  If, for instance, you're setting up an account for use in the classroom, you may want to turn off access to programs like Disk Utility, iChat, and Tomb Raider.

- **Limit the features.** When you first create Standard accounts, their holders are free to burn CDs or DVDs, modify what's on the Dock, change their passwords, and view the settings of all System Preferences panels (although they can't *change* all of these settings).

  Depending on your situation, you may find it useful to turn off some of these options. In a school lab, for example, you might want to turn off the ability to burn discs (to block software piracy). If you're setting up a Mac for a technophobe, you might want to turn off the ability to change the Dock (so your colleague won't accidentally lose access to his own programs and work).

Content (Dictionary and Web)

"Content," in this case, means "two options we really didn't have any other place to put." Actually, what it *really* means is Dictionary and Safari.

Hide profanity in Dictionary

As you will learn in Chapter 16, Mac OS X comes with a complete electronic copy of the *New Oxford American Dictionary.* And "complete," in this case, means "it even has swear words."

Turning on "Hide profanity in Dictionary" is like having an Insta-Censor™. It hides most of the naughty words from the dictionary whenever your young account holder is logged in (Figure 13-7).

Web Site Restrictions

This feature is designed to limit which Web sites your kid is allowed to visit.

Frankly, trying to block the racy stuff from the Web is something of a hopeless task; if your kid doesn't manage to get around this blockade by simply using a different browser, then he'll just see the dirty pictures at another kid's house. But at least you can enjoy the illusion of taking a stand, using approaches of three degrees of severity:

- **Allow unrestricted access to Web sites.** In other words, no filtering. Anything goes.

- **Try to limit access to adult Web sites automatically.** Those words—"try to"—are Apple's way of admitting that no filter is foolproof.

  In any case, Mac OS X comes with a built-in database of Web sites that it already knows may be inappropriate for children—and these sites won't appear in Safari while this account holder is logged in. By clicking Customize and then editing the "Always allow" and "Never allow" lists, you can override its decisions on a site-at-a-time basis.

- **Allow access to only these Web sites.** This is the most restrictive approach of all: It's a *whitelist*, a list of the *only* Web sites your youngster is allowed to visit. It's filled with kid-friendly sites like Disney and Discovery Kids, but of course you can edit the list by clicking the **+** and **−** buttons below the list.

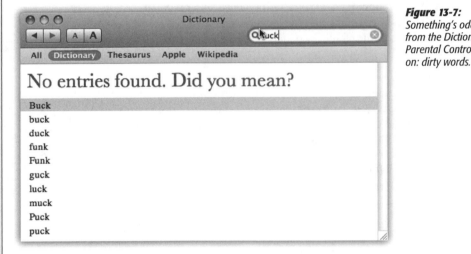

Figure 13-7:
Something's oddly missing from the Dictionary when Parental Controls are turned on: dirty words.

Mail & iChat

Here, you can build a list of email and chat addresses, corresponding to the people you feel comfortable letting your kid exchange emails and chat with. Click the **+** button below the list, type the address, press Return, lather, rinse, and repeat.

Tip: No, you can't drag cards in from your Address Book; that would be much too simple. But after clicking the **+** button to create a new row in the list (in Edit mode), you can drag just the email address out of an Address Book card you've opened up.

For reasons explained in a moment, turn on "Send permission emails to" and plug in your own email address.

For reasons explained in a moment, turn on "Send permission emails to" and plug in your own email address.

Now then: When your youngster uses Apple's Mail program to send a message to someone who's *not* on the approved list, or tries to iChat with someone not on the list, she gets the message shown at top in Figure 13-8. If she clicks Ask Permission, then *your* copy of Mail shortly receives a permission-request message (Figure 13-8, bottom); meanwhile, the outgoing message gets placed in limbo in her Drafts folder.

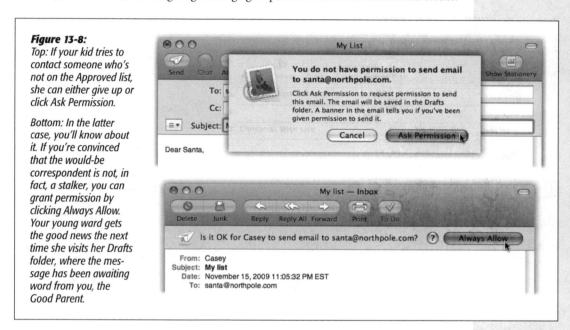

Figure 13-8:
Top: If your kid tries to contact someone who's not on the Approved list, she can either give up or click Ask Permission.

Bottom: In the latter case, you'll know about it. If you're convinced that the would-be correspondent is not, in fact, a stalker, you can grant permission by clicking Always Allow. Your young ward gets the good news the next time she visits her Drafts folder, where the message has been awaiting word from you, the Good Parent.

If you add that person's address to the list of approved correspondents, then the next time your young apprentice clicks the quarantined outgoing message in her Drafts folder, the banner across the top lets her know that all is well—and the message is OK to go out.

Note: This feature doesn't attempt to stop email or chat using other programs, like Microsoft Entourage or Skype. If you're worried about your efforts being bypassed, block access to those programs using the Forbidden Applications list described above.

When your underling fires up iChat or Mail, she'll discover that her Buddy List is empty except for the people you've identified.

Handling the teenage hissy fit is your problem.

Time Limits
Clever folks, those Apple programmers. They must have kids of their own.

They realize that some parents care about *how much* time their kids spend in front of the Mac, and that some also care about *which* hours (Figure 13-9).

Tip: When Time Limits have been applied, your little rugrats can now check to see how much time they have left to goof off on the Mac before your digital iron fist slams down. When they click the menu-bar clock (where it now says the current time), a menu appears, complete with a readout that says, for example, "Parental Controls: Time Remaining 1:29." Good parenting comes in all forms.

Figure 13-9:
Top: If this account holder tries to log in outside the time limits you specify here, she'll encounter only a box that says, "Computer time limits expired." She'll be offered a pop-up menu that grants her additional time, from 15 minutes to "Rest of the day"–but it requires your parental consent (actually, your parental password) to activate.

Bottom: Similarly, if she's using the Mac as her time winds down, she gets this message. Once again, you, the all-knowing administrator, can grant her more time using this dialog box.

Logs

The final tab of the Parental Controls panel is Big Brother Central. Here's a complete rundown of what your kids have been up to. Its four categories—Websites visited, Websites blocked, Applications, and iChat—are extremely detailed. For example, in

Applications, you can see exactly which programs your kids tried to use when, and how much time they spent in each one.

If you see something you really think should be off limits—a site in the Websites Visited list, an application, an iChat session with someone—click its name and then click Restrict. You've just nipped *that* one in the bud.

Conversely, if the Mac blocked a Web site that you think is really OK, click its name in the list, and then click Allow. (And if you're wondering what a certain Web page *is*, click it and then click Open.)

Editing Accounts

If you're an administrator, you can change your own account in any way you like.

If you have any other kind of account, though, you can't change anything but your picture and password. If you want to make any other changes, you have to ask an admin to log in, make the changes you want made to your account, and then turn the computer back over to you.

Deleting Accounts

Hey, it happens: Somebody graduates, somebody gets fired, somebody dumps you. Sooner or later, you may need to delete an account from your Mac.

When that time comes, click the account name in the Accounts list and then click the — button beneath the list. Mac OS X asks what to do with all the dearly departed's files and settings (Figure 13-10):

- **Save the home folder in a disk image.** This option represents the "I'll be back" approach. Mac OS X preserves the deleted account holder's folders on the Mac, in a tidy digital envelope that won't clutter your hard drive and can be reopened in case of emergency.

  In the Users→Deleted Users folder, you find a disk image file (.dmg). If you double-click it, a new, virtual disk icon named for the deleted account appears on your desktop. You can open folders and root through the stuff in this "disk," just as if it were a living, working Home folder.

  If fate ever brings that person back into your life, you can use this disk image to reinstate the deleted person's account. Start by creating a brand-new account. Then copy the contents of the folders in the mounted disk image (Documents, Pictures, Desktop, and so on) into the corresponding folders of the new Home folder.

- **Do not change the home folder.** This time, Mac OS X removes the *account,* in that it no longer appears in the Login list or in the Accounts panel of System Preferences—but it leaves the *Home folder* right where it is. Use this option if you don't intend to dispose of the dearly departed's belongings right here and now.

- **Delete the home folder.** This button offers the "Hasta la vista, baby" approach. The account and all its files and settings are vaporized forever, on the spot.

> ***Note:*** *If you delete a Shared Only account, you're not offered the chance to preserve the Home folder contents—because a Shared Only account doesn't have a Home folder.*

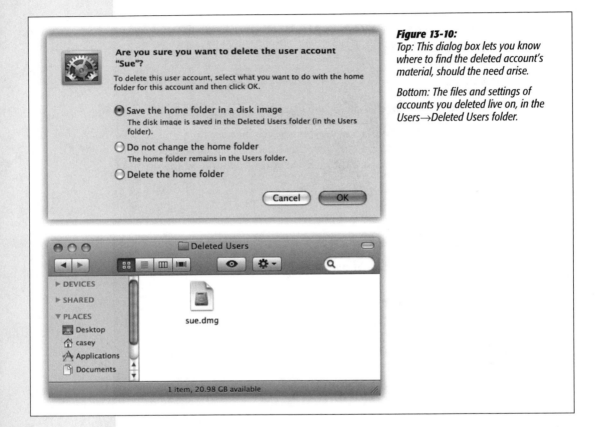

Figure 13-10:
Top: This dialog box lets you know where to find the deleted account's material, should the need arise.

Bottom: The files and settings of accounts you deleted live on, in the Users→Deleted Users folder.

Setting Up the Login Process

Once you've set up more than one account, the dialog box shown in Figure 13-1 appears whenever you turn on the Mac, whenever you choose →Log Out, or whenever the Mac logs you out automatically. But a few extra controls let you, an administrator, set up either more or less security at the login screen—or, put another way, build in less or more convenience.

Open System Preferences, click Accounts, and then click the Login Options button (Figure 13-11). Here are some of the ways you can shape the login experience for greater security (or greater convenience):

- **Automatic login.** This option eliminates the need to sign in at all. It's a timesaving, hassle-free arrangement if only one person uses the Mac, or uses it most of the time.

When you choose an account holder's name from this pop-up menu, you're prompted for his name and password. Type it and click OK.

From now on, the dialog box shown in Figure 13-1 won't appear *at all* at startup time. After turning on the machine, you, the specified account holder, zoom straight to your desktop.

Of course, everybody else must still enter their names and passwords. (And how can they, since the Mac rushes right into the Automatic person's account at startup time? Answer: The Automatic thing happens only at startup time. The usual login screen appears whenever the current account holder logs out—by choosing →Log Out, for example.)

Figure 13-11:
These options make it easier or harder for people to sign in, offering various degrees of security. By the way: Turning on "Name and password" also lets you sign in as >console, a troubleshooting technique described on page 560.

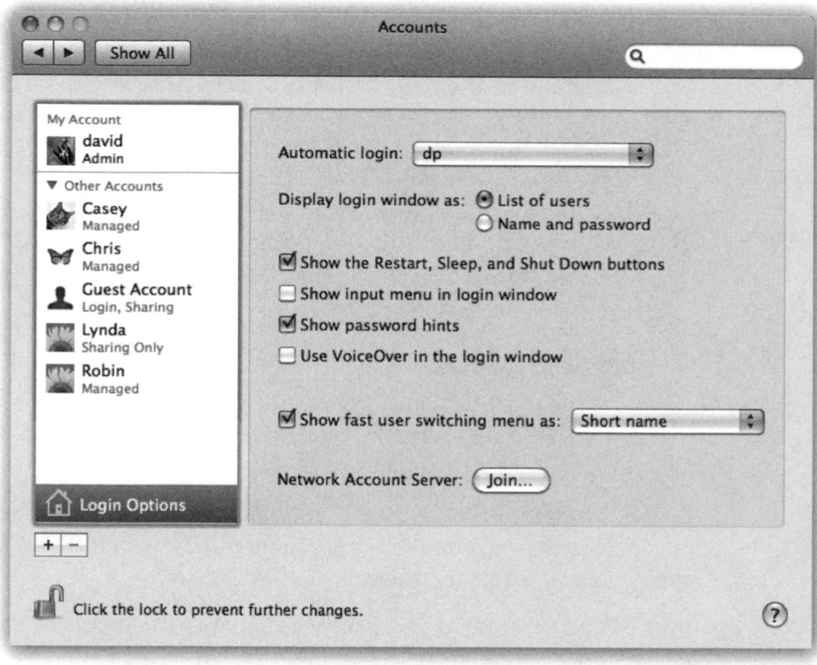

- **Display login window as.** Under normal circumstances, the login screen presents a list of account holders when you power up the Mac, as shown in Figure 13-1. That's the "List of users" option in action.

If you're especially worried about security, however, you might not even want that list to appear. If you turn on "Name and password," each person who signs in must type both his name (into a blank that appears) *and* his password—a very inconvenient, but more secure, arrangement.

- **Show the Restart, Sleep, and Shut Down buttons.** Truly devoted evildoers can bypass the standard login screen's security in a number of different ways: Restart in FireWire disk mode, restart at the Unix Terminal, and so on. One way to thwart them is to turn off this checkbox. Now there's no Restart or Shut Down button to tempt mischief-makers. That's plenty of protection in most homes, schools, and workplaces; after all, Mac people tend to be *nice* people.

- **Show password hints.** As described earlier, Mac OS X is kind enough to display your password hint ("middle name of the first person who ever kissed me") after you've typed it wrong three times when trying to log in. Or turn off this feature for an extra layer of security, and the hint will never appear.

- **Show fast user switching menu as:** The Fast User Switching feature lets you switch to another account without having to log out of the first one, as described on page 427.

  If you do turn on Fast User Switching, a new menu appears at the upper-right corner of your screen, listing all the account holders on the machine. Thanks to this pop-up menu, you can now specify what that menu looks like. It can display the current account holder's full name (Name), the short name (Short Name), or only a generic torso-silhouette icon (Icon) to save space on the menu bar.

Signing In, Logging Out

Once somebody has set up your account, here's what it's like getting into, and out of, a Mac OS X machine. (For the purposes of this discussion, "you" are no longer the administrator—you're one of the students, employees, or family members for whom an account has been set up.)

Identifying Yourself

When you first turn on the Mac—or when the person who last used this computer chooses →Log Out—the login screen shown in Figure 13-1 appears. At this point, you can proceed in any of several ways:

- **Restart.** Click if you need to restart the Mac for some reason. (The Restart and Shut Down buttons don't appear here if the administrator has chosen to hide them as a security precaution.)

- **Shut Down.** Click if you're done for the day, or if sudden panic about the complexity of user accounts makes you want to run away. The computer turns off.

- **Log In.** To sign in, click your account name in the list. If you're a keyboard speed freak, you can also type the first letter or two—or press the up or down arrow keys—until your name is highlighted. Then press Return.

  Either way, the password box appears now (if a password is required). If you accidentally click the wrong person's name on the first screen, you can click Back. Otherwise, type your password, and then press Return (or click Log In).

  You can try as many times as you want to type the password. With each incorrect guess, the entire dialog box shudders violently from side to side, as though shaking its head "No." If you try unsuccessfully three times, your hint appears—if you've set one up. (If you see a strange ⇪ icon in the password box, guess what? You've got your Caps Lock key on, and the Mac thinks you're typing an all-capitals password.)

Tip: So what happens if you forget your password, and even the Mac's administrator doesn't know it? On your third attempt to type the password correctly, the Mac shows you your password hint (unless the administrator has turned off the Hint option) and a button called Reset Password. When you click it, the Mac asks for the master password (page 400), which the administrator almost certainly knows.

Once that's typed in, you're allowed to make up a new password for your own account (and, presumably, a better hint this time). No harm done.

Once you're in, the world of the Mac looks just the way you left it (or the way an administrator set it up for you).

Logging Out

When you're finished using the Mac, choose →Log Out (or press Shift-⌘-Q). A confirmation message appears; if you click Cancel or press Esc, you return to whatever you were doing. If you click Log Out or press Return, you return to the screen shown in Figure 13-1, and the entire sign-in cycle begins again.

Tip: If you press Option as you choose →Log Out (or as you press Shift-⌘-Q), the confirmation box doesn't appear.

Sharing Across Accounts

It's all fine to say that every account is segregated from all *other* accounts. It's nice to know your stuff is safe from the prying eyes of your coworkers or family.

But what about collaboration? What if you *want* to give some files or folders to another account holder?

You can't just open up someone else's Home folder and drop it in there. Yes, every account holder has a Home folder (all in the Users folder on your hard drive). But if you try to open anybody else's Home folder, you'll see a tiny red ⊘ icon superimposed on almost every folder inside, telling you, "Look, but don't touch."

Fortunately, there are a couple of wormholes between accounts (Figure 13-12):

- **The Shared folder.** Sitting in the Users folder is one folder that doesn't correspond to any particular person: Shared. Everybody can freely access this folder, inserting and extracting files without restriction. It's the common ground among all the account holders on a single Mac. It's Central Park, the farmers market, and the grocery-store bulletin board.

- **The Public folder.** In your Home folder, there's a folder called Public. Anything you copy into it becomes available for inspection or copying (but not changing

---

or deleting) by any other account holder, whether they log into your Mac or sign in from across the network.

- **The Drop Box.** And *inside* your Public folder is another cool little folder: the Drop Box. It exists to let *other* people give files to *you*, discreetly and invisibly to anyone else. That is, people can drop files and folders into your Drop Box, but they can't actually *open* it. This folder, too, is available both locally (in person) and from across the network.

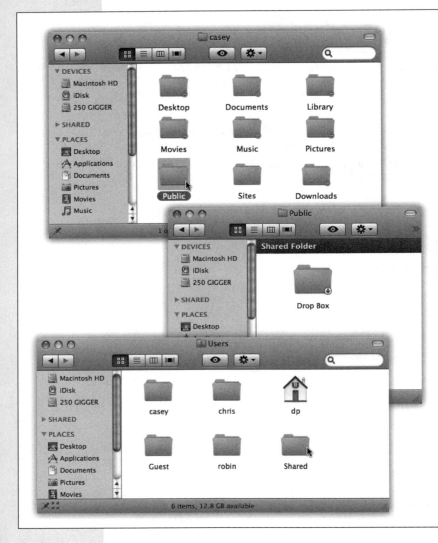

Figure 13-12:
Top: In other people's Home folders, the Public and Sites folders are available for your inspection. These two folders contain stuff that other people have "published" for the benefit of their coworkers.

Middle: In the Public folder is the Drop Box, which serves the opposite purpose. It lets anyone else who uses this Mac hand in files to you; they, however, can't see what's in it.

Bottom: Inside the Users folder (to get there from a Home folder, press ⌘-↑) is the Shared folder, a wormhole connecting all accounts. Everybody has full access to everything inside.

Fast User Switching

The account system described so far in this chapter has its charms. It keeps everyone's stuff separate, it keeps your files safe, and it lets you have the desktop picture of your choice.

Unfortunately, it can go from handy to hassle in one split second. That's when you're logged in, and somebody else wants to duck in just for a second—to check email or a calendar, for example. What are you supposed to do—log out completely, closing all your documents and quitting all your programs, just so the interloper can look something up? Then, afterward, you'd have to log back in and fire up all your stuff again, praying that your inspirational muse hasn't fled in the meantime.

Fortunately, that's all over now. Fast User Switching—a feature modeled on a similar Windows feature, which itself was modeled on a Unix feature—lets Person B log in and use the Mac for a little while. All *your* stuff, Person A, simply slides into the background, still open the way you had it; see Figure 13-13.

When Person B is finished working, you can bring your whole work environment back to the screen without having to reopen anything. All your windows and programs are still open, just as you left them.

To turn on this feature, open the Accounts panel of System Preferences (and click the 🔒, if necessary, to unlock the panel). Click Login Options, and turn on the "Show fast user switching menu as" checkbox. (You can see this option in Figure 13-11.)

The only change you notice immediately is the appearance of your own account name in the upper-right corner of the screen (Figure 13-13, top). You can change what this menu looks like by using the "Show fast user switching menu as" pop-up menu, also shown in Figure 13-11.

That's all there is to it. Next time you need a fellow account holder to relinquish control so you can duck in to do a little work, just choose your name from the Accounts menu. Type your password, if one is required, and feel guiltless about the interruption.

And now, the finer points of Fast User Switching:

- Depending on how many programs are open and how much memory the Mac has, switching accounts may entail a delay and a good deal of hard drive activity. That's Mac OS X's virtual memory scheme "setting down" what was in memory in *your* account to make room for the incoming account's stuff.

- To exit an open account, choose 🍎→Log Out as usual. Or just choose Login Window from the Accounts menu. It ensures that you can get to your own account no matter whose is running at the moment.

- Weirdly enough, a bunch of account holders can be using the same program simultaneously in their own parallel universes. Even if Microsoft Word was open in your account, Chris, Casey, and Robin can each open the same copy of the same program simultaneously when they fast-switch into their own accounts.

- You can't make changes to accounts (in System Preferences) that are still logged in. Nor, as you'd expect, can you turn off Fast User Switching while other people are logged in. Can't turn on FileVault, either.

- If you try to shut the Mac down or restart it while other people are logged in, a dialog box tells you, "There are currently logged in users who may lose unsaved changes if you shut down this computer." And you're asked to type in an administrator's name and password to establish that you know what the heck you're doing.

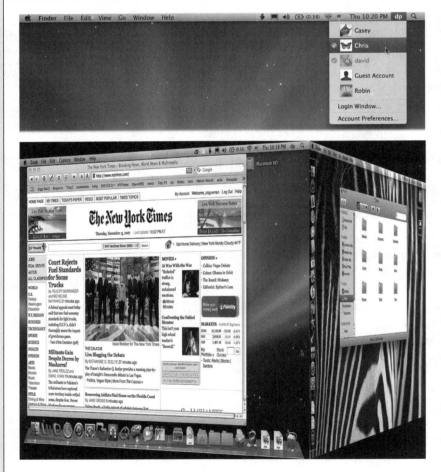

Figure 13-13:
Top: The appearance of the Accounts menu lets you know that Fast User Switching is turned on. The circled checkmark indicates people who are already logged in, including those who have been "fast user switched" into the background. The dimmed name shows who's logged in right now.

Bottom: When the screen changes from your account to somebody else's, your entire world slides visibly offscreen as though it's mounted on the side of a rotating cube—a spectacular animation made possible by Mac OS X's Quartz Extreme graphics software.

Here's a moral dilemma for the modern age. If you proceed by typing the password and clicking Shut Down, you shut down all accounts that were open in the background *and* any open documents—and if those documents hadn't been saved, any changes are gone forever. If you click Cancel, you can't shut down the Mac until you hunt down the account holders whose stuff is still open in the background so they can log out.

Tip: You can avoid this awkward situation in either of two ways: (1) Trust each other completely, or (2) save all your documents before you let anyone else cut in and send your account to the background.

- Remember the Shared folder (in the Users folder on the hard drive)? It's still the wormhole connecting all accounts. If you want to share a file with another account holder, put it there.

- Your account isn't anesthetized completely when it's switched into the background. In fact, it keeps on doing whatever you set it to doing. If you were downloading some big file, for example, it keeps right on downloading when the next guy logs in.

Five Mac OS X Security Shields

Mac OS X has a spectacular reputation for stability and security. At this writing, not a single Mac OS X virus has emerged. There's no Windows-esque plague of spyware, either (downloaded programs that do something sneaky behind your back). In fact, there isn't *any* Mac spyware.

The usual rap is, "Well, that's because Windows is a much bigger target. What virus writer is going to waste his time on a computer with 8 percent market share?"

That may be part of it. But Mac OS X has also been built more intelligently from the ground up. Listed below are a few of the many drafty corners of a typical operating system that Apple has solidly plugged:

- *Ports* are channels that remote computers use to connect to services on your computer: one for instant messaging, one for Windows's remote-control feature, and so on. It's fine to have them open if you're expecting visitors. But if you've got an open port that exposes the soft underbelly of your computer without your knowledge, you're in for a world of hurt. Open ports are precisely what permitted viruses like Blaster to infiltrate millions of PCs.

  Mac OS X has always come from the factory with all of them shut and locked. Microsoft didn't close those ports until the Windows XP Service Pack 2.

- Whenever a program tried to install itself in the original Windows XP, the operating system went ahead and installed it, potentially without your awareness.

  In Mac OS X, that never happens. You're notified at every juncture when anything is trying to install itself on your Mac. In fact, every time you try to download something, either in Safari or Mail, that contains *executable code* (a program, in other words), a dialog box warns you that it could conceivably harbor a virus—even if your download is compressed as a .zip or .sit file (Figure 13-14).

- Unlike certain other operating systems, Mac OS X doesn't even let an administrator touch the files that drive the operating system itself without pestering you to provide your password and grant it permission to do so. A Mac OS X virus (if there were such a thing) could theoretically wipe out all your files, but it wouldn't be able to access anyone else's stuff—and it couldn't touch the operating system itself.

- You probably already know about the Finder's Secure Empty Trash option (page 94). But an option on the Erase tab of the Disk Utility program can do the same super-erasing of *all free space* on your hard drive. We're talking not just erasing, but recording gibberish over the spots where your files once were—once, seven times, or *35* times—utterly shattering any hope any hard-disk recovery firm (or spy) might have had of recovering passwords or files from your hard drive.

- Safari's Private Browsing mode means that you can freely visit Web sites without leaving *any* digital tracks—no history, no nothing (page 376).

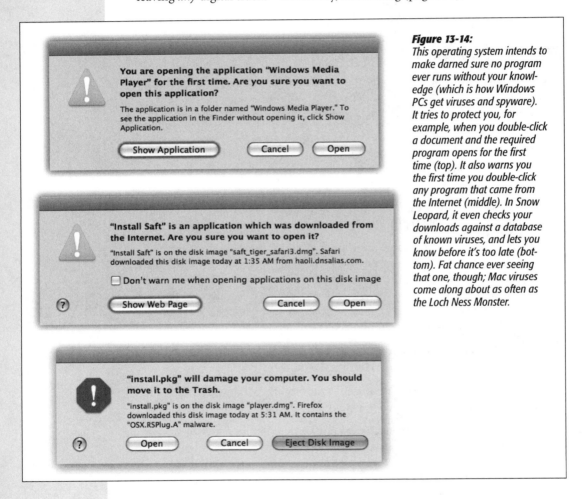

Figure 13-14:
This operating system intends to make darned sure no program ever runs without your knowledge (which is how Windows PCs get viruses and spyware). It tries to protect you, for example, when you double-click a document and the required program opens for the first time (top). It also warns you the first time you double-click any program that came from the Internet (middle). In Snow Leopard, it even checks your downloads against a database of known viruses, and lets you know before it's too late (bottom). Fat chance ever seeing that one, though; Mac viruses come along about as often as the Loch Ness Monster.

Those are only a few tiny examples. Here are a few of Mac OS X's big-ticket defenses.

The Firewall

If you have a broadband, always-on connection, you're open to the Internet 24 hours a day. It's theoretically possible for some cretin to use automated hacking software to flood you with files or take control of your machine. Snow Leopard's beefed-up *firewall* feature puts up a barrier to such mischief. To turn it on, click Start on this pane.

Note: You don't need to turn on this firewall if your Mac connects to the Internet through a wired or wireless router (including the AirPort base station). Virtually every router already has a built-in firewall that protects your entire network. (Similarly, if you're using the Mac's Internet Sharing feature, turn on the firewall only for the first Mac, the one connected right to the Internet.)

In short: Use the firewall only if your Mac is connected directly to a cable modem, DSL box, or dial-up modem.

Fortunately, it's not a *complete* barrier. One of the great joys of having a computer is its ability to connect to other computers. Living in a cement crypt is one way to avoid getting infected, but it's not much fun.

Therefore, you can turn the firewall on by opening System Preferences→Security→ Firewall tab and clicking Start. But in Snow Leopard, you can also fine-tune the blockade.

To do that, click Advanced; you see something like Figure 13-15 at middle. As you can sort of tell, Snow Leopard now lets you allow or block Internet connections individually for *each program* on your Mac. Here's what you'll find there:

DON'T PANIC

The Case of the Forgotten Password

Help—I forgot my password! And I never told it to anybody, so even the administrator can't help me!

No problem. Your administrator can simply open up System Preferences, click Accounts, click the name of the person who forgot the password, and then click Reset Password to re-establish the password.

But you don't understand. I am the administrator! And I'm the only account!

Ah—that's a different story. All right, no big deal. At the login screen, type a gibberish password three times. On the last attempt, the Mac will offer you the chance to reset the password. All you have to do is type in your master password (page 435) to prove your credentials.

Um—I never set up a master password.

All right then. That's actually good news, because it means you didn't turn on FileVault. (If you had, and you'd also forgotten the master password, your account would now be locked away forever.)

Insert the Mac OS X DVD. Restart the Mac while pressing down the letter C key, which starts up the Mac from the DVD and launches the Mac OS X installer. On the first screen, choose your language and then click the Next arrow (or hit Return).

On the Install screen, choose Utilities→Reset Password. When the Reset Password screen appears, click the hard drive that contains Mac OS X. From the first pop-up menu, choose the name of your account. Now make up a new password and type it into both boxes. Click Save, close the window, click the installer, and restart.

And next time, be more careful! Write down your password on a Post-it note and affix it to your monitor. (Joke—that's a joke!)

- **Block all incoming connections.** This option might be better known as Paranoid Mode. You're allowed to do email and basic Web surfing and a few other deep-seated services that Mac OS X needs to get by. But all other kinds of network connections are blocked, including screen sharing, iTunes music sharing, and so on. This is a hard-core, meat-fisted firewall that, for most people, is more trouble than it's worth.

- **[List of individual programs.]** If the firewall is on but you haven't turned on "Block all," then the Mac uses this list of individual programs and features to determine what's allowed to accept network connections.

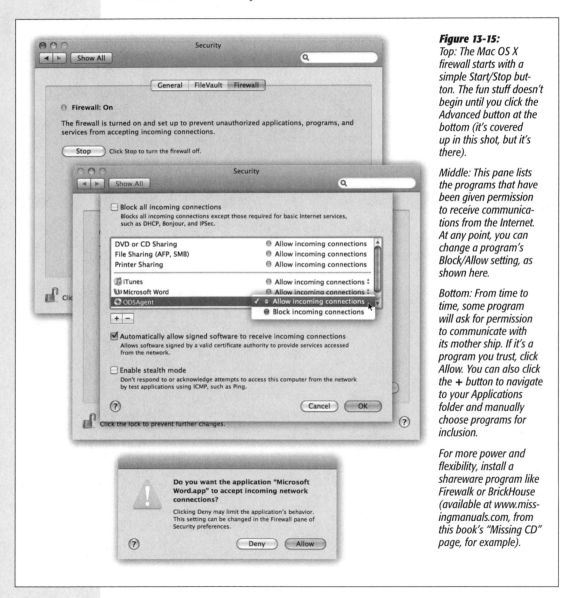

Figure 13-15:
Top: The Mac OS X firewall starts with a simple Start/Stop button. The fun stuff doesn't begin until you click the Advanced button at the bottom (it's covered up in this shot, but it's there).

Middle: This pane lists the programs that have been given permission to receive communications from the Internet. At any point, you can change a program's Block/Allow setting, as shown here.

Bottom: From time to time, some program will ask for permission to communicate with its mother ship. If it's a program you trust, click Allow. You can also click the + button to navigate to your Applications folder and manually choose programs for inclusion.

For more power and flexibility, install a shareware program like Firewalk or BrickHouse (available at www.missingmanuals.com, from this book's "Missing CD" page, for example).

Above the horizontal line (Figure 13-15, middle), features of Mac OS X itself are listed. They get added to this list automatically when you turn them on in System Preferences: File Sharing, Printer Sharing, and so on.

Non-Apple programs can gain passage through your firewall, too. You can add one to the list manually by clicking the **+** button below the list and choosing it by hand; or you can simply respond to the request box that pops up whenever a new program wants to connect to the Internet (Figure 13-15, bottom).

In fact, this bombardment of permission requests begins as soon as you turn on the firewall—one permission request for each of your *currently* open programs. Click Allow for each (unless, of course, you see a request for an app called Sneaky-PoisonVirus or something). As you do so, their names get added to the list of programs in this dialog box.

For each program, you can use the pop-up menu beside its name to specify either "Allow incoming connections" or "Block incoming connections," depending on your level of paranoia.

• **Automatically allow signed software to receive incoming connections.** *Signed* software means programs that Apple recognizes as coming from legitimate companies. Anything from Adobe or Microsoft, for example, has got to be OK, right? (Insert your own wisecrack here.)

Note: OK, technically, a signed program is one whose authenticity is confirmed by a third party—a "certificate authority" company like VeriSign or GoDaddy. A system of invisible keys (security numbers) confirms that the software did indeed come from the creators it claims it came from, no matter how many detours it took to reach you.

One more point: When you explicitly grant permission to a program as described below, you're signing that program.

If this checkbox is *not* turned on, then each time you run a new program for the first time, you'll be interrupted so the Mac can ask if it's OK to permit Internet connections. The "signed software" box cuts down on the interruptions, since well-known apps are assumed not to be viruses or spyware.

• **Enable Stealth Mode** is designed to slam shut the Mac's back door to the Internet. See, hackers often use automated hacker tools that send out "Are you there?" messages. They're hoping to find computers that are turned on and connected full time to the Internet. If your machine responds, and they can figure out how to get into it, they'll use it, without your knowledge, as a relay station for pumping out spam or masking their hacking footsteps.

Enable Stealth Mode, then, makes your Mac even more invisible on the network; it means your Mac won't respond to the electronic signal called a *ping*. (On the other hand, *you* won't be able to ping your machine, either, when you're on the road and want to know if it's turned on and online.)

FileVault

The Mac OS X accounts system is designed to keep people out of one another's stuff. Ordinarily, for example, Chris isn't allowed to go rooting through Robin's stuff.

Until FileVault came along, though, there were all kinds of ways to circumvent this protection system. A sneak or a showoff could start up the Mac in FireWire disk mode, for example, or even remove the hard drive and hook it up to a Linux machine or another Mac.

In each case, they'd then be able to run rampant through everybody's files, changing or trashing them with abandon. For people with sensitive or private files, the result was a security hole bigger than Steve Jobs's bank account.

FileVault is an extra line of defense. When you turn on this feature, your Mac automatically *encrypts* (scrambles) everything in your Home folder, using something called AES-128 encryption. (How secure is that? It would take a password-guessing computer *149 trillion years* before hitting pay dirt. Or, in more human terms, slightly longer than two back-to-back Kevin Costner movies.)

This means that unless someone knows (or can figure out) your password, FileVault renders your files unreadable for anyone but you and your computer's administrator—no matter what sneaky tricks they try to pull.

You won't notice much difference when FileVault is turned on. You log in as usual, clicking your name and typing your password. Only a slight pause as you log out indicates that Mac OS X is doing some housekeeping on the encrypted files: freeing up some space and/or backing up your home directory with Time Machine.

Tip: This feature is especially useful for laptop owners. If someone swipes or "borrows" your laptop, they can't get into your stuff without the password.

FREQUENTLY ASKED QUESTION

Shared Data Files

My wife and my 8-year-old kid share my Mac. Over the years, we've amassed a fabulous collection of MP3 files, but at the moment, I'm the only one who sees them in iTunes. This business of separate environments for every account holder is all well and good, but what about when we want to access the same files—like our iTunes Library?

The problem is that the iTunes Library is stored in the Music folder of just one person. Fortunately, the solution is easy enough.

Whoever is the administrator—probably your 8-year-old—should move the *iTunes Music* folder (currently inside

somebody's iTunes→Music folder) to the Users→Shared folder. Now it's available to everybody.

At this point, each account holder can log in, fire up iTunes, choose iTunes→Preferences→Advanced, and click the Change button to choose the relocated iTunes Music folder in the Shared folder.

From now on, each person will be able to see and access the entire library of iTunes tunes, but will still enjoy the flexibility to build individual playlists.

Here are some things you should know about FileVault's protection:

- **It's useful only if you've logged out.** Once you're logged in, your files are accessible. If you want the protection, log out before you wander away from the Mac. (Or let the screen saver close your account for you; see page 437.)

- **It covers only your Home folder.** Anything in your Applications, System, or Library folders is exempt from protection.

- **An administrator can access your files, too.** According to Mac OS X's caste system, anyone with an administrator's account can theoretically have unhindered access to his peasants' files—even with FileVault on—if that administrator has the master password described below.

- **It keeps other people from *opening* your files, not from deleting them.** It's still possible for someone to trash all your files, without ever seeing what they are. There's not much you can do about this with FileVault on *or* off—all a malicious person needs to do is start deleting the encrypted files, and your data is gone. (FileVault works by encrypting your Home folder into 8-megabyte chunks.)

- **Shared folders in your Home folder will no longer be available on the network.** That is, any folders you've shared won't be available to your coworkers *except* when you're at your Mac and logged in.

- **Backup programs may throw a tizzy.** FileVault's job is to "stuff" and "unstuff" your Home folder as you log in and out. Backup programs that work by backing up files and folders that have changed since the last backup may therefore get very confused.

  Even Time Machine (Chapter 9) doesn't always play well with FileVault. For one thing, it can copy the encrypted Home folder only when it's closed—that is, when you're logged off. So you don't get the continuous hourly backups that everyone else gets.

  Similarly, in times of tragedy, Time Machine can restore only your *entire* Home folder; you can't recover individual documents or folders in it.

- **If you forget your password *and* your administrator forgets the master password, you're toast.** If this happens, your data is *permanently lost*. You have no choice but to erase your hard drive and start from scratch.

To turn FileVault on, proceed like this:

1. **In System Preferences, click Security, and then click FileVault. Click Set Master Password.**

   If you're the first person to try to turn on FileVault, you need to create a *master* password first.

   The master password is an override password that gives an administrator full power to access any account, even without knowing the account holder's password, or to turn off FileVault for any account.

The thinking goes like this: Yeah, yeah, the peons with Standard accounts forget their *account* passwords all the time. But with FileVault, a forgotten password would mean *the entire Home folder is locked forever*—so Apple gave you, the technically savvy administrator, a back door. (And you, the omniscient administrator, would *never* forget the *master* password—right?)

When you click Set Master Password, the dialog box shown at top in Figure 13-16 appears.

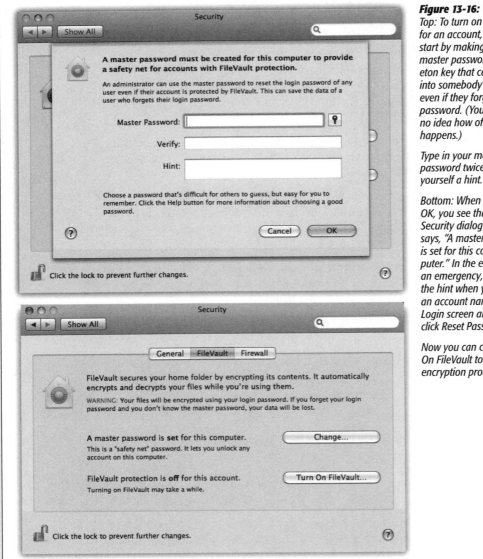

Figure 13-16:
Top: To turn on FileVault for an account, you must start by making up a master password: a skeleton key that can get you into somebody's account even if they forget their password. (You have no idea how often this happens.)

Type in your master password twice, and give yourself a hint.

Bottom: When you click OK, you see that the Security dialog box now says, "A master password is set for this computer." In the event of an emergency, you'll get the hint when you click an account name at the Login screen and then click Reset Password.

Now you can click Turn On FileVault to begin the encryption process.

2. **Click "Turn On FileVault."**

You'll see an error message if other account holders are simultaneously logged in (using Fast User Switching). Otherwise, you're asked to type your account password. An explanatory dialog box appears offering some options.

If you select the "Use secure erase" option, Mac OS X works harder when it erases files that you delete, and that makes it harder for the bad guys to obtain the encrypted data even if they kidnap your computer.

If you select "Use secure virtual memory," then Mac OS X also encrypts the contents of *virtual memory* (the hard-disk area a computer uses as a temporary shelf for what's in memory). (All accounts share the same virtual-memory files in Mac OS X, so an evil hacker with sophisticated tools could conceivably analyze the virtual-memory files Mac to see what's in the documents you have open on the screen.)

3. **Click "Turn On FileVault" again.**

Now Mac OS X logs you out of your own account. (It can't encrypt a folder that's in use.) Some time passes while it converts your Home folder into a protected state, during which you can't do anything but wait.

After a few minutes, you arrive at the standard login window, where you can sign in as usual, confident that your stuff is securely locked away from anyone who tries to get at it when you're not logged in.

Note: To turn off FileVault, open System Preferences, click Security, and then click Turn Off FileVault. Enter your password, and then click OK. (The master password sticks around once you've created it, however, in case you ever want to turn FileVault on again.)

Logout Options

As you read earlier in this chapter, the usual procedure for finishing up a work session is for each person to choose →Log Out. After you confirm your intention to log out, the Login screen appears, ready for the next victim.

But sometimes people forget. You might wander off to the bathroom for a minute, but run into a colleague there who breathlessly begins describing last night's date and proposes finishing the conversation over pizza. The next thing you know, you've left your Mac unattended but logged in, with all your life's secrets accessible to anyone who walks by your desk.

You can prevent that situation using either of two checkboxes, both in the Security→ General panel of System Preferences:

• **Require password immediately after sleep or screen saver begins.** This option gives you a password-protected screen saver that locks your Mac when you wander away. Now, whenever somebody tries to wake up your Mac after the screen saver has appeared (or when the Mac has simply gone to sleep according to your settings in the Energy Saver panel of System Preferences), the "Enter your password" dialog box appears. No password? No access.

Tip: The pop-up menu here (which starts out saying "immediately") is an awesome enhancement to this feature. Before Snow Leopard, the person most inconvenienced by the password requirement was you, not the evil snitch from Accounting; even if you'd just stepped away to the bathroom or the coffee machine, you'd have to unlock the screen saver with your password. It got old fast.

Now, the password requirement can kick in only after you've been away for a more serious amount of time—5 minutes, 15 minutes, an hour, whatever. You can still put the Mac to sleep, or you can still set up your screen saver to kick in sooner than that. But until that time period has passed, you'll be able to wake the machine without having to log in.

- **Disable automatic login.** This is just a duplicate of the Automatic Login on/off switch described on page 423.

- **Require a password to unlock each System Preferences pane.** Ordinarily, certain System Preferences changes require an administrator's approval—namely, the ones that affect the entire computer and everyone who uses it, like Date & Time, Accounts, Network, Time Capsule, and Security. If you're *not* an administrator, you can't make changes to these panels until an administrator has typed in his name and password to approve your change.

  However, once Mr. Teacher or Ms. Parent has unlocked *one* of those secure preference settings, they're *all* unlocked. Once the administrator leaves your desk, you can go right on making changes to the *other* important panels (Network *and* Time Machine *and* Security) without the administrator's knowledge.

  Unless this "Require a password" box is turned on, that is. In that case, an administrative-account holder has to enter his name and password to approve *each* of those System Preferences panes individually.

- **Log out after __ minutes of inactivity.** You can make the Mac sign out of your account completely if it figures out that you've wandered off (and it's been, say, 15 minutes since the last time you touched the mouse or keyboard). Anyone who shows up at your Mac will find only the standard Login screen.

Note: Beware! If there are open, unsaved documents at the moment of truth, the Mac can't log you out.

- **Use secure virtual memory.** *Virtual memory* is a trick that computers use to keep a lot of programs open at once—more, in fact, than they technically have enough memory (RAM) for. How do they manage to keep so many software balls in the air? Easy: They set some of them down on the hard drive.

  When you bring Photoshop to the front, Mac OS X frees up the necessary memory for it by storing some of the *background* programs' code on the hard drive. When you switch back to, say, Safari, Mac OS X swaps Photoshop for the Safari code it needs from the hard drive, so that the frontmost program always has full command of your actual memory.

  Sophisticated software snoopers could, in theory, sneak up to the Mac while you're logged in but away from your desk. Using a built-in Unix command called *strings,* the no-goodniks could actually *read* what's stored on the hard drive in that virtual-memory swap file—in particular, your passwords.

But this checkbox takes away all their fun; it encrypts your virtual memory swap file so nobody can read it. (You may also find that it slows down your Mac, though, especially when you switch from one program to another.)

- **Disable Location Services.** Location Services means "knowing where I am." It's the feature that lets a laptop figure out its own time zone, for example (page 479).

  Every time a program wants to use your current location for its own feature, you'll be asked about it. But if you want to rule out any possibility that someone, or some software, can find out where you are, then turn on this box.

- **Disable remote control infrared receiver.** You can operate the playback functions of laptops and iMacs with a remote control, like Apple's tiny white one. (For example, that's how you'd control movie, music, and slideshow playback in Front Row, a program described in Chapter 16.)

  If you're worried about some smart-aleck high-school kid interfering by, for example, summoning Front Row when you're trying to crunch some numbers, then turn this on. Now the Mac turns a deaf eye and ear to remote-control signals.

The Password Assistant

To prevent evildoers from guessing your passwords, Mac OS X comes with a password suggestion feature called the Password Assistant. It cheerfully generates one suggestion after another for impossible-to-guess passwords. (*recharges8@exchangeability,* anyone?)

Fortunately, *you* won't have to remember most of them, thanks to the Keychain password-memorizing feature described at the end of this chapter. (The only password you have to memorize is your account password.)

See Figure 13-17 for details on the Password Assistant.

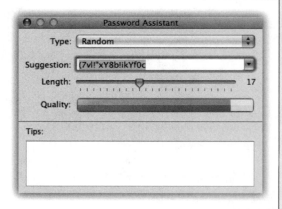

Figure 13-17:
Anyplace you're supposed to make up a password, including in the Accounts pane of System Preferences, a key icon appears. When you click it, the Password Assistant opens. Use the pop-up menu and the Length slider to specify how long and unguessable the password is. The Quality graph shows you just how tough it is to crack this password.

(In the Type pop-up menu, you might wonder about FIPS-181. It stands for the Federal Information Processing Standards Publication 181, which sets forth the U.S. government's standard for password-generating algorithms.)

The Keychain

The information explosion of the computer age may translate into bargains, power, and efficiency, but as noted above, it carries with it a colossal annoyance: the proliferation of *passwords* we have to memorize. Shared folders on the network, Web sites, your iDisk, FTP sites—each requires another password.

Apple has done the world a mighty favor with its *Keychain* feature. Whenever you log into Mac OS X and type in your password, you've typed the master code that tells the computer, "It's really me. I'm at my computer now." From that moment on, the Mac *automatically* fills in every password blank you encounter, whether it's a Web site in Safari, a shared disk on your network, a wireless network, an encrypted disk image, or an FTP program like Transmit or RBrowser. With only a few exceptions, you can safely forget *all* your passwords except your login password.

These days, all kinds of programs and services know about the Keychain and offer to store your passwords there. For example:

- In Safari, whenever you type your name and password for a certain Web page and then click OK, a dialog box asks: "Would you like to save this password?" (See Figure 13-18, top.)

Note: This offer is valid only if, in Safari→Preferences→AutoFill tab, "User names and passwords" is turned on. If not, the "Would you?" message never appears.

Note, too, that some Web sites use a nonstandard login system that also doesn't produce the "Would you?" message. Unless the Web site provides its own "Remember me" or "Store my password" option, you're out of luck; you'll have to type in this information with every visit.

FREQUENTLY ASKED QUESTION

Password Hell

With the introduction of the master password, you now have quite a few different passwords to keep straight. Each one, however, has a specific purpose:

Account password. You type this password in at the normal login screen. You can't get into anyone else's account with it—only yours. Entering this password unlocks FileVault, too.

Administrator password. You're asked to enter this password whenever you try to install new software or modify certain system settings. If you're the only one who uses your computer (or you're the one who controls it), your administrator password *is* your account password. Otherwise, you're

supposed to go find an administrator (the parent, teacher, or guru who set up your account to begin with) and ask that person to type in his name and password once he's assessed what you're trying to do.

Master password. Think of this password as a master key. If anyone with FileVault forgets her account password, the administrator who knows the master password can unlock the account. The master password also lets an administrator change an account's password right at the Login screen, whether FileVault is turned on or not.

Root password. This password is rarely useful for anything other than Unix hackery, and it's for geeks only.

- When you connect to a shared folder or disk on the network, the opportunity to save the password in your Keychain is equally obvious (Figure 13-18, bottom).

- You also see a "Remember password (add to Keychain)" option when you create an encrypted disk image using Disk Utility.

Figure 13-18:
Top: Safari is one of several Internet-based programs that offer to store your passwords in the Keychain; just click Yes. The next time you visit this Web page, you'll find your name and password already typed in.

Middle: At any time, you can see a complete list of the memorized Web passwords by choosing Safari→Preferences, clicking AutoFill, and then clicking the Edit button next to "User names and passwords." This is also where you can delete a password, thus making Safari forget it.

Bottom: When you connect to a server (a shared disk or folder on the network), just turn on "Remember this password in my keychain."

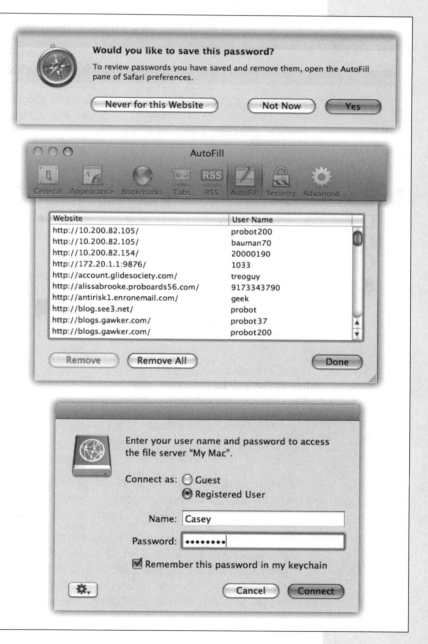

- Mac email programs, like Mail and Entourage, store your email account passwords in your Keychain. So do FTP (file-transfer) programs like RBrowser and Fetch; check their Preferences dialog boxes.

- Your MobileMe account information is stored in the Keychain, too (as you entered it on the MobileMe pane of System Preferences).

- A "Remember password" option appears when you type in the password for a wireless network or AirPort base station.

- The iTunes program memorizes your Apple Music Store password, too.

Tip: If you're a MobileMe subscriber (Chapter 10), the MobileMe service can even synchronize your Keychain with other Macs. (Open System Preferences→MobileMe→Sync to set it up.) All your Macs will contain the identical Keychain—so they will know and auto-enter your passwords, too. Life gets simpler yet.

Locking and unlocking the Keychain

If you work alone, the Keychain is automatic, invisible, and generally wonderful. Login is the only time you have to type a password. After that, the Mac figures, "Hey, I know it's you; you proved it by entering your account password. That ID is good enough for me. I'll fill in all your other passwords automatically." In Apple parlance, you've *unlocked* your Keychain just by logging in.

But there may be times when you want the Keychain to *stop* filling in all your passwords, perhaps only temporarily. Maybe you work in an office where someone else might sit down at your Mac while you're getting a candy bar.

Of course, you can have Mac OS X lock your Mac—Keychain and all—after a specified period of inactivity (page 437).

But if you want to lock the Keychain *manually,* so that no passwords are autofilled in until you unlock it again, you can use any of these methods. Each requires the Keychain Access program (in your Applications→Utilities folder):

- **Lock the Keychain manually.** In the Keychain Access program, choose File→Lock Keychain [Your Name] (⌘-L), or just click the big padlock at upper left. Click the 🔒 button in the toolbar of the Keychain Access window (Figure 13-19).

- **Choose Lock Keychain [Your Name] from the Keychain menulet.** To put the Keychain menulet on your menu bar, open Keychain Access, choose Keychain Access→Preferences→General. Turn on Show Status in Menu Bar.

- **Lock the Keychain automatically.** In the Keychain Access program, choose Edit→ Change Settings for Keychain [your name]. The resulting dialog box lets you set up the Keychain to lock itself, say, 5 minutes after the last time you used your Mac, or whenever the Mac goes to sleep. When you return to the Mac, you're asked to re-enter your account password in order to unlock the Keychain, restoring your automatic-password feature.

Whenever the Keychain is locked, Mac OS X no longer fills in your passwords.

Note: As noted above, you unlock your Keychain using the same password you use to log into Mac OS X, but that's just a convenience. If you're really worried about security, you can choose Edit→Change Password for Keychain [your name], thereby establishing a different password for your Keychain, so that it no longer matches your login password.

Of course, doing so also turns off the automatic-Keychain-unlocking-when-you-log-in feature.

Managing Keychain

To take a look at your Keychain, open the Keychain Access program. By clicking one of the password rows, you get to see its attributes—name, kind, account, and so on (Figure 13-19).

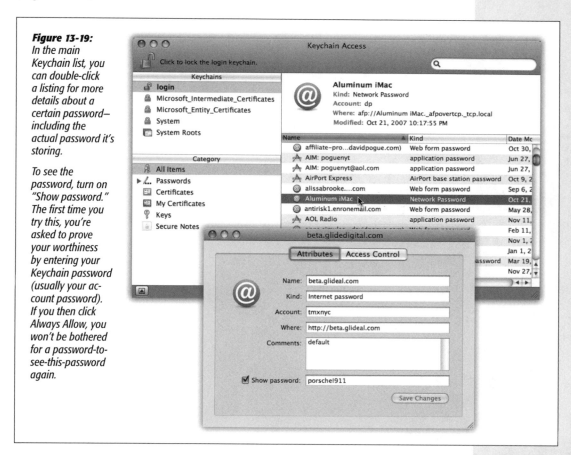

Figure 13-19:
In the main Keychain list, you can double-click a listing for more details about a certain password—including the actual password it's storing.

To see the password, turn on "Show password." The first time you try this, you're asked to prove your worthiness by entering your Keychain password (usually your account password). If you then click Always Allow, you won't be bothered for a password-to-see-this-password again.

Multiple Keychains

By choosing File→New Keychain, you can create more than one Keychain, each with its own master password. On one hand, this might defeat the simplicity goal of the Keychain. On the other hand, it's conceivable that you might want to encrypt all your business documents with one master password and all your personal stuff with another, for example.

If you do have more than one Keychain, you can view all of them by clicking the little Show Keychains button at the lower-left corner of the Keychain Access window; now you see a list of all your Keychains (including some maintained by Microsoft Office and Mac OS X itself). Click their names to switch among them.

Keychain files

Keychains are represented by separate files in your Home→Library→Keychains folder. Knowing that can be handy when you want to delete a Keychain or copy it to another Mac—your laptop, for example. (Then again, the File→Export command may be even more convenient.)

Networking, File Sharing, & Screen Sharing

Networks are awesome. Once you've got a network, you can copy files from one machine to another—even between Windows PCs and Macs—just as you'd drag files between folders a single computer. You can send little messages to other people's screens. Everyone on the network can consult the same database or calendar, or listen to the same iTunes music collection. You can play games over the network. You can share a single printer or cable modem among all the computers in the office. You can connect to the network from wherever you are in the world, using the Internet as the world's longest extension cord back to your office.

In Mac OS X, you can even do *screen sharing*, which means that you, the wise computer whiz, can see what's on the screen of your pathetic, floundering relative or buddy elsewhere on the network. You can seize control of the other Mac's mouse and keyboard. You can troubleshoot, fiddle with settings, and so on. It's the next best thing to being there—often, a lot *better* than being there.

This chapter concerns itself with *local* networking—setting up a network in your home or small office. But don't miss its sibling, Chapter 10, which is about hooking up to the somewhat larger network called the Internet.

Wiring the Network

Most people connect their computers using one of two connection systems: Ethernet or WiFi (which Apple calls AirPort).

Ethernet Networks

Every Mac (except the MacBook Air) and every network-ready laser printer has an Ethernet jack (Figure 14-1). If you connect all the Macs and Ethernet printers in your small office to a central *Ethernet hub* or *router*—a compact, inexpensive box with jacks for five, 10, or even more computers and printers—you've got yourself a very fast, very reliable network. (Most people wind up hiding the hub in a closet and running the wiring either along the edges of the room or inside the walls.) You can buy Ethernet cables, plus the hub, at any computer store or, less expensively, from an Internet-based mail-order house; none of this stuff is Mac-specific.

Tip: If you want to connect only two Macs—say, your laptop and your desktop machine—you don't need an Ethernet hub. Instead, you just need a standard Ethernet cable. Run it directly between the Ethernet jacks of the two computers. (You don't need a special crossover Ethernet cable, as you did with Macs of old.) Then connect the Macs as described in the box below.

Or don't use Ethernet at all; just use a person-to-person AirPort network.

Ethernet is the best networking system for many offices. It's fast, easy, and cheap.

Ethernet jack

Ethernet hub

Figure 14-1:
An Ethernet jack (left) looks like an overweight telephone jack. It connects to an Ethernet router or hub (right) via an Ethernet cable (also known as Cat 5 or Cat 6), which ends in what looks like an overweight telephone-wire plug (also known as an RJ-45 connector).

GEM IN THE ROUGH

Networking Without the Network

In a pinch, you can connect two Macs without any real network at all. You can create an Ethernet connection without a hub or a router—or an AirPort connection without a WiFi base station.

To set up the wired connection, just run a standard Ethernet cable between the Ethernet jacks of the two Macs. (You don't need to use an Ethernet *crossover* cable, as you did in days of old.)

To set up a wireless connection, from your 🛜 menulet, choose Create Network. Make up a name for your little

private network, and then click OK. On the second Mac, choose 🛜→Join Network, enter the same private network name, and click Join.

At this point, your two Macs belong to the same *ad hoc* micro-network. But that doesn't mean that you've started accessing their files yet.

To do that, in the Finder on one of the Macs, choose Go→ Connect to Server. The Network window opens, showing the icons for all the computers on the local network. Double-click the one you want, enter the account password, if necessary, and you're in.

AirPort Networks

WiFi, known to the geeks as 802.11 and to Apple fans as AirPort, means wireless networking. It's the technology that lets laptops the world over get online at high speed in any WiFi *hot spot*. Hot spots are everywhere these days: in homes, offices, coffee shops (notably Starbucks), hotels, airports, and thousands of other places.

Tip: At *www.jiwire.com*, you can type in an address or a city and learn exactly where to find the closest WiFi hot spots.

When you're in a WiFi hot spot, your Mac has a very fast connection to the Internet, as though it's connected to a cable modem or DSL.

AirPort circuitry comes preinstalled in every Mac. This circuitry lets your machine connect to your network and the Internet without any wires at all. You just have to be within about 150 feet of a *base station* or *access point* (as Windows people call it), which must in turn be physically connected to your network and Internet connection.

UP TO SPEED

AirPort a, b, g, and n: Regular or Supersized?

In the short history of wireless networking, WiFi gear has come in several variants, bearing the absurdly user-hostile names *802.11b, 802.11g, 802.11a, 802.11n,* and so on.

The difference involves the technical specs of the wireless signal. Original AirPort uses the 802.11b standard; AirPort Extreme uses 802.11g; the current AirPort cards and base stations use 802.11n.

So what's the difference? Equipment bearing the "b" label transfers data through the air at up to 11 megabits per second; the "g" system is almost five times as fast (54 megabits per second); and "n" is supposed to be four times as fast as *that*.

(Traditionally, geeks measure network speeds in mega*bits*, not mega*bytes*. If you're more familiar with megabytes, though, here's a translation: The older AirPort gear has a top speed of 1.4 megabytes per second, versus more than 6 megabytes per second for the AirPort Extreme stuff.)

(Oh, and while we're using parentheses here: The only place you'll get the quoted speeds out of this gear is when you're on the moon. Here on earth, signal strength is affected by pesky things like air, furniture, walls, floors, wiring, phone interference, and antenna angle. Speed and signal strength diminish proportionally as you move away from the base station.)

Now, each successive version of the WiFi base station/laptop circuitry standard is backward-compatible. For example, you can buy a new, 802.11n base station, and still connect to it from your ancient 802.11g PowerBook. You won't get any greater speed, of course—that would require a laptop with an 802.11n transmitter—but you'll enjoy the greater range in your house.

It's important to understand, though, that even the most expensive, top-tier cable modem or DSL service delivers Internet information at only about *half* a megabyte per second. The bottleneck is the Internet connection, not your network. Don't buy newer AirPort gear thinking that you're going to speed up your email and Web activity.

Instead, the speed boost you get with AirPort Extreme is useful *only* for transferring files between computers and gadgets on your own network (like the bandwidth-hungry Apple TV)—and playing networkable games.

And one more note: All WiFi gear works together, no matter what kind of computer you have. There's no such thing as a "Windows" wireless network or a "Macintosh" wireless network. Macs can use non-Apple base stations, PCs can use AirPort base stations, and so on.

If you think about it, the AirPort system is a lot like a cordless phone, where the base station is, well, the base station, and the computer is the handset.

The base station can take any of these forms:

- **AirPort base station.** Apple's sleek, white, squarish or rounded base stations ($100 to $180) permit as many as 50 computers to connect simultaneously.

  The less expensive one, the AirPort Express, is so small it looks like a small white power adapter. It also has a USB jack so you can share a USB printer on the network. It can serve up to 10 computers at once.

- **A Time Capsule.** This Apple gizmo is exactly the same as the AirPort base station except that it also contains a huge hard drive so that it can back up your Macs automatically over the wired or wireless network.

- **A wireless broadband router.** Lots of other companies make less expensive WiFi base stations, including Linksys (*www.linksys.com*) and Belkin (*www.belkin.com*). You can plug the base station into an Ethernet router or hub, thus permitting 10 or 20 wireless-equipped computers, including Macs, to join an existing Ethernet network without wiring. (With all due non-fanboyism, however, Apple's base stations and software are more polished and satisfying to use.)

Tip: It's perfectly possible to plug a WiFi base station into a regular router, too, to accommodate both wired and wireless computers.

- **Another Mac.** Using Internet Sharing (page 304), a Mac can also *impersonate* an AirPort base station. In effect, the Mac becomes a software-based base station, and you save yourself the cost of a separate physical base station.

Tip: If you connect through a modern router or AirPort base station, you already have a great firewall protecting you. You don't have to turn on Mac OS X's firewall. But remember to turn it on when you escape to the local WiFi coffee shop with your laptop.

For the easiest AirPort network setup, begin by configuring your Mac so that it can go online the wired way, as described in Chapter 10. Once it's capable of connecting to the Internet via wires, you can then use the AirPort Utility (in your Applications→Utilities folder) to transmit those Internet settings wirelessly to the base station itself. From then on, the base station's modem or Ethernet jack—not your Mac's—will do the connecting to the Internet.

Whether you've set up your own wireless network or want to hop onto somebody else's, Chapter 10 has the full scoop on *joining* WiFi networks.

File Sharing

When you're done wiring (or not wiring, as the case may be), your network is ready. Your Mac should "see" any Ethernet or shared USB printers, in readiness to print

(Chapter 14). You can now play network games or use a network calendar. And you can now turn on *File Sharing,* one of the most useful features of all.

In File Sharing, you can summon the icon for a folder or disk attached to another computer on the network, whether it's a Mac or a Windows PC. It shows up in a Finder window, as shown in Figure 14-2.

Figure 14-2:
Here's the master switch that makes your Public folder (and any other folders you designate) available to other people on the network. You can edit the Computer Name, if you like. Your Mac will appear on the network with this name. Make it nice and descriptive, such as Front Desk iMac.

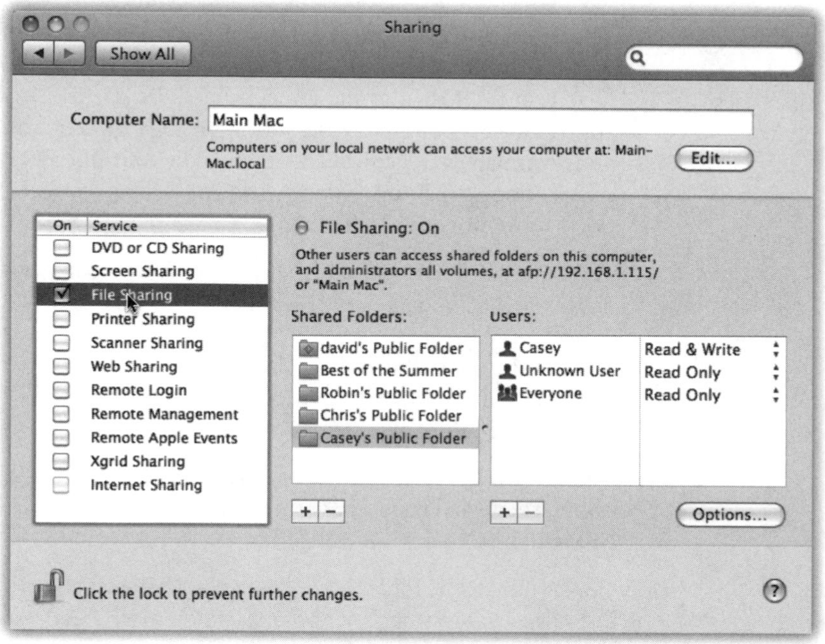

At this point, you can drag files back and forth, exactly as though the other computer's folder or disk is a hard drive connected to your own machine.

The thing is, it's not easy being Apple. You have to write *one* operating system that's supposed to please *everyone,* from the self-employed first-time computer owner to the network administrator for NASA. You have to design a networking system simple enough for the laptop owner who just wants to copy things to a desktop Mac when returning from a trip, yet secure and flexible enough for the network designer at a large corporation.

Clearly, different people have different attitudes toward the need for security and flexibility.

That's why Snow Leopard offers two ways to share files—a simple and limited way, and a more complicated and flexible way:

- **The simple way: the Public folder.** Every account holder has a Public folder. It's free for anyone else on the network to access. Like a grocery store bulletin board, there's no password required. Super-convenient, super-easy.

  There's only one downside, and you may not care about it: You have to move or copy files *into* the Public folder before anyone else can see them. Depending on how many files you want to share, this can get tedious, disrupt your standard organizational structure, and eat up disk space.

- **The flexible way: Any folder.** You can also make *any* file, folder, or disk available for inspection by other people on the network. This method means that you don't have to move files into the Public folder, for starters. It also gives you elaborate control over who is allowed to do what to your files. You might want to permit your company's executives to see *and* edit your documents, but allow the peons in Accounting just to see them. And Andy, that unreliable goofball in Sales? You don't want him even *seeing* what's in your shared folder.

  Of course, setting up all those levels of control means more work and more complexity.

Setup: The Public Folder

Inside your Home folder, there's a folder called Public. Inside *everybody's* Home folder is a folder called Public.

Anything you copy into this folder is automatically available to everyone else on the network. They don't need a password, they don't need an account on your Mac—they just have to be on the same network.

To make your Public folder available to your network mates, you have to turn on the File Sharing master switch. Choose →System Preferences, click Sharing, and turn on File Sharing (Figure 14-2).

Now round up the files and folders you want to share with all comers on the network, and drag them into your Home→Public folder. That's all there is to it.

Note: You may notice that there's already something in your Public folder: a folder called Drop Box. It's there so that other people can give *you* files from across the network, as described later in this chapter.

So now that you've set up Public folder sharing, how are other people supposed to *access* your Public folder? See page 454.

Setup: Sharing Any Folder

If the Public folder method seems too simple and restrictive, then you can graduate to the "share any folder" method. In this scheme, you can make *any* file, folder, or disk available to other people on the network.

This time, you don't have to move your files anywhere; they sit right where you have them. And this time, you can set up elaborate *sharing privileges* (also known as *permissions*) that grant individuals different amount of access to your files.

This method is more complicated to set up than that Public-folder business. In fact, just to underline its complexity, Apple has created two different setup procedures. You can share one icon at a time by opening its Get Info window; or you can work in a master list of shared items in System Preferences.

The following section covers both methods.

The Get Info method

Here's how to share a Mac file, disk, or folder disk using its Get Info window.

The following steps assume that you've opened →System Preferences, clicked Sharing, and then turned on File Sharing, as shown in Figure 14-2.

1. **Highlight the file, folder, or disk you want to share. Choose File→Get Info.**

   The Get Info dialog box appears (Figure 14-3). Expand the General panel, if it's not already visible.

Note: Sharing an entire disk means that every folder and file on it is available to anyone you give access to. On the other hand, by sharing only a folder or two, you can keep *most* of the stuff on your hard drive private, out of view of curious network comrades. Sharing only a folder or two does *them* a favor, too, by making it easier for them to find files you've made available. This way, they don't have to root through your entire drive looking for the folder they actually need.

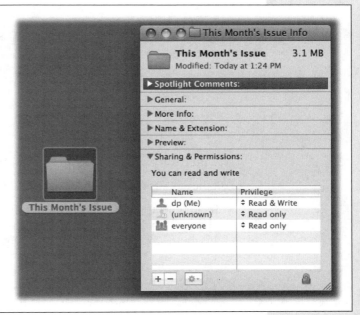

Figure 14-3:
The file-sharing permissions controls are back in the Get Info box for any file, folder, or disk—just as they are in the Properties dialog box of a folder in Windows.

2. **Turn on "Shared folder."**

   Enter your administrative password, if necessary.

OK, this disk or folder is now shared. But with whom?

3. **Expand the Sharing & Permissions panel, if it's not already visible. Click the 🔒 icon and enter your administrator's password.**

The controls in the Sharing & Permissions area spring to life and become editable. You wanted individual control over each account holder's access? You've got it.

At the bottom of the Info panel is a little table (Figure 14-4). The first column can display the names of individual account holders, like Casey or Chris, or *groups* of account holders, like Everyone or Accounting Dept. The second column lists the *privileges* each person or group has for this folder.

Now, the average person has no clue what "privileges" means, and this is why things

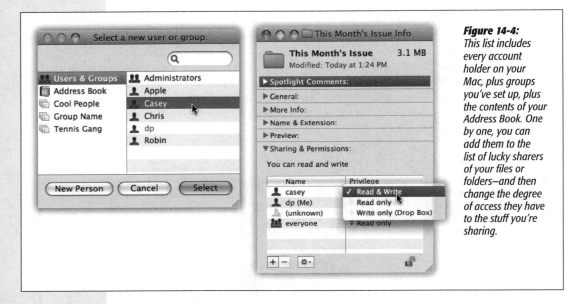

Figure 14-4:
This list includes every account holder on your Mac, plus groups you've set up, plus the contents of your Address Book. One by one, you can add them to the list of lucky sharers of your files or folders—and then change the degree of access they have to the stuff you're sharing.

get a little hairy when you're setting up folder-by-folder permissions.

4. **Edit the table by adding people's names. Then set their access permissions.**

At the moment, your name appears in the Name column, and it probably says Read & Write in the Privilege column. In other words, you're currently the master of this folder. You can put things in, and you can take things out.

But at the moment, the privileges for "Everyone" is probably "Read only." Other people can see this folder, but can't do anything with it.

Now your job is to work through this list of people, specifying *how much* control each person has over the file or folder you're sharing. To add the name of a person or group, click the **+** button below the list. The people list shown in Figure 14-4 at left appears.

Now click a name. From Privilege pop-up menu, choose a permissions setting.

Read & Write has the most access of all. This person, like you, can add, change, or delete any file in the shared folder, or make any changes you like to a document. Give Read & Write permission to people you trust not to mess things up.

Read only means "look, but don't touch." This person can see what's in the folder (or file) and can copy it, but can't delete or change the original. It's a good setting for distributing company documents or making source files available to your minions.

Write only (**drop box**) means that other people can't open the folder at all. They can drop things into it, but it's like dropping icons through a mail slot: The letter disappears into the slot, and then it's too late for them to change their minds. As the folder's owner, you can do what you like with the deposited goodies. This drop-box effect is great when you want students, coworkers, or family members to be able to *turn things in* to you—homework, reports, scandalous diaries—without running the risk that someone else might see those documents.

No access is an option only for "Everyone." It means that other people can see this file or folder's icon, but can't do a thing with it.

Tip: Usually, you'll want the privileges for the folder to also apply to everything *inside* it; it would be a real drag to have to change the sharing privileges of the contents one icon at a time. That's why the ✿ menu at the bottom of the Get Info box has a command called "Apply to enclosed items."

Figure 14-5:
Hiding in System Preferences is a list of every file, disk, and folder you've shared. To stop sharing something, click it and click the – button. To share something new, drag its icon off the desktop, or out of its window, directly into the Shared Folders list.

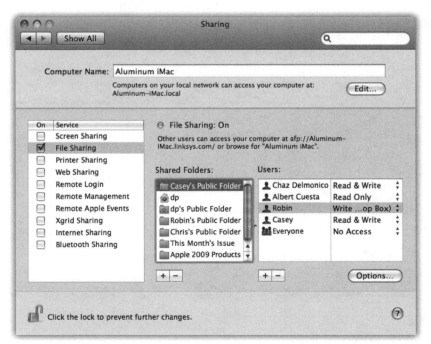

5. Close the Get Info window.

Now the folder is ready for invasion from across the network.

The System Preferences method

It's very convenient to turn on sharing one folder at a time, using the Get Info window. But there's another way in, too, one that displays *all* of your shared stuff in one handy master list.

To see it, choose →System Preferences. Click Sharing. Click File Sharing (and make sure it's turned on).

Now you're looking at a slightly different kind of permissions table, shown in Figure 14-5. It has *three* columns. The first lists the files, folders, and disks you've shared. The second shows *who* gets to work with a certain item from across the network. The third column lets you specify how much access each person in the *second* column has to this folder.

Accessing Shared Files

So far in this chapter, you've read about *setting up* a Mac so that people at other computers can access its files. Now comes the payoff: sitting at another computer and *connecting* to the one you set up. There are two ways to go about it.

Connection Method A: Use the Sidebar

Suppose, then, that you're seated in front of your Mac, and you want to see the files on another Mac on the network. Proceed like this:

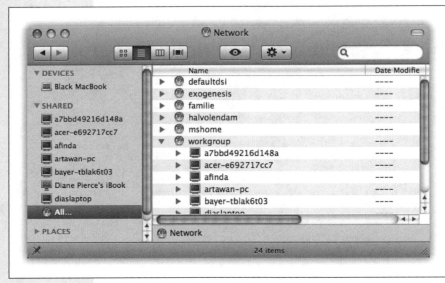

Figure 14-6:
Macs often appear in the Sidebar with model-specific names (MacBook, iMac, and so on). Other computers (like PCs) have generic blue monitors. When you click All in the Sidebar, you see both the icons of individual computers and the icons of network chunks (like AppleTalk zones and Windows workgroups).

1. **Open any Finder window.**

   In the Shared category of the Sidebar at the left side of the window, icons for all the computers on the network appear. See Figure 14-6.

Tip: The same Sidebar items show up in the Save and Open dialog boxes of your programs, too, making the entire network available to you for opening and saving files.

If you *don't* see a certain Mac's icon here, it might be turned off, it might not be on the network, or it might have File Sharing turned off.

If there are more than six icons in the Sidebar, or if you're on a corporate-style network that has sub-chunks like *nodes* or *workgroups*, you also see an icon called All. Click it to see the full list of network entities that your Mac can see: not just individual Mac, Windows, and Unix machines, but also any "network neighborhoods" (limbs of your network tree). For example, you may see the names of AppleTalk zones (clusters of machines, as found in big companies and universities).

Or, if you're trying to tap into a Windows machine, open the icon representing the *workgroup* (computer cluster) that contains the machine you want. In small office networks, it's usually called MSHOME or WORKGROUP. In big corporations, these workgroups can be called almost anything—as long as it's no more than 12 letters long with no punctuation. (Thanks, Microsoft.)

If you *do* see icons for workgroups or other network "zones," double-click your way until you're seeing the icons for individual computers.

2. **Click the computer whose files you want to open.**

   In the main window, you now see the icons for each account holder on that computer: Mom, Dad, Sissy, whatever. If you have an account on the other computer, you'll see a folder representing *your* stuff, too (Figure 14-7).

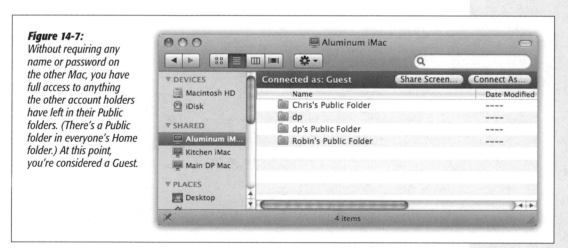

Figure 14-7:
Without requiring any name or password on the other Mac, you have full access to anything the other account holders have left in their Public folders. (There's a Public folder in everyone's Home folder.) At this point, you're considered a Guest.

At this point, the remaining instructions diverge, depending on whether you want to access *other* people's stuff or *your* stuff. That's why there are two alternative versions of step 3 here:

3a. **If you want to access the stuff that somebody *else* has left for you, double-click that person's Public folder.**

Instantly, the icon for that folder appears on your desktop, and an Eject button (⏏) appears beside the computer's name in the Sidebar. (You can turn off both of those visual signals in Finder→Preferences.)

In this situation, you're only a Guest. You don't have to bother with a password. On the other hand, the only thing you can generally see inside the other person's account folder is his Public folder.

If you see anything besides the Drop Box folder in the Public folder you've opened, then it's stuff that the account holder has copied there for the enjoyment of you and your network mates. You're not allowed to delete anything from the other person's Public folder or make changes to them.

You can, however, open those icons, read them, or even copy them to *your* Mac— and then edit *your* copies.

Figure 14-8:
Top: You can sign into your account on another Mac on the network (even while somebody else is actually using that Mac in person). Click Connect As (top right), and then enter your name and password. Turn on "Remember this password" to speed up the process for next time.

The Action (✿) pop-up menu offers a Change Password that gives you the opportunity to change your account password on the other machine, just in case you suspect someone saw what you typed.

No matter which method you use to connect to a shared folder or disk, its icon shows up in the Sidebar. It's easy to disconnect, thanks to the little ⏏ button.

3b. **To access your own Home folder on the other Mac, click it, and then click the
Connect As button (Figure 14-8). Sign in as usual.**

When the "Connect to the file server" box appears, you're supposed to specify
your account name and password (from the Mac you're tapping into). This is
the same name and password you'd use to log in if you were actually sitting at
that machine.

Tip: The dialog box shown in Figure 14-8 includes the delightful and timesaving "Remember this password
in my keychain" option, which makes the Mac memorize your password for a certain disk so you don't have
to type it—or even see this dialog box—every darned time you connect.

When you click Connect (or press Return), your own Home folder on the other
Mac appears. Its icon shows up on your desktop, and a little ⏏ button appears
next to its name. Click it to disconnect.

In the meantime, you can double-click icons to open them, make copies of them,
and otherwise manipulate them exactly as though they were icons on your own hard
drive. Depending on what permissions you've been given, you can even edit or trash
those files.

Connection Method B: Connect to Server

The Sidebar method of connecting to networked folders and disks is practically
effortless. But it doesn't let you type in a disk's network address. As a result, you can't
access any shared disk *on the Internet* (an FTP site, for example), or indeed anywhere
beyond your local subnet (your own small network).

Fortunately, there's another way. When you choose Go→Connect to Server, you get
the dialog box shown in Figure 14-9. You're supposed to type in the *address* of the
shared disk you want.

Figure 14-9:
*The Sidebar method of con-
necting to shared disks and
folders is quick and easy, but
it doesn't let you connect to
certain kinds of disks. The Connect to Server method entails
plodding through several
dialog boxes and doesn't let
you browse for shared disks,
but it can find just about every
kind of networked disk.*

Disconnecting Yourself

When you're finished using a shared disk or folder, you can disconnect from it by clicking the ⏏ icon next to its name in the Sidebar.

Networking with Windows

Mac OS X represents a historic moment in Mac-Windows relations: It lets Macs and Windows PCs see each other on the network, with no special software (or talent) required.

In fact, you can go in either direction. Your Mac can see shared folders on the Windows PCs, and a Windows PC can see shared folders on your Mac. Since a huge number of Mac "switchers" are actually Mac "adders" (meaning that you're keeping the old PC around), you might find these features especially useful.

It goes like this:

Seated at the Mac, Seeing the PC

Suppose you have a Windows PC and a Mac on the same wired or wireless network. Here's how you get the Mac and PC chatting:

1. **On your Windows PC, share some files.**

   This isn't really a book about Windows networking (thank heaven), but here are the basics.

   Just as on the Mac, there are two ways to share files in Windows. One of them is super-simple: You just copy the files you want to share into a central, fully accessible folder. No passwords, accounts, or other steps are required.

   In **Windows XP**, that special folder is the Shared Documents folder, which you can find by choosing Start→My Computer. Share it on the network as shown in Figure 14-10, top.

GEM IN THE ROUGH

Faster Ways to Connect Next Time

If you expect that you might want to access a shared disk or folder again later, take a moment to make an alias of it. (For example, right-click it and choose Make Alias from the shortcut menu.)

Next time, you can bring it back to your screen later just by double-clicking the alias. And if you turned on "Remember this password in my keychain," you won't even be asked for your name and password again.

Similarly, if you drag a shared folder into the Dock, you can bring it back to your screen later just by clicking its icon.

You can even drag its icon into the Login Items window described on page 413. Now the disk appears on your desktop *automatically* each time you log in—the most effortless arrangement of all.

In **Windows Vista,** it's the Public folder, which appears in the Navigation pane of every Explorer window. (In Vista, there's one Public folder for the whole *computer,* not one per account holder.)

In **Windows 7,** there's a Public folder in each of your libraries. That is, there's a Public Documents, Public Pictures, Public Music, and so on.

The second, more complicated method is the "share any folder" method. In XP or Vista, you right-click the folder you want to share, choose Properties from the shortcut menu, click the Sharing tab, and turn on "Share this folder on the network" (Figure 14-10, top). In Windows 7, use the Share With menu at the top of any folder's window. See the box on page 460 for more details.

Figure 14-10:
Top: To share a folder in Windows XP, right-click it, choose Properties, and then turn on "Share this folder on the network." In the "Share name" box, type a name for the folder as it will appear on the network. (No spaces are allowed).

Bottom: Back in the safety of Mac OS X, click the PC's name in the Sidebar. (If it's part of a workgroup, click All, and then your workgroup name first. And if you still don't see the PC's name, see the box on page 462.)

Next, click the name of the shared computer. If the files you need are in a Shared Documents or Public folder, no password is required. You see the contents of the PC's Shared Documents folder or Public folder, as shown here. Now it's just like file sharing with another Mac.

If you want access to any other shared folder, click Connect As, and see Figure 14-11.

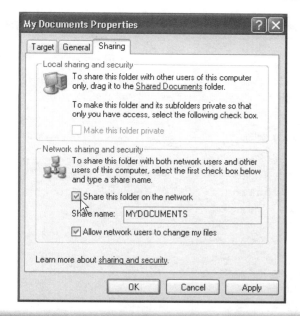

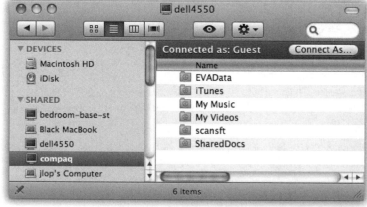

Repeat for any other folders you want to make available to your Mac.

2. On the Mac, open any Finder window.

The shared PCs may appear as individual computer names in the Sidebar, or you may have to click the All icon to see the icons of their *workgroups* (network clusters—an effect shown on page 454). Unless you or a network administrator changed it, the workgroup name is probably MSHOME or WORKGROUP. Double-click the workgroup name you want.

Tip: You can also access the shared PC via the Go→Connect to Server command in the Finder. You could type into it *smb://192.168.1.103* (or whatever the PC's IP address is) or *smb://SuperDell* (or whatever its name is) and hit Return—and then skip to step 5.

TROUBLESHOOTING MOMENT

Windows 7 Hell

In Windows 7, Microsoft gutted the networking software and replaced it with something it considers better. Unfortunately, it's also incompatible with Mac file sharing.

You can fix it, though.

First, make sure you've shared everything you want to share on the Windows 7 machine. For example, suppose you want to share your entire Personal folder (the equivalent of the Mac's Home folder).

To do that, choose Start→ [your name]. In the window that opens, choose "Share with"→"Specific people." In the resulting dialog box, you'll see that you are already permitted to access this folder, as shown here; unless you want to add someone else, just click Share, then Done.

Now, on the Mac, in the Finder, choose Go→Connect to Server. Type *smb://SuperDell,* or whatever your PC's name is. (And how do you find *that* out? Open the Start menu; right-click Computer; from the shortcut menu, choose

Properties. You'll see the Computer Name in the middle of the dialog box.)

On the Mac, after typing the PC's name, click Connect. After a moment, you're asked for your account name and password, as it appears on the *PC.* Enter these credentials— turn on "Remember my password" if you want to be spared this rigamarole the next time—and then click Connect.

Now you're shown a list of disks and folders you shared on the Windows PC. Double-click the one you want. Presto: It appears in a Finder window, ready to access!

(If you discover you can copy stuff *out* of these folders but can't put stuff *into* them, it's because you didn't turn on Full Control for yourself, as described above.)

Finally, for heaven's sake, make an alias of the Windows folder or disk on the Mac so you can just double-click to open it the next time!

Now the names of the individual PCs on the network appear in your Finder window. (If you're running Windows 7, see the box on page 463.)

3. **Double-click the name of the computer you want.**

   If you're using one of the simple file-sharing methods on the PC, as described above, that's it. The contents of the Shared Documents or Public folder now appear on your Mac screen. You can work with them just as you would your own files.

   If you're not using one of those simple methods, and you want access to individual shared folders, read on.

Note: In Windows XP Pro, the next step won't work unless you turn off Simple File Sharing. To do that, choose Tools→Folder Options in any Explorer window. Click the View tab and turn off "Use simple file sharing."

---

4. **Click Connect As.**

   This button appears in the top-right corner of the Finder window; you can see it at bottom in Figure 14-10. Now you're asked for your name and password (Figure 14-11, top).

Figure 14-11:
Top: The PC wants to make sure that you're authorized to visit it. If the terminology here seems a bit geeky by Apple standards, no wonder—this is Microsoft Windows' lingo you're seeing, not Apple's. Fortunately, you see this box only the very first time you access a certain Windows folder or disk; after that, you see only the box shown below.

Bottom: Here, you see a list of shared folders on the PC. Choose the one you want to connect to, and then click OK. Like magic, the Windows folder shows up on your Mac screen, ready to use!

5. **Enter the name and password for your account on the PC, and then click OK.**

At long last, the contents of the shared folder on the Windows machine appear in your Finder window, just as though you'd tapped into another Mac (Figure 14-11, bottom). The icon of the shared folder appears on your desktop, too, and an Eject button (⏏) appears next to the PC's name in your Sidebar.

From here, it's a simple matter to drag files between the machines, open Word documents on the PC using Word for the Mac, and so on—exactly like you're hooked into another Mac.

Seated at the PC, Seeing the Mac

Cross-platformers, rejoice: Mac OS X lets you share files in *both directions*. Not only can your Mac see other PCs on the network, but they can see the Mac, too.

On the Mac, open →System Preferences→Sharing. Click File Sharing (make sure File Sharing is turned on), and then click Options to open the dialog box shown in Figure 14-12.

Turn on "Share files and folders using SMB (Windows)." Below that checkbox, you see a list of all the accounts on your Mac. Turn on the checkboxes to specify *which* Mac user accounts you want to be able to access. You must type in each person's password, too. Click Done.

When Macs and PCs Don't See Each Other

If your Mac's icon doesn't show up on the PC at all, or vice versa, it's probably because the Mac doesn't know anything about Windows *workgroups*. And even a lowly home PC is part of a workgroup (a corporate cluster), whether it knows it or not. And until your Mac is part of that very tiny club, it won't be able to see your PCs, and they won't be able to see it.

So if you're having no luck with this whole Mac-PC thing, try this. Open System Preferences. Click Network. Click whatever connection you're on right now (like AirPort or Ethernet). Click Advanced. Click WINS.

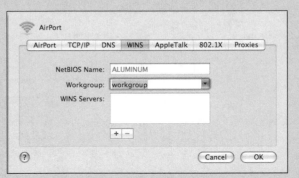

Now you see the peculiar set of controls shown here. The Workgroup pop-up menu already lists the workgroups that your Mac sees. Choose "workgroup" from the pop-up menu. Click OK, and then click Apply.

And marvel as your Windows PCs' names show up in the Sidebar, where they didn't before.

(Of course, your workgroup name might not be "workgroup," but that and mshome are the two most common Windows home-network workgroup names.)

Before you close System Preferences, study the line near the middle of the window, where it says something like: "Other users can access your computer at afp://192.168.1.108 or MacBook-Pro." You'll need one of these addresses shortly.

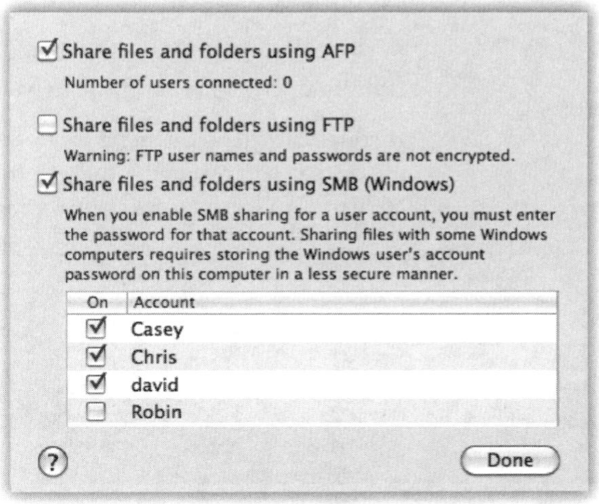

Figure 14-12:
Prepare your Mac for visitation by the Windows PC. It won't hurt a bit. The system-wide On switch for invasion from Windows is the third checkbox here, in the System Preferences→Sharing→File Sharing→Options box.

Next, turn on the individual accounts whose icons you'll want to show up on the PC. Enter their account passwords, too. Click Done when you're done.

☑ Share files and folders using AFP
   Number of users connected: 0

☐ Share files and folders using FTP
   Warning: FTP user names and passwords are not encrypted.

☑ Share files and folders using SMB (Windows)
   When you enable SMB sharing for a user account, you must enter the password for that account. Sharing files with some Windows computers requires storing the Windows user's account password on this computer in a less secure manner.

On	Account
☑	Casey
☑	Chris
☑	david
☐	Robin

(?)   (Done)

Now, on **Windows XP,** open My Network Places; in **Windows Vista,** choose Start→ Network; in **Windows 7,** expand the Network heading in the sidebar of any desktop window. If you've sacrificed the proper animals to the networking gods, your Mac's icon should appear by itself in the network window, as shown in Figure 14-13, top.

TROUBLESHOOTING MOMENT

When Windows 7 Can't See the Mac

If you're sitting at your PC and you want to bring the Mac onto your screen, things generally don't go quite as smoothly as they did with Windows XP or Vista. Windows 7 uses a different security method, which the Mac doesn't know about.

You can solve the problem, though, if you slog through an ugly but one-time procedure. It involves making some tweaky, geeky settings in a corner of Windows most people never see.

Click Start→Control Panel. Change the view to Small Icons; double-click Administrative Tools→Local Security Policy.

In the list at left, expand the Local Policies "folder"; click Security Options. In the list at right, hunt down the line called "Network security: LAN Manager authentication level."

Double-click it. In the resulting dialog box, change the pop-up menu to say "Send LM & NTLM - use NTLMv2 session if negotiated." (It's not necessary to understand what the hell Microsoft is talking about. Just do it.)

Click OK.

Now, in the same list, find and double-click "Network security: Minimum session security for NTLM SSP Based (including secure RPC) Clients." Turn off "Require 128-bit encryption," and then click OK.

Restart the PC. When it comes to, your Mac's icon shows up in the Sidebar of any desktop window on the PC. Click it to see what's in it.

Note: If you don't see your Mac here, proceed immediately to the boxes on pages 532 and 536.

Double-click the Mac's icon. Public-folder stuff is available immediately. Otherwise, you have to sign in with your Mac account name and password; Figure 14-13, middle, has the details.

In the final window, you see your actual Home folder—on a Windows PC! You're ready to open its files, copy them back and forth, or whatever (Figure 14-13, bottom).

If your Mac's icon *doesn't* appear, and you've read the box on page 462, wait a minute or two. Try restarting the PC. In Windows XP, try clicking "Microsoft Windows Network" or "View workgroup computers" in the task pane.

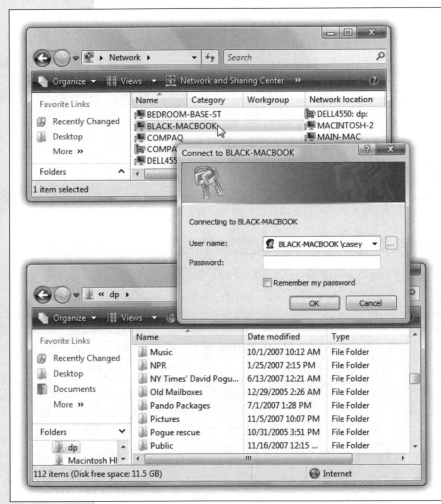

Figure 14-13:
Top: Double-click the icon of the Mac you want to visit from your Windows machine (Vista is shown here).

Middle: Type your Mac's name in all capitals (or its IP address), then a backslash, and then your Mac account short name. (You can find out your Mac's name on the Sharing pane of System Preferences.)

Enter your Mac account's password, too. Turn on "Remember my password" if you plan to do this again someday. Click OK.

Bottom: Here's your Mac Home folder—in Windows! Open it up to find all your stuff.

If your Mac still doesn't show up, you'll have to add it the hard way. In the address bar of any Windows window, type *macbook-pro**chris* (but substitute your Mac's actual computer name and your short account name), taking care to use backslashes, not normal / slashes. You can also type your Mac's IP address in place of its computer name.

In the future, you won't have to do so much burrowing; your Mac's icon should appear automatically in the My Network Places or Network window.

More Mac-Windows Connections

The direct Mac-to-Windows file-sharing feature of Mac OS X is by far the easiest way to access each other's files. But it's not the only way. Page 177 offers a long list of other options, from flash drives to the iDisk.

Screen Sharing

The prayers of baffled beginners and exasperated experts everywhere have now been answered. Now, when the novice needs help from the guru, the guru doesn't have to run all the way downstairs or down the hall to assist. Thanks to the Mac's screen-sharing feature, you can see exactly what's on the screen of another Mac, from across the network—and even seize control of the other Mac's mouse and keyboard (with the newbie's permission, of course).

(Anyone who's ever tried to help someone troubleshoot over the phone knows *exactly* what this means.)

Nor is playing Bail-Out-the-Newbie the only situation when screen sharing is useful. It's also great for collaborating on a document, showing something to someone for approval, or just freaking each other out. It can also be handy when *you* are the owner of both Macs (a laptop and a desktop, for example), and you want to run a program that you don't have on the Mac that's in front of you. You might want to adjust the playlist selection on the upstairs Mac that's connected to your sound system, for example. Or maybe you just want to keep an eye on what your kids are doing on the Macs upstairs in their rooms.

The controlling person can do *everything* on the controlled Mac, including running programs, messing around the folders and files, and even shutting down the controlled Mac.

Note: Mac OS X is crawling with different ways to use screen sharing. You can do it over a network, over the Internet, and even during an iChat chat.

That method, described in Chapter 12, is much simpler and better than the small-network method described here. It doesn't require names or passwords, it's easy to flip back between seeing the other guy's screen and your own, and you can transfer files by dragging them from your screen to the other guy's (or vice versa).

Then again, the small-network method described here is built right into the Finder, doesn't require logging into iChat, and doesn't require Leopard or Snow Leopard running on both computers.

As always, trying to understand meta concepts like seeing one Mac's screen on the monitor of another can get confusing fast. So in this example, suppose that you want to take control of Mac #1 while seated at Mac #2.

Mac #1: Give Permission in Advance

It would be a chaotic world (although greatly entertaining) if any Mac could randomly take control of any other Mac. Fortunately, though, nobody can see your screen without your explicit permission.

To give such permission, choose →System Preferences→Sharing, and then turn on Screen Sharing (Figure 14-14).

At this point, there are three levels of security to protect your Mac against unauthorized remote-control mischief:

- **Secure.** If you stop here, *anyone with an account on your Mac* will be able to tap in and take control any time they like, even when you're not around. They'll enter the same name and password they'd use if they were sitting at your machine.

    If "anyone" means "you and your spouse" or "you and the other two fourth-grade teachers," then that's probably perfectly fine.

- **Securer.** For greater security, though, you can limit who's allowed to stop in. Click "Only these users" and then click the **+** sign. A small panel appears, listing everyone

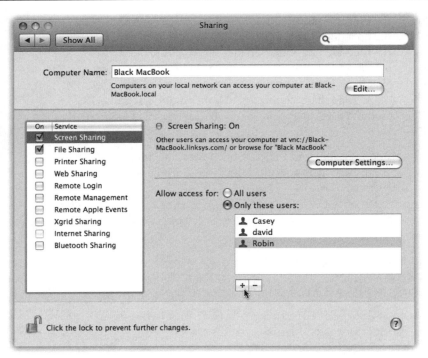

Figure 14-14:
Your Mac is now ready to be observed and even controlled by other machines across the network. The people listed here are allowed to tap in anytime they like, even when you're not at your machine.

with an account on your Mac. Choose the ones you trust not to mess things up while you're away from your Mac (Figure 14-14).

- **Securest.** If you click "Only these users" and then don't add *anyone* to the list, then *nobody* can tap into your screen.

Alternatively, if you're only a *little* bit of a Scrooge, you can set things up so that they can request permission to share your screen—as long as you're sitting in front of your Mac at the time and feeling generous.

To set this up, click Computer Settings and turn on "Anyone may request permission to share screen." Now your fans will have to request permission to enter, and you'll have to grant it (by clicking OK on the screen), in real time, while you're there to watch what they're doing.

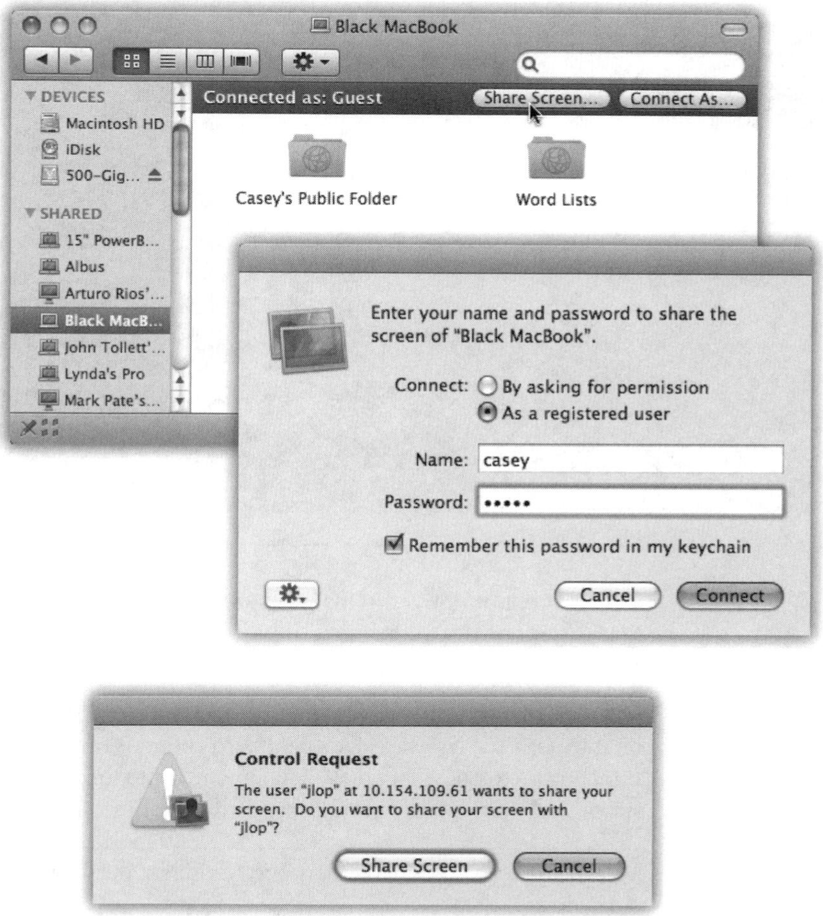

Figure 14-15:
Top: Start by clicking Share Screen in the strip at the top of the other Mac's window.

Middle: If you've been pre-added to the VIP list of authorized screen sharers, as described above, you can sign in with your name and password. If not, you can request permission to share Mac #1's screen. You'll be granted permission only if Mac #1's owner happens to be sitting in front of it at the moment, and has opted to accept such requests.

Bottom: If you request permission, the other person (sitting at Mac #1) sees your request in this form.

Mac #2: Take Control

All right, Mac #1 has been prepared for invasion. Now suppose you're the person on the other end. You're the guru, or the parent, or whoever wants to take control.

Sit at Mac #2 elsewhere on your home or office network. Open a Finder window. Expand the Sharing list in the Sidebar, if necessary, so that you see the icon of Mac #1.

When you click that Mac's icon, the dark strip at the top of the main window displays a button that wasn't there before: Share Screen. Proceed as shown in Figure 14-15.

If you signed in successfully, or if permission is granted, then a weird and wonderful sight appears. As shown in Figure 14-16, your screen now fills with a *second* screen—from the other Mac. You have full keyboard and mouse control to work with that other machine exactly as though you're sitting in front of it.

Figure 14-16:
Don't be alarmed. You're looking at the other Mac's desktop in a window on your *Mac desktop*. You have keyboard and mouse control, and so does the other guy (if he's there); when you're really bored, you can play King of the Cursor. (Note the Screen Sharing toolbar, which has been made visible by choosing View→Show Toolbar.)

Believe it or not, you can actually *copy and paste* material from the remote-controlled Mac to your own—or the other way—thanks to a freaky little wormhole in the timespace continuum.

Just make the toolbar visible (you can see it in Figure 14-16). Click the *second* button on it to copy the faraway Mac's clipboard contents onto *your* Clipboard. Or click the *third* button to put what's on *your* Clipboard onto the *other* Mac's Clipboard. Breathe slowly and drink plenty of fluids, and your brain won't explode.

Note: Unfortunately, there's no way to transfer *files* while screen sharing—only material you've copied *out* of documents.

- **Quitting.** When you hit the ⌘-Q keystroke, you *don't* quit Screen Sharing; you quit whatever program is *running* on the other Mac! So when you're finished having your way with the other computer, choose Screen Sharing→Quit Screen Sharing to return to your own desktop (and your own sanity).

Screen Sharing with Back to My Mac

"Back to My Mac" is intended to simplify the nightmare of remote networking. It works only if you're a MobileMe member, and you have at least two Macs, both running Leopard or Snow Leopard. On each one, you've entered your MobileMe information into the MobileMe pane of System Preferences, and logged in.

Once that's all in place, your Macs behave exactly as though they're on the same home network, even though they're thousands of miles apart across the network.

To set it up, open System Preferences on the first Mac. Click MobileMe, and then click Back to My Mac. Click Start. Close System Preferences. Repeat on each Mac, making sure that they all have the same MobileMe account information.

Now, on each Mac you'll want to "visit" from afar, open the System Preferences→Sharing pane and turn on File Sharing and/or Screen Sharing.

Then, on your laptop in New Zealand, you'll see an entry for Back to My Mac in the Sharing section of your Sidebar. Click to see the icon of your Mac back at home. At this point, you can connect to it for file sharing by clicking Connect As, or take control of it by clicking Share Screen (Figure 14-15).

GEM IN THE ROUGH

Screen Sharing with Windows and Other Oddball Machines

The beauty of Snow Leopard's screen-sharing technology is that it isn't *Snow Leopard's* screen-sharing technology. It's a popular, open standard called VNC (Virtual Network Computing).

Once you've turned on Screen Sharing on your Snow Leopard Mac, any computer on earth with a free VNC client program—sort of a viewer program—can pop onto your machine for a screen share. VNC clients are available for Windows, Linux, pre-Leopard Macs, and even some cellphones.

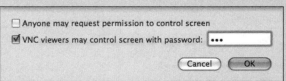

To prepare your Snow Leopard Mac for invasion, open the Sharing pane of System Preferences. Click Screen Sharing,

and click Computer Settings. Turn on "VNC viewers may control screen with password," and make up a password. (VNC doesn't know anything about Mac OS X account passwords, so you're making up one password for sharing your *whole* Mac.)

Give that password to the lucky few who have your trust. Let them plug your Mac's IP address into their VNC clients—or let them connect over your office network, using the address displayed on the Screen Sharing pane ("vnc://Black-MacBook," for example)—and let the sharing begin.

In theory, Back to My Mac spares you an awful long visit to networking hell, because Apple has done all the configuration work for you.

Note: Lots of people can't get Back to My Mac to work. Apple says that the problems are related to (a) this being a new service with some kinks to be worked out, (b) firewall problems, and (c) router incompatibilities.

All the technical details are available online. Go to *http://search.info.apple.com* and do a search for *306672*. (That's the article number that explains the Back to My Mac issues.)

System Preferences

The hub of Mac customization is System Preferences, the modern-day successor to the old Control Panel (Windows) or Control Panels (previous Mac systems). Some of its panels are extremely important, because their settings determine whether or not you can connect to a network or go online to exchange email. Others handle the more cosmetic aspects of customizing Mac OS X.

This chapter guides you through the entire System Preferences program, panel by panel.

Tip: Only a system administrator (page 407) can change settings that affect everyone who shares a certain machine: its Internet settings, Energy Saver settings, and so on. If you see a bunch of controls that are dimmed and unavailable, now you know why.

A tiny padlock in the lower-left corner of a panel is the other telltale sign. If you, a nonadministrator, would like to edit some settings, then call an administrator over to your Mac and ask him to click the lock, input his password, and supervise your tweaks.

The System Preferences Window

You can open System Preferences by choosing its name from the menu, clicking its "light-switch" icon in the Dock, or double-clicking its icon in the Applications folder. At first, the rows of icons are grouped according to function: Personal, Hardware, and so on (Figure 15-1, bottom).

But you can also view them in tidy alphabetical order, as shown at top in Figure 15-1. That can spare you the ritual of hunting through various rows just to find a certain panel icon whose name you already know. (Quick, without looking: Which row is Date & Time in?)

This chapter describes the various panels following this alphabetical arrangement.

Either way, when you click one of the icons, the corresponding controls appear in the main System Preferences window. To access a different preference pane, you have a number of options:

- **Fast:** When System Preferences first opens, the insertion point is blinking in the new System Preferences search box. (If the insertion point is *not* blinking there, press ⌘-F.) Type a few letters of *volume, resolution, wallpaper, wireless,* or whatever feature you want to adjust. In a literal illustration of Spotlight's power, the System Preferences window darkens *except* for the icons where you'll find relevant controls (Figure 15-2). Click the name or icon of the one that looks the most promising.

- **Faster:** Click the Show All icon in the upper-left corner of the window (or press ⌘-L, a shortcut worth learning). Then click the icon of the new panel you want.

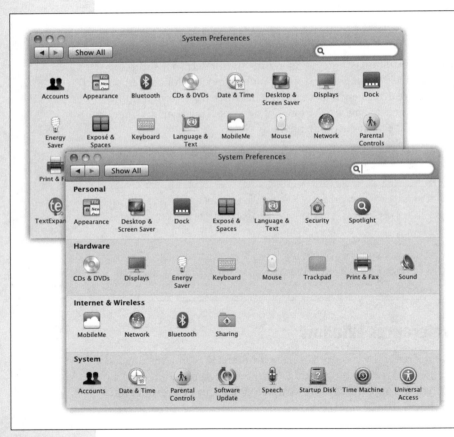

Figure 15-1:
You can view your System Preferences icons alphabetically (top), rather than in rows of arbitrary categories (bottom); just choose View→Organize Alphabetically. This approach not only saves space, but also makes finding a certain panel much easier, because you don't need to worry about which category it's in.

- **Fastest:** Choose any panel's name from the View menu—or from the System Preferences Dock icon pop-up menu described above.

Note: Once System Preferences is actually open, the click-and-hold thing no longer produces the list of all preference panes. Instead, you need to Control-click (or right-click) the System Preferences Dock icon to get that menu.

Here, then, is your grand tour of all 27 of Mac OS X's built-in System Preferences panes. (You may have a couple more or fewer, depending on whether you have a laptop or a desktop Mac. And if you've installed any non-Apple panes, they appear in their own row of System Preferences, called Other.)

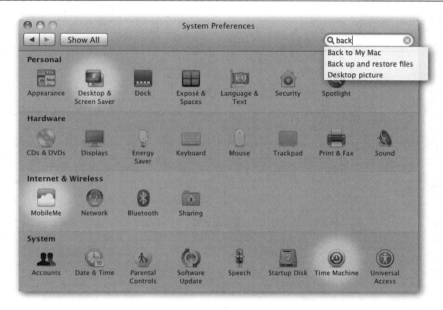

Figure 15-2:
Even if you don't know which System Preferences panel contains the settings you want to change, Spotlight can help. Type into the box at the top, and watch as the "spotlight" shines on the relevant icons. At that point, you can either click the icon, click the name in the pop-up menu, or arrow down the menu and press Return to choose.

Accounts

This is the master list of people who are allowed to log into your Mac, as described in Chapter 13.

Appearance

This panel is mostly about how things look on the screen: windows, menus, buttons, scroll bars, and fonts. Nothing you find here lets you perform any *radical* surgery on the overall Mac OS X look—but you can tweak certain settings to match your personal style.

Changing Colors

Two pop-up menus let you crank up or tone down Mac OS X's overall colorfulness:

- **Appearance.** Choose between Blue and Graphite. Blue refers to Mac OS X's factory setting—bright, candy-colored scroll-bar handles, progress bars, menu, and pulsing OK buttons—and those shiny red, yellow, and green buttons in the corner of every window. If you, like some graphics professionals, find all this circus-poster coloring a bit distracting, then choose Graphite, which renders all those interface elements in various shades of gray.

- **Highlight color.** When you drag your cursor across text, its background changes color to indicate that you've selected it. Exactly what color the background becomes is up to you—just choose the shade you want using the pop-up menu. The Highlight color also affects such subtleties as the lines on the inside of a window as you drag an icon into it.

If you choose Other, the Color Picker palette appears, from which you can choose any color your Mac is capable of displaying (page 167).

Tweaking the Scroll Bars

The two sets of radio buttons control the scroll-bar arrow buttons of all your windows. You can keep these arrows together at one end of the scroll bar, or you can split them up so the "up" arrow sits at the top of the scroll bar and the "down" arrow is at the bottom. (Horizontal scroll bars are similarly affected.) For details on the "Jump to the next page" and "Jump to here" options, see page 36.

You can also turn on these checkboxes:

- **Use smooth scrolling.** This option affects only one tiny situation: when you click (or hold the cursor down) inside the empty area of the scroll bar (not on the handle, and not on the arrow buttons). And it makes only one tiny change: Instead of jumping abruptly from screen to screen, the window lurches with slight accelerations and decelerations, so that the paragraph you're eyeing never jumps suddenly out of view.

- **Minimize when double-clicking a window title bar.** This option provides another way to minimize a window. In addition to the tiny yellow Minimize button at the upper-left corner of the window, you now have a much bigger target—the entire title bar.

Number of Recent Items

Just how many of your recently opened documents and applications do you want the Mac to show using the Recent Items command in the menu? Pick a number from the pop-up menus. For example, you might choose 30 for documents, 20 for programs, and 5 for servers.

Font Smoothing Style

The Mac's built in text-smoothing (*antialiasing*) feature is supposed to produce smoother, more commercial-looking text anywhere it appears on your Mac: in word processing documents, email messages, Web pages, and so on.

Experiment with the on/off checkbox—"Use LCD font smoothing when available," for example—to see how you like the effect. Either way, it's fairly subtle. (See Figure 15-3.) Furthermore, unlike most System Preferences, this one has no effect until the next time you open the program in question. In the Finder, for example, you won't notice the difference until you log out and log back in again.

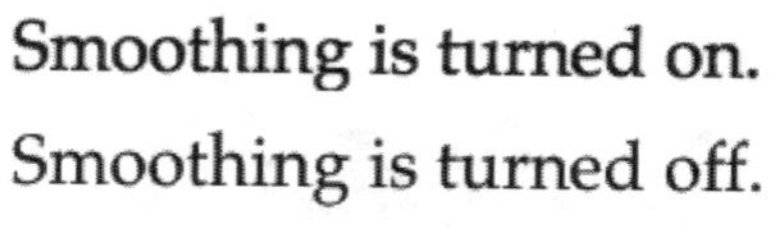

Figure 15-3:
Top: The same 24-point type with text smoothing turned on (top) and off, shown magnified for your inspection pleasure. In Snow Leopard, you no longer get a choice of degrees of smoothing—it's just on or off.

Smoothing is turned on.
Smoothing is turned off.

Turning Off Smoothing on Tiny Fonts

At smaller type sizes (10-point and smaller), you might find that text is actually *less* readable with font smoothing turned on. It all depends upon the font, the size, your monitor, and your taste. For that reason, this pop-up menu lets you choose a cutoff point. If you choose 12 here, for example, then 12-point (and smaller) type still appears crisp and sharp; only larger type, such as headlines, displays the graceful edge smoothing. You can choose a size cutoff as low as 4-point.

(None of these settings affect your printouts, only the onscreen display.)

Bluetooth

Bluetooth is a short-range, low-power, wireless *cable-elimination* technology. It's designed to connect gadgets in pairings that make sense, like cellphone+earpiece, wireless keyboard+Mac, or Mac+cellphone (to connect to the Internet or to transmit files).

Now, you wouldn't want the guy in the next cubicle to be able to operate *your* Mac using *his* Bluetooth keyboard. So the first step in any Bluetooth relationship is *pairing*, where you formally introduce the two gadgets that will be communicating. Here's how that goes:

1. **Open System Preferences→Bluetooth.**

   Make sure the On checkbox is turned on. (The only reason to turn it off is to save laptop battery power.) Also make sure Discoverable is turned on; that makes the Mac "visible" to other Bluetooth gadgets in range.

2. **Click the + button below the list at left.**

   The Bluetooth Setup Assistant opens. After a moment, it displays the names of all Bluetooth gadgets it can sniff out: nearby headsets, laptops, cellphones, and so on. Usually, it finds the one you're trying to pair.

3. Click the gadget you want to connect to, and then click Continue.

If you're pairing a mobile phone or something else that has a keypad or keyboard, the Mac now displays a large, eight-digit *passcode*. It's like a password, except you'll have to input it only this once, to confirm that *you* are the true owner of both the Mac and the gadget. (If it weren't for this passcode business, some guy next to you at the airport could enjoy free laptop Internet access through the cellphone in *your* pocket.)

At this point, your phone or palmtop displays a message to the effect that you have 30 seconds to type that passcode. Do it. When the gadget asks if you want to pair with the Mac and connect to it, say yes.

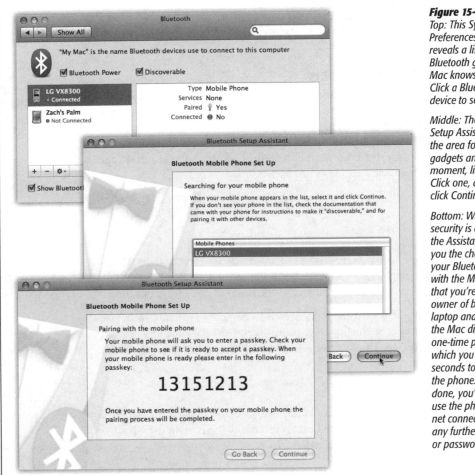

Figure 15-4:
Top: This System Preferences panel reveals a list of every Bluetooth gadget your Mac knows about. Click a Bluetooth device to see details.

Middle: The Bluetooth Setup Assistant scans the area for Bluetooth gadgets and, after a moment, lists them. Click one, and then click Continue.

Bottom: Where security is an issue, the Assistant offers you the chance to pair your Bluetooth device with the Mac. To prove that you're really the owner of both the laptop and the phone, the Mac displays a one-time password, which you have 30 seconds to type into the phone. Once that's done, you're free to use the phone's Internet connection without any further muss, fuss, or passwords.

If you're pairing a phone or palmtop, the Mac now asks *which* sorts of Bluetooth syncing you want to do. For example, it can copy your iCal appointments, as well as your Address Book, to the phone or palmtop.

(Or, if there are *no* kinds of Bluetooth syncing that your Mac can do with the gadget—for example, unless your cellphone offers Bluetooth file transfers, there may be nothing it can accomplish by talking to your Mac—an error message tells you that, too.)

When it's all over, the new gadget is listed in the left-side panel, in the list of Bluetooth cellphones, headsets, and other stuff that you've previously introduced to this Mac. Click the **+** button to open the Bluetooth Setup Assistant again, or the **−** button to delete one of the listed items.

And then there's the ✿ button. On first click, it's a pop-up menu that says only, "Show More Info." If you select that item and then click ✿ again, you get a pop-up menu with a few Bluetooth utility commands.

CDs & DVDs

This handy pane (Figure 15-5) lets you tell the Mac what it should do when it detects that you've inserted a CD or DVD. For example, when you insert a music CD, you probably want iTunes to open automatically so you can listen to the CD or convert its musical contents to MP3 or AAC files on your hard drive. Similarly, when you insert a picture CD (such as a Kodak Photo CD), you probably want iPhoto to open in readiness to import the pictures from the CD into your photo collection. And when you insert a DVD from Blockbuster, you want the Mac's DVD Player program to open.

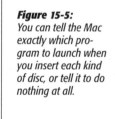

Figure 15-5:
You can tell the Mac exactly which program to launch when you insert each kind of disc, or tell it to do nothing at all.

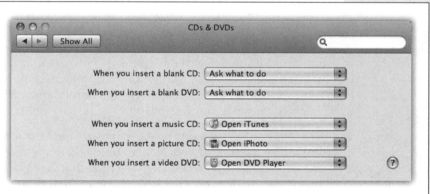

For each kind of disc (blank CD, blank DVD, music CD, picture CD, or video DVD), the pop-up menu lets you choose options like these:

- **Ask what to do.** A dialog box appears that asks what you want to do with the newly inserted disc.

- **Open (iDVD, iTunes, iPhoto, DVD Player…).** The Mac can open a certain program automatically when you insert the disc. When the day comes that somebody writes a better music player than iTunes, or a better digital shoebox than iPhoto, then you can use the "Open other application" option.

- **Run script.** If you someday become handy writing or downloading AppleScript programs (page 559), you can schedule one of your own scripts to take over from here. For example, you can set things up so that inserting a blank CD automatically copies your Home folder onto it for backup purposes.

- **Ignore.** The Mac won't do anything when you insert a disc except display its icon on the desktop. (If it's a blank disc, the Mac does nothing at all.)

Date & Time

Your Mac's conception of what time it is can be very important. Every file you create or save is stamped with this time, and every email you send or receive is marked with this time. As you might expect, setting your Mac's clock is what the Date & Time pane is all about.

Date & Time Tab

Click the Date & Time tab. If your Mac is online, turn on "Set date & time automatically" and be done with it. Your Mac sets its own clock by consulting a highly accurate scientific clock on the Internet. (No need to worry about daylight saving time, either; the time servers take that into account.)

Tip: If you have a full-time Internet connection (cable modem or DSL, for example), you may as well leave this checkbox turned on, so your Mac's clock is always correct. If you connect to the Internet by dial-up modem, however, turn off the checkbox, so your Mac won't keep trying to dial spontaneously at all hours of the night.

If you're not online and have no prospect of getting there, you can also set the date and time manually. To change the month, day, or year, click the digit that needs changing and then either (a) type a new number or (b) click the little arrow buttons. Press the Tab key to highlight the next number. (You can also specify the day of the month by clicking a date on the minicalendar.)

To set the time of day, use the same technique—or, for more geeky fun, you can set the time by dragging the hour, minute, or second hands on the analog clock. Finally, click Save. (If you get carried away with dragging the clock hands around and lose track of the *real* time, click the Revert button to restore the panel settings.)

Tip: If you're frustrated that the Mac is showing you the 24-hour "military time" on your menu bar (that is, 17:30 instead of 5:30 p.m.)—or that it isn't showing military time when you'd like it to—click the Clock tab and turn "Use a 24-hour clock" on or off.

Time Zone Tab

You'd be surprised how important it is to set the time zone for your Mac. If you don't do so, the email and documents you send out—and the Mac's conception of what documents are older and newer—could be hopelessly skewed.

You can teach your Mac where it lives by using what may be Snow Leopard's snazziest new feature: its ability to set its own time zone *automatically*. That's an especially useful feature if you're a laptop warrior who travels a lot.

Just turn on "Set time zone automatically using current location" (Figure 15-6). If possible—which means "if you're in an area populated enough to have a lot of WiFi hot spots, which the Mac triangulates to determine its location"—the Mac will think for a moment and then, before your eyes, drop a pin onto the world map to represent your location—and set the time zone automatically. (The world map goes black-and-white to show that you can no longer set your location manually.)

Often, you'll be told that the Mac is "Unable to determine current location at this time." In that case, specify your location manually, as shown in Figure 15-6.

Figure 15-6:
To set your time zone the quick and dirty way, click a section of the map to indicate your general region of the world. To teach the Mac more precisely where you are in that time zone, use the Closest City pop-up menu. (Or, instead of using the pop-up menu with the mouse, you can also highlight the text in the Closest City box. Then start typing your city name until the Mac gets it.)

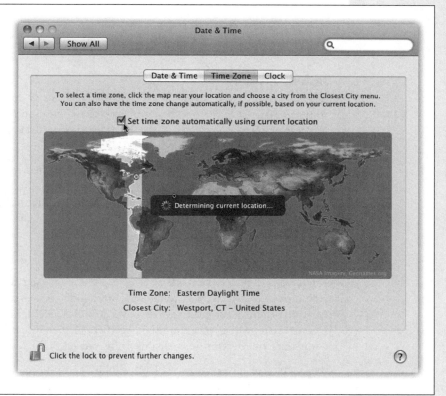

Clock Tab

In the Clock pane, you can specify whether or not you want the current time to appear, at all times, at the right end of your menu bar. You can choose between two different clock styles: digital (3:53 p.m.) or analog (a round clock face). You also get several other options that govern this digital clock display: the display of seconds, whether or not you want to include designations for a.m. and p.m., the day of the week, a blinking colon, and the option to use a 24-hour clock.

In Snow Leopard, the menu-bar clock can show not just the time, not just the day of the week, but also today's *date*. Turn on the "Show the day of the week" and "Show date" checkboxes if you want to see, for example, "Wed May 5 7:32 PM" on your menu bar.

If you decide you don't need all that information—if your menu bar is crowded enough as it is—you can always look up today's day and date just by *clicking* the time on your menu bar. A menu drops down revealing the complete date. The menu also lets you switch between digital and analog clock types and provides a shortcut to the Date & Time preferences pane.

Desktop & Screen Saver

This panel offers two ways to show off Mac OS X's glamorous graphics features: *desktop pictures* and *screen savers*.

Desktop Pictures

Mac OS X comes with several ready-to-use collections of desktop pictures, ranging from *National Geographic*–style nature photos to plain solid colors. To install a new background picture, first choose one of the image categories in the list at the left side of the window, as shown in Figure 15-7.

Your choices include Desktop Pictures (muted, soft-focus swishes and swirls), Nature (bugs, water, snow leopard, outer space), Plants (flowers, soft-focus leaves), Black & White (breathtaking monochrome shots), Abstract (swishes and swirls with wild colors), Patterns (a pair of fabric close-ups), or Solid Colors (simple grays, blues, and greens).

Using your own pictures

Of course, you may feel that decorating your Mac desktop is much more fun if you use one of your *own* pictures. You can use any digital photo, scanned image, or graphic you want in almost any graphics format (JPEG, PICT, GIF, TIFF, Photoshop, and—just in case you hope to master your digital camera by dangling its electronic instruction manual in front of your nose each morning—even PDF).

That's why icons for your own Pictures folder and iPhoto albums also appear here, along with a **+** button that lets you choose *any* folder of pictures. When you click one of these icons, you see thumbnail versions of its contents in the main screen to its right. Just click the thumbnail of any picture to apply it immediately to the desktop. (There's no need to remove the previously installed picture first.)

Tip: If there's one certain picture you like, but it's not in any of the listed sources, you can drag its image file onto the well (the miniature desktop displayed in the Desktop panel). A thumbnail of your picture instantly appears in the well and, a moment later, the picture is plastered across your monitor.

Making the picture fit

Unless you've gone to the trouble of editing your chosen photo so that it matches the precise dimensions of your screen (1280 × 854 pixels, for example), it probably isn't exactly the same size as your screen.

Figure 15-7:
Using the list of picture sources at left, you can preview an entire folder of your own images before installing one specific image as your new desktop picture. Use the + button to select a folder of assorted graphics—or, if you're an iPhoto veteran, click an iPhoto album name, as shown here. Clicking one of the thumbnails installs the corresponding picture on the desktop.

Fortunately, Mac OS X offers a number of solutions to this problem. Using the pop-up menu just to the right of the desktop preview well, you can choose Fit to Screen, Fill Screen, Stretch, Center, or Tile, each of which enlarges the picture (relative to your screen) in a different way.

Auto picture-changing

The novelty of any desktop picture, no matter how interesting, is likely to fade after several months of all-day viewing. That's why the randomizing function is so delightful.

Turn on "Change picture" at the bottom of the dialog box. From the pop-up menu, specify when you want your background picture to change: "Every day," "Every 15 minutes," or, if you're *really* having trouble staying awake at your Mac, "Every 5 seconds." (The option called "When waking from sleep" refers to the *Mac* waking from sleep, not its owner.)

Finally, turn on "Random order," if you like. If you leave it off, your desktop pictures change in alphabetical order by file name.

That's all there is to it. Now, at the intervals you specified, your desktop picture changes automatically, smoothly cross-fading between the pictures in your chosen source folder like a slideshow. You may never want to open another window, because you'll hate to block your view of the show.

Screen Saver

On the Screen Saver panel, you can create your own screen-saver slideshows—an absolute must if you have an Apple Cinema Display and a cool Manhattan loft apartment.

Tip: Of course, a screen saver doesn't really save your screen. LCD flat-panel screens, the only kind Apple sells, are incapable of "burning in" a stationary image of the sort that originally inspired the creation of screen savers years ago.

No, these screen savers offer two unrelated functions. First, they mask what's on your screen from passersby whenever you leave your desk. Second, they're kind of fun.

When you click a module's name in the Screen Savers list, you see a mini version of it playing back in the Preview screen. Click Test to give the module a dry run on your full monitor screen.

When you've had enough of the preview, just move the mouse or press any key. You return to the Screen Saver panel.

Apple provides a few displays to get you started, in two categories: Apple and Pictures.

Apple

Here are some of the best Apple screen savers:

- **Arabesque.** Your brain will go crazy trying to make sense of the patterns of small circles as they come and go, shrink and grow. But forget it; this module is all just drugged-out randomness.

- **iTunes Artwork.** Somebody put a lot of work into the album covers for the CDs whose music you own—so why not enjoy them as art? This module builds a gigantic mosaic of album art from *your* music collection, if you have one. The tiles periodically flip around, just to keep the image changing. (The Options button lets you specify how many rows of album-art squares appear, and how often the tiles flip.)

- **RSS Visualizer.** Here, buried 43 layers deep in the operating system, is one of Mac OS X's most spectacular and useful features: the RSS Visualizer. When this screen saver kicks in, it shows a jaw-dropping, 3-D display of headlines (news and other items) slurped in from the Safari Web browser's *RSS reader*. (RSS items, short for

Really Simple Syndication or Rich Site Summary, are like a cross between email messages and Web pages—they're Web items that get sent directly to you. Details in Chapter 11 and 12.)

After the introductory swinging-around-an-invisible-3-D-pole-against-a-swirling-blue-sky-background sequence, the screen saver displays one news blurb at a time. Each remains on the screen just long enough for you to get the point of the headline. Beneath, in small type, is the tantalizing instruction, "Press the '3' key to continue." (It's a different number key for each headline.) If you do, indeed, tap the designated key, you leave the screen saver, fire up Safari, and wind up on a Web page that contains the complete article you requested.

The whole thing is gorgeous, informative, and deeply hypnotic. Do not use while operating heavy equipment.

Tip: Click Options to specify which Web site's RSS feed you want displayed.

- **Word of the Day.** A parade of interesting words drawn from the Dictionary program. You're invited to tap the D key to open the dictionary to that entry to read more. Build your word power!

Tip: Click Options to specify which dictionary you want: the standard New Oxford American, or the Japanese one.

Pictures

The screen savers in this category are all based on the slideshowy presentation of photos. You can choose from three presentations of pictures in whatever photo group you choose, as represented by the three Display Style buttons just below the screen-saver preview.

- **Slideshow** displays one photo at a time; they slowly zoom and cut into each other.

- **Collage** sends individual photos spinning randomly onto the "table," where they lie until the screen is full.

Tip: The Options button here offers the "Present slides in random order" button, plus a "Collage style" pop-up menu that lets you add each photo's name and date to its white, Polaroid-style border.

- **Mosaic** will blow your mind; see Figure 15-8.

Tip: Click the Options button to specify the speed of the receding, the number of photos that become pixels of the larger photo, and whether or not you want the composite photos to appear in random order.

In any case, all these photo-show options are available for whatever photo set you choose from the list at left. These are your choices:

- **Abstract, Beach, Cosmos, Forest, Nature Patterns, Paper Shadow.** Abstract features psychedelic swirls of modern art. In the Beach, Cosmos, Forest, and Nature screen savers, you see a series of tropical ocean scenes, deep space objects, lush rain forests, and leaf/flower shots. Paper Shadow is a slideshow of undulating, curling, black-and-white shadowy abstract forms.

Each creates an amazingly dramatic, almost cinematic experience, worthy of setting up to "play" during dinner parties like the lava lamps of the '70s.

Figure 15-8:
This feeble four-frame sample will have to represent, on this frozen page, the stunning animated pull-out that is the Mosaic screen saver.

It starts with one photo (top); your "camera" pulls back farther and farther, revealing that that photo is just one in a grid—a huge grid— that's comprised of all your photos.

As you pull even further back, each photo appears so small that it becomes only one dot of another photo—from the same collection!

And then that one starts shrinking, and the cycle repeats, on and on into infinity.

- **iPhoto albums.** If you're using iPhoto to organize your digital photos, you'll see its familiar album and Event lists here, making it a snap to choose any of your own photo collections for use as a screen saver.

- **MobileMe albums.** One of the perks of paying $100 per year for a MobileMe membership is the ability to create slideshows online. If you've published some of them, their names show up here.

Weirder yet, you can also enjoy a screen saver composed of photos from *somebody else's* MobileMe gallery. ("Oh, look, honey, here's some shots of Uncle Jed's crops this summer!")

Click the **+** button and choose MobileMe Gallery. You're asked which member's slideshow collection you want to view and how you want it to appear (Figure 9-9).

Figure 15-9:
Once you enter a MobileMe member's name, you're shown that person's list of public photo albums. At this point, you can also specify how you want the screen saver to look: Turn off the crossfade between slides, crop the slides so they fit on the screen, present the slides in random order, and so on.

Whichever screen-saver module you use, you have two further options:

- **Use random screen saver.** If you can't decide which one of the modules to use, turn on this checkbox. The Mac chooses a different module each time your screen saver kicks in.

- **Show with clock.** This option just superimposes the current time on whatever screen saver you've selected. You'd be surprised at how handy it can be to use your Mac as a giant digital clock when you're getting coffee across the room.

Activating the screen saver

You can control when your screen saver takes over in a couple of ways:

- **After a period of inactivity.** Using the "Start screen saver" slider, you can set the amount of time that has to pass without keyboard or mouse activity before the screen saver starts. The duration can be as short as 3 minutes or as long as 2 hours, or you can drag the slider to Never to prevent the screen saver from ever turning on by itself.

Tip: The screen saver can auto-lock your Mac after a few minutes (and require the password to get back in)—a great security safety net when you wander away from your desk. See page 437.

- **When you park your cursor in the corner of the screen.** If you click the Hot Corners button, you see that you can turn each corner of your monitor into a *hot corner* (Figure 15-10).

Tip: You can find dozens more screen saver modules from Apple. To look them over, click the **+** button below the list; choose Browse Screen Savers. You're taken to *www.apple.com/downloads/macosx/icons_ screensavers*, where you can choose from a selection of amazing add-on screen-saver modules. (The older ones may not be compatible with Snow Leopard's new 64-bit design, however.)

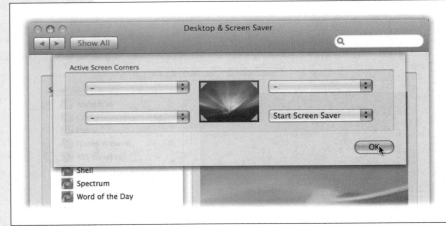

Figure 15-10:
Click the Hot Corners button to open this "sheet," which lets you designate certain corners of your screen as instant-activation spots, or never-come-on spots. Sliding the mouse to the Start Screen Saver corner, for example, turns on your screen saver right away.

Displays

Displays is the center of operations for all your monitor settings. Here, you set your monitor's *resolution*, determine how many colors are displayed onscreen, and calibrate color balance and brightness.

Tip: You can open up this panel with a quick keystroke from any program on the Mac. Just press Option as you tap one of the screen-brightness keys on the top row of your keyboard.

The specific controls depend on the kind of monitor you're using, but here are the ones you'll most likely see:

Display Tab

This tab is the main headquarters for your screen controls. It governs these settings:

- **Resolutions.** All Mac screens today can make the screen picture larger or smaller, thus accommodating different kinds of work. You perform this magnification or reduction by switching among different *resolutions* (measurements of the number of dots that compose the screen). The Resolutions list displays the various resolution settings your monitor can accommodate: 800 × 600, 1024 × 768, and so on.

  When you use a low-resolution setting, such as 800 × 600, the dots of your screen image get larger, thus enlarging (zooming in on) the picture—but showing a smaller slice of the page. Use this setting when playing a small QuickTime movie, for example, so that it fills more of the screen. (Lower resolutions usually look blurry on flat-panel screens, though.) At higher resolutions, such as 1280 × 800, the screen dots get smaller, making your windows and icons smaller, but showing more overall area. Use this kind of setting when working on two-page spreads in your page-layout program, for example.

Tip: You can adjust the resolution of your monitor without having to open System Preferences. Just turn on "Show displays in menu bar," which adds a Displays pop-up menu (a menulet) to the right end of your menu bar for quick adjustments. (If you choose Number of Recent Items—did Apple really mean for this command to say that?—then you can adjust how many common resolutions are listed in this menulet.)

- **Automatically adjust brightness as ambient light changes.** This option appears only if you have a Mac laptop with a light-up keyboard. In that case, your laptop's light sensor also dims the screen automatically in dark rooms—*if* this checkbox is turned on. (Of course, you can always adjust the keyboard lighting manually, by tapping the .☼. and .☼. keys.)

Arrangement Tab

From the dawn of the color-monitor era, Macs have had a terrific feature: the ability to exploit multiple monitors all plugged into the computer at the same time. Any Mac with a video-output jack (laptops, iMacs), or any Mac with a second or third video card (Power Macs, Mac Pros), can project the same thing on both screens (*mirror mode*); that's useful in a classroom when the "external monitor" is a projector.

But it's equally useful to make one monitor act as an *extension* of the next. For example, you might have your Photoshop image window on your big monitor but keep all the Photoshop controls and tool palettes on a smaller screen. Your cursor passes from one screen to another as it crosses the boundary.

You don't have to shut down the Mac to hook up another monitor. Just hook up the monitor or projector and then choose Detect Displays from the Displays *menulet.*

When you open System Preferences, you see a different Displays window on each screen, so that you can change the color and resolution settings independently for each. Your Displays menulet shows two sets of resolutions, too, one for each screen.

If your Mac can show different images on each screen, then your Displays panel offers an Arrangement tab, showing a miniature version of each monitor. By dragging these icons around relative to each other, you can specify how you want the second monitor's image "attached" to the first. Most people position the second monitor's image to the right of the first, but you're also free to position it on the left, above, below, or even directly on top of the first monitor's icon (the last of which produces a video-mirroring setup). For the least likelihood of going insane, consider placing the real-world monitor into the same position.

For committed multiple-monitor fanatics, the fun doesn't stop there. See the microscopic menu bar on the first-monitor icon? You can drag that tiny strip onto a different monitor icon, if you like, to tell Displays where you'd like your menu bar to appear. (And check out how most screen savers correctly show different stuff on each monitor!)

Color Tab

When you click Calibrate, the Display Calibrator Assistant opens to walk you through a series of six screens, presenting various brightness and color-balance settings in each screen. You pick the settings that look best to you; at the end of the process, you save your monitor tweaks as a ColorSync profile that ColorSync-savvy programs can use to adjust your display for improved color accuracy.

Dock

See Chapter 2 for details on the Dock and its System Preferences pane.

Energy Saver

The Energy Saver program helps you and your Mac in a number of ways. By blacking out the screen after a period of inactivity, it prolongs the life of your monitor. By putting the Mac to sleep half an hour after you've stopped using it, Energy Saver cuts down on electricity costs and pollution. On a laptop, Energy Saver extends the length of the battery charge by controlling the activity of the hard drive and screen.

Best of all, this pane offers the option to have your computer turn off each night automatically—and turn on again at a specified time in anticipation of your arrival at the desk.

Sleep Sliders

The Energy Saver controls are different on a laptop Mac and a desktop Mac, but both present a pair of sliders (Figure 15-11).

The top slider controls when the Mac will automatically go to sleep—anywhere from 1 minute after your last activity to Never. (Activity can be mouse movement, keyboard action, or Internet data transfer; Energy Saver won't put your Mac to sleep in the middle of a download.)

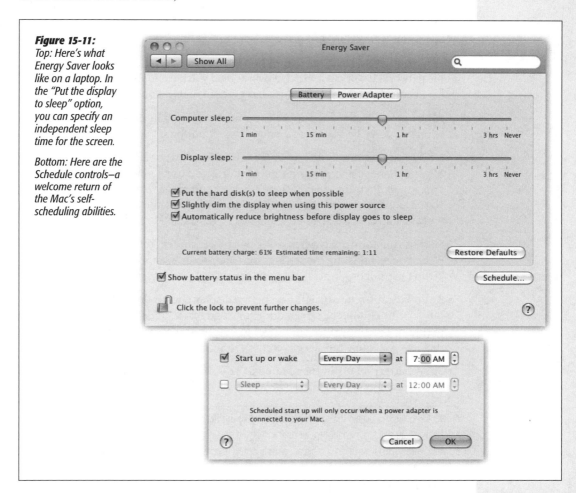

Figure 15-11:
Top: Here's what Energy Saver looks like on a laptop. In the "Put the display to sleep" option, you can specify an independent sleep time for the screen.

Bottom: Here are the Schedule controls—a welcome return of the Mac's self-scheduling abilities.

At that time, the screen goes dark, the hard drive stops spinning, and your processor chip slows to a crawl. Your Mac is now in *sleep* mode, using only a fraction of its usual electricity consumption. To wake it up when you return to your desk, press any key. Everything you were working on, including open programs and documents, is still onscreen, exactly as it was. (To turn off this automatic sleep feature entirely, drag the slider to Never.)

The second slider controls when the *screen* goes black to save power. These days, there's really only one good reason to put the screen to sleep independently of the Mac itself: so that your Mac can run its standard middle-of-the-night maintenance routines, even while the screen is off to save power.

Checkbox Options

Below the sliders, you see a selection of power-related options that may include:

- **Put the hard disk(s) to sleep when possible.** This saves even more juice—and noise—by letting your drives stop spinning when not in use. The downside is a longer pause when you return to work and wake the thing up, because it takes a few seconds for your hard drive to "spin up" again.

- **Wake for network access.** This option lets you access a sleeping Mac from across the network. It works on wired networks or, if you have an AirPort or Time Capsule base station and a 2008-or-later Mac, even on wireless ones.

- **Allow power button to put the computer to sleep.** On desktop Macs, it can be handy to sleep the Mac just by tapping its ⏻ button.

- **Start up automatically after a power failure.** This is a good option if you leave your Mac unattended and access it remotely, or if you use it as a network file server or Web server. It ensures that, if there's even a momentary blackout that shuts down your Mac, it starts itself right back up again when the juice returns. (On a laptop, it's available only when you're adjusting Power Adapter mode.)

- **Slightly dim the display when using this power source.** You see this checkbox only when you're adjusting the settings for battery-power mode on a laptop. It means "Don't use full brightness, so I can save power."

- **Automatically reduce brightness before display goes to sleep.** When this option is on for your laptop, the screen doesn't just go black suddenly after the designated period of inactivity; instead, it goes to half brightness as a sort of drowsy mode that lets you know full sleep is coming soon.

- **Show battery status in the menu bar.** This on/off switch (laptops only) controls the battery menulet at the top of your screen.

Note: On a laptop, notice the two tabs at the top of the dialog box. They let you create different settings for the two states of life for a laptop, when it's plugged in (Power Adapter) and when it's running on battery power (Battery). That's important, because on a laptop, every drop of battery power counts.

Scheduled Startup and Shutdown

By clicking the Schedule button, you can set up the Mac to shut itself down and turn itself back on automatically (Figure 15-11, bottom).

If you work 9 to 5, for example, you can set the office Mac to turn itself on at 8:45 a.m. and shut itself down at 5:30 p.m.—an arrangement that conserves electricity, saves money, and reduces pollution, but doesn't inconvenience you in the least. In fact, you may come to forget that you've set up the Mac this way, since you'll never actually see it turn itself off.

Note: The Mac doesn't shut down automatically if you've left unsaved documents open onscreen. It will go to sleep, though.

Exposé & Spaces

Exposé and Spaces, the two ingenious window- and screen-management features of Mac OS X, are described in detail in Chapter 4—and so is this joint-venture control panel.

Keyboard

This panel lets you do some frivolous fine-tuning of your keyboard. Here's a tour.

Keyboard

On this pane, you have:

- **Key Repeat Rate, Delay Until Repeat.** You're probably too young to remember the antique once known as the *typewriter.* On some electric versions of this machine, you could hold down the letter X key to type a series of XXXXXXXs—ideal for crossing something out in a contract, for example.

  On the Mac, *every* key behaves this way. Hold down any key long enough, and it starts spitting out repetitions, making it easy to type, for example, "No WAAAAAAAY!" or "You go, girrrrrrrrrl!" These two sliders govern this behavior. On the right: a slider that determines how long you must hold down the key before it starts repeating (to prevent triggering repetitions accidentally, in other words). On the left: a slider that governs how fast each key spits out letters once the spitting has begun.

- **Use all F1, F2, etc. keys as standard function keys.** This option appears *only* on laptops and aluminum-keyboard Macs. It's complicated, so read page 223 slowly.

- **Illuminate keyboard in low light conditions.** This setting appears only if your Mac's keyboard does, in fact, light up when you're working in the dark—a showy feature of many Mac laptops. You can specify that you want the internal lighting to shut off after a period of inactivity (to save power when you've wandered away, for example), or you can turn the lighting off altogether. (You can always adjust the keyboard brightness manually, of course, by tapping the ⚬ and ⚬ keys.)

- **Show Keyboard & Character Viewer in menu bar.** You can read all about these special symbol-generating windows on pages 169-170.

- **Modifier Keys.** This button lets you turn off, or remap, the functions of the Option, Caps Lock, Control, and ⌘ keys. It's for Unix programmers whose pinkies can't adjust to the Mac's modifier-key layout—and for anyone who keeps hitting Caps Lock by accident during everyday typing.

Keyboard Shortcuts

This pane lets you make up new keystrokes for just about any function on the Mac. You can come up with keyboard combinations that, for example, are easier to remember, harder to trigger by accident, or easier to hit with one hand.

Step-by-step instructions for using this pane appear on page 143.

Language & Text

The primary job of this pane, formerly called International, is to set up your Mac to work in other languages. Details appear on page 166.

MobileMe

This panel is of no value unless you've signed up for a MobileMe account. See Chapter 10 for details.

Mouse

This pane, newly split apart from the Keyboard & Mouse panel that kicked around the Mac OS for decades, looks different depending on what kind of mouse (if any) is attached to your Mac.

Tracking Speed, Double-Click Speed

It may surprise you that the cursor on the screen doesn't move 5 inches when you move the mouse 5 inches on the desk. Instead, the cursor moves farther when you move the mouse faster.

How *much* farther depends on how you set the first slider here. The Fast setting is nice if you have an enormous monitor, since you don't need an equally large mouse pad to get from one corner to another. The Slow setting, on the other hand, forces you to pick up and put down the mouse frequently as you scoot across the screen. It offers very little acceleration, but it can be great for highly detailed work like pixel-by-pixel editing in Photoshop.

The Double-Click Speed setting specifies how much time you have to complete a double-click. If you click too slowly—beyond the time you've allotted yourself with this slider—the Mac "hears" two *single* clicks instead.

Snow Leopard Spots: If you have a real mouse attached, you also see the magnificent "Zoom using scroll wheel while holding Control" checkbox at the bottom of this pane. What this means is that you can magnify the entire screen, zooming in, by turning the little ball or wheel atop your mouse while you press the Control key. It's great for reading tiny type, examining photos up close, and so on.

The Mighty Mouse and Magic Mouse

If you have an Apple Mighty Mouse (the white capsule-shaped mouse that came with desktop Macs from 2005 to 2009) or Magic Mouse (the winglike, multitouch-surface mouse that arrived in 2009)—then the Mouse pane is a much fancier affair (Figure 15-12).

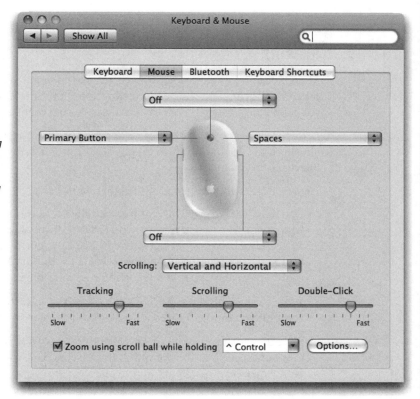

Figure 15-12:
This enormous photographic display shows up only if you have the Mighty Mouse, Apple's "two-button" mouse. The pop-up menus let you program the right, left, and side buttons. They offer functions like opening Dashboard, triggering Exposé, and so on.

This is also where you can turn the right-clicking feature on (just choose Secondary Button from the appropriate pop-up menu)—or swap the right- and left-click buttons' functions.

On a laptop without any mouse attached, the Mouse pane still appears in System Preferences—but its sole function is to help you "pair" your Mac with a wireless Bluetooth mouse.

Network

See Chapter 14 for the settings you need to plug in for networking.

Parental Controls

These controls are described at length in Chapter 12.

Print & Fax

Chapter 9 describes printing and faxing in detail. This panel offers a centralized list of the printers you've introduced to the Mac.

Security

See Chapter 13 for details on locking up your Mac.

Sharing

Mac OS X is an upstanding network citizen, flexible enough to share its contents with other Macs, Windows PCs, people dialing in from the road, and so on. On this panel, you'll find on/off switches for each of these sharing channels.

In this book, many of these features are covered in other chapters. For example, **Screen Sharing** and **File Sharing** are in Chapter 14; **Printer Sharing** is in Chapter 9; **Internet Sharing** is in Chapter 10.

Here's a quick rundown some of the other items here:

- **DVD or CD Sharing.** This feature was added to accommodate the MacBook Air laptop, which doesn't have a built-in CD/DVD drive. When you turn on this option, any MacBook Airs on the network can "see," and borrow, your Mac's DVD drive, for the purposes of installing new software or running Mac disk-repair software. (Your drive shows up under the Remote Disc heading in the Air's Sidebar.)

- **Web Sharing.** This single checkbox turns your Mac into a full-fledged Web server—a computer that provides Web pages to any visitors on the Internet.

  Place the actual Web pages (in HTML format) into your Home→Sites folder. Then give out the URL at the bottom of the Sharing pane to any prospective visitors: family members, neighbors, and so on.

Note: Unless you have an Internet connection that's on all the time (like a DSL or cable connection), your visitors will only be able to access the Web site when you are *also* online.

- **Bluetooth Sharing.** This pane lets you set up Bluetooth file sharing, a way for other people near you to shoot files over to (or receive files from) your laptop—without muss, fuss, or passwords. Page 560 has details.

Software Update

Whenever Apple improves or fixes some piece of Mac OS X or some Apple-branded program, the Software Update program can notify you, download the update, and install it into your system automatically. These updates may include new versions of programs like iPhoto and iMovie; drivers for newly released printers, scanners, cameras, and such; bug fixes and security patches; and so on.

Software Update doesn't download the new software without asking your permission first and explicitly telling you what it plans to install, as shown in Figure 15-13.

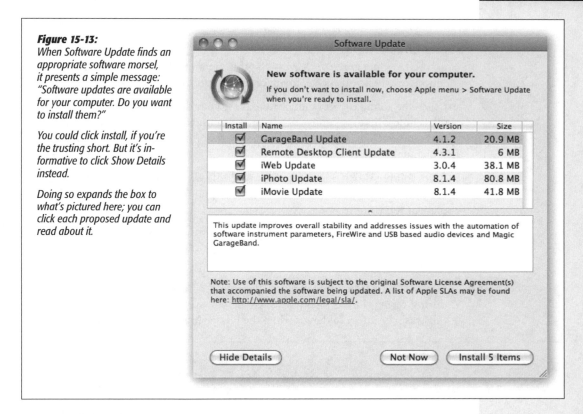

Figure 15-13:
When Software Update finds an appropriate software morsel, it presents a simple message: "Software updates are available for your computer. Do you want to install them?"

You could click install, if you're the trusting short. But it's informative to click Show Details instead.

Doing so expands the box to what's pictured here; you can click each proposed update and read about it.

Scheduled Check Tab

For maximum effortlessness, turn on the "Check for updates" checkbox and then select a frequency from the pop-up menu—daily, weekly, or monthly. If you also turn on "Download updates automatically," you'll still be notified before anything gets installed, but you won't have to wait for the downloading—the deed will already be done.

(If you've had "Check for updates" turned off, you can always click the Check Now button to force Mac OS X to report in to see if new patches are available.)

Installed Software

Software Update also keeps a meticulous log of everything it drops into your system. On this tab, you see them listed, for your reference pleasure.

Sound

Using the panes of the Sound panel, you can configure the sound system of your Mac in any of several ways.

Tip: Here's a quick way to jump directly to the Sound panel of System Preferences—from the keyboard, without ever having to open System Preferences or click Sound. Just press Option as you tap the ◄, ◄), or ◄)) key on the top row of your Apple keyboard.

Sound Effects Tab

"Sound effects" means *error beeps*—the sound you hear when the Mac wants your attention, or when you click someplace you shouldn't.

Just click the sound of your choice to make it your default system beep. Most of the canned choices here are funny and clever, yet subdued enough to be of practical value as alert sounds (Figure 15-14). As for the other controls on the Sound Effects panel, they include these:

- **Alert volume slider.** Some Mac fans are confused by the fact that even when they drag this slider all the way to the left, the sound from games and music CDs still plays at full volume.

  The actual *main* volume slider for your Mac is the "Output volume" slider at the bottom of the Sound pane. The "Alert volume" slider is *just* for error beeps; Apple was kind enough to let you adjust the volume of these error beeps independently.

- **Play user interface sound effects.** This option produces a few subtle sound effects during certain Finder operations: when you drag something off the Dock, into the Trash, or into a folder, or when the Finder finishes a file-copying job.

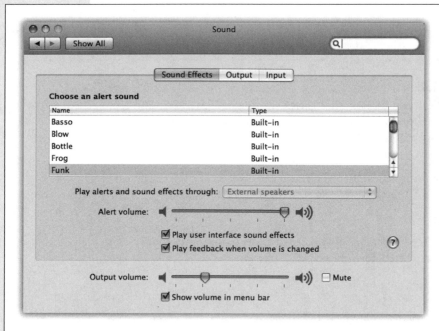

Figure 15-14:
You can adjust your overall speaker volume independently from the alert-beep volume, thank goodness. Tip nerds should note that you can also adjust the alert volume by holding down the Option key as you drag the handle in the speaker-volume menulet (on your menu bar).

- **Play feedback when volume is changed.** Each time you press one of the volume keys (◄, ◄◐, ◄》), the Mac beeps to help you gauge the current volume.

  That's all fine when you're working at home. But more than one person has been humiliated in an important meeting when the Mac made a sudden, inappropriately loud sonic outburst—and then amplified that embarrassment by furiously and repeatedly pressing the volume-down key, beeping all the way.

  If you turn off this checkbox, the Mac won't make any sound at all as you adjust its volume. Instead, you'll see only a visual representation of the steadily decreasing (or increasing) volume level.

Tip: The Shift key reverses the logic. So if you have "Play feedback" turned on, holding down Shift as you tap the volume keys makes them silent. If it's turned off, you can force the volume-gauging beeps to play by pressing Shift as you tap the volume keys.

- **Play Front Row sound effects.** You can read about Front Row, which turns your screen into a giant multimedia directory for your entire Mac, in Chapter 16. All this option does is silence the little clicks and whooshes that liven up the proceedings when you operate Front Row's menus.

Output Tab

"Output" means speakers or headphones. For most people, this pane offers nothing useful except the Balance slider, with which you can set the balance between your Mac's left and right stereo speakers. The "Select a device" wording seems to imply that you can choose which speakers you want to use for playback. But Internal Speakers is generally the only choice, even if you have external speakers. (The Mac uses your external speakers automatically when they're plugged in.)

A visit to this pane is necessary, however, if you want to use USB speakers or a Bluetooth or USB phone headset. Choose its name from the list.

Input Tab

This panel lets you specify which sound source you want the Mac to "listen to," if you have more than one connected: external microphone, internal microphone, line input, USB headset, or whatever. It also lets you adjust the sensitivity of that microphone—its *input volume*—by dragging the slider and watching the real-time Input level meter above it change as you speak. Put another way, it's a quick way to see if your microphone is working.

The "Use ambient noise reduction" is great if you make podcasts or use dictation software. It turns any mike into what amounts to a noise-canceling microphone, deadening the background noise while you're recording.

If you'd prefer even more control over your Mac's sound inputs and outputs, don't miss the rewritten Audio/MIDI Setup program in your Applications→Utilities folder.

Speech

The Mac can read any text out loud to you—a Web page, a Word document, whatever—and it can even take spoken commands (sort of). But it's a long story. To read it, consult the free downloadable PDF appendix to this chapter, "Speech on the Mac," from this book's "Missing CD" page at *www.missingmanuals.com*.

Spotlight

These options for the Mac's Spotlight search command are described in Chapter 3.

Startup Disk

Use this panel to pick the System Folder your Mac will use the next time it starts up—when you're swapping between Mac OS X and Windows (running with Boot Camp), for example. Check out the details in Chapter 8.

Time Machine

Here's the master on/off switch and options panel for Time Machine, which is described starting on page 277.

Trackpad

This panel, present only on laptops, keeps growing with each successive MacBook generation. (It's shown in Figure 1-3 on page 14.)

At the top, you find duplicates of the same Tracking Speed and Double-Click Speed sliders described under "Mouse" earlier in this chapter—but these let you establish independent tracking and clicking speeds for the *trackpad*. (There's even a new Scrolling slider, too, so you can control how fast the Mac scrolls a document when you drag two fingers down the trackpad.)

Trackpad Gestures

You may love your Mac laptop now, but wait until you find out about these special features. They make your laptop *crazy* better. It turns out you can point, click, scroll, right-click, rotate things, enlarge things, hide windows, and switch programs—all on the trackpad itself, without a mouse and without ever having to lift your fingers.

Apple keeps adding new "gestures" with each new laptop, so yours may not offer all these options. But here's what you might see. (If you point to one of these items without clicking, a movie illustrates each of these maneuvers right on the screen.)

One Finger
- **Tap to Click.** Usually, you touch your laptop's trackpad only to move the cursor. For clicking and dragging, you're supposed to use the clicking button *beneath* the trackpad (or, on the latest models, click the trackpad surface itself).

Many people find, however, that it's more direct to tap and drag directly on the trackpad, using the same finger that's been moving the cursor. That's the purpose of this checkbox. When it's on, you can tap the trackpad surface to register a mouse click at the location of the cursor. Double-tap to double-click.

- **Dragging.** This option lets you move icons, highlight text, or pull down menus—in other words, to drag, not just click—using the trackpad.

Start by tapping twice on the trackpad, then *immediately* after the second tap, begin dragging your finger. (If you don't start moving promptly, the laptop assumes that you were double-clicking.) You can stroke the trackpad repeatedly to continue your movement, as long as your finger never leaves the trackpad surface for more than about a second. When you "let go," the drag is considered complete.

- **Drag Lock.** If you worry that you're going to "drop" what you're dragging if you stop moving your finger, turn on this option instead. Once again, begin your drag by double-clicking, then move your finger immediately after the second click.

When this option is on, however, you can take your sweet time in continuing the movement. In between strokes of the trackpad, you can take your finger off the laptop for as long as you like. You can take a phone call, a shower, or a vacation; the Mac still thinks that you're in the middle of a drag. Only when you tap *again* does the laptop consider the drag a done deal.

Two Fingers

- **Scroll.** This one is *sweet.* You have to try it to believe it. It means that dragging *two* fingers across your trackpad scrolls whatever window is open, just as though you had slid over to the scroll bar and clicked there. Except doing it with your two fingers, right in place, is infinitely faster and less fussy. You even get a Scrolling *Speed* slider.

- **Rotate.** Place two fingers on the trackpad, and then twist them around an invisible center point, to rotate a photo or a PDF document. This doesn't work in all programs or in all circumstances, but it's great for turning images upright in the Finder, Preview, iPhoto, Image Capture, and so on.

- **Pinch Open & Close.** If you've used an iPhone, this one will seem familiar. What it means is, "Put two fingers on the trackpad and spread them apart to *enlarge* what's on the screen. Slide two fingers *together* to shrink it down again." It doesn't work in every program—it affects icons on the desktop, pictures in Preview and iPhoto, text in Safari, and so on—but it's great when it does.

- **Screen zoom.** Here's another irresistible feature. It lets you zoom into the screen image, magnifying the whole thing, just by dragging two fingers up or down the trackpad while you're pressing the Control key. You can zoom in so far that the word "zoom" in 12-point type fills the entire monitor.

This feature comes in handy with amazing frequency. It's great for reading Web pages in tiny type, or enlarging Web movies, or studying the dot-by-dot construction of a button or icon that you admire. Just Control-drag upward to zoom in, and Control-drag downward to zoom out again.

You can click Options to customize this feature. For example, you can substitute the Option or ⌘ key, if Control isn't working out for you. Furthermore, you can specify how you want to scroll around within your zoomed-in screen image. The factory setting, "Continuously with pointer," is actually pretty frustrating; the whole screen shifts around whenever you move the cursor. ("So the pointer is at or near the center of the image" is very similar.) "Only when the pointer reaches an edge" is a lot less annoying, and lets you *use* the cursor (to click buttons, for example) without sending the entire screen image darting away from you.

Tip: Also in the Options box: the ability to turn off the pixel-smoothing feature that adds a certain blurriness to the zoomed-in image—and a reminder that you can press Option-⌘-\ (backslash) to turn it on or off.

- **Secondary click.** This means "right-click." Right-clicking is a huge deal on the Mac; it unleashes useful features just about everywhere.

  On all Mac laptops, you can trigger a right-click by clicking with your thumb while resting your index and middle fingers on the trackpad.

  On the latest laptops—the ones with no separate clicker button—there's another option: a pop-up menu that lets you designate a certain trackpad corner (bottom right, for example) as the right-click spot. Clicking there triggers a right-click—to open a shortcut menu, for example. Weird, but wonderful.

Three Fingers
- **Swipe to Navigate.** Drag three fingers horizontally across the trackpad to skip to the next or previous page or image in a batch. Here again, this feature doesn't work in all programs, but it's great for flipping through images or PDF pages in Preview or iPhoto.

Four Fingers
- **Swipe Up/Down for Exposé.** A four-finger swipe *up* the trackpad triggers the "Show desktop" function of Exposé. A four-finger drag *downward* triggers the "Show all windows" function instead. Swipe the opposite direction to restore the windows.

- **Swipe Left/Right to Switch Applications.** A four-finger swipe left or right makes the ⌘-Tab program switcher appear so that you can point to a different program's icon and switch to it with a click.

Tip: If you have Apple's Magic Mouse, you can use similar gestures right on the surface of the mouse itself. *Drag one finger across the mouse* to scroll in any direction (even diagonally). *Swipe horizontally with two fingers* to go to the Previous/Next photo in iPhoto or Preview, Web page, or item in iTunes. *Drag one finger vertically while pressing the Control key* to zoom in or out of the screen.

Universal Access

The Universal Access panel is designed for people who type with one hand, find it difficult to use a mouse, or have trouble seeing or hearing. (These features can also be handy when the mouse is broken or missing.)

Accessibility is a huge focus for Apple, and in Snow Leopard, there are more features than ever for disabled people, including compatibility with Braille screens (yes, there is such a thing). In fact, there's a whole Apple Web site dedicated to explaining all these features: *www.apple.com/macosx/accessibility.*

Here, though, is an overview of the noteworthiest features.

Seeing Tab (Magnifying the Screen)

If you have trouble seeing the screen, then boy, does Mac OS X have features for you (Figure 15-15).

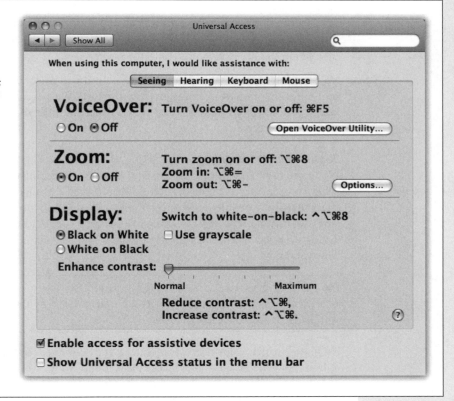

Figure 15-15:
You'll be amazed at just how much you can zoom into the Mac's screen using this Universal Access pane. In fact, there's nothing to stop you from zooming in so far that a single pixel fills the entire monitor. (That may not be especially useful for people with limited vision, but it can be handy for graphic designers learning how to reproduce a certain icon, dot by dot.)

VoiceOver

One option is VoiceOver, which makes the Mac *read out loud* every bit of text that's on the screen (See the free PDF "VoiceOver" appendix to this chapter on this book's "Missing CD" at *www.missingmanuals.com.*)

Zoom

Another quick solution is to reduce your monitor's *resolution*—thus magnifying the image—using the Displays panel described earlier in this chapter. If you have a 17-inch or larger monitor set to, say, 640 × 480, the result is a greatly magnified picture. That method doesn't give you much flexibility, however, and it's a hassle to adjust. If you agree, then try the Zoom feature that appears here; it lets you enlarge the area surrounding your cursor in any increment.

Tip: If you have a laptop, just using the Control-key trackpad trick described on page 499 is a far faster and easier way to magnify the screen. If you have a mouse, turning the wheel or trackpea (or dragging vertically on the Magic Mouse) while pressing Control is also much faster. Both of those features work even when this one is turned Off.

To make it work, press Option-⌘-8 as you're working. Or, if the Seeing panel is open, click On in the Zoom section. That's the master switch.

No zooming actually takes place, however, until you press Option-⌘-plus sign (to zoom in) or Option-⌘-minus sign (to zoom out). With each press, the entire screen image gets larger or smaller, creating a virtual monitor that follows your cursor around the screen.

Display (inverted colors)

While you're at it, pressing Control-Option-⌘-8, or clicking the "Switch to Black on White" button, inverts the colors of the screen, so that text appears white on black—an effect that some people find easier to read. (This option also freaks out many Mac fans who turn it on by *mistake*, somehow pressing Control-Option-⌘-8 by accident during everyday work. They think the Mac's expensive monitor has just gone loco. Now you know better.)

Tip: There's also a button called Use Grayscale, which banishes all color from your screen. This is another feature designed to improve text clarity, but it's also a dandy way to see how a color document will look when printed on a monochrome laser printer.

No matter which color mode you choose, the "Enhance contrast" slider is another option that can help. It makes blacks blacker and whites whiter, further eliminating in-between shades and thereby making the screen easier to see. (If the Universal Access panel doesn't happen to be open, you can always use the keystrokes Control-Option-⌘-< and Control-Option-⌘-> to decrease or increase contrast.)

Hearing Tab (Flashing the Screen)

If you have trouble hearing the Mac's sounds, the obvious solution is to increase the volume, which is why this panel offers a direct link to the Sound preferences pane.

Fortunately, hearing your computer usually isn't critical (except when working in music and audio, of course). The only time audio is especially important is when the Mac tries to get your attention by beeping. For those situations, turn on "Flash the screen when an alert sound occurs" (an effect you can try out by clicking the Flash Screen button). Now you'll see a white flash across the entire monitor whenever the Mac would otherwise beep—not a bad idea on laptops, actually, so that you don't miss beeps when you've got the speakers muted.

(The "Play stereo audio as mono" option is intended for people with hearing loss in one ear. This way, you won't miss any of the musical mix just because you're listening through only one headphone.)

Keyboard Tab (Typing Assistance)

This panel offers two clever features designed to help people who have trouble using the keyboard.

- **Sticky Keys** lets you press multiple-key shortcuts (involving keys like Shift, Option, Control, and ⌘) one at a time instead of all together.

  To make Sticky Keys work, first turn on the master switch at the top of the dialog box. Then go to work on the Mac, triggering keyboard commands as shown in Figure 15-16.

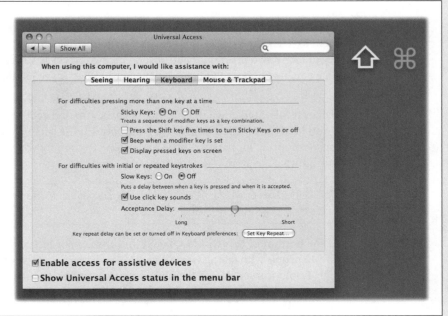

Figure 15-16:
Whenever you want to press a multiple-key keystroke like Shift-⌘-D, press them one at a time. You'll see ghost images of these keys superimposed on your screen, as though to show you which keystrokes you've added to your temporary collection. To "un-press" a key you've already pressed, press it again twice.

If you press a modifier key *twice,* meanwhile, you lock it down. (Its onscreen symbol gets brighter to let you know.) When a key is locked, you can use it for several commands in a row. For example, if a folder icon is highlighted, you could double-press ⌘ to lock it down—and then type O (to open the folder), look around, and then press W (to close the window). Press the ⌘ key a third time to "unpress" it.

Tip: The checkbox called "Press the Shift key five times to turn Sticky Keys on or off" gives you the flexibility of turning Sticky Keys on and off at will, without even taking a trip to System Preferences. Whenever you want to turn on Sticky Keys, press the Shift key five times in succession. You'll hear a special clacking sound effect alerting you that you just turned on Sticky Keys. (Repeat the five presses to turn Sticky Keys off again.)

- **Slow Keys,** on the other hand, doesn't register a key press at all until you've held down the key for more than a second or so—a feature designed to screen out accidental key presses.

  If "Use click key sounds" is turned on, you'll hear a little typing sound each time you press a key—but none of these key presses registers unless you hold the key down for a moment. (Use the Acceptance Delay slider to govern this threshold.)

  You hear a different sound when the Mac actually accepts the key press—and, of course, you see the letter you typed appear onscreen.

Mouse & Trackpad Tab (Cursor Control from the Keyboard)

Mouse Keys is designed to help people who can't use the mouse—or who want more precision when working in graphics programs. It lets you click, drag, and otherwise manipulate the cursor by pressing the keys on your numeric keypad. (It's not very useful on keyboards that don't *have* separate numeric keypads, like laptops.)

When Mouse Keys is turned on, the 5 key acts as the clicker—hold it down for a moment to "click the mouse," do that twice to double-click, and so on. Hold down the 0 key to lock down the mouse button, and the period key to unlock it. (The amount of time you have to hold them down depends on how you've set the Initial Delay slider.)

Move the cursor around the screen by pressing the eight keys that surround the 5 key. (For example, hold down the 9 key to move the cursor diagonally up and to the right.) If you hold one of these keys down continuously, the cursor, after a pause, begins to move smoothly in that direction—according to the way you've adjusted the sliders called Initial Delay and Maximum Speed.

Tip: The checkbox called "Press the Option key five times to turn Mouse Keys on or off" saves you the trouble of opening System Preferences.

At the bottom of this window, you'll find the Cursor Size slider. It's a godsend not only to people with failing vision, but also to anyone using one of Apple's large, super-high-resolution screens; as the pixel density increases, the arrow cursor gets smaller and smaller. This slider lets you make the arrow cursor larger—much larger, if you like—making it much easier to see.

The Free Programs

R ight out of the box, Mac OS X comes with a healthy assortment of nearly 50 freebies: programs for sending email, writing documents, doing math, even playing games. Some are dressed-up versions of Mac programs that have been around for years. Others, though, are new programs that not only show off some of Mac OS X's most dramatic new technologies, but also let you get real work done without having to invest in additional software.

These programs reside in two important folders on your hard drive: Applications (in the main hard drive window) and Utilities (within the Applications folder). The Applications folder houses the productivity programs; Utilities holds a couple of dozen maintenance programs for setting up printers and network connections, fixing problems on your hard disk, and so on.

Tip: You can jump straight to the Applications folder in the Finder by pressing Shift-⌘-A, or by clicking the Applications button in the Finder Sidebar (it's the icon that looks like an *A*). Similarly, Shift-⌘-U takes you to the Utilities folder.

You might consider adding the Application and Utilities folders' icons to the right side of your Dock, too, so that you can access them no matter what program you're in.

This chapter guides you through the most important Apple-supplied items in your new software library, one program at a time. (Of course, your Applications list may vary. Apple might have blessed your particular Mac model with some bonus programs, or you may have downloaded or installed some on your own.)

Address Book

The Address Book is a database that stores names, addresses, email addresses, phone numbers, and other contact information. See page 349.

Automator

Automator is another program that lets you teach your Mac what to do, step by step. But it's easier to use than AppleScript, because you don't have to type any commands. Instead, you assemble a series of visual building blocks called *actions*. Drag actions into the right order, click a big Run button, and your Mac faithfully runs through the list of steps you've given it.

This, too, is a program that most Mac fans will rarely explore. But if you're curious, by all means download the free appendix to this chapter, called "Automator.pdf." It's available on this book's "Missing CD" page at *www.missingmanuals.com*.

Calculator

The Calculator is much more than a simple four-function memory calculator. It can also act as a scientific calculator for students and scientists, a conversion calculator for metric and U.S. measures, and even a currency calculator for world travelers.

The little Calculator widget in the Dashboard is quicker to open, but the standalone Calculator program is far more powerful. For example:

- Calculator has three modes: Basic, Advanced, and Programmer (Figure 16-1). Switch among them by choosing from the View menu (or pressing ⌘-1 for Basic, ⌘-2 for Advanced, or ⌘-3 for Programmer).

Tip: You can also cycle among the three modes by repeatedly clicking what, on most windows, is the Zoom button (the green round dot at upper left). It's a first for the Mac—a Zoom button that changes function each time you click it—but it's kind of neat.

- You can operate Calculator by clicking the onscreen buttons, but it's much easier to press the corresponding number and symbol keys on your keyboard.

- As you go, you can make Calculator speak each key you press. The Mac's voice ensures that you don't mistype as you keep your eyes on the receipts in front of you, typing by touch.

  Just choose Speech→Speak Button Pressed to turn this feature on or off. (You choose *which* voice does the talking in the Speech panel of System Preferences.)

Tip: If you have a pre-2008 laptop, you probably have an embedded numeric keypad, superimposed on the right side of the keyboard and labeled on the keys in a different color ink. When you press the Fn key in the lower-left corner of the keyboard, typing these keys produces the numbers instead of the letters. (You can also press the NumLock key to stay in number mode, so you don't have to keep pressing Fn.)

- Press the C key to clear the calculator display.

- Once you've calculated a result, you can copy it (using Edit→Copy, or ⌘-C) and paste it directly into another program.

- Calculator even offers Reverse Polish Notation (RPN), a system of entering numbers that's popular with some mathematicians, programmers, and engineers, because it lets them omit parentheses. Choose View→RPN to turn it on and off.

Tip: How cool is this? In most programs, you don't need Calculator or even a Dashboard widget. Just highlight an equation (like 56*32.1-517) right in your document, and press ⌘-Shift-8. Presto—Mac OS X replaces the equation with the right answer. This trick works in TextEdit, Mail, Entourage, FileMaker, and many other programs.

And if you ever find that it doesn't work, remember that the Spotlight menu is now a calculator, too. Type or paste an equation into the Spotlight search box; instantly, the answer appears in the results menu.

Figure 16-1:
The Calculator program offers a four-function Basic mode, a full-blown scientific calculator mode, and a programmer's calculator (shown here, and capable of hex, octal, decimal, and binary notation). The first two modes offer a "paper tape" feature (View→Show Paper Tape) that lets you correct errors made way back in a calculation. To edit one of the numbers on the paper tape, drag through it, retype, and then click Recalculate Totals. You can also save the tape as a text file by choosing File→Save Tape As, or print it by selecting File→Print Tape.

Conversions

Calculator is more than a calculator; it's also a conversion program. No matter what units you're trying to convert—meters, grams, inches, miles per hour, money—Calculator is ready.

Now, the truth is, the Units Converter widget in Dashboard is simpler and better than this older Calculator feature. But if you've already got Calculator open, here's the drill:

1. **Clear the calculator (for example, type the letter C on your keyboard). Type in the starting measurement.**

   To convert 48 degrees Celsius to Fahrenheit, for example, type *48*.

2. **From the Convert menu, choose the kind of conversion you want.**

   In this case, choose Temperature. When you're done choosing, a dialog box appears.

3. **Use the pop-up menus to specify which units you want to convert to and from.**

   To convert Celsius to Fahrenheit, choose Celsius from the first pop-up menu, and Fahrenheit from the second.

4. **Click OK.**

   That's it. The Calculator displays the result—in degrees Fahrenheit, in this example.

The next time you want to make this kind of a calculation, you can skip steps 2, 3, and 4. Instead, just choose your desired conversion from the Convert→Recent Conversions submenu.

Calculator is especially amazing when it comes to *currency* conversions—from pesos to American dollars, for example—because it actually does its homework. It goes online to download up-to-the-minute currency rates to ensure that the conversion is accurate. (Choose Convert→Update Currency Exchange Rates.)

Tip: If you're working with big numbers, don't forget to turn on View→Show Thousands Separators. Calculator will add commas (like 1,242,939) to help you read your big numbers more easily.

Chess

Mac OS X comes with only one game, but it's a beauty (Figure 16-2). It's a traditional chess game played on a gorgeously rendered board with a set of realistic 3-D pieces.

Playing a Game of Chess

When you launch Chess, you're presented with a fresh, new game that's set up in Human vs. Computer mode—meaning that you, the Human (light-colored pieces) get to play against the Computer (your Mac, on the dark side). Drag the chess piece of your choice into position on the board, and the game is afoot.

If you choose Game→New Game, however, you're offered a pop-up menu with choices like Human vs. Computer, Human vs. Human, and so on. If you switch the pop-up menu to Computer vs. Human, you and your Mac trade places; the Mac takes the white side of the board and opens the game with the first move, and you play the black side.

Tip: The same New Game dialog box also offers a pop-up menu called Variant, which offers three other chess-like games: Crazyhouse, Suicide, and Losers. The Chess help screens (choose Help→Chess Help, and then click "Starting a new chess game") explain these variations.

On some night when the video store is closed and you're desperate for entertainment, you might also want to try the Computer vs. Computer option, which pits your Mac against itself. Pour yourself a beer, open a bag of chips, and settle in to watch until someone—either the Mac or the Mac—gains victory.

Figure 16-2:
You don't have to be terribly exact about grabbing the chess pieces when it's time to make your move. Just click anywhere within a piece's current square to drag it into a new position on the board (shown here in its Marble incarnation). And how did this chess board get rotated like this? Because you can grab a corner of the board and rotate it in 3-D space. Cool!

Dashboard

Dashboard, described in Chapter 5, is a true-blue, double-clickable application. As a result, you can remove its icon from your Dock, if you like.

Dictionary

For word nerds everywhere, the Dictionary (and Thesaurus) is a blessing—a handy way to look up word definitions, pronunciations, and synonyms. To be precise, Snow Leopard now comes with electronic versions of *seven* reference works in one:

- The entire *New Oxford American Dictionary*.

- The complete *Oxford American Writers Thesaurus*.

- A new dictionary of Apple terms, from A/UX to widget. (Apparently there aren't any Apple terms that begin with X, Y, or Z.)

- Wikipedia. Of course, this famous open-source, citizen-created encyclopedia isn't actually on your Mac. All Dictionary does is give you an easy way to search the *online* version, and display the results right in the comfy Dictionary window.

- A Japanese dictionary, thesaurus, and Japanese-to-English translation dictionary.

Tip: You don't ordinarily see the Japanese reference books. You have to turn them on in Dictionary→Preferences.

Mac OS X also comes with about a million ways to look up a word:

- **Double-click the Dictionary icon.** You get the window shown at top in Figure 16-3. As you type into the Spotlight-y search box, you home in on matching words; double-click a word, or highlight it and press Return, to view a full, typographically elegant definition, complete with sample sentence and pronunciation guide.

Tip: And if you don't recognize a word in the definition, click *that word* to look up *its* definition. (Each word turns blue and underlined when you point to it, as a reminder.) You can then double-click again in *that* definition—and on, and on, and on.

(You can then use the History menu, the ◄ and ► buttons on the toolbar, or the ⌘-[and ⌘-] keystrokes to go back and forward in your chain of lookups.)

It's worth exploring the Dictionary→Preferences dialog box, by the way. There, you can choose U.S. or British pronunciations and adjust the font size.

- **Press F12.** Yes, the Dictionary is one of the widgets in Dashboard (page 155).

- **Right-click a highlighted word in a Cocoa program.** From the shortcut menu, choose Look Up in Dictionary. The Dictionary program opens to that word. (Or visit the Dictionary's Preferences box and choose "Open Dictionary panel." Now you get a panel that pops out of the highlighted word instead.)

- **Point to a word in a Cocoa program, and then press Control-⌘-D.** That keystroke makes the definition panel sprout right from the word you were pointing to. (The advantage here, of course, is that you don't have to highlight the word first.)

Tip: Here's a trick for the informationally thirsty Mac fan (or speed reader). Once you've invoked the Control-⌘-D keystroke, keep the Control and ⌘ keys pressed. Now drag the cursor across the text. As you push the mouse around, the definition pops up for every word you touch.

Got a big screen or poor eyesight? Then bump up the type size. Dictionary's toolbar has bigger/smaller buttons, and there's a Font Size pop-up menu in the Preferences window.

DVD Player

DVD Player, your Mac's built-in movie projector, is described in Chapter 9.

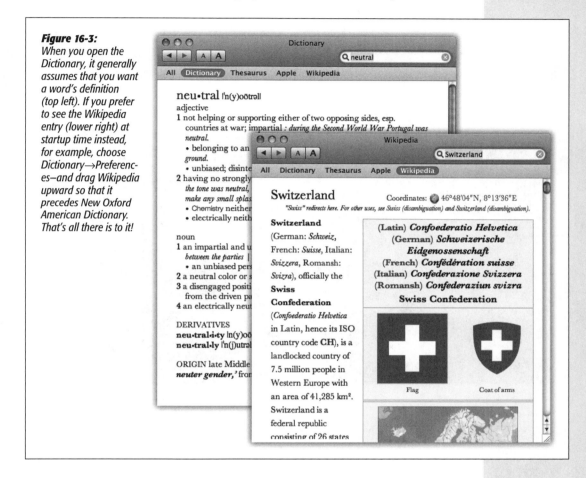

Figure 16-3:
When you open the Dictionary, it generally assumes that you want a word's definition (top left). If you prefer to see the Wikipedia entry (lower right) at startup time instead, for example, choose Dictionary→Preferences—and drag Wikipedia upward so that it precedes New Oxford American Dictionary. That's all there is to it!

Font Book

For details on this font-management program, see Chapter 9.

Front Row

For the last few years, most new Mac models have come with a peculiar accessory: a slim white remote control, looking for all the world like an iPod that's lost too much weight. If you point it at the Mac and press the remote's Menu button, you're catapulted into the magic world of Front Row, a special overlay that provides access to your music, photos, movies, and DVD player—with super-big fonts and graphics that are visible from the couch across the room.

It might seem a little bit weird, then, to hear that Front Row, the software, now comes on *all* Macs, even the ones that didn't come with a remote control and don't have an infrared sensor.

That's because you can operate Front Row entirely from the keyboard—even from across the room, if you have a Bluetooth wireless one. So now even infrared-less Macs like the Mac Pro are invited to the Front Row party.

As shown in Figure 16-4, Front Row is all about drilling down from one menu into another.

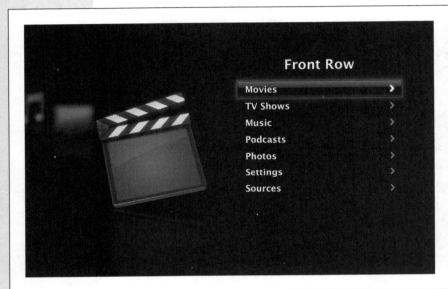

Figure 16-4:
Front Row is all about drilling down through the menu screens, exactly as on an iPod. Start here, on the main menu. Use the center button on the remote, or the space bar on your keyboard, to select a command or category and open the next screen. Keep going like that until you're watching your movies or slideshows, or listening to your music.

Use the arrow keys or the + and − buttons on the remote to choose the activity you're interested in: Music, Photos, DVD, or Videos. Use the space bar or the ▶ button as the Return key to choose that kind of entertainment. You'll find, to your delight, that Front Row lets you fire up not only all the music you've got in iTunes, all the photos in iPhoto, and so on, but also all the music, photos, and videos stored on other Macs on your network (assuming you've left iPhoto and iTunes running on those Macs).

Your Mac is now an entertainment center that can be operated from across the room.

Here, then, is the cheat sheet for navigating your Mac's entertainment collections—whether you have a Front Row remote or not.

How to	Using the Remote	Using the Keyboard
Open and close Front Row	Menu	⌘-Esc
Navigate menus and lists	+, −	↑, ↓
Return to a previous menu	Menu	Esc
Select an item in a menu or list	▶❚❚	space bar or Return

Play and pause audio or video	▶ ❚❚	space bar or Return
Change volume	**+, −**	↑, ↓
Go to the next/previous song, photo, or DVD chapter	◄◄/▶▶	→, ←
Rewind/fast-forward (DVD or movie)	◄◄/▶▶ (press and hold the button)	→, ← (hold down)

GarageBand

GarageBand, Apple's do-it-yourself music construction kit, isn't actually part of Mac OS X. If you have a copy, that's because it's part of the iLife suite that comes on every new Mac (along with iMovie, iPhoto, and iWeb). There's a crash-course bonus chapter on this book's "Missing CD" page at *www.missingmanuals.com*.

iCal

In many ways, iCal is not so different from those "Hunks of the Midwest Police Stations" paper calendars people leave hanging on the walls for months past their natural life span.

Tip: iCal's Dock icon displays today's date—even when iCal isn't running.

But iCal offers several advantages over paper calendars. For example:

- It can automate the process of entering repeating events, such as weekly staff meetings or gym workouts.

- iCal can give you a gentle nudge (with a sound, a dialog box, or even an email) when an important appointment is approaching.

- iCal can share information with your Address Book program, with Mail, with your iPod or iPhone, with other Macs, with "published" calendars on the Internet, or with a Palm organizer. Some of these features require one of those MobileMe accounts described in Chapter 10. But iCal also works fine on a single Mac, even without an Internet connection.

- iCal can subscribe to other people's calendars. For example, you can subscribe to your spouse's calendar, thereby finding out when you've been committed to after-dinner drinks on the night of the big game.

  iCal can display your company's Exchange calendar, too. For those details, see page 200.

Working with Views

When you open iCal, you see something like Figure 16-5. By clicking one of the View buttons above the calendar, you can switch among these views:

- **Day** shows the appointments for a single day in the main calendar area, broken down by time slot.

  If you choose iCal→Preferences, you can specify what hours constitute a workday. This is ideal both for those annoying power-life people who get up at 5 a.m. for two hours of calisthenics and the more reasonable people who sleep until 11 a.m.

Tip: iCal provides three quick ways to get to the current day's date. Click Today (upper-left corner), choose View→Go to Today, or press ⌘-T.

- **Week** fills the main display area with seven columns, reflecting the current week. (You can establish a five-day work week instead in iCal→Preferences.)

Tip: If you double-click the date above the calendar, you open the day view for that day.

- **Month** shows the entire month that contains the current date (Figure 16-5). Double-click a date number to open the day view for that date.

  To save space, iCal generally doesn't show you the *times* of your appointments in Month view. If you'd like to see them anyway, choose iCal→Preferences, click General, and turn on "Show time in month view."

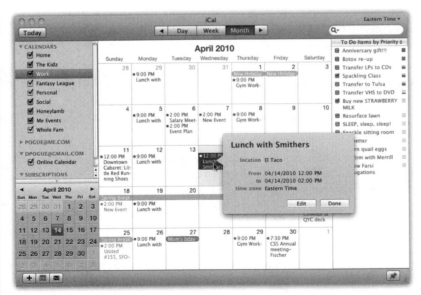

Figure 16-5:
In iCal, the miniature navigation calendar (lower left) provides an overview of adjacent months. You can jump to a different week or day by clicking the ◄ and ► buttons, and then clicking within the numbers. Double-click any appointment to see the summary balloon shown here. You can hide the To Do list either by using the View→Hide To Dos command or by clicking the thumbtack button in the lower-right corner.

Tip: If your mouse has a scroll wheel, you can use it to great advantage in iCal. For example, when entering a date, turning the wheel lets you jump forward or backward in time. It also lets you change the priority level of a To Do item you're entering, or even tweak the time zone as you're setting it.

In any of the views, *double-click* an appointment to see more about it. The very first time you do that, you get the summary balloon shown in Figure 16-5. If you want to make changes, you can then click the Edit button to open a more detailed view.

Tip: In Week or Day view, iCal sprouts a handy horizontal line that shows where you are in time right now. (Look in the hours-of-the-day "ruler" down the left side of the window to see this line's little red bulb.) A nice touch, and a handy visual aid that can tell you at a glance when you're already late for something.

Making an Appointment

The basic iCal calendar is easy to figure out. After all, with the exception of one unfortunate Gregorian incident, we've been using calendars successfully for centuries.

Even so, there are two ways to record a new appointment: a simple way and a more flexible, elaborate way.

The easy way

You can quickly record an appointment using any of several techniques, listed here in order of decreasing efficiency:

- In Month view, double-click a blank spot on the date you want. A pop-up info balloon appears (Figure 16-6), where you type the details for your new appointment.

- In Day or Week view, double-click the starting time to create a one-hour appointment. Or drag vertically through the time slots that represent the appointment's duration. Either way, type the event's name inside the newly created colored box.

- Choose File→New Event (or press ⌘-N). A new appointment appears on the currently selected day, regardless of the current view.

- In any view, Control-click or right-click a date and choose New Event from the shortcut menu.

Unless you use the drag-over-hours method, a new event believes itself to be one hour long. But in Day or Week view, you can adjust its duration by dragging the bottom edge vertically. Drag the dark top bar up or down to adjust the start time.

In many cases, that's all there is to it. You have just specified the day, time, and title of the appointment. Now you can get on with your life.

Tip: If this Edit balloon is blocking a part of the calendar you need to see, no biggie: Just drag the balloon out of the way, using any blank spot as a handle.

The long way

The information balloon shown in Figure 16-5 appears when you double-click a Month-view square, or double-click any existing appointment.

Tip: After you've already edited an appointment once, the full info balloon takes a little more effort to open; double-clicking an event produces only the summary balloon shown in Figure 16-5.

The short way to open the full balloon is to click the appointment and then press ⌘-E (which is short for Edit→Edit Event). The long way is to double-click the appointment to get the summary balloon and then click Edit inside it.

But the best solution to this problem is to avail yourself of an option in iCal→Preferences→Advanced. It's the checkbox called "Open events in separate windows." Now when you double-click an appointment in iCal, it opens immediately into a full-size Details window, saving you that intermediate step forever. (You can close the window with a quick ⌘-W.)

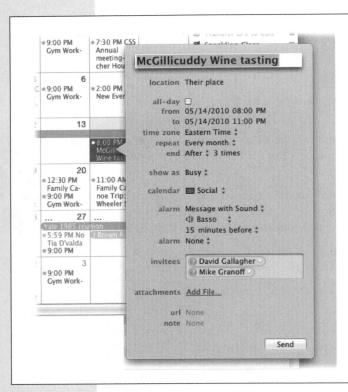

Figure 16-6:
All the details for an appointment sprout right out of the appointment itself in this balloon/box. Tab your way to an organized life.

For each appointment, you can Tab your way to the following information areas:

- **subject.** That's the large, bold type at the top—the name of your appointment. For example, you might type *Fly to Phoenix.*

- **location.** You might type a reminder for yourself like *My place,* a specific address like *212 East 23,* or some other helpful information like a contact phone number or flight number.

- **all-day.** An "all-day" event is something that has no specific time of day associated with it: a holiday, a birthday, a book deadline. When you turn on this box, you see the name of the appointment jump to the top of the iCal screen, in the area reserved for this kind of thing.

- **from, to.** You can adjust the times shown here by typing, clicking buttons, or both. Press Tab to jump from one setting to another, and from there to the hours and minutes of the starting time.

  For example, start by clicking the hour, then increase or decrease this number either by pressing ↑ and ↓ or by typing a number. Press Tab to highlight the minutes and repeat the arrow-buttons-or-keys business. Finally, press Tab to highlight the AM/PM indicator, and type either *A* or *P*—or press ↑ or ↓—to change it, if necessary.

Tip: If you specify a different ending date, a banner appears across the top of the calendar.

- **time zone.** This option appears only after you choose iCal→Preferences→Advanced and then turn on "Turn on time zone support." And you would do *that* only if you plan to be traveling on the day this appointment comes to pass.

  Once you've done that, a time zone pop-up menu appears. It starts out with "America/New York" (or whatever your Mac's usual time zone is); if you choose Other, a tiny world map appears. Click the time zone that represents where you'll be when this appointment comes due. From the shortcut menu, choose the major city that's in the same zone you'll be in.

Tip: The time zone pop-up menu remembers each new city you select. The next time you travel to a city you've visited before, you won't have to do that clicking-the-world-map business.

  Now, when you arrive in the distant city, use the time zone pop-up menu at the top-right corner of the iCal window to tell iCal where you are. You'll see all of iCal's appointments jump, like magic, to their correct new time slots.

- **repeat.** The pop-up menu here contains common options for recurring events: every day, every week, and so on. It starts out saying None.

  Once you've made a selection, you get an *end* pop-up menu that lets you specify when this event should *stop* repeating. If you choose "Never," you're stuck seeing this event repeating on your calendar until the end of time (a good choice for recording, say, your anniversary, especially if your spouse might be consulting the same calendar). You can also turn on "After" (a certain number of times), which is a useful option for car and mortgage payments. And if you choose "On date," you can specify the date that the repetitions come to an end; use this option to indicate the last day of school, for example.

"Custom" lets you specify repeat schedules like "First Monday of the month" or "Every two weeks."

- **show as (busy/free/tentative/"out of office")**. This little item shows up only if you've subscribed to an Internet-based calendar (in geek-speak, a CalDAV server) or you've hooked up to your company's Exchange calendar (Chapter 8). It communicates to your colleagues when you might be available for meetings.

> **Note:** If your calendar comes from a CalDAV server, then your only options are "busy" and "free." The factory setting for most appointments is "busy," but for all-day events it's "free." Which is logical; just because it's International Gecko Appreciation Day doesn't mean you're not available for meetings (rats!).

You might think: "Well, *duh*—if I've got something on the calendar, then I'm obviously busy!" But not necessarily. Some iCal entries might just be placeholders, reminders to self, TV shows you wanted to watch, appointments you'd be willing to change—not things that would necessarily render you unavailable if a better invitation should come along.

- **calendar**. A *calendar*, in iCal's confusing terminology, is a subset—a category—into which you can place various appointments. You can create one for yourself, another for family-only events, another for book-club appointments, and so on. Later, you'll be able to hide and show these categories at will, adding or removing them from iCal with a single click. Details begin on page 521.

UP TO SPEED

Inviting Guests

The truth is, this business of automatic invitations to iCal events hasn't really caught on yet. Unless you've hooked up iCal to your company's Exchange server (page 200), the invitations system is still fairly complicated, and it requires compatible software on the receivers' end.

When you click Send at the bottom of the info balloon, your guests receive your invitation. If they use iCal, the invitation appears in their Notifications panel. (To open the Notifications panel, click the tiny envelope icon in the lower-left corner of the window.) They can click Accept, Decline, or Maybe.

In *your* Notifications window, *you* then see the status of each invitee's name: a checkmark for Accepted, an X for Declined, a ? for Maybe, and an arrow for Not Yet Responded.

(Your guests, meanwhile, will be delighted to find that the appointment automatically appears on their calendars once they commit.)

Now, suppose you send an invitation to your sister, who doesn't have a Mac. She just gets an email message that says, "Chris Smith has invited you to the event: Company Hoedown, scheduled for February 02, 2010 at 3:00 PM. To accept or decline this invitation, click the link below." Unfortunately, there generally *is* no link. She just has to know to open the .ics attachment.

If she uses a calendar program that understands this attachment, the appointment appears on her calendar, and her RSVP shows up in your iCal Notification panel.

Tip: Use this same pop-up menu to change an appointment's category. If you filed something in "Company Memos" that should have been in "Sweet Nothings for Honey-Poo," then open the event's information balloon and reassign it. Quick.

- **alarm.** This pop-up menu tells iCal how to notify you when a certain appointment is about to begin. iCal can send any of four kinds of flags to get your attention. It can display a message on the screen (with a sound, if you like), send you an email, run a script (a min-program) you've written, or open a file on your hard drive. (You could use this unusual option to ensure that you don't forget a work deadline by flinging the relevant document open in front of your face at the eleventh hour.)

  Once you've specified an alarm mechanism, a new pop-up menu appears to let you specify how much advance notice you want for this particular appointment. If it's a TV show you'd like to watch, you might set up a reminder five minutes before airtime. If it's a birthday, you might set up a two-day warning to give yourself enough time to buy a present. In fact, you can set up more than one alarm for the same appointment, each with its own advance-warning interval.

Tip: In iCal→Preferences→Advanced, you can opt to prevent alarms from going off—a good checkbox to inspect before you give a presentation in front of 2,000 people. There's also an option to stifle alarms except when iCal is open. In other words, just quitting iCal is enough to ensure that those alarms won't interrupt whatever you're doing.

- **invitees.** If the appointment is a meeting or some other gathering, you can type the participants' names here. If a name is already in your Address Book program, iCal proposes autocompleting the name for you.

  If you separate several names with commas, iCal automatically turns each into a shaded oval pop-up button. You can click it for a pop-up menu of commands like Remove Attendee and Send Email. (That last option appears only if the person in your Address Book has an email address, or if you typed a name *with* an email address in brackets, like this: *Chris Smith <chris@yahoo.com>.*)

  Once you've specified some attendees, a Send button appears in the Info box. If you click it, iCal fires up Mail and prepares ready-to-send messages, each with an *iCal.ics* attachment: a calendar-program invitation file. See the box on page 518.

- **attachments.** This new option lets you fasten a file to the appointment. It can be anything: a photo of the person you're meeting, a document to finish by that deadline, the song that was playing the first time you met this person—whatever.

- **url.** A *URL* is a Uniform Resource Locator, better known as a Web address, like *www.apple.com.* If there's a URL relevant to this appointment, by all means type it here. Type more than one, if it'll help you; just be sure to separate them with a comma.

• **note.** Here's your chance to customize your calendar event. You can type, paste, or drag any text you like in the note area—driving directions, contact phone numbers, a call history, or whatever.

Your newly scheduled event now shows up on the calendar, complete with the color coding that corresponds to the calendar category you've assigned.

What to Do with an Appointment

Once you've entrusted your agenda to iCal, you can start putting it to work. iCal is only too pleased to remind you (via pop-up messages) of your events, reschedule them, print them out, and so on. Here are a few of the possibilities:

Editing events

To edit a calendar event's details, you have to open its Info balloon, as described in Figure 16-5.

Tip: If you just want to change an event's name, Option-double-click it right in place.

And if you want to change only an appointment's "calendar" category, Control-click (or right-click) anywhere on the appointment and, from the resulting shortcut menu, choose the category you want.

In both cases, you bypass the need to open the Info balloon.

You don't have to bother with this if all you want to do is *reschedule* an event, however, as described next.

Rescheduling events

If an event in your life gets rescheduled, you can drag an appointment block vertically in a day- or week-view column to make it later or earlier the same day, or horizontally to another date in any view. (If you reschedule a recurring event, iCal asks if you want to change only *this* occurrence, or this *and* all future ones.)

If something is postponed for, say, a month or two, you're in trouble, since you can't drag an appointment beyond its month window. You have no choice but to open the Info balloon and edit the starting and ending dates or times—or just cut and paste the event to a different date.

Lengthening or shortening events

If a scheduled meeting becomes shorter or your lunch hour becomes a lunch hour-and-a-half (in your dreams), changing the length of the representative calendar event is as easy as dragging the bottom border of its block in any column view (see Figure 16-7).

Tip: In week view, if you've grabbed the bottom edge of an appointment's block so that the cursor changes, you can drag horizontally to make an appointment cross the midnight line and extend into a second day.

Printing events

To commit your calendar to paper, choose File→Print, or press ⌘-P. The resulting Print dialog box lets you include only a certain range of dates, only events on certain calendars, with or without To Do lists or mini-month calendars, and so on.

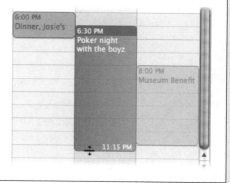

Figure 16-7:
You can resize any iCal calendar event just by dragging its bottom border. As your cursor touches the bottom edge of a calendar event, it turns into a double-headed arrow. You can now drag the event's edge to make it take up more or less time on your calendar.

Deleting events

To delete an appointment, just select it and then press the Delete key. If you delete a recurring event (like a weekly meeting), iCal asks whether you want to delete only that particular instance of the event, or the whole series from that point forward.

Searching for Events

You should recognize the oval text box at the top of the iCal screen immediately: It's almost identical to the Spotlight box. This search box is designed to let you hide all appointments except those matching what you type into it.

The "Calendar" Category Concept

Just as iTunes has *playlists* that let you organize songs into subsets and iPhoto has *albums* that let you organize photos into subsets, iCal has *calendars* that let you organize appointments into subsets. They can be anything you like. One person might have calendars called Home, Work, and TV Reminders. Another might have Me, Spouse 'n' Me, and Whole Family. A small business could have categories called Deductible Travel, R&D, and R&R.

To create a calendar, double-click any white space in the Calendar list (below the existing calendars), or click the + button at the lower-left corner of the iCal window. Type a name that defines the category in your mind.

Tip: Click a calendar name before you create an appointment. That way, the appointment will already belong to the correct calendar.

To change the color-coding of your category, Control-click (right-click) its name; from the shortcut menu, choose Get Info. The Calendar Info box appears. Here, you can change the name, color, or description of this category—or turn off alarms for this category.

You assign an appointment to one of these categories using the pop-up menu on its Info balloon, or by Control-clicking (right-clicking) an event and choosing a calendar name from the shortcut menu. After that, you can hide or show an entire category of appointments at once just by turning on or off the appropriate checkbox in the Calendars list.

Tip: iCal also has calendar *groups:* calendar containers, like folders, that consolidate the appointments from several *other* calendars. Super-calendars like this make it easier to manage, hide, show, print, and search subsets of your appointments.

To create a calendar group, choose File→New Calendar Group. Name the resulting item in the Calendar list; for the most part, it behaves like any other calendar. Drag other calendar names onto it to include them. Click the flippy triangle to hide or show the component calendars.

"Publishing" Calendars to the Web

One of iCal's best features is its ability to post your calendar on the Web, so that other people (or you, on a different computer) can subscribe to it, which adds *your* appointments to *their* calendars. If you have a MobileMe account, then anyone with a Web browser can also *view* your calendar, right online.

For example, you might use this feature to post the meeting schedule for a club that you manage, or to share the agenda for a series of upcoming financial meetings that all of your coworkers will need to consult.

Publishing

Begin by clicking the calendar category you want in the left-side list. (iCal can publish only one calendar category at a time. If you want to publish more than one calendar, create a calendar *group.*)

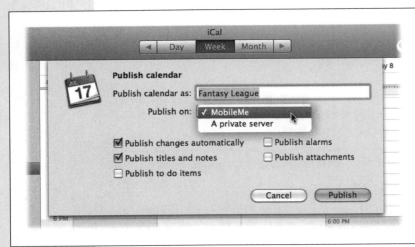

Figure 16-8:
If you click "Publish on: MobileMe," iCal posts the actual, viewable calendar on the Web. If you choose "a private server," you have the freedom to upload the calendar to your own personal Web site, if it's WebDAV-compatible (ask your Web-hosting company). Your fans will be able to download the calendar, but not view it online.

Then choose Calendar→Publish; the dialog box shown in Figure 16-8 appears. This is where you customize how your saved calendar is going to look and work. You can even turn on "Publish changes automatically," so whenever you edit the calendar, iCal connects to the Internet and updates the calendar automatically. (Otherwise, you'll have to choose Calendar→Refresh every time you want to update the Web copy.)

While you're at it, you can include To Do items, notes, and even alarms with the published calendar.

When you click Publish, your Mac connects to the Web and then shows you the Web address (the URL) of the finished page, complete with a Send Mail button that lets you fire the URL off to your colleagues.

Subscribing

If somebody else has published a calendar, you can subscribe to it by choosing Calendar→Subscribe. In the Subscribe to Calendar dialog box, type in the Internet address you received from the person who published the calendar. Alternatively, click the Subscribe button on any iCal Web page.

Either way, you can also specify how often you want your own copy to be updated (assuming you have a full-time Internet connection) and whether or not you want to be bothered with the publisher's alarms and notes.

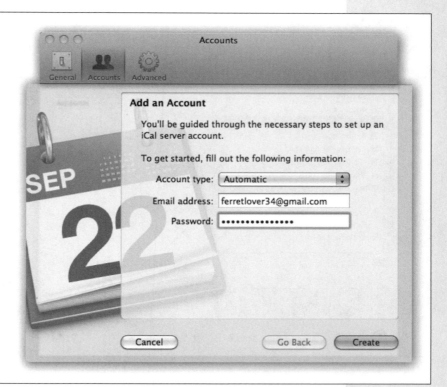

Figure 16-9:
To bring your Yahoo or Google calendar into iCal for free two-way syncing, choose iCal→Preferences→ Accounts. Click the + button below the list. Enter your Google or Yahoo address (for example, ferretlover34@ gmail.com) *and password, as shown here. Click Create.*

When it's all over, you see a new "calendar" category in your left-side list, representing the published appointments.

Google and Yahoo Calendars

If you maintain a calendar online—at *www.google.com/calendar* or *http://calendar.yahoo.com,* for example, you may take particular pleasure in discovering how easy it is to bring those appointments into iCal. It's one handy way to keep, for example, a husband's and wife's appointments visible on each other's calendars.

Setting this up is ridiculously easy in Snow Leopard (see Figure 16-9).

In a minute or so, you'll see all your Google or Yahoo appointments show up in iCal. (Each Web calendar has its own heading in the left-side list.) Better yet: It's a two-way sync; changes you make to these events in iCal show up on the Web, too.

To Do Lists

iCal's Tasks feature lets you make a To Do list and shepherds you along by giving you gentle reminders, if you so desire (Figure 16-10). What's nice is that Mac OS X maintains a single To Do list, which shows up in both iCal and Mail.

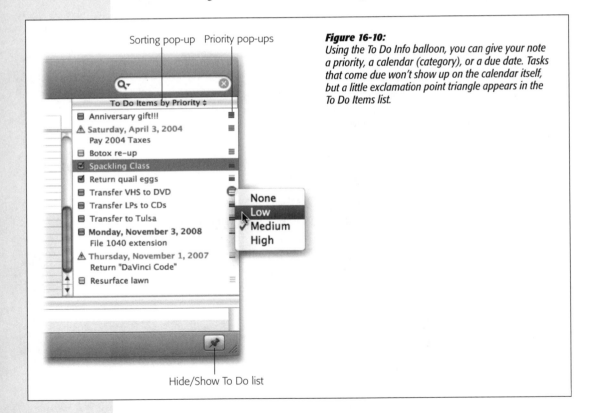

Figure 16-10:
Using the To Do Info balloon, you can give your note a priority, a calendar (category), or a due date. Tasks that come due won't show up on the calendar itself, but a little exclamation point triangle appears in the To Do Items list.

To see the list, click the pushpin button at the lower-right corner of the iCal screen. Add a new task by double-clicking a blank spot in the list that appears, or by choosing File→New To Do. After the new item appears, you can type to name it.

To change the task's priority, alarm, repeating pattern, and so on, double-click it. An Info balloon appears, just as it does for an appointment.

Tip: Actually, there's a faster way to change a To Do item's priority—click the tiny three-line ribbed handle at the right side of the list. Turns out it's a shortcut menu that lets you choose Low, Medium, or High priority (or None).

To sort the list (by priority, for example), use the pop-up menu at the top of the To Do list. To delete a task, click it and then press the Delete key.

Tip: You have lots of control over what happens to a task listing after you check it off. In iCal→Preferences, for example, you can make tasks auto-hide or auto-delete themselves after, say, a week or a month. (And if you asked them to auto-hide themselves, you can make them reappear temporarily using the Show All Completed Items command in the pop-up menu at the top of the To Do list.)

---

iChat

Details on the iChat instant-messaging program can be found in Chapter 12.

iDVD

iDVD isn't really part of Mac OS X, although you probably have a copy of it; as part of the iLife software suite, iDVD comes free on every new Mac. iDVD lets you turn your digital photos or camcorder movies into DVDs that work on almost any DVD player, complete with menus, slideshow controls, and other navigation features. iDVD handles the technology; you control the style.

For a primer on iDVD, see the free, downloadable iLife appendix to this chapter, available on this book's "Missing CD" page at *www.missingmanuals.com*.

Image Capture

This unsung little program was originally designed to download pictures from a camera and then process them automatically (turning them into a Web page, scaling them to emailable size, and so on). Of course, after Image Capture's birth, iPhoto came along, generally blowing its predecessor out of the water.

Even so, Apple includes Image Capture with Mac OS X for these reasons:

- Image Capture is a smaller, faster app for downloading all or only *some* pictures from your camera (Figure 16-11). iPhoto can do that nowadays, but sometimes that's like using a bulldozer to get out a splinter.

- Image Capture can grab images from Mac OS X–compatible scanners, too, not just digital cameras.

- Image Capture can download your *sounds* (like voice notes) from a digital still camera; iPhoto can't.

- Image Capture can share your camera or scanner on the network.

- Image Capture can turn a compatible digital camera into a Webcam, broadcasting whatever it "sees" to anyone on your office network—or the whole Internet. Similarly, it can share a scanner with all the networked Macs in your office.

You can open Image Capture in either of two ways: You can simply double-click its icon in your Applications folder, or you can set it up to open automatically whenever you connect a digital camera and turn it on. To set up that arrangement, open Image Capture manually. Using the "Connecting this camera opens:" pop-up menu, choose Image Capture.

Tip: You can specify which program on your Mac opens when you connect a camera independently for each camera. For example, you can set it up so that when you connect your fancy SLR camera, Aperture opens; when you connect your spouse's pocket camera, iPhoto opens; and when you connect your iPhone, Image Capture opens, so you can quickly grab the best shots and email them directly.

Figure 16-11:
Top: In some ways, Image Capture is like a mini iPhoto; use the slider in the lower right to change the thumbnail sizes. Use the "Delete after import" checkbox (lower-left) if you want your camera's card erased after you slurp in its photos. You can choose the individual pictures you want to download, rotate selected shots (using the buttons at the top), or delete shots from the camera.

Bottom: List view gives you a table of details about the photos to be imported.

Once Image Capture is open, it looks like Figure 16-11. Its controls, once buried in menus and Preferences dialog boxes, have, in Snow Leopard, all been brought out to the main window so they're readily available.

When you connect your camera, cellphone, or scanner, its name appears in the left-side list. To begin, click it. After a moment, Image Capture displays all the photos on the camera's card, in either list view or icon view (your choice).

Import To:

Use this pop-up menu to specify what happens to the imported pictures. Image Capture proposes putting photos, sounds, and movies from the camera into your Home folder's Pictures, Music, and Movies folders, respectively. But you can specify any folder (choose Other from the pop-up menu).

Furthermore, there are some other very cool options here:

- **iPhoto.** Neat that you can direct photos from your camera *to* iPhoto *via* Image Capture. Might come in handy when you didn't *expect* to want to load photos into your permanent collection, but change your mind when you actually look them over in Image Capture.

- **Preview** opens the fresh pictures in Preview so you can get a better (and bigger) look at them.

- **Mail** sends the pix directly into the Mac's email program, which can be very handy when the point of getting the photos off the camera is to send them off to friends.

- **Build web page** creates an actual, and very attractive, Web page of your downloaded shots. Against a dark gray background, you get thumbnail images of the pictures in a Web page document called index.html. Just click one of the small images to view it at full size, exactly as your Web site visitors will be able to do once this page is actually on the Web. (Getting it online is up to you.)

Note: Image Capture puts the Web page files in a Home folder→Pictures→Webpage on [today's date and time] folder. It contains the graphics files incorporated into this HTML document; you can post the whole thing on your Web site, if you like.

Image Capture automatically opens up this page in your Web browser, proud of its work.

- **MakePDF.** What is MakePDF? It's a little app you didn't even know you had.

When you choose this option, you wind up with what looks like a Preview window, showing thumbnails of your photos. If you choose Save right now, you'll get a beautiful full-color PDF of the selected photos, ready to print out and then, presumably, to cut apart with scissors or a paper cutter. But if you use the Layout menu, you can choose different layouts for your photos: 3×5, 4×6, 8×10, and so on.

And what if a photo doesn't precisely fit the proportions you've selected? The Crop commands in the Layout menu (for example, "Crop to 4×6") center each photo within the specified shape, and then trim the outer borders if necessary. The Fit commands, on the other hand, *shrink* the photo as necessary to fit into the specified dimensions, sometimes leaving blank white margins.

Note: The "crop" commands never touch the actual downloaded photos. The downloaded image files themselves retain their full sizes and resolutions.

When the downloading process is complete, a little green checkmark appears on the thumbnail of each imported photo.

Import Some, Import All

Clicking Import All, of course, begins the process of downloading the photos to the folder you've selected. A progress dialog box appears, showing you thumbnail images of each picture that flies down the wire.

If you prefer to import only *some* photos, select them first. (In icon view, you click and Shift-click to select a bunch of *consecutive* photos, and ⌘-click to add *individual* photos to the selection. In icon view, you can only click and *Shift*-click to select individual photos.) Then click Import.

Scanning

If you own a scanner, chances are good that you won't be needing whatever special scanning software came with it. Instead, Mac OS X gives you two programs that can operate any standard scanner: Image Capture and Preview. In fact, the controls are identical in both programs.

To scan in Image Capture, turn on your scanner and click its name in the left-side list. Put your photos or documents into the scanner.

Note: You can share a scanner on the network, if you like, by turning on the Share button in the lower-left corner of the window. That's sort of a weird option, though, for two reasons. First, what do you gain by sitting somewhere else in the building? Do you really want to yell or call up to whoever's sitting next to the scanner: "OK! Put in the next photo!"?

Second, don't forget that anyone else on the network will be able to see whatever you're scanning. Embarrassment may result. You've been warned.

Now you have a couple of decisions to make:

- **Separate and straighten?** If you turn on "Detect separate items," Snow Leopard will perform a nifty little stunt indeed: It will check to see if you've put *multiple* items onto the scanner glass, like several small photos. (It looks for rectangular images surrounded by empty white space, so if the photos are overlapping, this feature won't work.)

  If it finds multiple items, Snow Leopard automatically straightens them, compensating for haphazard placement on the glass, and then saves them as individual files.

- **Where to file.** Use the "Scan to" pop-up menu to specify where you want the newly scanned image files to land—in the Pictures folder, for example. You have some other cool options beyond sticking the scans in a folder; you can use the Web page, PDF, iPhoto, and other options described on page 251.

Once you've put a document onto it or into it, click Scan. The scanner heaves to life. After a moment, you see on the screen what's on the glass. It's simultaneously been sent to the folder (or post-processing task) you requested using the "Scan to" pop-up menu.

More power to you

As you can see, Apple has tried to make *basic* scanning as simple as possible: one click. That idiotproof method gives you very few options, however.

If you click Show Details before you scan, though, you get a special panel on the right side of the window that's filled with useful scanning controls (Figure 16-12).

Figure 16-12:
When you use the Show Details button, you get a new panel on the right, where you can specify all the tweaky details for the scan you're about to make: resolution, size, and so on. See how the three photos have individual dotted lines around them? That's because "Detect Separate Items" is turned on. These will be scanned into three separate files.

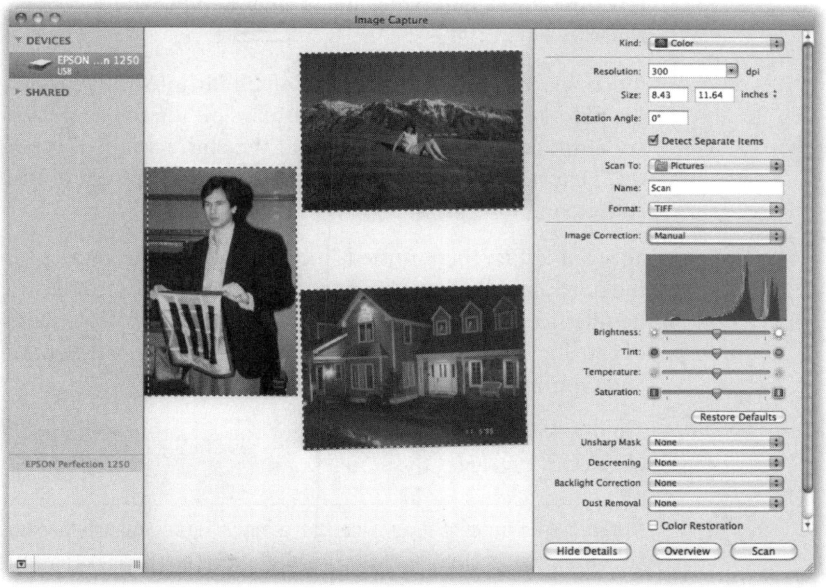

Here are some of the most useful options:

- **Resolution.** This is the number of tiny scanned dots per inch. 300 is about right for something you plan to print out; 72 is standard for graphics that will be viewed on the screen, like images on a Web page.

- **Name.** Here, specify how you want each image file named when it lands on your hard drive. If it says *Scan,* then the files will be called *Scan 1, Scan 2,* and so on.

- **Format.** Usually, the file format for scanned graphics is TIFF. That's a very high-res format that's ideal if you're scanning precious photos for posterity. But if these images are bound for the Web, you might want to choose JPEG instead; that's the standard Web format.

- **Image Correction.** If you choose Manual from this pop-up menu, then, incredibly, you'll be treated to a whole expando-panel of color correction tools: brightness, tint, saturation, a histogram, and so on.

- **Unsharp Mask.** This option sharpens up any slightly "soft" photos after scanning.

- **Descreening.** Sometimes, when you scan printed photos from a newspaper or magazine, you get a *moiré* effect: a weird rippling pattern in the scanned image that wasn't in the original. This option is supposed to get rid of that ugliness.

- **Dust Removal.** Dust is a common problem in scanned images. This option attempts to eliminate the specks of dust that might mar a photo.

Opening the Details panel has another handy benefit, too: It lets you scan only a *portion* of what's on the scanner glass.

Once you've put the document or photo into the scanner, click Overview. Snow Leopard does a quick pass and displays on the screen whatever's on the glass. You'll see a dotted-line rectangle around the entire scanned image—unless you'd turned on "Detect separate images," in which case you see a dotted-line rectangle around *each* item on the glass.

You can adjust these dotted-line rectangles around until you've enclosed precisely the portion of the image you want scanned. For example, drag the rectangles' corner handles to resize them; drag inside the rectangles to move them; drag the right end of the line inside the rectangle to rotate it; preview the rotation by pressing Control and Option.

Finally, when you think you've got the selection rectangle(s) correctly positioned, click Scan to trigger the actual scan.

Note: These instructions apply to the most common kind of scanner—the flatbed scanner. If you have a scanner with a document feeder—a tray or slot that sucks in one paper document after another from a stack—the instructions are only slightly different.

You may, for example, see a Mode or Scan Mode pop-up menu; if so, choose Document Feeder. You'll want to use the Show Details option described above. You may also be offered a Duplex command (meaning, "scan both sides of the paper"—not all scanners can do this).

---

iMovie, iPhoto

Here's another pair of the iLife apps—not really part of Mac OS X, but kicking around on your Mac because iLife comes with all new Macs.

A basic getting-started chapter for these programs awaits, in free downloadable PDF form, on this book's "Missing CD" page at *www.missingmanuals.com*.

Tip: If that basic guide isn't enough for you, keep in mind that masterfully written, in-depth guides are available in the form of *iMovie '09 & iDVD: The Missing Manual* and *iPhoto '09: The Missing Manual.* (Corresponding Missing Manual titles are available for earlier versions of these programs, too.)

---

iTunes

iTunes is Apple's beloved digital music–library program. Chapter 9 tells all.

Mail

See Chapter 11 for the whole story.

Photo Booth

It may be goofy, it may be pointless, but the Photo Booth program is a bigger time drain than Solitaire, the Web, and *Dancing with the Stars* put together.

It's a match made in heaven for Macs that have a tiny video camera above the screen, but you can also use it with a camcorder, iSight, or Webcam. Just be sure the camera is turned on and hooked up *before* you open Photo Booth. (Photo Booth doesn't even open if your Mac doesn't have *some* kind of camera.)

Open this program and then peer into the camera. Photo Booth acts like a digital mirror, showing whatever the camera sees—that is, you.

But then click the Effects button. You enter a world of special visual effects—and we're talking *very* special. Some make you look like a pinhead, or bulbous, or like a Siamese twin; others simulate Andy Warhol paintings, fisheye lenses, and charcoal sketches (Figure 16-13). In fact, there are *four pages* of effects, nine previews on a page; click the left or right arrow buttons, or press ⌘-← or ⌘-→, to see them all. (The last two pages hold *backdrop* effects, described below.)

Some of the effects have sliders that govern their intensity; you'll see them appear when you click the preview.

Still Photos

When you find an effect that looks appealing (or unappealing, depending on your goals here), click the camera button, or press ⌘-T. You see and hear a 3-second countdown, and then *snap!*—your screen flashes white to add illumination, and the resulting photo appears on your screen. Its thumbnail joins the collection at the bottom.

Tip: If that countdown is getting on your nerves, Option-click the camera button. You can get rid of the screen flash, too, by Shift-clicking. Needless to say, if you press Option and Shift, you get neither the countdown nor the flash.

4-Up Photos

If you click the 4-Up button identified in Figure 16-13, then when you click the Camera icon (or press ⌘-T), the 3-2-1 countdown begins, and then Photo Booth snaps *four* consecutive photos in 2 seconds. You can exploit the timing just the way you would in a real photo booth—make four different expressions, horse around, whatever.

Click an effect

Figure 16-13:
The Photo Booth effects must have been dreamed up one night in the midst of a serious beer party at Apple. They're disturbingly creative. If you decide that you really look best without any help from Apple's warped imagery, click the Normal icon in the center.

Still   4-Up   Movie   Effects pages   Finished shots (still, 4-up, movie)

The result is a single graphic with four panes, kind of like what you get at a shopping-mall photo booth. (In Photo Booth, they appear rakishly assembled at an angle; but when you export the image, they appear straight, like panes of a window.) Its icon plops into the row of thumbnails at the bottom of the window, just like the single still photos.

Movies

Photo Booth can also record *videos,* complete with those wacky distortion effects. Click the third icon below the screen, the Movie icon (Figure 16-13), and then click the camera button (or press ⌘-T). You get the 3-2-1 countdown—but this time, Photo Booth records a video, with sound, until you click the Stop button or the hard drive is full, whichever comes first. (The little digital counter at left reminds you that you're still filming.) When it's over, the movie's icon appears in the row of thumbnails, ready to play or export.

Or choose Edit→Auto Flip New Photos if you want Photo Booth to do the flipping for you from now on.

Exporting Shots and Movies

To look at a photo or movie you've captured, click its thumbnail in the scrolling row at the bottom of the screen. (To return to camera mode, click the camera button.)

GEM IN THE ROUGH

Still and Video Backdrops

Photo Booth and iChat are cousins, and they're closer than ever. One particular feature, in fact, is identical in each: custom backdrops. You can replace the actual, mundane background of your office or den with something far more exciting: a rushing waterfall, for example, or a rider's-eye view of a roller coaster. In fact, you can use any photo or video you want as the background.

It's just like the bluescreen or greenscreen technology that Hollywood uses to put their actors someplace they're not—but without the bluescreen or greenscreen.

To replace your back-ground in Photo Booth, click Effects. The third page of effects offers eight *canned* backgrounds, prepared by Apple for your enjoyment: various spectacular stills (cloudscape, color dots, the moon) and videos (Eiffel Tower plaza, aquarium, roller coaster, tropical beach, Yosemite waterfall).

The final page offers eight *empty* preview squares. You're supposed to drag a still or a video from your desktop (or iPhoto) into these empty squares, making them not so empty.

In any case, prepare the backdrop by clicking one of the preview squares. Photo Booth says, "Please step out of the frame." Do it. Photo Booth is going to memorize what its field of view looks like *without* you in it, so that when you reappear, it can tell *you* apart from your boring office background.

Now, when you record the movie or take the photo, you'll be amazed to discover that Photo Booth has just transplanted you to the far more exotic locale you selected. (Alas, blotches may result if the background includes movement or highly contrasting elements.)

Fortunately, these masterpieces of goofiness and distortion aren't locked in Photo Booth forever. You can share them with your adoring public in any of four ways:

- Drag a thumbnail out of the window to your desktop. Or use the File→Reveal in Finder command to see the actual picture or movie files.

Tip: They're in your Home→Pictures→Photo Booth folder. You'll find one JPEG apiece for single shots, four JPEG files for a 4-up, and a .mov movie file for videos.

- Click Mail to send the photo or movie as an outgoing attachment in Mail.
- Click the iPhoto button to import the shot or movie into iPhoto.
- Click Account Picture to make this photo represent you on the Login screen.

Tip: You can choose one frame of a Photo Booth movie to represent you. As the movie plays, click the Pause button, and then drag the scroll-bar handle to freeze the action on the frame you want. Then click Account Picture.

Similarly, you can click your favorite *one pane* of a 4-up image to serve as your account photo—it expands to fill the Photo Booth screen—before clicking Account Picture.

And speaking of interesting headshots: If you export a 4-up image and choose it as your buddy icon in iChat (Chapter 12), you'll get an *animated* buddy icon. That is, your tiny icon cycles among the four images, creating a crude sort of animation. It's sort of annoying, actually, but all the kids are doing it.

As you set off on your Photo Booth adventures, a note of caution: Keep it away from children. They won't move from Photo Booth for the next 12 years.

Preview

Preview is Mac OS X's scanning software, graphics viewer, fax viewer, and PDF reader. It's teeming with features that most Mac owners never even knew were there.

Importing Camera Photos

Preview can import pictures directly from a digital camera (or iPhone), meaning that there are now *three* Snow Leopard apps that can perform that duty. (iPhoto and Image Capture are the other two.) It's sometimes handy to use Preview for this purpose, though, because it has some great tools for photos: color-correction controls, size/resolution options, format conversion, and so on.

The actual importing process, though, is *exactly* like using Image Capture for this purpose. Connect your camera, choose File→Import from [Your Camera's Name], and carry on as described on page 527.

Operating Your Scanner

Preview can also operate a scanner, auto-straighten the scanned images, and export them as PDF files, JPEG graphics, and so on.

This, too, is exactly like using Image Capture to operate your scanner. Only the first step is different. Open Preview, choose File→Import from Scanner→[Your Scanner's Name], and proceed as described on page 528.

Clearly, Apple saved some time by reusing some code.

Multiple Pages, Multiple Views

One hallmark of Preview is its effortless handling of *multiples:* multiple fax pages, multiple PDF files, batches of photos, and so on. The key to understanding the possibilities is mastering the Sidebar, shown in Figure 16-14. The idea is that these thumbnails let you navigate pages or graphics without having to open a rat's nest of individual windows.

Tip: You can drag these thumbnails from one Preview window's Sidebar into another. That's a great way to mix and match pages from different PDF documents into a single new one, for example.

To hide or show the Sidebar, press Shift-⌘-D (or click the Sidebar button in the toolbar, or use the View→Sidebar submenu). Once the Sidebar is open, the four tiny icons at the bottom let you choose among four views: Contact Sheet, Thumbnails, Table of Contents, and Annotations (Figure 16-14). Each presents a different arrangement of PDF pages (or graphics) and navigation tools.

Tip: You can also change among these four views using the View→Sidebar submenu—or by pressing the keyboard shortcuts Option-⌘-1, 2, 3, and 4.

Figure 16-14:
The Sidebar can display thumbnails (left), a table of contents (right), or annotations, or it can appear as a full-screen array of thumbnail images. Drag the central scroll bar to make the Sidebar bigger; drag the lower-right corner of the Sidebar to make the whole Preview bigger.

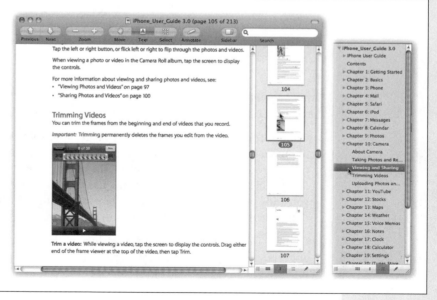

Preview as Graphics Viewer

Preview, as you're probably starting to figure out, is surprisingly versatile. It can display and manipulate pictures saved in a wide variety of formats, including common graphics formats like JPEG, TIFF, PICT, and GIF; less commonly used formats like BMP, PNG, SGI, TGA, and MacPaint; and even Photoshop, EPS, and PDF graphics. You can even open animated GIFs by adding a Play button to the toolbar (choose View→Customize Toolbar).

Bunches o' graphics

If you highlight a group of image files in the Finder and open them all at once (for example, by pressing ⌘-O), Preview opens the first one, but lists the thumbnails of the whole group in the Sidebar. You can walk through them with the ↑ and ↓ keys, or you can choose View→Slideshow (Shift-⌘-F) to open a full-screen slideshow. (You have to click through the pictures manually, though.)

Tip: You can change the order of the photos just by dragging them around in the Sidebar, in any of its views.

Cropping graphics

To crop graphics in Preview, drag across the part of the graphic that you want to keep. To redraw, drag the round handles on the dotted rectangle; or, to proceed with the crop, choose Tools→Crop. (The keyboard shortcut is ⌘-K.)

If you don't think you'll ever need the original again, save the document. Otherwise, choose File→Save As to spin the cropped image out as a separate file, preserving the original in the process.

Tip: You can also rotate an image—even a PDF document—in 90-degree increments and then flip it vertically or horizontally, using the commands in the Tools menu. In fact, if you select several thumbnails in the Sidebar first, you can rotate or flip them all simultaneously.

Fixing up photos

Preview is no Photoshop, but it's getting closer every year. Let us count the ways:

- **Choose Tools→Inspector.** A floating palette appears. Click the first tab to see the photo's name, when it was taken, its pixel dimensions, and so on. Click the second one for even more geeky photo details, including camera settings like the lens type, ISO setting, focus mode, whether the flash was on, and so on. The third tab lets you add keywords, so you'll be able to search for this image later using Spotlight. (The fourth is for PDF documents only, not photos; it lets you add annotations.)

- **Choose Tools→Adjust Color.** A translucent, floating color-adjustment palette appears, teeming with sliders for brightness, contrast, exposure, saturation (color intensity), temperature and tint (color cast), sharpness, and more. See Figure 16-15.

- **Choose Tools→Adjust Size.** This command lets you adjust a photo's resolution, which comes in handy a lot. For example, you can scale an unwieldy 10-megapixel, gazillion-by-gazillion-pixel shot down to a nice 640 × 480 JPEG that's small enough to send by email. Or you can shrink a photo down so it fits within a desktop window, for use as a window background.

There's not much to it. Type in the new print dimensions you want for the photo, in inches or whatever units you choose from the pop-up menu. If you like, you can also change the resolution (the number of pixels per inch) by editing the Resolution box.

Figure 16-15:
Humble little Preview has grown up into a big, strong mini-Photoshop. You can really fix up a photo if you know what you're doing, using these sliders. Or you can just click the Auto Levels button. It sets all those sliders for you, which generally does an amazing job of making almost any photo look better.

Converting file formats

Preview doesn't just open all these file formats—it can also convert between most of them. You can pop open some old Mac PICT files and turn them into BMP files for a Windows user, pry open some SGI files created on a Silicon Graphics workstation and turn them into JPEGs for use on your Web site, and so on.

Tip: What's even cooler is you can open raw PostScript files right into Preview, which converts them into PDF files on the spot. You no longer need a PostScript laser printer to print out high-end diagrams and page layouts that come to you as PostScript files. Thanks to Preview, even an inkjet printer can handle them.

All you have to do is open the file you want to convert and choose File→Save As. In the dialog box that appears, choose the new format for the image using the Format pop-up menu (JPEG, TIFF, PNG, or Photoshop, for example). Finally, click Save to export the file.

Preview as PDF Reader

Preview is a nearly full-blown equivalent of Acrobat Reader, the free program used by millions to read PDF documents. It lets you search PDF documents, copy text out of them, add comments, fill in forms, click live hyperlinks, add highlighting, circle certain passages, type in notes—features that used to be available only in Adobe's Acrobat Reader.

Here are the basics:

• Zoom in and out using ⌘-plus and ⌘-minus.

• Use the View→PDF Display submenu to control how the PDF document appears: as two-page spreads, as single scrolling sheets of "paper towel," with borders that indicate ends of pages, and so on.

• Press the space bar to page through a document (add Shift to page *upward*. The Page Up and Page Down keys do the same thing.)

Tip: Some PDF documents include a table of contents, which you'll see in Preview's Sidebar, complete with flippy triangles that denote major topics or chapter headings (Figure 16-17, right). You can use the ↑ and ↓ keys alone to walk through these chapter headings, and then expand one that looks good by pressing the → key. Collapse it again with the ← key.

In other words, you expand and collapse flippy triangles in Preview just as you do in a Finder list view.

• Bookmark your place by choosing Bookmarks→Add Bookmark (⌘-D); type a clever name. In the future, you'll be able to return to that spot by choosing its name

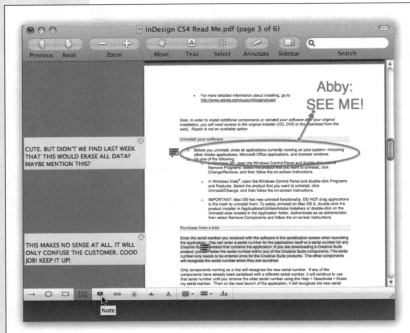

Figure 16-16:
The new Annotation strip at the bottom edge of the Preview window makes it incredibly easy to add different kinds of annotations. This strip appears when you click the Annotate button on the top toolbar, or whenever you've added a marking or a note manually using the Tools→Annotate submenu.

Click the button you want, then drag diagonally to define a rectangle, oval, arrow, or link. Or click to place a Note icon and edit that note in the left margin. You can drag or delete the annotation's little icon, or adjust its look using the Tools→Inspector palette.

from the Bookmarks menu.

- You can type in notes, add clickable links (to Web addresses or other spots in the document), or use circles, arrows, rectangles, strikethrough, underlining, or yellow highlighting to draw your readers' attention to certain sections, as shown in Figure 16-16.

Tip: Preview ordinarily stamps each text note with your name and the date. If you'd rather not have that info added, choose Preview→Preferences, click PDF, and then turn off "Add name to annotations."

These remain living, editable entities even after the document is saved and re-opened. These are full-blown Acrobat annotations; they'll show up when your PDF document is opened by Acrobat Reader, even on Windows PCs.

Tip: You can add circles, arrows, rectangles, and text boxes, even on image files like photos.

- Turn smoothing on or off to improve readability. To find the on/off switch, choose Preview→Preferences, and click the PDF tab. Turn on "Smooth line art and text." (Though antialiased text generally looks great, it's sometimes easier to read very small type with antialiasing turned off. It's a little jagged, but clearer nonetheless.)

- Turn on View→PDF Display→Single Page (or Double Page) Continuous to scroll through multipage PDF documents in one continuous stream, instead of jumping from page to page when you use the scroll bars.

- To find a word or phrase somewhere in a PDF document, press ⌘-F (or choose Edit→Find→Find) to open the Find box—or just type into the ٩ box at the top of the Sidebar, if it's open. Proceed as shown in Figure 16-17.

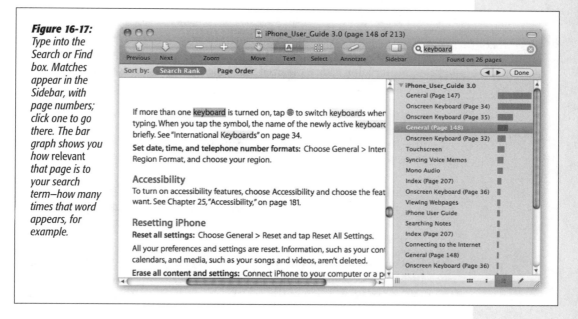

Figure 16-17:
Type into the Search or Find box. Matches appear in the Sidebar, with page numbers; click one to go there. The bar graph shows you how relevant that page is to your search term—how many times that word appears, for example.

- If you want to copy some text out of a PDF document—for pasting into a word processor, for example, where you can edit it—click the Text tool (the letter A on the toolbar) or choose Tools→Text Tool. Now you can drag through some text and then choose Edit→Copy, just as though the PDF document were a Web page. You can even drag across page boundaries.

Tip: Ordinarily, dragging across text selects the text from one edge of the page to the other, even if the PDF document is laid out in columns. But in Mac OS X, Preview is a bit smarter. It can tell if you're trying to get the text in only one column, and highlights just that part automatically.

- You can save a single page from a PDF as a TIFF file to use it in other graphics, word processing, or page layout programs that might not directly recognize PDF.

  To extract a page, use the usual File→Save As command, making sure to choose the new file format from the pop-up menu. (If you choose a format like Photoshop or JPEG, Preview converts only the currently selected page of your PDF document. That's because there's no such thing as a multipage Photoshop or JPEG graphic. But you already knew that.)

- Add keywords to a graphic or PDF (choose Tools→Show Inspector, click the ९ tab, click the **+** button). Later, you'll be able to call up these documents with a quick Spotlight search for those details.

QuickTime Player

A QuickTime movie is a video file. Like any movie, it creates the illusion of motion by flashing many individual frames (photos) per second before your eyes, while also playing a synchronized soundtrack.

Thousands of Mac OS X programs can open QuickTime movies, play them back, and sometimes even incorporate them into documents. Among them: Word, FileMaker, Keynote, PowerPoint, Safari, and even the Finder (when you use Quick Look, column view, or Cover Flow view; see Chapter 2).

But the cornerstone of Mac OS X's movie-playback software is QuickTime Player, which sits in your Applications folder (and even comes factory-installed in the Dock). This program is designed not only to play movies and sounds, but also to record and trim them, post them to YouTube or MobileMe, and so on.

Playing movies with QuickTime Player

You can open a movie file by double-clicking it. When QuickTime Player first opens, you get a very cool, borderless playback window. If you just hit the space bar, you play the movie.

There's a control toolbar at the bottom of the window (Figure 16-18), but it fades away after a few seconds—or immediately, if you push the cursor out of the frame. The toolbar reappears anytime your mouse moves back where it used to be. These are the controls:

- **Volume slider** (◐...◀》). Click in the slider, or drag the dot, to adjust the volume—although it's actually easier to just tap the ↑ or ↓ keys. Click the ◐ to mute the audio; click it again to unmute.

Tip: To mute the sound, click the ◐ icon, or press Option-↓. Press Option-↑ to make the volume slider jump to full-blast position.

Figure 16-18:
QuickTime Player displays this control bar only when you move your mouse into its window, or whenever playback is stopped.

- **Rewind, Fast-forward** (◀◀, ▶▶). By clicking one of these buttons, you get to speed through your movie at double speed, backward or forward, complete with sound. Click again for 4× speed, again for 8×.

Tip: You don't have to keep your mouse button pressed on these buttons. Just click once and let QuickTime Player do the work. Click ▶ or tap the space bar to stop scanning.

- **Play/Pause** (▶/❙❙). Click ▶ to start playback, ❙❙ to pause/stop. Or just tap the space bar for both functions.

- **Scroll bar.** Drag the little diamond, or just click inside its track, to jump to a different spot in the movie. The counters at the beginning and end of the scroll bar tell you, in "hours:minutes:seconds" format, how far your playhead cursor has moved into the movie, and how far you are from the end. (Click the right-hand readout to see the total movie duration.)

Tip: You can also press the ← and → keys to step through the movie one frame at a time. If you press Option-← or Option-→, you jump to the beginning or end of the movie.

- **Resize handle.** Drag diagonally to make the window bigger or smaller. QuickTime Player always maintains the same *aspect ratio* (relative dimensions) of the original movie, so you won't accidentally squish it.

- **Share button** (☎). Click for a pop-up menu of three choices for passing on this video to your adoring fans: iTunes, YouTube, or MobileMe. The Trim command is here, too. All four of these options are described below.

- **Full Screen** (⬛). Click to make the video fill your entire monitor, just as though you'd chosen View→Enter Full Screen.

Snow Leopard Spots: When you enter Full Screen, the movie doesn't begin playing automatically, as it did in the old QuickTime Player. You have to tap the space bar to get the show under way.

Changing the screen size

As noted above, you can drag the window to any size using the lower-right handle. But the View menu commands—Fit to Screen, Actual Size, Enter Full Screen, and so on—are handy, too.

- **Actual size** represents the movie on your screen at its real size—no larger. (If it's truly huge, larger than your screen, it may be scaled *smaller* to fit. But that's a rarity.)

- **Fit to Screen** fills your screen without cropping or distorting; the menu bar and other windows remain visible.

- **Enter Full Screen** is especially satisfying, because it turns your entire monitor into a movie playback area; even the menu bar is hidden. And what if the proportions of the movie don't quite match your screen? If you make the menu bar return by pointing to the top of your screen, you can handle this problem using one of the three choices in the View menu:

- **Fit to Screen,** as before, enlarges the video as much as possible *without chopping off the edges.* So you might get black letterbox bars at top/bottom or left/right. **Fill Screen** enlarges the movie to fill your screen completely, even if the edges get chopped off. **Panoramic** squishes the outer edges of the video, distorting them slightly, so that nothing gets chopped off *and* the movie fills the screen.

Tip: These same options are available via keyboard shortcuts—⌘-3, ⌘-4, and ⌘-5. There's even a little button on the control bar, second from right, that switches back and forth between Fit to Screen and Fill Screen. (This button appears only when you're already in Full Screen mode.)

Making the window larger may also make the movie coarser, because QuickTime Player simply enlarges every dot that was present in the original. Still, when you want to show a movie to a group of people more than a few feet back from the screen, these larger sizes are perfectly effective.

Tip: You can make the movie window bigger or smaller by pressing ⌘-plus (+) or ⌘-minus (-).

Recording Movies with QuickTime Player

QuickTime Player does more than *play* movies; it can also *record* them. Yes, your Mac is now a camcorder, and a darned handy one; you can pop out quick video greetings, gross out your former roommates, impress your coworkers with a dress rehearsal of your pitch, and so on.

Laptops and iMacs, of course, have a video camera built right in, above the screen. If you have another model, you can attach a Web cam, an old iSight camera, or even a FireWire camcorder.

Then open QuickTime Player and choose File→New Video Recording. The preview window appears. Use the pop-up menu shown in Figure 16-19 to specify what mike and camera you want to use (in the unlikely event that you have more than one), what video quality you want, and where you want to store the result.

Figure 16-19:
Use the pop-up menu to set up your flick; check the audio level (reflected by the "sound waves" at the bottom of the control bar). Press space when you're ready to roll!

Then, to record, click the red Record button, or just tap the space bar. Do your schtick. Press space again to stop the recording.

Your new video appears in its own playback window. Check it out, trim it if necessary, then shoot it off to iTunes, MobileMe, or YouTube!

Recording Screen Movies

Now here's a feature *nobody* saw coming: You can also record movies *of the screen.*

Why is it useful to capture screen activity as a video? Because you can give little lessons to techno-clueless relatives by sending a mini-tutorial. You can make video podcasts that show how to do things in your software programs. You can preserve Web animations that you used to think you had no way to capture.

There are limitations. QuickTime Player can record only the *entire screen,* not just a part of it. Your movies don't include the sound from the Mac's own speakers, so forget about capturing YouTube videos. (It can record from the *mike,* though, so you can narrate what you're doing.) In other words, it's no match for a dedicated screen-movie-making program like Snapz Pro X.

But who cares? It's fantastically handy.

Tip: If you do want to isolate only part of the screen, you can do that later in iMovie, which came with your Mac. It has a very cool video-cropping tool.

To make a screen recording, choose File→New Screen Recording. Use the pop-up menu on the resulting Screen Recording panel to turn the microphone on or off, to choose a quality setting, and to indicate where you want the finished movie stored.

Finally, click the red Record button, or tap the space bar, then proceed as shown in Figure 16-20.

When you finally click Stop Recording in the menu bar, or press ⌘-Control-Esc, your movie appears in a regular playback window—a *really big* one—ready to trim or send away to your fans.

Figure 16-20:
This odd little warning appears when you tap the space bar. It lets you know that it's going to hide itself so that it won't mess up your screen movie, but that a Stop Recording button will appear in your menu bar. Try the Show Me button. Weird! (Yes, the Stop Recording button will appear in your video.) Click Start Recording once you understand the deal.

Trimming Video

Like it or not, we live in a short-attention-span world. In this culture of YouTube and digital camera videos, the world has become one gigantic highlights reel.

Maybe that's why the new QuickTime Player comes equipped with a handy Trim command. You still can't cut anything out of the *middle* of a video, but you can very easily trim dead space off the *ends*. Figure 16-21 shows how.

Tip: Once you're in Trim mode, the Edit menu sprouts a very cool command: Select All Excluding Silence. It automatically adjusts the yellow trim handles so that they cut out any silent portions of the video (at the beginning or end). That's a handy shortcut if you, like many impromptu videographers, let the camera roll a bit before and after the main event.

Figure 16-21:
To trim a video, choose Edit→Trim, or press ⌘-T. Drag the yellow handles inward to isolate the chunk you want to preserve. (You can click ▶ or tap the space bar to check your work.) When everything looks good, click Trim or press Return.

Supertip: It's often useful to "see the audio" as you trim, so you can end the clip after someone's final word, for example. No problem. If you hold down the Option key, you see a graph of the audio (bottom).

You don't have to worry about damaging the original video when trimming—you couldn't modify the original if you tried, because there's no Save command. (But if you've just recorded fresh video, save it before you trim; otherwise, the trim is permanent!)

You can, however, export or upload the shortened video, as described next.

Four Ways to Export Your Video

One of the new QuickTime Player's most important talents is *sharing* a video: posting it directly to YouTube or MobileMe, converting it to the right format for an iPod, iPhone or cellphone, stashing it in iTunes for easy transfer to your iPod/iPhone, or saving it to the hard drive as a double-clickable movie.

Let us count the ways.

Send to iTunes

The main reason you'd want to send your video to iTunes is because you have an iPod, iPhone, or Apple TV. Once it's in iTunes, you can sync your video easily to that other Apple gadget and have it ready to view at all times.

To make this transfer happen, choose Share→iTunes. Or click the 🖼 icon on the control bar and choose iTunes from the pop-up menu.

Either way, you see the dialog box in Figure 16-22. Click the appropriate gadget/screen size, and then click Share. When it's all over, your video will appear safely nestled in iTunes, in the Movies category, ready to watch or sync.

Figure 16-22:
This dialog box gives you three size choices for the movie you're exporting, which correspond to the screen sizes of the three Apple gadgets available. (The Computer option is just there in case you like to play videos right in iTunes, right on the screen. It's dimmed if the original movie isn't big enough to fill the screen.)

Post to MobileMe Gallery

If you have a MobileMe account (Chapter 10), a better alternative awaits: You can post your video to your own online gallery. Advantages over YouTube? Simpler, quicker uploading. No 10-minute, 1-gig length or size limit. A much classier presentation online, without blinking ads and juvenile comments. Control over who can see it. Higher quality (even high definition).

Choose Share→MobileMe, or click 🖼 on the control bar and choose MobileMe Gallery from the pop-up menu. Type a name and description, and consider these three options:

- **Include a movie compatible with iPhone and iPod Touch.** The big-screen movie you're about to post isn't in the right format for people who tune into your MobileMe Gallery on their iPhones and Touches. But if you turn on this checkbox, you generate a shadow version that's correctly sized and formatted for those popular gadgets.

- **Hide movie on my Gallery home page.** In other words, "Don't make this movie public." Nobody will even know this movie exists online unless you send them the unguessable Web address.

- **Allow movie to be downloaded.** Just what it says. If you want to retain control of your movie, leave this off; people will be able to watch it only on your Me gallery. If you want your creation to go viral, on the other hand, then turn this on and hope for the best.

Finally, click Share. QuickTime Player gets right to work sending your video to your MobileMe Gallery. When the progress bar finishes its crawl across the status dialog box, you see a tiny link (Figure 16-23) to the posted video.

Figure 16-23:
When the video is finished uploading to MobileMe, a tiny Web address appears in the progress box. Click it to view your masterpiece online, or send the Web address around to your fans.

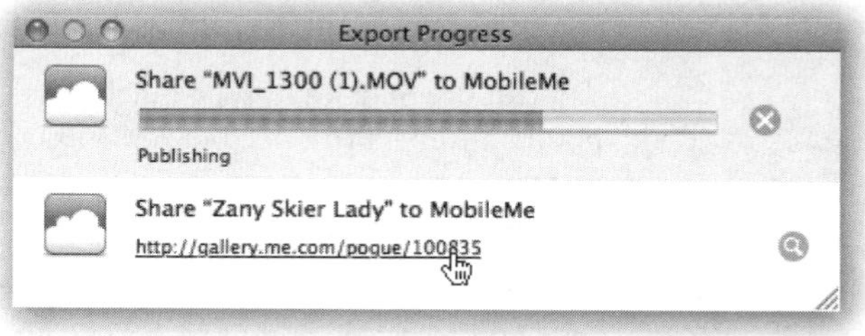

Post to YouTube

When you consider your movie ready for prime time, you can post it to YouTube, the world's most popular and famous Web site for short videos, with a single command. (The movie can't be longer than 10 minutes, or larger than 1 gigabyte.)

Before you begin, though, you have to sign up for a YouTube *account*. It's free, but you have to do it at YouTube.com, and remember the name and password you choose.

Then, with your movie open in QuickTime Player, choose Share→YouTube. (Or click the 📧 icon on the control bar and then choose YouTube from the pop-up menu.) You're asked for your YouTube name and password. If you turn on "Remember this password in my keychain," you won't have to enter it the next time.

Finally, click Sign In. On the next screen, type a title and description for the movie. Enter keywords (search categories like "funny" or "sports") so people on YouTube will find your video when they search.

Finally, click Next. A final screen appears, warning you not to be naughty. Click Share to finish process. In a few minutes, your video will be live for the whole world to see—no charge.

Saving the finished movie

After you've trimmed a movie (or not), you can choose File→Save As to specify a new name for your edited masterpiece. All you have to do is specify, using the Format pop-up menu, what *size* you want the finished file to be: iPhone, iPod, HD 480p (meaning "standard TV screen"), HD 720p (meaning "hi-def TV"), and so on. Keep in mind that big size on the screen = huge video file that's slow and awkward to transmit online.

Safari

Apple's Web browser harbors enough tips and tricks lurking inside to last you a lifetime. Details in Chapter 12.

Stickies

Stickies (Figure 16-24) lets you create virtual Post-it notes that you can stick anywhere on your screen—a triumphant software answer to the thousands of people who stick notes on the edges of their *actual* monitors. If you're a fan of the Windows Notepad, you might find yourself getting heavily into Stickies instead.

You can use Stickies to type quick notes and to-do items, paste in Web addresses or phone numbers you need to remember, or store any other little scraps and snippets of text you come across. Your electronic Post-its show up whenever the Stickies program is running.

You can use a mix of fonts, text colors, and styles within each note. You can even copy and paste (or drag) *pictures, movies, and sounds* into your notes, producing the world's most elaborate reminders and to-do lists. You can even spell check your notes and search-and-replace text.

Figure 16-24:
In the old days of the Mac, the notes you created with Stickies were text-only, single-font deals. Today, however, you can use a mix of fonts, text colors, and styles within each note. You can even paste in graphics, sounds, and movies (like PICT, GIF, JPEG, QuickTime, AIFF, whole PDF files, and so on), creating the world's most elaborate reminders and to-do lists.

Creating Sticky Notes

The first time you launch Stickies, a few sample notes appear automatically, describing some of the program's features. You can quickly dispose of each sample by clicking the close button in the upper-left corner of each note or by choosing File→Close (⌘-W). Each time you close a note, a dialog box asks if you want to save the note. If you click Don't Save, the note disappears permanently.

Note: The Stickies module that's part of Dashboard is extremely similar, and it's arguably quicker to open (just press F12). But it's also far more limited.

To create a new note, choose File→New Note (⌘-N) and start typing, pasting, or dragging text (or graphics, movies, or sounds) in from other programs.

Organizing Stickies

Once you start plastering your Mac with notes, it doesn't take long to find yourself plagued with desktop clutter. Fortunately, Stickies includes a few built-in tricks for managing a deskful of notes:

- There's a small resize handle on the lower-right corner of each note. Drag it to make notes larger or smaller onscreen.

- Use the small triangle in the upper-right corner of each note to zoom and shrink note windows with a single click. The first click collapses a note down to a more compact size. Another click pops the note back open to normal size.

- The best option: Double-click anywhere along the dark strip at the top of each note to miniaturize it into a compact one-line mini-note, as shown in Figure 16-25. You also can miniaturize a selected note by choosing Window→Miniaturize Window (⌘-M).

- If your notes are scattered randomly across the desktop, you can bring them all forward with the Window→Bring All to Front command.

Tip: The most efficient way to use Stickies is to keep the notes in their miniaturized state, as shown in Figure 16-25. When a note is miniaturized, the first line of text shows up in tiny type right in the collapsed title bar of the note, so you don't have to expand the note to remember what's in it. And since many—if not most—of your notes can probably be summed up in a couple of words ("pick up dry cleaning," "call Mom"), it's perfectly possible to keep your sticky notes in their miniaturized state permanently.

Figure 16-25:
If the first line of text gets truncated, as in the third note shown here, you can tug the right corner of the note and drag it wider without de-miniaturizing it.

Formatting Notes

The Stickies menus offer several word processor–like commands for creating designer sticky notes, with any combination of fonts, colors, and styles. (You can also choose from six different background colors from the Color menu.)

Saving Sticky Notes

The notes you create in Stickies last only as long as you keep them open. If you close a note to get it out of the way, it vanishes permanently.

If you want to preserve the information you've stuffed into your notes in a more permanent form, use File→Export Text to save each note as a standalone text document. When you use the Export Text command, you can save the file as a plain text file, RTF (a special format recognized by most word processors), and RTFD (a strange and powerful variant of RTF that can contain *attachments*—graphics, files, and even programs you've dragged into the note).

System Preferences

This program opens the door to the nerve center of Mac OS X's various user preferences, settings, and options. Chapter 15 covers every option in detail.

TextEdit

TextEdit is a word processor (Figure 16-26)—a pretty darn powerful one, at that, considering you didn't have to pay a cent extra for it. You can create real documents with real formatting, using style sheets, colors, automatic numbering and bullets, tables, and customized line spacing, and—get this—even save the result as a Microsoft Word document. If you need to use Word files, but you can't stand bloated Microsoft interfaces, welcome.

TextEdit's Two Personalities

The one confusing aspect of TextEdit is that it's both a *plain text editor* (no formatting; globally compatible) and a true *word processor* (fonts, sizes, styles; compatible with other word processors). You need to keep your wits about you as you edit, because the minute you add formatting to your document, TextEdit no longer lets you save it as a plain text file.

Here's the scheme:

- You can change a plain text document to a formatted one by choosing Format→ Make Rich Text. The ruler appears automatically to remind you that a new world of formatting has just become available.

- Conversely, you can change a formatted document (a Word file you've opened, for example) to a plain text document by choosing Format→Make Plain Text. An alert message appears to point out that you're about to lose all formatting.

- If you know what kind of document you *always* want to open, go to the TextEdit→Preferences dialog box; on the New Document tab, select Rich Text or Plain Text. That's what you'll get each time you choose File→New.

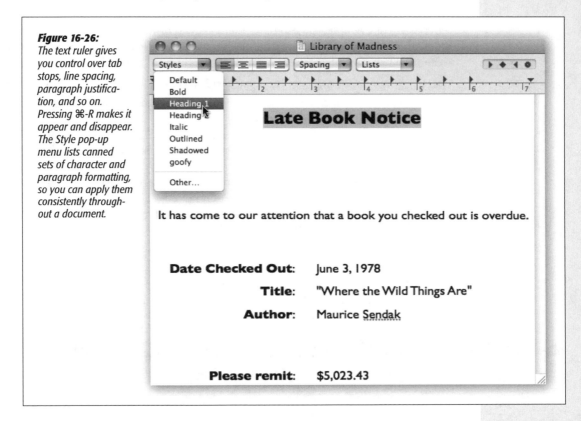

Figure 16-26:
The text ruler gives you control over tab stops, line spacing, paragraph justification, and so on. Pressing ⌘-R makes it appear and disappear. The Style pop-up menu lists canned sets of character and paragraph formatting, so you can apply them consistently throughout a document.

Working in TextEdit

As you begin typing, all the usual word processing rules apply, with a few twists:

- Choose Bold, Italic, and font sizes using the Format→Font submenu, or choose Format→Font→Show Fonts (⌘-T) to open up the standard Mac OS X Font panel. You can even create subscript or superscript, change the color of the text (Format→Font→Show Colors), and so on.

- Common paragraph-alignment options—Align Left, Align Right, Center, Justify—are all available as ruler buttons and also reside in the Format→Text submenu. Adjust the line spacing (single, double, or any fraction or multiple) using the Spacing pop-up menu in the ruler.

- The ruler also offers automatic bulleting and numbering of paragraphs. Just choose the numbering style you prefer from the Lists pop-up menu.

- You can select several non-adjacent bits of text *simultaneously.* To pull this off, highlight your first piece of text by dragging, and then press ⌘ as you use the mouse to select more text. Bingo: You've highlighted two separate chunks of text.

When you're done selecting bits of text here and there, you can operate on them en masse. For example, you can make them all bold or italic with one fell swoop. You can even use the Cut, Copy, and Paste commands, as described in the next section. When you cut or copy, the command acts upon all your selections at once.

You can also drag any *one* of the highlighted portions to a new area, confident that the other chunks will come along for the ride. All of the selected areas wind up consolidated in their new location.

Tip: If you *Option*-drag one of the highlighted bits, you *copy* it, leaving the original in place.

- Similarly, you can use the Find command to highlight a certain term everywhere it appears in a document. To do that, choose Edit→Find→Find (or just press ⌘-F). Fill in the "Find" and "Replace with" boxes—and then press the Control key. The Replace All button changes to say Select All.

- If you Option-drag vertically, you can freely select an arbitrary column of text (not necessarily the entire page width). This technique is very useful when you want to select only one column in a multicolumn layout, or when you want to select the numbers in a list ("1.," "2.," and so on) and format them all at once. (As noted earlier, this trick also works in Preview PDF documents.)

UP TO SPEED

The Deal with Microsoft Word

Yes, you read that correctly: Humble TextEdit can open and create Microsoft Word documents! Your savings: the $400 price of Microsoft Office!

Well, sort of.

When you open a Microsoft Word document in TextEdit, most of the formatting comes through alive: bold, italic, font choices, colors, line spacing, alignment, and so on. Even very basic tables make it into TextEdit, although with different column widths.

A lot of Word-specific formatting does not survive crossing the chasm, however: borders, style sheets, footnotes, and the like. Bullets and numbered lists don't make it, either, even though TextEdit can create its own versions of these. And TextEdit doesn't recognize the comments and tracked changes your collaborators might use to mark up your manuscript.

Saving a TextEdit document as a Word document (File→Save As) is a better bet, because Word understands the many kinds of formatting that TextEdit can produce—including bullets, numbering, and tables. The one disappointment is that Word doesn't recognize any style sheets you've set up in TextEdit. The formatting applied by those style names survives—just not the style names themselves.

Even so, a built-in Word-document editor is a huge, huge step for the Mac OS. It means that in many cases, you can be a first-class citizen on the playing field of American business. Nobody ever needs to know that you're (a) using a Mac, and (b) not using the real Microsoft Word.

Style Sheets

A *style* is a prepackaged collection of formatting attributes that you can apply and reapply with a click of the mouse (bold, 24-point Optima, double-spaced, centered, for instance). You can create as many styles as you need: chapter headings, sidebar styles, and so on. You end up with a collection of custom-tailored styles for each of the repeating elements of your document.

Once you've created your styles, you can apply them as you need them, safe in the knowledge that they'll be consistent throughout the document. During the editing process, if you notice you accidentally styled a *headline* using the *Subhead* style, you can fix the problem by simply reapplying the correct style.

Note: Unlike a real word processor, TextEdit doesn't let you *change* a style's formatting and thereby update every occurrence of it. You can't search and replace by style, either.

- **Creating a named style.** To create a style, format some text so that it looks the way you like it, complete with font, color, line spacing, tab settings, and so on.

  Then, from the Styles pop-up menu in the ruler, choose Other (Figure 16-27, top). Click Add to Favorites, type a name for the style, turn on both checkboxes (Figure 16-27, bottom), and click Add.

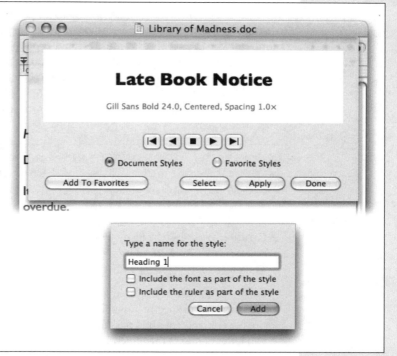

Figure 16-27:
Top: Highlight the text you want to format. Then, from the Styles pop-up menu in the ruler, choose Other. With each click of the ▶ button, you summon a snippet of the next chunk of formatting. When you find one you like, you can either click Apply (to zap the highlighted text into submission) or Add To Favorites (to reuse this canned style later). In the latter case, you can give the new style a name (bottom).

- **Applying a style.** Later, when you want to reuse the formatting you set up, highlight some text and then choose the appropriate name from the Styles pop-up menu. TextEdit applies the formatting immediately.

Tip: If you simply click *inside a paragraph,* applying a style affects only *paragraph* attributes like line spacing, tab stops, and alignment. If you *highlight a random chunk of text* instead, applying a style affects only *character* attributes like the font and type size. If you highlight an *entire* paragraph, however, both text and paragraph formatting appear.

- **Deleting a style.** To delete a superfluous style, choose Other from the Styles pop-up menu on the ruler. Click the Favorite Styles button, choose the unwanted style's name from the pop-up menu, and then click Remove From Favorites. (Deleting a style doesn't affect any formatting that's already in your document; it just removes the name from the Styles menu.)

- **Copying by example.** In Word and most other "serious" word processors, the routines above correctly describe how you use styles. In TextEdit, however, you can use Option-⌘-C and Option-⌘-V (Format→Copy Style and Format→Paste Style) to grab formatting from one place in your document and reuse it elsewhere. (Of course, you can't apply styles in text-only documents.)

Tables

Tables can make life a heck of a lot easier when you want to create a resumé, agenda, program booklet, list, multiple-choice test, Web page, or another document where numbers, words, and phrases must be aligned across the page. In the bad old days, people did it by pressing the Tab key to line up columns—a technique that turned into a nightmare as soon as you tried to add or delete text. But using a word processor's *table* feature is light-years easier and more flexible, because each row of a table expands infinitely to contain whatever you put into it. Everything else on its row remains aligned.

Tip: Tables are also critical for designing Web pages, as any Web designer can tell you. Even though you can't see the table outlines, many a Web page is filled with columns of text that are aligned invisibly by tables. And now that TextEdit can save your work as an HTML document, it's suddenly a viable candidate for designing basic Web pages.

- **Create a table** by choosing Format→Text→Table. The floating Table palette appears (Figure 16-28). Use it to specify how many rows and columns you want. The placeholder table in your document adjusts itself in real time.

- **Format the table** using the other controls in the Table palette. The Alignment controls let you specify how the text in one of the table cells hugs its border. Cell Border controls the thickness of the line around the selected cells' borders (or, if you enter 0, makes the table walls invisible). The color swatch next to Cell Border specifies the color of the solid lines. The Cell Background controls let you color in the table cells with colors of your choice. (Choose Color Fill from the pop-up menu, and then click the color swatch.) This is an especially valuable option for Web designers.

- **Adjust the rows and columns** by dragging the cell borders.

- **Merge two selected cells** by clicking Merge Cells in the Table palette. Once you've done that, you can use the Split Cell button to split them apart again. (Split Cell doesn't work except in cells you've previously merged.)

- **Nest one table inside a cell of another** by clicking in the cell and then clicking Nest Table. Change the numbers in the Rows and Columns boxes to set up its dimensions.

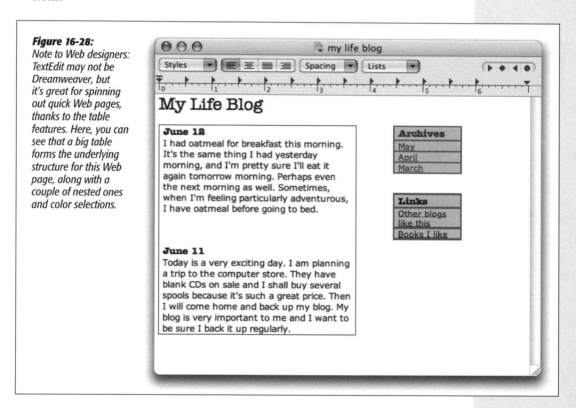

Figure 16-28:
Note to Web designers: TextEdit may not be Dreamweaver, but it's great for spinning out quick Web pages, thanks to the table features. Here, you can see that a big table forms the underlying structure for this Web page, along with a couple of nested ones and color selections.

TextEdit as Web Designer

The Table palette isn't the only clue that Apple intends TextEdit to be a quick-and-dirty Web page design program. Consider these other tools:

- You can easily add graphics to the page by dragging or pasting them into a document. The program understands TIFF, PICT, JPG, and GIF formats.

- You can add Web-style hyperlinks by highlighting "Click here" (or whatever the link says), choosing Format→Text→Link, and entering the Web address in the resulting dialog box. Or just drag a link in from Safari, Mail, or another program. (To edit the link later, right-click it, and then choose Edit Link.)

- To save a document as an HTML (Web page) file, choose File→Save As; from the File Format pop-up menu, choose Web Archive.

- Don't miss the HTML options in TextEdit→Preferences. On the "Open and Save" tab, you can specify what kind of HTML document you want to produce, what cascading style sheets (CSS) setting you want, and whether or not you want TextEdit to include code to preserve blank areas (white space) in your layout.

Tip: When you *open* a Web page document—that is, an HTML document—TextEdit is faced with a quandary. Should it open up the page as though it's a Web page, interpreting the HTML code as though it's a browser? Or should it reveal the underlying HTML code itself?

Actually, that's up to you. When you choose File→Open, turn on "Ignore rich text commands" to make the document open up as HTML code. (To make this change permanent, turn on the same checkbox on the "Open and Save" pane of the TextEdit→Preferences dialog box.)

Time Machine

This marquee feature of Mac OS X is described starting on page 277.

Utilities: Your Mac OS X Toolbox

The Utilities folder (inside your Applications folder) is home to another batch of freebies: a couple of dozen tools for monitoring, tuning, tweaking, and troubleshooting your Mac.

The truth is, you're likely to use only about six of these utilities. The rest are very specialized gizmos primarily of interest to network administrators or Unix geeks who are obsessed with knowing what kind of computer-code gibberish is going on behind the scenes.

Activity Monitor

Activity Monitor is designed to let the technologically savvy Mac fan see how much of the Mac's available power is being tapped at any given moment.

The Processes table

Even when you're only running a program or two on your Mac, dozens of computational tasks (*processes*) are going on in the background. The top half of the dialog box, which looks like a table, shows you all the different processes—visible and invisible—that your Mac is handling at the moment.

Check out how many items appear in the Process list, even when you're just staring at the desktop. It's awesome to see just how busy your Mac is! Some are easily recognizable programs (such as Finder), while others are background system-level operations you don't normally see. For each item, you can see the percentage of CPU being used, who's using it (either your account name, someone else's, or *root*, meaning the Mac itself), and how much memory it's using.

Or use the pop-up menu above the list to see:

- **All Processes.** This is the complete list of running processes; you'll notice that the vast majority are little Unix applications you never even knew you had.

- **My Processes.** This list shows only the programs that pertain to *your* world—your login. There are still plenty of unfamiliar items, but they're all running to serve *your* account.

- **Windowed Processes.** Now *this* is probably what you were expecting: a list of actual programs with actual English names, like Activity Monitor, Finder, Safari, and Mail. These are the only ones running in actual windows, the only ones that are *visible*, which is what most people probably think of as programs.

The System monitor tabs

At the bottom of Activity Monitor, you're offered five tabs that reveal intimate details about your Mac and its behind-the-scenes efforts (Figure 16-29):

- **CPU.** As you go about your usual Mac business, opening a few programs, dragging a playing QuickTime movie across the screen, playing a game, and so on, you can see the CPU graph rise and fall, depending on how busy you're keeping the CPU. On multiple-processor Macs, you see a different bar for each chip, enabling you to see how efficiently Mac OS X is distributing the work among them.

Tip: You may also want to watch this graph right in your Dock (choose View→Dock Icon→Show CPU History) or in a bar at the edge of your screen (choose Window→Floating CPU Window→Horizontally).

Finally, there's the weirdly uncapitalized command View→"Show CPU monitors on top of other windows." It makes the little bar float on top of all your other programs, so you can't miss it.

- **System Memory.** Here's a colorful graph that reveals the state of your Mac's RAM at the moment.

  The number below the graph shows how much memory is installed in your Mac. If, when your Mac is running a typical complement of programs, the Wired number plus the Active number nearly equals your total RAM amount, it's time to consider buying more memory. You're suffocating your Mac.

- **Disk Activity.** Even when you're not opening or saving a file, your Mac's hard drive is frequently hard at work, shuffling chunks of program code into and out of memory, for example. Here's where the savvy technician can see exactly how frantic the disk is at the moment.

- **Disk Usage.** This little graph offers one of the quickest ways to check out how full your hard drive is at the moment. (If you have more than one drive—say, a flash drive, tape-backup drive, or whatever—choose another drive's name from the pop-up menu.)

- **Network.** Keep an eye on how much data is shooting across your office network with this handy EKG-ish graph.

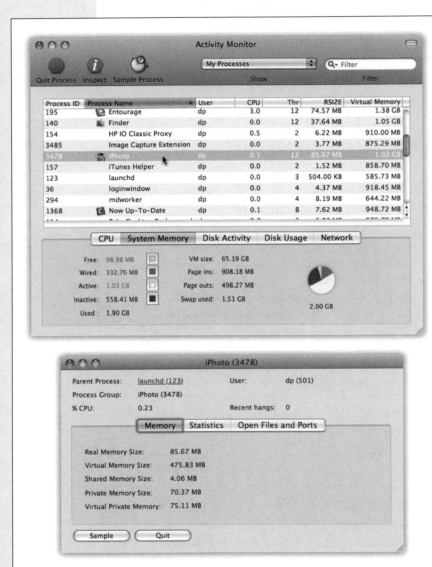

Figure 16-29:
The many faces of Activity Monitor.

Top: It can be a graph of your processor (CPU) activity, your RAM usage at the moment, your disk capacity, and so on. For most people, only the processes listed here with tiny icons beside their names are actual windowed programs—those with icons in the Finder, the ones you actually interact with.

Don't miss the top-left Quit Process button. It's a convenient way to jettison a locked-up program when all else fails.

Bottom: If you double-click a process's name, you get a three-tab dialog box that offers stunningly complete reams of data (mostly of interest only to programmers) about what that program is up to. (The Open Files and Ports tab, for example, shows you how many files that program has opened, often invisibly.)

AirPort Utility

You use the AirPort Utility to set up and manage AirPort base stations (Apple's line of wireless WiFi networking routers).

If you click Continue, it presents a series of screens, posing one question at a time: what you want to name the network, what password you want for it, and so on. Once you've followed the steps and answered the questions, your AirPort hardware will be properly configured and ready to use.

AppleScript Editor

AppleScript may be hard for a Windows switcher to grasp right away, because there's simply nothing like it in Windows. It's a programming language that's both very simple and very powerful, because it lets Mac programs send instructions or data to *each other*.

A simple AppleScript program might perform some simple daily task for you: backing up your Documents folder, for example. A more complex script can be pages long. In professional printing and publishing, where AppleScript enjoys its greatest popularity, a script might connect to a photographer's hard drive elsewhere on the Internet, download a photo from a predetermined folder, color-correct it in Photoshop, import it into a specified page-layout document, print a proof copy, and send a notification email to the editor—automatically.

This little program is the gateway to all of the scripts and tools pertaining to Apple-Script. For details on using Apple's included AppleScripts and writing your own, check out the free downloadable Appendix to this chapter, "AppleScript." It's available on this book's "Missing CD" at *www.missingmanuals.com*.

Audio MIDI Setup

This program, which is aimed primarily at musicians and audio geeks, has two halves:

- **Audio.** When you first open Audio MIDI Setup, you see a complete summary of the audio inputs and outputs available on your Mac right now. It's a lot like the Sound pane of System Preferences, but with a lot more geeky detail. Here, for example, you can specify the recording level for your Mac's microphone, or even change the audio quality it records.

  For most people, this is all meaningless, because most Macs have only one input (the microphone) and one output (the speakers). But if you're sitting in your darkened music studio, which is humming with high-tech audio gear whose software has been designed to work with this little program, you'll smile when you see this tab.

- **MIDI.** MIDI stands for Musical Instrument Digital Interface, a standard "language" for inter-synthesizer communication. It's available to music software companies who have written their wares to capitalize on these tools.

  When you choose Window→Show MIDI Window, you get a window that represents your recording-studio configuration. By clicking Add Device, you create a new icon that represents one of your pieces of gear. Double-click the icon to specify its make and model. Finally, by dragging lines from the "in" and "out" arrows, you teach your Mac and its MIDI software how the various components are wired together.

Bluetooth File Exchange

One of the luxuries of using a Mac that has Bluetooth is the ability to shoot files (to colleagues who own similarly clever gadgets) through the air, up to 30 feet away. Bluetooth File Exchange makes it possible.

Boot Camp Assistant

This program helps you create (or destroy) a partition of your hard drive to hold a copy of Microsoft Windows. Details in Chapter 8.

ColorSync Utility

If you use ColorSync, then you probably know already that this configuration utility is for people in the high-end color printing business.

Console

Console is a viewer for all of Mac OS X's text logs—the behind-the-scenes, internal Unix status messages being passed between the Mac OS X and other applications. These messages can be of significant value to programmers who are debugging software or troubleshooting a messy problem, or, occasionally, to someone you've called for tech support.

DigitalColor Meter

DigitalColor Meter can grab the exact color value of any pixel on your screen, which can be helpful when matching colors in Web page construction or other design work.

Disk Utility

This important program serves two key functions:

- It serves as Mac OS X's own little Norton Utilities: a powerful hard drive administration tool that lets you repair, erase, format, and partition disks. In everyday life, you'll probably use Disk Utility most often for its *Repair Permissions* feature, which solves an uncanny number of weird little Mac OS X glitches. But it's also worth keeping in mind in case you ever find yourself facing a serious disk problem.

- Disk Utility also creates and manages *disk images,* electronic versions of disks or folders that you can exchange electronically with other people.

The following discussion tackles the program's two personalities one at a time.

Disk Utility, the hard drive repair program

Here are some of the tasks you can perform with this half of Disk Utility:

- Repair folders, files, and programs that don't work because you supposedly don't have sufficient "access privileges." Using the Repair Disk Permissions button fixes an *astonishing* range of bizarre Mac OS X problems, from programs that won't open to menulets that freeze up the works.

- Get size and type information about any disks attached to your Mac.

- Fix disks that won't appear on your desktop or behave properly.

- Completely erase disks—including rewritable CDs and DVDs (such as CD-RW and DVD-RW discs).

- Partition a disk into multiple *volumes* (that is, subdivide a drive so that its segments appear on the desktop with separate disk icons).

- Set up a *RAID array* (a cluster of separate disks that acts as a single volume).

Note: Disk Utility can perform some of its magic on the startup disk—the disk that's running Mac OS X at the moment. For example, it can check the disk for damage, fix the permissions of the disk, or even adjust its partitions.

But any other operation, like reformatting, erasing, or actually repairing the disk, still requires the Mac to start up from a different disk (your Snow Leopard DVD, for example). Otherwise, it'd be like a surgeon performing an appendectomy on himself—not a great idea.

The left Disk Utility panel lists your hard drive and any other disks in or attached to your Mac at the moment. When you click the name of your hard drive's mechanism, like "74.5 GB Hitachi iC25N0…" (not the "Macintosh HD" partition label below it), you see a panel with five tabs, one for each of the main Disk Utility functions:

- **First Aid.** This is the disk-repair part of Disk Utility, and it does a terrific job at fixing many disk problems. When you're troubleshooting, Disk Utility should always be your first resort.

  To use it, click the icon of a disk and then click either Verify Disk (to get a report on the disk's health) or Repair Disk (which fixes whatever problems the program finds). In other words, First Aid attempts to perform the same healing effects on a sick hard drive as, say, a program like the old Norton Utilities.

  If Disk First Aid reports that it's unable to fix the problem, *then* it's time to invest in a program like DiskWarrior (*www.alsoft.com*).

  You may wind up using the Verify and Repair Disk *Permissions* buttons even more often. Their function is to straighten out problems with the invisible Unix file permissions that keep you from moving, changing, or deleting files or folders. (The occasional software installer can create problems like this.) You'd be surprised how often running one of these permission checks solves little Mac OS X glitches.

  Chapter 14 has more details on permissions.

- **Erase.** Select a disk, choose a format (*always* Mac OS Extended [Journaled], unless you're formatting a disk for use on a Windows machine or an ancient Mac running Mac OS 8.1 or earlier), give it a name, and then click Erase to wipe a disk clean.

• **Partition.** With the Partition tools, you can erase a hard drive in such a way that you subdivide its surface. Each chunk is represented on your screen by another hard drive icon (Figure 16-30).

There are some very good reasons *not* to partition a drive these days: A partitioned hard drive is more difficult to resurrect after a serious crash, requires more navigation when you want to open a particular file, and offers no speed or safety benefits.

On the other hand, there's one very good reason *to* do it: Partitioning is the only way to use Boot Camp, described in Chapter 8. When you're using Boot Camp, your Mac is a Mac when running off of the first partition, and a Windows PC when starting up from the second one. (But you don't use Disk Utility in that case; use Boot Camp Assistant.)

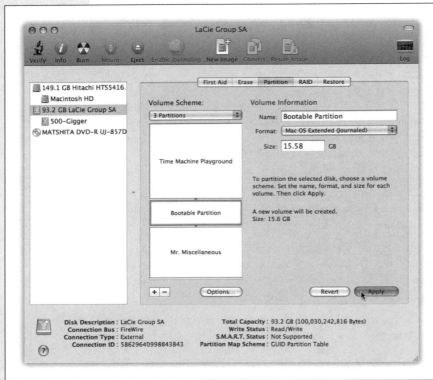

Figure 16-30:
Partitioning your drive with Disk Utility no longer involves erasing it completely. Select the drive you want to partition from the list on the left, and then click the Partition tab. Click the + button for each new partition you want.

Now drag the horizontal dividers in the Volumes map to specify the relative sizes of the partitions you want to create. Assign a name and a format for each partition in the Volume Information area, and then click Apply.

• **RAID.** RAID stands for Redundant Array of Independent Disks, and refers to a special formatting scheme in which a group of separate disks are configured to work together as one very large, very fast drive. In a RAID array, multiple disks share the job of storing data—a setup that can improve speed and reliability.

Most Mac owners don't use or set up RAID arrays, probably because most Mac owners have only one hard drive (and Disk Utility can't make your startup disk part of a RAID array).

If you're using multiple external hard disks, though, you can use Apple RAID to merge them into one giant disk. Just drag the icons of the relevant disks (or disk partitions) from the left-side list of disks into the main list (where it says, "Drag disks or volumes here to add to set"). Use the RAID Type pop-up menu to specify the RAID format you want to use (Stripe is a popular choice for maximizing disk speed), name your new mega-disk, and then click Create. The result is a single "disk" icon on your desktop that actually represents the combined capacity of all the RAID disks.

- **Restore.** This tab lets you make a perfect copy of a disk or a disk image, much like the popular shareware programs Carbon Copy Cloner and SuperDuper. You might find this useful when, for example, you want to make an exact copy of your old Mac's drive on your new one. You can't do that just by copying your old files and folders manually. If you try, you won't get the thousands of *invisible* files that make up Mac OS X. If you use the Restore function, they'll come along for the ride.

Start by dragging the disk or disk image you want to copy *from* into the Source box. Then drag the icon of the disk you want to copy *to* into the Destination box.

Tip: If you want to copy an online disk image onto one of your disks, you don't have to download it first. Just type its Web address into the Source field. You might find this trick convenient if you keep disk images on your iDisk, for example.

POWER USERS' CLINIC

Partition Adjustments on the Fly

You can expand, shrink, or create partitions without having to erase the whole hard drive. If you're into partitioning at all, this is a *huge* convenience.

Expanding a partition. Suppose, for example, that your main hard drive has two partitions: a main one (200 gigs) and a secondary one (50 gigs) that used to hold all your photos and movies. But you've outgrown the second partition and have moved all those photos and movies to their own external hard drive. Wouldn't it be nice to add the newly unoccupied 50 gigs to your main partition?

You can do that without having to erase the whole hard drive. (This process, however, nukes everything on the *second* partition, so make sure you're prepared to lose it all.)

Open Disk Utility. Click the name of the hard drive (for example, "Hitachi HTS541616J9SA00"—*not* "Macintosh HD"). Click Partition. You see a display like the one in Figure 16-30.

Click the second partition (or third, or whatever partition is *just after* the one you want to expand) and then click the − button below the list. Poof! It's gone.

Now you can drag the main partition's bottom edge downward (or type a new size into the Size box), expanding it into the free area. Take a deep breath, and then click Apply.

Shrinking a partition. In Figure 16-30, you can see that a portion of the first partition is lightly shaded. (It's blue in real life.) The blue represents data; you can't shrink a partition so much that it crowds out your files. You can, however, shrink the partition to eliminate empty space. Just drag the lower edge of its map chunk upward.

Creating new partitions. Anytime there's leftover space on the drive, you can create *new* partitions from it.

To do that, click the **+** button, and proceed as described in Figure 16-30.

If you turn on Erase Destination, Disk Utility obliterates all the data on your target disk before copying the data. If you leave this checkbox off, however, Disk Utility simply copies everything onto your destination, preserving all your old data in the process. (The Skip Checksum checkbox is available only if you choose to erase your destination disk. If you're confident all the files on the source disk are 100 percent healthy and whole, turn on this checkbox to save time. Otherwise, leave it off for extra safety.)

Finally, click the Restore button. (You might need to type in an administrator password.) Restoring can take a long time for big disks, so go ahead and make yourself a cup of coffee while you're waiting.

Tip: Instead of clicking a disk icon and then clicking the appropriate Disk Utility tab, you can just Control-click (or right-click) a disk's name and choose Information, First Aid, Erase, Partition, RAID, or Restore from the shortcut menu.

Disk Utility, the disk-image program

Disk images are very cool. Each one is a single icon that behaves precisely like an actual disk—a flash drive or hard drive, for example—but can be distributed electronically. For example, a lot of Mac OS X add-on software arrives from your Web download in disk-image form, as shown below.

Disk images are popular for software distribution for a simple reason: Each image file precisely duplicates the original master disk, complete with all the necessary files in all the right places. When a software company sends you a disk image, it ensures that you'll install the software from a disk that *exactly* matches the master disk.

It's important to understand the difference between a *disk-image file* and the *mounted disk* (the one that appears when you double-click the disk image). If you flip back to page 153 and consult Figure 4-17, this distinction should be clear.

You can create disk images, too. Doing so can be very handy in situations like these:

- You want to create a backup of an important CD. By turning it into a disk-image file on your hard drive, you'll always have a safety copy, ready to burn back onto a *new* CD. (This is an essential practice for educational CDs that kids will be handling soon after eating peanut butter and jelly.)

- You want to replicate your entire hard drive—complete with all of its files, programs, folder setups, and so on—onto a new, bigger hard drive (or a new, better Mac), using the Restore feature described earlier.

- You want to back up your entire hard drive, or maybe just a certain chunk of it, onto an iPod or another disk. (Again, you can later use the Restore function to complete the transaction.)

- You bought a game that requires its CD to be in the drive at all times. Many programs like these run equally well off of a mounted disk image that you made from the original CD.

- You want to send somebody else a copy of a disk via the Internet. You simply create a disk image, and then send *that*—preferably in compressed form.

Here's how you make a disk image:

- **To image-ize a disk or partition.** Click the name of the disk in the left-panel list, where you see the disks currently in, or attached to, your Mac. (The topmost item is the name of your *drive*, like "484.0 MB MATSHITA DVD-R" for a DVD drive or "74.5 GB Hitachi" for a hard drive. Beneath that entry, you generally see the name of the actual partition, like "Macintosh HD," or the CD's name as it appears on the screen.)

  Then choose File→New→Disk Image from [whatever the disk or partition's name is].

- **To image-ize a folder.** Choose File→New→Disk Image from Folder. In the Open dialog box, click the folder you want, and then click Image.

Tip: Disk Utility can't turn an individual file into a disk image. But you can put a single file into a folder, and then make a disk image of it.

Either way, the next dialog box (Figure 16-31) offers some fascinating options.

- **Image Format.** If you choose "read/write," your disk image file, when double-clicked, turns into a superb imitation of a hard drive. You can drag files and folders onto it, drag them off of it, change icons' names on it, and so on.

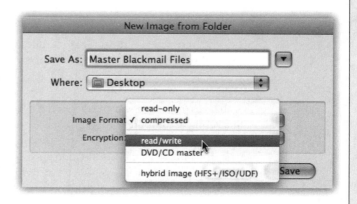

Figure 16-31:
These two pop-up menus let you specify (a) what kind of disk image you want, and (b) whether or not you want it password-protected. The latter option is great when you want to password-protect one folder, without bothering with your entire Home folder.

If you choose "read-only," however, the result behaves more like a CD. You can copy things off of it, but not make any changes to it.

The "compressed" option is best if you intend to send the resulting file by email, post it for Web download, or preserve the disk image on some backup disk for a rainy day. It takes a little longer to create a simulated disk when you double-click the disk image file, but it takes up a lot less disk space than an uncompressed version.

Finally, choose "DVD/CD master" if you're copying a CD or a DVD. The resulting file is a perfect mirror of the original disc, ready for copying onto a blank CD or DVD when the time comes.

- **Encryption.** Here's an easy way to lock private files away into a vault that nobody else can open. If you choose one of these two AES encryption options (choose AES-128, if you value your time), you're asked to assign a password to your new image file. Nobody can open it without the password—not even you. On the other hand, if you save it into your Keychain (page 440), it's not such a disaster if you forget the password.

- **Save As.** Choose a name and location for your new image file. The name you choose here doesn't need to match the original disk or folder name.

When you click Save (or press Return), if you opted to create an encrypted image, you're asked to make up a password at this point.

Otherwise, Disk Utility now creates the image and then *mounts* it—that is, turns the image file into a simulated, yet fully functional, disk icon on your desktop.

When you're finished working with the disk, eject it as you would any disk (Control-click it and choose Eject, for example). Hang onto the .dmg disk image file itself, however. This is the file you'll need to double-click if you ever want to recreate your "simulated disk."

Turning an image into a CD

One of the other most common disk-image tasks is turning a disk image *back* into a CD or DVD—provided your Mac has a CD or DVD burner, of course.

All you have to do is drag the .dmg file into the Disk Utility window, select it, and click the Burn icon on the toolbar (or, alternatively, Control-click the .dmg icon and choose Burn from the shortcut menu). Insert a blank CD or DVD, and then click Burn.

Grab

Grab takes pictures of your Mac's screen, for use when you're writing up instructions, illustrating a computer book, or collecting proof of some secret screen you found buried in a game. You can take pictures of the entire screen (press ⌘-Z, which for once in its life does *not* mean Undo) or capture only the contents of a rectangular selection (press Shift-⌘-A). When you're finished, Grab displays your snapshot in a new window, which you can print, close without saving, copy, or save as a TIFF file, ready for emailing or inserting into a manuscript.

Now, as experienced Mac enthusiasts already know, the Mac OS has long had its *own* built-in shortcuts for capturing screenshots: Press Shift-⌘-3 to take a picture of the whole screen, and Shift-⌘-4 to capture a rectangular selection.

Tip: Don't forget that you can choose different, easier to remember keyboard shortcuts for these functions, if you like. Just open System Preferences→Keyboard→Keyboard Shortcuts, click where it now says Shift-⌘-3 (or whatever), and press the new key combo.

So why use Grab instead? In many cases, you shouldn't. The Shift-⌘-3 and Shift-⌘-4 shortcuts work like a dream. But there are some cases in which it might make more sense to opt for Grab. Here are three:

- Grab can make a *timed* screen capture (choose Capture→Timed Screen, or press Shift-⌘-Z), which lets you enjoy a 10-second delay before the screenshot is actually taken. After you click the Start Timer button, you have an opportunity to activate windows, pull down menus, drag items around, and otherwise set up the shot before Grab shoots the picture.

- When you capture a screenshot using Grab's Selection command, the *size* of your selection is displayed, in pixels, right under the pointer as you drag. If you need to capture a 256-pixel-wide square, for example, you can do so with pinpoint accuracy. (Choose Edit→Inspector to read the dimensions of a screenshot *after* you capture it.)

- With Grab, you have the option of including the cursor in the picture, which is extremely useful when you're showing a menu being pulled down or a button being clicked. (Mac OS X's screenshot keystrokes, by contrast, always eliminate the pointer.) Use the technique described in Figure 16-32 to add the pointer style of your choice to a Grab screenshot.

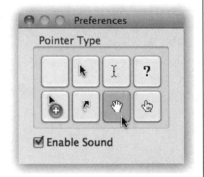

Figure 16-32:
Unlike the Shift-⌘-3 or Shift-⌘-4 keystrokes, Grab lets you include the pointer/cursor in the picture—or hide it. Choose Grab→Preferences and pick one of the eight pointer styles, or choose to keep the pointer hidden by activating the blank button in the upper-left corner.

Grapher

This little unsung app lets you create 2-D or 3-D graphs of staggering beauty and complexity.

When you first open Grapher, you're asked to choose what kind of virtual "graph paper" you want: two-dimensional (standard, polar, logarithmic) or three-dimensional (cubic, spherical, cylindrical). Click a name to see a preview; when you're happy with the selection, click Open.

Now the main Grapher window appears (Figure 16-33). Do yourself a favor: Spend a few wow-inducing minutes choosing canned equations from the Examples menu, and watching how Grapher whips up gorgeous, colorful, sometimes animated graphs on the fly.

When you're ready to plug in an equation of your own, type it into the text box at the top of the window. (If you're not such a math hotshot, or you're not sure of the equation format, work from the canned equations and mathematical building blocks that appear when you choose Equation→New Equation from Template or Window→Show Equation Palette.)

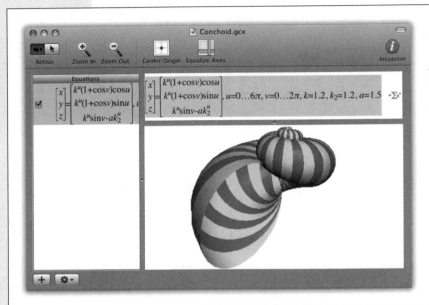

Figure 16-33:
In general, you type equations into Grapher just as you would on paper (like z=2xy). If in doubt, check the online help, which offers enough hints on functions, constants, differential equations, series, and periodic equations to keep the A Beautiful Mind guy busy for days.

Once the graph is up on the screen, you can tailor it like this:

- To move a 2-D graph in the window, choose View→Move Tool and then drag; to move a 3-D graph, ⌘-drag it.

- To rotate a 3-D graph, drag it around.

- To change the colors, line thicknesses, 3-D "walls," and other graphic elements, click the ❶ button (or choose Window→Show Inspector) to open the formatting palette. The controls you find here vary by graph type, but rest assured that Grapher can accommodate your every visual whim.

- To change the fonts and sizes, choose Grapher→Preferences. On the Equations panel, the four sliders let you specify the relative sizes of the text elements. If you click the sample equation, the Fonts panel appears (page 255), so you can fiddle with the type.

- Add your own captions, arrows, ovals, or rectangles using the Object menu.

Java Preferences

Programmers generally use the Java programming language to create small programs that they then embed into Web pages—animated effects, clocks, calculators, stock tickers, and so on. Your browser automatically downloads and runs such applets (assuming that you have "Enable Java" turned on in your browser).

Your Java folder contains several Java-related tools, which exist primarily for the benefit of Web programmers and Web programs (including Safari).

Keychain Access

Keychain Access memorizes and stores all your secret information—passwords for network access, file servers, FTP sites, Web pages, and other secure items. For instructions on using Keychain Access, see page 440.

Migration Assistant

This little cutie automates the transfer of all your stuff from one Mac to another—your Home folder, network settings, programs, and more. This comes in extremely handy when you buy a newer, better Mac—or when you need Time Machine to recover an entire dead Mac's worth of data. (It can also copy everything over from a secondary hard drive or partition.) The instructions on the screen guide you through the process (see page 585).

Network Utility

The Network Utility gathers information about Web sites and network citizens. It offers a suite of standard Internet tools like NetStat, Ping, Traceroute, Finger, and Whois—advanced tools, to be sure, but ones that even Mac novices may be asked to fire up when calling a technician for Internet help.

Podcast Capture

This program is a front end for Podcast Producer, a professional-league podcast recording and publishing program that's part of Apple's Mac OS X Server software suite. Unless you work in an office where a Mac OS X Server hums away in a back room, you can toss this program.

RAID Utility

Useful only if your office has Mac OS X Server, and only if your Mac has a RAID (multiple-disk system) card installed.

Remote Install Mac OS X

OK, so you bought a MacBook Air laptop. It has no CD/DVD drive. How are you supposed to install Snow Leopard on it, or run a disk testing/repair program?

By "borrowing" another Mac's DVD drive, that's how. To use this little utility, put the CD or DVD into the other Mac; then run Remote Install Mac OS X (on the same

Mac). Click Continue. You'll be walked through the process of installing Mac OS X or running your utility program, remotely, across the network to your Air.

Spaces

Double-clicking this icon is another way of triggering Spaces, the Mac's virtual-screen feature; it's described on page 129.

System Profiler

System Profiler is a great tool for learning exactly what's installed on your Mac and what's not—in terms of both hardware and software. The people who answer the phones on Apple's tech-support line are particularly fond of System Profiler, since the detailed information it reports can be very useful for troubleshooting nasty problems.

There are three ways to open System Profiler:

- **Slow.** Burrow into your Applications→Utilities folder; double-click System Profiler.

- **Medium.** Choose →About This Mac. In the resulting dialog box, click More Info.

Tip: If you click your Mac OS X version number twice in the About box, you get to see your Mac's serial number!

- **Fast.** Hold down the Option key, which makes the →About This Mac command *change* to say System Profiler. Choose it.

When you launch System Profiler, it reports information about your Mac in a categorized list down the left side (Figure 16-34).

Tip: If any of these screens is showing you more or less technical information than you'd like, use the View menu to choose Mini Profile, Basic Profile, or Full Profile.

Saving a report

To create a handsomely formatted report that you can print or save, choose File→Save, and then choose Rich Text Format from the File Format pop-up menu. Note, however, that the resulting report can be well over 100 pages long. In many cases, you're better off simply making a screenshot of the relevant Profiler screen, as described on page 566, or saving the thing as a PDF file (page 251).

Terminal

Mac OS X's resemblance to an attractive, mainstream operating system like Windows is just an optical illusion; the engine underneath the pretty skin is Unix, one of the oldest and most respected operating systems in use today. And Terminal is the rabbit hole that leads you—if you're technically bold—straight down into the Mac's powerful Unix world.

The first time you see it, you'd swear that Unix has about as much in common with the Mac OS X illustrated in the other chapters of this book as a Jeep does with a watermelon. It's a *command line interface:* a place where you can type out instructions to the computer itself. This is a world without icons, menus, or dialog boxes; even the mouse is almost useless.

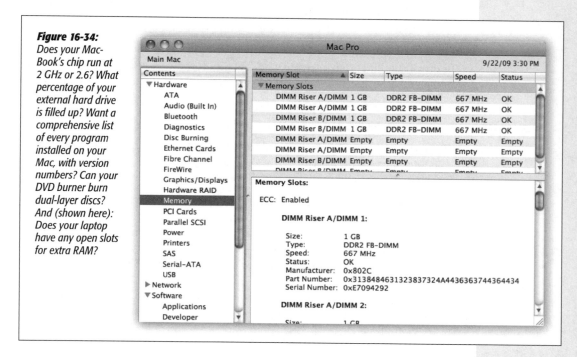

Figure 16-34:
Does your Mac-Book's chip run at 2 GHz or 2.6? What percentage of your external hard drive is filled up? Want a comprehensive list of every program installed on your Mac, with version numbers? Can your DVD burner burn dual-layer discs? And (shown here): Does your laptop have any open slots for extra RAM?

Surely you can appreciate the irony: The brilliance of the original 1984 Macintosh was that it *eliminated* the command line interface that was still the ruling party on the computers of the day (like Apple II and DOS machines). Most non-geeks sighed with relief, delighted that they'd never have to memorize commands again. Yet here's Mac OS X, Apple's supposedly ultramodern operating system, complete with a command line! What's going on?

Actually, the command line never went away. At universities and corporations worldwide, professional computer nerds kept right on pounding away at the little *C:* or % prompts, appreciating the efficiency and power such direct computer control afforded them.

Now, you never *have* to use Mac OS X's command line. In fact, Apple has swept it far under the rug, obviously expecting that most people will use the beautiful icons and menus of the regular desktop.

For intermediate or advanced computer fans with a little time and curiosity, however, the command line opens up a world of possibilities. It lets you access corners of Mac OS X that you can't get to from the regular desktop. It lets you perform certain tasks with much greater speed and efficiency than you'd get by clicking and dragging icons. And it gives you a fascinating glimpse into the minds and moods of people who live and breathe computers.

A Terminal crash course

The first time you open Terminal, you'll notice that there's not much in its window except the date and time of your last login, a welcome message, and the "$" (the command line prompt).

For user-friendliness fans, Terminal doesn't get off to a very good start—this prompt looks about as technical as computers get. It breaks down like this (see Figure 16-35):

- **office-mac:** is the name of your Mac (at least, as Unix thinks of it), as recorded in the Sharing panel of System Preferences.

- **~.** The next part of the prompt indicates what folder you're "in" (Figure 16-35). It denotes the *working directory*—the current folder. (Remember, there are no icons in Unix.) Essentially, this notation tells you where you are as you navigate the Mac.

  The very first time you try out Terminal, the working directory is set to the symbol ~, which is shorthand for "your own Home folder." It's what you see the first time you start up Terminal, but you'll soon be seeing the names of other folders here—*[office-mac: /Users]* or *[office-mac: /System/Library]*, for example. (The slashes show you which folders are inside which other folders.)

Note: Before Apple came up with the user-friendly term *folder* to represent an electronic holding tank for files, folders were called *directories*. (Yes, they mean the same thing.) But in any discussion of Unix, "directory" is the correct term.

Working directory
(current folder)　　　What you type　　　What Unix
types back

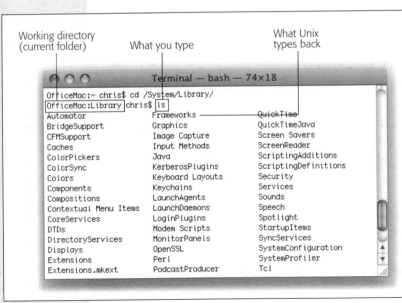

Figure 16-35:
On the Web, Mac OS X's Terminal is one of the most often-discussed elements of Mac OS X. Dozens of step-by-step tutorials for performing certain tasks circulate online, usually without much annotation as to why you're typing what you're typing. As you read this chapter, remember that capitalization matters in Terminal, even though it doesn't in the Finder. As far as most Unix commands are concerned, Hello and hello are two different things.

- **chris$** begins with your short user name. It reflects whoever's logged into the *shell* (the current terminal "session"), which is usually whoever's logged into the *Mac* at the moment. As for the $ sign: Think of it as a colon. In fact, think of the whole prompt shown in Figure 16-35 as Unix's way of asking, "OK, Chris, I'm listening. What's your pleasure?"

The insertion point—the rectangle at the end of the line—trots along as you type.

Unix programs

Each Unix command generally calls up a single application (or *process*, as geeks call it) that launches, performs a task, and closes. Many of the best-known such applications come with Mac OS X.

Here's a fun one: Just type *uptime* (capitalization counts in Unix) and press Return. That's how you run a Unix program: Just type its name and press Return. On the next line, Terminal shows you how long your Mac has been turned on continuously. It shows you something like: "6:00PM up 8 days, 15:04, 1 user, load averages: 1.24, 1.37, 1.45"—meaning your Mac has been running for 8 days, 15 hours nonstop.

You're finished running the *uptime* program. The $ prompt returns, suggesting that Terminal is ready for whatever you throw at it next.

Try this one: Type *cal* at the prompt, and then press Return. Unix promptly spits out a calendar of the current month.

```
OfficeMac:~ chris$ cal
    September 2009
Su Mo Tu We Th Fr Sa
       1  2  3  4  5
 6  7  8  9 10 11 12
13 14 15 16 17 18 19
20 21 22 23 24 25 26
27 28 29 30


OfficeMac:~ chris$
```

This time, try typing *cal 4 2010, cal -y,* or *cal -yj.* These three commands make Unix generate a calendar of April 2010, a calendar of the current year, and a calendar of *Julian* days of the current year, respectively.

Navigating in Unix

If you can't see any icons for your files and folders, how are you supposed to work with them?

You use Unix commands like *pwd* (tells you what folder you're looking at), *ls* (lists what's *in* the current folder), and *cd* (changes to a different folder).

Tip: As you can tell by these examples, Unix commands are very short. They're often just two-letter commands, and an impressive number of those use *alternate hands* (ls, cp, rm, and so on).

Getting help

Mac OS X comes with over 1,200 Unix programs. How are you supposed to learn what they all do? Fortunately, almost every Unix program comes with a help file. It may not appear within an elegant, gradient-gray Snow Leopard window—in fact, it's pretty darned plain—but it offers much more material than the regular Mac Help Center.

These user-manual pages, or *manpages*, hold descriptions of virtually every command and program available. Mac OS X, in fact, comes with manpages on almost 9,000 topics—over 30,000 printed pages' worth.

Unfortunately, manpages rarely have the clarity of writing or the learner-focused approach you'll find in the Mac Help Center. They're generally terse, just-the-facts descriptions. In fact, you'll probably find yourself needing to reread certain sections again and again. The information they contain, however, is invaluable to new and experienced users alike, and the effort spent mining them is usually worthwhile.

To access the manpage for a given command, type *man* followed by the name of the command you're researching. For example, to view the manpage for the *ls* command, enter: *man ls.* Now the manual appears, one screen at a time.

For more information on using *man,* view its *own* manpage by entering—what else?—*man man.*

Tip: The free program ManOpen, available for download from the "Missing CD" page of *www.missing manuals.com,* is a Cocoa manual-pages reader that provides a nice-looking, easier-to-control window for reading manpages.

Learning more

Unix is, of course, an entire operating system unto itself. If you get bit by the bug, here are some sources of additional Unix info:

- *www.ee.surrey.ac.uk/Teaching/Unix.* A convenient, free Web-based course in Unix for beginners.

- *www.megazone.org/Computers/manual.shtml.* A fast-paced, more advanced introduction.

- *Learning Unix for Mac OS X Tiger,* by Dave Taylor & Brian Jepson (O'Reilly Media). A compact, relatively user-friendly tour of the Mac's Unix base.

Tip: Typing *unix for beginners* into a search page like Google.com nets dozens of superb help, tutorial, and reference Web sites. If possible, stick to those that feature the *bash shell.* That way, everything you learn online should be perfectly applicable to navigating Mac OS X via Terminal.

VoiceOver Utility

The Mac has always been able to read stuff on the screen out loud. But VoiceOver is a full-blown *screen reader* for the benefit of people who can't see. VoiceOver doesn't just read every scrap of text it finds on the screen, it also lets you control everything on the screen (menus, buttons, and so on) without ever needing the mouse.

As you can guess, learning VoiceOver means learning a *lot* of new keyboard shortcuts. (Most of them involve the same two modifier keys pressed together: Control-Option.) Click "Open VoiceOver Utility" to configure this feature's settings. You'll want to spend a good deal of time with the online help screens reading about how VoiceOver works (choose Help→Mac Help, and search for *voiceover*). Or you can download the free PDF Appendix to this chapter, "VoiceOver," from this book's "Missing CD" page at *www.missingmanuals.com.*

SWITCHING TO THE MAC: THE MISSING MANUAL

Part Five:
Appendixes

5

Installation & Troubleshooting

If you're lucky, this is a wasted chapter. After all, you'll probably never have to install Mac OS X (assuming it came preinstalled on your Mac), and in the best of all technological worlds, you won't have to do much troubleshooting, either. But here's this appendix, anyway—just in case.

Getting Ready to Install

For starters, you need to make sure you and your Mac have what it takes to handle Mac OS X—specifically:

- **A Macintosh with an Intel processor.** Those old PowerPC Macs (PowerBooks, iBooks, Power Macs, eMacs, and pre-2006 iMacs and Mac minis) have finally fallen off the Mac OS X upgrade path. Basically, most Macs manufactured since 2006 are eligible.

- **Free hard disk space.** You need 5 GB free to install Mac OS X 10.6. (Believe it or not, that's *half* the space requirements of the previous Mac OS X version. Doesn't Apple know how the world works?!)

- **A lot of memory.** Apple recommends at least 1 GB of memory, but Mac OS X absolutely *loves* memory. For the greatest speed, install 2 gigabytes—more if you can afford it. (And these days, you probably can.)

- **The latest firmware.** *Firmware* describes the low-level, underlying software instructions that control the actual circuitry of your Mac. Every now and then, Apple updates it for certain Mac models, and it's very important that your Mac have the absolute latest. If yours doesn't, a message will appear to let you know during the installation. Some Macs might just spit the DVD right out. Quit the installer and grab the latest updater from *http://support.apple.com/kb/HT1237*.

- **A copy of Snow Leopard to install.** Apple sells Mac OS X Snow Leopard in two ways. There's the regular Snow Leopard DVD ($30), for example, and there's the Family Pack ($50), which authorizes you to install Mac OS X on up to five Macs in the same household. (Neither version is copy-protected; only the honor system stops you from installing it on a sixth Mac.)

  Technically, the $30 price of Snow Leopard is available only if you already have Mac OS X 10.5 (Leopard) installed. If you have Tiger (10.4), for example, you're supposed to buy the Mac Box Set, which costs $170 and includes Snow Leopard, iLife '09 (iPhoto, iMovie, GarageBand, iWeb, and iDVD), and iWork '09 (Pages, Numbers, and Keynote).

  But—don't tell anyone—it turns out that the $30 version also installs just fine if you have an earlier Mac OS X version. It's against Apple's rules, but it works.

- **A full backup.** It's a really, *really* good idea to back up your entire Mac before you begin this, or any, upgrade. Even if things go wrong for only, say, 0.01 percent of Mac owners, that's still thousands of people. If you don't have a second hard drive, this is your excuse to buy one; they're dirt cheap these days. If you have Mac OS X Leopard already, you can use it to make a complete, automatic backup of your Mac as it is now.

Two Kinds of Installation

The Mac OS X installer can perform two kinds of installations; it's much simpler than previous installers. Here they are:

- **Automatic.** Double-click it and forget it. This kind of installation preserves everything on your Mac. Every program, setting, and file will be exactly as you had it. In essence, this kind of installation just works through your System folder, updating each component and disturbing nothing else.

- **Erase & Install.** There aren't many reasons to opt for this power-user technique, but it's here if you want it. This version erases your entire hard drive. When it's finished installing Snow Leopard, it then offers you the chance to reinstall all your programs and files from a backup (which you did make, right?).

The Automatic Installation

The installation process takes about 45 minutes, but for the sake of your own psyche, set aside a whole afternoon. Once the installation is over, you'll want to play around, organize your files, and learn the lay of the land.

1. **Insert the Mac OS X DVD.**

   If you're installing Snow Leopard on a MacBook Air, you'll have to use the Remote Disc trick described on page 569.

2. **Double-click the Install Mac OS X icon in the disc's main window (Figure A-1).**

The Mac takes you directly to the first Installer screen, featuring two buttons: Utilities and Continue.

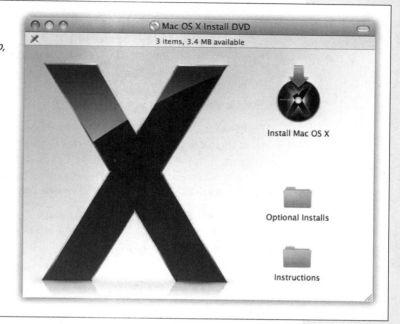

Figure A-1:
Your installation adventure is about to begin. The very first step, though, is restarting the Mac, which the installer invites you to do.

The Utilities, if you were to click that button, include programs like Disk Utility (to erase or partition your hard drive), Terminal (to do some Unixy preparatory steps), System Profiler (to see how much memory this machine has), Reset Password (if you've forgotten yours), and more.

If you do decide to take that detour to another program, then when you quit it, you'll return to the Installer program, right where you left off

As you're seeing already, the installer follows a pattern: Read the instructions, make a couple of choices, and click Continue to advance to the next screen. As you go, the list on the left side of the screen reveals where you are in the overall procedure.

Tip: You can back out of the installation at any time before step 6, just by choosing Installer→Quit Installer. When the Restart button appears, click it. Then eject the Mac OS X disc, either by holding down the mouse button while the computer restarts or, if you have a tray-loading CD drive, by pushing its Eject button during the moment of darkness during the restart.

---

3. **Click Agree to pass the Software License Agreement screen.**

The Software License Agreement requires you to agree with whatever Apple's lawyers say.

4. **Choose the disk or partition where you want to install Mac OS X.**

   The installer proposes the screamingly obvious hard drive: the main one inside your Mac.

   If you have other drives, you can click Show All Disks to see their icons and choose one. (Yellow exclamation-mark icons mean, "You can't install here," for one technical reason or another.)

   The easiest way to proceed from here is to click Install. But don't.

   Instead, take the time to click Customize.

5. **Click Customize.**

   The Installer shows you a list of the various chunks that constitute Mac OS X. A few of them are easily dispensable. For example, if you turn off Additional Fonts, Language Translations (for Japanese, German, French, and so on), and the X11 Unix kit, you save a staggering *400 megabytes*. It's like getting a whole mini-hard drive for free (ka-ching!). Click Done when you're finished gloating.

   On the other hand, do turn on Rosetta (page 95)— although if you ever need this component, the Mac will download and install it for you automatically from the Internet. And you can always install it later from the Optional Installs folder on your Mac OS X DVD.

6. **Click OK, then Install.**

   Now you're in for a 30- to 45-minute wait as the Installer copies software onto your hard drive. (That's why, if you're using a laptop and it's not plugged in, you'll be encouraged to plug it in.) At one point, it restarts the Mac from the DVD and carries right on.

   When the installer's finished, you see a message indicating that your Mac will restart in 30 seconds. If you haven't wandered off to watch TV, click the Restart button to end the countdown and get on with it.

Tip: If the installer found a bit of startup software that's incompatible with Snow Leopard, a message on the screen lets you know at this point. It informs you that the offending software has been moved into a folder on your desktop called Incompatible Software, just so you know what's going on.

Mac OS X 10.6 is now installed on your Mac—but you're not quite ready to use it yet. See "The Setup Assistant" on the facing page.

The Erase & Install Option

If Mac OS X version 10.0 through 10.5-point-anything is on your hard drive, the Snow Leopard installer can neatly nip and tuck its software code, turning it *into* version 10.6. Everything remains just as you had it: your accounts, folders, files, email, network settings, everything-else settings, and so on.

In the olden days, this sophisticated surgery *very occasionally* left behind a minor gremlin here and there: peculiar cosmetic glitches, a checkbox that didn't seem to work, and so on. In the popular lore of Mac, therefore, gurus suggested that a clean install—a "nuke 'n' pave," where you *erase the hard drive completely* and then install Mac OS X afresh—was a safer way to go.

That option is still available in Snow Leopard. You might use it when you're about to sell your Mac and want to ensure that no trace of your former stuff is still there. Otherwise, there's little good reason to opt for this more dramatic purging.

If you're absolutely certain that you won't regret *completely erasing the computer*, follow the previously outlined steps 1 and 2. On the first screen, though, click Utilities, then Restart. Enter your administrator's name and password; click OK to restart from the DVD.

Select your language (a screen that now appears only when you start up from the Snow Leopard DVD) and click the right-arrow button. This time, click on the Install screen, and choose Utilities→Disk Utility. Click your hard drive's name, click Erase, confirm that the format is Mac OS Extended (Journaled), click Erase, and click Erase again. (By the way, you're about to *erase your entire hard drive*.)

When the erasing is complete, choose Disk Utility→Quit Disk Utility. You return to the installer screen, and you can resume from step 3 above.

Of course, you'll wind up with a factory-fresh, nearly empty Mac. You'll have to restore all your files and programs from your backup.

The Setup Assistant

When the Mac restarts after the installation, the first thing you experience is one of the most visually stunning post-installation OS startup movies in history: a fly-through of deep space, accompanied by scooby-dooby music and a fancy parade of 3-D, computer-generated translations of the word "Welcome." Once Apple has quite finished showing off its multimedia prowess, you arrive at a Welcome screen.

FREQUENTLY ASKED QUESTION

Selective Installs

Whoops! I accidentally trashed my copy of the Calculator. How can I get it back? Do I have to reinstall the whole, seething mass of Mac OS X?

Fortunately, no. If you know the secret, you can install only specific components of Mac OS X without having to install the whole darned thing.

What you need is Pacifist, a shareware program that lets you install individual files and folders from the archipelago that

is the collection of Mac OS X installation discs.

Technically, the Mac OS X installer is composed of dozens of subinstallers known as .pkg package files, which the installer opens one after another. That's the point of Pacifist—it lets you open an individual .pkg file.

Pacifist can also check existing installations and find missing or altered files. You can download it from this book's "Missing CD" page at *www.missingmanuals.com*.

Note: You also hear a man's voice letting you know that if you're blind, you can press Esc to hear audio guidance for setting up the Mac and learning VoiceOver.

If you do so, you're treated to a crash course in VoiceOver, the Mac's screen-control/screen-reading software. This, by the way, is the only time you'll be offered this tutorial, so pay attention. (Hint: Here are the basics. Hold down the Control and Option keys and press the arrow keys to highlight different elements of the screen, hearing them pronounced. When a new window opens, press Control-Option-Shift-W to read the contents of the window. Press Control-Option-space bar to "click.")

Once again, you're in for a click-through-the-screens experience, this time with the aim of setting up your Mac's various options. After answering the questions on each screen, click Continue.

The number and sequence of information screens you encounter depend on whether you've upgraded an existing Mac or started fresh. Most of them are self-explanatory, but here are a few that may throw you:

- **Do you already own a Mac?** If you choose "Transfer my information from another Mac," the installer will assist you in sucking all your old programs, files, folders, and settings from the old Mac to the new one.

   You can connect your Mac to the other one over a network—even a wireless one—or using FireWire Disk Mode (page 184).

   You're using the Mac OS X Migration Assistant, shown in Figure A-2. The bottom of the screen lets you know how much stuff you've tagged for transferring, and how much disk space remains on the new Mac.

   When you click Transfer, the data-copying process begins.

- **Select a Wireless Service.** This is your chance to introduce the Mac to any wireless networks in the vicinity. Click the network name you want to join, if you see it. Or if there's no wireless hot spot at all—hey, it could happen—click Different Network Setup.

   In that event, you're offered choices like AirPort wireless, Cable modem/DSL modem, Local network (Ethernet), and "My computer does not connect to the Internet" (bummer!). When you click Continue, you may be asked for specific information—the local access number, account name, and password, and so on—regarding your Internet account. See Chapter 10 for advice on filling in these settings.

- **Enter Your Apple ID.** Here, you're offered the chance to type in, or create, an Apple ID—which is your email address. An Apple ID doesn't cost anything, but it makes life easier if you want to buy songs from the iTunes Store, order gift books or prints from iPhoto, and so on. (If you have a MobileMe account—see Chapter 10—put that account info here.)

- **Create Your Account.** Most of the steps up to this point have been pretty inconsequential, but this is a big moment. You're about to create your *account*—your Administrator account, in fact, as described in Chapter 13.

  All you have to do is make up a name, usually a short variation of your name, and a password. Choose carefully, because you can't easily change your account name later.

  What you come up with here is extremely important, especially if several people use this Mac at different times, or if other people connect to it on a network. See page 411 for details on creating a password and a hint that will help you remember it.

  If you're the only one who uses your Mac, it's perfectly OK to leave the password blank empty.

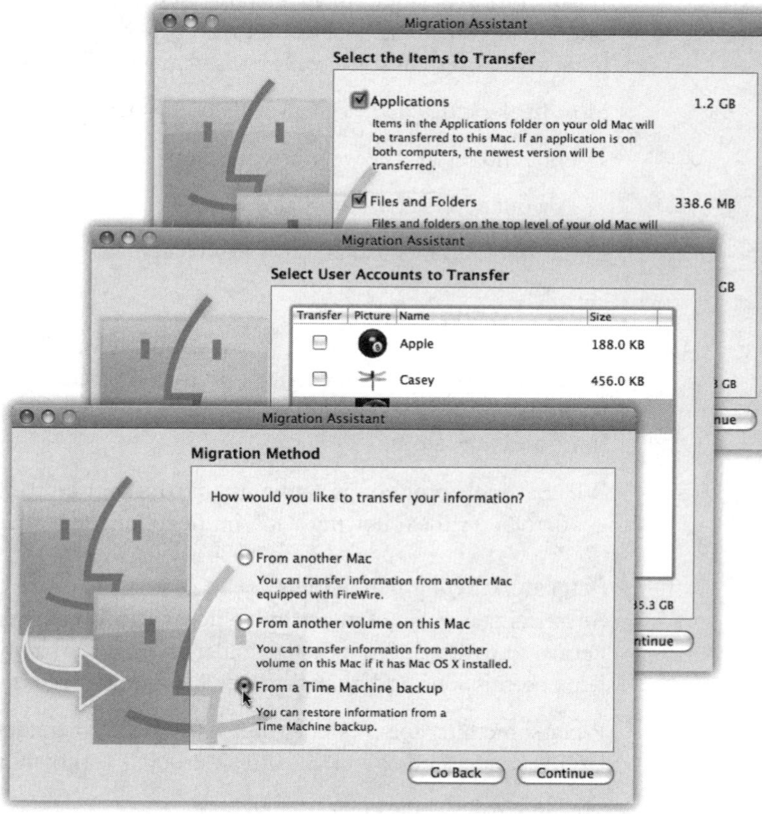

Figure A-2:
The Migration Assistant is actually pretty amazing. It brings over to your new Mac (or new Mac OS X installation) all the files, settings, folders, and even installed programs from an older Mac—or, in times of tragedy, from a Time Machine backup.

Along the way, you'll be asked whose account folder(s) you want brought over, which other stuff (like applications, files, and folders) to copy, and which sorts of settings.

When it's all over, you might have to reactivate a couple of Adobe programs, but otherwise, you should be ready to roll on your new (or new-feeling) Mac.

- **Select a Picture For This Account.** If your Mac has a built-in camera (laptops and iMacs do), you can take a photo of yourself to use as your account icon. Just click "Take a video snapshot." You get a 3-second countdown, and then the Mac snaps your photo. (You can always reshoot it.) Adjust the cropping by dragging inside the photo, and adjust the size by dragging the slider beneath it.

If you're camera-shy, of course, you can choose "Choose from the picture library" and find an Apple-provided icon instead.

- **Your MobileMe Information.** If you have a MobileMe membership, Apple cheerfully lets you know when it will expire.

- **Thanks for being a MobileMe member.** Aw, shucks.

- **Thank You.** When you click Go, you wind up at the Mac OS X desktop, just as described in Chapter 1.

Troubleshooting

Whether it's a car engine or an operating system, anything with several thousand parts can develop the occasional technical hiccup. Mac OS X is far more resilient than its predecessors, but it's still a complex system with the potential for occasional glitches.

Most freaky little glitches go away if you just try these two steps, one at a time:

- Quit and restart the wayward program.

- Log out and log back in again.

It's the *other* problems that'll drive you batty.

Minor Eccentric Behavior

All kinds of glitches may befall you, occasionally, in Mac OS X. Your desktop picture doesn't change when you change it in System Preferences. A menulet doesn't open when you click it. A program won't open—it just bounces in the Dock a couple of times and then stops.

When a single program is acting up like this, but quitting and restarting it does no good, then try the following steps, in the following sequence.

First resort: Repair permissions

An amazing number of mysterious glitches arise because the *permissions* of either that item or something in your System folder—that is, the complex mesh of interconnected Unix permissions underlying a Mac's files—have become muddled.

When something doesn't seem to be working right, therefore, open your Applications→ Utilities folder and open Disk Utility. Proceed as shown in Figure A-3.

This is a really, *really* great trick to know.

Second resort: Look for an update

If a program starts acting up immediately after you've installed Mac OS X 10.6, chances are good that it has some minor incompatibility. Chances are also good that you'll find an updated version on the company's Web site.

Third resort: Toss the prefs file

A corrupted preference file can bewilder the program that depends on it.

Before you go on a dumpfest, however, take this simple test. Log in using a *different account* (perhaps a dummy account that you create just for testing purposes). Run the problem program. Is the problem gone? If so, then the glitch exists only when *you* are logged in—which means it's a problem with *your* copy of the program's preferences.

Return to your own account. Open your Home folder→Library→Preferences folder, where you'll find neatly labeled preference files for all the programs you use. Each ends with the file name suffix *.plist*. For example, com.apple.finder.plist is the Finder's preference file, com.apple.dock.plist is the Dock's, and so on.

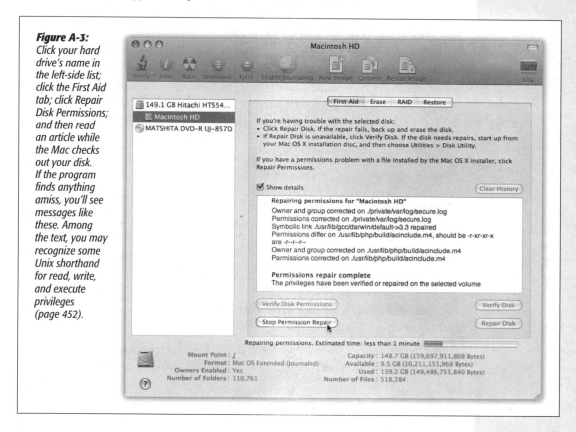

Figure A-3:
Click your hard drive's name in the left-side list; click the First Aid tab; click Repair Disk Permissions; and then read an article while the Mac checks out your disk. If the program finds anything amiss, you'll see messages like these. Among the text, you may recognize some Unix shorthand for read, write, and execute privileges (page 452).

Put the suspect preference file into the Trash, but don't empty it. The next time you run the recalcitrant program, it will build itself a brand-new preference file that, if you're lucky, lacks whatever corruption was causing your problems.

If not, quit the program. You can reinstate its original .plist file from the Trash, if you find that helpful as you pursue your troubleshooting agenda.

Remember, however, that you actually have *three* Preferences folders. In addition to your own Home folder's stash, there's a second one in the Library folder in the main hard drive window (which administrators are allowed to trash), and a third in the System→Library folder in the main hard drive window (which nobody is allowed to trash).

In any case, the next time you log in, the Mac creates fresh preference files.

Fourth resort: Restart

Often, you can give Mac OS X or its programs a swift kick by restarting the Mac. It's an inconvenient step, but not nearly as time-consuming as what comes next. And it can fix problems that cropped up when you started up the computer.

Last resort: Trash and reinstall the program

Sometimes reinstalling the problem program clears up whatever the glitch was.

First, however, throw away all traces of it. Open the Applications folder and drag the program's icon (or its folder) to the Trash. In most cases, the only remaining pieces to discard are its .plist file (or files) in your Home→Library→Preferences folder, and any scraps bearing the program's name in your Library→Application Support folder. (You can do a quick Spotlight search to round up any other pieces.)

Then reinstall the program from its original disc or installer—after first checking the company's Web site to see if there's an updated version, of course.

Frozen Programs (Force-Quitting)

The occasional unresponsive application has become such a part of Mac OS X life that, among the Mac cognoscenti online, the dreaded, endless "please wait" cursor has been given its own acronym: SBOD (Spinning Beachball of Death, not to be confused with the Blue Screen of Death in Windows). When the SBOD strikes, no amount of mouse clicking and keyboard pounding will get you out of the program.

Here are the different ways you can go about *force-quitting* a stuck program (the equivalent of pressing Ctrl+Alt+Delete in Windows), in increasing order of desperation:

- **Force-quit the usual way.** Choose →Force Quit to terminate the stuck program, or use one of the other force-quit methods described on page 119.

- **Force-quit the sneaky way.** Some programs, including the Dock, don't show up at all in the usual Force Quit dialog box. Your next attempt, therefore, should be to open the Activity Monitor program (in Applications→Utilities), which shows *everything* that's running. Double-click a program and then, in the resulting dialog box, click Quit to force-quit it.

Tip: If all this seems like a lot to remember, you can always force-restart the Mac. On most Macs, you do that by holding down the power button for 5 seconds. If that doesn't work, press Control-⌘-power button.

Application Won't Open

If a program won't open (if its icon bounces merrily in the Dock for a few seconds, for instance, but then nothing happens), begin by trashing its preference file, as described on page 587. If that doesn't solve it, reinstalling the program, or installing the Snow Leopard-compatible update for it, usually does.

Startup Problems

Not every problem you encounter is related to running applications. Sometimes trouble strikes before you even get that far. The following are examples:

Kernel panic

When you see the cheerful, multilingual dialog box shown in Figure A-4, you've got yourself a *kernel panic*—a Unix nervous breakdown.

(In such situations, *user panic* might be the more applicable term, but that's programmers for you.)

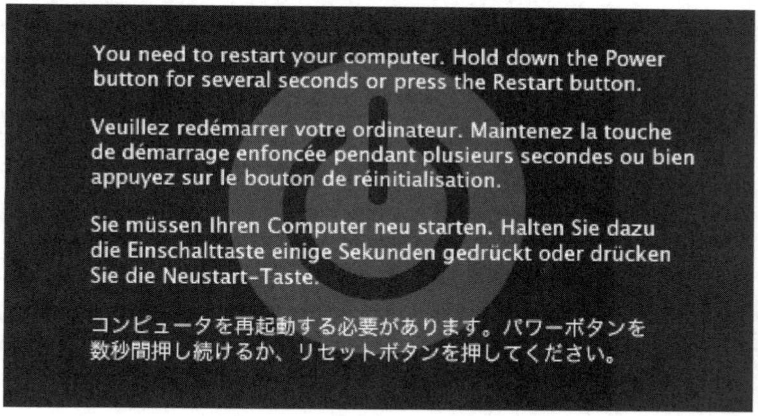

Figure A-4:
A kernel panic is almost always related to some piece of add-on hardware. And look at the bright side: At least you get this handsome dialog box in Snow Leopard. That's a lot better than the Mac OS X 10.0 and 10.1 effect—random text gibberish super-imposing itself on your screen.

You need to restart your computer. Hold down the Power button for several seconds or press the Restart button.

Veuillez redémarrer votre ordinateur. Maintenez la touche de démarrage enfoncée pendant plusieurs secondes ou bien appuyez sur le bouton de réinitialisation.

Sie müssen Ihren Computer neu starten. Halten Sie dazu die Einschalttaste einige Sekunden gedrückt oder drücken Sie die Neustart-Taste.

コンピュータを再起動する必要があります。パワーボタンを数秒間押し続けるか、リセットボタンを押してください。

If you experience a kernel panic, it's almost always the result of a *hardware* glitch—most often a bad memory (RAM) board, but possibly an accelerator card, graphics card, SCSI gadget, or USB hub that Mac OS X doesn't like. A poorly seated AirPort card can bring on a kernel panic, too, and so can a bad USB or FireWire cable.

If simply restarting the machine doesn't help, detach every shred of gear that didn't come from Apple. Restore these components to the Mac one at a time until you find out which one was causing Mac OS X's bad hair day. If you're able to pinpoint the culprit, seek its manufacturer (or its Web site) on a quest for updated drivers, or at least try to find out for sure whether the add-on is compatible with Mac OS X.

> **_Tip:_** This advice goes for your Macintosh itself. Apple periodically updates the Mac's _own_ "drivers" in the form of a _firmware update._ You download these updates from the Support area of Apple's Web site (if indeed Mac OS X's own Software Update mechanism doesn't alert you to their existence).

There's one other cause for kernel panics, by the way, and that's moving, renaming, or changing the access permissions for Mac OS X's essential system files and folders—the Applications or System folder, for example. (See Chapter 13 for more on permissions.) This cause isn't even worth mentioning, of course, because nobody would be that foolish.

Safe Mode (safe boot)

In times of troubleshooting, Windows fans press an F-key to start up in Safe Mode. That's how you turn off all nonessential system-software nubbins in an effort to get a sick machine at least powered up.

Although not one person in a hundred knows it, Mac OS X offers the same kind of emergency keystroke. It can come in handy when you've just installed some new piece of software and find that you can't even start up the machine, or when one of your fonts is corrupted, or when something you've designated as a Login Item turns out to be gumming up the works. With this trick, you can at least turn on the computer so that you can uninstall the cranky program.

The trick is to _press the Shift key_ as the machine is starting up. Hold it down from the startup chime until you see the words "Safe Boot," in red lettering, on the login screen.

Welcome to Safe Mode.

What have you accomplished?

- **Checked your hard drive.** The Shift-key business makes the startup process seem to take a very long time; behind that implacable Apple logo, Mac OS X is actually scanning your entire hard drive for problems.

- **Brought up the login screen.** When you do a safe boot, you must click your name and enter your password, even if you normally have Automatic Login turned on.

- **Turned off your kernel extensions.** All kinds of software nuggets load during the startup process. Some of them, you choose yourself: icons you add to the Login Items list in the System Preferences→Accounts pane. Others are normally hidden: a large mass of _kernel extensions,_ which are chunks of software that add various features to the basic operating system. (Apple's kernel extensions live in your System→Library→Extensions folder; others may be in your Library→StartupItems folder.)

  If you're experiencing startup crashes, some non-Apple installer may have given you a kernel extension that doesn't care for Mac OS X 10.6—so in Safe Mode, they're all turned off.

- **Turned off your fonts.** Corrupted fonts are a chronic source of trouble—and because you can't tell by looking, they're darned difficult to diagnose. So just to make sure you can at least get into your computer, Safe Mode turns them all off (except the authorized, Apple-sanctioned ones that it actually needs to run, which are in your System→Library→Fonts folder).

- **Trashed your font cache.** The font cache is a speed trick. Mac OS X stores the visual information for each of your fonts on the hard drive so the system won't have to read every single typeface off your hard drive when you open your Font menus or the Font panel.

  When these files get scrambled, startup crashes can result. That's why a Safe Boot moves all these files into the Trash. (You'll even see them sitting there in the Trash after the startup process is complete, although there's not much you can do with them except walk around holding your nose and pointing.)

- **Turned off your login items.** Safe Mode also prevents any Finder windows from opening *and* prevents your own handpicked startup items from opening—that is, whatever you've asked Snow Leopard to auto-open by adding them to the System Preferences→Accounts→Login Items list.

  This, too, is a troubleshooting tactic. If some login item crashes your Mac every time it opens, you can squelch it just long enough to remove it from your Login Items list.

Tip: If you don't hold down the Shift key until you click the Log In button (after entering your name and password at the login screen), you squelch *only* your login items but *not* the fonts and extensions.

Once you reach the desktop, you'll find a long list of standard features inoperable. You can't use DVD Player, capture video in iMovie, use a wireless network, use certain microphones and speakers, or use your modem. (The next time you restart, all this goodness will be restored, assuming you're no longer clutching the Shift key in a sweaty panic.)

In any case, the beauty of Safe Mode is that it lets you get your Mac going. You have access to your files, so at least the emergency of crashing-on-startup is over. And you can start picking through your fonts and login items to see if you can spot the problem.

Gray screen during startup

Confirm that your Mac has the latest firmware, as described earlier. Detach and test all your non-Apple add-ons. Finally, perform a disk check, as described earlier.

Blue screen during startup

Most of the troubleshooting steps for this problem (which is usually accompanied by the Spinning Beachball of Death cursor) are the same as those described under "Kernel panic" on page 589.

Forgotten password

If you or someone else who uses your Mac have forgotten the corresponding account password, no worries: Just read the box on page 431.

Fixing the Disk

The beauty of Mac OS X's design is that the operating system itself is frozen in its perfect, pristine state, impervious to conflicting system extensions, clueless Mac users, and other sources of disaster.

That's the theory, anyway. But what happens if something goes wrong with the complex software that operates the hard drive itself?

Fortunately, Mac OS X comes with its own disk-repair program. It takes the form of a program in Applications→Utilities called Disk Utility. It's a powerful and useful troubleshooting tool that can cure all kinds of strange ills, including these problems, among others:

- Your Mac freezes during startup, either before or after the Login screen.

- The startup process stalls and presents a text-only command line.

- You get the "applications showing up as folders" problem.

Disk Utility can't fix the disk it's *on* (except for permissions repairs, described at the beginning of this appendix). That's why you have to restart the computer from the Snow Leopard installation disc (or another startup disk), and run Disk Utility from there. The process goes like this:

1. **Start up the Mac from the Mac OS X DVD.**

   The best way to do that is to insert the disc and then restart the Mac while holding down the C key.

   You wind up, after some time, at the Mac OS X Installer screen. Don't be fooled— installing Mac OS X is *not* what you want to do here. Don't click Continue!

2. **Click Utilities. Then choose Utilities→Disk Utility.**

   That's the unexpected step. After a moment, the Disk Utility screen appears.

Tip: You could also skip steps 1 and 2 by starting up from an external hard drive. Just run its own copy of Disk Utility to check your Mac's hard drive.

---

3. **Click the disk or disk partition you want to fix, click the First Aid tab, and then click Repair Disk.**

   The Mac whirls into action, checking a list of very technical disk-formatting parameters.

If you see the message, "The volume 'Macintosh HD' appears to be OK," that's meant to be *good* news. Believe it or not, that cautious statement is as definitive an affirmation as Disk Utility is capable of making about the health of your disk.

Disk Utility may also tell you that the disk is damaged but that it can't help you. In that case, you need a more heavy-duty disk-repair program like DiskWarrior (*www. alsoft.com*).

Where to Get Troubleshooting Help

If the basic steps described in this chapter haven't helped, the universe is crawling with additional help sources. In general, this is the part in any Mac book where you're directed to Apple's Support Web site, to various discussion forums, and so on—and, indeed, those help sources are listed below.

But the truth is, the mother of all troubleshooting resources is not any of those—it's Google. You'll find more answers faster using Google than you ever will using individual help sites. That's because Google includes all those help sites in its search!

Suppose, for example, that you've just installed the 10.6.2 software update for Snow Leopard, and it's mysteriously turned all your accounts into Standard accounts. And without any Administrator account, you can't install new programs, change network settings, add or edit other accounts, and so on.

You could go to one Web site after another, hunting for a fix, repeating your search— or you could just type *Snow Leopard 10.6.2 standard accounts* into Google and hit Return. You'll get your answers after just a few more seconds of clicking and exploring the results.

Help Online

These Web sites contain nothing but troubleshooting discussions, tools, and help:

- **Apple Discussion Groups** (*http://discussions.apple.com*). The volume and quality of question-and-answer activity here dwarfs any other free source. If you're polite and concise, you can post questions to the multitudes here and get more replies from them than you'll know what to do with.

- **Apple's help site** (*www.apple.com/support*). Apple's help site includes downloadable manuals, software updates, frequently asked questions, and many other resources.

  It also has a Search box. It's your ticket to the Knowledge Base, a collection of 100,000 individual technical articles, organized in a searchable database, that the Apple technicians themselves consult when you call for help. You can search it either by typing in keywords or by using pop-up menus of question categories.

- **MacFixIt** (*www.macfixit.com*). The world's one-stop resource for Mac trouble-shooting advice; alas, you have to pay to access the good stuff.

Help by telephone

Finally, consider contacting whoever sold you the component that's making your life miserable: the printer company, scanner company, software company, or whatever.

If it's a Mac OS problem, you can call Apple at 800-275-2273 (that's 800-APL-CARE). For the first 90 days after your purchase of Mac OS X, the technicians will answer your questions for free.

After that, unless you've paid for AppleCare for your Mac (a 3-year extended warranty program), Apple will charge you to answer your questions. Fortunately, if the problem turns out to be Apple's fault, they won't charge you.

The "Where'd It Go?" Dictionary

A ll the words and pictures so far in this book are just great for leisure reading. But in a crisis of helplessness on your new Mac, this appendix may be more useful. It's an alphabetical listing of every common Windows function and where to find it in Mac OS X. After all, an operating system is an operating system. The actual functions are pretty much the same—they're just in different places.

About [This Program]

To find out the version number of the program you're using, don't look in the Help menu. Instead, look in the *application* menu next to the menu—the one that bears the name of the program you're in. That's where you find the About command for Macintosh programs.

Accessibility Options Control Panel

The special features that let you operate the computer even with impaired vision, hearing, or motor control are called Universal Access in Mac OS X. It's in System Preferences (Chapter 15).

Active Desktop

The Mac never displays Web pages directly on the desktop—and knowing Apple, that's probably a point of pride. But Dashboard (Chapter 4) keeps Internet information only a keystroke away.

Add Hardware Control Panel

The Mac requires no program for installing the driver for a new external gadget. The drivers for most printers, mice, keyboards, cameras, camcorders, and other accessories are preinstalled. If you plug something into the Mac and find that it doesn't work immediately, just install the driver from the included CD (or the manufacturer's Web site).

Add or Remove Programs Control Panel

Here's another one you just don't need on the Macintosh. Installing a program onto the Mac is described on page 151. Removing a program simply involves dragging its icon to the Trash. (For a clean sweep, inspect your Home→Library→Preferences and Library→Application Support folders to see if any preference files got left behind.)

All Programs

There's no Programs menu built into Mac OS X, like the one on the Windows Start menu. If you'd like one, drag your Applications folder into the end of the Dock. Now its icon is a tidy pop-up menu of every program on your machine.

Alt Key

On the Mac, it's the Option key. You can substitute Option for Alt in any keystroke in most popular programs. The Option key has a number of secondary features on the Mac, too: It hides the windows of one program when you click into another, for example.

Automatic Update

On the Mac, it's called Software Update, and it does exactly the same thing.

Backspace key

It's in the same place on the Macintosh keyboard, but it's called the Delete key.

Battery Level

The status of the battery in your Mac laptop appears in the menu bar. (If you don't see it, open ☰→System Preferences→Energy Saver and turn it on.)

BIOS

You'll never have to update or even think about the ROM of your Macintosh (the approximate equivalent of the BIOS on the PC). It's permanent and unchanging. The very similar *firmware* of your Macintosh does occasionally have to be updated in order to work with a new version of the Mac operating system or some dramatic new feature—once every four years, perhaps. You'll be notified on the screen when the time comes.

Briefcase

Mac OS X doesn't have anything like the Briefcase, a Windows invention designed to help you keep your files in sync between a laptop and a desktop computer. On the other hand, if you sign up for a MobileMe account (Chapter 10), you get something even better: automatic syncing between multiple Macs and PCs, using the Internet as an intermediary.

Calculator

The Calculator program in Mac OS X is almost identical to the one in Windows, except that it can also perform conversions (temperature, distance, currency, and so on) and features an editable "paper tape." It sits in your Applications folder and is described in Chapter 16. (There's a simpler Calculator in Dashboard, too, and of course you can do quick computations right in the Spotlight box in your menu bar [page 102]).

Camera and Scanner Wizard

When you connect a digital camera or scanner to your Mac, iPhoto opens automatically and prepares to download the pictures automatically. Details on iPhoto are in this book's free online iLife Appendix.

Character Map

This Windows program helps you find out what keys you need to press to trigger trademark symbols, copyright symbols, and other special characters. The equivalent on the Mac is called Keyboard Viewer (page 170)—but the Character Palette (page 169) is even easier to use.

Clean Install

The Mac OS X installer can give you a fresh, virginal copy of the operating system, just as the Windows installer can. Instructions are in Appendix A.

Clipboard

The Macintosh Clipboard works almost exactly like the one in Windows. In the Finder, you can choose Edit→Show Clipboard to see whatever you have most recently copied or cut.

Command Line

In Mac OS X, the command line is alive and well—but it speaks Unix, not DOS. You get to it by opening Terminal (page 570).

Control Panel

The Control Panel in Mac OS X is called System Preferences, and it's represented on the Dock by a little light-switch icon. As in Windows XP and later, you can view these icons either by category or in a simple alphabetical list: Just choose either Organize by Categories or Organize Alphabetically from the View menu.

Copy, Cut, Paste

When you're editing in a word processor or graphics program, the Mac OS X Cut, Copy, and Paste commands work exactly as they do in Windows.

At the desktop, however, there are a few differences. You can indeed copy icons and paste them into a new window using the Copy and Paste commands—you just can't *cut* them out of a window, as you can in Windows. On the other hand, Mac OS X offers a handy secondary feature: If you paste into a word or text processor instead of into another desktop window, you get a tidy list of the names of the icons you copied.

Ctrl+Alt+Delete

Instead of pressing the "three-fingered salute" (Ctrl+Alt+Delete) to jettison a stuck program on the Mac, you press Option-⌘-Esc. A Force Quit dialog box appears. Click the program you want to toss, click Force Quit, confirm your choice, and then relaunch the program to get on with your day.

Ctrl Key

On the Macintosh, you generally substitute the ⌘ key in keystrokes that would normally involve the Ctrl key. In other words, the Save command is now ⌘-S instead of Ctrl+S, Open is ⌘-O instead of Ctrl+O, and so on.

Date and Time

You set your Mac's calendar and clock in the Date & Time pane of System Preferences (Chapter 15).

Delete Key (Forward Delete)

Desktop Mac keyboards have a forward-delete key (labeled *Del*) exactly like the ones on PCs. On Mac laptops, you trigger the forward-delete function by pressing the regularly scheduled Delete key while pressing the Fn key in the lower-left corner of the keyboard.

Desktop

The Macintosh desktop is pretty much the same idea as the Windows desktop, with a few key differences:

- Disk icons show up on the Mac desktop as soon as they are inserted or connected. You don't have to open a window to see their icons.

- You change the desktop picture using the Desktop & Screen Saver pane of System Preferences.

- The Trash is an icon on the Dock, not loose on the desktop.

Directories

Most people call them *folders* on the Mac.

Disk Defragmenter

There's no such utility included with Mac OS X; the Mac defragments important files on its own hard drive automatically. (A *defragmenting* program moves around the pieces of files on your hard drive in an effort to optimize their placement and speed of opening.)

Disks

Working with disks is very different on the Mac. Every disk inside, or attached to, a Macintosh is represented on the screen by an icon. Mac OS X does have something like the My Computer window (choose Go→Computer), but the icons on the desktop, the Sidebar, and the Computer window reflect only the disks currently inserted in your

Mac. You'll never see an icon for an empty drive, as you do on Windows, and there's no such thing as drive letters (because the Mac refers to *disks,* not to *drives*—and refers to them by name).

Display Control Panel

The functions of the Windows Display Control Panel lurk in the Mac OS X System Preferences program—just not all in one place. You set a desktop picture and choose a screen saver using the Desktop & Screen Saver pane, and adjust your monitor settings using the Displays pane. (Mac OS X offers no equivalent to the Appearance tab in Windows, for changing the system-wide look of your computer.)

DLL Files

The Macintosh equivalent of DLL files—shared libraries of programming code—are invisible and off-limits. As a result, no Macintosh user ever experiences DLL conflicts or out-of-date DLL files.

DOS Prompt

There's a command line in Mac OS X, but it's Unix, not DOS. See page 570.

Drivers

See "Add or Remove Programs."

Eject

Hold down the ⏏ key on your Mac keyboard for a moment to open the CD/DVD drawer, or, if you have a slot-loading CD drive, to spit out the disc that's in it. There are various other ways to eject a disk, but the point is that you never do so by pushing the Eject button on the disk drive itself.

End Task Dialog Box

If some Macintosh program is hung or frozen, you escape it pretty much the same way you would in Windows: by forcing it to quit. To bring up the Force Quit dialog box, you press Option-⌘-Esc, or choose Force Quit from the menu.

Exiting Programs

You can quit a program either by choosing Quit from the menu bearing its name (next to the menu), or by right-clicking its Dock icon and then choosing Quit from the pop-up menu.

Explorer

The Mac has its own "tree" view of the files and folders on your hard drive: list view. By expanding the "flippy triangles" of your folders, you build a hierarchy that shows you as much or as little detail as you like.

If you prefer the Explorer effect of clicking a folder in *one* pane to see its contents in the next, try column view instead. Both views are described in Chapter 2.

Favorites

In Mac OS X, there isn't one single Favorites menu that lists both favorite Web sites and favorite icons. The Bookmarks menu of Safari, the Web browser, lists only Web sites. In the Finder, you can use the Sidebar to list favorite files.

Faxing

Faxing is built into Mac OS X; it's described on page 247. (Hint: Choose File→Print; from the PDF button at the bottom of the print dialog box, choose Fax PDF.)

File Sharing

See Chapter 14 for an in-depth look at the Macintosh networking and file-sharing system.

Floppy Disks

Floppy drives on Macs disappeared in about 1998. According to Apple, it's much more efficient to transfer files between machines using an Ethernet cable, a wireless network, a CD that you burned, a flash drive, or email.

Of course, you can buy an external USB floppy drive for any Mac for about $45.

Folder Options

The Folder Options control panel in Windows is a crazy collection of unrelated settings that boil down to this:

- **General tab.** Exactly as in Windows, it's up to you whether or not double-clicking a folder opens up a second window—or just changes what's in the first one. On the Mac, you make these changes using the Finder→Preferences command. There you'll find the option called "Always open folders in a new window."

- **View tab.** Most of the options here don't exist on the Mac. For example, you can't opt to make all the invisible system files visible (at least not without add-on shareware). You can, however, choose whether or not you want to see the file name extensions in your desktop windows (like .doc and .html). Choose Finder→Preferences, and turn "Show all file extensions" on or off.

- **File Types tab.** Just as in Windows, you can reassign certain document types so that double-clicking opens them up in the program of your choice. But on the Mac, you can reassign either a whole class of files at once, as on Windows, *or* one file at a time. To do it, use the Get Info window as described on page 138.

- **Offline Files.** The closest equivalent feature on the Mac is the MobileMe syncing feature described on page 307.

Fonts

The Mac and Windows both use TrueType, PostScript, and Open Type fonts. (In fact, your Mac can even use the exact font files you had on Windows.) A complete discussion is on page 252.

FTP (File Transfer Protocol)

You can pull up FTP servers right on your screen (just type their addresses into the Go→Connect to Server dialog box). To put files *onto* an FTP server, though, you need a shareware program like RBrowser or Fetch.

Help and Support

At the desktop, choose Help→Mac Help. In other programs, the Help command is generally at the right end of your menus, exactly as in Windows.

Hibernation

When you use the Hibernate command on a modern PC, you cut all power, but Windows memorizes what programs and documents you had open—and stores that information on the hard drive—for a faster restart later. The Mac can enter hibernation mode, too, but only automatically—on laptops, when the battery dies. Otherwise, Sleep mode is the closest it gets (see "Standby Mode" in this appendix).

Internet Explorer

Microsoft abandoned Internet Explorer for Mac years ago—right after Apple introduced its own, better, faster browser called Safari. If you come across a site that *requires* Internet Explorer, you can still download the ancient Mac version of this program from *www.mactopia.com*.

Internet Options

You find the options for your Web browser by choosing Safari→Preferences.

IRQs

They don't exist on the Mac.

Java

This interpreter of tiny programs written in the Java programming language is alive and well in Mac OS X. Java programs run fine in all Mac Web browsers.

Keyboard Control Panel

You can make exactly the same kinds of settings—and more—on the Keyboard pane of System Preferences.

Logging In

As it turns out, the multiple-accounts feature of Mac OS X is extremely similar to that of Windows. In either case, you can, if you wish, create a requirement to login with a name and password before using the computer. This arrangement keeps separate the documents, email, and settings of each person who uses the computer. (Chapter 13 tells all.)

Mail Control Panel

Mac OS X comes with its own email program (see Chapter 11); all of its settings are contained within the program.

Maximize Button

On the Mac, clicking the Zoom button (the green button at the upper-left corner of a window) does something like the Maximize button in Windows: It makes your window larger. On the Mac, however, clicking the Zoom button rarely makes the window expand to fill the entire screen. Instead, the window grows—or *shrinks*—precisely enough to enclose its contents.

Menus

Here's one of the biggest differences between the Mac and Windows: On the Macintosh, there's only one menu bar, always at the very top of the screen. The menus change depending on the program and the window you're using, but the point is that the menu bar is no longer inside each window you open.

Tip: Just because you don't see the little underlines in the menus doesn't mean you can't operate all the menus from the keyboard, as in Windows. See page 141 for details.

Minimize Button

You can minimize a Mac OS X window to the Dock, just the way you would minimize a Windows window to the taskbar. You do so by double-clicking its title bar, pressing ⌘-M, choosing Window→Minimize Window, or clicking the yellow Minimize button at the top left of a window. (Restore the window by clicking its icon on the Dock.)

Mouse Control Panel

The equivalent settings await you in the Keyboard & Mouse pane of System Preferences.

My Computer

The Mac's Computer window is very similar (choose Go→Computer), in that it shows the icons of all disks (hard drive, CD, and so on). On the other hand, it shows *only* the disks that are actually inserted or connected (see "Disks").

My Documents, My Pictures, My Music

The equivalent buckets for your everyday documents, music files, and pictures are the Documents, Pictures, and Music folders in your Home folder.

My Network Places

To see your "network neighborhood," just open any Finder window; all the Macs and PCs on your network show up in the Sidebar at the left side.

Network Neighborhood

See the previous entry.

Notepad

There's no Mac OS X Notepad program. But give Stickies a try (page 548).

Personal Web Server

If you're technically proficient, you can turn your Mac into a Web site. On the Sharing pane of System Preferences, turn on Personal Web Sharing. Any HTML documents you put into your Home→Sites folder are now available on your network or the Web.

Phone and Modem Options Control Panel

To find the modem settings for your Mac, open System Preferences. Click Network, click Internal Modem (or External Modem) in the list at left, and then click Advanced.

Power Options

To control when your Mac goes to sleep and (if it's a laptop) how much power it uses, use the Energy Saver panel of System Preferences (Chapter 15).

Printer Sharing

To share a USB inkjet printer with other Macs on the network, open the Sharing pane of System Preferences on the Mac with the printer. Turn on Printer Sharing.

To use the shared printer from across the network, open the document you want to print, choose File→Print, and choose the name of the shared printer from the first pop-up menu.

Printers and Faxes

For a list of your printers, open the Printer Setup Utility in your Aplications→Utilities folder. For details on faxing, see "Faxing."

PrntScrn Key

You capture pictures of your Mac screen by pressing Shift-⌘-3 (for a full-screen grab) or Shift-⌘-4 (to grab a selected portion of the screen). Details on page 566.

Program Files Folder

The Applications folder (Go→Applications) is like the Program Files folder in Windows—except that you're not discouraged from opening it and double-clicking things. On the Macintosh, every program bears its true name. Microsoft Word is called Microsoft Word, not WINWORD.EXE.

Properties Dialog Box

You can call up something very similar for any *icon* (file, folder, program, disk, printer) by highlighting its icon and then choosing File→Get Info. But objects in Macintosh *programs* generally don't contain Properties dialog boxes.

Recycle Bin

Mac OS X has a Trash icon at the end of the Dock. In general, it works exactly like the Windows Recycle Bin—and why not, since the Macintosh Trash was Microsoft's inspiration?—but there are a couple of differences. The Macintosh never auto-empties it, for example. That job is up to you (the simplest way is to right-click it and choose Empty Trash from the shortcut menu).

The Mac never bothers you with an "Are you sure?" message when you throw something into the Trash, either. In fact, it doesn't even ask for confirmation when you *empty* the Trash (at least, not when you empty it by right-clicking). The Mac interrupts you for permission only when you choose File→Empty Trash—and you can even turn that confirmation off, if you like (in Finder→Preferences).

To put icons into the Trash, drag them there, or just highlight them and then press ⌘-Delete.

Regional and Language Options Control Panel

The equivalent is the International pane of System Preferences (Chapter 15).

Registry

There is no registry. Let the celebration begin!

Run Command

The equivalent command line is Terminal (page 570).

Safe Mode

You can press the Shift key during startup to suppress the loading of certain software libraries, but Mac OS X's "safe mode" (page 590) isn't quite as stripped-down as Windows' Safe Mode.

ScanDisk

Just like Windows, the Mac automatically scans and, if necessary, repairs its hard drive every time your machine starts up. To run such a check on command, open Disk Utility (located in the Applications→Utilities folder), and then click the First Aid tab.

Scheduled Tasks

To schedule a task to take place unattended, use the *launchd* command in Terminal (geeks only), or one of the scheduling programs listed at *www.versiontracker.com*.

Scrap Files

On the Mac, they're called *clipping files,* and they're even more widely compatible. You create them the same way: Drag some highlighted text, or a graphic, out of a program's window and onto the desktop. There it becomes an independent clipping file that you can drag back in—to the same window, or a different one.

Screen Saver

The Mac's screen savers are impressive. Open System Preferences and click the Desktop & Screen Saver icon.

Search

In Mac OS X, you have the ultimate file-searching tool: Spotlight (Chapter 3). Get psyched!

To find Web sites, use the Google Search box at the top of the Safari browser.

Shortcut Menus

They work exactly the same as they do in Windows. You produce a shortcut menu by right-clicking things like icons, list items, and so on.

Shortcuts

On the Mac, they're known as *aliases*. See page 88.

Sounds and Audio Devices

Open System Preferences; click the Sound icon. You may also want to explore the Audio MIDI Setup program in Applications→Utilities.

Speech Control Panel

The Mac's center for speech recognition and text-to-speech is the Speech pane of System Preferences. The Mac can read aloud any text in any program, and it lets you operate all menus, buttons, and dialog boxes by voice alone.

Standby Mode

On the Mac, it's called Sleep, but it's the same idea. You make a Mac laptop sleep by closing the lid. You make a Mac desktop sleep by choosing →Sleep, or just walking away; the Mac will go to sleep on its own, according to the settings in the Energy Saver pane of System Preferences.

Start Menu

There's no Start menu in Mac OS X. Instead, you stash the icons of the programs, documents, and folders you use frequently onto the Dock at the edge of the screen, or into the Sidebar at the left edge of every Finder window.

Exactly as with the Start menu, you can rearrange these icons (drag them horizontally), or remove the ones you don't use often (drag them away from the Dock and then release). To add new icons of your own, just drag them into place (applications go to the left of the Dock's divider line, documents and folders to the right).

StartUp Folder

To make programs launch automatically at startup, include them in the list of Login Items in the System Preferences→Accounts pane.

System Control Panel

The Mac has no central equivalent of the System window on a Windows PC. But its functions have analogs here:

- **General tab.** To find out your Mac OS X version number and the amount of memory on your Mac, choose →About This Mac.

- **Computer Name tab.** Open System Preferences, click Sharing, and edit your computer's network names here.

- **Hardware tab.** The closest thing the Mac has to the Device Manager is System Profiler (in your Applications→Utilities folder). See page 570.

- **Advanced tab.** In Mac OS X, you can't easily adjust your virtual memory, processor scheduling, or user profile information.

- **System Restore tab.** This feature isn't available in Mac OS X.

- **Automatic Updates tab.** Open System Preferences and click Software Updates.

- **Remote tab.** Mac OS X Snow Leopard excels at remote control of other computers. See the description, for example, of screen sharing on page 465.

System Tray

The perfect Mac OS X equivalent of the system tray (also called the notification area) is the row of *menulets* at the upper-right corner of your screen; see page 16.

Taskbar

Mac OS X doesn't have a taskbar, but it does have something very close: the Dock (Chapter 2). Open programs are indicated by a small glowing dot beneath their icons on the Dock. If you hold down your cursor on one of these icons (or right-click it), you get a pop-up list of the open windows in that program, exactly as in Windows XP.

Clicking a folder or disk icon on the Dock is even more useful. It produces a pop-up display of everything inside that disk or folder—a terrific form of X-ray vision that has no equivalent in Windows.

On the other hand, some conventions never die. Much as on Windows, you cycle through the various open programs on your Dock by holding down the ⌘ key and pressing Tab repeatedly.

Taskbar and Start Menu Control Panel

To configure your Dock (the equivalent of the taskbar and Start menu), choose → Dock→Dock Preferences, or click the Dock icon in System Preferences.

ToolTips

Small, yellow identifying balloons pop up on the Mac just as they do in Windows. Just point to a toolbar icon or truncated file name without clicking. (There's no way to turn these labels off.)

TweakUI

The closest equivalent for this free, downloadable, but unsupported Microsoft utility for tweaking the look of your PC is TinkerTool for Mac OS X. You can find it at, and download it from, *www.versiontracker.com*.

User Accounts Control Panel

Like Windows 2000 and later, Mac OS X was designed from square one to be a multiuser operating system, keeping the files, mail, and settings of each person separate. You set up and manage these accounts in System Preferences→Accounts (Chapter 13).

Window Edges

You can enlarge or shrink a Mac OS X window only by dragging its lower-right corner—not its edges.

Windows (or WINNT) Folder

Mac OS X's operating system resides in a folder simply called System, which sits in your main hard drive window. Exactly as in recent Windows versions, you're forbidden to add, remove, or change anything inside. Also as in Windows, most of it is invisible anyway.

Windows Logo Key

The Mac has no equivalent for the ⊞ key on most PC keyboards.

Tip: If you hook up a Windows keyboard to your Mac, the ⊞ key behaves like the Mac's ⌘ key.

Windows Media Player

The Mac comes with individual programs for playing multimedia files:

- **QuickTime Player** (page 540) to play back movies and sounds.

- **iTunes** (page 263) to play CDs, Internet radio, MP3 files, and other audio files. (iTunes for Mac, like its Windows brother, can even *create* MP3 files.)

- **DVD Player** (page 273) for playing DVDs. If your Mac does, in fact, have a DVD player built in, this program is in the Applications folder.

Windows Media Player *is,* however, available in a Macintosh version, paradoxical though that may sound. For details, see page 222.

Windows Messenger

Mac OS X's voice and videoconferencing software is called iChat, and it's described in Chapter 12. But if you really want the actual Microsoft experience, Windows Messenger is available in a Mac version. You can download it from *www.microsoft.com/mac*.

WordPad

The TextEdit program (in the Applications folder) is a bare-bones word processor like WordPad. It can even open and save Word files, as WordPad can.

Zip Files

Zip files exist on the Mac, too, and you create them almost the same way: right-click a file or folder and choose Compress from the shortcut menu.

The Master Mac OS X Secret Keystroke List

H ere it is, by popular, frustrated demand: The master list of every secret (or not-so-secret) keystroke in Mac OS X Snow Leopard, including all the keys you can press during startup. Clip and post to your monitor (unless, of course, you got this book from the library).

Note: For the most part, the following list doesn't include the keystrokes already listed in your menus, like ⌘-P for Print, ⌘-S for Save, and so on.

Startup Keystrokes

Keys to Hold Down	Effect
C	Starts up from a CD
D	Starts up from the first partition
N	Starts up from network server
R	Resets the laptop screen
T	Puts the Mac into FireWire Target Disk mode
Option	Shows icons of all startup disks and partitions, so you can choose one for starting up
Shift-Option-⌘-Delete	Starts up from external drive (or CD)
Option-⌘-P-R	Zaps the parameter RAM (PRAM). (Hold down until you hear the second chime.)
Option-⌘-O-F	Brings up Open Firmware screen (pre-Intel Macs).

⌘-V	Shows Unix console messages during startup, logout, and shutdown
⌘-S	Starts up in single-user (Unix command-line) mode
Mouse down	Ejects a stuck CD or DVD
6 and 4 keys	Starts up in 64-bit mode
Shift	Just after powering up: Turns off *kernel extensions*
Shift	Just after logging in: Prevents Finder windows and startup items from opening. (They'll return the next time you start up.)

In the Finder

⌘-space	Highlights Spotlight box
Option-⌘-space	Opens Spotlight window
→, ←	Expands or collapses a selected folder in list view
Option-→	Expands a folder in a list view *and* all folders inside it
Option-←	Collapses folder *and* all folders inside it
⌘-↑	Opens parent folder
Shift-Option-⌘-↑	Selects the Desktop
⌘-↓ (or ⌘-O)	Opens the selected icon
Option-click the flippy triangle	Expands or collapses all folders within that window
Tab	Selects next icon alphabetically
Shift-Tab	Selects previous icon alphabetically
space bar	Opens Quick Look preview of highlighted icon(s)
space bar	During a spring-loaded folder drag, opens the disk or folder under mouse immediately
Option-click Zoom button	Enlarges the window to full screen
Option-click Close button	Closes all Finder windows
Option-click Minimize button	Minimizes all windows (works in most apps)
⌘-drag an icon	Moves it into, or out of, the System folder (administrator password required)
Option	Changes Quick Look button to Slideshow button
⌘-drag	Rearranges or removes menulets or toolbar icons

⌘-click window title	Opens a pop-up menu showing the folder path

🍎 Menu

Option	Changes "About This Mac" to "System Profiler"
Option	Eliminates confirmation box from Restart, Shut Down, and Log Out

Finder Menu

Option	Eliminates confirmation box from Empty Trash and Secure Empty Trash
Shift-⌘-Q	Logs out
Shift-Option-⌘-Q	Logs out without confirmation box
Shift-⌘-Delete	Empties the Trash
Shift-⌘-Delete	Puts back a highlighted icon in the Trash
Shift-Option-⌘-Delete	Empties the Trash without confirmation box
Option-"Empty Trash"	Empties the Trash without confirmation box
⌘-comma	Opens Preferences
⌘-H	Hide this program
Shift-⌘-H	Hide other programs

File Menu

⌘-N	New Finder window
Shift-⌘-N	New folder
Option-⌘-N	New smart folder
⌘-O or ⌘-↓	Open
Control-⌘-O	Open in new window
Option-click File menu	Changes "Open With" to "Always Open With"
⌘-W	Close window
Option-⌘-W	Close All
⌘-I	Get Info
Option-⌘-I	Show Inspector
Control-⌘-I	Summary Info (of selected icons)
⌘-D	Duplicate
⌘-L	Make Alias
⌘-Y	Quick Look
Option-⌘-Y	Slideshow (of selected icons)
⌘-R	Show Original (of alias)
⌘-T	Add to Sidebar

Shift-⌘-T	Add to Favorites
⌘-Delete	Move to Trash
⌘-E	Eject
⌘-F	Find
Shift-⌘-F	Find by Name

Edit Menu

⌘-Z	Undo
⌘-C, ⌘-X, ⌘-V	Copy, Cut, Paste
⌘-A	Select All
Option-⌘-A	Deselect All

View Menu

⌘-1, -2, -3, -4	Icon, list, column, Cover Flow views
Control-⌘-1, -2, -3, -4, -5, -6	Arrange by Name, Date Modified, Date Created, Size, Kind, Label
Option	Changes "Clean Up Selection" to "Clean Up"
Option	Changes "Keep Arranged By" to "Arrange By"
Option-⌘-T	Show/Hide Toolbar
⌘-J	Show/Hide View Options palette

Go Menu

⌘-[, ⌘-]	Back, Forward
⌘-↑	Enclosing folder
Control-⌘-↑	Enclosing folder in new window
Shift-⌘-C	Computer window
Shift-⌘-H	Home window
Shift-⌘-D	Desktop window
Shift-⌘-K	Network window
Shift-⌘-I	Open iDisk
Shift-⌘-A	Applications window
Shift-⌘-G	Go to Folder
⌘-K	Connect to Server

Window Menu

⌘-M	Minimize
Option-⌘-M	Minimize All
Option	Changes "Bring All to Front" to "Arrange in Front"

Help Menu

Shift-⌘-?   Opens help search box

Power Keys

Control-⏏   Brings up dialog box for shutdown, sleep, or
                                             restart

Option-⌘-⏏   Sleep

Control-Option-⌘-⏏   Shut Down

Control-⌘-power   Restart

The Dock

Option-click a Dock icon   Switches to new program and hides previous
                                             one

Option-⌘-D   Hides/shows the Dock

⌘-click a Dock or Stacks icon   Reveals its actual Finder icon

Option-⌘-click a Dock icon   Switches to this program and hides all others

Control-click a Dock icon   Opens a shortcut menu

Hold mouse down on Dock app icon   Triggers Exposé (shows all windows of that app
                                             in miniature)

⌘-drag an icon onto a Dock icon   Prevents Dock icons from moving, so you can
                                             drop your icon onto one of them

⌘-drag a Dock icon   Drags the actual item

Option-⌘-drag an icon onto the Dock   Forces Dock program icon to open the icon
                                             you're dropping

Managing Programs

Option-click a Dock icon   Switches to new program and hides previous
                                             one

Option-click in a window   Switches to new program and hides previous
                                             one

⌘-H   Hide this program's windows (works in most
                                             apps)

Option-⌘-H   Hide all *other* programs' windows (most apps)

F8   Spaces: Enters "big picture" view of your virtual
                                             screens (if you've turned on Spaces)

Shift-F8   Spaces: Enters "big picture" view in slow motion

Control-1, 2, 3, 4...   Jump to a specific Spaces screen

Control-↑, ↓, ←, →   Next Spaces screen in this direction

F9   Exposé: Shrinks and tiles all windows in all
                                             programs

Shift-F9	Exposé: Shrinks and tiles all windows in slow motion
F10	Exposé: Shrinks and tiles all windows in frontmost program
F11	Exposé: Flings all windows in all programs to edges of screen, revealing desktop
F12	Dashboard widgets
⌘-Tab	Press and release: Switches back and forth between current and previous open program
⌘-Tab	Hold down ⌘: Displays floating icons of open programs. Press Tab repeatedly to cycle through them. (Add Shift to cycle *backward* through open programs on the Dock.)
⌘-~	Switches to next open window in this program. (Add Shift to cycle in the opposite direction.)
Option-⌘-Esc	Opens the Force Quit dialog box (to close a stuck program)
Shift-⌘-3	Captures the screen image as a PDF file on your desktop
Shift-⌘-4	Produces a crosshairs; drag to capture a selected portion of the screen as a PDF graphics file. (Press space to get the "camera" cursor that snips out just a menu, icon, or window.)
⌘-space	Switches keyboard layout (if more than one is installed). (If you use Spotlight, you must choose a different keystroke for this function.)

Dialog Boxes

⌘-comma	Opens Preferences dialog box (any Apple program)
Esc	"Clicks" the Cancel button in a dialog box
Enter or Return	"Clicks" the OK button (or other blue, highlighted button) in a dialog box
Option-⌘-F	Moves insertion point to the Search box in most Apple programs
⌘-D, ⌘-R	"Clicks" the Don't Save or Replace button

Index

Index

Colophon

This book was written on a black MacBook laptop that remained attached to David Pogue like an appendage. It was typed in Microsoft Word, with substantial assistance from the typing-shortcut program TypeIt4Me (*www.typeit4me.com*) and the macro program QuicKeys (*www.quickeys.com*).

The screenshots were captured with Snapz Pro X (*www.ambrosiasw.com*), edited in Adobe Photoshop CS3 (*www.adobe.com*), and overlaid with labels, lines, and circles in Macromedia Freehand Mac OS X (*www.adobe.com*).

The author wrote the index, entry by entry, using a highly tweaked FileMaker database (*www.filemaker.com*) and a clever Perl script that converted FileMaker's output into a fully formatted index.

The book was designed and laid out in Adobe InDesign CS4 on a MacBook Pro and Mac Pro. The fonts include Formata (as the sans-serif family) and Minion (as the serif body face). To provide the symbols (, ⌘, ⏏, and so on), Phil Simpson designed two custom fonts using Macromedia Fontographer.

The book was then exported as Adobe Acrobat PDF files for final transmission to the printing plant in Michigan.

Get even more
for your money.

Buy this book and get access to the online edition for 45 days—for free!

"Pogue, the *New York Times* computer columnist, is among the world's best explainers."
—KEVIN KELLY, CO-FOUNDER OF *WIRED*

Switching to the Mac
the missing manual®
The book that should have been in the box

Snow Leopard Edition

O'REILLY®   David Pogue

Switching to the Mac: The Missing Manual,
Snow Leopard Edition

By David Pogue
December 2009, $29.99
ISBN 9780596153281

With Safari Books Online, you can:

Access the contents of thousands of technology and business books

- Quickly search over 7000 books and certification guides
- Download whole books or chapters in PDF format, at no extra cost, to print or read on the go
- Copy and paste code
- Save up to 35% on O'Reilly print books
- **New!** Access mobile-friendly books directly from cell phones and mobile devices

Stay up-to-date on emerging topics before the books are published

- Get on-demand access to evolving manuscripts.
- Interact directly with authors of upcoming books

Explore thousands of hours of video on technology and design topics

- Learn from expert video tutorials
- Watch and replay recorded conference sessions

To try out Safari and the online edition of this book FREE for 45 days,
go to **www.oreilly.com/go/safarienabled** and enter the coupon code OMNJZAA.
To see the complete Safari Library, visit safari.oreilly.com.

Spreading the knowledge of innovators   safari.oreilly.com